STERLING
Test Prep

DAT

Biology

Practice Questions

9th edition

Customer Satisfaction Guarantee

Your feedback is important because we strive to provide the highest quality prep materials. Email us questions, comments or suggestions.

info@sterling–prep.com

We reply to emails – check your spam folder

9 8 7 6 5 4 3 2 1

ISBN-13: 979-8-8855714-1-8

Sterling Test Prep materials are available at quantity discounts.

Contact info@sterling–prep.com

Sterling Test Prep
6 Liberty Square #11
Boston, MA 02109

© 2023 Sterling Test Prep

Published by Sterling Test Prep

 Printed in the U.S.A.

STERLING
Test Prep

Thousands of students use our study aids to achieve high DAT scores!

Scoring well on the DAT is essential for dental school admission to pursue your dream of practicing dentistry. This book helps you develop and apply knowledge to quickly choose the correct answers to biology questions on the Survey of the Natural Sciences section. Solving targeted practice questions builds your understanding of fundamental biology concepts and is a more effective strategy than merely memorizing terms.

This book has 1,292 high-yield practice questions covering DAT biology topics. Life sciences instructors with years of teaching experience prepared these questions by analyzing the test content and developing practice material that builds your knowledge and skills crucial for success on the DAT. Our editorial team reviewed and systematized the content to match the current ADA test requirements. We are experts on preparing students for standardized tests and admissions into competitive dental schools.

The detailed explanations describe why an answer is correct and – more important for your learning – why another attractive choice is wrong. They teach the scientific foundations and details of essential biology topics needed to answer conceptual test questions. Read the explanations carefully to understand how they apply to the question and learn important biology principles and the relationships between them. With the practice material contained in this book, you will significantly improve your DAT score.

We wish you great success in dental school admissions and look forward to being an important part of your DAT preparation!

230730akp

DAT Biology Subject Review provides a comprehensive review of biology topics tested on the DAT. The content covers foundational principles and theories necessary to answer test questions.

This review book will increase your score.

Visit our Amazon store

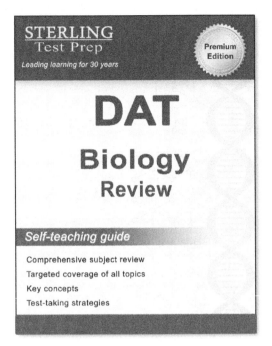

DAT online practice questions

Our advanced online testing platform allows you to practice these and other DAT questions on the computer and generate Diagnostic Reports for each test.

Assess your knowledge of subjects and topics via Diagnostics Reports with your performance analysis

Learn important scientific topics and concepts for comprehensive DAT preparation

Improve your test-taking skills by simulating testing under time constraints

To access these and other DAT questions online
at a special pricing for book owners, see page 589

If you benefited from this book, we would appreciate if you left a review on Amazon, so others can learn from your input. Reviews help us understand our customers' needs and experiences while keeping our commitment to quality.

Table of Contents

Table of Contents (*Continued*)

DAT Preparation and Test-Taking Strategies

Test preparation strategies

The best way to do well on DAT Survey of Natural Sciences section is to be good at tested subjects. There is no way around knowing the subject; proper preparation is the key to success. Prepare for the test to answer with confidence as many questions as possible.

Study in advance

Devote 3 to 6 months studying. The information is manageable by studying regularly during the weeks before the test.

Cramming is not a successful tactic. However, do not study too far in advance. Studying more than six months ahead is not advised and may result in fatigue and poor knowledge retention.

Develop a realistic study and practice schedule

Cramming eight hours a day is unfeasible and leads to burnout, detrimental to performance.

Commit to a realistic study and practice schedule.

Remove distractions

During this preparation period, temporarily eliminate distractions.

However, balance is key, and it is crucial not to neglect physical well-being and social or family life. Prepare with full intensity but do not jeopardize your health or emotional well-being.

Develop an understanding over memorization

When studying, devote time to each topic.

After a study session, write a short outline of the concept to clarify relationships and increase knowledge retention.

Make flashcards

Avoid commercial flashcards because making cards helps build and retain knowledge.

Consider using self-made flashcards to develop knowledge retention and quiz what you know.

Find a study partner

Occasionally studying with a friend preparing for the test can motivate and provide accountability.

Explaining concepts to another improves and fine-tunes your understanding, integrates knowledge, bolsters competence, and identifies deficiencies in comprehension.

Take practice tests

Do not take practice tests too early. First, develop a broad and detailed understanding of concepts. In the last weeks, use practice tests to fine-tune your final preparation. If you are not scoring well on practice tests, you want time to improve without undue stress.

Alternate studying and practicing to increase knowledge retention and identify areas for further study. Taking practice tests accustoms you to the challenges of test-taking.

Test day strategies

Be well-rested and eat the right foods

Get a full night's sleep before the test for proper mental and physical capacity. If you are up late the night before, you will have difficulty concentrating and focusing on the test.

Avoid foods and drinks that lead to drowsiness (carbohydrates and protein). Avoid drinks high in sugar, causing glucose to spike and crash.

Pack in advance

Check what you are allowed to bring to the test. Pay attention to the required check-in items (e.g., printed confirmation, identification).

Pack the day before to avoid the stress of not frantically looking for things on test day.

Arrive at the testing center early

Starting off right is an advantage. Allow time to check in and remain calm before the test begins.

Map and test your route to the center in advance and determine parking locations, if applicable. If you are not familiar with the test location, visit before the test day to practice and avoid travel errors. Plan your route correctly to arrive at the center without additional challenges and unnecessary stress.

Maintain a positive attitude

Avoid falling into a mental spiral of negative emotions. Too much worry leads to underperformance.

If you become anxious, chances are higher for lower performance in preparation and during the test. Inner peace helps during preparation and the high-stakes test.

To do well on the test requires logical, systematic, and analytical thinking, so relax and remain calm.

Focus on your progress

Do not be concerned with other test-takers. Someone proceeding rapidly through the exam may be rushing or guessing on questions.

Take breaks and breathe deeply

Do not skip the available timed breaks. Refreshing breaks help you finish strong.

If time allows, eat a light snack to replenish your energy. Your mind and body will appreciate the available breaks.

The best approach to any test is *not* to keep your head down the whole session. While there is no time to waste, take a few seconds between questions to breathe deeply.

Momentarily clear your thoughts to relax your mind and muscles.

Time management strategies

Timing

Besides good preparation, time management is the critical strategy for the exam.

Timed practice is not the objective at this stage. While practicing, note how many questions you would have completed in the allotted time.

Average time per question

In advance, determine the average time allotted for each question.

Use two different approaches depending on which preparation phase you are working on.

During the first preparation phase, acquire, fortify, and refine your knowledge.

During your final practice stage, use the time needed to develop analytical and thought processes related to specific questions.

Work systematically

Note your comprehension compared to the correct answers to learn the material and identify conceptual weaknesses. Do not overlook the value of explanations to questions; these can be a great source of content, analysis, and interdependent relationships.

During the second preparation phase, do not spend more than the average allotted time on each question when taking practice tests.

Pace your response time to develop a consistent pace and complete the test within the allotted time. If you are time-constrained during the final practice phase, work more efficiently, or your score will suffer.

Focus on the easy questions and skip the unfamiliar

Easy or difficult questions are worth the same points. Score more points for three quickly answered questions than one hard-earned victory.

Answer all familiar and easy questions to maximize points if time runs out.

Identify strengths and weaknesses

Skip unfamiliar questions on the first round as challenging questions require more than the average allotted time.

On the second review, questions that you cannot approach systematically or lack fundamental knowledge will likely not be answered through analysis.

Use the elimination and educated guessing strategy to select an answer and move on to another question

Do not overinvest in any question

Some questions consume more time than the average and make you think of investing more time. Stop thinking that investing more time in challenging questions is productive.

Do not get entangled with questions while losing track of time. The test is timed, so you cannot spend too much time on any question.

Look at every question on the exam

It is unfortunate not to earn points for a question you could have quickly answered because you did not see it.

If you are in the first half of the test and spending more than the average on a question, select the best option, note the question number, and move on. You do not want to rush through the remaining questions, causing you to miss more answers.

If time allows, return to marked questions and take a fresh look. However, do not change the original answer unless you have a reason to change it. University studies show that hastily changing answers often replace correct and incorrect answers.

Multiple-choice questions

Answer all questions

How many questions are correct, not how much work went into selecting the answers matters. An educated guess earns the same points as an answer known with confidence.

On the test, you need to think and analyze information quickly. The skill of analyzing information quickly cannot be gained from a college course, prep course, or textbook. Working efficiently and effectively is a skill developed through focused effort and applied practice.

Strategic approach

There are strategies, approaches, and perspectives to answer multiple-choice questions and help maximize points.

Many strategies are known by you and seem like common sense. However, these helpful approaches might be overlooked under the pressure of a timed test.

While no strategy replaces comprehensive preparation, apply probability for success on unfamiliar questions.

Understand the question

Know what the question is asking before selecting an answer. It is surprising how many students do not read (and reread) carefully and rush selecting the wrong answer.

The test-makers anticipate these hasty mistakes, and many enticing answers include the specious choices. A successful student reads the question and understands it precisely before looking at the answers.

Focus on the answer

Separate the vital information from distracters and understand the design and thrust of the question.

Answer the question posed and not merely pick a factually accurate statement or answer a misconstrued question.

Rephrasing the question helps articulate what precisely the correct response requires. When rephrasing, do not change the meaning of the question; assume it is direct and to the point as written.

After selecting the answer, review the question and verify that the choice selected answers the question.

Answer the question before looking at choices

This valuable strategy is applicable if the question asks for generalized factual details. Form a thought response first, then look for the choice that matches your preordained answer.

Select the predetermined statement as it is likely correct.

Factually correct, but wrong

Questions often have incorrect choices that are factually correct but do not answer the question.

Predetermine the answer and do not choose merely a factually correct statement. Verify that the choice answers the question.

Do not fall for the familiar

When in doubt, it is comforting to choose what is familiar. If you recognize a term or concept, you may be tempted to pick that choice impetuously.

However, do not go with familiar answers merely because they are familiar. Think through the answer and how it relates to the question before selecting it.

Words of caution

The words *"all," "none,"* and *"except"* require attention. Be alert with questions containing these words, as the answer may not be apparent on the first read of the question.

Double-check the question

After selecting an answer, return to the question to ensure the selected choice answers the question as asked.

Fill the answers carefully

Many mistakes happen when filling in answers. Filling the answers correctly is simple but crucial. Be attentive to the question number and enter the answer accordingly. If you skip a question, skip it on the answer sheet.

Quantitative multiple-choice questions

Know the equations

Many exam questions require scientific equations, so understand when to use each. As you work with this book, learn to apply formulas and equations and use them in many questions.

Manipulate the formulas

Know how to rearrange the formulas. Many questions require manipulating equations to calculate the correct answer.

Familiarity includes manipulating the terms, understanding relationships, and isolating variables.

Estimating

Estimating helps choose the answer quickly for quantitative questions with a sense of the order of magnitude. Often, estimation enables the correct answer to be identified quickly compared to the time needed for calculations.

Estimating is especially applicable to questions where the answer choices have different orders of magnitude. It saves time to estimate instead of computing the solution.

Evaluate the units

For quantitative problems, analyze the units to build relationships between the question and the correct answer. Understand what value is sought and eliminate wrong choices with improper units.

Make visual notes

Write, draw, or graph the question to determine the information provided, the objective, and the concept tested. Even if a question does not require a graphic answer, a chart or table often allows a solution to become apparent.

Experiments questions

Determine the purpose, methods, variables, and controls of the experiment. Understanding the presented information helps answer the question.

With multiple experiments, understand variations of the same experiment by focusing on the differences. For example, focus on the changes between the first and second experiments, second and third, and first and third. Direct comparison between experiments helps organize the information and apply it to the answer.

Elimination strategies

If the correct answer is not immediately apparent, use the process of elimination.

Use the strategy of educated guessing by eliminating one or two answers. Usually, at least one answer choice is easily identified as wrong. Eliminating even one choice increases the odds of selecting the correct one.

Process of elimination

Eliminate choices:

- Use proportional estimations for quantitative questions to eliminate choices that are too high or low.

- Eliminate answers that are *almost right* or *half right*. Consider *half right* as *wrong* since these distractor choices are purposely included.

- If two answers are direct opposites, the correct answer is likely one of them. However, note if they are direct opposites or another reason to consider them correct. Therefore, eliminate the other choices and narrow the search for the correct one.

- For numerical questions, eliminate the smallest and largest numbers (unless for a reason).

Roman numeral questions

Roman numeral questions present several statements and ask which is/are correct. These questions are tricky for most test-takers because they present more than one potentially correct statement.

Roman numeral questions are often included in combinations with more than one answer. Eliminating a wrong Roman numeral statement eliminates all choices that include it.

Educated guessing

Correct ways to guess

Do not assume you must get every question right; this will add unnecessary stress during the exam. You will (most likely) need to guess some questions.

Answer as many questions correctly as possible without wasting time that should be used to maximize your score.

For challenging questions, random guessing does not help. Use educated guessing after eliminating one or two choices.

Playing the odds

Guessing is a form of "partial credit" because while you might not be sure of the correct answer, you have the relevant knowledge to identify some wrong choices.

There is a 20% chance of correctly guessing for random responses since questions have five choices. Therefore, the odds are guessing 1 question correctly to 4 incorrectly.

Guessing after elimination of answers

After eliminating one answer as wrong, you have a 25% chance for a lucky guess. Therefore, your odds move to 1 question right to 3 questions wrong.

While this may not seem like a dramatic increase, it can make an appreciable difference in your score.

Confidently eliminating two wrong choices increases the chances of guessing correctly to 33%!

When using elimination:

- Do not rely on gut feelings alone to answer questions quickly.

  Understand and recognize the difference between *knowing* and *gut feeling* about the answer. Gut feelings should sparingly be used after the process of elimination.

- Do not fall for answers that sound "clever," and choose "bizarre" answers. Choose them only with a reason to believe they may be correct.

Eliminating Roman numeral choices

A workable strategy for Roman numeral questions is to guess the wrong statement.

For example:

> A. I only
>
> B. III only
>
> C. I and II only
>
> D. I and III only

Notice that statement II does not have an answer dedicated to it. This indicates that statement II is likely wrong and eliminates choice C, narrowing your search to three choices. However, if you are confident that statement II is the answer, do not apply this strategy.

DAT study aids by Sterling Test Prep

Biology Review

Biology Practice Questions

General Chemistry Review

General Chemistry Practice Questions

Organic Chemistry Practice Questions

Visit our Amazon store

DAT Biology

Practice Questions

Page intentionally left blank

Cell and Molecular Biology

Eukaryotic Cell: Structure and Function

1. Facilitated transport can be differentiated from active transport because:

    A. active transport requires a symport

    B. facilitated transport displays saturation kinetics

    C. active transport displays sigmoidal kinetics

    D. active transport requires an energy source

    E. active transport only occurs in the mitochondrial inner membrane

2. The cell is the basic unit of function and reproduction because:

    A. subcellular components cannot regenerate whole cells

    B. cells can move in space

    C. single cells can sometimes produce an entire organism

    D. cells can transform energy to do work

    E. new cells can arise by the fusion of two cells

3. Which is/are NOT able to readily diffuse through plasma membranes without a transport protein?

    I. water

    II. small hydrophobic molecules

    III. small ions

    IV. neutral gas molecules

    A. I only   **C.** I and IV only

    B. I and II only   **D.** III and IV only

                                E. I and III only

4. During a hydropathy analysis of a recently sequenced protein, a researcher discovers that the protein has several regions containing 20-25 hydrophobic amino acids. What conclusion would she draw from this finding?

    A. Protein would be specifically localized in the mitochondrial inner membrane

    B. Protein would be targeted to the mitochondrion

    C. Protein is likely an integral protein

    D. Protein is likely involved in glycolysis

    E. Protein is likely secreted from the cell

5. If a membrane-bound vesicle that contains hydrolytic enzymes is isolated, it is likely a:

    A. vacuole

    B. microbody

    C. chloroplast

    D. phagosome

    E. lysosome

6. A DNA damage checkpoint arrests cells in:

    A. M/G2 transition

    B. G1/G2 transition

    C. G1/S transition

    D. anaphase

    E. S/G1 transition

7. If a segment of double-stranded DNA has a low ratio of guanine-cytosine (G-C) pairs relative to adenine-thymine (A-T) pairs, it is reasonable to assume that this nucleotide segment:

    A. requires less energy to separate the two DNA strands than a comparable segment with a high C-G ratio

    B. requires more energy to separate the two DNA strands than a comparable segment with a high C-G ratio

    C. requires the same energy to separate the two DNA strands as a comparable segment with a high C-G ratio

    D. contains more adenine than thymine

    E. contains more cytosine than guanine

8. In general, phospholipids contain:

    A. a glycerol molecule

    B. saturated fatty acids

    C. unsaturated fatty acids

    D. a cholesterol molecule

    E. a glucose molecule

9. The overall shape of a cell is determined by its:

    A. cell membrane

    B. cytoskeleton

    C. nucleus

    D. cytosol

    E. endoplasmic reticulum

10. Which molecule generates the greatest osmotic pressure when placed into water?

    A. 300 mM NaCl

    B. 250 mM CaCl$_2$

    C. 500 mM glucose

    D. 600 mM urea

    E. 100 mM KCl

11. Which cellular substituent is produced within the nucleus?

    A. Golgi apparatus

    B. lysosome

    C. ribosome

    D. rough endoplasmic reticulum

    E. cell membrane

12. In the initial stages of the cell cycle, progression from one phase to the next is controlled by:

    A. p53 transcription factors   **C.** origin recognition complexes

    B. anaphase-promoting complexes   **D.** pre-replication complexes

                                         E. cyclin–CDK complexes

13. Which is the correct sequence occurring during polypeptide synthesis?

    A. DNA generates tRNA → tRNA anticodon binds to the mRNA codon in the cytoplasm → tRNA is carried by mRNA to the ribosomes, causing amino acids to join in a specific order

    B. DNA generates mRNA → mRNA moves to the ribosome → tRNA anticodon binds to the mRNA codon, causing amino acids to join in their appropriate order

    C. Specific RNA codons cause amino acids to line up in a specific order → tRNA anticodon attaches to mRNA codon → rRNA codon causes the protein to cleave into specific amino acids

    D. DNA regenerates mRNA in the nucleus → mRNA moves to the cytoplasm and attaches to the tRNA anticodon → operon regulates the sequence of amino acids in the appropriate order

    E. DNA generates mRNA → mRNA anticodon binds to tRNA codon causing amino acids to join together in their appropriate order

14. Both prokaryotes and eukaryotes contain:

       I. a plasma membrane   II. ribosomes   III. peroxisomes

    A. I only   **C.** I and II only

    B. II only   **D.** II and III only

                                       E. I, II and III

15. RNA is NOT expected to be in a:

    A. nucleus   **C.** prokaryotic cell

    B. mitochondrion   **D.** ribosome

                                       E. vacuole

16. Phosphotransferase is needed to form the mannose-6-phosphate tag that targets hydrolase enzymes to their lysosomal destination. Defective phosphotransferase causes I-cell disease, whereby the defective organelle which gives rise to this condition is the:

    A. nucleus   **C.** Golgi apparatus

    B. cell membrane   **D.** smooth ER

                                       E. nucleolus

17. Mitochondria and chloroplasts are unusual organelles because they:

    A. synthesize all their ATP using substrate-level phosphorylation

    B. contain cytochrome C oxidase

    C. are devoid of heme-containing proteins

    D. contain nuclear-encoded and organelle-encoded proteins

    E. degrade macromolecules using hydrolytic enzymes

18. All statements are true about cytoskeleton EXCEPT that it:

    A. is not required for mitosis

    B. maintains the cell's shape

    C. gives the cell mechanical support

    D. is composed of microtubules and microfilaments

    E. is important for cell motility

19. Inside the cell, several key events in the cell cycle include:

    I. DNA damage repair and replication completion

    II. centrosome duplication

    III. assembly of the spindle and attachment of the kinetochores to the spindle

    A. I only

    B. I, II and III

    C. I and II only

    D. II and III only

    E. I and III only

20. A researcher labeled *Neurospora* mitochondria with a radioactive phosphatidylcholine membrane component and followed cell division by autoradiography in an unlabeled medium, allowing enough time for one cell division. What results did this scientist observe before concluding that pre-existing mitochondria give rise to new mitochondria?

    A. Daughter mitochondria are labeled equally

    B. Daughter mitochondria are all unlabeled

    C. One-fourth of daughter mitochondria are labeled

    D. Some of the daughter mitochondria are unlabeled, while some are labeled

    E. Daughter mitochondria are all labeled

21. Which involves the post-translational modification of proteins?

    A. peroxisomes

    B. vacuoles

    C. Golgi complex

    D. lysosomes

    E. smooth ER

22. The width of a typical animal cell is closest to:

A. 1 millimeter

B. 20 micrometers

C. 1 micrometer

D. 10 nanometers

E. 100 micrometers

23. Which organelle is identified by the sedimentation coefficient – S units (Svedberg units)?

A. peroxisome

B. nucleus

C. mitochondrion

D. nucleolus

E. ribosome

24. Which is NOT involved in osmosis?

A. H_2O spontaneously moves from a hypertonic to a hypotonic environment

B. H_2O spontaneously moves from an area of high solvent to a low solvent concentration

C. H_2O spontaneously moves from a hypotonic to a hypertonic environment

D. Transport of H_2O

E. Diffusion of H_2O

25. During cell division, cyclin B is marked for destruction by the:

A. p53 transcription factor

B. anaphase-promoting complex

C. CDK complex

D. pre-replication complex

E. maturation promoting factor

26. When a female mouse with a defect in a mitochondrial protein required for fatty acid oxidation is crossed with a wild-type male, all progeny (both male and female) have the wild-type phenotype. Which statement is likely correct?

A. Mice do not exhibit maternal inheritance

B. The defect is a result of an autosomal X-linked recessive trait

C. The defect is a result of an X-linked recessive trait

D. The defect is a result of a recessive mitochondrial gene

E. The defect is a result of a nuclear gene mutation

27. The smooth ER participates in:

A. substrate-level phosphorylation

B. exocytosis

C. synthesis of phosphatidylcholine

D. allosteric activation of enzymes

E. synthesis of cytosolic proteins

28. What type of organelle is in plants but not in animals?

    A. ribosomes   **C.** nucleus

    B. mitochondria   **D.** plastids

                                          E. nucleolus

29. Mitochondrial mutations are often limited to one tissue type. If an individual does not produce blood calcium-decreasing hormone calcitonin, which tissue is likely to carry the mitochondrial mutation?

    A. thyroid   **C.** parathyroid

    B. kidney   **D.** liver

                                          E. spleen

30. The rough ER participates in:

    A. oxidative phosphorylation   **C.** endocytosis

    B. synthesis of plasma membrane proteins   **D.** post-translational modification of enzymes

                                          E. synthesis of lipids

31. The best definition of active transport is the movement of:

    A. solutes across a semipermeable membrane down an electrochemical gradient

    B. solutes across a semipermeable membrane up a concentration gradient

    C. substances across a membrane per the Donnan equilibrium

    D. solutes via osmosis across a semipermeable membrane from high to low concentration

    E. H_2O via diffusion across a semipermeable membrane

32. Overexpression of cyclin D:

    A. increases contact inhibition   **C.** activates apoptosis

    B. decreases telomerase activity   **D.** promotes unscheduled entry into the S phase

                                          E. promotes the transition from G1 to the S phase

33. A failure in which stage of spermatogenesis produces nondisjunction and males with XXY karyotype?

    A. prophase I   **C.** prophase II

    B. metaphase   **D.** telophase

                                          E. anaphase I

34. Protein targeting occurs during the synthesis of which type of proteins?

    A. nuclear proteins   **C.** cytosolic proteins

    B. secreted proteins   **D.** mitochondrial proteins

                                    E. chloroplast proteins

35. The difference between "free" and "attached" ribosomes is that:

    I. Free ribosomes are in the cytoplasm, while attached ribosomes are anchored to the endoplasmic reticulum

    II. Free ribosomes produce proteins in the cytosol, while attached ribosomes produce proteins that are inserted into the ER lumen

    III. Free ribosomes produce proteins that are exported from the cell, while attached ribosomes make proteins for mitochondria and chloroplasts

    A. I only   **C.** I and II only

    B. II only   **D.** I, II and III

                              E. I and III only

36. The concentration of growth hormone receptors will significantly reduce after selective destruction of which structure?

    A. nucleolus   **C.** cytosol

    B. nucleus   **D.** plasma membrane

                              E. peroxisomes

37. All these processes are ATP-dependent, EXCEPT:

    A. export of Na^+ from a neuron

    B. influx of Ca^{2+} into a muscle cell

    C. influx of K^+ into a neuron

    D. exocytosis of neurotransmitter at a nerve terminus

    E. movement of urea across a cell membrane

38. The loss of function of p53 protein results in:

    A. blockage in activation of the anaphase-promoting complex

    B. increase of contact inhibition

    C. elimination of the DNA damage checkpoint

    D. activation of apoptosis

    E. suppression of spindle fiber assembly

39. Which organelle is most closely associated with exocytosis of newly synthesized secretory protein?

    A. peroxisome

    B. ribosome

    C. lysosome

    D. Golgi apparatus

    E. nucleus

40. Plant membranes are more fluid than animal membranes because plant membranes:

    A. contain substantial amounts of cholesterol

    B. have higher amounts of unsaturated fatty acids compared to the membranes of animals

    C. have lower amounts of unsaturated fatty acids compared to the membranes of animals

    D. are only found in the inner membrane of the mitochondria

    E. do not contain glycosylated proteins

41. Which organelles are enclosed in a double membrane?

    I. nucleus   II. chloroplast   III. mitochondrion

    A. I and II only

    B. II and III only

    C. I and III only

    D. I, II and III

    E. I only

42. Proteins are marked and delivered to specific cell locations through:

    A. specific protein transport channels

    B. regulation signals released by the cell's cytoskeleton

    C. post-translational modifications occurring in the Golgi

    D. compartmentalization of the rough ER during protein synthesis

    E. post-translational modifications occurring in the nucleus

43. The presence of which element differentiates a protein from a carbohydrate molecule?

    A. carbon

    B. hydrogen

    C. nitrogen

    D. oxygen

    E. nitrogen and oxygen

44. What change occurs in the capillaries when arterial blood is infused with the plasma protein albumin?

    A. Decreased movement of H_2O from the capillaries into the interstitial fluid

    B. Increased movement of H_2O from the capillaries into the interstitial fluid

    C. Decreased movement of H_2O from the interstitial fluid into the capillaries

    D. Increased permeability to albumin

    E. Decreased permeability to albumin

45. The retinoblastoma protein controls:

A. contact inhibition

B. transition from G1 to S phase

C. activation of apoptosis

D. expression of cyclin D

E. A and C

46. All processes take place in the mitochondrion, EXCEPT:

A. oxidation of pyruvate

B. Krebs cycle

C. electron transport chain

D. reduction of FADH into $FADH_2$

E. glycolysis

47. Which is the most abundant lipid in the human body?

A. teichoic acid

B. peptidoglycan

C. glycogen

D. triglycerides

E. glucose

48. What is the secretory sequence in the flow of newly synthesized protein for export from the cell?

A. Golgi → rough ER → smooth ER → plasma membrane

B. Golgi → rough ER → plasma membrane

C. smooth ER → rough ER → Golgi → plasma membrane

D. rough ER → smooth ER → Golgi → plasma membrane

E. rough ER → Golgi → plasma membrane

49. Digestive lysosomal hydrolysis would affect all the following EXCEPT:

A. proteins

B. minerals

C. nucleotides

D. lipids

E. carbohydrates

50. Recycling of organelles within the cell is accomplished through autophagy by:

A. mitochondria

B. peroxisomes

C. nucleolus

D. lysosomes

E. rough endoplasmic reticulum

51. All are lipid derivatives EXCEPT:

A. carotenoids

B. albumins

C. waxes

D. steroids

E. lecithin

52. Defective attachment of a chromosome to the spindle:

    A. blocks activation of the anaphase-promoting complex

    B. activates exit from mitosis

    C. prevents overexpression of cyclin D

    D. activates sister chromatid separation

    E. promotes the transition from G1 to the S phase

53. Which stage is when human cells with a single unreplicated copy of the genome are formed?

    A. mitosis   **C.** meiosis I

    B. meiosis II   **D.** interphase

                                    E. G1

54. Which organelle in the cell is the site of fatty acid, phospholipid, and steroid synthesis?

    A. endosome   **C.** rough endoplasmic reticulum

    B. peroxisome   **D.** smooth endoplasmic reticulum

                                      E. chloroplast

55. Which eukaryotic organelle is NOT membrane-bound?

    A. nucleus   **C.** centriole

    B. plastid   **D.** chloroplast

                                    E. C and D

56. Which phase of mitotic division do spindle fibers split the centromere and separate the sister chromatids?

    A. interphase   **C.** prophase

    B. telophase   **D.** metaphase

                                  E. anaphase

57. All are correct about cyclic AMP (cAMP), EXCEPT:

    A. the enzyme that catalyzes the formation of cAMP is in the cytoplasm

    B. membrane receptors can activate the enzyme that forms cAMP

    C. ATP is the precursor molecule in the formation of cAMP

    D. adenylate cyclase is the enzyme that catalyzes the formation of cAMP

    E. cAMP is a second messenger that triggers a cascade of intracellular reactions when a peptide hormone binds to a receptor on the cell membrane

Molecular Biology of Eukaryotes

1. Which primers should be used to amplify the DNA shown in the figure below via PCR?

A. 5'-CCCC-3' and 5'-AAAA-3'

B. 5'-GGGG-3' and 5'-TTTT-3'

C. 5'-AAAA-3' and 5'-GGGG-3'

D. 5'-TTTT-3' and 5'-CCCC-3'

E. none of the above

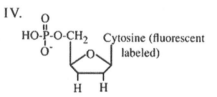

2. The major phenotypic expression of a genotype is in:

A. rRNA

B. tRNA

C. mRNA

D. nucleic acids

E. proteins

3. Which molecule is used in DNA sequencing to cause termination when the template strand is G?

I. $HO-P-O-P-O-P-O-CH_2$ Guanine (fluorescent labeled)

III. $HO-P-O-P-O-P-O-CH_2$ Cytosine (fluorescent labeled)

II. $HO-P-O-P-O-P-O-CH_2$ Cytosine (fluorescent labeled)

IV. $HO-P-O-CH_2$ Cytosine (fluorescent labeled)

A. molecule I & III

B. molecule III & IV

C. molecule II

D. molecule IV

E. molecule III

4. Which is NOT a part of the post-translational modification of protein?

A. addition of a 3' poly-A tail

B. phosphorylation

C. methylation

D. glycosylation

E. acetylation

5. A chromosome with its centromere in the middle is:

A. acrocentric

B. telocentric

C. metacentric

D. holocentric

E. midcentromeric

6. Which is NOT an example of an environmental factor affecting how a gene is expressed?

A. Heat shock proteins are synthesized in cells after a temperature increase

B. *Drosophila* with specific genes develop bent wings when incubated at low temperatures and straight wings when incubated at elevated temperatures

C. Himalayan hares change hair color after cooling in the naturally warm regions

D. Shivering occurs after a decrease in body temperature

E. All the above

7. cDNA libraries contain:

A. promoters

B. intron portions of expressed genes

C. exon portions of expressed genes

D. non-expressed retrotransposons

E. both introns and exons of expressed genes

8. Individual genes often encode for:

    I. enzymes with tertiary structure

    II. enzymes with quaternary structure

    III. complex polysaccharides

A. I only

B. II only

C. I and II only

D. I, II and III

E. I and III only

9. What enzyme is often used to make a genomic library?

A. RNA polymerase

B. reverse transcriptase

C. deoxyribonuclease

D. DNA polymerase

E. restriction endonuclease

10. Attachment of glycoprotein side chains and amino acid hydroxylation are post-translational modifications. What is the site for protein glycosylation?

    I. Lysosomes

    II. Golgi apparatus

    III. Rough endoplasmic reticulum

A. II only

B. III only

C. I and II only

D. II and III only

E. I, II and III

11. The enzyme used for restoring the ends of the DNA in a chromosome is:

    A. telomerase   **C.** polymerase

    B. helicase   **D.** gyrase

                                 E. ligase

12. A cDNA library is made using:

    A. DNA from the region where the gene of interest is expressed

    B. mRNA from the region where the gene of interest is expressed

    C. mRNA from the region where the gene of interest is not expressed

    D. rRNA from the region where the gene of interest is expressed

    E. all the above

13. Which statement is the *central dogma* of molecular biology?

    A. Information flow between DNA, RNA, and protein is reversible

    B. Information flow in the cell is unidirectional, from protein to RNA to DNA

    C. The genetic code is ambiguous but not degenerate

    D. The DNA sequence of a gene can be predicted from the amino acid sequence of the protein

    E. Information flow in the cell is unidirectional, from DNA to RNA to protein

14. What is alternative splicing?

    A. Cleavage of peptide bonds to create different proteins

    B. Cleavage of DNA to make different genes

    C. Cleavage of hnRNA to make different mRNAs

    D. A new method of splicing that does not involve snRNPs

    E. None of the above

15. This compound is synthesized by the nucleolus and is necessary for ribosomal function.

    A. ribozyme   **C.** liposome

    B. riboflavin   **D.** rRNA

                                 E. tRNA

16. *E. coli* RNA polymerase:

        I. synthesizes RNA in the 5' to 3' direction   III. copies a DNA template

        II. synthesizes RNA in the 3' to 5' direction   IV. copies an RNA template

    A. I and III only   **C.** I and IV only

    B. II and III only   **D.** II and IV only

                                 E. I only

17. Within primary eukaryotic transcripts, introns are:

A. often functioning as exons in other genes

B. different in size and number among different genes

C. joined to form mature mRNA

D. highly conserved in nucleotide sequence

E. absent from the primary eukaryotic transcript because they are not transcribed

18. Which statement(s) is/are TRUE for eukaryotic protein synthesis?

    I. exons of mRNA are spliced together before translation

    II. proteins must be spliced soon after translation

    III. prokaryotic ribosomes are smaller than eukaryotic ribosomes

A. I only

B. II only

C. I and II only

D. I, II and III only

E. I and III only

19. Which would decrease the transcription of retrotransposons?

    I. Acetylation of histones associated with the retrotransposon

    II. Deacetylation of histones associated with the retrotransposon

    III. Methylation of retrotransposon DNA

    IV. Loss of methylation of retrotransposon DNA

A. I and II only

B. I and III only

C. II and III only

D. III and IV only

E. II and IV only

20. Which is an exception to the principle of the *central dogma*?

A. yeast

B. retroviruses

C. bread mold

D. skin cells

E. onion cells

21. miRNA is generated from the cleavage of:

A. double-stranded RNA

B. single-stranded RNA

C. double-stranded DNA

D. single-stranded DNA

E. None of the above

22. The DNA polymerase cannot fully replicate the 3' DNA end, which results in shorter DNA with every division cycle. The new strand synthesis mechanism that follows prevents the loss of the DNA coding region.

Which structure is present at the location of the new strand synthesis?

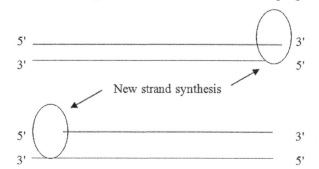

A. kinetochore

B. centrosome

C. telomere

D. centromere

E. chromatid

23. The cell structure composed of a core particle of 8 histones is:

A. telomere

B. nucleosome

C. kinetochore

D. centrosome

E. spindle

24. Which statement is CORRECT about miRNA? (interference RNA):

    I. It is a backup system for tRNA in the regulation of translation

    II. It base pairs with mRNA and causes it to be cleaved

    III. It base pairs with mRNA and prevents its translation

A. II only

B. I and II only

C. II and III only

D. I, II and III

E. I and III only

25. The region of DNA in prokaryotes to which RNA polymerase binds most tightly is the:

A. promoter

B. poly C center

C. enhancer

D. operator site

E. minor groove

26. Genomic libraries contain:

    I. promoters

    II. intron portions of genes

    III. exon portions of genes

    IV. retrotransposons

A. I and II only

B. I and III only

C. I, II and III only

D. II and III only

E. I, II, III and IV

27. Which RNA molecules have a common secondary structure called cloverleaf and are relatively small?

 A. hnRNA

 B. mRNA

 C. rRNA

 D. tRNA

 E. miRNA

28. A chromosome when the linear sequence of a group of genes is reverse of typical sequences has undergone:

 A. translocation

 B. inversion

 C. duplication

 D. deletion

 E. position effect variegation

29. If a drug inhibits ribosomal RNA synthesis, which eukaryotic organelle is most affected by this drug?

 A. Golgi apparatus

 B. lysosome

 C. mitochondria

 D. nucleus

 E. nucleolus

30. What evidence shows that the AG gene is vital for forming reproductive organs in *Arabidopsis* flowers?

 A. The AG gene encodes a miRNA

 B. RNA blot experiments show that the AG gene is strongly expressed in flowers, leaves, and roots

 C. The AG gene is in all flowering Arabidopsis plants

 D. AG mutant flowers do not have reproductive organs

 E. None of the above

31. Which statement about the glycocalyx is FALSE?

 A. May be composed of polysaccharide

 B. May be composed of polypeptide

 C. Protects from osmotic lysis

 D. Is used to adhere to surfaces

 E. May be responsible for virulence

32. Which does NOT affect chromatin structure?

 A. tandem repeats

 B. DNA acetylation

 C. histone acetylation

 D. chromatin remodeling proteins

 E. DNA methylation

33. Which enzyme maintains and regulates normal DNA coiling?

A. ligase

B. helicase

C. DNA polymerase I

D. DNA polymerase III

E. topoisomerase

34. RNA polymerase uses the two ribonucleotide triphosphates shown below to make 5'-CG-3'. Which of the indicated phosphorous atoms participates in phosphodiester bond formation?

A. phosphorous atom A

B. phosphorous atom B

C. phosphorous atom C

D. phosphorous atom D

E. phosphorous atom E

35. When eukaryotic mRNA hybridizes with its corresponding DNA coding strand (i.e., heteroduplex analysis) and is visualized by electron microscopy, the looping strands of nucleic acid which are seen represent:

A. introns

B. exons

C. lariat structures

D. inverted repeats

E. overlapping genes

36. Which statement does NOT accurately describe an aspect of the nucleosome?

A. has an octet of proteins

B. has a histone H1

C. is the first step in compacting the DNA in the nucleus

D. has DNA wrapped on the outside

E. has a histone H3

37. Which is NOT a bacterial cell wall chemical component?

A. N-acetylmuramic acid

B. peptidoglycan

C. teichoic acids

D. peptide chains

E. cellulose

38. Combinatorial control of gene transcription in eukaryotes is when:

I. each transcription factor regulates only one gene

II. a single transcription factor regulates a combination of genes

III. presence or absence of a combination of transcription factors is required

A. I only

B. II only

C. II and III only

D. III only

E. I, II and III

39. Which post-transcriptional modifications have matured eukaryotic mRNAs undergone before being transported into the cytoplasm?

    A. addition of 3' G-cap and 5' poly-A-tail, removal of introns, and splicing of exons

    B. RNA splicing together of exons and removal of introns

    C. RNA addition of 5' cap and 3' poly-A-tail

    D. addition of 5' G-cap and 3' poly-A-tail, removal of introns, and splicing of exons

    E. RNA splicing together introns and removal of exons

40. Which statement about gene expression is correct?

    A. The ribosome binding site lies at the 3' end of the mRNA

    B. The second round of transcription can begin before the preceding transcript is completed

    C. Only one gene can be present within a given DNA sequence

    D. Mistakes in transcription are corrected by RNA polymerase

    E. Change in genotype always results in a changed phenotype

41. Considering that in vitro, the transcription factor SP1 binds nucleic acids with high affinity, where would the radio-labeled SP1 likely NOT be found?

    A. Golgi apparatus   **C.** nucleolus

    B. mitochondria   **D.** ribosomes

                                      E. nucleus

42. During splicing, the snRNA base pairs with:

    A. mRNA sequences in the intron   **C.** DNA sequences in the intron

    B. hnRNA sequences in the exon   **D.** DNA sequences in the exon

                                      E. hnRNA sequences in the intron

43. Which macromolecule would be repaired rather than degraded?

    A. triglyceride   **C.** polypeptide

    B. polynucleotide   **D.** polysaccharide

                                        E. proteins

44. The poly-A tail of RNA is:

    A. encoded in the DNA sequence of the gene

    B. added by the ribosome during translation

    C. base paired with tRNA during translation initiation

    D. enzymatically added soon after transcription is finished

    E. in the cytoplasm of the cell

45. Which type of histone is not part of the nucleosome core particle?

A. H3

B. H2B

C. H2A

D. H4

E. H1

46. During splicing, the phosphodiester bond at the upstream exon/intron boundary is hydrolyzed by:

A. protein within the snRNP complex

B. 2'-OH of a base within the intron

C. 3'-OH of a base within the intron

D. RNA polymerase III

E. 3'-OH of a base within the exon

47. What is the expected charge, if any, on a histone that binds to DNA?

A. neutral

B. depends on the DNA conformation

C. positive

D. negative

E. neutral or negative

48. RNA polymerase uses the two ribonucleotide triphosphates shown below to make 5'-CG-3'. Which of the indicated oxygen atoms participates in phosphodiester bond formation?

A. oxygen atom A

B. oxygen atom B

C. oxygen atom C

D. oxygen atom D

E. either oxygen atom B or D

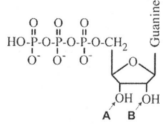 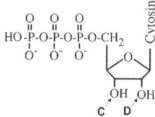

49. Chromosome regions with very few functional genes are:

A. heterochromatin

B. mid-repetitive sequences

C. euchromatin

D. chromatids

E. nucleosomes

50. Which is characteristic of prokaryotes only?

A. primary transcripts of RNA have introns

B. the processed RNA has a poly-A

C. the processed RNA has a 5'-cap

D. transcription of the RNA occurs simultaneously with translation for the RNA

E. the primary transcript is longer than the mRNA

51. What is the product of combining DNA from different sources?

    A. recombinant DNA

    B. clone

    C. hybrid DNA

    D. mutant

    E. plasmid

52. Transformation of a plant cell is successful when:

    A. plasmid cannot enter the cell

    B. cell produces daughter cells that subsequently produce other daughter cells

    C. cell goes through programmed cell death (apoptosis)

    D. cell's enzymes destroy the plasmid after it enters the cell

    E. foreign DNA is integrated into one of the plant cell's chromosomes

53. The figure shown illustrates:

    A. PCR making a copy of the DNA

    B. enzyme cutting the DNA

    C. use of hybridization in genetic engineering

    D. DNA sequencing via gel electrophoresis

    E. insertion of a genetic marker

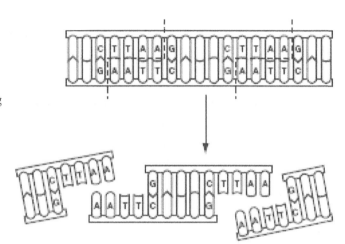

54. Between which two nucleotides are DNA cut in the figure?

    A. thymine and adenine

    B. adenine and guanine

    C. adenine and cytosine

    D. thymine and guanine

    E. thymine and cytosine

Cellular Metabolism & Enzymes

1. The atom that generates a hydrogen bond to stabilize the α-helical configuration of a polypeptide is:

A. peptide bond atom

B. atom in the R-groups

C. hydrogen of carbonyl oxygen

D. hydrogen of the amino nitrogen

E. two of the above

2. The ATP molecule contains three phosphate groups, two of which are:

A. bound as phosphoanhydrides

B. bound to adenosine

C. never hydrolyzed from the molecule

D. cleaved off during most biochemical reactions

E. equivalent in energy for the hydrolysis of each of the phosphates

3. Which attractive force is used by side chains of nonpolar amino acids to interact with nonpolar amino acids?

A. ionic bonds

B. hydrogen bonds

C. hydrophobic interaction

D. disulfide bonds

E. dipole-dipole

4. Fermentation yields less energy than aerobic respiration because:

A. it requires a greater expenditure of cellular energy

B. glucose molecules are not completely oxidized

C. it requires more time for ATP production

D. oxaloacetic acid serves as the final H^+ acceptor

E. it occurs in H_2O

5. How would the reaction kinetics of an enzyme and its substrate change if an anti-substrate antibody is added?

A. The antibody binds to the substrate, which increases the V_{max}

B. The antibody binds to the substrate, which decreases K_m

C. No change because K_m and V_{max} are independent of antibody concentration

D. The antibody binds the substrate, which decreases V_{max}

E. The antibody binds to the substrate, which increases K_m

6. Metabolism is:

    A. consumption of energy

    B. release of energy

    C. all conversions of matter and energy taking place in an organism

    D. production of heat by chemical reactions

    E. exchange of nutrients and waste products with the environment

7. During alcoholic fermentation, all occur EXCEPT:

    A. release of CO_2

    B. oxidation of glyceraldehyde-3-phosphate

    C. oxygen is not consumed in the reaction

    D. ATP synthesis as a result of oxidative phosphorylation

    E. NAD^+ is produced

8. When determining a protein's amino acid sequence, acid hydrolysis causes partial destruction of tryptophan, conversion of asparagine into aspartic acid, and conversion of glutamine into glutamic acid. Which statement is NOT correct?

    A. Glutamine concentration is related to the level of aspartic acid

    B. Glutamic acid levels are an indirect indicator of glutamine concentration

    C. Tryptophan levels cannot be estimated accurately

    D. Asparagine levels cannot be estimated accurately

    E. Tryptophan and asparagine levels cannot be estimated accurately

9. What is the correct sequence of energy sources used by the body?

    A. fats → glucose → other carbohydrates → proteins

    B. glucose → other carbohydrates → fats → proteins

    C. glucose → other carbohydrates → proteins → fats

    D. glucose → fats → proteins → other carbohydrates

    E. fats → proteins → glucose → other carbohydrates

10. Enzymes act by:

    A. lowering the overall free energy change of the reaction

    B. decreasing the distance reactants must diffuse to find each other

    C. increasing the activation energy

    D. shifting equilibrium towards product formation

    E. decreasing the activation energy

11. For the following reaction, which statement is TRUE?

$$ATP + Glucose \rightarrow Glucose\text{-}6\text{-}phosphate + ADP$$

A. reaction results in the formation of a phosphodiester bond

B. reaction is endergonic

C. reaction is part of the Krebs cycle

D. free energy change for the reaction is approx. –4 kcal

E. reaction does not require an enzyme

12. Which is the correct cAMP classification because cAMP-dependent protein phosphorylation activates hormone-sensitive lipase?

A. DNA polymerase

B. lipoproteins

C. glycosphingolipids

D. second messenger

E. phospholipids

13. Which statement is NOT true about the Krebs cycle?

A. Krebs cycle occurs in the matrix of the mitochondria

B. Citrate is an intermediate in the Krebs cycle

C. Krebs cycle produces nucleotides such as NADH and $FADH_2$

D. Krebs cycle is linked to glycolysis by pyruvate

E. Krebs cycle is the single greatest direct source of ATP in the cell

14. The rate of V_{max} is directly related to:

I. Enzyme concentration

II. Substrate concentration

III. Concentration of a competitive inhibitor

A. I, II, and III

B. I and III only

C. I and II only

D. I only

E. II and III only

15. A reaction in which the substrate glucose binds to the enzyme hexokinase, and the conformation of both molecules changes, is an example of:

A. lock and key mechanism

B. induced-fit mechanism

D. allosteric inhibition

E. covalent bond formation at the active site

C. competitive inhibition

16. You are studying an enzyme that catalyzes a reaction with a free energy change of +5 kcal. If you double the amount of enzyme in a reaction mixture, what would be the free energy change for the reaction?

    A. −10 kcal

    B. −5 kcal

    C. 0 kcal

    D. +5 kcal

    E. +10 kcal

17. Glucokinase and hexokinase catalyze the first glycolysis reaction; glucokinase has a higher K_m. Which is a correct statement if K_m is equal to [Substrate] = $1/2 V_{max}$?

    A. hexokinase is always functional and is not regulated by negative feedback

    B. hexokinase and glucokinase are not isozymes

    C. glucokinase is not a zymogen

    D. glucokinase becomes active from elevated levels of fructose

    E. none of the above

18. α-helices and β-pleated sheets are characteristic of which level of protein folding?

    A. primary

    B. secondary

    C. tertiary

    D. quaternary

    E. secondary & tertiary

19. Coenzymes are:

    A. minerals such as Ca^{2+} and Mg^{2+}

    B. small inorganic molecules that work with an enzyme to enhance the reaction rate

    C. linking together of two or more enzymes

    D. small molecules that do not regulate enzymes

    E. small organic molecules that work with an enzyme to enhance the reaction rate

20. Hemoglobin is an example of a protein that:

    A. is initially inactive in cell

    B. has a quaternary structure

    C. conducts a catalytic reaction

    D. has only a tertiary structure

    E. has a signal sequence

21. The site of the TCA cycle in eukaryotic cells, as opposed to prokaryotes, is:

    A. mitochondria

    B. endoplasmic reticulum

    C. cytosol

    D. nucleolus

    E. intermembrane space of the mitochondria

22. All are metabolic waste products, EXCEPT:

A. lactate
B. pyruvate

C. CO_2
D. H_2O
E. ammonia

23. When measuring the reaction velocity as a function of substrate concentration, what is likely to occur if the enzyme concentration changes?

A. V_{max} changes, while K_m remains constant
B. V_{max} remains constant, while V changes
C. V_{max} remains constant, while K_m changes
D. V_{max} remains constant, while V and K_m change
E. Not possible to predict without experimental data

24. A holoenzyme is:

A. inactive enzyme without its cofactor
B. inactive enzyme without its coenzyme

C. active enzyme with its organic moiety
D. active enzyme with its coenzyme
E. active enzyme with its cofactor

25. *Clostridium butyricum* is a heterotrophic anaerobe that grows on glucose, converting it to butyric acid as a product. If the free energy for this reaction is –50 kcal, the maximum number of ATP that this organism can synthesize from one molecule of glucose is approximately:

A. 5 ATP
B. 36 ATP

C. 7 ATP
D. 38 ATP
E. 0 ATP

26. Which amino acid is directly affected by dithiothreitol (DTT), known to reduce and break disulfide bonds?

A. methionine
B. leucine

C. glutamine
D. cysteine
E. proline

27. Which answer represents a correct pairing of aspects for cellular respiration?

A. Krebs cycle – cytoplasm
B. fatty acid degradation – lysosomes
C. electron transport chain – inner mitochondrial membrane
D. glycolysis – inner mitochondrial membrane
E. ATP synthesis – outer mitochondrial membrane

28. An apoenzyme is:

A. active enzyme with its organic moiety

B. inactive enzyme without its inorganic cofactor

C. active enzyme with its cofactor

D. active enzyme with its coenzyme

E. inactive enzyme without its cofactor

29. Several forces stabilize tertiary structure of a protein. Which is likely involved in this stabilization?

A. glycosidic bonds

B. disulfide bonds

C. peptide bonds

D. anhydride bonds

E. phosphodiester bonds

30. In the non-oxidative branch of the pentose phosphate pathway, transketolase is a reaction catalyst enzyme, and its activity depends on a prosthetic group. Which bond is used by a prosthetic group to attach to its target?

A. van der Waals interactions

B. covalent bond

C. ionic bond

D. hydrogen bond

E. dipole-dipole interactions

31. The process of $C_6H_{12}O_6 + O_2 \rightarrow CO_2 + H_2O$ is completed in the:

A. plasma membrane

B. cytoplasm

C. ribosome

D. nucleus

E. mitochondria

32. In hyperthyroidism, oxidative metabolism rates measured through basal metabolic rate (BMR) will be:

A. indeterminable

B. below normal

C. above normal

D. normal

E. between below normal to normal

33. Cofactors are:

    I. small inorganic molecules that work with an enzyme to enhance the reaction rate

    II. small organic molecules that work with an enzyme to enhance the reaction rate

    III. small molecules that regulate enzyme activity

A. I only

B. I and II only

C. II and III only

D. I, II and III

E. I and III only

34. All proteins:

A. are post-translationally modified

B. have a primary structure

C. have catalytic activity

D. contain prosthetic groups

E. contain disulfide bonds

35. After being gently denatured with the denaturant removed, proteins can recover significant activity because recovery of the structure depends on?

A. $4°$ structure of the polypeptide

B. $3°$ structure of the polypeptide

C. $2°$ structure of the polypeptide

D. $1°$ structure of the polypeptide

E. interactions between the polypeptide and its prosthetic groups

36. All statements about glycolysis are true, EXCEPT:

A. end-product can be lactate, ethanol, CO_2, and pyruvate

B. $FADH_2$ is produced during glycolysis

C. a molecule of glucose is converted into two molecules of pyruvate

D. net total of two ATPs are produced

E. NADH is produced

37. Vitamins are:

A. necessary components in the human diet

B. present in plants but not in animals

C. absent in bacteria within the gastrointestinal tract

D. all water-soluble

E. inorganic components of the diet

38. Hemoglobin is a protein that contains a:

A. site where proteolysis occurs

B. phosphate group at its active site

C. bound zinc atom

D. prosthetic group

E. serine phosphate at its active site

39. Which amino acid is nonoptically active, lacking four different groups bonded to the α carbon?

A. valine

B. aspartic acid

C. glutamate

D. cysteine

E. glycine

40. Which statement is TRUE for the glycolytic pathway?

   A. glucose produces a net of two molecules of ATP and two molecules of NADH

   B. glucose produces one molecule of pyruvate

   C. O_2 is a reactant for glycolysis

   D. glucose is partially reduced

   E. pyruvate is the final product of the Krebs cycle and is intermediate for the next series of reactions in cellular respiration

41. Which metabolic process occurs in the mitochondria?

     I. Krebs cycle   II. glycolysis   III. electron transport chain

   A. II only   **C.** II and III only

   B. I and III only   **D.** I, II and III

                             E. I and II only

42. Which statement below best describes the usual relationship of the inhibitor molecule to the allosteric enzyme in feedback inhibition of enzyme activity?

   A. The inhibitor is the substrate of the enzyme

   B. The inhibitor is the product of the enzyme-catalyzed reaction

   C. The inhibitor is the final product of the metabolic pathway

   D. The inhibitor is a metabolically unrelated signal molecule

   E. The inhibitor binds to a tertiary protein

43. *Clostridium butyricum* is an obligate anaerobe that grows on glucose and converts it to butyric acid. If the ΔG for this reaction is –50 kcal, the synthesis of ATP occurs through:

   A. substrate-level phosphorylation

   B. oxidative phosphorylation

   C. neither substrate-level nor oxidative phosphorylation

   D. both substrate-level and oxidative phosphorylation

   E. electron transport cascade

44. While covalent bonds are the strongest bonds of protein structure, which are connected by a peptide bond?

   A. ammonium group and ester group   **C.** the α carbons

   B. two amino groups   **D.** two carboxylate groups

                               E. amino group and carboxylate group

45. All statements apply to oxidative phosphorylation, EXCEPT:

   A. it can occur under anaerobic conditions

   B. it produces two ATPs for each $FADH_2$

   C. it involves O_2 as the final electron acceptor

   D. it occurs on the inner membrane of the mitochondrion

   E. it involves a cytochrome electron transport chain

46. Like other catalysts, enzymes:

   I. increase the rate of reactions without affecting ΔG

   II. shift the chemical equilibrium from more reactants to more products

   III. do not alter the chemical equilibrium between reactants and products

   A. I only   **C.** I and III only

   B. I and II only   **D.** III only

                        E. II and III only

47. Enzyme activity can be regulated by:

   I. zymogen proteolysis

   II. changes in substrate concentration

   III. post-translational modifications

   A. I only   **C.** I, II and III

   B. II and III only   **D.** I and II only

                        E. I and III only

48. Which interactions stabilize parallel and non-parallel beta-pleated sheets?

   A. hydrophobic interactions   **C.** van der Waals interactions

   B. hydrogen bonds   **D.** covalent bonds

                        E. dipole-dipole interactions

49. Glycogen is:

   A. degraded by glycogenesis   **C.** unbranched molecule

   B. synthesized by glycogenolysis   **D.** in both plants and animals

                        E. the storage polymer of glucose

50. If $[S] = 2\,K_m$, what portion of active sites of the enzyme is filled by substrate?

   A. 3/4   **C.** 1/2

   B. 2/3   **D.** 1/3

                        E. 1/4

51. In allosteric regulation, how is enzyme activity affected by binding a small regulatory molecule to the enzyme?

    A. It is inhibited

    B. It is stimulated

    C. Can be either stimulated or inhibited

    D. Is neither stimulated nor inhibited

    E. The rate increases to twice K_m and then plateaus

52. All biological reactions:

    A. are exergonic

    B. have an activation energy

    C. are endergonic

    D. occur without a catalyst

    E. are irreversible

53. In eukaryotes, energy is trapped in a high-energy phosphate group during oxidative phosphorylation in the:

    A. nucleus

    B. mitochondrial matrix

    C. inner mitochondrial membrane

    D. outer mitochondrial membrane

    E. cytoplasmic face of the plasma membrane

54. All statements about enzymes are true, EXCEPT:

    A. They function optimally at a particular temperature

    B. They function optimally at a particular pH

    C. They may interact with non-protein molecules to achieve biological activity

    D. Their activity is not affected by a genetic mutation

    E. They are almost always proteins

55. The Gibbs free-energy change (ΔG) of a reaction is determined by:

    I. intrinsic properties of the reactants and products

    II. concentrations of the reactants and products

    III. the temperature of the reactants and products

    A. I only

    B. I and III only

    C. II and III only

    D. I, II and III

    E. I and II only

Biomolecules

1. The linear sequence of amino acids along a peptide chain determines its:

A. primary structure

B. secondary structure

C. tertiary structure

D. quaternary structure

E. none of the above

2. There are [ ] different types of major biomolecules used by humans.

A. a few dozen

B. four

C. several thousand

D. several million

E. a few hundred

3. Amino acids are linked to one another in a protein by which of the following bonds?

A. amide bonds

B. carboxylate bonds

C. ester bonds

D. amine bonds

E. glycosidic bonds

4. What type of protein structure corresponds to a spiral alpha-helix of amino acids?

A. primary

B. secondary

C. tertiary

D. quaternary

E. none of the above

5. Proteins are characterized by the fact that they:

A. always have quaternary structures

B. retain their conformation above 35-40 °C

C. have a primary structure formed by covalent linkages

D. are composed of a single peptide chain

E. none of the above

6. Members of which class of biomolecules is the building blocks of proteins?

A. fatty acids

B. amino acids

C. glycerols

D. monosaccharides

E. nucleic acids

7. Proteins are polymers consisting of which monomer units?

A. keto acids

B. amide

C. amino acids

D. ketones

E. polyaldehydes

8. Why might a change in pH cause a protein to denature?

A. The hydrogen bonds between the hydrophobic portions of the protein collapse due to extra protons

B. The disulfide bridges open

C. The functional groups that give the protein its shape becomes protonated or deprotonated

D. The water hardens and causes the protein's shape to change

E. All the above

9. Collagen is an example of a(n):

A. storage protein

B. transport protein

C. enzyme

D. structural protein

E. hormone

10. The coiling of a chain of amino acids describes a protein's:

A. primary structure

B. secondary structure

C. tertiary structure

D. quaternary structure

E. none of the above

11. What is the name given to the localized bending and folding of a polypeptide backbone of a protein molecule?

A. primary structure

B. secondary structure

C. tertiary structure

D. quaternary structure

E. zymogen structure

12. Which of the following macromolecules are composed of polypeptides?

A. amino acids

B. proteins

C. carbohydrates

D. fats

E. steroids

13. What is the purpose of the plasma membrane?

A. Storing of the genetic material of the cell

B. Retaining water in the cell to prevent it from dehydrating

C. Acting as a cell wall to give the cell structure and support

D. Acting as a boundary, but letting molecules in and out

E. None of the above

14. It is important to have cholesterol in one's body because:

    A. it breaks down extra fat lipids

    B. it serves as the starting material for the biosynthesis of most other steroids

    C. it is the starting material for the building of glycogen

    D. the brain is made almost entirely of cholesterol

    E. it mainly serves as an energy reserve

15. Cholesterol belongs to the [   ] group of lipids.

    A. prostaglandin

    B. triacylglycerol

    C. saccharides

    D. steroid

    E. wax

16. The function of cholesterol in a cell membrane is to:

    A. act as a precursor to steroid hormones

    B. take part in the reactions that produce bile acids

    C. maintain structure due to its flat rigid characteristics

    D. attract hydrophobic molecules to form solid deposits

    E. none of the above

17. The biochemical roles of lipids are:

    A. short-term energy storage, transport of molecules, and structural support

    B. storage of excess energy, component of cell membranes, and chemical messengers

    C. catalysis, protection against outside invaders, motion

    D. component of cell membranes, catalysis, and structural support

    E. neurotransmitters, hormones, transport of molecules

18. Which of the following molecules is an omega-3 fatty acid?

    A. oleic acid

    B. linolenic acid

    C. linoleic acid

    D. palmitic acid

    E. none of the above

19. Which of the following is a lipid?

    A. lactose

    B. aniline

    C. nicotine

    D. estradiol

    E. collagen

20. Lipids are compounds soluble in:

A. glucose solution

B. organic solvents

C. distilled water

D. normal saline solution

E. oxygen

21. Which statement regarding fatty acids is NOT correct? Fatty acids:

A. are always liquids

B. are long-chain carboxylic acids

C. are usually unbranched chains

D. usually have an even number of carbon atoms

E. none of the above

22. Unsaturated triacylglycerols are usually [   ] because [   ]?

A. liquids … they have relatively short fatty acid chains

B. liquids … the kinks in their fatty acid chains prevent their fitting closely

C. liquids … they contain impurities from their natural sources

D. solids … they have relatively long fatty acid chains

E. solids … the similar zig-zag shape of their fatty acid chains allows them to fit closely

23. Oils are generally [   ] at room temperature and are obtained from [   ]:

A. liquids … plants

B. liquids … animals

C. solids … plants

D. solids … animals

E. none of the above

24. Lipids are naturally occurring compounds which all:

A. contain fatty acids as structural units

B. are water-insoluble but soluble in nonpolar solvents

C. contain ester groups

D. contains cholesterol

E. are unsaturated

25. Saturated fats are [   ] at room temperature and are obtained from [   ]?

A. liquids; plants

B. liquids; animals

C. solids; plants

D. solids; animals

E. solids; plants and animals

26. How many molecules of fatty acid are needed to produce one molecule of fat or oil?

A. 1

B. 1.5

C. 2

D. 3

E. 6

27. How many fatty acids are in a phospholipid molecule?

A. 0

B. 1

C. 2

D. 3

E. variable

28. Which of the following is NOT a function of lipids within the body?

A. cushioning to prevent injury

B. insulation

C. energy reserve

D. precursor for glucose catabolism

E. precursor for the synthesis of androgens

29. Which of the following statements describes most monosaccharides?

A. They are unsaturated compounds

B. They are rarely monomers in nature

C. They are composed of carbon, hydrogen, and oxygen, with each carbon bound to at least one oxygen

D. They are insoluble

E. None of the above

30. The three elements in carbohydrates are [ ], [ ] and [ ]:

A. nitrogen, oxygen, hydrogen

B. carbon, hydrogen, oxygen

C. carbon, hydrogen, water

D. nitrogen, oxygen, carbon

E. carbon, nitrogen, hydrogen

31. Fructose does not break apart into smaller units because it is a(n):

A. monosaccharide

B. polysaccharide

C. hexose

D. aldose

E. disaccharide

32. Which of the following molecules is a disaccharide?

A. fructose

B. cellulose

C. amylose

D. glucose

E. lactose

33. What is the major biological function of the glycogen biomolecule?

A. It is used to synthesize disaccharides

B. It is the building block of proteins

C. It stores glucose in animal cells

D. It is a storage form of sucrose

E. It stores glucose in plant cells

34. A carbohydrate that gives two molecules when it is completely hydrolyzed is a:

A. polysaccharide

B. starch

C. monosaccharide

D. disaccharide

E. trisaccharide

35. Which group of carbohydrates CANNOT be hydrolyzed to give smaller molecules?

A. oligosaccharides

B. trisaccharides

C. disaccharides

D. monosaccharides

E. polysaccharides

36. Carbohydrate can be defined as a molecule:

A. composed of carbon atoms bonded to water molecules

B. composed of amine groups and carboxylic acid groups bonded to a carbon skeleton

C. composed mostly of hydrocarbons and soluble in non-polar solvents

D. that is an aldehyde or ketone and has more than one hydroxyl group

E. ending in ~*ase*

37. Disaccharides are best characterized as:

A. two monosaccharides linked by a nitrogen bond

B. two peptides linked by a hydrogen bond

C. two monosaccharides linked by an oxygen bond

D. two amino acids linked by a peptide bond

E. two glycogens linked by a fatty acid

38. The two strands of DNA in the double helix are held by:

A. dipole–dipole attractions

B. metallic bonds

C. ionic bonds

D. covalent bonds

E. none of the above

39. What happens to DNA when placed into an aqueous solution at physiological pH?

A. Individual DNA molecules repel each other due to the presence of positive charges

B. DNA molecules bind to negatively charged proteins

C. Individual DNA molecules attract each other due to the presence of positive and negative charges

D. Individual DNA molecules repel each other due to the presence of negative charges

E. DNA molecules bind to neutral proteins

40. The nucleotide sequence, T-A-G, stands for

A. threonine-alanine-glutamine

B. thymine-adenine-guanine

C. tyrosine-asparagine-glutamic acid

D. thymine-adenine-glutamine

E. none of these

41. If one strand of a DNA double helix has the sequence AGTACTG, what is the sequence of the other strand?

A. GACGTCA

B. AGTACTG

C. GTCATGA

D. TCATGAC

E. AGUACUG

42. The main role of DNA is to provide instructions on how to build:

I. lipids   II. carbohydrates   III. proteins

A. I only

B. II only

C. III only

D. I and II only

E. I, II and III

43. Nucleic acids are polymers of [   ] monomers.

A. monosaccharide

B. fatty acid

C. DNA

D. nucleotide

E. none of the above

44. During DNA transcription, a guanine base on the template strand codes for which base on the growing RNA strand?

A. guanine

B. thymine

C. adenine

D. cytosine

E. uracil

45. What type of biological compound is a polymer composed of sugar, a base, and phosphoric acid?

A. nucleic acid

B. lipid

C. carbohydrate

D. protein

E. none of the above

46. The number of adenines in a DNA molecule is equal to the number of thymines because:

A. adenines are paired opposite of guanine in a DNA molecule

B. of the strong attraction between the nucleotides of adenine and thymine

C. the structure of adenine is similar to uracil

D. adenine is paired to cytosine in a DNA molecule

E. none of the above

47. What is the sugar component in RNA called?

A. fructose

B. galactose

C. glucose

D. ribose

E. deoxyribose

48. During DNA replication, an adenine base on the template strand codes for which base on the complementary strand?

A. thymine

B. guanine

C. cytosine

D. adenine

E. uracil

49. Which of the following is NOT part of a nucleotide?

A. cyclic nitrogenous base

B. fatty acid

C. phosphate group

D. cyclic sugar

E. oxygen

50. Which of the following linkage is in a nucleic acid?

A. phosphate linkage

B. ester linkage

C. glycoside linkage

D. peptide linkage

E. amide linkage

51. The one cyclic amine base that occurs in DNA but not in RNA is:

A. cystine

B. guanine

C. thymine

D. uracil

E. adenine

52. In the synthesis of mRNA, an adenine in the DNA pairs with:

A. guanine

B. thymine

C. uracil

D. adenine

E. cytosine

53. Nucleic acids determine the:

A. quantity and type of prions

B. number of mitochondria in a cell

C. sequence of amino acids

D. pH of the cell nucleus

E. catabolism rate for food

Structure and Function of Systems

Endocrine System

1. HMG-CoA reductase is the key enzyme in cholesterol biosynthesis. If a patient takes statins, a potent inhibitor of this enzyme, production of which hormone will not decrease?

   A. insulin

   B. cortisol

   C. testosterone

   D. aldosterone

   E. progesterone

2. Which hormone is NOT produced by the anterior pituitary gland?

   A. growth hormone

   B. prolactin

   C. luteinizing hormone

   D. thyroxine

   E. FSH

3. Molecular signals that travel to distant cells are:

   A. paracrine signals

   B. parasitic signals

   C. autocrine signals

   D. hormones

   E. responders

4. The class of hormones affecting cellular targets by starting or ending transcription is:

   A. steroids

   B. eicosanoids

   C. peptides

   D. amino acids

   E. neurotransmitters

5. Which is expected in a patient with acromegaly, a condition from oversecreting growth hormone, considering that growth hormone decreases cellular receptors' sensitivity to insulin?

   A. decreased urine volume

   B. decreased cardiac output

   C. low blood glucose concentration

   D. high blood glucose concentration

   E. decreased osmolarity of urine

6. Which endocrine gland releases vasopressin, a hormone involved in water balance?

   A. posterior pituitary

   B. hypothalamus

   C. thyroid

   D. adrenal cortex

   E. adrenal medulla

7. Which is TRUE about hormones?

    A. Most hormones operate by activation of cyclic cAMP

    B. The circulating level is held constant through a series of positive feedback loops

    C. Both lipid-soluble and water-soluble hormones bind to intracellular protein receptors

    D. The ducts of endocrine organs release their contents into the bloodstream

    E. They regulate cellular functions and are generally controlled via negative feedback

8. Which regulates temperature?

    A. cerebrum

    B. hypothalamus

    C. medulla oblongata

    D. pons

    E. pineal gland

9. In the last mile of a long-distance run, physiological and hormonal effects of stress would be observed in a runner, EXCEPT:

    A. decreased ACTH secretion

    B. decreased blood flow to the small intestine

    C. increased glucagon secretion

    D. increased heart rate

    E. pupil dilation

10. In general, cell signaling causes:

    A. increased expression of genes

    B. an influx of ions

    C. protein kinase activity

    D. G protein activation

    E. a change in receptor conformation

11. What kind of messenger is produced by all endocrine cells?

    A. intracellular second messenger

    B. extracellular messenger carried by the lymph

    C. extracellular neurotransmitter released from nerve endings

    D. extracellular or intracellular messenger carried by blood

    E. a messenger molecule secreted into a duct

12. Parathyroid hormone is vital for the control of blood Ca^{2+} ion levels; it is essential for:

    I.   bone density

    II. renal calcium reabsorption

    III. blood calcium concentration

    A. I only

    B. I and II only

    C. I and III only

    D. II and III only

    E. I, II and III

13. All statements are characteristic of peptide hormone activity, EXCEPT:

    A. hormone is transmitted via blood circulation

    B. the target organ is at a distant site from the release of the hormone

    C. cellular effects within cells often require the activity of a protein kinase

    D. hormones pass into the target cell's membrane and enter the nucleus

    E. cellular effects within cells often are mediated by second messengers

14. A hormone released by the posterior pituitary is:

    A. TSH   **C.** oxytocin

    B. prolactin   **D.** progesterone

                             E. calcitonin

15. Deficiency of which hormone causes female infertility due to the ovulation of immature ova?

    A. oxytocin   **C.** FSH

    B. estrogen   **D.** LH

                             E. prolactin

16. The receptor of estrogen is:

    A. an ion channel receptor

    B. a protein kinase receptor

    C. a G protein

    D. on the extracellular side of the membrane

    E. within the cytoplasm

17. Which endocrine gland synthesizes ACTH?

    A. hypothalamus   **C.** anterior pituitary

    B. thalamus   **D.** medulla

                             E. posterior pituitary

18. All the following hormones utilize a second messenger system, EXCEPT:

    A. TSH   **C.** cAMP

    B. estrogen   **D.** insulin

                             E. epinephrine

19. Why do some cells respond differently to the same peptide hormones?

    A. Different target cells have different genes

    B. Each cell knows how it fits into the body's overall plan

    C. A signal transduction pathway determines a target cell's response

    D. The circulatory system regulates responses to hormones by routing them to specific targets

    E. The hormone is chemically altered in different ways as it travels in the bloodstream

20. The thyroid secretes all the following EXCEPT:

    A. triiodothyronine   **C.** thyroxine

    B. TSH   **D.** all the above

                              E. none of the above

21. Which clinical manifestations would be expected of a mouse with a partial deletion of both IGF-1 genes?

    A. Decreased Ca^{2+} levels and brittle bones

    B. Anemia

    C. Deficiency in the digestion of lipids

    D. Deficiency in growth

    E. Increased heart rate and no thyroid hormone release

22. Vitamin A is a small, lipid-soluble molecule that can behave like a hormone. Which is predicted about its receptor?

    A. It would be an ion channel receptor

    B. It would be a protein kinase receptor

    C. It would involve a G protein

    D. It would not exist; vitamin A would not have a receptor

    E. It would not be connected to the plasma membrane

23. GH, PRL and ACTH hormones are secreted by:

    A. hypothalamus   **C.** posterior pituitary

    B. anterior pituitary   **D.** adrenal glands

                              E. medulla

24. Serum auto-antibody binding to TSH receptors of the thyroid gland causes a patient to have:

    A. low thyroid hormone levels because autoantibodies suppress the thyroid gland

    B. high thyroid hormone levels because the thyroid is over-stimulated by the autoantibodies

    C. low thyroid hormone levels because autoantibodies block TSH from binding to its receptor

    D. asymptomatic condition because negative feedback regulates thyroid hormone levels

    E. an unchanged basal level of thyroid hormone

25. If a hormone administered to mice intravenously accumulates rapidly inside renal cells without endocytosis, this hormone is likely a:

A. neurotransmitter

B. second messenger

C. steroid

D. polypeptide

E. amine

26. A gland that produces both exocrine and endocrine secretions is:

A. adrenal

B. pancreas

C. parathyroid

D. pituitary

E. parotid

27. Female infertility caused by a failure to ovulate is the result of:

A. low levels of LH

B. a dilation of the cervix

C. high levels of FSH

D. high levels of LH

E. high levels of LH and low levels of FSH

28. From start to finish, the order of the basic steps of a signal transduction pathway is:

A. signal → responder → receptor → effects

B. receptor → signal → responder → effects

C. signal → receptor → responder → effects

D. signal → receiver → responder → effects

E. signal → effects → receiver → responder

29. During stress, the adrenal cortex responds by secreting:

A. adrenaline

B. norepinephrine

C. ACTH

D. acetylcholine

E. cortisol

30. A neuroendocrine tumor of the adrenal glands releases epinephrine at abnormally high levels. Which symptoms would be observed in a patient with such a tumor?

A. pupil constriction

B. abnormally low heart rate

C. reduced blood pressure

D. elevated blood pressure

E. decreased blood flow to skeletal muscles

31. The hypothalamus controls the anterior pituitary using:

A. cytokines

B. second messengers

C. releasing hormones

D. antibodies

E. bidirectional nervous inputs

32. The concentration of blood Ca^{2+} is raised by:

A. calcitonin

B. parathyroid hormone

C. aldosterone

D. glucagon

E. antidiuretic hormone

33. Which is an example of antagonistic endocrine relationships that maintain homeostasis?

A. ACTH — TSH

B. oxytocin — prolactin

C. vitamin D — parathyroid hormone

D. insulin — glucagon

E. estrogen — insulin

34. Which signals do cells receive?

A. light

B. sound

C. hormones

D. odorants

E. all the above

35. Which endocrine gland synthesizes PTH?

A. adrenal

B. anterior pituitary

C. kidneys

D. parathyroid

E. thyroid

36. What is the immediate response by adrenal glands to modulate elevated blood levels of K^+ in blood?

A. block the secretion of aldosterone and increase the release of corticotrophins

B. stimulate the secretion of aldosterone from the adrenal gland

C. stimulate the secretion of aldosterone from the anterior pituitary gland

D. no response because aldosterone only increases Na^+ reabsorption in the nephron

E. decrease blood Na^+ levels

37. What is the classification of a feedback system where a response enhances the original stimulus?

A. enhancing

B. responsive

C. negative

D. intermittent

E. positive

38. Which hormone directly affects blood sugar?

A. calcitonin

B. estrogen

C. glucagon

D. oxytocin

E. thyrotropin

39. Which hormone inhibits the *hormone-sensitive lipase* cascade, releasing fatty acids from adipose tissue?

A. insulin

B. epinephrine

C. estrogen

D. glucagon

E. norepinephrine

40. The molecular signals that bind to receptors of the same cell that made them are referred to as:

A. paracrine signals

B. responders

C. autocrine signals

D. hormones

E. second messengers

41. Which endocrine gland synthesizes melatonin?

A. pineal

B. hypothalamus

C. anterior pituitary

D. posterior pituitary

E. thalamus

42. Which paracrine hormone is secreted by the pancreatic islets of Langerhans to inhibit the release of insulin and glucagon (also secreted by the islets)?

A. cortisol

B. trypsin

C. somatostatin

D. pepsin

E. epinephrine

43. During exercise, a person perspires profusely. Sweat glands are which component of the feedback loop?

A. controlled condition

B. receptors

C. stimulus

D. effectors

E. control center

44. Which statement is true for epinephrine?

A. It causes bronchial constriction

B. It is released during parasympathetic stimulation

C. It is a steroid hormone

D. The adrenal cortex synthesizes it

E. The adrenal medulla releases it

45. Which gland produces the growth-hormone-releasing hormone (GHRH) that stimulates the transcription of the growth hormone gene?

    A. parathyroid

    B. anterior pituitary

    C. hypothalamus

    D. liver

    E. adrenal

46. In what way do ligand-receptor interactions differ from enzyme-substrate reactions?

    A. The ligand signal is not metabolized into useful products

    B. The enzyme-substrate reactions and the ligand-receptor interactions are similar

    C. Inhibitors never bind to the ligand-binding site

    D. Reversibility does not occur in the ligand-receptor interactions

    E. Receptor-ligand interactions do not obey the laws of mass action

47. Which is associated with steroid hormone activity?

    A. enzyme activity

    B. gene expression

    C. neural activity

    D. extracellular receptors

    E. second messenger

48. Which basic categories are the correct chemical classification for hormones?

    A. female and male hormones

    B. peptides and steroids

    C. carbohydrates, proteins, and steroids

    D. steroid, peptide, and amines

    E. stimulator and receptor hormones

49. One of the most common second messengers is:

    A. ATP

    B. growth hormone

    C. acetylcholine

    D. adrenaline

    E. cyclic AMP

50. Which is NOT a pancreatic exocrine secretion?

    A. glucagon

    B. amylase

    C. lipase

    D. protease

    E. bicarbonate ions

Nervous System

1. Which is NOT a function of astrocytes?

   A. Guiding migration of developing neurons

   B. Controlling the chemical environment around neurons

   C. Assisting in the maturation of Schwann cells

   D. Anchoring neurons to blood vessels

   E. Providing nutrients to the neurons

2. All are correct regarding the occurrence of a sensation, EXCEPT:

   A. stimulus energy must be converted into threshold energy

   B. generator potential in the associated sensory neuron must reach threshold

   C. stimulus energy must match the specificity of the receptor

   D. stimulus energy must occur within the receptor's receptive field

   E. all are true statements

3. Which effect would result from stimulating the parasympathetic nervous system?

   A. Relaxation of the bronchi

   B. Dilation of the pupils

   C. Increased gut motility

   D. Increased heart rate

   E. Increased respiratory volume

4. The autonomic nervous system is comprised of the following:

   A. sensory neurons that supply the digestive tract

   B. sensory neurons that convey information from somatic receptors for special senses of vision, hearing, taste, and smell

   C. CNS motor fibers that conduct nerve impulses from the CNS to skeletal muscles

   D. motor fibers that conduct nerve impulses from CNS to smooth muscle, cardiac muscle, and glands

   E. motor fibers that supply the digestive tract

5. The specific molecule in the eye that must absorb photons for the perception of vision to occur is the:

   A. opsin

   B. retinal

   C. cGMP

   D. G-protein

   E. cAMP

6. The central nervous system determines the strength of a stimulus by the:

    A. amplitude of action potentials

    B. wavelength of action potential

    C. type of stimulus receptor

    D. origin of the stimulus

    E. frequency of action potentials

7. In a myopic eye, the inverted image formed by the lens falls:

    A. on the optic nerve

    B. in front of the retina

    C. behind the retina

    D. on the retina

    E. on the optic disc

8. Bipolar neurons are:

    A. not in ganglia

    B. in the organ of Corti

    C. motor neurons

    D. called neuroglial cells

    E. in the retina of the eye

9. The smallest distance that can be resolved with the unaided eye is:

    A. 200 mm

    B. 0.2 mm

    C. 20 mm

    D. 0.2 nm

    E. 2 micrometers

10. The blood-brain barrier is effective against:

    A. metabolic waste such as urea

    B. nutrients such as glucose

    C. alcohol

    D. anesthetics

    E. psychotropics

11. Which structure of the brain controls the breathing rate?

    A. cerebrum

    B. cerebellum

    C. medulla oblongata

    D. hypothalamus

    E. pituitary gland

12. An excitatory neurotransmitter secreted by motor neurons innervating skeletal muscle is:

    A. gamma amine

    B. acetylcholine

    C. norepinephrine

    D. epinephrine

    E. alpha peptide

13. The partial decussation (i.e., crossing) of axons in the optic chiasm results in:

    A. both sides of the visual field are represented together in each hemisphere of the primary visual cortex

    B. representation of the left side of the visual field remaining ipsilateral

    C. both visual fields have the same representation

    D. the left side of the visual field is represented on the left hemisphere of the primary visual cortex

    E. the left side of the visual field is represented on the right hemisphere of the primary visual cortex

14. All are correct about neurons, EXCEPT that they:

    A. are mitotic

    B. have high metabolic rates

    C. conduct impulses

    D. have extreme longevity

    E. have a greater concentration of Na^+ outside

15. The autonomic nervous system's motor pathway contains:

    A. three neurons

    B. many neurons

    C. a single long neuron

    D. two neurons

    E. a single short neuron

16. Which ion channel opens in response to a change in membrane potential and participates in generating and conducting action potentials?

    A. leakage channel

    B. ligand-gated channel

    C. mechanically gated channel

    D. voltage-gated channel

    E. all the above

17. Which is most characteristic of an accident victim who sustained isolated damage to the cerebellum?

    A. loss of coordination of smooth muscle contractions

    B. loss of speech

    C. loss of voluntary muscle contraction

    D. loss of sensation in the extremities

    E. loss of muscular coordination

18. The somatic nervous system:

    A. innervates skeletal muscles

    B. innervates glands

    C. innervates cardiac muscle

    D. innervates smooth muscle of the digestive tract

    E. innervates peristalsis of the gastrointestinal tract

19. The fovea has an extremely high concentration of:

A. cones

B. axons leaving the retina for the optic nerve

C. rods

D. blood vessels

E. ganglions

20. All are chemical classes of neurotransmitters EXCEPT:

A. ATP and other purines

B. biogenic amines

C. amino acids

D. nucleic acids

E. acetylcholine

21. Somatic sensory nerve cell bodies are in the:

A. brain

B. ventral horn

C. dorsal root ganglion

D. spinal cord

E. nerve plexus

22. Which is the most correct statement?

A. Ganglia are collections of neuron cell bodies in the spinal cord that are associated with efferent fibers

B. Ganglia are associated with afferent nerve fibers containing cell bodies of sensory neurons

C. The dorsal root ganglion is only a motor neuron structure

D. The cell bodies of afferent ganglia are in the spinal cord

E. The dorsal root ganglion contains both sensory and motor neurons

23. All these matches of brain structure to its function are correct, EXCEPT:

A. reticular activating system – sensory processing

B. hypothalamus – appetite

C. cerebellum – motor coordination

D. cerebral cortex – higher intellectual function

E. medulla oblongata – basic emotional drives

24. Which is a FALSE statement?

    I. An excitatory postsynaptic potential occurs if the excitatory effect is less than the inhibitory effect and lower than threshold

    II. A nerve impulse occurs if the inhibitory and excitatory stimuli are equal

    III. An inhibitory postsynaptic potential occurs if the inhibitory effect is greater than the excitatory effect

A. I only

B. II only

C. III only

D. I and II only

E. I and III only

25. Being able to make out objects 5-10 min after bright lights are turned off is due to:

    A. sudden bleaching of cones

    B. sudden bleaching of rods

    C. sudden bleaching of rhodopsin

    D. slow unbleaching of rods

    E. fast adaptation from the bleaching of rods

26. Which statement about synapses is correct?

    A. The synaptic cleft prevents an impulse from being transmitted directly between neurons

    B. Neurotransmitter receptors are not on the axon terminal of the cell

    C. Release of neurotransmitter molecules gives cells the property of being electrically coupled

    D. Cells with gap junctions use chemical synapses

    E. Calcium is not required for the release of the vesicles containing the neurotransmitter

27. Which results from parasympathetic stimulation?

    A. Piloerection of the hair of the skin

    B. Contraction of the abdominal muscles during exercise

    C. Production of saliva

    D. Increased heart rate

    E. Dilation of the pupils

28. A graded potential:

    A. is a voltage stimulus to initiate an action potential

    B. is voltage-regulated repolarization

    C. is long-distance signaling

    D. is the amplitude of various sizes

    E. does not use summation

29. Which would occur from ingesting the insecticide Diazinon, known to block acetylcholinesterase function?

    A. decrease in postsynaptic receptors

    B. decrease in ACh concentration in synapses

    C. decrease in postsynaptic depolarization

    D. all synaptic nervous transmission ceases

    E. increase in ACh concentration in synapses

30. Which cells are functionally like Schwann cells?

    A. oligodendrocytes

    B. astrocytes

    C. ependymal cells

    D. microglia

    E. glutamate transporters

31. Most refraction (bending of light in the eye) is accomplished by:

    A. the pupil
    B. photoreceptors

    C. the vitreous humor
    D. the cornea
    E. rod cells

32. Which is correct regarding the movement of ions across excitable membranes?

    A. Ions move from an area of higher concentration to an area of lower concentration
    B. Sodium gates in the membrane can open in response to electrical potential changes
    C. Ions move passively across membranes
    D. Ions move actively across membranes through leakage channels
    E. The Na^+ ion is concentrated inside the cell during a resting potential

33. The release of which hormone most closely resembles a response to sympathetic stimulation?

    A. aldosterone
    B. dopamine

    C. acetylcholine
    D. insulin
    E. epinephrine

34. Which is NOT a location where the white matter would be found?

    A. pyramidal tracts
    B. outer portion of the spinal cord

    C. corpus callosum
    D. cerebral cortex
    E. all the above

35. Which function would be significantly impaired by destroying the cerebellum?

    A. thermoregulation
    B. coordinated movement

    C. sense of smell
    D. urine formation
    E. blood pressure

36. A second nerve impulse cannot be generated until:

    A. proteins have been resynthesized
    B. all sodium gates are closed

    C. the membrane potential has been reestablished
    D. Na^+ ions are pumped back into the cell
    E. K^+ ions are pumped back out of the cell

37. Which is the *correct pathway* for a beam of light entering the eye?

    A. lens → pupil → vitreous humor → retina
    B. lens → pupil → retinal ganglion cells → photoreceptor outer segments
    C. pupil → vitreous humor → bipolar cells → retinal ganglion cells
    D. lens → retinal ganglion cells → photoreceptor outer segments → bipolar cells
    E. cornea → aqueous humor → lens → vitreous humor

38. Compared to the external surface of a cell membrane for a resting neuron, the interior surface is:

   A. positively charged and contains more sodium
   B. negatively charged and contains more sodium
   C. negatively charged and contains less sodium
   D. positively charged and contains less sodium
   E. positively charged and contains more potassium

39. Detection of sound involves air pressure waves that are converted into neural signals in the:

   A. semicircular canals
   B. cochlea
   C. tympanic membrane
   D. retina
   E. sclera

40. If an electrode is placed at the midpoint along the length of the axon, the impulse would:

   A. move bidirectionally
   B. move to the axon terminal and muscle contraction would not occur
   C. not move to the axon terminal, but muscle contraction would not occur
   D. not move to the axon terminal, but muscle contraction would occur
   E. not move because of the phase change in amplitudes

41. Which systems, when stimulated, results in increased heart rate, blood pressure, and blood glucose levels?

   A. central nervous system
   B. somatic nervous system
   C. sympathetic nervous system
   D. parasympathetic nervous system
   E. motor nervous system

42. Which neurotransmitters inhibit pain in a manner similar to morphine?

   A. acetylcholine
   B. norepinephrine
   C. serotonin
   D. nitric oxide
   E. endorphin

43. When light strikes the eye, photoreceptors:

   A. depolarize
   B. enter refractory
   C. hyperpolarize
   D. release neurotransmitter
   E. contract

44. The brain stem consists of the following:

   A. midbrain
   B. pons, medulla, midbrain, and cerebellum
   C. pons, medulla, and midbrain
   D. cerebrum, pons, and medulla
   E. medulla, cerebellum, and midbrain

45. Which portion of the brain do nerve cells controlling thermoregulation concentrate?

    A. medulla

    B. hypothalamus

    C. cerebellum

    D. cerebrum

    E. substantia nigra

46. All are in normal cerebrospinal fluid, EXCEPT:

    A. potassium

    B. protein

    C. glucose

    D. red blood cells

    E. sodium

47. Which condition is NOT an eye disorder?

    A. glaucoma

    B. amblyopia

    C. myopia

    D. hyperopia

    E. otitis

48. Which area of the brain contains the primary auditory cortex?

    A. temporal lobe

    B. parietal lobe

    C. prefrontal lobe

    D. frontal lobe

    E. occipital lobe

49. Which statement is correct about a reflex arc?

    A. Responses do not involve the central nervous system

    B. It involves inhibition along with excitation of muscles

    C. It involves motor neurons exiting the dorsal side of the spinal cord

    D. Cerebral cortex provides fine motor control for the muscle responses

    E. The brain processes sensory inputs prior to a standard response

50. Cell bodies of the sensory neurons of the spinal nerves are in the:

    A. sympathetic ganglia

    B. thalamus

    C. ventral root ganglia of the spinal cord

    D. dorsal root ganglia of the spinal cord

    E. nerve plexus

51. Which statement is true regarding a reflex arc?

    A. There are two types of reflex arc: autonomic and somatic

    B. The motor response occurs without synaptic delay

    C. A minimum of three neurons must participate

    D. Sensory and motor neurons can synapse outside of the spinal cord

    E. Reflex arc neurons synapse in the brain

52. The white matter of the spinal cord contains:

    A. myelinated nerve fibers

    B. neither myelinated nor unmyelinated nerve fibers

    C. myelinated and unmyelinated nerve fibers

    D. unmyelinated nerve fibers

    E. unmyelinated nerve fibers and glial cells

53. The one place where a physician can directly observe blood vessels is the:

    A. eardrum

    B. pointer finger

    C. skin of the eyelid

    D. retina

    E. lumen of the digestive system

54. Which statement is true regarding Broca's area?

    A. It is considered a motor speech area

    B. It serves for the recognition of complex objects

    C. It is in the right hemisphere

    D. It serves for auditory acuity

    E. It serves for visual acuity

55. Which structure contains hair cells that detect motion?

    I. the skin   II. the organ of Corti   III. the semicircular canals

    A. I only

    B. III only

    C. II only

    D. I, II and III

    E. II and III only

56. The part of the cerebral cortex involved in cognition, personality, intellect, and recall is:

    A. the limbic association area

    B. combined primary somatosensory cortex and somatosensory association

    C. the prefrontal cortex

    D. the cortex posterior association area

    E. Broca's area

Notes for active learning

Circulatory System

1. What cell is the precursor of all elements of blood?

   A. polymorphonuclear cell
   B. hemocytoblast
   C. normoblast
   D. megakaryocyte
   E. platelet

2. Which is correct about the hemoglobin molecule of the red blood cell?

   A. At physiological conditions, it exists in the more oxidized form of Fe(II) rather than Fe(III)
   B. It has a higher O_2 affinity in adults compared with fetal hemoglobin
   C. It does not bind CO
   D. It exhibits positive, cooperative binding for O_2
   E. It does not bind CO_2

3. The osmotic pressure at the arterial end of a capillary bed:

   I. results in a net outflow of fluid
   II. is less than the hydrostatic pressure
   III. is greater than the hydrostatic pressure

   A. I only
   B. II only
   C. III only
   D. I and III only
   E. I and II only

4. Comparing two liquids with a pH of 2 and 7, which liquid has the highest $[H^+]$?

   A. Both liquids have the same $[H^+]$
   B. A pH 2 liquid has a greater $[H^+]$ than a pH 7 liquid
   C. A pH 7 liquid has a greater $[H^+]$ than a pH 2 liquid
   D. Neither liquid contains $[H^+]$
   E. None of the above

5. All are functions of blood, EXCEPT:

   A. transport of salts to maintain blood volume
   B. transport of hormones to their target organs
   C. transport of metabolic waste from cells
   D. delivery of O_2 to body cells
   E. transport of CO_2 to the lungs

6. Hill coefficient measures cooperativity, where a Hill coefficient greater than 1 signifies positive cooperativity, less than 1 signifies negative cooperativity, and equal to 1 signifies the absence of cooperativity. What is the Hill coefficient of hemoglobin?

    A. 2.3
    B. 1

    C. 0
    D. −1.5
    E. between −1 and 1

7. All statements about the circulatory system are true, EXCEPT:

    A. the ventricles are the pumping chambers of the heart
    B. oxygenated blood is typically transported in arteries
    C. mammals have a four-chambered heart
    D. the thoracic duct returns lymphatic fluid to the circulatory system
    E. veins have a strong pulse

8. Which is the *correct* blood flow path through the heart?

    A. Superior/inferior vena cava → left atrium → left ventricle → pulmonary artery → lungs → pulmonary vein → right atrium → right ventricle → aorta
    B. Superior/inferior vena cava → right atrium → left ventricle → pulmonary artery → lungs → pulmonary vein → left atrium → right ventricle → aorta
    C. Superior/inferior vena cava → right atrium → right ventricle → pulmonary vein → lungs → pulmonary artery → left atrium → left ventricle → aorta
    D. Superior/inferior vena cava → right atrium → right ventricle → pulmonary artery → lungs → pulmonary vein → left atrium → left ventricle → aorta
    E. Superior/inferior vena cava → right atrium → left atrium → pulmonary vein → lungs → pulmonary artery → right ventricle → left ventricle → aorta

9. Which is a protective role of blood?

    A. maintenance of pH in body tissue
    B. maintenance of body temperature

    C. prevention of blood loss
    D. maintenance of adequate fluid volume
    E. maintenance of osmolarity

10. Which statement is correct for myoglobin, considering that myoglobin accepts O_2 from hemoglobin and releases it to the cytochrome c oxidase system?

    A. myoglobin has a lower affinity for O_2 than hemoglobin
    B. myoglobin has a higher affinity for O_2 than hemoglobin
    C. cytochrome oxidase c system has a lower affinity for O_2 than hemoglobin
    D. cytochrome oxidase c system has a lower affinity for O_2 than myoglobin
    E. hemoglobin has a higher affinity for O_2 than myoglobin

11. Which blood component participates in clot formation?

   A. erythrocytes   **C.** B cells

   B. macrophages   **D.** T cells

                             E. platelets

12. A patient with AB-type blood is considered the *universal recipient* because this patient's blood:

   A. contains neither antibody   **C.** is the most common

   B. contains both antibodies   **D.** is the least common

                           E. is not able to agglutinate

13. All statements are true regarding blood, EXCEPT:

   A. It contains albumins to regulate osmolarity   **C.** It varies from bright red to a dark red color

   B. Its pH is between 7.34 and 7.45   **D.** It is denser and more viscous than water

                             E. It carries body cells to injured areas for repair

14. What is the functional human myoglobin protein structure with 154 amino acid residues in a single chain?

   A. 1°   **C.** 3°

   B. 2°   **D.** 4°

                           E. 5°

15. When inhaled, carbon monoxide can be lethal because it:

   A. irritates the pleura

   B. blocks electron transport within the cytochrome system

   C. binds with a strong affinity to hemoglobin

   D. is insoluble in the bloodstream

   E. inhibits the Na^+/K^+ pump

16. Which statement correctly describes the relationship between osmotic and hydrostatic pressure differentials necessary for exchanging fluid between blood in the capillaries and the surrounding tissues?

   A. Osmotic pressure causes solutes and fluid to move out of the capillaries and into the tissues

   B. Hydrostatic pressure causes fluid to move out of the capillaries and into the tissues

   C. Osmotic pressure forces fluid to move out of the capillaries and into the tissues

   D. Hydrostatic pressure forces fluid to move out of the tissue and into the capillaries

   E. Both osmotic and hydrostatic pressure cause fluid to move out of the capillaries and into the tissues

17. Which statement is NOT true regarding the formation of blood cells?

A. Platelets form from myeloblasts

B. Lymphocytes form from lymphoblasts

C. Eosinophils form from myeloblasts

D. Erythrocytes form from erythroblasts

E. None of the above

18. T and B-cell abnormalities can be caused by severe combined immunodeficiency (SCID), which develops due to a genetic disease where adenosine deaminase is deficient. Which organs would be underdeveloped in a patient with SCID?

A. bone marrow only

B. bone marrow and thymus

C. thymus only

D. bone marrow and spleen

E. liver and spleen

19. Which is characteristic of a capillary?

　　I. hydrostatic pressure is higher at the arteriole end than at the venule end

　　II. osmotic pressure is higher in blood plasma than in the interstitial fluid

　　III. hydrostatic pressure results from heart contractions

A. I only

B. II only

C. II and III only

D. I, II and III

E. I and III only

20. What is the numerical difference in [H^+] between a liquid at pH 4 and 6?

A. 2 times

B. 10 times

C. 20 times

D. 100 times

E. 50% increase

21. Which plasma protein is the major contributor to osmotic pressure?

A. fibrinogen

B. albumin

C. alpha globulin

D. gamma globulin

E. hemoglobin

22. What is the primary function of the angiotensin-converting enzyme (ACE) produced in the lungs?

A. to increase levels of angiotensinogen

B. to decrease levels of angiotensin II

C. to increase parathyroid hormone

D. to increase calcitonin synthesis

E. to increase levels of angiotensin II

23. All statements about blood are correct, EXCEPT:

    A. mature erythrocytes lack a nucleus

    B. blood platelets participate in the clotting process

    C. erythrocytes develop in the adult spleen

    D. leukocytes undergo phagocytosis of foreign matter

    E. new red blood cells are constantly developing in the bone marrow

24. A patient has a blood clot forming in one of the large veins of his leg due to infection. What would be this patient's initial problem if the clot dislodges and moves?

    A. Cerebral stroke because the clot has moved to the brain

    B. Coronary thrombosis because the clot has moved to the coronary circulation

    C. Pulmonary embolism because the clot has moved to the pulmonary capillaries

    D. Renal shutdown because the clot has moved to the kidney

    E. Liver ischemia because the clot has moved to the hepatic portal circulation

25. Which cell has no visible cytoplasmic granules?

    A. monocyte   **C.** eosinophil

    B. basophil   **D.** neutrophil

                                E. none of the above

26. Given that surfactant is produced by pneumocytes and is fully functional when it forms *micelles*, which property describes a surfactant?

    A. acidic molecule   **C.** neutral molecule

    B. hydrophilic molecule   **D.** basic molecule

                                E. hydrophobic molecule

27. Which is a normal blood flow pathway?

    A. inferior vena cava to left atrium   **C.** pulmonary veins to left ventricle

    B. right ventricle to aorta   **D.** pulmonary veins to left atrium

                                  E. left ventricle to pulmonary artery

28. A patient with O-type blood is considered the *universal donor* because this patient's blood:

    A. contains neither antigen   **C.** is the least common

    B. contains both antigens   **D.** is the most common

                                E. is not able to physically agglutinate

29. Which property is shared by leukocytes?

    A. They are the most numerous of the formed elements in the blood

    B. They are phagocytic

    C. They have cytoplasmic granules

    D. They are nucleated

    E. They lack a nucleus

30. Interfacial tension between liquids is reduced by a soluble compound, surfactant, found in the:

    A. larynx   **C.** trachea

    B. alveoli   **D.** epiglottis

                         E. nasopharynx

31. The site of O_2 absorption in the capillaries of the lungs is:

    A. alveoli   **C.** bronchi

    B. pleura   **D.** bronchioles

                         E. trachea

32. In an infant born with a congenital heart defect, which results from mixing blood between the right and left ventricles?

    A. recurrent fever   **C.** myoglobin deficiency

    B. hemoglobin deficiency   **D.** low blood pressure

                         E. poor oxygenation of the tissues

33. Which statement is accurate regarding blood plasma?

    A. It is over 90% water

    B. It contains about 20 dissolved components

    C. It is the same as serum but without the clotting proteins

    D. The main protein component is hemoglobin

    E. Erythrocytes lack a nucleus

34. Which organelle must be well developed within plasma cells for effective antibody synthesis?

    A. storage vacuole   **C.** smooth ER

    B. rough ER   **D.** mitochondria

                         E. lysosome

35. Which vessel has the highest partial pressure of oxygen in a healthy person?

A. aorta

B. coronary veins

C. superior vena cava

D. pulmonary arteries

E. inferior vena cava

36. The pH of cellular fluids (as well as blood fluids) is approximately:

A. 5

B. 6

C. 7

D. 8

E. 10

37. Which sequence of events is correct?

A. prothrombin → thrombin; formation of thromboplastin; fibrinogen → fibrin; clot retraction

B. formation of thromboplastin; clot retraction, fibrinogen → fibrin; prothrombin → thrombin

C. formation of thromboplastin; prothrombin → thrombin; fibrinogen → fibrin; clot retraction

D. fibrinogen → fibrin; clot retraction; formation of thromboplastin; prothrombin → thrombin

E. prothrombin → thrombin; fibrinogen → fibrin; clot retraction → formation of thromboplastin

38. Class II Major Histocompatibility Complex (MHC) proteins are on the surface of leukocyte cells. Which cells does MHC II cell-mediated immunity require?

A. neutrophils

B. antibody-producing cells

C. erythrocytes

D. macrophages

E. T-helper cells

39. Which structure would be reached LAST by a tracer substance injected into the superior vena cava?

A. left atrium

B. pulmonary veins

C. left ventricle

D. right ventricle

E. tricuspid valve

40. In the mammalian heart, semi-lunar valves are:

A. where blood goes from the atria to the ventricles

B. on the right side of the heart, only

C. where the pulmonary veins attach to the heart

D. where blood leaves via the aorta and pulmonary arteries

E. at locations where the anterior and posterior venae cavae enter

41. Erythrocyte production is regulated by the following:

A. liver

B. pancreas

C. kidney

D. brain

E. spleen

42. Which statement is correct about the atrioventricular node?

A. It regulates the contraction rhythm of cardiac cells

B. It delays the contraction of the heart ventricles

C. It is the parasympathetic ganglion in the left atrium of the heart

D. It conducts action potentials from the vagus nerve to the heart

E. It is the parasympathetic ganglion in the right atrium of the heart

43. Stenosis is when the valve's opening is narrowed, resulting in decreased blood flow. If diagnosed with mitral valve stenosis, where would a patient experience the greatest blood pressure increase?

A. right atrium

B. aorta

C. left ventricle

D. left atrium

E. right ventricle

44. A difference of 1 pH unit (e.g., pH 6 *vs.* 7) corresponds to what change in the $[H^+]$?

A. 1

B. 2

C. 10

D. doubling

E. 100

45. Which would result from a large blood loss due to a hemorrhage?

A. No change in blood pressure but a slower heart rate

B. No change in blood pressure but a change in respiration

C. Vasodilation

D. Rise in blood pressure due to change in cardiac output

E. Lowering blood pressure due to change in cardiac output

46. What is the correct order for the cardiac conduction pathway?

A. Purkinje fibers → SA node→ AV node → bundle of His

B. SA node → bundle of His → Purkinje fibers → AV node

C. SA node → AV node → bundle of His → Purkinje fibers

D. AV node → SA node → bundle of His → Purkinje fibers

E. AV node → SA node → Purkinje fibers → bundle of His

47. Which heart structure has blood with the greatest O_2 content?

A. right atrium

B. left ventricle

C. pulmonary artery

D. thoracic duct

E. superior vena cava

48. When a swimmer holds their breath, which blood gas changes first and creates the urge to breathe?

A. rising O_2

B. falling O_2

C. rising CO_2

D. falling CO_2

E. rising CO_2 and falling O_2

49. The left ventricular wall of the heart is thicker than the right wall because it:

A. pumps blood through a smaller valve

B. pumps blood with greater pressure

C. expands the thoracic cage during diastole

D. accommodates a greater volume of blood

E. undergoes isotonic contractions

50. At high altitudes, the H_2O vapor pressure in the lungs remains constant while O_2 and CO_2 pressures fall. All physiological changes assist a rock climber during low O_2 levels, EXCEPT:

A. increased diffusion capacity of the lungs

B. increased pulmonary ventilation

C. increased blood flow to the tissues

D. increased number of erythrocytes

E. decreased BPG synthesis

51. Which heart structure has blood with the lowest O_2 content?

A. thoracic duct

B. left ventricle

C. pulmonary artery

D. inferior vena cava

E. right atrium

52. Which vessel would be expected to have the highest protein concentration?

A. proximal tubule

B. afferent arteriole

C. inferior vena cava

D. vasa recta

E. efferent arteriole

53. Which statement regarding the heart valves is accurate?

    A. Aortic valves control the flow of blood into the heart

    B. AV valves are supported by chordae tendineae to prevent the regurgitation of blood into the atria during ventricular contraction

    C. Mitral valve separates the right atrium from the right ventricle

    D. Tricuspid valve divides the left atrium from the left ventricle

    E. Pulmonary valves control the flow of blood into the heart

54. Which thermoregulation mechanism is NOT involved in heat conservation?

    A. blood vessel constriction

    B. shivering

    C. perspiration

    D. piloerection

    E. none of the above

55. Which blood cell is responsible for coagulation?

    A. leukocyte

    B. erythrocyte

    C. lymphocyte

    D. platelet

    E. macrophage

56. Which is NOT correct about the hepatic portal system?

    A. It branches off the inferior vena cava

    B. It consists of a vein connecting two capillary beds

    C. Its major vessels are the superior mesenteric, inferior mesenteric, and splenic veins

    D. It carries nutrients to the liver for processing

    E. It carries toxins and microorganisms to the liver for processing

57. When directed in right-to-left circulation in a fetus, blood travels directly from the:

    A. right atrium to the aorta

    B. superior vena cava to the aorta

    C. right lung to the left lung

    D. pulmonary vein to the pulmonary artery

    E. right atrium to the left atrium

Lymphatic and Immune Systems

1. All statements regarding the thymus are correct, EXCEPT:

   A. its stroma consists of epithelial tissue

   B. it is smaller and less active in children than in adults

   C. it functions strictly in T lymphocyte maturation

   D. it does not fight antigens

   E. all the above are true

2. All the following cell lines might be elevated in a patient exposed to an antigen, EXCEPT:

   A. plasma cells

   B. macrophages

   C. T-cells

   D. monocytes

   E. erythrocytes

3. All participate in lymph transport EXCEPT:

   A. lymph capillary mini valve action

   B. smooth muscle contraction in the lymph capillary walls

   C. thoracic pressure changes during breathing

   D. milking action of active muscle fibers

   E. lymph fluid rejoins the circulation at the superior vena cava

4. A person lacking gamma globulins would have the following:

   A. diabetes

   B. hemophilia

   C. severe allergies

   D. low resistance to infection

   E. none of the above

5. Which digestive system organ is the site of absorption of amino acids, fatty acids, and sugars?

   A. large intestine

   B. small intestine

   C. gallbladder

   D. stomach

   E. colon

6. The thymus has levels of high activity during:

    I. neonatal development

    II. pre-adolescence

    III. middle age

A. I only

B. II only

C. III only

D. I and III only

E. I and II only

7. Humoral immunity depends on the function of:

A. erythrocytes

B. cytotoxic T cells

C. immunoglobulins

D. albumin

E. fibrin

8. The lymphatic capillaries are:

A. completely impermeable

B. as permeable as blood capillaries

C. less permeable than blood capillaries

D. more permeable than blood capillaries

E. smaller in diameter than blood capillaries

9. Which cell produces antibodies?

A. neurons

B. T cells

C. B cells

D. macrophages

E. natural killer cells

10. Antibodies that function against a particular foreign substance are released by:

A. lymph nodes

B. medullary cords

C. T lymphocytes

D. plasma cells

E. natural killer cells

11. Through which process, like phagocytosis, do cells engulf liquid droplets?

A. apoptosis

B. necrosis

C. exocytosis

D. endocytosis

E. pinocytosis

12. Lymph leaves a lymph node through:

A. the subcapsular sinus

B. the cortical sinus

C. afferent lymphatic vessels

D. efferent lymphatic vessels

E. capillaries

13. Based on the diagram showing the relationship between lymph flow and interstitial (extracellular) fluid pressure, would increased interstitial fluid protein increase lymph flow?

    A. No, because fluid movement into the capillaries decreases interstitial fluid pressure

    B. No, because the subsequent increase in interstitial fluid pressure reduces lymph flow

    C. Yes, because fluid movement out of the capillaries increases interstitial fluid pressure

    D. Yes, because the increased interstitial fluid protein reduces interstitial fluid volume

    E. Yes, because fluid movement out of the capillaries decreases interstitial fluid pressure

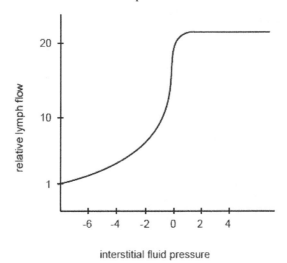

interstitial fluid pressure

14. Inflammatory responses may include:

    A. clotting proteins migrating away from the site of infection

    B. increased activity of phagocytes in an inflamed area

    C. reduced permeability of blood vessels to conserve plasma

    D. release of substances that decrease blood supply to an inflamed area

    E. inhibiting the release of white blood cells from bone marrow

15. Which statement about lymph transport is correct?

    A. It depends on the movement of adjacent tissues, such as skeletal muscles

    B. It only occurs when illness causes tissue swelling

    C. It is faster than transport via veins

    D. Lymph vessels are high-pressure conduits

    E. It is rapid and continuous

16. The capsule of *B. vulgatus* bacteria is a significant factor in its virulence because it inhibits phagocytosis by preventing the activity of:

    A. monocytes   **C.** T-cells

    B. platelets   **D.** B-cells

                               E. fibrin

17. Which statement about lymphocytes is correct?

    A. T cells are the precursors of B cells

    B. T cells are the only form of lymphocytes in lymphoid tissue

    C. The two main types are T cells and macrophages

    D. B cells differentiate into plasma cells that secrete antibodies into the blood

    E. B cells are the precursors of T cells

18. Which will likely result in erythroblastosis fetalis?

    A. Rh^- mother and Rh^- fetus   **C.** Rh^+ mother and Rh^- fetus

    B. Rh^+ mother and Rh^- father   **D.** Rh^+ mother and Rh^+ fetus

                                           E. Rh^- mother and Rh^+ fetus

19. Functions of the spleen include all the following, EXCEPT:

        I. storage of iron   III. storage of blood platelets

        II. forming crypts that trap bacteria   IV. removal of old blood cells from the blood

    A. I only   **C.** III and IV only

    B. II only   **D.** I and II only

                                 E. II and III only

20. The thymus gland is primarily responsible for:

    A. lymphoid T cell maturation

    B. removal and replacement of erythrocytes

    C. production of humoral immunity cells

    D. immunity only after a child matures into adulthood

    E. production of erythrocytes

21. Which structure(s) is/are the location of Peyer's patches?

        I. large intestine

        II. jejunum of the small intestine

        III. ileum of the small intestine

    A. I only   **C.** I and II only

    B. II only   **D.** II and III only

                                 E. I, II and III

22. If erythrocytes from a person with type A blood are added to three test tubes, each containing a different blood type (AB, B, and O), which test tube(s) will NOT agglutinate?

      I. type AB blood   II. type B blood   III. type O blood

A. I only

B. II only

C. III only

D. I and III only

E. II and III only

23. Which would NOT be classified as a lymphatic structure?

      I. Peyer's patches of the intestine   III. tonsils

      II. spleen   IV. pancreas

A. I only

B. II only

C. III only

D. IV only

E. I and IV only

24. Lymph capillaries are in:

      I. digestive organs   III. bones

      II. bone marrow   IV. CNS

A. I only

B. I and II only

C. III only

D. I and IV only

E. II and III only

25. Which innate immune response is exhibited by a patient initially exposed to a pathogen?

A. T killer cells

B. neutrophils

C. T helper cells

D. B lymphocytes

E. immunoglobulin proliferation

26. The thymus is the only lymphoid organ that does NOT:

A. directly fight antigens

B. have a cortex

C. produce hormones

D. have lymphocytes

E. have a medulla

27. Which blood type could be inherited by a child of a father with type AB and a mother with type O blood?

      I. type A   II. type B   III. type AB   IV. type O

A. III only

B. I and IV only

C. II and IV only

D. I and III only

E. I and II only

28. Which is NOT lymphatic tissue associated with the digestive tract?

    A. islets of Langerhans

    B. lingual tonsils

    C. palatine tonsils

    D. Peyer's patches

    E. all the above

29. Which would be impaired due to the HIV infecting and killing helper CD4$^+$ T lymphocytes?

    I. humoral immunity

    II. cell-mediated immunity

    III. non-specific immunity

    A. I only

    B. I and II only

    C. I and III only

    D. II and III only

    E. I, II and III

30. Which is a function of lymphoid tissue?

    I. To be involved in lymphocyte and macrophage activities

    II. To store and provide a proliferation site for lymphocytes

    III. To store and provide a proliferation site for neutrophils

    A. I only

    B. II only

    C. III only

    D. I and II only

    E. I and III only

31. What is the function of lymph nodes?

    A. breaking down hemoglobin

    B. filtering of lymph

    C. facilitating the absorption of amino acids

    D. increasing glucose concentrations in the blood

    E. carrying oxygen

32. What are antigens?

    A. proteins in blood that cause foreign blood cells to clump

    B. proteins embedded in B cell membranes

    C. proteins that consist of two light and two heavy polypeptide chains

    D. foreign molecules that trigger the production of antibodies

    E. proteins released during an inflammatory response

33. All are functions of lymph nodes, EXCEPT:

   A. producing lymph fluid and cerebrospinal fluid
   B. serving as antigen surveillance areas
   C. acting as lymph filters
   D. producing lymphoid cells and storing granular leukocytes
   E. activating the immune system

34. Which cells are responsible for secreting virus-neutralizing antibodies?

   A. T cells
   B. erythrocytes
   C. macrophages
   D. thymus cells
   E. plasma cells

35. Which statement is correct regarding antibodies?

   A. There are three binding sites per antibody monomer
   B. They are incapable of being transferred from one person to another
   C. They contain a prominent carbohydrate structure
   D. They are composed of heavy and light polypeptide chains
   E. They are held together by hydrophobic interactions

36. Which is absorbed by lacteals?

   A. salts
   B. fatty acids
   C. proteins
   D. carbohydrates
   E. sugars

37. All are NOT associated with passive immunity, EXCEPT:

   A. booster shot of vaccine
   B. differentiation of plasma cells
   C. infusion of weakened viruses
   D. exposure to an antigen
   E. passage of IgG antibodies from a pregnant mother to her fetus

38. Hyperactivity of which organ causes anemia?

   A. adenoids
   B. spleen
   C. parathyroid
   D. thymus
   E. thyroid

39. All are a T cell type EXCEPT:

    A. memory

    B. regulatory

    C. cytotoxic

    D. antigenic

    E. helper

40. All are functions of the lymphatic system, EXCEPT:

    A. regulation of erythropoiesis

    B. destruction and removal of foreign particles

    C. removal of proteins from interstitial spaces

    D. absorption of lipids from the small intestine

    E. transport of white blood cells to and from the lymph nodes into the bones

41. Which is normally NOT a function of the adult liver?

    A. synthesis of red blood cells

    B. deamination of amino acids

    C. conversion of carbohydrates to fats

    D. storage of glycogen

    E. metabolism of alcohol

42. B lymphocytes develop immunocompetence in:

    A. lymph nodes

    B. bone marrow

    C. the spleen

    D. the thymus

    E. the liver

43. Antibodies act by:

    A. aiding in phagocytosis of antigens

    B. binding to antigens via the variable portion

    C. inhibiting stem cell production in the bone marrow

    D. binding to plasma cells and marking them for destruction via phagocytosis

    E. converting fibrinogen into fibrin

44. The inflammatory response participates in the following processes EXCEPT:

    A. disposing of cellular debris and pathogens

    B. setting the stage for repair processes

    C. preventing the spread of the injurious agent to nearby tissue

    D. replacing injured tissues with connective tissue

    E. increasing blood flow to the site of injury

45. According to the theory of blood groups, all statements are true, EXCEPT:

   A. agglutination is caused by antibodies

   B. type O blood does not undergo agglutination

   C. Rh factor is a type of antigen in human blood

   D. type B blood contains antibodies for type A antigen

   E. agglutinins can be antibodies

46. Which bond holds antibody molecules together?

   A. hydrophobic   **C.** van der Waals

   B. ionic   **D.** hydrogen

                                         E. disulfide

47. Fluid absorbed from the interstitial spaces by lymphatic vessels is carried to the:

   A. kidneys, where it is excreted as urine

   B. lungs, where the fluid is expired during exhalation

   C. lymphatic ducts, where it returns to the circulation

   D. large intestine, where it is absorbed and returned to the bloodstream

   E. aorta, where it returns to the circulation

48. During clonal selection of B cells, which substance determines what cells will eventually become cloned?

   A. complement   **C.** interferon

   B. antibody   **D.** antigen

                                         E. major histocompatibility complex (MHC)

49. B cells are dormant in lymph nodes and other lymphoid tissues until activated by specific lymphocyte antigens. When activated, B cells produce:

   A. cytotoxic T cells   **C.** antibodies

   B. lymphokines   **D.** macrophages

                                         E. monocytes

50. In which situation will helper T cells be activated?

   A. When natural killer (NK) cells encounter a tumor cell

   B. When a cytotoxic T cell releases cytokine

   C. In the bone marrow during the self-tolerance test

   D. When B cells respond to T-independent antigens

   E. When an antigen is displayed by a dendritic cell

51. The correct sequence of events in phagocytosis is:

    A. ingestion → adherence → chemotaxis → digestion → killing

    B. chemotaxis → adherence → ingestion → digestion → killing

    C. chemotaxis → ingestion → digestion → adherence → killing

    D. adherence → digestion → killing → ingestion → chemotaxis

    E. adherence → chemotaxis → digestion → killing → ingestion

52. All are examples of innate immunity, EXCEPT:

    A. phagocytic cells

    B. digestive enzymes and stomach acid

    C. memory B cells

    D. skin as a physical barrier to antigens

    E. neutrophils

Digestive System

1. All processes take place in the liver EXCEPT:

A. glycogen storage

B. detoxification of poisons

C. synthesis of adult erythrocytes

D. conversion of amino acids to urea

E. regulation of blood sugar levels

2. Glycogenolysis is the breakdown of glycogen stored in the liver and skeletal muscles. Which hormone inhibits glycogenolysis?

A. aldosterone

B. glucagon

C. adrenaline

D. cortisol

E. insulin

3. Which statement is true of mammals?

A. All foods begin their enzymatic digestion in the mouth

B. The epiglottis prevents food from entering the trachea

C. After leaving the oral cavity, the bolus enters the larynx

D. Enzyme production continues in the esophagus

E. The trachea leads to the esophagus and then to the stomach

4. What cartilaginous structure prevents food from going down the trachea?

A. tongue

B. larynx

C. glottis

D. epiglottis

E. esophageal sphincter

5. The chemical and mechanical receptors that control digestion are:

A. pons and medulla

B. oral cavity

C. glandular tissue that lines the organ lumen

D. walls of the tract organs

E. hypothalamus

6. Herbivores have longer alimentary canals to body size than carnivores because herbivores need:

A. reduced oxygen consumption

B. more time for digestion

C. a more robust hepatic portal vein

D. more surface area for absorption of nutrients

E. microorganisms to metabolize nutrients

7. What structure does food enter as it is swallowed and leaves the mouth?

A. glottis

B. esophagus

C. trachea

D. larynx

E. fundus

8. What is a function of the hepatic portal circulation?

A. Returning glucose to the general circulation when blood sugar is low

B. Distributing hormones throughout the body

C. Carrying nutrients to the spleen

D. Carrying toxins to the venous system for disposal through the urinary tract

E. Collecting absorbed nutrients for metabolic processing or storage

9. Which organ is the main site of fatty acid synthesis?

A. smooth muscle

B. spleen

C. kidney

D. liver

E. adrenal glands

10. Which organ is the site of bile production?

A. large intestine

B. small intestine

C. liver

D. gallbladder

E. pancreas

11. Which is the correct order (from the lumen) of the four basic layers comprising the walls of every organ in the alimentary canal?

A. mucosa → submucosa → muscularis externa → serosa

B. submucosa → serosa → muscularis externa → mucosa

C. serosa → mucosa → submucosa → muscularis externa

D. muscularis externa → serosa → mucosa → submucosa

E. mucosa→ serosa → submucosa → muscularis externa

12. What would be observed about a patient with type 1 diabetes and low blood insulin concentration?

A. decreased levels of blood glucose

B. increased insulin levels from thyroid stimulation

C. decreased levels of circulating erythrocytes

D. presence of glucose in the urine

E. increased hematocrit

13. The primary site of water absorption is the:

    A. duodenum   **C.** jejunum

    B. large intestine   **D.** ileum

                           E. mouth

14. The hormone that increases the output of enzyme-rich pancreatic juice and stimulates contraction of the gallbladder to release bile is:

    A. gastric inhibitor peptide   **C.** secretin

    B. trypsin   **D.** gastrin

                           E. cholecystokinin

15. Which molecule has the highest lipid density?

    A. very-low-density lipoprotein (VLDL)   **C.** high-density lipoprotein (HDL)

    B. low-density lipoprotein (LDL)   **D.** chylomicron

                           E. all have the same lipid density

16. Which process does NOT occur in the mouth?

    A. moistening of food   **C.** bolus formation

    B. mechanical digestion   **D.** chemical digestion of proteins

                           E. chemical digestion of starch

17. All statements about bile are correct, EXCEPT that it:

    A. functions to carry bilirubin formed from the breakdown of worn-out RBCs

    B. contains enzymes for digestion

    C. is both an excretory product and a digestive secretion

    D. functions to emulsify fats

    E. is synthesized in the liver and stored in the gallbladder

18. An electrolyte is a compound that dissociates well in water; an example of a poor electrolyte would be:

    A. H_2SO_4 **C.** glucose

    B. NaBr   **D.** KCl

                           E. $MgCl_2$

19. The principal function of $NaHCO_3$ is to:

    A. inactivate bile

    B. combines with CO_2 in alveoli

    C. dissolve CO_2

    D. combines with O_2 when hemoglobin is saturated

    E. buffer a solution

20. Saliva includes the following solutes:

    A. mucin, lysozyme, electrolytes, salts, and minerals

    B. electrolytes, digestive enzyme, mucin, lysozyme, and IgA

    C. digestive enzyme and electrolytes only

    D. proteases and amylase only

    E. salts and minerals only

21. Structures at the esophagus-stomach, stomach-duodenum, and ileum-colon junction sites are:

    A. sphincters

    B. regions of dense villi

    C. junction points for enzyme release

    D. sites for peristalsis

    E. Peyer's patches

22. Which statement is NOT true about the digestive system?

    A. Peristalsis is a wave of smooth muscle contractions that proceeds along the digestive tract

    B. Digestive enzymes from the pancreas are released via a duct into the duodenum

    C. Low pH of the stomach is essential for the functioning of carbohydrate digestive enzymes

    D. Villi in the small intestine absorbs nutrients into both the lymphatic and circulatory systems

    E. The hormone cholecystokinin triggers the release of bile from the gallbladder

23. In addition to mechanical breakdown and storage of food, the stomach:

    A. initiates protein digestion and denatures proteins

    B. is the first site where absorption occurs

    C. is the site of lipid digestion

    D. is the site of carbohydrate and lipid digestion

    E. is the site of carbohydrate digestion

24. What would be expected in a patient after administering Tagamet, a drug that is an antagonist of gastric parietal cell H_2-receptors?

    A. increased $[H^+]$ in the stomach

    B. increased pH in the stomach

    C. increased ATP consumption by gastric parietal cells

    D. decreased pepsin release

    E. increased levels of pepsin

25. All the following match nutrients to the specific digestive enzymes correctly, EXCEPT:

A. fats – pancreatic lipase

B. proteins – chymotrypsin

C. proteins – carboxypeptidase

D. carbohydrates – pancreatic amylase

E. proteins – ptyalin (salivary amylase)

26. The acid secretions in the stomach are stimulated by:

A. lipids and fatty acids

B. simple carbohydrates and alcohols

C. protein and peptide fragments

D. starches and complex carbohydrates

E. carbohydrates and lipids

27. For laboratory use, cellulose is a neutral polymer of glucose that can become either positive or negative by attaching cationic or anionic groups. What plasma compound will be filtered from blood during dialysis with anionic groups on the cellulose?

A. negatively charged compounds

B. positively charged compounds

C. all compounds are filtered uniformly

D. neutral charged compounds

E. no compounds are filtered with efficiency

28. Which enzyme functions to convert disaccharides into monosaccharides?

A. kinase

B. lactase

C. lipase

D. zymogen

E. phosphatase

29. The digestive enzyme pepsinogen is secreted by:

A. Brunner's glands

B. goblet cells of the duodenum

C. foveolar cells of the stomach

D. parietal cells of the stomach

E. chief cells of the stomach

30. The gastrointestinal tract comprises three layers: mucosa, submucosa, and muscularis mucosae. The latter is composed of which type of muscle?

A. voluntary skeletal

B. voluntary smooth

C. involuntary smooth

D. involuntary skeletal

E. voluntary smooth and skeletal

31. Which is a correct statement about lipids?

    A. They are composed of elements C, O, N & H

    B. Their secondary structure is composed of α helices and β pleated sheets

    C. They are molecules used for long-term energy storage in animals

    D. Elements of C:H:O are in the ratio of 1:2:1

    E. Maltose is an example of a lipid

32. All are functions of hepatocytes, EXCEPT:

    A. producing digestive enzymes

    B. processing nutrients

    C. storing fat-soluble vitamins

    D. detoxifying chemicals

    E. synthesizing cholesterol

33. Which enzyme is secreted as an inactive precursor and converted into its active form in the lumen of the small intestine?

    A. protease

    B. salivary amylase

    C. lipase

    D. bicarbonate

    E. trypsinogen

34. What is the site of amino acid absorption?

    A. stomach

    B. gallbladder

    C. large intestine

    D. small intestine

    E. rectum

35. Which vitamin requires an intrinsic factor for absorption?

    A. A

    B. C

    C. B_{12}

    D. K

    E. E

36. What is the function of bicarbonate in mucus secreted into the gastrointestinal tract by epithelium?

    I. Digestion of proteins

    II. Functioning as a buffer for the contents within the gastrointestinal tract

    III. Preventing the gastrointestinal tract from becoming acidic

    A. I only

    B. I and II only

    C. I and III only

    D. I, II and III

    E. II and III only

37. Which nutrients yield 4 calories per gram?

A. glucose and proteins

B. fats and glucose

C. proteins and lipids

D. lipids and sugars

E. glucose, proteins, and fats

38. What is a function of goblet cells?

A. Protects against invading disease-causing organisms (e.g., bacteria) in the digestive tract by food

B. Secretion of buffers to keep the pH of the digestive tract close to neutral

C. Produces mucus to protect digestive organs from the effects of protease enzymes needed for digestion

D. Absorption of nutrients from digested food

E. Storing nutrients for future use

39. Which is NOT an end product of digestion?

A. amino acids

B. lactose

C. fructose

D. fatty acids

E. glucose

40. Which vitamin is needed for the hepatic production of prothrombin?

A. vitamin A

B. vitamin B_{12}

C. vitamin D

D. vitamin K

E. vitamin E

41. Bacteria of the large intestine are essential role in:

A. synthesizing vitamin K and some B vitamins

B. synthesizing vitamin C

C. producing gas

D. absorption of bilirubin

E. synthesizing vitamin D

42. Which enzyme is secreted by both saliva and the pancreas?

A. chymotrypsin

B. lipase

C. pepsin

D. trypsin

E. secretin

43. Which controls the flow of material from the esophagus into the stomach?

A. gallbladder

B. pyloric sphincter

C. epiglottis

D. cardiac sphincter

E. appendix

44. For normal hemoglobin production in RBCs, the necessary stomach secretion is:

A. gastric lipase

B. intrinsic factor

C. pepsinogen

D. HCl

E. vitamin K

45. Cholecystokinin (CCK) is released by I cells of the small intestine in response to dietary fat and protein. What substance would NOT be released in response to CCK?

A. trypsin

B. pancreatic lipase

C. pancreatic chymotrypsin

D. bile

E. salivary amylase

46. Which enzymes would be most affected in a patient with a peptic ulcer after an antacid overdose?

A. procarboxypeptidase

B. trypsin

C. pepsin

D. lipase

E. amylase

47. Most nutrients are absorbed through the mucosa of the intestinal villi by:

A. active transport

B. bulk flow

C. simple diffusion

D. facilitated diffusion

E. osmosis

48. Which organ secretes intrinsic factors and absorbs caffeine?

A. liver

B. pancreas

C. duodenum

D. ileum

E. stomach

49. Lactic acid buildup results from continuous muscle contractions because it is a:

A. breakdown product of fatty acid degradation

B. metabolic product of anaerobic metabolism

C. product of phosphocreatine degradation

D. breakdown product of ADP hydrolysis

E. contraction induced by the lactic acid released from actin-myosin cross-bridges

50. In the small intestine, chemical digestion needs:

    A. secretions from the spleen containing enzymes necessary for complete digestion

    B. bile salts that emulsify carbohydrates so that they can be easily digested by enzymatic action

    C. a significant amount of enzyme secretion by the intestinal mucosa

    D. cholecystokinin (CCK), an intestinal hormone that stimulates gallbladder contraction

    E. pancreatic lipase that digests proteins

51. Which stomach cell secretes intrinsic factors?

    A. parietal cell   **C.** chief cell

    B. G cell   **D.** mucous cell

                              E. Peyer's patches

52. Which statement is true for bile?

    A. It is a protease   **C.** It is an enzyme

    B. It is a protein   **D.** It is a hormone

                              E. It is an emulsifying agent

53. As chyme passes from the stomach into the small intestine, the catalytic activity of pepsin:

    A. decreases because of increased pH

    B. decreases because pancreatic amylase degrades pepsin

    C. decreases because the pH decreases

    D. decreases because pepsinogen is converted into pepsin

    E. increases because of increased pH

54. Which statement is correct about hormonal regulation of digestion?

    A. Secretin targets the pancreas to release bile

    B. Secretin targets the gallbladder to release digestive enzymes

    C. Cholecystokinin (CCK) targets the pancreas to release digestive enzymes

    D. Cholecystokinin (CCK) targets the pancreas to release sodium bicarbonate

    E. Gastrin stimulates the gallbladder to contract

55. Most digestion of food in humans occurs in the:

    A. liver   **C.** mouth

    B. small intestine   **D.** stomach

                              E. pancreas

Notes for active learning

Excretory System

1. The kidneys are stimulated to produce renin when:

   A. blood pressure decreases

   B. specific gravity of urine rises above 1.05

   C. peritubular capillaries are dilated

   D. pH of the urine decreases

   E. aldosterone levels are high

2. A structure originating from the renal pelvis and extending to the urinary bladder is:

   A. urethra

   B. major calyx

   C. ureter

   D. vas deferens

   E. collecting duct

3. All these statements about aldosterone are correct, EXCEPT that it:

   A. stimulates reabsorption of Na^+

   B. stimulates the secretion of K^+

   C. results in concentrated urine

   D. is produced by the adrenal cortex

   E. stimulates the secretion of Na^+

4. Permeability properties of which structure allow the kidney to establish the medullary osmotic gradient?

   A. collecting duct

   B. distal convoluted tubule

   C. loop of Henle

   D. glomerular filtration membrane

   E. proximal convoluted tubule

5. Which results from increased hydrostatic pressure in Bowman's capsule due to the excretory system blockage by a calcified deposit in the urethra?

   A. Increased filtration of blood toxins

   B. Decreased filtration of blood toxins

   C. Vasoconstriction of renal blood vessels

   D. Increased filtrate production

   E. No physiological effect because humans have two kidneys

6. If a concentrated NaCl solution is infused into the renal tubules of a healthy person, what is the effect?

   A. Urine volume decrease because of decreased filtrate osmolarity

   B. Urine volume increases because of decreased filtrate osmolarity

   C. Urine volume is unchanged

   D. Urine volume decreases because of increased filtrate osmolarity

   E. Urine volume increases because of increased filtrate volume

7. In the collecting tubule, the permeability of the cells to water increases because of a(n):

    A. increase in the plasma levels of aldosterone

    B. decrease in the osmolarity of blood plasma

    C. decrease in the plasma levels of ADH

    D. increase in the plasma levels of ADH

    E. decrease in the plasma levels of cortisol

8. Which is NOT reabsorbed by secondary active transport in the proximal convoluted tubule?

    A. phosphate   **C.** glucose

    B. urea   **D.** amino acids

                            E. all are reabsorbed

9. Certain mammals have unusually long loops of Henle to maintain a steep osmotic gradient, allowing the animal to excrete:

    A. insoluble nitrogenous wastes   **C.** less Na^+ across the membrane

    B. isotonic urine   **D.** hypertonic urine

                            E. hypotonic urine

10. Which of the choices is NOT a urinary system function?

    A. Eliminates solid undigested wastes and salts and excretes CO_2 and H_2O

    B. Maintains blood osmolarity

    C. Regulates blood glucose levels and produces hormones

    D. Helps maintain homeostasis by controlling blood volume

    E. Helps maintain homeostasis by controlling blood pressure

11. Bowman's capsule functions to filter urea from the blood by:

    A. ATP-hydrolysis for pumping urea into the filtrate via active transport

    B. conversion of urea into amino acids

    C. diffusion of urea into the filtrate via hydrostatic pressure

    D. antiport exchange of urea for glucose

    E. antiport exchange of urea for water

12. Which statement is true about the descending limb of the nephron loop?

    A. It draws water by osmosis into the lumen of the tubule

    B. It contains filtrate that becomes more concentrated as it moves down into the medulla

    C. It is not permeable to water

    D. It is permeable to sodium

    E. It is permeable to urea

13. Which is NOT typically in blood after it has been filtered through the glomerulus in the kidney?

A. sodium ions

B. blood cells

C. amino acids

D. glucose

E. potassium ions

14. Which statement about ureters is correct?

A. Only parasympathetic nerves innervate the ureters

B. Ureters are capable of peristalsis

C. The epithelium is stratified squamous-like skin, which allows distensibility

D. Ureters contain sphincters at the entrance to the bladder to prevent the backflow of urine

E. The detrusor muscle is a layer of the urinary bladder wall made of skeletal muscle

15. A presence of glucose in a patient's urine indicates that:

A. the proximal tubule is impervious to glucose

B. the collecting ducts are defective

C. glucose transporters in the loop of Henle are defective

D. no clinical significance because glucose in the urine is normal

E. glucose is entering the filtrate at a higher rate than it is being reabsorbed

16. What major force moves solutes and water out of the blood across the filtration membrane?

A. Glomerular hydrostatic pressure

B. Size of the pores in the basement membrane of the capillaries

C. Ionic electrochemical gradient

D. Protein-regulated diffusion

E. Osmotic pressure

17. Fish living in seawater drink large amounts of saltwater and use cells in their gills to pump excess salt out in response to:

A. loss of salt into their surroundings

B. loss of H_2O by active transport to their hypertonic surroundings

C. the need to maintain their tissues in a hypotonic state

D. the influx of H_2O by osmosis into their tissues

E. the need to maintain their tissues in a hypertonic state

18. Water reabsorption by the descending limb of the loop of Henle occurs through:

    A. cotransport with sodium ions

    B. filtration

    C. osmosis

    D. active transport

    E. facilitated transport

19. Gout is manifested by decreased excretion of uric acid. Which organ is responsible for the elimination of uric acid?

    A. spleen

    B. large intestine

    C. kidney

    D. liver

    E. duodenum

20. Most electrolyte reabsorption by the renal tubules is:

    A. in the proximal convoluted tubule

    B. in the descending loop of Henle

    C. not limited by a transport maximum

    D. in the distal convoluted tubule

    E. in the ascending loop of Henle

21. The lowest solute concentration in which region of the kidney:

    A. cortex

    B. nephron

    C. pelvis

    D. medulla

    E. epithelia

22. Fluid in Bowman's (glomerular) capsule is similar to plasma but does NOT contain significant amounts of:

    A. urea

    B. electrolytes

    C. hormones

    D. glucose

    E. plasma protein

23. Which is true of urea?

    A. It is insoluble in water

    B. It is more toxic to human cells than ammonia

    C. It is the primary nitrogenous waste product of humans

    D. It is the primary nitrogenous waste product of most birds

    E. It is the primary nitrogenous waste product of most aquatic invertebrates

24. Alcohol acts as a diuretic because it:

    A. increases secretion of ADH

    B. inhibits the release of ADH

    C. is not reabsorbed by the tubule cells

    D. increases the rate of glomerular filtration

    E. decreases the rate of glomerular filtration

25. Which area of the kidney is the site of the passive diffusion of Na^+?

   A. thick segment of ascending limb   **C.** loop of Henle

   B. distal convoluted tubule   **D.** proximal convoluted tubule

                                        E. collecting ducts

26. Angiotensin II functions to:

   A. decrease water absorption   **C.** decrease aldosterone production

   B. decrease arterial blood pressure   **D.** constrict arterioles and increase blood pressure

                                        E. decrease plasma pH

27. The primary mechanism of removing Na^+ ions from urine is the nephron sodium-hydrogen exchange carrier (an anti-port carrier). What is the approximate pH of the urine when the carrier is functioning?

   A. 5.8   **C.** 7.6

   B. 8.2   **D.** 11.1

                                        E. 2

28. Inadequate secretion of ADH causes symptoms of polyuria in a disease known as:

   A. diabetic acidosis   **C.** diabetes mellitus

   B. nephrogenic diabetes insipidus   **D.** diabetes insipidus

                                        E. diabetic alkalosis

29. Hydrolysis results in the production of nitrogenous waste in urea, uric acid, or ammonia?

   A. vitamins   **C.** sugars

   B. fats   **D.** carbohydrates

                                        E. proteins

30. The above normal hydrostatic pressure in Bowman's capsule would result in:

   A. filtration increases in proportion to the increase in Bowman's capsule pressure

   B. osmotic pressure compensating so that filtration does not change

   C. net filtration increased above normal

   D. net filtration decreased below normal

   E. no effect on filtration rate

31. The concentration of which compound is controlled by the respiratory system and maintains pH of fluids?

A. oxygen

B. bicarbonate

C. carbon dioxide

D. HCl

E. pepsin

32. All statements regarding tubular reabsorption are true, EXCEPT that:

A. it involves hormonal signals in the collecting ducts

B. it is only a passive transport process

C. it occurs via transcellular or paracellular routes

D. it is a reclamation process

E. the transport mechanism of the components depends on their location within the nephron

33. Which is part of the excretory and reproductive systems of male mammals?

A. urethra

B. ureter

C. prostate

D. vas deferens

E. epididymis

34. High levels of glucose and amino acids are reabsorbed in the filtrate through:

A. counter-transport

B. primary active transport

C. facilitated diffusion

D. passive transport

E. secondary active transport

35. Which statement most accurately describes the expected levels of aldosterone and vasopressin in the blood of a dehydrated patient compared to a healthy individual?

A. Aldosterone levels are higher, and vasopressin levels are lower

B. Aldosterone levels are lower, and vasopressin levels are higher

C. Aldosterone and vasopressin levels are higher

D. Aldosterone and vasopressin levels are lower

E. Aldosterone and vasopressin levels are not related

36. Compared to the human kidney, the kidney of an animal living in an arid environment is capable of producing more concentrated urine because it:

   A. produces urine that is isotonic compared to the blood
   B. maintains a greater osmolarity gradient in the medulla
   C. maintains a greater hydrostatic pressure for filtration at the glomerulus
   D. increases the rate of filtration
   E. maintains a lower osmolarity gradient in the medulla

37. Which is a function of the loop of Henle?

   A. Absorption of water into the filtrate
   B. Absorption of electrolytes by active transport and water by osmosis in the same segments
   C. Forming a small volume of very concentrated urine
   D. Forming a large volume of very concentrated urine
   E. Absorption of electrolytes into the filtrate

38. Which nephron structure is a site for removing H_2O to concentrate the urine?

   I. ascending loop of Henle
   II. descending loop of Henle
   III. proximal convoluted tubule

   A. III only
   B. I and III only
   C. II only
   D. I, II and III
   E. II and III only

39. If an amino acid has a T_m of 140 mg/100 ml and its concentration in blood is 230 mg/100 ml, this amino acid will:

   A. be entirely reabsorbed by secondary active transport
   B. appear in the urine
   C. be entirely reabsorbed into the filtrate by facilitated transport
   D. be entirely reabsorbed by primary active transport
   E. be entirely reabsorbed into the filtrate by diffusion

40. Which would be the result of increased plasma osmolarity?

   A. dehydration
   B. increased ADH secretion
   C. decreased H_2O permeability in the nephron
   D. excretion of dilute urine
   E. increased calcitonin release

41. If the renal clearance value of substance X is zero, it means that:

    A. usually, all substance X is reabsorbed

    B. the value is relatively high in a healthy adult

    C. the substance X molecule is too large to be filtered via the kidneys

    D. most of substance X is filtered via the kidneys and is not reabsorbed in the convoluted tubules

    E. substance X is mainly excreted in the urine

42. Which sequence correctly represents the pathway of anatomical structures passed by a probe being inserted into the urethra of a female patient?

    A. urethra → bladder → opening to the ureter → ureter → prostate → renal pelvis

    B. ureter → opening to the ureter → prostate → vas deferens → epididymis

    C. urethra → bladder → opening to the ureter → ureter → renal pelvis

    D. kidney → ureter → opening to the bladder → bladder → urethra

    E. opening to the ureter → bladder → ureter → prostate → renal pelvis

43. Which is observed for chronic adrenal insufficiency caused by decreased adrenal cortex activity?

    A. high sex hormone concentrations

    B. high plasma control

    C. increased resistance to stress

    D. high urinary output

    E. decreased rate of filtration

44. Which sequence correctly represents the pathway of anatomical structures passed by a probe being inserted into the urethra of a male patient?

    A. urethra → vas deferens → prostate → ejaculatory duct → seminiferous tubules → epididymis

    B. urethra → prostate → vas deferens → ejaculatory duct → seminiferous tubules → epididymis

    C. urethra → ejaculatory duct → prostate → vas deferens → epididymis → seminiferous tubules

    D. urethra → ejaculatory duct → vas deferens → epididymis → seminiferous tubules

    E. urethra → prostate → ejaculatory duct → vas deferens → epididymis → seminiferous tubules

45. Renin is a polypeptide hormone that:

    A. is produced in response to increased blood volume

    B. is produced in response to decreased blood pressure

    C. acts on the pituitary gland

    D. is produced in response to concentrated urine

    E. is secreted in the proximal convoluted tubules of the kidney

46. What is unique about transport epithelial cells in the ascending loop of Henle in humans?

    A. They are the largest epithelial cells in the body

    B. They are not in contact with interstitial fluid

    C. They are membranes that are impermeable to water

    D. 50% of their cell mass is comprised of smooth endoplasmic reticulum

    E. They are not affected by high levels of nitrogenous wastes

47. Which symptom is characteristic of a patient with *Nephrogenic diabetes insipidus*, whereby kidneys are unresponsive to ADH hormone?

    A. dilute urine

    B. decreased levels of plasma ADH

    C. detection of glucose in urine

    D. elevated plasma glucose levels

    E. concentrated urine

48. Excretion of dilute urine requires the:

    A. presence of vasopressin

    B. transport of sodium ions out of the descending nephron loop

    C. impermeability of the collecting tubule to water

    D. relative permeability of the distal tubule to water

    E. transport of chloride ions out of the descending nephron loop

49. All are reabsorbed from the glomerular filtrate in the ascending loop of Henle, EXCEPT:

    A. K^+

    B. Cl^-

    C. Na^+

    D. glucose

    E. amino acids

50. The epithelial cells of the proximal convoluted tubule contain a brush border; the primary purpose is to:

    A. slow the rate of movement of the filtrate through the nephron

    B. move the filtrate via cilia action through the nephron

    C. increase the volume of urine produced

    D. increase the amount of filtrate entering the loop of Henle

    E. increase the absorptive surface area

51. Which structure within the nephron is the site of aldosterone function?

    A. Bowman's capsule

    B. distal convoluted tubule

    C. ascending loop of Henle

    D. descending loop of Henle

    E. glomerulus

52. Which would NOT be observed in a child with acute inflammation of the glomerulus, causing its failure to filter adequate quantities of fluid?

A. high urine [Na$^+$]

B. decreased urine output

C. high plasma [urea]

D. excess interstitial fluid

E. low urine [Na$^+$]

53. In the ascending limb of the nephron loop, the:

A. thin segment is not permeable to chloride

B. thin segment is not permeable to sodium

C. thick segment is permeable to water

D. thin segment is freely permeable to water

E. thick segment moves ions out into interstitial spaces for reabsorption

54. What is the clinical result of administering a pharmaceutical that selectively binds and inactivates renin?

A. Decreased Na$^+$ reabsorption by the distal tubule

B. Increase in the amount of filtrate entering Bowman's capsule

C. Increased Na$^+$ reabsorption by the distal tubule

D. Increase in blood pressure

E. Excretion of platelets in the urine

55. An example of a properly functioning homeostatic control system is seen when:

A. core body temperature of a runner rises gradually from 37° to 45 °C

B. kidneys excrete salt into the urine when dietary salt levels rise

C. blood cell shrinks when placed in a solution of salt and water

D. blood pressure increases in response to an increase in blood volume

E. the level of glucose in the blood is abnormally high whether or not a meal has been eaten

56. Within the kidney:

A. filtration of blood begins at the glomerulus and ends at the loop of Henle

B. glucose and H$_2$O are actively reabsorbed from the glomerular filtrate

C. ammonia is converted to urea

D. nephrons are only in the cortex of the kidney

E. antidiuretic hormone causes the collecting tubule to reabsorb H$_2$O

Muscle System

1. What part of the sarcolemma contains acetylcholine receptors?

   A. the part contiguous to another muscle cell   **C.** motor endplate

   B. entire sarcolemma   **D.** distal end of the muscle fiber

      E. presynaptic membrane

2. How are cardiac muscle cells different from smooth and skeletal muscle cells?

   A. It is often branched   **C.** It is under involuntary control

   B. It lacks actin and myosin fibers   **D.** It has a striated appearance

      E. It has T tubules

3. The energy for muscle contraction is supplied by:

   A. lactose   **C.** lactic acid

   B. ADP   **D.** phosphocreatine and ATP

      E. cAMP and ATP

4. The role of tropomyosin in skeletal muscles is to:

   A. serve as a contraction inhibitor by blocking the actin-binding sites on the myosin molecules

   B. be the receptor for the motor neuron neurotransmitter

   C. be the chemical that activates the myosin heads

   D. provide the energy for myosin heads to dissociate from the actin filaments

   E. serve as a contraction inhibitor by blocking myosin-binding sites on the actin molecules

5. Which occurs during muscular contraction?

   A. Neither the thin nor the thick filament contracts

   B. Both the thin and thick filaments contract

   C. The thin filament contracts while the thick filament remains constant

   D. The thin filament remains constant while the thick filament contracts

   E. Both the thin and thick filaments undergo depolymerization

6. At the neuromuscular junction, the depression on the sarcolemma is:

   A. motor endplate   **C.** synaptic knob

   B. junctional folds   **D.** synaptic vesicle

      E. boundary of the sarcomere

7. Most skeletal muscles consist of:

    A. predominantly slow oxidative fibers

    B. predominantly fast oxidative fibers

    C. muscle fibers of the same type

    D. a mixture of fiber types

    E. predominantly fast glycolytic fibers

8. Irreversible sequestering of Ca^{2+} in the sarcoplasmic reticulum likely results in:

    A. depolymerization of actin filaments within the sarcomere

    B. permanent contraction of the muscle filaments analogous to *rigor mortis*

    C. increased bone density as Ca^{2+} is resorbed from bones to replace sequestered Ca^{2+}

    D. prevention of actin cross-bridges to myosin thin filaments

    E. prevention of myosin cross-bridges to actin thin filaments

9. Which does NOT happen during muscle contraction?

    A. H band shortens or disappears

    B. I band shortens or disappears

    C. A band shortens or disappears

    D. sarcomere shortens

    E. Z disks approach each other

10. The strongest muscle contractions are typically achieved by:

    A. increasing the stimulation up to the maximal stimulus

    B. recruiting small and medium muscle fibers

    C. increasing stimulus above the threshold

    D. increasing stimulus above the *treppe* stimulus

    E. all the above

11. The SA node, innervated by the vagus nerve, is a collection of cardiac muscle cells with the capacity for self-excitation. The effect of the vagus nerve on the frequency of the heartbeat for self-excitation is likely:

    A. slower because innervation decreases heart rate

    B. faster because innervation decreases heart rate

    C. slower because innervation increases heart rate

    D. faster because innervation increases heart rate

    E. no effect on heart rate because cardiac cells maintain auto-rhythmicity

12. Continuous repetitive muscle contraction results in a buildup of lactic acid because it is the:

    A. degradation product of ADP

    B. degradation product of phosphocreatine

    C. organic product of anaerobic metabolism

    D. degradation product of fatty acid degradation

    E. releasing factor for hydrolysis actin-myosin crosslinking

13. The point of attachment of a nerve to muscle fiber is the:

A. contraction point   C. relaxation point

B. synapse   D. neuromuscular junction

     E. Z disc

14. Which is used later in muscle stimulation when contractile strength increases?

A. Motor units with larger, less excitable neurons

B. Large motor units with small, highly excitable neurons

C. Many small motor units with the ability to stimulate other motor units

D. Motor units with the longest muscle fibers

E. Large motor units with small, less excitable neurons

15. The reason for sudden vasodilation, manifested by flush skin, before the onset of frostbite is:

A. blood shunting via sphincters within the smooth muscle

B. rapid contractions of skeletal muscles

C. paralysis of skeletal muscle encapsulating the area

D. onset of tachycardia from the increase in blood pressure

E. paralysis of smooth muscle in the area

16. Which is NOT correct regarding cardiac muscle?

A. The ANS is required for stimulation

B. Large mitochondria fill about 25% of the cell

C. It is rich in glycogen and myoglobin

D. It has one or possibly two nuclei

E. It is repaired primarily by fibrosis

17. In the muscle cell, the function of creatine phosphate is:

A. to induce a conformational change in the myofilaments

B. to induce energy that will be transferred to ADP to synthesize ATP

C. to form a temporary chemical compound with myosin

D. to form a chemical compound with actin

E. to bind to the troponin

18. Shivering functions to increase core body temperature because it:

   A. increases the contractile activity of skeletal muscles

   B. signals the hypothalamus that body temperature is higher than actual

   C. causes bones to rub together to generate heat

   D. signals the body that the core temperature is low and encourages behavioral modification

   E. increases the contractile activity of smooth muscles

19. Which is NOT a property of muscle tissue?

   A. extensibility

   B. contractility

   C. communication

   D. excitability

   E. all the above

20. The individual muscle cell is surrounded by:

   A. fascicle

   B. epimysium

   C. periosteum

   D. perimysium

   E. endomysium

21. Which muscle types are involuntary muscles?

   A. cardiac and smooth

   B. cardiac, smooth, and skeletal

   C. skeletal and smooth

   D. only smooth

   E. cardiac and skeletal muscle

22. Myoglobin:

   A. phosphorylates ADP directly

   B. stores oxygen in muscle cells

   C. produces the endplate potential

   D. breaks down glycogen

   E. transports carbon dioxide in the blood

23. During an action potential, a cardiac muscle cell remains depolarized much longer than a neuron to:

   A. prevent a neuron from depolarizing twice in rapid succession

   B. permit adjacent cardiac muscle cells to contract at different times

   C. prevent the initiation of another action potential during contraction of the heart

   D. ensures that Na^+ voltage-gated channels remain open, so Na^+ exits the cell

   E. ensures that K^+ voltage-gated channels remain open, so K^+ exits the cell

24. A characteristic of cardiac muscle that can be observed with the light microscope is:

    A. somatic motor neurons

    B. no nuclei

    C. intercalated discs

    D. single cells

    E. none of the above

25. Rigor mortis (stiffness of the corpse's limbs after death) occurs because:

    A. no ATP is available to release attached actin and myosin molecules

    B. proteins are beginning to hydrolyze and break down

    C. the cells are dead

    D. sodium ions leak into the muscle causing continued contractions

    E. calcium ions are prevented from flowing to their target

26. Muscles undergo movement at joints by:

    A. increasing in length and pushing the origin and insertion of the muscle together

    B. filling with blood and increasing the distance between the ends of a muscle

    C. increasing in length and pushing the origin and insertion of the muscle apart

    D. depolarizing neurons, which initiate electrical twitches at the tendons

    E. decreasing in length and moving the origin and insertion of the muscle closer

27. The plasma membrane of a muscle cell is:

    A. sarcolemma

    B. sarcoplasmic reticulum

    C. titin

    D. myofibril

    E. periosteum

28. T tubules function to:

    A. hold cross-bridges in place in a resting muscle

    B. synthesize ATP to provide energy for muscle contraction

    C. stabilize the G and F actin

    D. facilitate cellular communication during muscle contraction

    E. store calcium when the muscle is at rest

29. What is the role of Ca^{2+} in muscle contraction?

    A. Transmitting the action potential across the neuromuscular junction

    B. Reestablishing the polarization of the plasma membrane after an action potential

    C. Propagation of the action potential through the transverse tubules

    D. Binding to troponin, changing the conformation of tropomyosin for myosin to bind to actin

    E. Binding to troponin, which changes the conformation of tropomyosin and permits the actin heads to bind to the myosin thin filament

30. Wavelike contraction produced by a smooth muscle is:

A. vasoconstriction

B. myoblastosis

C. vasodilation

D. circulitus

E. peristalsis

31. The striations of a skeletal muscle cell are due to:

A. T tubules

B. sarcoplasmic reticulum

C. arrangement of myofilaments

D. thickness of the sarcolemma

E. repetition of actin thick filaments

32. For the movement of a pair of antagonistic muscles, one of the muscles:

A. contracts in an isometric action

B. acts synergistically by contracting to stabilize the moving bone

C. contracts in an isotonic action

D. relaxes

E. establishes an insertion point to slide along the bone to allow a larger range of movement

33. Which skeletal muscle fiber type is most resistant to fatigue?

A. no-twitch

B. fast glycolytic

C. intermediate

D. fast-oxidative

E. slow-oxidative

34. During muscle contraction, the thick filament cross-bridges attach to:

A. Z discs

B. T tubules

C. myosin filaments

D. actin filaments

E. M line

35. What structure connects the biceps muscle to the radius bone?

A. biceps cartilage

B. biceps ligament

C. biceps muscle

D. annular ligament of the radius

E. biceps tendon

36. Which is the correct sequence of events for muscle contractions?

A. Motor neuron action potential → muscle cell action potential → neurotransmitter release → release of calcium ions from SR → sliding of myofilaments → ATP-driven power stroke

B. Neurotransmitter release → motor neuron action potential → muscle cell action potential → release of calcium ions from SR → ATP-driven power stroke

C. Motor neuron action potential → neurotransmitter release → muscle cell action potential → release of calcium ions from SR → ATP-driven power stroke → sliding of myofilaments

D. Neurotransmitter release → muscle cell action potential → motor neuron action potential → release of calcium ions from SR → sliding of myofilaments → ATP-driven power stroke

E. Muscle cell action potential → neurotransmitter release → ATP-driven power stroke → calcium ion release from SR → sliding of myofilaments

37. The release of which molecule from the sarcoplasmic reticulum is typically required to contract a muscle?

A. calcium

B. potassium

C. water

D. sodium

E. magnesium

38. The enteric nervous system controls which action of the muscle?

A. Contraction of the diaphragm

B. Peristalsis of the gastrointestinal tract

C. Conduction of cardiac muscle action potentials

D. The reflex arc of the knee-jerk response when the patella is struck

E. Contraction of the bicep and the opposing relaxation of the triceps

39. Which molecule breaks the bonding between the two contractile proteins for the myosin-actin cross-bridges?

A. ATP

B. sodium

C. acetylcholine

D. calcium

E. potassium

40. The contraction of smooth muscle is different from skeletal muscle because smooth muscle contraction:

A. ATP energizes the sliding process

B. the site of calcium regulation differs

C. the trigger for contraction is a rise in intracellular calcium

D. actin and myosin interact through the sliding filament mechanism

E. none of the above

41. Which is NOT present in a skeletal muscle?

    A. sarcoplasmic reticulum

    B. multinucleated cells

    C. individual innervations of each muscle fiber

    D. intercellular conductivity of action potentials

    E. regular array of molecular components

42. Excitation-contraction coupling requires which substance(s)?

    I. ATP   II. glucose   III. Ca^{2+}

    A. I only

    B. III only

    C. I and II only

    D. I and III only

    E. I, II and III

43. All statements are true for smooth muscle, EXCEPT:

    A. Its contractions are involuntary

    B. It does not require Ca^{2+} for contraction

    C. Its contractions produce a chemical change near the smooth muscle

    D. Its contractions are longer than the contractions in skeletal muscle

    E. Its contractions are slower than the contractions in skeletal muscle

44. Which molecule is released by synaptic vesicles into the synaptic cleft for skeletal muscles?

    A. water

    B. sodium

    C. acetylcholine

    D. calcium

    E. calcitonin

45. Which statement about smooth muscle is correct?

    A. Smooth muscle cannot stretch as much as skeletal muscle

    B. Smooth muscle has well-developed T tubules at the site of invagination

    C. Smooth muscle stores sodium in the sarcoplasmic reticulum

    D. Smooth muscle contains troponin as a calcium-binding site

    E. Certain smooth muscle cells can divide to increase their numbers

46. Which muscle is under voluntary control?

    A. smooth muscle in the gastrointestinal tract

    B. iris of the eye

    C. diaphragm

    D. cardiac tissue

    E. vasodilation

47. The thick filament of skeletal muscle fibers is composed of:

A. myosin   **C.** tropomyosin

B. troponin   **D.** actin

                                  E. none of the above

48. Which is NOT a characteristic of a smooth muscle?

A. Noncontractile intermediate filaments attach to dense bodies within the cell

B. There are no sarcomeres

C. Calmodulin is a regulatory protein to regulate cellular calcium levels

D. It lacks troponin

E. There are more thick filaments than thin filaments

49. Which statement describes the structure of smooth muscle?

A. Multicellular units of muscle tissue are under voluntary control

B. Peristalsis results from single-unit muscle cells within the gastrointestinal tract

C. Ca^{2+} distribution occurs via an extensive network of T-tubules

D. Ca^{2+} binds to troponin and changes the conformation of the tropomyosin

E. Sarcomeres are visible as repeating motifs of actin and myosin

50. Which molecule abundant in the sarcoplasm provides stored energy for the muscle to use during exercise?

A. glycogen   **C.** water

B. calcium   **D.** myosin

                                  E. actin

51. Which is a true statement about muscle?

A. Skeletal muscle cells are long and cylindrical with many nuclei

B. Cardiac muscle cells are in the heart and large blood vessels

C. Cardiac muscle cells have four nuclei

D. Smooth muscle cells have T tubules

E. Smooth muscles have extensive gap junctions for rapid communication

52. Which statement is true for cardiac muscle?

A. It is multi-nucleated

B. It is not striated

C. It does not require Ca^{2+}

D. It is innervated by the somatic motor nervous system

E. It is under involuntary control

53. A typical skeletal muscle:

    A. is innervated by the somatic nervous system

    B. is innervated only by the autonomic nervous system

    C. lines the walls of glands and organs

    D. has myosin and actin that lack a striated appearance

    E. is innervated only by the parasympathetic and sympathetic nervous system

54. A muscle type that has only one nucleus, no sarcomeres, and rare gap junctions:

    A. cardiac muscle

    B. skeletal muscle

    C. visceral smooth muscle

    D. multiunit smooth muscle

    E. cardiac and skeletal muscle

55. A protein in muscle cells that binds oxygen is:

    A. tropomyosin

    B. glycogen

    C. calmodulin

    D. myosin

    E. myoglobin

56. The muscle type characterized by multinucleated cells?

    A. cardiac muscle

    B. smooth muscle

    C. skeletal muscle

    D. cardiac and skeletal muscle

    E. smooth and skeletal muscle

57. In skeletal muscle cells, the structure that functions in calcium storage is:

    A. intermediate filament network

    B. myofibrillar network

    C. calmodulin

    D. sarcoplasmic reticulum

    E. mitochondria

58. Which statement is correct about cardiac muscle?

    I. It acts as a functional syncytium

    II. It is under the control of the autonomic nervous system

    III. It is striated due to the arrangement of actin and myosin filaments

    A. I only

    B. III only

    C. II and III only

    D. I, II, and III

    E. I and II only

Skeletal System

1. The vertebral curves function to:

   A. improve the cervical center of gravity

   B. accommodate the weight of the pelvic girdle

   C. provide resilience and flexibility

   D. accommodate muscle attachment

   E. provide a route for blood distribution

2. Which connective tissue attaches a muscle to the bone?

   A. origin

   B. ligament

   C. aponeurosis

   D. tendon

   E. cartilage

3. The purpose of synovial fluid in a synovial joint is to:

   A. hydrate osteocyte cells

   B. create a rigid connection between opposing flat bones

   C. reduce friction between the ends of opposing bones

   D. create the structure for the necessary morphology of joints and bones

   E. create a physical barrier, so cells do not migrate from the region

4. Which region of the human vertebral column bears the most body weight and receives the most stress?

   A. thoracic region

   B. lumbar region

   C. cervical region

   D. sacral region

   E. cranial

5. During bone maturation, osteoblasts are trapped in their matrix and become which cells when they stop producing matrix?

   A. matrixocytes

   B. trabeculocytes

   C. osteoclasts

   D. spiculoclasts

   E. osteocytes

6. Which is characteristic of short bones?

   A. Consist mainly of hyaline cartilage

   B. Consist mostly of dense bone

   C. Consist of both spongy and dense bone

   D. Consist mostly of spongy bone

   E. Consist mostly of hyaline cartilage and dense bone

7. The primary function of the axial skeleton is to:

    A. provide central support for the body and protect internal organs

    B. provide a space for the major digestive organs

    C. provide a conduit for the peripheral nerves

    D. provide an attachment point for muscles to allow movement

    E. give the body resilience

8. The skeletal system performs the following functions EXCEPT:

    A. removal of toxins from the blood   **C.** protection of the viscera

    B. storage and release of minerals   **D.** production of the blood

                                           E. production of Vitamin C

9. Which tissue would result in the LEAST amount of pain when surgically cut?

    A. skin   **C.** bone

    B. smooth muscle   **D.** cartilage

                                         E. skeletal muscle

10. Which bone tissue is most adapted to support weight and withstand tension stress?

    A. compact bone   **C.** spongy bone

    B. trabecular bone   **D.** irregular bone

                                         E. long bone

11. What disease in children results in soft and pliable bones due to the lack of vitamin D?

    A. Paget's disease   **C.** Rickets

    B. Brittle bones   **D.** osteoporosis

                                         E. Turner's syndrome

12. All structures are made of cartilage EXCEPT:

    A. larynx   **C.** middle ear

    B. nose   **D.** outer ear

                                         E. skeletal joint

13. Yellow bone marrow contains a significant percentage of:

    A. collagen fibers   **C.** blood-forming cells

    B. elastic tissue   **D.** fat

                                         E. hydroxyapatite

14. The parathyroid hormone can increase the production of:

    A. osteoblasts

    B. osteoclasts

    C. osteocytes

    D. osseous tissue

    E. cartilage

15. The structural unit of compact bone is:

    A. lamellar bone

    B. spongy bone

    C. canaliculi

    D. osseous matrix

    E. osteon

16. Which hormone maintains the appropriate calcium levels in the blood, often at the expense of bone loss?

    A. vitamin D

    B. parathyroid hormone

    C. androgens

    D. calcitonin

    E. estrogen

17. Which connective tissue has a flexible and strong matrix?

    A. cartilage

    B. dense regular connective tissue

    C. reticular tissue

    D. areolar tissue

    E. collagenous tissue

18. During bone formation, a deficiency of growth hormone can cause:

    A. decreased proliferation of the epiphyseal plate cartilage

    B. increased osteoclast activity

    C. inadequate calcification of bone

    D. decreased osteoclast activity

    E. decreased formation of hydroxyapatite

19. Connective tissue holding the bones together in a synovial joint is:

    A. osteocyte

    B. tendons

    C. cartilage

    D. periosteum

    E. ligament

20. Which statement is correct regarding the ossification of the ends of long bones?

    A. It takes twice as long as diaphysis ossification

    B. Secondary ossification centers produce it

    C. It involves medullary cavity formation

    D. It is a characteristic of intramembranous bone formation

    E. none of the above

21. The abnormal curvature of the thoracic spine from compression fractures of weakened vertebrae is:

A. kyphosis

B. calluses

C. stooping

D. menopausal atrophy

E. scoliosis

22. Which substance is NOT involved in bone remodeling?

A. calcitonin

B. vitamin D

C. melanin

D. thyroxine

E. parathyroid hormone

23. Until adolescence, the diaphysis of the bone can increase in length due to the:

A. epiphyseal plate

B. epiphyseal line

C. lacunae

D. Haversian system

E. canaliculi

24. Which is NOT the function of bone?

A. storage of lipids

B. facilitate muscle contraction

C. structural support

D. storage of minerals

E. regulation of blood temperature

25. Which is the most important stimulus for epiphyseal plate activity during infancy and childhood?

A. cortisol

B. growth hormone

C. calcium

D. parathyroid hormone

E. thyroid hormone

26. The normal histological makeup of bone is concentric lamellae called:

A. periosteum

B. endosteum

C. osteon

D. trabeculae

E. canaliculi

27. Parathyroid hormone elevates blood calcium levels by:

A. increasing the number and activity of osteoblasts

B. decreasing the number and activity of osteoblasts

C. decreasing the number and activity of osteoclasts

D. increasing the number and activity of osteoclasts

E. does not affect bone cells

28. The inner osteogenic layer of the periosteum consists primarily of:

A. hyaline and cartilage

B. chondrocytes and osteocytes

C. cartilage and compact bone

D. marrow and osteons

E. progenitor cells

29. Which is NOT in compact bone?

A. yellow marrow

B. canaliculi

C. Haversian canals

D. Volkmann's canals

E. osteons

30. The Haversian canal runs through the core of each osteon and is the site of:

A. yellow marrow and spicules

B. blood vessels and nerve fibers

C. cartilage and interstitial lamellae

D. adipose tissue and nerve fibers

E. adipose tissue and cartilage

31. The process when bone develops from hyaline cartilage is:

A. periosteal ossification

B. intramembranous ossification

C. intermembranous ossification

D. endochondral ossification

E. none of the above

32. Connective tissue that connects bones is:

A. synovium

B. osteoprogenitor cells

C. ligaments

D. sockets

E. muscles

33. A failure of the lamina of the vertebrae to fuse correctly in the lumbar region during development can produce an exposed spinal cord called:

A. spondylosis

B. spina bifida

C. stenosis

D. scoliosis

E. kyphosis

34. The process of bones increasing in width is:

A. concentric growth

B. long bone growth

C. epiphyseal plate opening

D. closing of the epiphyseal plate

E. appositional growth

35. Hydroxyapatite is the mineral portion of bone and does NOT contain:

A. hydrogen

B. calcium

C. phosphate

D. sulfur

E. all are in bone

36. Osteoclast activity to release more calcium ions into the bloodstream is stimulated by:

A. cortisol

B. parathyroid hormone

C. thyroxine

D. calcitonin

E. estrogen

37. Which tissue is bone classified as?

A. epithelial

B. endothelial

C. muscle

D. skeletal

E. connective

38. What connective tissue stores calcium?

A. muscle

B. tendon

C. ligament

D. bone

E. calyx of the kidneys

39. Bone growth and healing from a fracture are impossible without:

A. osteoclasts

B. osteoblasts

C. dietary intake of calcium and vitamin D

D. osteocytes

E. chondrocytes

40. The precursor of an osteoclast, the cell responsible for bone resorption, is:

A. erythrocyte

B. chondrocyte

C. osseous tissue

D. macrophage

E. canaliculi

41. Which statement regarding interstitial growth is correct?

A. Unspecialized mesenchymal cells develop into chondrocytes that divide and form cartilage

B. Chondrocytes in the lacunae divide and secrete a matrix allowing the cartilage to grow from within

C. Growth occurs in the lining of the long bones

D. Fibroblasts give rise to chondrocytes that differentiate and form cartilage

E. Chondrocytes in the lacunae divide and secrete a matrix allowing cartilage to grow by depositing new layers onto the surface of the bone

42. The shaft of long bones is:

A. cortex

B. medulla

C. epiphysis

D. diaphysis

E. endochondral ossification

43. The concentration of blood calcium is raised by which hormone?

A. insulin

B. glucagon

C. antidiuretic hormone

D. aldosterone

E. parathyroid hormone

44. In the epiphyseal plate, cartilage grows:

A. in a circular fashion

B. from the edges inward

C. by pushing the epiphysis away from the diaphysis

D. by pulling the diaphysis toward the epiphysis

E. by pulling the epiphysis toward the diaphysis

45. Which is the most important function of the spongy bone of the hips?

A. storage of fats

B. synthesis of lymph fluid

C. degradation of leukocytes

D. storage of erythrocytes

E. synthesis of erythrocytes

46. The structural unit of spongy bone is:

A. trabeculae

B. osseous lamellae

D. lamellar bone

C. osteons

E. Haversian canals

47. If a thyroid tumor secreted an excessive amount of calcitonin, this would result in:

A. increase in blood calcium concentration

B. reduction in the rate of endochondral ossification

C. increase in the level of osteoblast activity

D. increase in the level of osteoclast activity

E. decrease in bone density

48. Which can NOT contribute to osteoporosis (i.e., decreased bone mass and density)?

   A. menopause

   B. high blood levels of calcitonin hormone

   C. high sensitivity to endogenous parathyroid hormone

   D. high blood levels of parathyroid hormone

   E. impaired intestinal Ca^{2+} absorption

49. Connective tissue sacs lined with synovial membranes that act as cushions where friction develops are:

   A. tendons

   B. ligaments

   C. bursae

   D. menisci

   E. Haversian canal

50. The narrow space of hyaline cartilage that is the site of long bone growth until the end of puberty is:

   A. chondrocyte line

   B. epiphyseal plate

   C. medullary cavity

   D. mineralization

   E. endochondral ossification

Respiratory System

1. Which is NOT a respiratory system function?

   A. Helping to expel abdominal contents during defecation and childbirth
   B. Helping to transport gases to tissues
   C. Allowing the exchange of O_2 between blood and air
   D. Contributing to the maintenance of the pH balance
   E. Allowing the exchange of CO_2 between blood and air

2. The loudness of a person's voice depends on:

   A. force of air as it rushes across the vocal folds
   B. strength of the intrinsic laryngeal muscles
   C. length of the vocal folds
   D. thickness of vestibular folds
   E. all the above

3. Which nervous system controls vasoconstriction of arterioles involved in heat conduction to the skin?

   A. motor
   B. somatic
   C. sensory
   D. sympathetic
   E. central

4. The function of type I cells of the alveoli is to:

   A. form the structure of the alveolar wall
   B. protect the lungs from bacterial invasion
   C. secrete surfactant
   D. trap dust and other debris
   E. replace mucus in the alveoli

5. Where in the brain is the inspiratory and expiratory center located?

   A. cerebral hemispheres
   B. substantia nigra
   C. pons
   D. cerebellum
   E. medulla oblongata

6. Air moves out of the lungs when the pressure inside the lungs is:

   I. greater than the intra-alveolar pressure
   II. greater than the pressure in the atmosphere
   III. less than the pressure in the atmosphere

   A. I only
   B. II only
   C. III only
   D. I and II only
   E. I and III only

7. Which factors are necessary for expiration?

   A. Negative feedback of expansion fibers during inspiration and outward pull of surface tension due to surfactant
   B. The combined amount of CO_2 in blood and air in the alveoli
   C. The recoil of elastic fibers that were stretched during inspiration and the inward pull of surface tension due to the film of alveolar fluid
   D. Expansion of respiratory muscles that were contracted during inspiration and the lack of surface tension on the alveolar wall
   E. The combined amount of O_2 in blood and CO_2 in the alveoli

8. During breathing, inhalation results from:

   A. forcing air from the throat into the lungs
   B. contracting the abdominal muscles
   C. relaxing the muscles of the rib cage
   D. muscles of the lungs expanding the alveoli
   E. contracting the diaphragm

9. In a panting animal that breathes in and out rapidly, a substantial portion of new air comes into contact with the upper regions of the respiratory passages to:

   A. decrease body heat via evaporation
   B. rapidly increase CO_2 expiration
   C. moisten the mucosa of the respiratory passages
   D. minimize the movement of respiratory muscles
   E. decrease CO_2 expiration

10. What maintains the openness (i.e., patency) of the trachea?

    A. relaxation of smooth muscle
    B. C-shaped cartilage rings
    C. surfactant production
    D. surface tension of water
    E. relaxation of skeletal muscle

11. Why are there rings of hyaline cartilage in the trachea?

    A. To prevent choking
    B. To keep the passageway open for the continuous flow of air
    C. To provide support for the mucociliary escalator
    D. To provide support for the passage of food through the esophagus
    E. To provide the surface for gas exchange

12. Intrapulmonary pressure is:

    A. negative pressure in the intrapleural space
    B. the difference between atmospheric pressure and respiratory pressure
    C. pressure within the pleural cavity
    D. pressure within the alveoli of the lungs
    E. difference between the pressure in the pleural cavity and the atmospheric pressure

13. The gas exchange between blood and tissues occurs in:

   A. arteries, arterioles, and capillaries

   B. the entire systemic circulation

   C. pulmonary arteries only

   D. pulmonary veins only

   E. capillaries only

14. Surfactant helps to prevent the alveoli from collapsing by:

   A. protecting the surface of alveoli from dehydration

   B. disrupting the cohesiveness of H_2O, thereby reducing the surface tension of the alveolar fluid

   C. warming the air before it enters the lungs

   D. humidifying the air before it enters the lungs

   E. protecting the surface of alveoli from environmental variations

15. Through the Bohr effect, more oxygen is released to the tissue because:

   A. an increase in pH weakens the hemoglobin-oxygen bond

   B. an increase in pH strengthens the hemoglobin-oxygen bond

   C. the tissue-oxygen bond is stronger

   D. a decrease in pH strengthens the hemoglobin-oxygen bond

   E. a decrease in pH weakens the hemoglobin-oxygen bond

16. In a healthy person, the most potent respiratory stimulus for breathing is:

   A. acidosis

   B. alkalosis

   C. a decrease of oxygen in tissues

   D. an increase of carbon dioxide in the blood

   E. an increase in oxygen in the lungs

17. Which cells produce pulmonary surfactant?

   A. type II alveolar cells

   B. goblet cells

   C. alveolar macrophages

   D. type I alveolar cells

   E. none of the above

18. Ductus arteriosus connects the aorta and the pulmonary arteries during fetal development and closes at birth. Patent ductus arteriosus, a congenital heart defect when the ductus arteriosus fails to close, would NOT increase:

   A. cardiac output by the left ventricle

   B. cardiac output by the right ventricle

   C. pulmonary plasma $[O_2]$

   D. systemic plasma $[O_2]$

   E. heart rate

19. The graph shows the relationship between total alveolar ventilation (the rate at which air reaches the alveoli) and O_2 consumption during exercise.

What is the net effect of exercise on the arterial partial pressure of oxygen (P_{O_2})?

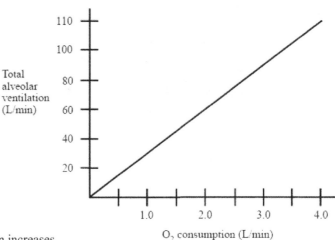

A. P_{O_2} decreases because O_2 consumption increases

B. P_{O_2} initially decreases and then rebounds because ventilation increases

C. P_{O_2} remains the same because ventilation increases as metabolism increases

D. P_{O_2} increases significantly because ventilation increases as metabolism decreases

E. P_{O_2} increases because O_2 consumption decreases

20. After inhalation, lungs pull away from the thoracic wall during elastic recoil due to:

A. natural tendency for the lungs to recoil and transpulmonary pressure

B. compliance and the surface tension of the alveolar fluid

C. elastic fibers of the connective tissue and the surface tension of the alveolar fluid

D. compliance and transpulmonary pressure

E. none of the above

21. Which would cause an increased breathing rate?

A. Low partial pressure of CO_2 in blood

B. High partial pressure of CO_2 in blood

C. High partial pressure of O_2 in blood

D. High pH of blood

E. High number of red blood cells

22. Lung compliance is determined by:

A. alveolar surface tension

B. muscles of inspiration

C. flexibility of the thoracic cage

D. airway opening

E. muscles of expiration

23. What would cause bronchodilation?

A. inspiratory center of the medulla

B. asthma

C. vagus nerve

D. sympathetic nerves

E. parasympathetic nerves

24. Tidal volume is the amount of air:

A. forcibly inhaled after normal inspiration

B. forcibly expelled after normal expiration

C. remaining in the lungs after forced expiration

D. equal to total lung capacity

E. exchanged during normal breathing

25. Working muscles produce lactic acid that lowers blood pH. For homeostasis, the lungs alter the blood ratio of CO_2 to HCO_3^- as shown in the reaction: $CO_2 + H_2O \leftrightarrow H^+ + HCO_3^-$

Which mechanism is utilized by the lungs as a compensatory action?

A. increased production of O_2

B. increased exhalation of CO_2

C. decreased ventilation rate

D. increased conversion of CO_2 to H^+ and CO_3^-

E. decreased exhalation of CO_2

26. The direction of respiratory gas movement is determined by:

A. molecular weight of the gas molecule

B. average mean temperature

C. partial pressure gradient

D. density

E. size of the gas molecule

27. Since fetal lungs are nonfunctional prior to birth, they are supplied with only enough blood to nourish the lung tissue itself. Obstruction of which structure would increase blood supply to fetal lungs?

A. ductus venosus

B. pulmonary artery

C. aorta

D. ductus arteriosus

E. pulmonary vein

28. What is a cause of hypoxia?

A. taking several rapid, deep breaths

B. very cold climate

C. low atmospheric oxygen levels

D. obstruction of the esophagus

E. none of the above

29. All are stimuli for breathing EXCEPT:

I. decrease in plasma pH

III. elevated blood pressure

II. decreased O_2 levels

IV. elevated CO_2 levels

A. I only

B. II only

C. III only

D. I and IV only

E. II and III only

30. Where does the lower respiratory tract begin?

A. bronchioles

B. primary bronchi

C. choanae

D. glottis

E. trachea

31. Which structure would NOT be affected by a respiratory tract infection?

A. alveoli

B. bronchi

C. esophagus

D. trachea

E. bronchioles

32. Respiratory control centers are in the:

A. pons and midbrain

B. upper spinal cord and medulla

C. midbrain and medulla

D. medulla and pons

E. upper spinal cord and pons

33. Which sequence is correct for air movement during exhalation?

A. alveoli → trachea → bronchi → bronchioles → larynx → pharynx

B. alveoli → bronchi → bronchioles → trachea → pharynx

C. alveoli → bronchi → lungs → bronchioles → trachea → pharynx

D. alveoli → bronchi → trachea → bronchioles → pharynx → larynx

E. alveoli → bronchioles → bronchi → trachea → larynx → pharynx

34. All statements about CO_2 are correct, EXCEPT:

A. more is carried by erythrocytes than is dissolved in blood plasma as bicarbonate

B. its concentration is greater in venous blood than in arterial blood

C. its concentration in the blood decreases by hyperventilation

D. its accumulation in the blood is associated with increased plasma acidity

E. it stimulates breathing

35. The projection from the inside of the nose into the breathing passage is:

A. meatus

B. concha

C. vibrissae

D. naris

E. nasopharynx

36. In the lungs and through cell membranes, oxygen and carbon dioxide are exchanged through the process of:

A. active transport

B. filtration

C. diffusion

D. osmosis

E. facilitated transport

37. In a healthy individual, the highest blood pressure would be in the:

A. superior vena cava

B. aorta

C. pulmonary capillaries

D. systemic capillaries

E. inferior vena cava

38. The majority of CO_2 is transported in the blood:

A. combined with the heme portion of hemoglobin

B. as carbonic acid in plasma

C. as bicarbonate ions in plasma after first entering the erythrocytes

D. combined with the amino acids of hemoglobin as carbaminohemoglobin in the erythrocytes

E. combined with albumin

39. Which physiological process is generally passive?

I. gas exchange   II. inhalation   III. exhalation

A. I only

B. I and II only

C. III only

D. I, II and III

E. I and III only

40. All are mechanisms of CO_2 transport EXCEPT:

A. attached to the heme part of hemoglobin

B. as bicarbonate ion in the plasma

C. about 10% of CO_2 is carried in the form of carbaminohemoglobin

D. about 7-10% of CO_2 is dissolved directly into the plasma

E. all are mechanisms of CO_2 transport

41. The point of division of the trachea into the right and left primary bronchi is the:

A. trachea

B. esophagus

C. carina

D. glottis

E. alveoli

42. All factors promote oxygen binding to and dissociation from hemoglobin, EXCEPT:

A. partial pressure of CO_2

B. number of erythrocytes

C. partial pressure of O_2

D. pH of the blood

E. BPG

43. Hypovolemic shock occurs when a patient's blood volume falls abruptly and is the result of:

    A. depleted Na^+ consumption

    B. excessive Na^+ consumption

    C. venous bleeding

    D. high levels of aldosterone

    E. arterial bleeding

44. An individual moves from a low to a high altitude, erythrocyte counts increase after a few days because:

    A. concentration of O_2 or total atmospheric pressure is lower at high altitudes

    B. concentration of O_2 or total atmospheric pressure is higher at higher altitudes

    C. basal metabolic rate is higher at high altitudes

    D. temperature is lower at higher altitudes

    E. the concentration of CO_2 is higher at high altitudes

45. These statements regarding the respiratory system are true, EXCEPT:

    A. when the pulmonary pressure is less than atmospheric pressure, air flows out of the lungs

    B. thoracic cavity enlargement causes the pressure of air within the lungs to decrease

    C. contraction of the diaphragm enlarges the thoracic cavity

    D. ciliated nasal membranes warm, moisten and filter inspired air

    E. respiratory process is a cycle of repetitive inspirations and expirations

46. Most inhaled particles (e.g., dust) do not reach the lungs because of the:

    A. action of epiglottis

    B. porous structure of turbinate bones

    C. abundant blood supply to the nasal mucosa

    D. ciliated mucous lining in the nose

    E. ciliated lining of the alveoli

47. Which is NOT a part of the pharynx?

    A. laryngopharynx

    B. oropharynx

    C. nasopharynx

    D. mesopharynx

    E. vertebropharynx

48. Which statement regarding the physical factors influencing pulmonary ventilation is correct?

    A. Surfactant helps increase alveolar surface tension

    B. As alveolar surface tension increases, additional muscle action is required

    C. A lung that is less elastic requires less muscle action to perform adequate ventilation

    D. A decrease in compliance causes an increase in ventilation

    E. None are correct

Integumentary System

1. The primary role of melanin in the skin is to:

   A. provide a waterproof layer for the skin

   B. shield the nucleus from damage by UV radiation

   C. be an integral component of collagen fibers

   D. keep the body cool via evaporation

   E. provide a "healthy tan look" for the person

2. Which layer is NOT part of the skin?

   A. hypodermis

   B. papillary

   C. dermis

   D. epidermis

   E. keratinocytes

3. Most of the sensations of the skin are due to nerve endings in the:

   A. medulla

   B. hypodermis

   C. dermis

   D. epidermis

   E. subcutaneous layer

4. The touch sensors of the epidermis are:

   A. nociception

   B. dendritic cells

   C. melanocytes

   D. keratinocytes

   E. tactile cells

5. Which is the site for apocrine glands?

   A. Palms of the hands and soles of the feet

   B. Under arms and in the external genitalia areas

   C. Beneath the flexure lines

   D. All body regions deep in the dermis

   E. All body superficial regions of the dermis

6. Which layer of the skin is composed of dense, irregular connective tissue?

   A. reticular layer of the dermis

   B. hypodermis

   C. epidermis

   D. papillary layer of the dermis

   E. subcutaneous layer

7. The most important function of the eccrine sweat gland is:

   A. sebum production

   B. earwax production

   C. milk production

   D. stress-induced sweating

   E. body temperature regulation

8. What causes "goosebumps" (the hair standing on end)?

   A. contraction of the epidermal papillae

   B. contraction of the epidermal ridges

   C. contraction of the arrector pili

   D. contraction of the dermal papillae

   E. none of the above

9. In addition to waterproofing and lubricating skin, sebum protects against:

   A. abrasions or cuts to the skin

   B. harmful bacteria

   C. overheating

   D. overexposure to UV light

   E. changes in pH of the integumentary

10. Which part of the hair cells has pigment granules responsible for hair color?

   A. cuticle

   B. bulb

   C. medulla

   D. cortex

   E. eccrine

11. Loss of skin, such as with a severe burn, leads to an increased risk of:

    I. dehydration

    II. bacterial infection

    III. inadequate body temperature maintenance

   A. I only

   B. II only

   C. III only

   D. I, II and III

   E. I and II only

12. Which glands are numerous throughout most of the body and produce a watery sweat that cools the body?

   A. merocrine (eccrine) glands

   B. apocrine glands

   C. ceruminous glands

   D. sebaceous glands

   E. holocrine

13. Which contributes to skin color?

       I. carotene   II. melanin   III. keratin   IV. hemoglobin

  A. II only
  B. I and II only

  C. II and IV only
  D. I, II and IV only
  E. I, II, III and IV

14. Which degree of burn destroys the epidermis and dermis and frequently requires a skin graft?

  A. first-degree burn
  B. second-degree burn

  C. third-degree burn
  D. fourth-degree burn
  E. fifth-degree burn

15. Which layer of the skin has no blood vessels?

  A. papillary
  B. hypodermis

  C. epidermis
  D. dermis
  E. none of the above

16. Which is NOT a function of the integument?

  A. thermoregulation
  B. vitamin E synthesis

  C. water retention
  D. infection resistance
  E. barrier to UV energy

17. Which is NOT associated with the dermis?

  A. elastin
  B. extrafibrillar matrix

  C. blood vessels
  D. collagen
  E. keratin

18. The outside layer of the skin is the:

  A. epidermis
  B. dermis

  C. apocrine layer
  D. lamellar layer
  E. hypodermis

19. Sweat is mainly composed of:

  A. electrolytes
  B. metabolic wastes

  C. sodium chloride
  D. antibodies
  E. water

20. The inside layer of the two main layers of the skin is the:

    A. dermis

    B. epidermis

    C. lamellar layer

    D. apocrine layer

    E. hypodermis

21. Which skin glands are an essential role in body temperature regulation?

    A. sebaceous

    B. ceruminous

    C. apocrine

    D. eccrine

    E. all the above

22. Which kind of cells comprise 30 or more stratum corneum layers?

    A. keratinized

    B. tactile "Merkel"

    C. non-keratinized

    D. stem

    E. melanocytes

23. Which skin gland is a holocrine gland?

    A. eccrine

    B. sudoriferous

    C. endocrine

    D. ceruminous

    E. sebaceous

24. The factor in the hue of the skin is the amount of:

    A. oxygen in the blood

    B. blood vessels

    C. keratin

    D. melanin

    E. lamellar layer

25. All are accessory glands of the skin EXCEPT:

    A. sebaceous

    B. mammary

    C. ceruminous

    D. all are accessory glands

    E. none are accessory glands

26. The distinctive fingerprints of humans are due to the following:

    A. friction ridges

    B. hypodermal channels

    C. oily hair

    D. sudoriferous glands

    E. keratin

27. The principal tissue in the dermal layer is:

    A. dense regular connective tissue

    B. dense irregular connective tissue

    C. areolar connective tissue

    D. stratified squamous epithelium

    E. stratified irregular connective tissue

28. Which is NOT a derivative of the epidermis?

    A. nails

    B. glands

    C. adipose tissue

    D. hair

    E. all the above

29. Which protein provides the epidermis with protective properties?

    A. elastin

    B. carotene

    C. melanin

    D. collagen

    E. keratin

30. Which is NOT a zone of hair along its length?

    A. cuticle

    B. shaft

    C. bulb

    D. root

    E. all the above

31. Which is NOT associated with hair?

    A. medulla

    B. lunula

    C. cuticle

    D. keratin bundles

    E. matrix

32. What layer of the integumentary system contains adipose tissue?

    A. dermis

    B. hypodermis

    C. epidermis

    D. muscular layer

    E. reticular dermis

33. When people gain weight, they often accumulate fat in:

    A. hypodermis

    B. reticular dermis

    C. papillary dermis

    D. epidermis

    E. dermis

34. The apocrine sweat glands are in specific locations on the body in association with:

   A. soles of the hand and feet   **C.** hair

   B. nails   **D.** exposed areas to the sun

                                       E. none of the above

35. Which statement regarding skin cancer is the most accurate?

   A. Basal cell carcinomas are the least common but most malignant

   B. Melanomas are rare but must be removed quickly to prevent them from metastasizing

   C. Most tumors that arise on the skin are malignant

   D. Squamous cell carcinomas arise from the stratum corneum

   E. Basal cell carcinomas often metastasize

36. Skin cancer is most often due to exposure to:

   A. UV light   **C.** infrared light

   B. chemicals   **D.** x-rays

                                       E. gamma rays

37. In which order would a needle pierce the epidermal layers of the skin?

   A. granulosum → basale → spinosum → corneum → lucidum

   B. corneum → lucidum → granulosum → spinosum → basale

   C. basale → spinosum → lucidum → granulosum → corneum

   D. basale → spinosum → granulosum → lucidum → corneum

   E. corneum → lucidum → basale → granulosum → spinosum

38. Which layer of the epidermis is affected first by a drug that inhibits cell division (e.g., chemotherapy drug)?

   A. stratum spinosum   **C.** stratum corneum

   B. stratum granulosum   **D.** stratum lucidum

                                       E. stratum basale

39. Mitosis occurs primarily in which stratum of the epidermis?

   A. spinosum   **C.** corneum

   B. granulosum   **D.** basale

                                       E. lucidum

40. Which layer of the skin is responsible for fingerprints?

    A. hypodermis
    B. papillary dermis

    C. reticular dermis
    D. epidermis
    E. stratum corneum

41. Which cutaneous receptor detects touch or light pressure?

    A. Ruffini endings
    B. endbulbs of Krause

    C. Meissner's corpuscles
    D. Pacinian corpuscles
    E. free nerve endings

42. The aging of the integumentary system involves changes in the following:

    I. hair   II. sebaceous glands   III. blood vessels

    A. I only
    B. II only

    C. I and III only
    D. I, II and III
    E. I and II only

43. Which statement is correct about the integument functions?

    A. Epidermal blood vessels serve as a blood reservoir
    B. Body cools by increasing the action of sebaceous glands during high-temperature conditions
    C. Dermis provides the major mechanical barrier to chemicals and other external substances
    D. Dermis provides the major mechanical barrier to water
    E. Resident macrophage-like cells ingest antigenic invaders and present them to the immune system

44. Glands only in the auditory canal are:

    A. mammary glands
    B. apocrine glands

    C. sebaceous glands
    D. cerumen glands
    E. eccrine glands

45. All are the major regions of a hair shaft, EXCEPT:

    A. medulla
    B. cortex

    C. external root sheath
    D. cuticle
    E. all the above

46. Oil glands associated with hair shafts and providing lubrication for hair and skin are:

A. apocrine glands

B. mammary glands

C. cerumen glands

D. sebaceous glands

E. eccrine glands

47. Which glands produce ear wax?

A. ceruminous glands

B. eccrine glands

C. merocrine glands

D. apocrine glands

E. sudoriferous

48. What is typically associated with the hair shaft for tactile sensations?

A. sebaceous glands

B. keratin

C. oil glands

D. muscle

E. free nerve endings

Reproductive System

1. Which event is essential for the menstrual cycle?

> I.   adrenal medulla releases norepinephrine
> II. FSH stimulates ovarian follicle development
> III. progesterone stimulates the formation of the endometrial lining

A. II only
B. III only
C. I and II only
D. II and III only
E. I and III only

2. All the following about human gamete production is true, EXCEPT:

A. meiosis in females produces four egg cells
B. sperm develops in the seminiferous tubules within the testes
C. eggs develop in the ovarian follicles within the ovaries
D. FSH stimulates gamete production in both males and females
E. gametes arise via meiosis

3. All these statements regarding the menstrual cycle are true, EXCEPT:

A. Graafian follicle, under the influence of LH, undergoes ovulation
B. follicle secretes estrogen as it develops
C. corpus luteum develops from the remains of the post-ovulatory Graafian follicle
D. FSH causes the development of the primary follicle
E. FSH and LH are both secreted by the posterior pituitary

4. Which is the initial site of spermatogenesis?

A. seminiferous tubules
B. seminal vesicles
C. vas deferens
D. epididymis
E. prostate

5. Which event occurs first?

A. formation of corpus luteum
B. rupture of the Graafian follicle
C. secretion of estrogen
D. release of progesterone
E. decrease in FSH release by the pituitary

6. Which statement correctly describes the role of LH in the menstrual cycle?

    A. stimulates the ovary to increase LH secretions

    B. inhibits secretions of GnRH

    C. stimulates the development of the endometrium for implantation of the zygote

    D. induces the corpus luteum to secrete estrogen and progesterone

    E. stimulates milk production after birth

7. What causes the testes not fully to descend into the scrotum due to abnormal testicular development?

    A. cortisol deficiency

    B. testosterone deficiency

    C. excess LH

    D. excess estrogen

    E. excess FSH

8. Testosterone is synthesized primarily by:

    A. sperm cells

    B. hypothalamus

    C. Leydig cells

    D. anterior pituitary gland

    E. seminiferous tubules

9. Which condition is the LEAST probable cause of male infertility?

    A. acrosomal enzymes denaturation

    B. immotility of cilia

    C. abnormal mitochondria

    D. testosterone deficiency

    E. abnormal flagellum

10. The surgical removal of the seminiferous tubules would likely cause:

    A. sterility, because sperm would not be produced

    B. sterility, because sperm would not be able to exit the body

    C. reduced volume of semen

    D. enhanced fertilization potency of sperm

    E. testes to migrate back into the abdominal cavity

11. Which results from scars in women's reproductive system with an elevated risk of infections (e.g., chlamydia)?

    A. elevated levels of estrogen

    B. decreased ovulation

    C. infertility

    D. reduced gamete production

    E. decreased levels of estrogen

12. The surgical removal of the seminal vesicles would likely cause:

　　A. sterility, because sperm would not be produced

　　B. sterility, because sperm would not be able to exit the body

　　C. testes to migrate back into the abdominal cavity

　　D. enhanced fertilization potency of sperm

　　E. reduced volume of semen

13. The primary difference between estrous and menstrual cycles is that:

　　A. in estrous cycle, the endometrium is shed and reabsorbed by the uterus, while in the menstrual cycle the shed the endometrium is excreted from the body

　　B. behavioral changes during estrous cycles are much less apparent than those during menstrual cycles

　　C. season and climate have less pronounced effects on the estrous cycle than they do on menstrual cycles

　　D. copulation typically occurs across the estrous cycle, whereas in menstrual cycles, copulation only occurs during the period surrounding ovulation

　　E. most estrous cycles are much longer in duration compared to menstrual cycles

14. One function of estrogen is to:

　　A. induce the ruptured follicle to develop into the corpus luteum

　　B. stimulate testosterone synthesis in males

　　C. maintain female secondary sex characteristics

　　D. promote the development and release of the follicle

　　E. lower blood glucose

15. Increasing estrogen levels during the female menstrual cycle trigger which feedback mechanism?

　　A. positive, which stimulates LH secretion by the anterior pituitary

　　B. positive, which stimulates FSH secretion by the anterior pituitary

　　C. negative, which stimulates the uterine lining to be shed

　　D. negative, which inhibits progesterone secretion by the anterior pituitary

　　E. none of the above

16. The epididymis functions to:

　　A. synthesize and release testosterone

　　B. store sperm until they are released during ejaculation

　　C. initiate the menstrual cycle by secreting FSH and LH

　　D. provide a conduit for the ovum as it moves from the ovary into the uterus

　　E. provide most of the fluid that comprises semen

17. What is the purpose of the cilia covering the inner linings of the Fallopian tubes?

   A. Preventing polyspermy by immobilizing additional incoming sperm after fusion
   B. Facilitating movement of the ovum toward the uterus
   C. Removing particulate matter that becomes trapped in the mucus layer
   D. Protecting the ovum from pH fluctuations
   E. Protecting the ovum from temperature fluctuations

18. Which endocrine structure initiates the production of testosterone?

   A. adrenal medulla   **C.** pancreas
   B. hypothalamus   **D.** anterior pituitary
                                           E. posterior pituitary

19. Decreasing progesterone during the luteal phase of the menstrual cycle results from:

   A. increased secretion of estrogen in the follicle followed by the menstruation phase
   B. degeneration of the corpus luteum in the ovary
   C. increased secretion of LH, which produces the luteal surge and onset of ovulation
   D. thickening of the endometrial lining in preparation for implantation of the zygote
   E. none of the above

20. Vasectomy prevents the following:

   A. movement of sperm along the vas deferens
   B. transmission of sexually transmitted disease
   C. production of sperm via spermatogenesis
   D. production of semen in seminal vesicles
   E. synthesis of seminal fluid

Genetics

Mechanisms of Reproduction

1. How many double-stranded DNA molecules are in a single mouse chromosome after gametes form?

A. 0   **C.** 2

B. 1   **D.** 4

                                          E. 8

2. Common red-green color blindness is an X-linked trait. When a woman whose father is color blind has a son with a non-afflicted man, what is the probability that their son will be color blind?

A. 0   **C.** 1/2

B. 1/4   **D.** 3/4

                                          E. 1

3. The likely gamete cell to be produced from meiosis in the seminiferous tubules is:

A. diploid 2° spermatocytes   **C.** haploid spermatids

B. haploid 1° spermatocytes   **D.** diploid spermatids

                                          E. none of the above

4. At birth, a woman possesses a finite number of ova. In oogenesis, the meiotic division is arrested at which stage until she reaches menarche?

A. ovum   **C.** ova

B. oogonium   **D.** secondary oocytes

                                          E. primary oocytes

5. A human cell after the first meiotic division is:

A. 2N and 2 chromatids   **C.** 1N and 2 chromatids

B. 2N and 4 chromatids   **D.** 1N and 1 chromatid

                                          E. None of the above

6. What distinguishes meiosis from mitosis?

      I. Genetic recombination

      II. Failure to synthesize DNA between successive cell divisions

      III. Separation of homologous chromosomes into distinct cells

A. I only   **C.** I and III only

B. II only   **D.** II and III only

                                          E. I, II and III

7. Oocytes within primordial follicles of the ovary are arrested in:

A. interphase

B. prophase II of meiosis

C. prophase I of meiosis

D. prophase of mitosis

E. G1

8. SRY gene encoding for the testis-determining factor is the primary sex-determining gene that resides on:

A. pseudoautosomal region of the Y chromosome

B. short arm of the Y chromosome, but not in the pseudoautosomal region

C. X chromosome

D. pseudoautosomal region of the X chromosome

E. autosomes

9. The number of chromosomes contained in the human primary spermatocyte is:

A. 23

B. 23, X/23, Y

C. 92

D. 184

E. 46

10. Which process does NOT contribute to genetic variation?

A. Random segregation of homologous chromosomes during meiosis

B. Random segregation of chromatids during mitosis

C. Recombination

D. Mutation

E. All the above

11. In human females, secondary oocytes do not complete meiosis II until:

A. menarche

B. menstruation

C. puberty

D. menopause

E. fertilization

12. 47, XXY is a condition known as:

A. Turner syndrome

B. double Y syndrome

C. trisomy X syndrome

D. Klinefelter syndrome

E. fragile X syndrome

13. All cells contain diploid (2N) numbers of chromosomes EXCEPT:

A. primary oocyte

B. spermatogonium

C. spermatid

D. zygote

E. oogonium

14. The probability that all children in a four-children family will be males is:

   A. 1/2   **C.** 1/8

   B. 1/4   **D.** 1/16

                         E. 1/64

15. Unequal cytoplasm division is characteristic of:

   A. binary fission of bacteria   **C.** production of sperm

   B. mitosis of a kidney cell   **D.** production of an ovum

                         E. none of the above

16. All are clinical manifestations of Kartagener's syndrome, resulting from defective dynein that causes paralysis of cilia and flagella, EXCEPT:

   A. chronic respiratory disorders   **C.** male infertility

   B. cessation of ovulation   **D.** ectopic pregnancy

                         E. middle ear infections

17. Translation, transcription, and replication occur in which phase of the cell cycle?

   A. G1   **C.** metaphase

   B. G2   **D.** anaphase

                         E. S

18. Progesterone is primarily secreted by the:

   A. primary oocyte   **C.** corpus luteum

   B. hypothalamus   **D.** anterior pituitary gland

                         E. endometrial lining

19. All statements are true for a normal human gamete, EXCEPT it:

   A. originates via meiosis from a somatic cell

   B. contains genetic material that has undergone recombination

   C. contains a haploid number of genes

   D. always contains an X or Y chromosome

   E. forms from the meiotic process

20. Which cell division results in four genetically different daughter cells with 1N chromosomes?

   A. interphase   **C.** cell division

   B. somatic cell regeneration   **D.** mitosis

                         E. meiosis

21. A genetically important event of crossing over occurs during:

A. metaphase II

B. telophase I

C. anaphase I

D. prophase I

E. telophase II

22. Which does NOT describe events occurring in prophase I of meiosis?

A. chromosomal migration

B. genetic recombination

C. formation of a chiasma

D. spindle apparatus formation

E. tetrad formation

23. The difference between spermatogenesis and oogenesis is:

A. spermatogenesis produces haploid cells, while oogenesis produces diploid cells

B. spermatogenesis produces gametes, while oogenesis does not produce gametes

C. oogenesis is a mitotic process, while spermatogenesis is a meiotic process

D. spermatogenesis is a mitotic process, while oogenesis is a meiotic process

E. spermatogenesis produces 4 1N sperms, while oogenesis produces 1 egg cell and polar bodies

24. How many Barr bodies are present in the white blood cells of a 48, XXYY individual?

A. 0

B. 1

C. 2

D. 3

E. 4

25. Polar bodies are the products of:

A. meiosis in females

B. meiosis in males

C. mitosis in females

D. mitosis in males

E. two of the above

26. Turner syndrome results from:

A. extra chromosome number 13

B. absence of the Y chromosome

C. presence of an extra Y chromosome

D. trisomy of the X chromosome

E. monosomy of an X chromosome

27. A sheep in 1996 named Dolly was different from animals produced by sexual reproduction because:

A. her DNA is identical to the DNA of her offspring

B. she was carried by a surrogate mother, while her DNA came from two other individuals

C. all her cells' DNA are identical

D. her DNA was taken from a somatic cell of an adult individual

E. her DNA was taken from a gamete of a neonatal individual

Development

1. Which statement is true regarding respiratory exchange during fetal life?

  A. Respiratory exchanges are made through the placenta

  B. Since lungs develop later in gestation, a fetus does not need a mechanism for respiratory exchange

  C. The respiratory exchange is made through the ductus arteriosus

  D. The respiratory exchange is not necessary

  E. The respiratory exchange is made through the ductus venosus

2. When each cell in an early stage of embryonic development still has the ability to develop into a complete organism, it is known as:

  A. gastrulation

  B. blastulation

  C. determinate cleavage

  D. indeterminate cleavage

  E. none of the above

3. Mutations in *Drosophila*, resulting in the transformation of one body segment into another, effect:

  A. maternal-effect genes

  B. homeotic genes

  C. execution genes

  D. segmentation genes

  E. gastrulation genes

4. Which structure is developed from embryonic ectoderm?

  A. connective tissue

  B. bone

  C. rib cartilage

  D. epithelium of the digestive system

  E. hair

5. The placenta is a vital metabolic organ made from a contribution by the mother and fetus. The portion of the placenta contributed by the fetus is:

  A. amnion

  B. yolk sac

  C. umbilicus

  D. chorion

  E. none of the above

6. What occurs when an embryo lacks human chorionic gonadotropin (hCG) synthesis?

  A. The embryo does not support the maintenance of the corpus luteum

  B. The embryo increases the production of progesterone

  C. The embryo develops immunotolerance

  D. The placenta forms prematurely

  E. Conception does not occur

7. Which germ layer gives rise to smooth muscle?

    A. ectoderm   **C.** mesoderm

    B. epidermis   **D.** endoderm

                                E. hypodermis

8. In early embryogenesis, the most critical morphological change in the development of cellular layers is:

    A. epigenesis   **C.** conversion of morula to blastula

    B. gastrulation   **D.** acrosomal reaction

                                E. fertilization membrane

9. During the first eight weeks of development, all events occur EXCEPT:

    A. myelination of the spinal cord   **C.** formation of a functional cardiovascular system

    B. presence of all body systems   **D.** beginning of ossification

                                E. limb buds appear

10. Which structures derive from the ectoderm germ layers?

    A. blood vessels, tooth enamel, and epidermis   **C.** nails, epidermis, and blood vessels

    B. heart, kidneys, and blood vessels   **D.** epidermis and adrenal cortex

                                E. epidermis and neurons

11. A diagram of the blastoderm that identifies regions from which specific adult structures are derived is a:

    A. phylogenetic tree   **C.** fate map

    B. pedigree diagram   **D.** linkage map

                                E. lineage diagram

12. Which tissue is the precursor of long bones in the embryo?

    A. hyaline cartilage   **C.** dense fibrous connective tissue

    B. fibrocartilage   **D.** elastic cartilage

                                E. costal cartilage

13. What changes are observed in cells as development proceeds?

    A. Cytoskeletal elements involved in forming the mitotic spindle

    B. Energy requirements of each cell

    C. Genetic information that was duplicated with each round of cell division

    D. Composition of polypeptides within the cytoplasm

    E. Composition of nucleotides within the nucleus

14. During fertilization, what is the earliest event in the process?

    A. sperm contacts the cortical granules around the egg

    B. sperm nucleic acid enters the egg's cytoplasm to form a pronucleus

    C. acrosome releases hydrolytic enzymes

    D. sperm contacts the vitelline membrane around the egg

    E. hyaluronic acid forms a barrier to prevent polyspermy

15. The embryonic ectoderm layer gives rise to all the following EXCEPT:

    A. eyes

    B. fingernails

    C. integument

    D. nervous system

    E. blood vessels

16. All are correct matches of a fetal structure with what it becomes at birth, EXCEPT:

    A. ductus venosus—ligamentum venosum

    B. umbilical arteries—medial umbilical ligament

    C. foramen ovale—fossa ovalis

    D. ductus arteriosus—ligamentum teres

    E. all choices are correct

17. All statements regarding gastrulation are true, EXCEPT:

    A. the primitive gut that results from gastrulation is the archenteron

    B. for amphibians, gastrulation is initiated at the gray crescent

    C. after gastrulation, the embryo consists of two germ layers of endoderm and ectoderm

    D. for amphibians, blastula cells migrate during gastrulation by an invagination region of the blastopore

    E. the mesoderm develops as the third primary germ layer during gastrulation

18. A homeobox is a:

    A. protein involved in the control of meiosis

    B. transcriptional activator of other genes

    C. DNA binding site

    D. sequence responsible for post-transcriptional modifications

    E. sequence that encodes for a DNA binding motif

19. After the gastrulation's completion, the embryo undergoes the following:

    A. cleavage

    B. blastulation

    C. blastocoel formation

    D. neurulation

    E. dedifferentiation

20. Shortly after implantation:

    A. trophoblast forms two distinct layers

    B. embryo undergoes gastrulation within 3 days

    C. maternal blood sinuses bathe the inner cell mass

    D. myometrial cells cover and seal off the blastocyst

    E. the umbilical cord forms within 48 hours

21. What is the anatomical connection between the placenta and embryo?

    A. chorion

    B. umbilical cord

    C. endometrium

    D. corpus luteum

    E. vas deferens

22. Which statement correctly illustrates the principle of induction during vertebrate development?

    A. Neural tube develops into the brain, the spinal cord, and the nervous system

    B. Secretion of TSH stimulates the release of thyroxine hormone

    C. Ectoderm develops into the nervous system

    D. Neurons synapse with other neurons via neurotransmitters

    E. Presence of a notochord beneath the ectoderm results in the formation of a neural tube

23. The acrosomal reaction by the sperm is:

    A. a transient voltage change across the vitelline envelope

    B. the jelly coat blocking penetration by multiple sperms

    C. the consumption of yolk protein

    D. hydrolytic enzymes degrading the plasma membrane

    E. the inactivation of the sperm acrosome

24. Which primary germ layer gives rise to the cardiovascular system, bones, and skeletal muscles?

    A. endoderm

    B. blastula

    C. mesoderm

    D. ectoderm

    E. gastrula

25. The dorsal surface cells of the inner cell mass form:

    A. notochord

    B. placenta

    C. one of the fetal membranes

    D. structure called the embryonic disc

    E. primitive streak

26. All occur in a newborn immediately after birth, EXCEPT:

    A. the infant completely stops producing fetal hemoglobin

    B. resistance in the pulmonary arteries decreases

    C. pressure in the left atrium increases

    D. pressure in both the inferior vena cava and the right atrium increase

    E. ductus arteriosus constricts

27. Homeobox sequences are present in:

    A. introns

    B. exons

    C. 3'-untranslated regions

    D. 5'-untranslated regions

    E. exon-intron boundaries

28. After 30 hours of incubation, the ectoderm tissue within the gastrula differentiates into different specific tissues, which supports the conclusion that:

    I. cells become either endoderm or mesoderm

    II. cells contain a different genome from their parental cells

    III. gene expression is altered

    A. III only

    B. I and III only

    C. I only

    D. I and II only

    E. II and III only

29. What is the function of the yolk sac in humans?

    A. forms into the placenta

    B. secretes progesterone in the fetus

    C. gives rise to blood cells and gamete-forming cells

    D. stores embryonic waste

    E. stores nutrients for the embryo

30. The trophoblast is mostly responsible for forming:

    A. placental tissue

    B. lining of the endometrium

    C. allantois

    D. archenteron

    E. chorion

31. Certain lesions to the mesodermal embryonic primary germ layer may stimulate the development of *spina bifida*, a congenital fissure in the lower vertebrae. Besides the spinal column, what other structures would be affected by such lesions?

I. intestinal epithelium	III. blood vessels
II. skin and hair	IV. muscles

A. I and II only

B. II and III only

C. III and IV only

D. I, III and IV only

E. IV only

32. The homeotic genes encode for:

A. repressor proteins

B. transcriptional activator proteins

C. helicase proteins

D. single-strand binding proteins

E. restriction enzymes

33. Which cells give rise to muscles in a frog embryo?

A. neural tube

B. ectoderm

C. endoderm

D. mesoderm

E. notochord

34. Which is NOT involved in the implantation of the blastocyst?

A. Settling of the blastocyst onto the prepared uterine lining

B. Adherence of the trophoblast cells to the uterine lining

C. Phagocytosis by the trophoblast cells

D. Inner cell mass giving rise to primitive streak

E. Endometrium proteolytic enzymes produced by the trophoblast cells

35. During labor, which hormone stimulates contractions of uterine smooth muscle?

A. oxytocin

B. prolactin

C. luteinizing hormone

D. hCG

E. estrogen

36. In a chick embryo, specific ectoderm cells give rise to wing feathers, while others develop into thigh feathers or foot claws. The ectodermal cells that develop into wing feathers were transplanted to an area that develops into thigh feathers or feet claws. It was observed that the transplanted cells developed into claws. Which best explains the experimental results?

A. ectoderm cells possess positional information

B. destiny of the cells was already determined

C. ectoderm cells can develop into any tissue

D. the underlying mesoderm-induced cells

E. ectoderm released growth factors

37. The *slow block* to polyspermy is due to the following:

A. transient voltage changes across membranes

B. jelly coat blocking sperm penetration

C. consumption of yolk protein

D. formation of the fertilization envelope

E. inactivation of the sperm acrosome

38. Polyspermy in humans results in:

A. mitotic insufficiency

B. interruption of meiosis

C. nonviable zygote

D. multiple births

E. formation of multiple placentas

39. Mesoderm gives rise to:

A. intestinal mucosa

B. nerves

C. skin

D. lung epithelium

E. heart

40. Genomic imprinting is:

A. inactivation of a gene by interruption of its coding sequence

B. organization of molecules in the cytoplasm to provide positional information

C. DNA modification in gametogenesis that affects gene expression in the zygote

D. suppression of a mutant phenotype because of a mutation in a different gene

E. mechanism by which enhancers distant from the promoter can still regulate transcription

41. Comparing a developing frog embryo and an adult, cells of which have a greater rate of translation?

A. Adult, because ribosomal production is more efficient in a mature organism

B. Adult, because a mature organism has more complex metabolic requirements

C. Embryo, because a developing organism requires more protein production than an adult

D. Embryo, because ribosomal production is not yet under regulatory control by DNA

E. Embryo, because the proteins must undergo more extensive post-translation processing

42. Which structure is the first to form during fertilization in humans?

A. blastula

B. morula

C. neural tube

D. ectoderm

E. zygote

43. It is impossible for sperm to be functional (i.e., able to fertilize the egg) until after:

    I. they undergo capacitation   III. they have been in the uterus for several days

    II. the tail disappears   IV. they become spermatids

A. I only

B. II and IV only

C. I and IV only

D. I and III only

E. IV only

44. Where is the deformity if a teratogen affects the endoderm development shortly after gastrulation?

A. nervous system

B. lens of the eye

C. liver

D. skeleton

E. connective tissue

45. Mutations that cause cells to undergo developmental fates of other cell types are:

A. heterochronic mutations

B. loss-of-function mutants

C. transection mutations

D. execution mutations

E. homeotic mutations

46. Each is true for the cells of an early gastrula's eye field, EXCEPT that they are:

A. terminally differentiated

B. competent

C. derived from the ectoderm layer

D. capable of becoming other ectoderm structures

E. undifferentiated ectoderm

47. What is the role of proteases and acrosin enzymes in reproduction?

A. They degrade the nucleus of the egg and allow the sperm to enter

B. They degrade the protective barriers around the egg and allow the sperm to penetrate

C. They direct the sperm to the egg through chemotaxis messengers

D. They neutralize the mucous secretions of the uterine mucosa

E. They degrade the protective barriers around the sperm and allow the egg to penetrate

48. When does the human blastocyst implant in the uterine wall?

A. about a week past fertilization

B. at blastulation

C. a few hours past fertilization

D. at primary germ formation

E. at primitive streak formation

49. Which primary layer develops into the retina of the eye?

    I. endoderm   II. ectoderm   III. mesoderm

A. I only   **C.** III only
B. II only   **D.** II and III
                           E. I and III

50. What changes must occur in a newborn's cardiovascular system after the infant takes its first breath?

A. Ductus arteriosus constricts and is converted to the ligamentum arteriosum
B. The urinary system is activated at birth
C. Ductus venosus is severed from the umbilical cord, and visceral blood enters the vena cava
D. Foramen ovale between the atria of the fetal heart closes at the moment of birth
E. Foramen ovale becomes the medial umbilical ligament

51. Early activation of the mammalian zygote nucleus may be necessary because:

A. most developmental decisions are made under the influence of the paternal genome
B. mammalian oocytes are too small to store molecules needed to support the cleavage divisions
C. in gametogenesis, specific genes undergo imprinting
D. mammals do not have maternal-effect genes
E. none of the above

52. In reptiles, the aquatic environment necessary for the embryonic development of amphibians is replaced by:

A. use of lungs instead of gills   **C.** shells which prevent the escape of gas
B. humid atmospheric conditions   **D.** intrauterine development
                                 E. amniotic fluid

53. What would be expected to form from a portion of cells destined to become the heart if it was excised from an early gastrula and placed in a culture medium?

A. undifferentiated mesoderm   **C.** differentiated endoderm
B. undifferentiated ectoderm   **D.** undifferentiated endoderm
                                 E. differentiated ectoderm

54. During gestation, when can an ultrasound determine the sex of the fetus?

A. at the midpoint of the first trimester   **C.** at the end of the first trimester
B. about 18 weeks after fertilization   **D.** at the midpoint of the second trimester
                                 E. at the midpoint of the third trimester

55. How long is the egg viable and able to be fertilized after ovulation?

A. 36-72 hours

B. a full week

C. up to 6 hours

D. 24-36 hours

E. 12-24 hours

56. Which stage of embryonic development has a hollow ball of cells surrounding a fluid-filled center?

A. 3-layered gastrula

B. blastula

C. morula

D. zygote

E. 2-layered gastrula

57. Which statement describes the acrosome of a sperm cell?

A. It contains nucleic acid

B. It contains hydrolytic enzymes, which are released when the sperm encounters the jelly coat of the egg

C. It fuses with the egg's cortical granules

D. It functions to prevent polyspermy

E. It is used for the motility of the sperm along the Fallopian tubes (oviducts)

58. Which statement about fertilization is correct?

A. Most sperm cells are protected and remain viable once inside the uterus

B. If estrogen is present, the pathway through the cervical opening is blocked from sperm entry

C. The vagina's acidic environment destroys millions of sperm cells

D. Spermatozoa remain viable for about 72 hours in the female reproductive tract

E. The ovulated secondary oocyte is viable for about 72 hours in the female reproductive tract

DNA and Protein Synthesis

1. DNA and RNA differ because:

    A. only DNA contains phosphodiester bonds

    B. only RNA contains pyrimidines

    C. DNA is in the nucleus, and RNA is in the cytosol

    D. RNA is associated with ribosomes, and DNA is associated with histones

    E. RNA contains a phosphate group in its ribose ring

2. In the 1920s, circumstantial evidence indicated that DNA was the genetic material. Which experiments led to the acceptance of this hypothesis?

    A. Griffith's experiments with *Streptococcus pneumoniae*

    B. Avery, MacLeod and McCarty's work with isolating the transforming principle

    C. Hershey and Chase's experiments with viruses and radioisotopes

    D. A, B and C were used to support this hypothesis

    E. Darwin's theory of natural selection

3. The N-glycosidic bond is relatively unstable within a guanine molecule and can be hydrolyzed through depurination. Which molecule is likely to undergo depurination?

    A. sterols   **C.** phospholipids

    B. lipids   **D.** proteins

                               E. DNA

4. What process duplicates a single gene?

    A. Unequal recombination at repeated sequences that flank the gene

    B. Equal recombination at repeated sequences that flank the gene

    C. Unequal recombination within a single gene

    D. Equal recombination within a single gene

    E. All the above

5. Which element is NOT within nucleic acids?

    A. nitrogen   **C.** phosphorus

    B. oxygen   **D.** sulfur

                               E. carbon

6. Which RNA molecule is translated?

A. miRNA

B. tRNA

C. rRNA

D. mRNA

E. C and D

7. The aging of normal cells is associated with:

A. loss of telomerase activity

B. a decrease in contact inhibition

C. an increase in mutation rate

D. activation of the maturation-promoting factor

E. extranuclear inheritance

8. Protein synthesis in eukaryotic cells initiates in which structures?

A. nucleus

B. Golgi

C. cytoplasm

D. rough endoplasmic reticulum

E. smooth endoplasmic reticulum

9. When a gene is duplicated on one chromatid, the gene on the other chromatid is:

A. duplicated

B. inverted

C. transposed to another site

D. maintained as a single gene

E. deleted

10. Experiments designed by Avery, McLeod, and McCarty to identify the transforming principle were based on:

I. purifying each of the macromolecule types from a cell-free extract

II. removing each of the macromolecules from a cell, then testing its type

III. selectively destroying the different macromolecules in a cell-free extract

A. I only

B. II only

C. III only

D. I, II and III

E. I and II only

11. What is the term for a blotting method where proteins are transferred from a gel to membranes and probed by antibodies to specific proteins?

A. Eastern blotting

B. Western blotting

C. Northern blotting

D. Southern blotting

E. both Northern and Western blotting

12. The figure shows a nucleotide. At what position will the incoming nucleotide be attached in the figure?

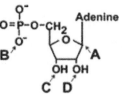

A. position A

B. position B

C. position C

D. position D

E. none of the above

13. All are correct about DNA, EXCEPT:

A. the strands are anti-parallel

B. the basic unit is nucleotide

C. the sugar molecule is deoxyribose

D. guanine binds to cytosine via three hydrogen bonds

E. adenine and guanine are pyrimidines

14. Tumor-suppressor genes normally control:

A. cell differentiation

B. necrosis

C. cell proliferation or activation of apoptosis

D. sister chromatid separation

E. protein degradation

15. Select the correct statement for aminoacyl tRNA synthetase.

A. It binds several different amino acids

B. It is an enzyme that uses energy from ATP to attach a specific amino acid to a tRNA

C. It is a tRNA that covalently binds amino acids

D. It synthesizes tRNA

E. It synthesizes rRNA

16. Griffith's experiment with pneumococcus demonstrated that:

A. smooth bacteria can survive heating

B. DNA, not protein, is the genetic molecule

C. materials from dead organisms can affect and change living organisms

D. nonliving viruses can change living cells

E. the virus injects its DNA into the host cell

17. The genetic code deciphered by Noble laureate Marshall W. Nirenberg (1927-2020) in 1964 encodes each amino acid by three nucleotides (codons). How many possible codons exist in nature that encode 20 amino acids in polypeptides?

A. 4

B. 20

C. 27

D. 64

E. 16

18. What mechanism targets proteins to organelles (e.g., chloroplast, mitochondrion)?

    A. Addition of phosphate groups to the protein

    B. Synthesizing the proteins as zymogens

    C. Adding prosthetic groups to the protein

    D. Cysteine bond formation

    E. The signal sequence at the N-terminus of the polypeptide

19. When DNA is treated with 2-aminopurine, adenine is replaced by guanine on one strand. During replication, the complementary strand will have a substitution of:

    A. guanine for adenine

    B. adenine for guanine

    C. cytosine for thymine

    D. thymine for cytosine

    E. adenine for cytosine

20. Before Nobel laureate Marshall W. Nirenberg *et al.* in 1964 determined the genetic code experimentally, why was it hypothesized that each codon would contain at least three bases?

    A. Three bases are needed to produce a stable codon structure

    B. There were three known nucleotide bases

    C. There were more proteins than nucleotide bases

    D. Three bases can form $4^3 = 64$ pairs, which is enough to encode 20 amino acids

    E. There were twenty known amino acids

21. DNA of bacteria grown in a heavy (^{15}N) medium was isolated and added to an *in vitro* synthesis system. Then the bacteria are grown in a light (^{14}N) medium. After several hours, a sample of DNA was taken and analyzed for differing densities. How many DNA densities were in the sample after 2 generations?

    A. 1

    B. 2

    C. 4

    D. 8

    E. 12

22. Which experimental procedure(s) simultaneously measure(s) the level of all mRNAs in a tissue?

    I. Northern blot   II. *In situ* hybridization   III. Microarray experiment

    A. I only

    B. II only

    C. III only

    D. I, II and III

    E. I and III only

23. To demonstrate that DNA is the "transforming principle," Avery, MacLeod, and McCarty showed that DNA could transform nonvirulent strains of pneumococcus. Their hypothesis was strengthened by their demonstration:

    A. enzymes that destroyed proteins destroyed transforming activity

    B. enzymes that destroyed nucleic acids destroyed transforming activity

    C. enzymes that destroyed complex carbohydrates destroyed transforming activity

    D. the transforming activity was destroyed by boiling

    E. other strains of bacteria were transformed successfully

24. Which components of codon-anticodon hybridization on ribosomes determine the fidelity of protein synthesis?

    A. mRNA & tRNA

    B. mRNA & rRNA

    C. tRNA & rRNA

    D. DNA & RNA polymerase

    E. RNA polymerase

25. Which procedure measures mRNA levels from only a single gene?

    I. Northern blot   II. *In situ* hybridization   III. Microarray experiment

    A. II only

    B. I and II only

    C. II and III only

    D. I, II and III

    E. I and III only

26. Which stage of cell division is the stage when chromosomes replicate?

    A. prophase

    B. telophase

    C. anaphase

    D. metaphase

    E. interphase

27. If the transcript's sequence is 5'-CUAAGGGCUAC-3', what is the sequence of the DNA template?

    A. 3'-GUAGCCCUUAG-5'

    B. 3'-GTACGCCTTAG-5'

    C. 5'-GTAACCCTTAG-3'

    D. 5'-GUTACCUGUAG-3'

    E. 5'-GTAGCCCTTAG-3'

28. Duplicated genes:

    A. are more common in prokaryote genomes than in eukaryote genomes

    B. are closely related but diverged in sequence and function over evolutionary time

    C. never encodes for essential proteins, such as transcription factors

    D. encode for proteins that catalyze different steps of a biochemical pathway

    E. all the above

29. The Hershey–Chase experiment:

    A. proved that DNA replication is semiconservative

    B. used ^{32}P to label protein

    C. used ^{35}S to label DNA

    D. supported the hypothesis that DNA is the transforming molecule

    E. both A and C

30. Which statement is NOT correct about DNA replication?

    A. DNA polymerase synthesizes and proofreads the DNA

    B. RNA primers are necessary for the hybridization of the polymerase

    C. Ligase relaxes positive supercoils that accumulate as the replication fork opens

    D. DNA polymerase adds Okazaki fragments in a 5' → 3' direction

    E. DNA polymerase adds deoxynucleotides in a 5' → 3' direction

31. Which structures represent a peptide bond between adjacent amino acids?

    A. structure A

    B. structure B

    C. structure C

    D. structure D

    E. structures A and D

32. All these statements apply to proteins, EXCEPT:

    A. they regulate cell membrane trafficking

    B. they catalyze chemical reactions

    C. they can be hormones

    D. they undergo self-replication

    E. they bind antigens

33. Eukaryote RNA polymerase usually:

    A. binds to the TATAA promoter sequence and initiates transcription

    B. needs general transcription factors to bind to the promoter and initiate basal-level transcription

    C. needs specific regulatory transcription factors to bind to the promoter and initiate basal-level transcription

    D. transcribes tRNA genes

    E. transcribes mRNA genes

34. If an RNA sequence has a cytosine content of 25%, what is its adenine content?

A. 50%

B. 37.5%

C. 12.5%

D. 25%

E. cannot be determined

35. If a portion of prokaryotic mRNA has the base sequence 5′-ACUACUA<u>U</u>GCGUCGA-3′, what could result from a mutation where the underlined base is changed to A?

    I. truncation of the polypeptide

    II. inhibition of initiation of translation

    III. no effect on protein synthesis

A. I and II only

B. I and III only

C. II and III only

D. III only

E. II only

36. Which statement is INCORRECT about the genetic code?

A. Many amino acids are specified by more than one codon

B. Most codons specify more than one amino acid

C. There are multiple stop codons

D. Codons are 3 bases in length

E. The start codon inserts methionine at the amino end of the polypeptide

37. In bacteria, the enzyme that removes the RNA primers is:

A. DNA ligase

B. primase

C. reverse transcriptase

D. DNA polymerase I

E. helicase

38. Okazaki fragments are:

A. synthesized in a 5'→ 3' direction by DNA polymerase I

B. covalently linked by DNA polymerase I

C. components of the leading strand

D. components of DNA synthesized to fill in gaps after excision of the RNA primer

E. synthesized in a 5'→ 3' direction by DNA polymerase III

39. Peptide bond synthesis is catalyzed by:

A. tRNA in the cytoplasm

B. ribosomal proteins

C. ribosomal RNA

D. mRNA in the ribosome

E. none of the above

40. Which statement does NOT apply to protein synthesis?

    A. The process does not require energy

    B. rRNA is required for proper binding of the mRNA message

    C. tRNA molecules shuttle amino acids assembled into polypeptides

    D. The amino acid is bound to the 3' end of the tRNA

    E. The mRNA is synthesized from $5' \rightarrow 3'$

41. All statements about PCR are correct, EXCEPT:

    A. PCR can be used to obtain large quantities of a particular DNA sequence

    B. PCR does not require knowledge of the terminal DNA sequences of the region to be amplified

    C. PCR uses a DNA polymerase to synthesize DNA

    D. PCR uses short synthetic oligonucleotide primers

    E. PCR involves heating the DNA sample to denature complementary base pairing

42. The shape of a tRNA is determined primarily by:

    A. its number of bases

    B. proteins that bind it

    C. tRNA and aminoacyl tRNA synthetase interactions

    D. intramolecular base pairing

    E. hydrophobic interactions

43. In prokaryotic cells, methylated guanine contributes to:

    A. increased rate of DNA replication   **C.** correcting the separation of DNA strands

    B. decreased rate of DNA replication   **D.** proofreading the replicated strands

                                                       E. correcting mismatched pairs of bases

44. In the polymerization reaction by DNA polymerase, what is the function of magnesium?

$$\text{Primer (free 3' OH)} + 5' \text{ PPP} \xrightarrow{\text{Mg}^{+2}, \text{ 4 dNTPs, DNA polymerase}} \text{Primer 3'O-P-5'} + \text{PPi}$$

    A. cofactor   **C.** substrate

    B. monovalent metal ion   **D.** enzyme

                                           E. coenzyme

45. The structure of the ribosome is created by:

    I. internal base pairing of rRNA   III. internal base pairing of mRNA

    II. ribosomal proteins   IV. internal base pairing of tRNA

  A. I only   **C.** I and II only

  B. II only   **D.** I, II and IV only

                                     E. I, II and III only

46. Which statement is true for tRNA?

  A. It has some short double-stranded segments   **C.** It is produced in the nucleolus

  B. It has a poly-A tail   **D.** It is a long molecule of RNA

                                     E. It is the template for protein synthesis

47. Which chemical group is at the 5' end of a single polynucleotide strand?

  A. diester group   **C.** hydroxyl group

  B. purine base   **D.** phosphate group

                                       E. nitrogen group

48. The drug aminoacyl-tRNA is an analog of puromycin. Both have an amino group capable of forming a peptide bond, but puromycin lacks a carboxyl group to form another peptide bond. What is the possible effect of adding puromycin to bacteria undergoing protein synthesis?

  A. Inhibition of initiation of protein synthesis

  B. Inhibition of entry of aminoacyl-tRNA into the P site during elongation

  C. Inability to form a complete ribosome

  D. Substitution of puromycin for another amino acid in the protein, yielding a normal-length protein

  E. Termination of protein synthesis via covalent attachment of puromycin

49. In *E. coli* cells, DNA polymerase I:

    I.   synthesizes most of the Okazaki fragments

    II.   simultaneously copies both strands of DNA

    III. degrades the RNA primer portion of Okazaki fragments

  A. I only   **C.** III only

  B. II only   **D.** I and III only

                                       E. I and II only

50. During DNA synthesis, the error rate is on the order of one mismatched nucleotide per:

A. 100

B. 1,000

C. 10,000

D. 1,000,000

E. 10,000,000

51. All are contained within a molecule of DNA, EXCEPT:

A. nitrogenous bases

B. phosphodiester bonds

C. polypeptide bonds

D. deoxyribose sugars

E. phosphate groups

52. In *E. coli* cells, DNA polymerase III:

A. synthesizes most of the Okazaki fragments

B. removes the RNA primer

C. is the only DNA polymerase used by *E. coli* during replication

D. degrades the RNA portion of an Okazaki fragment

E. synthesizes DNA in the 3' to 5' direction

53. Which molecule belongs to a different chemical category than the others?

A. uracil

B. guanine

C. adenine

D. thymine

E. cysteine

54. The enzyme that cleaves DNA at the sequence-specific site is:

A. restriction endonuclease

B. exonuclease

C. DNA polymerase

D. ligase

E. integrase

55. *E. coli* RNA polymerase-initiated transcription and synthesized one phosphodiester bond. Which molecule shown is RNA polymerase made from?

56. What rate does PCR increase the amount of DNA during each cycle?

A. additively

B. exponentially

C. linearly

D. systematically

E. gradually

57. Which is present in RNA but absent in DNA?

A. additional hydroxyl group

B. hydrogen bonds

C. thymine

D. double helix

E. phosphodiester bonds

58. After DNA strands are synthesized, which enzyme completes the process of DNA replication?

A. primase

B. ligase

C. helicase

D. reverse transcriptase

E. both B and D

59. When a base is paired with its complementary strand, which strand would have the highest melting point?

A. TTAGTCTC

B. TTTTAAAA

C. AGCTTCGT

D. CGCGTATA

E. GCCAGTCG

60. A technique that investigates gene function by mutating wildtype genes is:

A. contig building

B. transgenetics

C. reverse genetics

D. gene therapy

E. gene mapping

61. How many high-energy phosphate bonds are needed to translate a 50-amino acid polypeptide (starting with mRNA, tRNA, amino acids, and the necessary enzymes)?

A. 49

B. 50

C. 101

D. 199

E. 150

62. The mRNA in *E. coli* cells is composed primarily of:

A. four bases – A, T, C, G

B. phosphodiester linkages connecting deoxyribonucleotide molecules

C. two strands that base pair in an anti-parallel orientation

D. processed RNA molecule containing introns

E. phosphodiester linkages connecting ribonucleotide molecules

63. Which statement about DNA mismatch repair is correct?

A. DNA is scanned for any base-pairing mismatches after methyl groups are added to guanines

B. Errors in replication made by DNA polymerase are corrected on the unmethylated strand

C. The proofreading mechanism removes all abnormal bases

D. Repairs from high-energy radiation damage are made

E. Mismatch repair occurs on each strand of DNA during replication

64. What is the first amino acid of each protein of eukaryotic cells?

A. methionine

B. glutamate

C. valine

D. proline

E. isoleucine

Genetics and Inheritance Patterns

1. Which characteristic makes an organism unsuitable for genetic studies?

   A. Large number of chromosomes

   B. Short generation time

   C. Ease of cultivation

   D. Ability to control crosses

   E. Availability of a variation for traits

2. People with the sex-linked genetic disease hemophilia suffer from excessive bleeding because their blood will not clot. Tom, Mary, and their four daughters do not exhibit symptoms of hemophilia. However, their son exhibits symptoms of hemophilia because:

   A. Tom is heterozygous

   B. Tom is homozygous

   C. Mary is heterozygous

   D. Mary is homozygous

   E. All the above are equally probable

3. Several eye colors are characteristic of *Drosophila melanogaster*. Red eyes are dominant over sepia or white eyes. What percent of offspring of a sepia-eyed fly will have sepia eyes if mated with a red-eyed fly that was a cross of red-eyed and sepia-eyed parents?

   A. 0%

   B. 25%

   C. 50%

   D. 75%

   E. 100%

4. Color blindness mutations in humans result from:

   A. fragile X syndrome

   B. chromosome nondisjunction

   C. reciprocal translocation

   D. dosage compensation

   E. unequal crossing-over

5. Which method was NOT used by Mendel to study the genetics of garden peas?

   A. Maintenance of true-breeding lines

   B. Cross-pollination

   C. Microscopy

   D. Production of hybrid plants

   E. Quantitative analysis of results

6. Crossing AAbbCc × AaBbCc where A, B and C are unlinked genes, what is the probability of obtaining offspring with the AaBbCc genotype?

   A. 1/4

   B. 1/16

   C. 1/64

   D. 1/32

   E. 1/8

7. What is the probability of having a child affected by a disease with an autosomal recessive inheritance if the mother and father are carriers of the disease?

    A. 0%
    B. 25%

    C. 50%
    D. 75%
    E. 66%

8. For the multi-step progression of cancer, the major mutational target(s) is/are:

    A. telomerase
    B. X-linked traits

    C. tumor suppressor gene
    D. trinucleotide repeats
    E. transcription factors

9. Since the gene responsible for color blindness is on the X chromosome, what is the probability that a son of a colorblind man and a woman carrier will be colorblind?

    A. 75%
    B. 100%

    C. 25%
    D. 50%
    E. 66%

10. If two strains of true-breeding plants with alleles for a specific character are crossed, their progeny are:

    A. P generation
    B. F_1 generation

    C. F_2 generation
    D. F_1 crosses
    E. F_2 progeny

11. The Arabidopsis plant has five pairs of homologous chromosomes. Suppose an Arabidopsis is heterozygous for five mutations, and each mutation is on a different chromosome. How many genetically distinct gametes will this plant make after meiosis?

    A. 5
    B. 10

    C. 32
    D. 64
    E. 25

12. An unknown inheritance pattern has the following characteristics:

    • 25% probability of having a homozygous unaffected child

    • 25% probability of having a homozygous affected child

    • 50% probability of having a heterozygous child

Which Mendel's inheritance pattern best matches the above observations?

    A. autosomal recessive
    B. autosomal dominant

    C. X-linked recessive
    D. X-linked dominant
    E. cannot be determined without more information

13. What is the frequency of heterozygotes within a population in Hardy-Weinberg equilibrium if the frequency of the dominant allele D is three times that of the recessive allele d?

    A. 7.25%

    B. 12.75%

    C. 33%

    D. 37.5%

    E. 50%

14. A recessive allele may appear in a phenotype due to:

    A. gain-of-function mutation

    B. acquired dominance

    C. senescence

    D. processivity

    E. the loss of heterozygosity

15. Which observations would support the theory of maternal inheritance for the spunky phenotype?

    A. Spunky female x wild-type male → progeny all spunky

    B. Wild-type female x spunky male → progeny all spunky

    C. Wild-type female x spunky male → progeny 1/2 spunky, 1/2 wild-type

    D. Spunky female x wild-type male → progeny 1/2 spunky, 1/2 wild-type

    E. Spunky female x wild-type male → progeny all wild-type

16. Mendel concluded that each pea has two units for each characteristic, and each gamete contains one unit. Mendel's "unit" is now referred to as:

    A. genome

    B. hnRNA

    C. codon

    D. transcription factor

    E. gene

17. Which leads to a complete loss of gene function?

    A. A missense mutation that causes the nonpolar methionine to be replaced with glycine

    B. GC base pair being converted to an AT base pair in the promoter

    C. A mutation in the third codon of the open reading frame

    D. A base pair change that does not affect the amino acid sequence

    E. All the above

18. All effects are possible after a mutation, EXCEPT:

    A. abnormal lipid production

    B. abnormal protein production

    C. gain of enzyme function

    D. loss of enzyme function

    E. no change in protein production

19. Which cross must produce all green, smooth peas if green (G) is dominant over yellow (g) and smooth (S) is dominant over wrinkled (s)?

A. GgSs × GGSS

B. GgSS × ggSS

C. Ggss × GGSs

D. GgSs × GgSs

E. None of the above

20. Retinoblastoma is inherited as:

A. a multifactorial trait

B. X-linked recessive

C. Mendelian dominant

D. Mendelian recessive

E. an extranuclear trait

21. Tay-Sachs disease is a rare autosomal recessive genetic disorder. If a male heterozygous carrier and a female heterozygous carrier have a first child who is homozygous wild type, what is the probability that the second child develops Tay-Sachs?

A. 1/3

B. 1/2

C. 1/16

D. 1/8

E. 1/4

22. Mendel's crossing of spherical-seeded pea plants with wrinkled-seeded pea plants resulted in progeny that all had spherical seeds. This indicates that the wrinkled-seed trait is:

A. codominant

B. dominant

C. recessive

D. penetrance

E. codominant and recessive

23. The result of mitosis is the production of:

A. two (1N) cells identical to the parent cell

B. two (2N) cells identical to the parent cell

C. four (1N) cells identical to the parent cell

D. four (2N) cells identical to the parent cell

E. four (1N) unique cells that are genetically different from the parent cell

24. The degree of genetic linkage is often measured by the:

A. frequency of nonsense mutations

B. histone distribution

C. frequency of missense mutations

D. probability of crossing over

E. AT/GC ratio

25. Cancers associated with defects in mismatch repair are inherited via:

    A. dominant inheritance

    B. maternal inheritance

    C. X-linked inheritance

    D. epigenetic inheritance

    E. recessive inheritance

26. Given that color blindness is a recessive trait inherited through a sex-linked gene on the X chromosome, what probability will a daughter born to a colorblind father and a mother carrier be a carrier?

    A. 0%

    B. 25%

    C. 50%

    D. 100%

    E. 12.5%

27. What is the probability that a cross between a true-breeding pea plant with a dominant trait and a true-breeding pea plant with a recessive trait will result in all F_1 progeny having the dominant trait?

    A. 50%

    B. 25%

    C. 0%

    D. 100%

    E. 12.5%

28. The tall allele is dominant to short. True-breeding tall plants were crossed with true-breeding short plants. The F_1 plants were self-crossed to produce F_2 progeny. What are the phenotypes of the F_1 and F_2 progeny?

    A. All F_1 and 1/4 of the F_2 are short

    B. All F_1 are short, and 1/4 of the F_2 are tall

    C. All F_1 and 3/4 of the F_2 are tall

    D. All F_1 are tall, and 3/4 of the F_2 plants are short

    E. All the above are equally probable

29. All DNA lesions result in a frameshift mutation, EXCEPT:

    A. 1 inserted base pair

    B. 2 substituted base pairs

    C. 4 inserted base pairs

    D. 2 deleted base pairs

    E. 5 deleted base pairs

30. If two species with the AaBbCc genotype reproduce, what is the probability that their progeny have the AABBCC genotype?

    A. 1/2

    B. 1/4

    C. 1/16

    D. 1/64

    E. 1/8

31. At the hypoxanthine-guanine phosphoribosyltransferase (HPRT) locus, an average amount of mRNA is present, but no protein is observed. This phenotype is caused by the following:

  A. frameshift mutation

  B. mutation in the gene-altering the restriction pattern but not affecting the protein; for instance, the mutated nucleotide is in the third codon position of the open reading frame

  C. point mutation leading to an amino acid substitution necessary for enzyme function

  D. gene deletion or mutation affecting the promoter

  E. nonsense mutation affecting message translation

32. Hemophilia is a recessive X-linked trait. Knowing that females with Turner's syndrome have a high incidence of hemophilia, it can be concluded that these females have:

  A. lost an X and gained a Y   **C.** gained an X

  B. lost an X   **D.** gained a Y

                                           E. none of the above

33. What is the pattern of inheritance for a rare recessive allele?

  A. Every affected person has an affected parent

  B. Unaffected parents can produce children who are affected

  C. Unaffected mothers have affected sons and daughters who are carriers

  D. Every affected person produces an affected offspring

  E. None of the above

34. True-breeding plants with large purple flowers were crossed with true-breeding plants with small white flowers. The F_1 progeny all had large purple flowers. The F_1 progeny were crossed to true-breeding plants with small white flowers. Among 1000 progeny:

Number of progeny	Flower size	Flower color
250	small	white
250	small	purple
250	large	white
250	large	purple

Most likely, the genes for flower size and color:

  A. are unlinked

  B. are sex-linked

  C. are linked and separated by no more than 25 centimorgans

  D. require determination of the cross of the F_2 progeny

  E. cannot be determined

35. If tall height and brown eye color are dominant, what is the probability for a heterozygous tall, heterozygous, brown-eyed mother and a homozygous tall, homozygous, blue-eyed father to have a tall child with blue eyes? Note: the genes for eye color and height are unlinked.

A. 3/4
B. 1/8

C. 1/4
D. 1/2
E. None of the above

36. Recombination frequencies:

A. are the same for *cis*- and *trans*-heterozygotes
B. arise from completely random genetic exchanges
C. decrease with distance
D. are the same for all genes
E. are the same for all chromosomes

37. How many different gametes can be produced from the genotype AaBbCc, assuming independent assortment?

A. 4
B. 6

C. 8
D. 16
E. 3

38. What is the pattern of inheritance for a rare dominant allele?

A. Every affected person has an affected parent
B. Unaffected parents can produce children who are affected
C. Unaffected mothers have affected sons and daughters who are carriers
D. Every affected person produces an affected offspring
E. All the above

39. Individuals homozygous for an autosomal recessive mutation accumulate harmful amounts of lipids. Jane and her parents are not afflicted. However, Jane's sister accumulates lipids. What is the probability that Jane is heterozygous for the mutation?

A. 1/4
B. 1/3

C. 2/3
D. 1/2
E. 3/4

40. A genetic disease with early-onset and severe symptoms with every generation is an example of:

A. codominance
B. penetrance

C. heterozygous advantage
D. gain-of-function mutations
E. anticipation

41. For a trait with two alleles, if the recessive allele frequency is 0.6 in a population, what is the frequency of individuals expressing the dominant phenotype?

A. 0.48

B. 0.64

C. 0.16

D. 0.36

E. 0.12

42. The maximum recombination frequency between two genes is:

A. 100%

B. 80%

C. 50%

D. 10%

E. 1%

43. In mice, short hair is dominant over long hair. If a short-haired individual is crossed with a long-haired individual, and both long and short-haired offspring result, what can be concluded?

A. Short-haired individual is homozygous

B. Short-haired individual is heterozygous

C. Long-haired individual is homozygous

D. Long-haired individual is heterozygous

E. More information is required

44. The result of meiosis in males is the production of:

A. two (1N) cells genetically identical to the parent cell

B. two (2N) cells genetically identical to the parent cell

C. four (1N) cells genetically identical to the parent cell

D. four (1N) unique cells genetically different from the parent cell

E. four (2N) cells genetically identical to the parent cell

45. Which is a type of genetic mutation?

I. insertion   II. frameshift   III. nonsense   IV. missense

A. I and II only

B. I, II and III only

C. II and IV only

D. I, II, III and IV

E. II, III and IV only

46. Two reciprocal crossing-over events appear in the progeny at an approximate ratio of:

A. 4:1

B. 3:1

C. 2:1

D. 2:3

E. 1:1

47. In dogs, phenotype A (erect ears and barking while following a scent) is caused by dominant alleles; recessive alleles cause phenotype B (droopy ears and silent while following a scent). A dog that is homozygous dominant for both traits is mated with a dog that is homozygous recessive for both traits. If the two genes are unlinked, which is the expected F_1 phenotypic ratio?

A. 9:3:3:1

B. 1:1

C. 16:0

D. 1:2:1

E. None of the above

48. Mutations:

A. always cause severe mutant phenotypes

B. never cause severe mutant phenotypes

C. are not inherited by the progeny

D. may cause premature termination of translation

E. are none of the above

49. What is the probability of having a child affected by a disease with autosomal dominant inheritance if both the mother and father have one mutant gene for that disease?

A. 0%

B. 25%

C. 50%

D. 12.5%

E. 75%

50. Given the recombinant frequencies below, what is the sequence of linked genes D, E, F and G?

GE: 23%	ED: 15%	EF: 8%
GD: 8%	GF: 15%	DF: 7%

A. FGDE

B. EFGD

C. GFDE

D. GDFE

E. DEFG

Questions **51** through **57** are based on the following:

The pedigree illustrated by the schematic shows the inheritance of albinism, a homozygous recessive condition manifested in a lack of pigment. Specify the genotypes using *A* and *a* to indicate dominant and recessive alleles.

Note: solid figures are albino individuals.

51. Individual A-1 in the pedigree shown is:

  A. *AA*

  B. *aa*

  C. *Aa*

  D. any of the above

  E. none of the above

52. Individual A-2 in the pedigree shown is:

  A. *AA*

  B. *aa*

    C. *Aa*

    D. any of the above

    E. none of the above

53. Individual B-1 in the pedigree shown is:

  A. *AA*

  B. *aa*

    C. *Aa*

    D. any of the above

    E. none of the above

54. Individual B-2 in the pedigree shown is:

  A. *AA*

  B. *aa*

    C. *Aa*

    D. any of the above

    E. none of the above

55. Individual C-3 in the pedigree shown is:

  A. *AA*

  B. *aa*

    C. *Aa*

    D. any of the above

    E. none of the above

56. Individual C-4 in the pedigree shown is:

A. *AA*

B. *aa*

C. *Aa*

D. any of the above

E. none of the above

57. Individual D-4 in the pedigree shown is:

A. *AA*

B. *aa*

C. *Aa*

D. any of the above

E. none of the above

58. In cocker spaniels, black color (B) is dominant over red (b), and solid color (S) is dominant over spotted (s). If the genes are unlinked and the offspring of BBss and bbss individuals are mated, what fraction of their offspring will be black and spotted?

A. 1/16

B. 9/16

C. 1/9

D. 3/16

E. 3/4

59. Why do genes that cause disease often appear to skip generations in an X-linked recessive inheritance?

A. The disease is primarily transmitted through unaffected carrier females

B. Males with an affected gene are carriers but do not show the disease

C. X-linked diseases are only expressed in males

D. All X-linked diseases display incomplete penetrance

E. none of the above

60. The "calico" coat pattern of a female cat is a result of:

A. endoreduplication

B. unequal crossing-over

C. random X chromosome inactivation

D. Turner syndrome

E. trisomy of the X chromosome

61. Which statement is true for an autosomal dominant inheritance?

    I. A single allele of the mutant gene is needed to exhibit the phenotype

    II. Transmission to the son by the father is not observed

    III. Autosomal dominant traits do not skip generations

A. II only

B. I, II and III

C. I only

D. I and III only

E. II and III only

Notes for active learning

Diversity of Life

Microbiology

1. What is the *major* distinction between prokaryotic and eukaryotic cells?

   A. prokaryotic cells do not have DNA, and eukaryotic cells do

   B. prokaryotic cells cannot obtain energy from their environment

   C. eukaryotic cells are smaller than prokaryotic cells

   D. prokaryotic cells have not prospered, while eukaryotic cells are evolutionary "successes."

   E. prokaryotic cells do not have a nucleolus, but eukaryotic cells do

2. Which statement describes the actions of penicillin?

   A. it is a reversible competitive inhibitor

   B. it is an irreversible competitive inhibitor

   C. it activates transpeptidase that digests the bacterial cell wall

   D. it is an effective antiviral agent

   E. it acts as a noncompetitive inhibitor

3. Which statement applies to all viruses?

   A. They have an RNA genome

   B. They have a DNA genome

   C. They have chromosomes

   D. They cannot replicate outside of a host cell

   E. They have reverse transcriptase

4. The replica plating technique of Joshua and Esther Lederberg demonstrated that:

   A. mutations are usually beneficial

   B. mutations are usually deleterious

   C. streptomycin caused the formation of streptomycin-resistant bacteria

   D. streptomycin revealed the presence of streptomycin-resistant bacteria

   E. the frequency of mutations is proportional to the concentration of streptomycin

5. Operons:

   A. are a common feature of the eukaryote genome

   B. often coordinate the production of enzymes that function in a single pathway

   C. have multiple translation start and stop sites used by ribosomes

   D. usually undergo alternative splicing

   E. both B and C

6. Which is TRUE for the life cycle of sexually reproducing *Neurospora* fungus?

    A. Only mitosis occurs

    B. Fertilization and meiosis are separated

    C. Meiosis quickly follows fertilization

    D. Fertilization immediately follows meiosis

    E. Mitosis quickly follows fertilization

7. Which is in prokaryotic cells?

    A. mitochondria

    B. chloroplasts

    C. nuclei

    D. enzymes

    E. extensive endomembrane system

8. Which organelle is the site of protein modification and carbohydrate synthesis?

    A. Golgi apparatus

    B. lysosomes

    C. peroxisomes

    D. smooth ER

    E. nucleolus

9. What is likely to occur if a suspension of Hfr cells is mixed with excess F^- cells?

    A. Most of the F^- cells are transformed into F^+ cells

    B. The F^- cells produce sex pili that attach to the Hfr cells

    C. Hfr chromosomal DNA is transferred to F^- cells by conjugation

    D. Hfr cells replicate the F factor independently of their chromosomes

    E. Most of the F^+ cells become F^- cells

10. What carcinogen and mutagen test looks for an increased reversion frequency in a His^- bacteria strain?

    A. *Salmonella* reversion test

    B. auxotrophic reversion test

    C. mutagen test

    D. amber test

    E. Ames test

11. The type of bacteria NOT able to grow on minimal media due to mutations affecting metabolism:

    A. auxotrophs

    B. chemotrophs

    C. heterotrophs

    D. prototrophs

    E. all are able to grow

12. Which statement is TRUE?

   A. Endospores are for reproduction
   B. Endospores allow a cell to survive environmental changes
   C. Endospores are easily stained with Gram stain
   D. Cell produces one endospore and keeps growing
   E. Cell produces many endospores and keeps growing

13. Most fungi spend the biggest portion of their life cycle as:

   A. neither haploid nor diploid
   B. both haploid and diploid
   C. diploid
   D. polyploidy
   E. haploid

14. An aerobic bacteria culture that has been exposed to cyanide gas is infected by a bacteriophage strain. However, replication of viruses does not occur. What is cyanide's action mechanism?

   A. Binding to viral nucleic acid
   B. Denaturing bacteriophage enzymes
   C. Inhibiting aerobic ATP production
   D. Destroying bacteriophage binding sites on the bacterial cell wall
   E. Denaturing viral enzymes needed for replication

15. Recipient cells acquire genes from free DNA molecules in the surrounding medium by:

   A. generalized transduction
   B. conjugation
   C. transduction
   D. recombination
   E. transformation

16. Viruses can have a genome that is:

   A. single-stranded DNA
   B. single-stranded RNA
   C. double-stranded RNA
   D. double-stranded DNA
   E. all the above

17. Which assumption must be true to map the order of bacterial genes on the chromosome in a Hfr strain?

   A. Bacterial genes are polycistronic
   B. A given Hfr strain always transfers its genes in the same order
   C. The rate of chromosome transfer varies between bacteria of the same strain
   D. Different mechanisms replicate the inserted F factor and bacterial genes
   E. All the above statements are true

18. Which statement about prokaryotic cells is generally FALSE?

A. They have a semirigid cell wall
B. They are motile using flagella

C. They possess 80S ribosomes
D. They reproduce by binary fission
E. They lack membrane-bound nuclei

19. All events have a role in the life cycle of a typical retrovirus, EXCEPT:

A. injection of viral DNA into the host cell
B. integration of viral DNA into the host genome
C. reverse transcriptase gene is transcribed, and mRNA is translated inside the host cell
D. viral DNA incorporated into the host genome may be replicated along with the host DNA
E. none of the above

20. All are true for viruses EXCEPT:

A. Genetic material may be either single-stranded or double-stranded RNA
B. A virus may replicate in a bacterial or eukaryotic host
C. A virus may replicate without a host
D. The protein coat of the virus does not enter a host bacterial cell
E. Genetic material may be either single-stranded or double-stranded DNA

21. DNA transfer from a bacterial donor cell to a recipient cell by cell-to-cell contact is:

A. conjugation
B. transformation

C. transduction
D. recombination
E. transposons

22. On the overnight agar plates with *E. coli*, replication of a virus is marked by:

A. no visible change
B. bacterial colonies on the agar surface
C. growth of a smooth layer of bacteria across the plate
D. growth of bacteria across the entire plate except for small clear patches
E. absence of any growth on the plate

23. Which statement about gram-negative cell walls is FALSE?

A. They protect the cell in a hypotonic environment
B. They have an extra outer layer of lipoproteins, lipopolysaccharides, and phospholipids
C. They are toxic to humans
D. They have a thinner outer membrane
E. They are sensitive to penicillin

24. All the following may be present in a mature virus outside the host cell, EXCEPT:

    A. core proteins

    B. both RNA and DNA

    C. protein capsid

    D. phospholipid bilayer envelope

    E. none of the above are necessary

25. All are correct about *lac* operon, EXCEPT:

    A. Repressor protein binds to the operator, halting gene expression

    B. The promoter is the binding site of RNA polymerase

    C. There is not a gene that encodes for a repressor protein

    D. Three structural genes code for functional proteins

    E. *Lac* operon is in eukaryotes

26. Phage DNA integrated into the chromosome is:

    A. lytic phage

    B. specialized transducing phage

    C. lysogenic phage

    D. prophage

    E. insertion sequence

27. Many RNA copies of the retrovirus RNA genome are made by:

    A. host cell DNA polymerases

    B. reverse transcriptase

    C. host cell RNA polymerases

    D. host cell ribosomes

    E. none of the above

28. In the laboratory, *E. coli* are grown at a temperature of 37 °C because:

    A. *E. coli* strain is a 37 °C temperature-sensitive mutant

    B. *E. coli* reproduces most rapidly at this temperature

    C. lower temperatures inhibit conjugation

    D. *E. coli* are obligate aerobes

    E. *E. coli* obtains energy from the temperature of the growth medium

29. Some bacteria can propel themselves through liquid using:

    A. flagellum

    B. centriole

    C. centrosome

    D. peptidoglycan

    E. cell wall

30. When most viruses infect eukaryotic cells:

    A. their capsid does not enter the host cell

    B. they replicate independently of the host cell during a lysogenic infection

    C. they can enter the cell via endocytosis

    D. they do not need to have host-specific proteins to infect the target cell

    E. they replicate as the host cell replicates during a lytic infection

31. Which organelle(s) is/are NOT present in bacteria?

    I. peroxisomes   II. nucleolus   III. ribosomes   IV. flagellum

    A. I only   **C.** I and II only

    B. II only   **D.** I, II, and III

                                     E. III and IV only

32. A bacterial cell carrying a prophage is:

    A. virulent   **C.** exconjugant

    B. temperate   **D.** transformant

                                     E. lysogen

33. All are true of prokaryotic translation, EXCEPT:

    A. mRNA is not spliced before initiation

    B. N-terminal amino acid of nascent polypeptides is formylated

    C. mRNA chain being translated may not be fully transcribed before translation begins

    D. Hydrogen bonds between amino acids and mRNA codons are necessary for translation

    E. Translation and transcription both happen in the same location within the cell

34. Prokaryotes are about how many times smaller in diameter than a typical eukaryote?

    A. two   **C.** 100

    B. ten   **D.** 10,000

                                     E. zero

35. Which structures are in prokaryotes?

    I. A cell wall containing peptidoglycan

    II. A plasma membrane with cholesterol

    III. Ribosomes

    A. I only   **C.** I and II only

    B. II only   **D.** I and III only

                                     E. II and III only

36. Which is characteristic of viruses?

    A. membrane-bound organelles

    B. genetic material not made of nucleic acids

    C. peptidoglycan cell wall

    D. phospholipid bilayer membrane

    E. protein coat

37. An F-plasmid that can integrate into the bacterial chromosome by homologous recombination is:

    A. episome

    B. virion

    C. endoconjugate

    D. lytic

    E. virulent

38. The RNA genome of a retrovirus is converted to double-stranded DNA by:

    A. host cell DNA polymerases

    B. reverse transcriptase

    C. host cell RNA polymerases

    D. host cell ribosomes

    E. none of the above

39. Which statement is true about T4 infection of *E. coli*?

    A. T4 mRNA is translated by bacterial ribosomes while still being transcribed from DNA

    B. One of the first genes expressed during viral infection is a lysozyme that facilitates cell lysis

    C. The final stage for lytic cycles of infection is the viral assembly after the virus leaves the cell

    D. T4 buds via endocytosis through the plasma membrane to leave the cell

    E. T4 exits the cell through protein pores in the plasma membrane to leave the cell

40. Which statement about a gram-positive cell wall is FALSE?

    A. It maintains the shape of cells

    B. It is sensitive to lysozyme

    C. It protects the cell in a hypertonic environment

    D. It contains teichoic acids

    E. It is sensitive to penicillin

41. Which statement is correct about the lipopolysaccharide layer outside the peptidoglycan cell wall of a Gram-negative bacterium?

    A. It allows the bacterium to attach to solid objects

    B. It does not contain a phospholipid membrane

    C. It protects the bacterium against antibiotics

    D. It absorbs and holds Gram stain

    E. It appears deep purple from Gram stain

42. DNase added to a bacterial cell causes hydrolysis of the cell's DNA, preventing protein synthesis and cell death. Regardless, some viruses pretreated with DNase produce new proteins following infection because:

   A. viral genome contains multiple copies of their genes

   B. viruses are homozygous for necessary genes

   C. viral genome contains multiple reading frames

   D. icosahedral protein coat of the virus denatures DNase

   E. viral genome is comprised of RNA

43. In a mating between Hfr and F⁻ cells, the F⁻ recipient:

   A. becomes Hfr   **C.** remains F⁻

   B. becomes F′   **D.** becomes F⁺

                              E. cannot establish lysogeny

44. The unique feature of the methionine residue used for prokaryotic initiation of translation is that it is:

   A. formylated   **C.** methylated

   B. hydrophilic   **D.** acetylated

                              E. hydrophobic

45. Which statement describes a bacterial cell placed in a 35% large polysaccharide solution (e.g., dextran)?

   A. NaCl moves into the cell from a higher to a lower concentration

   B. The cell undergoes plasmolysis

   C. H_2O moves out of the cell

   D. H_2O moves into the cell

   E. No change result because the solution is isotonic

46. If the Gram stain method is used to stain a Gram-positive bacterium, it appears?

   A. deep purple because of a thicker peptidoglycan cell wall

   B. deep purple because of a thinner peptidoglycan cell wall

   C. red or pink because of a thicker peptidoglycan cell wall

   D. red or pink because of a thinner peptidoglycan cell wall

   E. red or pink, because of the absence of a peptidoglycan cell wall

47. Which enzyme replicates the F factor in F⁺ bacteria prior to conjugation?

   A. DNA polymerase   **C.** DNA ligase

   B. reverse transcriptase   **D.** integrase

                                E. RNA polymerase

48. In a mating between Hfr and F⁻ cells, the Hfr donor:

A. becomes F′

B. remains Hfr

C. becomes F⁺

D. becomes F⁻

E. loses part of the chromosome

49. Which statement(s) is/are TRUE regarding retrotransposons?

   I. They are never between genes in the human genome

   II. They comprise close to half of the human genome

   III. They can cause mutations by inserting themselves into genes

A. I and II only

B. II only

C. I and III only

D. I, II and III

E. II and III only

50. Which is TRUE about plasmids?

   I. They are small organelles in the bacterial cytoplasm

   II. They are transcribed and translated simultaneously

   III. Bacterial enzymes replicate them

A. I only

B. II and III only

C. I and III only

D. I, II, and III

E. I and II only

51. Which has a cell wall?

A. protoplasts

B. fungi

C. L forms

D. viruses

E. mycoplasmas

52. Which statement about a prokaryotic cell is correct?

A. It contains a range of different organelles

B. It has a nucleolus within the cytoplasm

C. It contains cell walls composed of chitin

D. It has a nuclear membrane that encloses a nucleus

E. It uses glycolysis to produce ATP

53. Which statement applies to both a bacteriophage and retrovirus?

    A. They are capable of infecting human cells

    B. They function as immunosuppressive agents

    C. They integrate their genetic material into the genome of the host cell

    D. They have genes that encode reverse transcriptase

    E. They have a genome of RNA

54. Integration of the phage DNA into the bacterial chromosome is facilitated by:

    A. DNA polymerase encoded in the host genome

    B. topoisomerase encoded in the phage

    C. several proteins, some of them encoded in the phage and some in the host genome

    D. site-specific recombinase encoded in the host genome

    E. site-specific recombinase encoded in the phage

55. After being digested by restriction enzymes, how is DNA ligated into a plasmid in two different directions?

    A. Both ends of a DNA fragment produced by a restriction enzyme are identical if rotated 180°

    B. The existing DNA strands serve as primers for DNA polymerase

    C. DNA ligase enzymes can link any two pieces of DNA together

    D. Plasmid DNA is single-stranded, so the ligated strands form double-stranded segments

    E. DNA polymerase links any two pieces of DNA together

56. Virulent phage:

    I. is capable only of lytic growth

    II. can only undergo a process called lysogeny

    III. needs several different proteins to be incorporated into the bacterial chromosome

    A. I and II only   **C.** II only

    B. III only   **D.** I only

                                E. I, II, and III

Classification and Diversity

1. The *Canis lupus* is a wolf in the Canidae family. Which statement is accurate about its members?

    A. They may be classified as *lupus* but not *Canis*

    B. They may be classified as *Canis* but not Canidae

    C. More are classified as *lupus* than *Canis*

    D. More are classified as Canidae than *Canis*

    E. None of the above

2. Two species of the same order must be members of the same:

    A. class

    B. habitat

    C. genus

    D. family

    E. subfamily

3. Homology serves as the evidence of:

    A. balancing selection

    B. biodiversity

    C. genetic mutation

    D. sexual selection

    E. common ancestry

4. Which statement is correct about orthologous genes?

    A. They are related through speciation

    B. They are house-keeping genes

    C. They are repetitive

    D. They are related via gene duplication within species

    E. They are viral oncogenes

5. Which given pair represents homologous structures?

    A. Mouth of a fly and beak of a hummingbird

    B. Wings of a dragonfly and a blue jay

    C. Forelimb of a human and of a dog

    D. Wings of a pigeon and a bat

    E. Forelimb of a raccoon and the hind limb of a wolf

6. Humans belong to the order:

    A. hominidae

    B. primata

    C. chordata

    D. vertebrata

    E. sapiens

7. All are members of the phylum Chordata EXCEPT:

A. birds   **C.** tunicates

B. ants   **D.** apes

     E. snakes

8. All statements regarding the phylum Echinodermata are true, EXCEPT:

A. echinoderms are heterotrophs

B. echinoderms are invertebrates

C. echinoderms reproduce sexually

D. phylum includes starfish and sea urchins

E. phylum includes crayfish

9. Two species of the same phylum must be members of the same:

A. order   **C.** genus

B. kingdom   **D.** class

     E. family

10. *Homo sapiens* belong to the phylum:

A. Vertebrata   **C.** Mammalia

B. Homo   **D.** Chordata

     E. sapiens

11. Which organism is a chordate but not a vertebrate?

A. lizard   **C.** shark

B. lancelet   **D.** lamprey eel

     E. none of the above

12. Which represents the levels of complexity at which life is studied, from the simplest to the most complex?

A. cell, tissue, organ, organism, population, community

B. community, population, organism, organ, tissue, cell

C. cell, organ, tissue, organism, population, community

D. cell, tissue, organ, population, organism, community

E. tissue, organ, cell, population, organism, community

13. Which statement is TRUE for the notochord?

    A. It is present in chordates during embryological development

    B. It is always a vestigial organ in chordates

    C. It is present in all adult chordates

    D. It is present in all echinoderms

    E. It is part of the nervous system of all vertebrates

14. All are present in members of the phylum Chordata at some point in their life cycle, EXCEPT:

    A. pharyngeal slits   **C.** notochord

    B. tail   **D.** dorsal neural tube

                          E. backbone

15. Which are likely two organisms of the same species?

    A. Two South American iguanas which mate in different seasons

    B. Two migratory birds nesting on the different Indonesian Islands

    C. Cabbage in Alabama and Texas mate and produce fertile progeny only in seasons of extreme climate conditions

    D. Two fruit flies on the island of Bali with distinct courtship behaviors

    E. All the above

16. What is a reason sponges are classified as animals?

    A. Sponges form partnerships with photosynthetic organisms

    B. Sponges are autotrophic

    C. Their cells have cell walls

    D. Sponges are heterotrophic

    E. Sponges are omnivores

17. What is a protostome?

    A. outermost germ layer

    B. animal whose mouth is formed from the blastopore

    C. animal whose anus is formed from the blastopore

    D. embryo just after fertilization

    E. innermost germ layer

18. Arthropods have:

  A. spiny skin and an internal skeleton

  B. flattened body with an external shell

  C. segmented body and an exoskeleton

  D. soft body and an internal shell

  E. segmented body and an endoskeleton

19. A medical student examines a tissue slice on an unlabeled microscope slide. The student concludes the tissue is not from an animal because the cells in the tissue have:

  A. flagella

  B. cell membranes

  C. nuclei

  D. membrane-bound organelles

  E. cell walls

20. Which is true about annelids?

  A. Each body segment contains several pairs of antennae

  B. Annelids rely on diffusion to transport oxygen and nutrients to their tissues

  C. Annelids have segmented bodies and a true coelom

  D. Annelids are acoelomates

  E. Annelids have segmented bodies and a pseudocoelom

21. Ancient chordates are thought to be most closely related to:

  A. octopi

  B. sea anemones

  C. spiders

  D. earthworms

  E. none of the above

22. Which is true about echinoderms?

  A. Echinoderms have one pair of antennae and unbranched appendages

  B. Adult echinoderms have an exoskeleton

  C. Most adult echinoderms exhibit radial symmetry

  D. Echinoderm's body is divided into a head, thorax, and abdomen

  E. Most adult echinoderms lack radial symmetry

23. The simplest animals to have body symmetry are:

  A. cnidarians

  B. echinoderms

  C. sponges

  D. algae

  E. bacteria

24. In chordates whose pharyngeal pouches develop slits for breathing, leading outside the body, adults use:

A. pharynx

B. nose

C. gills

D. lungs

E. larynx

25. In a chordate embryo, nerves branch in intervals from:

A. spinal column

B. notochord

C. pharyngeal pouches

D. tail

E. hollow nerve cord

26. Each is an essential function performed by animals, EXCEPT:

A. circulation

B. cephalization

C. excretion

D. respiration

E. all are required

27. Which animals are deuterostomes?

A. mollusks and arthropods

B. arthropods and chordates

C. annelids and arthropods

D. cnidarians and mollusks

E. echinoderms and chordates

28. In fishes, pharyngeal pouches may develop into:

A. gills

B. tails

C. lungs

D. fins

E. larynx

29. What is true about corals?

A. The polyp form of corals is restricted to a small larval stage

B. Corals only reproduce by asexual means

C. Corals have only the medusa stage in their life cycles

D. Coral polyps secrete an underlying skeleton of calcium carbonate

E. One coral polyp forms a balloon-like float that keeps the entire colony afloat

30. Amphibians evolved from:

A. jawless fishes

B. lobe-finned fishes

C. ray-finned fishes

D. cartilaginous fishes

E. none of the above

31. The notochord is responsible for which function in an embryo?

A. respiration

B. processing nerve signals

C. processing wastes

D. cognitive abilities

E. structural support

32. A flexible, supporting structure found only in chordates is the:

A. pharyngeal slits

B. dorsal fin

C. nerve net

D. notochord

E. vertebrates

33. Which is NOT true about earthworms?

A. Earthworms are hermaphrodites that reproduce sexually

B. Earthworms have a digestive tract that includes a mouth and an anus

C. Earthworms have a pseudocoelom

D. Their tunnels allow for the growth of oxygen-requiring soil bacteria

E. Earthworms feed on live and dead organic matter

34. Skeletons of early vertebrates were composed of cartilage instead of bone. Which characteristic does cartilage share with notochords?

A. Oxygen can diffuse through it

B. It contracts

C. It is soft and flexible

D. It is hard and rigid

E. It contains hydroxyapatite

35. Which do NOT exhibit bilateral symmetry?

A. arthropods

B. cnidarians

C. mollusks

D. annelids

E. primates

36. Which chordate characteristic is visible on the outside of an adult cat?

A. a tail that extends beyond the anus

B. pharyngeal pouches

C. hollow nerve cord

D. notochord

E. nerve plexus

37. Fewer than 5 percent of animal species have:

A. cell membranes

B. vertebral columns

C. a protostome development pattern

D. eukaryotic cells

E. membrane-bound organelles

38. The eggs of ovoviviparous fish are:

A. released from the female before they are fertilized

B. nourished by a structure similar to a placenta

C. released from the female immediately after being fertilized

D. retained and nourished by the female

E. held inside the female's body as they develop

39. Which statement about chordates is true?

A. All chordates are vertebrates

B. All chordates have paired appendages

C. All chordates have a notochord

D. All chordates have backbones

E. Chordates include protostomes and deuterostomes

40. Which pairs of modern chordate groups are most closely related?

A. birds and crocodilians

B. sharks and the coelacanth

C. hagfishes and lungfishes

D. lampreys and ray-finned fishes

E. crocodilians and sharks

41. The hominoid group of primates includes:

A. anthropoids only

B. apes and hominines

C. New World monkeys and Old World monkeys

D. lemurs, lorises and anthropoids

E. apes and anthropoids

42. What fossil evidence indicates the order for these three vertebrates: a bony fish with a jaw, a jawless fish, and a fish with leglike fins?

A. The jawless fish was the last to evolve

B. The fish with leglike fins evolved before the jawless fish

C. The bony fish evolved before the jawless fish

D. The fish with leglike fins was the last to evolve

E. The bony fish was the last to evolve

43. Jaws and limbs are characteristic of:

    A. reptiles only

    B. invertebrates only

    C. all chordates

    D. worms

    E. vertebrates only

44. Which structure in the amniotic egg provides nutrients for the embryo as it grows?

    A. yolk

    B. allantois

    C. chorion

    D. amnion

    E. shell

45. Which trend in reproduction is evident when following vertebrate groups?

    A. progressively fewer openings in the digestive tract

    B. closed circulatory system becomes open

    C. internal fertilization evolves into external fertilization

    D. endothermy evolves into ectothermy

    E. external fertilization evolves into internal fertilization

46. A tail that is adapted for grasping and holding objects is:

    A. prehensile

    B. radial

    C. bipedal

    D. binocular

    E. symmetrical

47. Which is NOT a characteristic of mammals?

    A. hair

    B. endothermy

    C. ability to nourish their young with milk

    D. lack of pharyngeal pouches during development

    E. three middle ear bones

48. The group that includes gibbons and humans but does not include tarsiers is the:

    A. mollusks

    B. hominines

    C. primates

    D. anthropoids

    E. hominoids

49. All are examples of cartilaginous fishes, EXCEPT:

A. rays

B. sharks

C. hagfishes

D. skates

E. sturgeons

50. Old World monkeys can be distinguished from New World monkeys by observing:

A. how the monkeys use their tails

B. when the monkeys are most active

C. what the monkeys eat

D. how the monkeys interact with their troop

E. how the monkeys gather food

51. Compared with that of a reptile, a bird's body temperature is:

A. lower and more constant

B. lower and more variable

C. higher and more constant

D. higher and more variable

E. the same

52. Which internal characteristic would an earthworm have?

A. prostomium

B. notochord

C. pseudocoelom

D. paired organs

E. blastopore

53. Mammals that lay eggs are called:

A. reptiles

B. placentals

C. marsupials

D. amphibians

E. monotremes

54. The presence of legs or other limbs indicates that the animal is:

A. protostome

B. segmented

C. acoelomate

D. radially symmetrical

E. deuterostome

55. A primatologist finds a new species of primate in a Madagascar forest. The primate has a long snout and is active at night. A primatologist would classify this primate as a:

A. bush baby

B. hominoid

C. anthropoid

D. lemur

E. none of the above

56. The vertebrate group with the most complex respiratory system is:

A. fish

B. amphibians

C. mammals

D. reptiles

E. birds

57. Having a thumb that can move against the other fingers makes it possible for a primate to:

A. judge the locations of tree branches

B. display elaborate social behaviors

C. merge visual images

D. hold objects firmly

E. develop elaborate social communications

58. Which is NOT a characteristic of chordates?

A. pharyngeal pouches

B. vertebrae

C. tail that extends past the anus

D. dorsal, hollow nerve cord

E. none of the above

59. An animal that has body parts that extend outward from its center shows:

A. bilateral symmetry

B. radial symmetry

C. segmentation

D. several planes of symmetry

E. protostome development

Ecosystems and Biomes

1. The lowest level of environmental complexity that includes living and nonliving factors is:

A. ecosystem

B. biosphere

C. biome

D. community

E. population

2. How does an area's weather differ from the area's climate?

A. Weather does not change very much, and an area's climate may change many times

B. Weather is the area's daily conditions, while climate is the area's average conditions

C. Weather involves temperature and precipitation, while climate involves only temperature

D. Weather depends on where it is on Earth, while the area's climate does not

E. Weather involves temperature and precipitation, while climate involves only precipitation

3. One type of symbiosis is:

A. parasitism

B. predation

C. competition

D. succession

E. none of the above

4. Climate zones are the result of differences in:

A. thickness of the ozone layer

B. greenhouse gases

C. angle of the sun's rays

D. heat transport

E. altitude of the observer

5. The greenhouse effect is:

A. an unnatural phenomenon that causes heat energy to be radiated back into the atmosphere

B. the result of the differences in the angle of the sun's rays

C. primarily related to the levels of ozone in the atmosphere

D. a phenomenon that has only occurred in the last 50 years

E. a natural phenomenon that maintains Earth's temperature range

6. The tendency for warm air to rise and cool air to sink results in:

A. regional precipitation

B. the seasons

C. ocean upwelling

D. global wind patterns

E. regional temperature

7. An ecosystem with water covering the soil or near the surface of the soil for part of the year is a(n):

    A. estuary

    B. salt marsh

    C. mangrove swamp

    D. pond

    E. wetland

8. Which is the biological aspect of an organism's niche?

    A. composition of soil

    B. amount of sunlight

    C. predators

    D. the water in the area

    E. availability of minerals

9. An organism's niche is:

    A. the range of temperatures that the organism needs to survive

    B. a complete description of the place an organism lives

    C. the range of physical and biological conditions in which an organism lives and the way it obtains what it needs to survive and reproduce

    D. all the physical factors in the organism's environment

    E. all the biological factors in the organism's environment

10. No two species can occupy the same niche in the same habitat at the same time:

    A. unless the species require different biotic factors

    B. because of the competitive exclusion principle

    C. unless the species requires different abiotic factors

    D. because of the interactions that shape the ecosystem

    E. unless the species require different biotic and the same abiotic factors

11. Plants are:

    A. omnivores

    B. herbivores

    C. primary consumers

    D. primary producers

    E. detritivores

12. How do most primary producers make their food?

    A. By breaking down remains into carbon dioxide

    B. By converting water into carbon dioxide

    C. By using chemical energy to make carbohydrates

    D. By using heat energy to make nutrients

    E. By using light energy to make carbohydrates

13. Compared to land, the open oceans:

A. are nutrient-poor environments

B. are rich in silica and iron

C. have less zooplankton

D. contain abundant oxygen

E. are nutrient-rich environments

14. Several species of warblers can live in the same spruce tree ONLY because they:

A. can find different temperatures within the tree

B. occupy different niches within the tree

C. have different habitats within the tree

D. do not eat food from the tree

E. can find different amounts of direct sunlight within the tree

15. All the interconnected feeding relationships in an ecosystem make up the food:

A. web

B. network

C. chain

D. framework

E. scheme

16. A symbiotic relationship in which both species benefit is:

A. predation

B. parasitism

C. commensalism

D. omnivorism

E. mutualism

17. A wolf pack hunts, kills and feeds on a moose. In this interaction, the wolves are:

A. predators

B. mutualists

C. prey

D. hosts

E. symbionts

18. The total amount of living tissue within a given trophic level is:

A. energy mass

B. biomass

C. organic mass

D. trophic mass

E. abiotic

19. An interaction in which an animal feeds on plants is:

A. symbiosis

B. predation

C. herbivory

D. carnivory

E. parasitism

20. A symbiotic relationship in which one organism is harmed, and another benefits is:

A. synnecrosis

B. predation

C. mutualism

D. parasitism

E. commensalism

21. Which animals eat, both producers and consumers?

A. autotrophs

B. chemotrophs

C. omnivores

D. herbivores

E. heterotrophs

22. Ecosystem services include:

A. food production

B. production of oxygen

C. solar energy

D. all the above

E. none of the above

23. Organisms that can capture energy and produce food are:

A. omnivores

B. heterotrophs

C. herbivores

D. consumers

E. autotrophs

24. What is one difference between primary and secondary succession?

A. Secondary succession begins with lichens, and primary succession begins with trees

B. Primary succession modifies the environment, while secondary succession does not

C. Secondary succession begins on the soil, while primary succession begins on newly exposed surfaces

D. Primary succession is rapid and secondary succession is slow

E. Both primary succession and secondary succession are rapid

25. A term that means the same thing as a *consumer* is:

A. carbohydrate

B. heterotroph

C. autotroph

D. producer

E. detritivore

26. Primary succession would likely occur after:

A. severe storm

B. farmland is abandoned

C. earthquake

D. forest fire

E. lava flow

27. Which organism is a detritivore?

A. fungus

B. snail

C. crow

D. caterpillar

E. mouse

28. Matter can be recycled through the biosphere because:

A. biological systems do not deplete matter but transform it

B. biological systems use only carbon, oxygen, hydrogen, and nitrogen

C. matter does not change into new compounds

D. matter is assembled into chemical compounds

E. biological systems do not change matter into new compounds

29. A tropical rainforest may not return to its original climax community after which type of disturbances?

A. volcanic eruption

B. flooding after hurricane

C. burning of a forest fire

D. clearing and farming

E. earthquake

30. A collection of the organisms living in a place, together with their nonliving environment, is a(n):

A. ecosystem

B. biome

C. population

D. community

E. biomass

31. Which biome is characterized by very low temperatures, little precipitation, and permafrost?

A. tropical dry forest

B. tundra

C. temperate forest

D. desert

E. savannah

32. A bird stalks, kills, and eats an insect. Based on its behavior, which ecological terms describe the bird?

A. herbivore ↔ decomposer

B. autotroph ↔ herbivore

C. carnivore ↔ consumer

D. producer ↔ heterotroph

E. herbivore ↔ consumer

33. Which two biomes have the least precipitation?

A. boreal forest and temperate woodland

B. tundra and desert

C. tropical savanna and tropical dry forest

D. tundra and temperate shrubland

E. tropical rainforest and temperate grassland

34. Which represents box 5 of the food web in the figure?

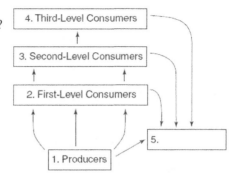

A. decomposers

B. carnivores

C. scavengers

D. herbivores

E. omnivores

35. The average, year-after-year conditions of temperature and precipitation in a region are:

A. zonation

B. microclimate

C. weather

D. climate

E. weather and climate

36. Nitrogen fixation is carried out primarily by:

A. producers

B. consumers

C. humans

D. plants

E. bacteria

37. The rate at which producers create organic matter is:

A. primary succession

B. nitrogen fixation

C. primary productivity

D. nutrient limit

E. secondary succession

38. Which landforms are NOT classified into a major biome?

A. coastlines

B. islands

C. prairies

D. mountain ranges

E. deserts

39. The North Pole and the South Poles are:

A. not classified into major biomes

B. part of aquatic ecosystems

C. classified as tundra biomes

D. not home to any animals

E. classified as temperate biomes

40. The interaction in which one organism captures and feeds on another is:

A. mutualism

B. symbiosis

C. competition

D. parasitism

E. predation

41. Are zooplankton in the aphotic, benthic zone of an ocean?

A. No, zooplankton cannot undergo chemosynthesis in the dark without oxygen in the water

B. No, zooplankton feed on phytoplankton that cannot photosynthesize without light

C. No, zooplankton cannot photosynthesize in the dark without oxygen in the water

D. Yes, zooplankton is a chemosynthetic autotroph

E. Yes, zooplankton can photosynthesize in the dark

42. Carbon cycles through the biosphere in the following processes EXCEPT:

A. decomposition of plants

B. burning of fossil fuels

C. transpiration

D. photosynthesis

E. decomposition of animals

43. The nutrient availability of aquatic ecosystems is the:

A. number of different animal species living in the water

B. amount of rainfall the water receives

C. number of other organisms present in the water

D. amount of nitrogen, oxygen, and other elements dissolved in the water

E. amount of salinity of the water

44. What organism forms the base of many aquatic food webs?

A. phytoplankton

B. mangrove trees

C. secondary consumers

D. plants

E. zooplankton

45. The movements of energy and nutrients through living systems are different because:

A. nutrients flow in two directions, while energy recycles

B. energy forms chemical compounds while nutrients are lost as heat

C. energy flows in one direction while nutrients are recycled

D. energy is limited in the biosphere while nutrients are always available

E. nutrients are lost as heat while energy is limited in the biosphere

46. Boreal Forest biomes are:

A. near the equator

B. known as taiga

C. home to more species than all other biomes combined

D. hot and wet year-round

E. made up of mostly hardwood

47. Freshwater ecosystems that often originate from underground sources in mountains or hills are:

A. lakes

B. wetlands

C. estuaries

D. ponds

E. rivers and streams

48. Which is how a wetland differs from a lake or pond?

A. Water does not always cover a wetland as it does a lake or pond

B. Wetlands are salty, while lakes and ponds are freshwater

C. Water flows in a lake or pond but never flows in a wetland

D. Wetlands are nesting areas for birds, while lakes and ponds are not nesting areas

E. None of the above are differences

49. A wetland that contains a mixture of fresh water and saltwater is:

A. pond

B. river

C. stream

D. estuary

E. wetland

50. The permanently dark zone of the ocean is the:

A. aphotic zone

B. intertidal zone

C. photic zone

D. coastal zone

E. intercoastal zone

51. Each is an abiotic factor in the environment, EXCEPT:

A. temperature

B. rainfall

C. plant life

D. soil type

E. pH

52. Estuaries are commercially important because:

A. fossil fuels are found in estuaries

B. lumber trees grow in estuaries

C. hotels are often built in estuaries

D. abundant fish species live in estuaries

E. the shoreline of estuaries attracts tourists

53. Animals that get energy by eating the carcasses of animals killed by predators or died by natural causes are:

A. detritivores

B. heterotrophs

C. omnivores

D. autotrophs

E. scavengers

Evolution and Ecology

Evolution and Natural Selection

1. During his trip to the Galapagos Islands in 1835, Darwin discovered that:

    A. local fossils were not related to contemporary organisms of that region

    B. all organisms were related

    C. organisms in tropical regions were closely related and independent of the region

    D. several species of finches varied from island to island

    E. organisms had no relationship with others

2. In evolutionary terms, organisms belonging to which category would be the most similar?

    A. genus   **C.** order

    B. family   **D.** kingdom

                             E. class

3. What is the source of genetic variation for natural selection?

    A. gene duplication   **C.** meiosis

    B. mitosis   **D.** heterozygosity

                             E. mutation

4. In modern evolutionary theory, chloroplasts probably descended from:

    A. free-living cyanobacteria   **C.** mitochondria

    B. red algae   **D.** aerobic prokaryote

                             E. eukaryotic cells

5. Speciation is the evolution of new, genetically distinct populations from a common ancestral stock by:

        I. random mutation   II. geographic isolation   III. reduction of gene flow

    A. I and III only   **C.** I and II only

    B. II and III only   **D.** I, II, and III

                             E. III only

6. Darwin (1809-1882) hypothesized that the mechanism of evolution involves:

    A. selective pressure   **C.** natural selection

    B. epigenetics   **D.** selective breeding

                             E. random selection

7. The complexity of the organisms that exist on earth today is the result of:

        I. multicellularity   II. photosynthesis   III. eukaryotic cell development

A. I only

B. II only

C. I and II only

D. II and III only

E. I, II and III

8. The Archaean Eon contains the oldest known fossil record dating to about:

A. 1.5 billion years

B. 2.0 million years

C. 7,000 years

D. 3.5 billion years

E. 7 billion years

9. Urey-Miller experiment in 1952 demonstrates that:

A. life may have evolved from inorganic precursors

B. humans have evolved from photosynthetic cyanobacteria

C. life existed on prehistoric earth

D. small biological molecules cannot be synthesized from inorganic material

E. the early earth lacked oxygen

10. To ensure the survival of their species, animals that do not care for their young:

A. have protective coloring

B. produce many offspring

C. lay eggs

D. can live in water and on land

E. have internal fertilization

11. Which best describes the relationship between nitrogen-fixing bacteria that derive their nutrition from plants and the plants that benefit from the nitrogen supplied by the bacteria?

A. parasitism

B. commensalism

C. mutualism

D. mimicry

E. amensalism

12. Which selection type is likely to lead to speciation?

A. sexual selection

B. stabilizing selection

C. directional selection

D. disruptive selection

E. nondirectional selection

13. The similarity among the embryos of fish, amphibians, reptiles, and humans is evidence of:

A. genetic drift

B. sexual selection

C. analogous traits

D. common ancestry

E. genetic equilibrium

14. Selective breeding of soybeans by humans has genetically altered the soybean so that it could not survive in the wild without human intervention. The soybean population is controlled, and most soybean seeds are eaten or become spoiled. The relationship between humans and soybeans is best described as follows:

A. commensalism, because both species benefit

B. parasitism, because humans benefit, and soybeans are harmed

C. commensalism, because there is no benefit to either species

D. commensalism, because humans benefit, and soybeans are neither benefited nor harmed

E. mutualism, because both species benefit

15. Natural selection leads to:

A. larger population

B. population most adapted to its present environment

C. phenotypic diversity

D. broad genetic variation

E. population well adapted to changes in the environment

16. From an evolutionary perspective, which cell property is paramount?

A. passing genetic information to progeny

B. containing a nucleus

C. containing mitochondria

D. interacting with other cells

E. extracting energy from the environment

17. Inherited traits determined by elements of heredity are:

A. crossing over

B. homologous chromosomes

C. locus

D. p elements

E. genes

18. Which statement is correct about the evolutionary process?

A. Organisms develop traits that they need for survival

B. Mutations decrease the rate of evolution

C. Natural selection works on traits that cannot be inherited

D. Natural selection works on existing genetic variation within a population

E. Organisms evolve due to natural selection

19. Genetic drift results from:

A. environmental change

B. genetic diversity

C. probability

D. sexual selection

E. genetic mutation

20. The likely result of polygenic inheritance is:

A. human height

B. blood type

C. freckles

D. polydactyly (extra digits)

E. color of the iris

21. Which is the earliest form of life to evolve on Earth?

A. plants

B. eukaryotes

C. prokaryotes

D. protists

E. fish

22. If two animals produce viable, fertile offspring under natural conditions, it can be concluded that:

A. for any given allele, they both have the same gene

B. their blood types are compatible

C. they both have haploid somatic cells

D. they both are from the same species

E. none of the above

23. The population's total collection of alleles at any one time makes up its:

A. phenotype

B. biodiversity

C. gene pool

D. genotype

E. genetic mutations

24. A pivotal point in Darwin's explanation of evolution is that:

A. biological structures inherited are better suited to the environment through constant use

B. mutations that occur are those that help future generations fit into their environments

C. mutations develop based on the use/disuse of physical traits

D. genes change to help organisms cope with problems encountered within their environments

E. any trait that confers even a slight increase in the probability that its possessor will survive and reproduce will be strongly favored and will spread throughout the population

25. If the allele frequency in a population is 0.7, what is the alternate allele frequency?

A. 0.14

B. 0.21

C. 0.30

D. 0.4

E. 0.42

26. Which statement about evolution is CORRECT?

A. Darwin's theory of natural selection relies solely on environmental conditions

B. Darwin's theory explains the evolution of man from present-day apes

C. Darwin's theory of natural selection relies solely on genetic mutation

D. Lamarck's theory of use and disuse adequately describes why giraffes have long necks

E. Natural selection is when random mutations are selected for survival by the environment

27. A significant genetic drift may be prevented by:

A. random mutations

B. large population size

C. small population size

D. genetic variation

E. lack of migration

28. Which statement would apply to a population that survived a bottleneck and recovered to its original size?

A. It is subject to genetic drift

B. It is less likely to become extinct than before the bottleneck

C. It has more genetic variation than before the bottleneck

D. It has less genetic variation than before the bottleneck

E. None of the above applies

29. The difference between the founder effect and a population bottleneck is that the founder effect:

A. only occurs in island populations

B. requires the isolation of a small group from a larger population

C. requires a large gene pool

D. involves sexual selection

E. always follows genetic drift

30. Which compound was likely unnecessary for the origin of life on Earth?

A. carbon

B. O_2

C. hydrogen

D. H_2O

E. nitrogen

31. In a population of humans, there is a higher rate of polydactyly (extra fingers or toes) than in the human population. The likely explanation is:

    A. bottleneck effect

    B. founder effect

    C. sexual selection

    D. natural selection

    E. missense mutation

32. Gene flow occurs through:

    A. random mutations

    B. bottleneck effect

    C. founder effect

    D. directional selection

    E. migration

33. The first living organisms on Earth derived their energy from:

    A. eating dead organisms

    B. eating organic molecules

    C. the sun

    D. eating each other

    E. all the above

34. Evolutionary fitness measures:

    A. population size

    B. reproductive success

    C. gene pool size

    D. genetic load

    E. migration rate

35. Which scientist would explain the hawk's lost flying ability with a theory that "since the hawk stopped using its wings, the wings became smaller, and this acquired trait was passed on to the offspring"?

    A. Lamarck

    B. de Vries

    C. Mendel

    D. Darwin

    E. Morgan

36. Which example is a likely result of directional selection?

    A. Increased number of cat breeds

    B. Python snakes with assorted color patterns exhibit different behavior when threatened

    C. Female *Drosophila* select usual yellowish-grey colored males over less common, yellow-colored males

    D. Non-poisonous butterflies evolving color changes to look like poisonous butterflies

    E. None of the above

37. The genetic variation would be decreased by:

A. genetic drift

B. balancing selection

C. directional selection

D. sexual selection

E. stabilizing selection

38. Asexually reproducing species have a selective disadvantage over sexually reproducing species because sexual reproduction:

A. always decreases an offspring's survival ability

B. decreases the likelihood of mutations

C. creates novel genetic recombination

D. is more energy efficient

E. always increases an offspring's survival ability

39. Which example is a likely result of stabilizing selection?

A. Female *Drosophila* select yellowish-grey colored male mates over less common, yellow-colored males

B. Increased number of different breeds within one species

C. Non-poisonous butterflies evolving color changes to look like poisonous butterflies

D. Female birds that lay an intermediate number of eggs have the highest reproductive success

E. none of the above

40. According to one theory about the origins of life, these molecules were formed by purines, pyrimidines, sugars, and phosphates combining:

A. lipids

B. carbohydrates

C. nucleosides

D. proteins

E. nucleotides

41. Which example is a likely result of sexual selection?

A. Female deer choosing to mate with males that have the biggest antlers

B. Python snakes with distinct color patterns exhibit different behavior when threatened

C. Non-poisonous butterflies evolving color changes to look like poisonous butterflies

D. Increased number of different breeds within one species

E. Lions experience a founder effect

42. Some fossils from before the Cambrian Explosion are embryos, suggesting that the organisms:

A. reproduce sexually

B. exhibit cephalization

C. reproduce asexually

D. have bilateral symmetry

E. are protostomes

43. The Cambrian Explosion resulted in the evolution of the first:

A. bacteria

B. land animals

C. dinosaurs and mammals

D. representatives of most animal phyla

E. plants

44. A primate's ability to hold objects in its hands or feet is an evolutionary development necessary for it to:

A. create elaborate social systems

B. consume food

C. use simple tools

D. walk upright

E. escape predation

45. Suppose a paleontologist discovers a fossil skull that he believes might be distantly related to primates. Unlike true primates, the face is not flat, and the eyes do not face entirely forward. The paleontologist would conclude that the animal lacked the ability to:

A. manipulate tools

B. judge the location of tree branches

C. form extended family groups

D. grip branches precisely

E. harvest crops

46. When an animal's environment changes, sexual reproduction improves a species' ability to:

A. increase its numbers rapidly

B. produce genetically identical offspring

C. react to new stimuli

D. adapt to new living conditions

E. reduce genetic diversity

47. Researchers have concluded that Dikika Baby was a better climber than modern humans. This evidence suggests that Dikika Baby's relatives may have spent part of their time:

A. hunting in groups

B. waging war on other troops

C. using tools

D. in trees

E. in Rocky Mountains

48. Fossil evidence indicates that *Australopithecus afarensis:*

A. was bipedal

B. appeared later than *Homo ergaster*

C. was primarily a meat-eater

D. had a large brain

E. was a hunter and gatherer

49. One way in which reptiles are adapted to fully terrestrial life is:

A. endothermy

B. viviparous development

C. external fertilization

D. placenta

E. amniotic egg

50. Researchers concluded from the leg bones of the fossil known as Lucy that it was bipedal. Which of the following indicates that this hominine was bipedal?

A. bowl-shaped pelvis

B. opposable thumbs

C. skull with a flat face

D. broad rib cage

E. flexible spinal column

51. Which statement is true of *Homo sapiens?*

A. They replaced *Homo habilis* in the Middle East

B. They became extinct about 1 million years ago

C. They have been Earth's only hominine for the last 24,000 years

D. They evolved after the Cro-Magnons

E. They replaced *Homo habilis* in Europe

52. Which was a unique characteristic of Neanderthals?

A. Producing tools from bones and antlers

B. Burying their dead with simple rituals

C. Making sophisticated stone blades

D. Producing cave paintings

E. Members joined into groups

53. Which factor would NOT favor an *r-selection* over a *K-selection* reproductive strategy?

A. Commercial predation by humans

B. Limited space

C. Shorter growing season

D. Frequent and intense seasonal flooding

E. None of the above

54. A small subpopulation of flies with a slightly advantageous modification in the structure was extinct after a locally isolated decimating fire. A geneticist would attribute the loss of this advantageous gene to:

A. differential reproduction

B. natural selection

C. Hardy-Weinberg principle

D. genetic drift

E. high genetic mutation rate

Notes for active learning

Animal Behavior

1. Which behavior must be learned from another animal?

   A. potato washing in macaques

   B. suckling of newborn mammals

   C. web building in spiders

   D. nest building in birds

   E. location identity in pigeons

2. A cat hears a rustling in the leaves that sounds like a mouse digging for food. The cat crouches, becoming very still and focused on the leaves as it waits for the right moment to pounce. This combination of movements is an example of:

   A. courtship

   B. stimulus

   C. imprinting

   D. circadian rhythm

   E. behavior

3. For a behavior to evolve under the influence of natural selection, that behavior must be:

   A. acquired through learning

   B. influenced by genes

   C. related to predator avoidance

   D. neither adaptive nor harmful

   E. independent of reproductive success

4. If a dog that barks when indoors is always let outside immediately, it learns to bark when it wants to go outside. This change in the dog's behavior is an example of:

   A. imprinting

   B. insight learning

   C. operant conditioning

   D. classical conditioning

   E. acquired behavior

5. A behavior is innate, rather than learned, when:

   A. all individuals perform the behavior the same way each time

   B. individuals become better at performing the behavior the more they practice it

   C. some individuals perform the behavior, and some do not

   D. the behavior is different in individuals that have had different experiences

   E. different individuals perform the behavior at different stages of development

6. The terms "inborn behavior" and "instinct" have the same meaning as:

   A. courtship behavior

   B. imprinting

   C. learned behavior

   D. innate behavior

   E. operant conditioning

7. When disturbed, certain moths lift their front wings to expose eyelike markings on their hind wings. This behavior would be most effective against predators that hunt by:

    A. touch

    B. sight

    C. smell

    D. sound

    E. innate predation

8. The learning that occurs when a stimulus produces a particular response because it is associated with a positive or negative experience is:

    A. trial-and-error learning

    B. habituation

    C. operant conditioning

    D. classical conditioning

    E. imprinting

9. Certain behaviors are innate in animals because they are essential for:

    A. acquiring other behaviors

    B. developing a circadian rhythm

    C. survival immediately after birth

    D. guarding territory

    E. maintenance of homeostasis

10. Imprinting is a form of behavior that:

    A. requires practice for the animal to become good at the activity

    B. always involves the sense of sight

    C. is restricted to birds

    D. is often used in the training of adult animals

    E. occurs during a specific time in young animals

11. When people first move into an apartment near railroad tracks, they are awakened when they hear a train. Which response to the sound of the train would result from habituation?

    A. People begin to sleep through the sound of the train over the next few nights

    B. People learn that they can cover the sound of the train by sleeping with the radio on

    C. People associate the sound of the train with the arrival of the morning newspaper

    D. People learn they can sleep between the times that the train travels by their home

    E. People learn they will be given a reward if they wake up when the train goes by

12. Aquarium fish often swim to the water's surface when a person approaches. Their behavior has probably formed through:

    A. imprinting

    B. insight learning

    C. instinct

    D. classical conditioning

    E. habituation

13. What are specific chemical signals that insects use that affect the behavior or development of other individuals of the same species?

    A. cilia

    B. spiracles

    C. pheromones

    D. peptidoglycans

    E. glycolipids

14. The ability of salmon to recognize their home stream at spawning time is an example of:

    A. communication

    B. imprinting

    C. competition

    D. insight learning

    E. classical conditioning

15. Learning occurs whenever:

    A. a stimulus does not affect an animal the first time the animal encounters the stimulus

    B. an animal leaves a chemical scent on its territory

    C. an animal ignores the stimulus

    D. an animal performs a task perfectly without prior experience

    E. a stimulus causes an animal to change its behavior

16. The appearance of fireflies at dusk is an example of a circadian rhythm because it:

    A. happens daily

    B. happens seasonally

    C. is related to the phase of the moon

    D. is related to the temperature of the air

    E. is related to the organism's reproductive cycle

17. During migration, animals:

    A. search for new permanent habitats

    B. enter a sleep-like state

    C. repeat their daily cycle of behavior

    D. conduct seasonal movement

    E. change types of foods consumed

18. The theory that states helping family members survive increases the probability that some of one's genes will be passed along to offspring is:

    A. competition

    B. classical conditioning

    C. kin selection

    D. imprinting

    E. operant conditioning

19. In winter, bears settle into dens and enter a sleep-like state until spring. This state is:

A. imprinting

B. aggression

C. new permanent habitats

D. migration

E. hibernation

20. When a bird learns to press a button to get food, it has learned by:

A. insight learning

B. operant conditioning

C. classical conditioning

D. habituation

E. imprinting

21. To survive during winter, when resources are scarce, some animals enter a sleep-like state called:

A. reproductive rhythm

B. territoriality

C. ritual

D. circadian rhythm

E. dormancy

22. In some species of balloon flies, males spin balloons of silk and carry them while flying. If a female approaches a male and accepts his balloon, the two will fly off to mate. This behavior is an example of:

A. courtship

B. language

C. aggression

D. territorial defense

E. operant conditioning

23. Members of a society:

A. act independently for each's benefit

B. are usually unrelated to one another

C. belong to at least two species

D. belong to the same species and interact closely with each other

E. develop no direct relations with other members

24. Animals that use language are likely those that have the greatest capacity for:

A. habituation

B. insight learning

C. behavioral cycles

D. innate behavior

E. imprinting

25. An animal can benefit the most by defending a territory if:

    A. the animals it defends against do not use the same resources

    B. there are more than enough resources in that territory for all competitors

    C. that territory has more resources than surrounding areas

    D. that territory has many predators

    E. the territory is a temporary location for the members

26. An innate behavior:

    A. requires reasoning

    B. occurs with trial and error

    C. requires habituation

    D. appears in fully functional form the first time it is performed

    E. improves in function with each additional practice

27. It is advantageous for grazing mammals to gather in groups because groups:

    A. must travel less distance to locate food compared to individuals

    B. are more difficult for predators to locate than are individuals

    C. can migrate more easily than individuals can

    D. can make the available food resources last longer

    E. offer greater protection from predation

28. Nocturnal animals that have a poorly developed sense of smell are likely to communicate by:

    A. pheromones   **C.** auditory signals

    B. chemical signals   **D.** visual displays

                           E. olfactory signals

29. Many cat species mark their territory by rubbing glands on their faces against surfaces such as tree trunks. This form of communication relies on the following:

    A. chemical messenger   **C.** visual signal

    B. defensive display   **D.** sound signal

                           E. predatory behavior

30. When an animal associates a stimulus with a reward or a punishment, it has learned by:

    A. imprinting   **C.** habituation

    B. operant conditioning   **D.** classical conditioning

                           E. insight

31. Cephalopods (i.e., squid and octopi) can communicate by changing skin colors and patterns. This type of communication is an example of the following:

A. visual signal

B. language

C. sound signal

D. chemical signal

E. touch signal

32. Dolphins communicate with one another mainly through:

A. chemical signals

B. pheromones

C. auditory signals

D. visual displays

E. touch signals

33. When newly hatched ducklings separate from their mother, following a person swimming in a pond is:

A. imprinting

B. instrumental conditioning

C. discrimination

D. response to pheromones

E. none of the above

Populations and Community Ecology

1. A developer wants to build a new housing development in or around a large city. Which plans would be LEAST harmful to the environment?

- **A.** Building a neighborhood in a meadow at the edge of the city
- **B.** Filling a wetland area and building oceanfront condominiums
- **C.** Clearing a forested area outside of the city to build houses
- **D.** Building apartments at the site of an abandoned factory in the city
- **E.** Building apartments on an abandoned farm

2. Assemblages of different populations that live together in a defined area are:

- **A.** communities
- **B.** species
- **C.** ecosystems
- **D.** habitats
- **E.** biodiversity

3. There are over 165 Saguaro cactus plants per square kilometer in an area of the Arizona desert. To which population characteristic does this information refer?

- **A.** age structure
- **B.** population density
- **C.** growth rate
- **D.** geographic range
- **E.** death rate

4. Using resources in a way that does not cause long-term environmental harm is:

- **A.** subsistence hunting
- **B.** biological magnification
- **C.** monoculture
- **D.** sustainable development
- **E.** none of the above

5. What does the range of a population teach the observer that density does not?

- **A.** The deaths per unit area
- **B.** The births per unit area
- **C.** The areas inhabited by a population
- **D.** The number that lives in an area
- **E.** The migrations per unit area

6. Which ecological inquiry method is an ecologist using when she enters an area periodically to count the population numbers of a particular species?

- **A.** modeling
- **B.** experimenting
- **C.** hypothesizing
- **D.** questioning
- **E.** observing

7. Which is NOT a factor for population growth rates?

    A. demography   **C.** death rate

    B. emigration   **D.** Immigration

                                 E. birth rate

8. What is an example of population density?

    A. number of deaths per year   **C.** number of births per year

    B. number of bacteria per square millimeter   **D.** number of frogs in a pond

                                 E. immigration rate per year

9. An example of a biotic factor is:

    A. sunlight   **C.** competing species

    B. soil type   **D.** average temperature

                                 E. average monthly rainfall

10. An example of a non-renewable resource is:

    A. wood   **C.** sunlight

    B. fish   **D.** wind

                                 E. coal

11. A mathematical formula designed to predict population fluctuations in a community is:

    A. ecological model   **C.** biological experiment

    B. ecological observation   **D.** biological system

                                 E. population experiment

12. The 1930s Dust Bowl in the Great Plains was caused by:

    A. using renewable resources   **C.** deforestation

    B. poor farming practices   **D.** contour plowing

                                 E. using non-renewable resources

13. The movement of organisms into a range is:

    A. population shift   **C.** immigration

    B. carrying capacity   **D.** emigration

                                 E. bottleneck effect

14. Which is NOT a basic method ecologists use to study the living world?

A. modeling

B. observing

C. experimenting

D. animal training

E. hypothesizing

15. If immigration and emigration numbers remain equal, which is the most important contributing factor to a slowed growth rate?

A. decreased death rate

B. constant birth rate

C. increased birth rate

D. constant death rate

E. decreased birth rate

16. When farming, overgrazing, climate change, or seasonal drought change farmland into land that cannot support plant life, it is:

A. deforestation

B. monoculture

C. extinction

D. depletion

E. desertification

17. Which factor might NOT contribute to an exponential growth rate in a given population?

A. reduced resources

B. less competition

C. higher birth rates

D. lower death rates

E. increased longevity

18. Which is NOT a sustainable development strategy for managing Earth's resources?

A. selective harvesting of trees

B. crop rotation

C. desertification

D. contour plowing

E. none of the above

19. Which are two ways a population can decrease in size?

A. Emigration and increased birth rate

B. Decreased birth rate and emigration

C. Increased death rate and immigration

D. Immigration and emigration

E. Increased birth rate and death rate

20. Farmers can reduce soil erosion by:

A. plowing up roots

B. grazing cattle on the land

C. contour plowing

D. increasing irrigation

E. planting monocultures

21. Which age structure is likely for a population that has not completed the demographic transition?

    A. 10 percent of people aged 50–54

    B. 5 percent of people aged 10–14

    C. 15 percent of people under age 15

    D. 50 percent of people under age 15

    E. 20 percent of people above age 60

22. Which two factors increase population size?

    A. births and immigration

    B. deaths and emigration

    C. births and emigration

    D. deaths and immigration

    E. none of the above

23. In a logistic growth curve, exponential growth is the phase in which the population:

    A. growth begins to slow down

    B. growth stops

    C. reaches carrying capacity

    D. death rate exceeds the growth rate

    E. grows quickly

24. An example of sustainable resource use is the use of predators and parasites to:

    A. control pest insects

    B. eat unwanted plants

    C. harm natural resources

    D. pollinate plants

    E. feed livestock

25. The graph shows the growth of a bacterial population. Which describes the growth curve?

    A. demographic

    B. exponential

    C. logistic

    D. limiting

    E. linear

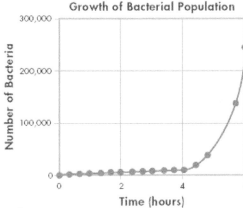

26. DDT was used to:

    A. form ozone

    B. feed animals

    C. kill insects

    D. fertilize the soil

    E. form greenhouse gases

27. All renewable resources:

    A. are living

    B. can be recycled or reused

    C. are unlimited in supply

    D. can regenerate or be replenished

    E. once were living

28. Density-dependent limiting factors include:

A. blizzards

B. damming of rivers

C. disease

D. earthquakes

E. average temperature

29. If a population grows larger than the carrying capacity of the environment:

A. birth rate must fall

B. death rate must fall

C. birth rate may rise

D. birth rate and death rate may rise

E. death rate may rise

30. One property that makes DDT hazardous is that it is:

A. deadly to herbivores

B. subject to biological magnification

C. volatile pesticide

D. insecticide

E. organic pesticide

31. As the population gets larger, it grows more quickly because the size of each generation of offspring is larger than the generation before, resulting in:

A. multiple growth

B. exponential growth

C. growth density

D. logistic growth

E. linear growth

32. The gray-brown haze often observed over large cities is:

A. vapor

B. particulates

C. greenhouse gases

D. ozone layer

E. smog

33. Compounds that contribute to the formation of acid rain contain:

A. nitrogen and sulfur

B. ammonia and nitrates

C. carbon dioxide and oxygen

D. calcium and phosphorus

E. carbon dioxide and ammonia

34. The various growth phases through which most populations go are represented on:

A. normal curve

B. population curve

C. logistic growth curve

D. exponential growth curve

E. linear growth curve

35. Water lilies do not grow in desert sand because water availability to these plants in a desert is:

A. competition factor

B. logistic growth curve

C. limiting factor

D. carrying capacity

E. none of the above

36. The sulfur and nitrogen compounds in smog combine with water to form:

A. acid rain

B. chlorofluorocarbons

C. ozone

D. ammonia

E. greenhouse gases

37. Air and water pollution have been reduced by:

A. raising more cattle for food

B. increasing biological magnification

C. using fossil fuels in factories

D. using only unleaded gasoline

E. using more effective pesticides

38. Which would be least likely affected by a density-dependent limiting factor?

A. population with a high immigration rate

B. large, dense population

C. population with a high birth rate

D. small, scattered population

E. population with a low death rate

39. Raising cattle and farming rice contribute to air pollution by:

A. releasing ozone into the atmosphere

B. producing smog which reacts to form dangerous ozone gas

C. producing particulates into the air

D. releasing sulfur compounds that form acid rain

E. releasing the greenhouse gas methane into the atmosphere

40. For most populations that are growing, as resources become less available, the population:

A. enters a phase of exponential growth

B. reaches carrying capacity

C. increases more rapidly

D. declines rapidly

E. enters a phase of linear growth

41. Which term best describes the number of distinct species in the biosphere or a particular area?

A. species diversity

B. genetic diversity

C. ecosystem diversity

D. biodiversity

E. homogeneity

42. Which density-dependent factors other than the predator/prey relationship affect the populations of moose and wolves on an island?

  A. A hurricane for both moose and wolves
  B. Food availability for the moose and disease for the wolf
  C. Extreme temperatures for the moose and flooding for the wolves
  D. Parasitic wasps for the wolves and clear-cut forest for the moose
  E. A drought for both moose and wolves

43. How are species diversity and genetic diversity different?

  A. Species diversity measures the number of individuals of a species, while genetic diversity measures the total variety of species
  B. Conservation biology is concerned with species diversity but not with genetic diversity
  C. Species diversity is evaluated in ecosystems, while genetic diversity is evaluated in the entire biosphere
  D. Species diversity measures the number of species in the biosphere, while genetic diversity measures the variety of genes in the biosphere, including genetic variation within species
  E. Species diversity results from natural selection, while genetic diversity results from genetic engineering

44. Which is NOT likely to be a limiting factor on the sea otter population living in the ocean?

  A. prey availability   **C.** disease
  B. predation   **D.** competition
                                    E. drought

45. Introduced species can threaten biodiversity because they can:

  A. crowd out native species   **C.** cause desertification of land
  B. reduce the fertility of native species   **D.** cause biological magnification
                                            E. mate with native species

46. Which is a density-independent limiting factor?

  A. parasitism and disease   **C.** predator/prey relationships
  B. eruption of a volcano   **D.** struggle for food
                                          E. available water or sunlight

47. Which would reduce competition within a species' population?

  A. higher population density   **C.** higher birth rate
  B. fewer resources   **D.** fewer individuals
                                            E. lower death rate

48. A significant factor that negatively affects biodiversity is:

A. non-renewable resources

B. contour plowing

C. habitat fragmentation

D. biological magnification

E. preservation of ecosystems

49. All are threats to biodiversity EXCEPT:

A. habitat fragmentation

B. desertification

C. habitat preservation

D. biological magnification of toxic compounds

E. all the above are threats

50. The graph shows the changes in the mosquito population. What caused the changes in the graph?

A. increase in resources

B. density-dependent limiting factor

C. reduction in resources

D. increase in predation

E. density-independent limiting factor

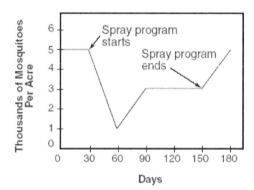

51. Each is a density-dependent limiting factor, EXCEPT:

A. crowding

B. disease

C. competition

D. temperature

E. predation

52. The "hot spot" strategy seeks to protect species in danger of extinction due to the following:

A. human activity

B. biological magnification

C. captive breeding programs

D. expanding national parks

E. preservation of ecosystems

53. About 500 years ago, the world's population started to:

A. level off

B. grow more rapidly

C. reach carrying capacity

D. decrease

E. grow sporadically

DAT Biology

Answer Keys
&
Detailed Explanations

If you benefited from this book, we would appreciate if you left a review on Amazon, so others can learn from your input. Reviews help us understand our customers' needs and experiences while keeping our commitment to quality.

Answer Keys

Chapter 1. Eukaryotic Cell: Structure and Function

1: D	11: C	21: C	31: B	41: D	51: B
2: A	12: E	22: B	32: D	42: C	52: A
3: E	13: B	23: E	33: E	43: C	53: B
4: C	14: C	24: A	34: B	44: A	54: D
5: E	15: E	25: B	35: C	45: B	55: C
6: C	16: C	26: E	36: D	46: E	56: E
7: A	17: D	27: C	37: E	47: D	57: A
8: A	18: A	28: D	38: C	48: E	
9: B	19: B	29: A	39: D	49: B	
10: B	20: A	30: B	40: B	50: D	

Chapter 2. Molecular Biology of Eukaryotes

1: A	11: A	21: A	31: C	41: A	51: A
2: E	12: B	22: C	32: A	42: E	52: E
3: C	13: E	23: B	33: E	43: B	53: B
4: A	14: C	24: C	34: B	44: D	54: B
5: C	15: D	25: A	35: A	45: E	
6: D	16: A	26: E	36: B	46: B	
7: C	17: B	27: D	37: E	47: C	
8: A	18: E	28: B	38: D	48: C	
9: E	19: C	29: E	39: D	49: A	
10: D	20: B	30: D	40: B	50: D	

Chapter 3. Cellular Metabolism and Enzymes

1: D	11: A	21: A	31: E	41: B	51: C
2: A	12: D	22: B	32: C	42: C	52: B
3: C	13: E	23: A	33: D	43: A	53: C
4: B	14: D	24: E	34: B	44: E	54: D
5: E	15: B	25: C	35: D	45: A	55: D
6: C	16: D	26: D	36: B	46: C	
7: D	17: C	27: C	37: A	47: C	
8: A	18: B	28: E	38: D	48: B	
9: B	19: E	29: B	39: E	49: E	
10: E	20: B	30: B	40: A	50: B	

Chapter 4. Biomolecules

1: A	11: B	21: A	31: A	41: D	51: C
2: B	12: B	22: B	32: E	42: C	52: C
3: A	13: D	23: A	33: C	43: D	53: C
4: B	14: B	24: B	34: D	44: D	
5: C	15: D	25: D	35: D	45: A	
6: B	16: C	26: D	36: D	46: B	
7: C	17: B	27: C	37: C	47: D	
8: C	18: B	28: D	38: A	48: A	
9: D	19: D	29: C	39: D	49: B	
10: B	20: B	30: B	40: B	50: A	

Chapter 5. Endocrine System

1: A	11: D	21: D	31: C	41: A
2: D	12: E	22: E	32: B	42: C
3: D	13: D	23: B	33: D	43: D
4: A	14: C	24: B	34: E	44: E
5: D	15: C	25: C	35: D	45: C
6: A	16: E	26: B	36: B	46: A
7: E	17: C	27: A	37: E	47: B
8: B	18: B	28: C	38: C	48: D
9: A	19: C	29: E	39: A	49: E
10: E	20: B	30: D	40: C	50: A

Chapter 6. Nervous System

1: C	11: C	21: C	31: D	41: C	51: A
2: A	12: B	22: B	32: B	42: E	52: A
3: C	13: E	23: E	33: E	43: C	53: D
4: D	14: A	24: D	34: D	44: C	54: A
5: B	15: D	25: D	35: B	45: B	55: E
6: E	16: D	26: A	36: C	46: D	56: C
7: B	17: E	27: C	37: E	47: E	
8: E	18: A	28: D	38: C	48: A	
9: B	19: A	29: E	39: B	49: B	
10: A	20: D	30: A	40: A	50: D	

Chapter 7. Circulatory System

1: B	11: E	21: B	31: A	41: C	51: C
2: D	12: A	22: E	32: E	42: B	52: E
3: E	13: E	23: C	33: A	43: D	53: B
4: B	14: C	24: C	34: B	44: C	54: C
5: A	15: C	25: A	35: A	45: E	55: D
6: A	16: B	26: E	36: C	46: C	56: A
7: E	17: A	27: D	37: C	47: B	57: E
8: D	18: B	28: A	38: E	48: C	
9: C	19: D	29: D	39: C	49: B	
10: B	20: D	30: B	40: D	50: E	

Chapter 8. Lymphatic and Immune Systems

1: B	11: E	21: D	31: B	41: A	51: B
2: E	12: D	22: A	32: D	42: B	52: C
3: B	13: C	23: D	33: A	43: B	53: A
4: D	14: B	24: D	34: E	44: D	
5: B	15: A	25: B	35: D	45: B	
6: E	16: A	26: A	36: B	46: E	
7: C	17: D	27: E	37: E	47: C	
8: D	18: E	28: A	38: B	48: D	
9: C	19: B	29: B	39: D	49: C	
10: D	20: A	30: D	40: A	50: E	

Chapter 9. Digestive System

1: C	11: A	21: A	31: C	41: A	51: A
2: E	12: D	22: C	32: A	42: B	52: E
3: B	13: B	23: A	33: E	43: D	53: A
4: D	14: E	24: B	34: D	44: B	54: C
5: D	15: D	25: E	35: C	45: E	55: B
6: E	16: D	26: C	36: E	46: C	
7: B	17: B	27: B	37: A	47: A	
8: E	18: C	28: B	38: C	48: E	
9: D	19: E	29: E	39: B	49: B	
10: C	20: B	30: C	40: D	50: D	

Chapter 10. Excretory System

1: A	11: C	21: A	31: C	41: A	51: B
2: C	12: B	22: E	32: B	42: C	52: A
3: E	13: E	23: C	33: A	43: D	53: E
4: C	14: B	24: B	34: E	44: E	54: A
5: B	15: E	25: C	35: C	45: B	55: B
6: E	16: A	26: D	36: B	46: C	56: E
7: D	17: C	27: A	37: C	47: A	
8: B	18: C	28: D	38: E	48: C	
9: D	19: C	29: E	39: B	49: D	
10: A	20: A	30: D	40: B	50: E	

Chapter 11. Muscle System

1: C	11: A	21: A	31: C	41: D	51: A
2: A	12: C	22: B	32: D	42: D	52: E
3: D	13: D	23: C	33: E	43: B	53: A
4: E	14: A	24: C	34: D	44: C	54: D
5: A	15: E	25: A	35: E	45: E	55: E
6: A	16: A	26: E	36: C	46: C	56: C
7: D	17: B	27: A	37: A	47: A	57: D
8: E	18: A	28: D	38: B	48: E	58: D
9: C	19: C	29: D	39: A	49: B	
10: A	20: E	30: E	40: B	50: A	

Chapter 12. Skeletal System

1: C	11: C	21: A	31: D	41: B	51: A
2: D	12: C	22: C	32: C	42: D	52: D
3: C	13: D	23: A	33: B	43: E	53: B
4: B	14: B	24: E	34: E	44: C	
5: E	15: E	25: B	35: D	45: E	
6: D	16: B	26: C	36: B	46: A	
7: A	17: A	27: D	37: E	47: C	
8: E	18: A	28: E	38: D	48: B	
9: D	19: E	29: A	39: B	49: C	
10: A	20: B	30: B	40: D	50: B	

Chapter 13. Respiratory System

1: B	11: B	21: B	31: C	41: C
2: A	12: D	22: A	32: D	42: B
3: D	13: E	23: D	33: E	43: E
4: A	14: B	24: E	34: A	44: A
5: E	15: E	25: B	35: B	45: A
6: B	16: D	26: C	36: C	46: D
7: C	17: A	27: D	37: B	47: E
8: E	18: D	28: C	38: C	48: B
9: A	19: C	29: C	39: E	
10: B	20: C	30: E	40: A	

Chapter 14. Integumentary System

1: B	11: D	21: D	31: B	41: C
2: A	12: A	22: A	32: B	42: D
3: C	13: D	23: E	33: A	43: E
4: E	14: C	24: D	34: C	44: D
5: B	15: C	25: D	35: B	45: C
6: A	16: B	26: A	36: A	46: D
7: E	17: E	27: B	37: B	47: A
8: C	18: A	28: C	38: E	48: E
9: B	19: E	29: E	39: D	
10: D	20: A	30: A	40: B	

Chapter 15. Reproductive System

1: D	11: C
2: A	12: E
3: E	13: A
4: A	14: C
5: C	15: A
6: D	16: B
7: B	17: B
8: C	18: B
9: B	19: B
10: A	20: A

Chapter 16. Mechanisms of Reproduction

1: B	11: E	21: D
2: C	12: D	22: A
3: C	13: C	23: E
4: E	14: D	24: B
5: C	15: D	25: A
6: D	16: B	26: E
7: C	17: E	27: D
8: B	18: C	
9: E	19: A	
10: B	20: E	

Chapter 17. Development

1: A	11: C	21: B	31: C	41: C	51: C
2: D	12: A	22: E	32: B	42: E	52: E
3: B	13: D	23: D	33: D	43: A	53: A
4: E	14: C	24: C	34: D	44: C	54: C
5: D	15: E	25: E	35: A	45: E	55: E
6: A	16: D	26: D	36: D	46: A	56: B
7: C	17: C	27: B	37: D	47: B	57: B
8: B	18: E	28: A	38: C	48: A	58: C
9: A	19: D	29: C	39: E	49: B	
10: E	20: A	30: A	40: C	50: A	

Chapter 18. DNA and Protein Synthesis

1: D	11: B	21: B	31: A	41: B	51: C	61: D
2: D	12: C	22: C	32: D	42: D	52: A	62: E
3: E	13: E	23: B	33: B	43: E	53: E	63: B
4: A	14: C	24: A	34: E	44: A	54: A	64: A
5: D	15: B	25: B	35: A	45: C	55: C	
6: D	16: C	26: E	36: B	46: A	56: B	
7: A	17: D	27: E	37: D	47: D	57: A	
8: C	18: E	28: B	38: E	48: E	58: B	
9: E	19: C	29: D	39: C	49: C	59: E	
10: C	20: D	30: C	40: A	50: D	60: C	

Chapter 18. Genetics and Inheritance Patterns

1: A	11: C	21: E	31: E	41: B	51: C	61: D
2: C	12: A	22: C	32: B	42: C	52: C	
3: C	13: D	23: B	33: B	43: B	53: C	
4: E	14: E	24: D	34: A	44: D	54: B	
5: C	15: A	25: A	35: D	45: D	55: C	
6: E	16: E	26: C	36: A	46: E	56: B	
7: B	17: B	27: D	37: C	47: C	57: B	
8: C	18: A	28: C	38: A	48: D	58: E	
9: D	19: A	29: B	39: C	49: E	59: A	
10: B	20: C	30: D	40: E	50: D	60: C	

Chapter 20. Microbiology

1: E	11: A	21: A	31: C	41: C	51: B
2: B	12: B	22: D	32: E	42: E	52: E
3: D	13: E	23: E	33: D	43: C	53: C
4: D	14: C	24: B	34: B	44: A	54: E
5: B	15: E	25: E	35: D	45: C	55: A
6: C	16: E	26: D	36: E	46: A	56: D
7: D	17: B	27: C	37: A	47: A	57: C
8: A	18: C	28: B	38: B	48: B	
9: C	19: A	29: A	39: A	49: E	
10: E	20: C	30: C	40: C	50: B	

Chapter 21. Classification and Diversity

1: D	11: B	21: B	31: E	41: B	51: C
2: A	12: A	22: C	32: D	42: D	52: D
3: E	13: A	23: A	33: C	43: E	53: E
4: A	14: E	24: C	34: C	44: A	54: B
5: C	15: B	25: E	35: B	45: E	55: D
6: B	16: D	26: B	36: A	46: A	56: E
7: B	17: B	27: E	37: B	47: D	57: D
8: E	18: C	28: A	38: E	48: E	58: B
9: B	19: E	29: D	39: C	49: C	59: B
10: D	20: C	30: B	40: A	50: A	

Chapter 22. Ecosystems and Biomes

1: A	11: D	21: C	31: B	41: B	51: C
2: B	12: E	22: D	32: C	42: C	52: D
3: A	13: A	23: E	33: B	43: D	53: E
4: C	14: B	24: C	34: A	44: A	
5: E	15: A	25: B	35: D	45: C	
6: D	16: E	26: E	36: E	46: B	
7: E	17: A	27: B	37: C	47: E	
8: C	18: B	28: A	38: B	48: A	
9: C	19: C	29: D	39: A	49: D	
10: B	20: D	30: A	40: E	50: A	

Chapter 23. Evolution and Natural Selection

1: D	11: C	21: C	31: B	41: A	51: C
2: A	12: D	22: D	32: E	42: A	52: B
3: E	13: D	23: C	33: C	43: D	53: B
4: A	14: E	24: E	34: B	44: C	54: D
5: D	15: B	25: C	35: A	45: B	
6: C	16: A	26: E	36: D	46: D	
7: E	17: E	27: B	37: E	47: D	
8: D	18: D	28: D	38: C	48: A	
9: A	19: C	29: B	39: D	49: E	
10: B	20: A	30: B	40: E	50: A	

Chapter 24. Animal Behavior

1: A	11: A	21: E	31: A
2: E	12: D	22: A	32: C
3: B	13: C	23: D	33: A
4: C	14: B	24: B	
5: A	15: E	25: C	
6: D	16: A	26: D	
7: B	17: D	27: E	
8: D	18: C	28: C	
9: C	19: E	29: A	
10: E	20: B	30: B	

Chapter 25. Populations and Community Ecology

1: D	11: A	21: D	31: B	41: A	51: D
2: A	12: B	22: A	32: E	42: B	52: A
3: B	13: C	23: E	33: A	43: D	53: B
4: D	14: D	24: A	34: C	44: E	
5: C	15: E	25: B	35: C	45: A	
6: E	16: E	26: C	36: A	46: B	
7: A	17: A	27: D	37: D	47: D	
8: B	18: C	28: C	38: D	48: C	
9: C	19: B	29: E	39: E	49: C	
10: E	20: D	30: B	40: B	50: E	

Notes for active learning

Cell and Molecular Biology

Eukaryotic Cell: Structure and Function – Detailed Explanations

1. D is correct.

Facilitated transport (or *passive transport*) uses a protein pore (or channel) but is differentiated from *active transport, which requires energy.*

2. A is correct.

Cell is the unit of function and reproduction because subcellular components cannot regenerate whole cells.

3. E is correct.

I: water relies on *aquaporins* to readily diffuse across a plasma membrane.

Without aquaporins, only a small fraction of water molecules can diffuse through the cell membrane per unit of time because of the polarity of water molecules.

II: *small hydrophobic molecules* readily diffuse through the hydrophobic tails of the plasma membrane.

III: *small ions* rely on ion channel transport proteins to diffuse across the membrane.

IV: *neutral gas molecules* (e.g., O_2, CO_2) readily diffuse through the hydrophobic tails of the plasma membrane.

4. C is correct.

Integral proteins often span the plasma membrane.

Plasma membrane is a phospholipid bilayer with an inner span of hydrophobic (or *water-fearing*) regions.

Diameter of a plasma membrane is 20 to 25 amino acids thick.

Spans of 20-25 hydrophobic residues prefer to be embedded in the plasma membrane and isolated from water.

Hydropathy analysis determines the degree of *hydrophobicity* (i.e., nonpolar or *water-fearing*) or *hydrophilicity* (i.e., polar or *water-loving*) of amino acids in a protein. It characterizes the possible structures of a protein.

Each residue (i.e., individual amino acid) has a hydrophobicity value (analogous to electronegativity).

Hydropathy analysis plots the degree of hydrophobicity (or *hydrophilicity*) on the *y*-axis and the amino acid sequence on the *x*-axis, *hydrophobicity vs. amino acid* position.

Amino acids have lower energy when polar amino acids occupy a polar environment (e.g., cytoplasm) and nonpolar amino acids occupy a nonpolar environment (e.g., the interior of the plasma membrane).

5. E is correct.

Lysosome is the digestive region of the cell and is a membrane-bound organelle with a low pH (around 5) that stores hydrolytic enzymes.

A: *vacuoles* and *vesicles* are membrane-bound sacs involved in the transport and storage of materials ingested, secreted, processed, or digested by cells.

Vacuoles are larger than vesicles and are in plant cells (e.g., central vacuole).

C: *chloroplasts* are the site of photosynthesis and are only in algae and plant cells.

Like mitochondria, chloroplasts contain circular DNA and ribosomes and may have evolved similarly via endosymbiosis.

D: *phagosomes* are vesicles for transporting and storing materials ingested by the cell through phagocytosis. Vesicles form by the fusion of the cell membrane around the particle.

Phagosome is a cellular compartment in which pathogenic microorganisms are digested.

Phagosomes *fuse with lysosomes* in their maturation process to form *phagolysosomes*.

6. C is correct.

DNA damage checkpoints are *signal transduction pathways* that block cell cycle progression in G1, G2, and metaphase and slow the S phase progression rate when DNA is damaged.

Pausing cell cycle allows the cell to repair the damage before dividing.

Cell cycle divides into interphase (G1. S, G2) and mitosis (prophase, metaphase, anaphase, and telophase)

7. A is correct.

(C≡G) base pairs are linked in the double helix by *three hydrogen bonds*.

(A=T) base pairs are linked in the double helix by *two hydrogen bonds*.

Therefore, it takes more energy to separate G-C base pairs.

Less G–C rich strands of double-stranded DNA require less energy to separate (i.e., denature).

Chargaff's rule specifies complementary base pairing; double-stranded DNA has equal G and C (and A and T).

8. A is correct.

Phospholipids are lipids as major components of cell membranes; they form lipid bilayers.

Phospholipids contain a glycerol backbone, a phosphate group, and a simple organic molecule (e.g., choline).

The 'head' is *hydrophilic* (i.e., attracted to water), while the 'tails' are *hydrophobic* (i.e., repelled by water), and the tails aggregate (via hydrophobic forces).

Hydrophilic heads contain negatively charged phosphate groups and glycerol.

Hydrophobic tails usually consist of 2 long fatty acids (saturated or unsaturated) hydrocarbon chains.

Cholesterol is embedded within animal lipid bilayers but is absent in plant cell membranes. Embedded cholesterol in the phospholipid bilayer in eukaryotic animal cells allows for protective cell membranes that can also change shape.

Plant and bacterial cell walls are primarily composed of cellulose and peptidoglycan glucose polymers, respectively, which are rigid and restrict movement.

9. B is correct.

Cytoskeleton determines the *overall shape* of a cell and is composed of:

> *Microtubules* help synthesize cell walls in plants which primarily contribute to shape; centrosomes organize microtubules, cilia, and flagella (9+2).

> Microtubules form *mitotic spindles* and *centrioles* (non-membrane-bound organelles).

> *Intermediate filaments*: anchor organelles (e.g., nucleus) and bear tension, contributing to cell shape.

> *Microfilaments:* resist compression, thus contributing to cell shape.

10. B is correct.

Osmolarity is determined by the total concentration of dissolved particles in the solution.

Compounds that dissociate into ions (i.e., electrolytes) increase the concentration of particles and produce a higher osmolarity.

To determine which molecule (after dissociation into ions) generates the highest osmolarity, determine the number of individual ions each molecule dissociates into in H_2O.

> $CaCl_2$ dissociates into 1 Ca^{2+} and 2 Cl^-

As a result, $CaCl_2$ generates the greatest osmolarity, which equals 250 mOsmoles for Ca^{2+} + 500 mOsmoles for Cl^- = 750 mOsmoles when $CaCl_2$ dissociates into ions within the solution.

A: NaCl dissociates in water with an osmolarity of 600 mOsmoles because it dissociates into 1 Na^+ and 1 Cl^-.

Na^+ cations and Cl^- anions are added: 300 mOsmoles for Na^+ + 300 mOsmoles for Cl^- = 600 mOsmoles.

C: glucose does *not* dissociate in water and has the same osmolarity as the starting molecule—500 mOsmoles.

D: urea does *not* dissociate in water and has the same osmolarity as the starting molecule— 600 mOsmoles.

11. C is correct.

The two ribosomal subunits are synthesized in the nucleolus, a region within the nucleus. The ribosomes are the sites of protein production.

Prokaryotic ribosomes (30S small + 50S large subunit = 70S complete ribosome) are smaller than *eukaryotic ribosomes* (40S small + 60S large subunit = 80S complete ribosome).

A: *Golgi apparatus* is a membrane-bound organelle that modifies (e.g., glycosylation), sorts, and packages proteins synthesized by the ribosomes.

B: *lysosomes* have a low pH of about 5 and contain hydrolytic enzymes involved in digestion.

D: *rough endoplasmic reticulum* (RER) is part of the endomembrane extending from the nuclear envelope.

RER has ribosomes associated with its membrane and is the site of the production and folding of proteins.

Misfolded proteins exit the rough ER and are sent to the *proteasome* for degradation.

E: *cell membrane* is a barrier between the interior and exterior of the cell.

12. E is correct.

Cyclins are phosphorylated proteins responsible for specific events during cycle division, such as microtubule formation and chromatin remodeling.

Cyclins are four classes based on their behavior in the cell cycle: G1/S, S, M, and G1 cyclins.

p53 is not a transcription factor but is a tumor suppressor gene. The p53 protein is crucial in multicellular organisms, where it regulates the cell cycle and functions as a tumor suppressor (preventing cancer).

p53 is *the guardian of the genome* because it conserves stability by preventing genome mutation.

13. B is correct.

Codon is a three-nucleotide segment of an mRNA that hybridizes (via complementary base pairing) with the appropriate anticodon on the tRNA to encode one amino acid in a polypeptide chain during protein synthesis.

The tRNA molecule interacts with the mRNA codon after the ribosomal complex binds the mRNA.

A: tRNA molecules interact with the mRNA codon after (not before) the ribosomal complex binds mRNA

C: *translation* involves the conversion of mRNA into protein.

D: *operons* regulate the transcription of genes into mRNA and are not involved in translating mRNA into proteins.

14. C is correct.

Peroxisomes are organelles in most eukaryotic cells; a significant function is the breakdown of very-long-chain fatty acids through *beta-oxidation*.

Peroxisomes convert the very long fatty acids to medium-chain fatty acids in animal cells, subsequently shuttled to the mitochondria. Medium-chain fatty acids are degraded, via oxidation, into CO_2 and H_2O.

Peroxisomes are membrane-bound, while ribosomes are non-membrane-bound organelles.

15. E is correct.

Vacuole is a membrane-bound organelle in plant and fungal cells and some protist, animal, and bacterial cells.

Vacuoles are enclosed compartments filled with water. They contain inorganic and organic molecules (including enzymes in solution) and may contain solids that have been engulfed.

Function and significance of vacuoles vary by cell type, with much greater prominence in plants, fungi, and certain protists than in animals or bacteria.

Mitochondria and chloroplasts have circular DNA resembling DNA in prokaryotes, as supported by the endosymbiotic *theory* for the evolution of mitochondria and chloroplasts from prokaryotes.

Ribosomes are the site of protein synthesis.

16. C is correct.

I-cell disease patients cannot correctly direct newly synthesized peptides to their target organelles. The Golgi apparatus is part of the endomembrane system and serves as a cellular distribution center.

Golgi apparatus packages proteins before they are sent to their destination. It modifies, sorts, and packages proteins for cell secretion (i.e., exocytosis) or use within the cell.

A: *nucleus* is the largest organelle, contains genetic material (i.e., DNA), and is the site of rRNA synthesis (within the nucleolus).

D: *smooth ER* (endoplasmic reticulum) forms the endomembrane system, is connected to the nuclear envelope, and functions in several metabolic processes. It synthesizes lipids, phospholipids, and steroids.

Cells secreting lipids, phospholipids, and steroids (e.g., testes, ovaries, and skin oil glands) have an extensive smooth endoplasmic reticulum.

Smooth ER conducts the metabolism of carbohydrates and drug detoxification.

It is responsible for the attachment of receptors on cell membrane proteins and steroid metabolism.

E: *nucleolus* is the organelle within the nucleus responsible for synthesizing ribosomal RNA (rRNA).

17. D is correct.

Cytochrome c oxidase is a large transmembrane protein complex in bacteria and the mitochondrion of eukaryotes. It receives an electron from each of four cytochrome c molecules and transfers the electrons to an O_2 molecule, converting molecular oxygen to two molecules of H_2O.

Cytochrome c oxidase is the *last enzyme in the electron transport chain* (ETC) of mitochondria (or bacteria) in the mitochondrial (or bacterial) inner membrane.

Mitochondria and chloroplasts have circular DNA resembling DNA in prokaryotes.

Endosymbiotic theory illustrates the evolution of mitochondria and chloroplasts from prokaryotes, thus explaining the resemblance.

18. A is correct.

Cytoskeleton is integral to proper cell division because it forms the mitotic spindle and separates sister chromatids during cell division.

Cytoskeleton comprises microtubules and microfilaments, provides mechanical cell support to maintain shape, and functions in cell motility.

19. B is correct.

Biochemical events during the cell cycle include DNA damage repair and replication completion, centrosome duplication, spindle assembly, and attachment of the kinetochores to the spindle.

20. A is correct.

Mitochondria divide autonomously (i.e., independent of the genome) to produce daughter mitochondria that incorporate new nonradioactive phosphatidylcholine and inherit radioactive phosphatidylcholine from the parent via *semiconservative replication*.

Therefore, the daughter mitochondria have equal radioactivity.

B: mitochondria divide *autonomously*, and daughter mitochondria retain parental (original) radioactive label.

C: original sample was 100% radiolabeled.

DNA replication is *semiconservative*, whereby one strand of parental DNA (radiolabeled) and one strand of newly replicated (non-radiolabeled) are in each daughter cell after the first round of division.

D: requires the daughter mitochondria to be synthesized *de novo* (i.e., new) with newly synthesized, nonradioactive phosphatidylcholine.

If the mitochondria divide autonomously, the daughter mitochondria retain the radioactive label evenly via *semiconservative replication*.

21. C is correct.

Golgi apparatus (i.e., Golgi complex) is a eukaryotic cell organelle.

Golgi apparatus processes proteins via *post-translational modifications* for three destinations:

> 1) *secreted* from the cell,
>
> 2) transported into *organelles,* or
>
> 3) targeted to the *plasma membrane*.

Golgi complex mainly processes proteins synthesized by the ER

In plant cells, the central vacuole functions as a lysosome, stores nutrients and maintains osmotic balance.

Peroxisomes are like lysosomes in size, are bound by a single membrane, and are filled with enzymes.

However, peroxisomes *bud from* the endoplasmic reticulum.

22. B is correct.

Prokaryotic cells (bacteria) have a typical cell width of 0.2 to 2.0 micrometers in diameter.

Eukaryotic cells (animal cells) have a typical cell width of 10-100 micrometers in diameter.

$$1 \text{ millimeter} = 1 \times 10^{-3} \text{ m}$$

$$1 \text{ micrometer} = 1 \times 10^{-6} \text{ m}$$

$$1 \text{ nanometer} = 1 \times 10^{-9} \text{ m}$$

Light microscopes visualize objects from 1 millimeter (10^{-3} m) to 0.2 micrometers (2×10^{-7} m).

Electron microscopes visualize objects as small as an atom (1 angstrom or 10^{-10} m).

Microscopic scale ranges from 1 millimeter (10^{-3} m) to a ten-millionth of a millimeter (10^{-10} m). There are immense variations in objects' sizes, even within the microscopic scale.

10^{-3} m is 10 million times larger than 10^{-10} m, equivalent to the Earth's size *vs.* a beach ball.

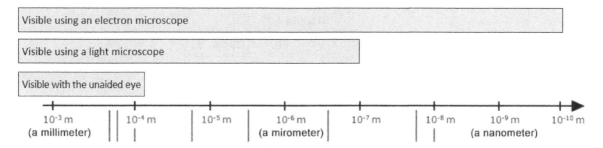

Comparison of resolution by unaided eyes, light, and electron microscopes

23. E is correct.

Ribosomes are composed of specific rRNA molecules and associated proteins.

Ribosomes are identified by the sedimentation coefficients (i.e., S units for Svedberg units) for density.

Prokaryotes have a 30S small and a 50S large subunit (i.e., complete ribosome = 70S; based on density).

Eukaryotes have a 40S small and 60S large subunit (i.e., complete ribosome = 80S).

A: *peroxisomes* are organelles involved in hydrogen peroxide (H_2O_2) synthesis and degradation. They function in cell detoxification and contain the catalase that decomposes H_2O_2 into H_2O and O_2.

C: *mitochondria* are organelles as the site of cellular respiration (i.e., oxidation of glucose to yield ATP) and plentiful in cells with high demands for ATP (e.g., muscle cells).

The number of mitochondria within a cell varies widely by organism and tissue type.

Many cells have a single mitochondrion, whereas others contain several thousand mitochondria.

Nucleus is the largest membrane-bound organelle in eukaryotes, containing the genetic code (i.e., DNA).

It directs the storing and transmitting of genetic information. Cells can contain multiple nuclei (e.g., skeletal muscle cells), one nucleus, or none (e.g., red blood cells).

24. A is correct.

Osmosis is a type of diffusion involving water and is a form of passive transport.

Hypertonic means a solution of high solute and low solvent concentrations.

Hypotonic means a solution of high solvent and low solute concentrations.

Solvents flow spontaneously from an area of high solvent to a low solvent concentration.

During *osmosis*, water flows from a hypotonic to a hypertonic environment.

25. B is correct.

Complex of Cdk and cyclin B is a maturation or mitosis-promoting factor (MPF).

Cyclin B is necessary to progress cells into and out of the M phase of the cell cycle.

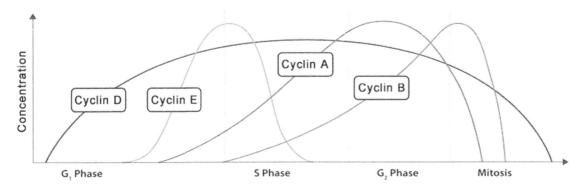

26. E is correct.

Mitochondria have their DNA genetic material and machinery to manufacture their RNAs and proteins.

For example, the trait is recessive (not observed in limited number of offspring) and encoded by a nuclear gene.

A: like organisms that reproduce sexually, mice inherit the *mitochondrial organelle* from their mother and display maternal inheritance of mitochondrial genes.

C: if X-linked, selectively male (not female) progeny would display the trait.

D: mitochondrial genes cannot be *recessive* because mitochondria are *inherited from the mother*.

27. C is correct.

Smooth endoplasmic reticulum (smooth ER) participates in synthesizing phosphatidylcholine.

Smooth ER functions include:

   1) synthesis of lipids, phospholipids, and steroids

   2) metabolism of carbohydrates and steroids

   3) detoxifying alcohol and drugs

   4) regulating Ca^{2+} concentration in muscle cells

Phosphatidylcholine is a class of phospholipids.

28. D is correct.

Plastids (e.g., chloroplast and chromoplast) are major organelles in plants and algae.

Plastids are the site of manufacturing and storing critical chemical compounds used by cells.

They often contain pigments used in photosynthesis. Pigments change to determine cell color.

Plastids, like prokaryotes, contain a circular double-stranded DNA molecule.

29. A is correct.

Thyroid gland synthesizes calcitonin in response to high blood calcium levels. It acts to reduce blood calcium (Ca^{2+}), opposing the effects of parathyroid hormone (PTH).

Calcitonin lowers blood Ca^{2+} levels in three ways:

> 1) inhibiting Ca^{2+} absorption by the intestines,
>
> 2) inhibiting osteoclast activity in bones, and
>
> 3) inhibiting renal tubular cell reabsorption of Ca^{2+}, allowing it to be excreted in the urine.

B: *kidneys* serve several essential regulatory roles. They are essential in the urinary system and serve homeostatic functions such as regulating electrolytes, maintaining acid-base balance, and regulating blood pressure (maintaining salt and water balance).

Kidneys secrete *renin* (involved in blood pressure regulation) that induces the release of aldosterone from the adrenal cortex (it increases blood pressure via sodium reabsorption, increasing blood pressure).

C: *parathyroid glands* synthesize parathyroid hormone (PTH), which increases blood calcium.

PTH increases calcium concentration in blood by acting upon the parathyroid hormone receptor (elevated levels in bone and kidney) and the parathyroid hormone receptor (elevated levels in the central nervous system, pancreas, testes, and placenta).

D: *liver* is the largest organ with many functions, including detoxification, protein synthesis, and the production of biomolecules necessary for digestion. The liver synthesizes bile, which is necessary for dietary lipid emulsification (in the small intestine).

E: *spleen* is a *reservoir* for red blood cells and *filters* the blood.

30. B is correct.

Rough endoplasmic reticulum (rough ER) participates in synthesizing plasma membrane proteins.

Oxidative phosphorylation is a series of redox reactions in the electron transport chain (ETC), leading to the production of ATP. In Eukaryotes, this occurs in the *mitochondrial inner membrane* and in prokaryotes in the intermembrane space.

Endocytosis is when a cell membrane invaginates, forming a vacuole to store molecules from the extracellular space actively transported across the cell's plasma membrane.

Post-translational modification is after ribosomes translate mRNA into polypeptide chains; the polypeptide chains become a mature protein by undergoing biochemical reactions (e.g., cleavage, folding).

31. B is correct.

Active transport uses a carrier protein and energy to move a substance across a membrane against (i.e., up) a concentration gradient: from low solute to a region of high solute concentration.

Donnan equilibrium refers to some ionic species passing through the barrier while others cannot.

Charged substances that cannot pass through the membrane create an uneven electrical charge.

Donnan potential is the electric potential arising between the solutions.

32. D is correct.

Cyclin D synthesis is initiated during G1 and drives the G1/S phase transition.

Apoptosis is programmed cell death (PCD) that may occur in multicellular organisms. Biochemical events lead to characteristic cell changes (morphology) and death.

Apoptotic changes include blebbing (i.e., an irregular bulge in the plasma membrane), cell shrinkage, chromatin condensation, nuclear fragmentation, and chromosomal DNA fragmentation.

In contrast to necrosis, traumatic cell death resulting from acute cellular injury, apoptosis confers advantages during an organism's life cycle.

For example, the differentiation of fingers and toes in a developing human embryo occurs because cells between the fingers undergo apoptosis, and the digits are separated.

Unlike necrosis, apoptosis produces cell fragments called *apoptotic bodies* that phagocytic cells can engulf and quickly remove before the cell's contents can spill out onto surrounding cells and cause damage.

33. E is correct.

During meiosis I, *homologous chromosomes* separate.

Sister chromatids (identical copies, except for recombination) separate during meiosis II.

Klinefelter syndrome (XXY karyotype) contains two X and one Y chromosome.

X and Y would be "homologous chromosomes" and typically separate during meiosis I.

Failure to separate during meiosis I could create a sperm containing an X and a Y, causing Klinefelter syndrome.

Anaphase is when the *centromere splits*, and the *homologous chromosomes / sister chromatids* are drawn away (via spindle fibers) from each other toward opposite sides of the two cells.

Homologous chromosomes separate during anaphase I, while sister chromatids separate during anaphase II.

In females, Turner's syndrome is due to the single X karyotype (single X chromosome and lacking a Y).

34. B is correct.

Most proteins that are secretory, membrane-bound, or targeted to an organelle use the *N-terminal signal sequence* (i.e., 5 to 30 amino acids) to target the protein.

Signal sequence of the polypeptide is recognized by a signal recognition particle (SRP), while the protein is synthesized on ribosomes.

Synthesis pauses while the ribosome-protein complex transfers to an SRP receptor on the ER (in eukaryotes) or plasma membranes (in prokaryotes) before polypeptide translation resumes.

35. C is correct.

Ribosomes anchored to the endoplasmic reticulum create the *rough endoplasmic reticulum* "studded" with ribosomes in contrast to the *smooth endoplasmic reticulum*, which lacks ribosomes.

"*Free*" and "*attached*" ribosome comparisons:

> 1) *free ribosomes* are in the cytoplasm, while *attached ribosomes* are anchored to the endoplasmic reticulum (ER), and

> 2) *free ribosomes* produce proteins in the cytosol, while *attached ribosomes* produce proteins inserted into the ER lumen (i.e., interior space).

36. D is correct.

Anterior pituitary hormones (including GH) are peptides.

Peptide hormones are *hydrophilic* and *cannot* cross the hydrophobic phospholipid bilayer; peptide hormones bind to receptors on the plasma membrane.

Destruction of the plasma membrane dramatically *reduces* the concentration of GH receptors.

37. E is correct.

Urea, a byproduct of amino acid metabolism, is a small uncharged molecule that crosses cell membranes by simple diffusion – a passive process that does not require energy.

A and C: export of Na^+ from a neuron is coupled with the *import of K^+*; the sodium-potassium-ATPase pump is an ATP-dependent process necessary to maintain a voltage potential across the neuron membrane.

B: movement of Ca^{2+} into a muscle cell occurs against the concentration gradient, and Ca^{2+} enters cells by *active transport*, which requires ATP.

D: *synaptic vesicles* contain neurotransmitters, and their exocytosis at a nerve terminus is an ATP-dependent process triggered by an action potential propagating along the neuron.

Vesicle fusion requires Ca^{2+} to enter the cell upon axon depolarization reaching the terminus.

38. C is correct.

p53 is a *tumor suppressor protein* that regulates the cell cycle and prevents cancer in multicellular organisms.

p53 is *the guardian of the genome* because of its role in conserving genetic stability by inhibiting genome mutations. The name p53 refers to its apparent molecular mass of 53 kDa.

Dalton is defined as 1/12 the mass of carbon and is a unit of a convention for expressing (i.e., often in kilodaltons or kDa) the molecular mass of proteins.

39. D is correct.

Newly synthesized secretory protein pathway:

rough ER → Golgi → secretory vesicles → exterior of the cell (via exocytosis)

Peroxisomes and *lysosomes* are destinations for proteins but do not involve secretory path exocytosis.

Ribosomes synthesize proteins, but the Golgi is the final organelle before exocytosis.

40. B is correct.

Plant cell membranes have higher amounts of unsaturated fatty acids.

The ratio of saturated and unsaturated fatty acids determines membrane fluidity.

Unsaturated fatty acids have kinks in their tails (due to double bonds) that push the phospholipids apart so the membrane retains its fluidity.

A: some textbooks state that plant membranes lack cholesterol, but a small amount is present, which is negligible compared to animal cells.

Cholesterol is usually dispersed in varying amounts throughout animal cell membranes in the irregular spaces between the hydrophobic lipid tails of the membrane.

Cholesterol functions as a *bidirectional buffer.*

At *elevated temperatures*, cholesterol *decreases membrane fluidity* because it confers stiffening and strengthening effects on the membrane.

At *low temperatures*, cholesterol *intercalates* between the phospholipids, preventing clustering and *stiffening the membrane.*

41. D is correct.

Nucleus, chloroplast, and mitochondria are organelles enclosed in a double membrane.

Endosymbiotic theory illustrates the evolution of mitochondria and chloroplasts from prokaryotes, thus explaining the resemblance.

42. C is correct.

Golgi apparatus processes *secretory proteins* via post-translational modifications.

Proteins targeted to the Golgi (from the rough ER) have three destinations:

1) secreted out of the cell,

2) transported into organelles, or

3) targeted to the plasma membrane (as a receptor, channel, or pore).

43. C is correct.

Carbon, hydrogen, and oxygen are in macromolecules (i.e., proteins, carbohydrates, nucleic acids, and lipids).

Nitrogen is in nucleic acids and proteins, which may contain sulfur or phosphorus.

Amino acids are *monomers* (building blocks) of proteins, and *nitrogen* is an *amino acid* and *urea* component.

Organic nitrogen is a nitrogen compound originating from a living organism.

Carbohydrates and lipids are made of only carbon, hydrogen, and oxygen

Carbohydrates have about 2 H and 1 O atom for every C atom.

Proteins are composed of C, H, O, N, and sometimes S.

Nucleic Acids are composed of: nucleotides composed of C, H, O, N, and P.

44. A is correct.

Albumin is the most abundant plasma protein; primarily responsible for *osmotic pressure* in circulatory systems.

Albumin is too large to pass from the circulatory system into the interstitial space.

Osmotic pressure is the force of H_2O flowing from an area of a lower solute to a higher solute concentration.

If a membrane is impermeable to a solute, H_2O flows across the membrane (i.e., osmosis) until the differences in solute concentrations have equilibrated.

Capillaries are impermeable to albumin (i.e., solute).

Increasing albumin concentration in the arteries and capillaries increases the movement of H_2O from the interstitial fluid to reduce the osmotic pressure in the arteries and capillaries.

45. B is correct.

Retinoblastoma protein (i.e., pRb or *RB1*) is a dysfunctional tumor suppressor protein.

pRb inhibits excessive cell growth by regulating the cell cycle through G1 (first gap phase) into S (DNA synthesis) phase.

pRb recruits chromatin-remodeling enzymes, such as methylases and acetylases.

46. E is correct.

Glycolysis occurs in the *cytoplasm.*

Krebs (TCA) cycle and *pyruvate oxidation* to acetyl-CoA occurs in the mitochondrial *matrix.*

Electron transport chain (ETC) uses cytochromes in the inner mitochondrial membrane and a proton (H$^+$) gradient in the intermembrane space).

A: *pyruvate* is oxidized to acetyl-CoA and transported from the cytoplasm into the matrix before joining oxaloacetate in the Krebs cycle.

B: Krebs cycle is the second stage of cellular respiration and occurs in the matrix of the mitochondrion.

C: *electron transport chain* is the final stage of cellular respiration occurring in the inner membrane (i.e., cytochromes) / intermembrane space (i.e., H$^+$ proton gradient) of the mitochondrion.

D: *reduction* (i.e., a gain of electrons) of FADH into FADH$_2$ occurs during the Krebs cycle.

47. D is correct.

Triglycerides are derived from glycerol and three fatty acids, commonly called "fats" and lipids, and are the most abundant lipid.

Teichoic acids are bacterial copolymers of carbohydrates and phosphate.

Peptidoglycan is formed by monosaccharide and amino acid polymers in bacterial cell walls.

Glycogen is a polysaccharide of glucose, a monosaccharide.

48. E is correct.

Secretory sequence in the flow of newly synthesized protein for export from the cell is:

       rough ER → Golgi → plasma membrane

49. B is correct.

Minerals (e.g., potassium, sodium, calcium, and magnesium) are essential nutrients because they must be consumed in the diet and function as cofactors (i.e., nonorganic components) for enzymes.

Lysosomes do not digest minerals.

Organic molecules, such as nucleotides, proteins, and lipids, are hydrolyzed (i.e., degraded) into monomers.

Nucleotides have phosphate, sugar, and base; proteins have amino acids; lipids have glycerol and fatty acids.

50. D is correct.

Recycling of organelles within the cell is accomplished through autophagy by *lysosomes.*

51. B is correct.

Albumins are globular proteins in the circulatory system.

Carotenoids are organic pigments in chloroplasts of plants and photosynthetic organisms, such as some bacteria and fungi.

Carotenoids are fatty acid-like carbon chains containing *conjugated double bonds* and sometimes have six-membered carbon rings at ends.

Under visible light, they produce red, yellow, orange, and brown colors in plants and animals as pigments.

Waxes (esters of fatty acids and alcohols) are protective coatings on the skin, fur, leaves of higher plants, and on the exoskeleton cuticle of many insects.

Steroids (e.g., cholesterol, estrogen) have three fused cyclohexane rings and one cyclopentane ring.

Lecithin is an example of a phospholipid that contains glycerol, two fatty acids, a phosphate group, and nitrogen-containing alcohol.

52. A is correct.

Defective attachment of a chromosome to the spindle blocks activation of the *anaphase-promoting complex*.

Spindle checkpoint prevents anaphase onset in mitosis and meiosis until all chromosomes are attached to the spindle with the proper bipolar orientation.

53. B is correct.

Human gametes, formed during meiosis, are cells with a single copy (1N) of the genome.

After the second meiotic division, cells have a single unreplicated copy (i.e., devoid of a sister chromatid).

54. D is correct.

Smooth endoplasmic reticulum is the organelle for fatty acid, phospholipid, and steroid synthesis.

Smooth endoplasmic reticulum (SER) synthesizes lipids, phospholipids, and steroids; metabolism of carbohydrates and steroids; detoxification of alcohol and drugs; regulates Ca^{2+} concentration in muscle cells.

Endosome is a transport pathway starting at the Golgi.

Peroxisome undergoes beta-oxidation of long-chain fatty acids, which eventually yields $CO_2 + H_2O$.

Rough endoplasmic reticulum (RER) assembles proteins.

55. C is correct.

Centrioles are cylindrical structures mainly of *tubulin* in eukaryotic cells (except flowering plants and fungi).

Centrioles participate in the organization of the *mitotic spindle* and the completion of *cytokinesis*. They contribute to the structure of centrosomes and organize microtubules in the cytoplasm.

Centriole position determines the location of the nucleus and is crucial in the spatial arrangement of cells.

continued…

Plastid (e.g., chloroplast and chromoplast) are major organelles in plants and algae.

Plastids are the site of manufacturing and storing critical chemical compounds used by cells.

They often contain pigments used in photosynthesis. Pigments change to determine cell color.

Plastids, like prokaryotes, contain a circular double-stranded DNA molecule.

56. E is correct.

Centrioles are the organizational sites for microtubules (i.e., spindle fibers) that assemble during cell division (e.g., mitosis and meiosis).

Four phases of mitosis are *prophase*, *metaphase*, *anaphase*, and *telophase*.

Mitotic phases are followed by cytokinesis, which physically divides cells into two identical daughter cells.

Condensed chromosomes align along the *equatorial plane* in metaphase before the centromere (i.e., heterochromatin region of DNA) splits.

The two sister chromosomes begin their journey to the respective poles of the cell.

57. A is correct.

cAMP is a second messenger triggered when a ligand (e.g., peptide hormone or neurotransmitter) binds a membrane-bound receptor.

Adenylate cyclase (enzyme) is activated through a G-protein intermediate and converts ATP into cAMP.

Adenylate cyclase is attached to the inner layer of the phospholipid bilayer and is not in the cytoplasm.

cAMP   ATP

Molecular Biology of Eukaryotes – Detailed Explanations

1. A is correct.

5'-CCCC-3' and 5'-AAAA-3' primers should be used to amplify the DNA shown via PCR.

$$5' \xrightarrow{\text{AAAA} \qquad\qquad\qquad \text{GGGG}} 3'$$
$$3' \xleftarrow{\text{TTTT} \qquad\qquad\qquad \text{CCCC}} 5'$$

Polymerase chain reaction (PCR) requires the sequence at the ends of the fragment to be amplified.

From the ends, primers use complementary base pairing to anneal the target fragment and permit amplification.

Regions between ends are not required as the parent strands are the template used by the DNA polymerase.

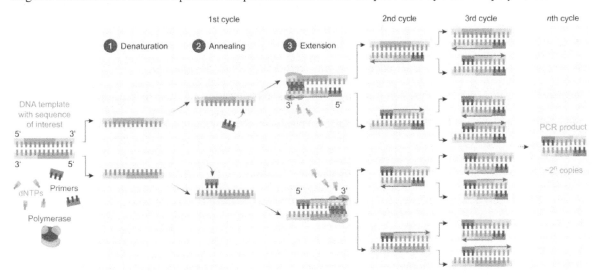

Polymerase chain reaction (PCR) with exponential product amplification during each cycle. Step one heats DNA to separate the two strands of the double helix. Step 2 cools the sample for annealing by complementary primers. Step 3 is chain elongation for the synthesis of DNA by polymerase anchored to the primers.

2. E is correct.

Proteins are the major phenotypic expression of a genotype.

3. C is correct.

Dideoxy (without ~OH at 2' and 3' positions) cytosine is used in DNA sequencing to cause termination when the template strand is G.

4. A is correct.

Adding a 3' poly-A tail to mRNA (not proteins) is a *post-transcription* event.

Post-transcription events include adding a 5' cap and splicing exons (removing introns) from RNA molecules.

5. C is correct.

Centromeres are chromosomal regions of highly coiled DNA (i.e., *heterochromatin*) at the point of attachment of the sister chromatids, replicated during the S phase of interphase.

6. D is correct.

Genes provide hereditary information for the organism, but the environment (to a degree) influences the phenotypic pattern of proteins resulting from gene expression.

Genetic and environmental factors interact to produce the phenotype. These are examples of the environment affecting gene activation.

Shivering is an example of a change in the environment causing a physiological (i.e., behavioral) change to maintain homeostasis. Homeostasis is achieved because shivering generates heat when muscles contract rapidly.

7. C is correct.

Library refers to DNA molecules inserted into cloning vectors (e.g., bacterial plasmid).

Complementary DNA (cDNA) is created from mRNA in a eukaryotic cell using reverse transcriptase.

In eukaryotes, a poly-A tail (i.e., a sequence of 100-250 adenosine (A) nucleotides) distinguishes mRNA from tRNA and rRNA.

Only mRNA has the poly-A tail bind (i.e., mRNA is isolated from the other RNA molecules).

Poly-A tail can be used as a primer site for *reverse transcription* (i.e., mRNA → cDNA).

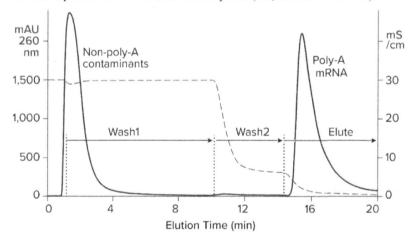

mRNA is purified by column chromatography using oligomeric dT nucleotide resins

mRNA is isolated by oligo-dT and used as a complementary primer to bind the poly-A tail and extend the primer molecule by reverse transcriptase to create the cDNA strand.

The original mRNA templates are removed using RNAse, leaving a *single-stranded* cDNA (sscDNA).

cDNA is converted into double-stranded DNA by DNA polymerase for double-stranded cDNA.

cDNA is cloned in bacterial plasmids.

8. A is correct.

Quaternary protein structure requires two or more polypeptide chains whereby different genes specify each polypeptide.

Complex polysaccharides are linked to monomers of sugar. Complex polysaccharides include sugar monomers such as lactose (e.g., glucose and galactose).

The presence of more than one monomer requires additional genes.

9. E is correct.

Genomic library is a set of clones representing a given organism's entire genome. Among the tools making recombinant DNA technology possible are *restriction enzymes*.

Restriction endonucleases (i.e., *restriction enzymes*) cut DNA at specific nucleotide sequences, often inverted repeat sequences (i.e., palindromes that read the same if the DNA strand is rotated 180°).

After cutting, the ends of some restriction-digested double-stranded DNA fragments have several nucleotide overhangs of single-stranded DNA as "sticky ends."

Restriction enzymes cut similarly, so the sticky end from one fragment anneals via hydrogen bonding with the sticky end from another fragment cut by the same enzyme.

After annealing, DNA ligase covalently closes the plasmid into circular DNA for transformation into bacteria.

10. D is correct.

Attachment of glycoprotein side chains is a post-translational modification.

Rough endoplasmic reticulum (RER) and the *Golgi apparatus* are two organelles modifying proteins as a post-translational event.

Lysosomes are organelles with low pH that function to digest intracellular molecules.

11. A is correct.

Telomerase (i.e., enzyme ending in ~*ase*) restores the ends of the DNA in a chromosome.

Telomeres are maintained by *telomerase*, an enzyme that (during embryogenesis) adds repeats to chromosomal ends. A measure of telomerase activity in adults indicates one marker for cancer activity (i.e., uncontrolled cell growth) within the cell.

DNA polymerase cannot fully replicate the 3' DNA end, resulting in shorter DNA with each division.

The new strand synthesis mechanism prevents the loss of the DNA coding region.

New strand synthesis prevents the loss of the terminal DNA at the coding region during replication and represents telomere function.

Telomeres are at chromosomal ends and consist of nucleotide repeats that provide stability and prevent the loss of the ends of the DNA coding region during DNA replication.

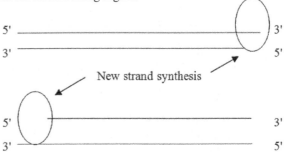

12. B is correct.

Unlike a genomic library that reflects the entire DNA of the organism, a *cDNA library* uses mRNA from *expressed genes after processing* (i.e., removal of introns and ligating of exons).

13. E is correct.

Central dogma of molecular biology proposes that information flow in the cell is unidirectional.

Schematically,

> DNA → RNA → protein

14. C is correct.

Alternative splicing occurs in the nucleus with three stages of RNA processing:

> 1) adding a G-modified cap to the 5' end of the primary transcript,
>
> 2) adding a 3' poly-A tail, and
>
> 3) removing introns (intervening sequences) and ligating exons (expressed sequences).

This process cleavages hnRNA to make corresponding mRNAs transported in the cytoplasm.

15. D is correct.

Ribosomal RNA (rRNA) binds the small and large ribosomal subunits (i.e., 30S & 50S in prokaryotes and 40S & 60S in eukaryotes) to create the functional ribosome (i.e., 70S in prokaryotes and 80S in eukaryotes).

Ribosomes are complex assemblies of RNA molecules and several associated proteins. rRNAs are the only RNA molecules (others being mRNA and tRNA) synthesized in the nucleolus (within the nucleus).

16. A is correct.

E. coli RNA polymerase synthesizes RNA in the 5' to 3' direction and copies a DNA template.

17. B is correct.

Introns (intervening sequences) vary in size and number among different genes.

18. E is correct.

I: eukaryotes *splice* hnRNA (*primary transcript*) by *removing introns* (intervening sequences) and *ligating exons* (expressed sequences) in the nucleus before exporting the modified mRNA transcript to the cytoplasm for translation.

A poly-A tail to the mRNA is added before export from the nucleus.

II: after protein synthesis in the ER, they may be modified in the Golgi apparatus (e.g., glycosylation), but this is different from the required *splicing* of mRNA molecules (i.e., removal of introns) before the mRNA can pass through the nuclear pores and enter the cytoplasm.

III: *prokaryotic ribosomes* (30S small & 50S large subunit = 70S complete ribosome) are smaller than *eukaryotic ribosomes* (40S small & 60S large subunit = 80S complete ribosome).

19. C is correct.

Deacetylation of histones associated with the retrotransposon and methylation of retrotransposon DNA decreases the transcription of retrotransposons.

20. B is correct.

Central dogma of molecular biology refers to the direction of genetic information flow.

DNA → RNA → protein

Central dogma of molecular biology is violated by *retroviruses* with RNA genomes and reverse transcriptase to copy viral RNA into DNA within the infected host cell.

21. A is correct.

miRNA (*interference mRNA*) is generated from the cleavage of double-stranded RNA. miRNA is a small non-coding RNA molecule (about 22 nucleotides) in plants, animals, and some viruses, which functions in transcriptional and post-transcriptional regulation of gene expression.

miRNA hybridizes to mRNA and inactivates its ability as a template for translation into protein.

22. C is correct.

DNA polymerase cannot fully replicate the 3' DNA end, resulting in shorter DNA with each division. The new strand synthesis mechanism prevents the loss of the DNA coding region.

The process of new strand synthesis prevents the loss of the terminal DNA at the coding region during replication by *telomeres*. Telomeres are at chromosomal ends and consist of nucleotide repeats that provide stability and prevent the loss of the ends of the DNA coding region during DNA replication.

Telomeres are generated by *telomerase*, an enzyme that (during embryogenesis) adds repeats to chromosomal ends. A measure of telomerase activity in adults indicates one marker for cancer activity (i.e., uncontrolled cell growth) within the cell.

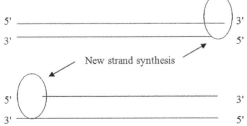

A: *kinetochore* is a protein collar around the centromere on the chromosome as the site of attachment of the spindle fiber to the chromosome during cell division.

Kinetochore attaches to the spindle fibers (microtubulin) and is anchored to chromosomes by centromeres. The other end of the spindle fibers is attached at the poles (centromere region) of the cell to the centrioles.

B: *centrosome* (*~some* means body) is a region at the poles of the cell giving rise to the asters (microtubules projecting past the centrioles) of the centrioles.

D: *centromeres* are on the chromosomes consisting of highly coiled DNA (i.e., heterochromatin) at the point of attachment of the sister chromatids.

23. B is correct.

Core particle of 8 *histones* (i.e., positively charged DNA-binding proteins) is the *nucleosome* (i.e., octamer).

octamer of core histones:
H2A, H2B, H3, H4 (each one ×2)

core DNA

histone H1

linker DNA

Nucleosome of 8 histones joined by a linker region with histone H1 permit efficient coiling of DNA

24. C is correct.

miRNA (or *interference RNA*) is a small non-coding RNA molecule (~22 nucleotides) in plants, animals, and some viruses, which functions in transcriptional and post-transcriptional regulation of gene expression.

miRNA hybridizes to mRNA and inactivates its ability to be used as a template for protein translation.

25. A is correct.

Promoter is the region of DNA in prokaryotes to which *RNA polymerase binds* most tightly.

Promoter is a region of 100–1000 base pairs long on the DNA that initiates gene transcription.

Promoters are nucleotides near the genes they transcribe, on the same strand, and upstream on the DNA (towards the 3' region of the antisense strand – template and non-coding strands).

Promoters contain specific DNA sequences and response elements that provide a secure initial binding site for RNA polymerase and transcription factors proteins.

Transcription factors have specific activator (or repressor) sequences of nucleotides that attach to specific promoters and regulate gene expressions.

In bacteria, the promoter is recognized by RNA polymerase and an associated sigma factor (i.e., a protein needed only for initiation of RNA synthesis), which are often brought to the promoter DNA by an activator protein's binding to its own nearby DNA binding site.

In eukaryotes, the process is complicated, and at least seven factors are necessary for binding an RNA polymerase II to the promoter.

26. E is correct.

Genomic libraries reflect the entire DNA of the organism and, unlike a cDNA library, do not use mRNA, which corresponds to expressed genes after processing (i.e., removal of introns).

Retrotransposons are genetic elements that can amplify themselves in a genome and are ubiquitous components of the DNA of many eukaryotic organisms.

27. D is correct.

tRNA has a *cloverleaf secondary structure* and is the smallest single-stranded RNA.

tRNA contains the *anticodon* and delivers individual amino acids to the growing peptide chain based on the *codon* specified by mRNA.

A: hnRNA (*heteronuclear RNA* or *primary transcript*) has not yet undergone post-transcriptional modification (i.e., 5' Guanine cap, removal of introns and ligation of exons, and the addition of a 3' poly-A tail).

Once three modifications occur, the hnRNA becomes a mature mRNA and is transported through the nuclear pores (in the nuclear envelope).

mRNA enters the cytoplasm for translation into proteins.

B: mRNA is a single-stranded RNA molecule from its genesis and is shorter than hnRNA (i.e., the primary transcript before post-transcriptional processing).

mRNA does not contain introns (exons are joined) and has a 5' G-cap and a 3' poly-A tail.

C: rRNA is synthesized in the *nucleolus* (organelle in nucleus) and is the most abundant single-stranded RNA molecule.

rRNA (and associated proteins) are necessary for *ribosome* assembly in protein synthesis (i.e., translation).

E: miRNA (*interference mRNA*) is generated from the cleavage of double-stranded RNA.

miRNA is a small non-coding RNA molecule (about 22 nucleotides) in plants, animals, and some viruses, which functions in transcriptional and post-transcriptional regulation of gene expression.

miRNA hybridizes to mRNA and inactivates its ability as a template for translation into protein.

28. B is correct.

Inversion is a chromosomal rearrangement when a chromosome segment is reversed and occurs when a single chromosome undergoes breakage and rearrangement.

Inversions do not cause abnormalities if rearrangement is balanced with no extra or missing DNA.

Heterozygous individuals for an inversion have increased production of abnormal chromatids resulting from crossing over within inversion spans.

Heterozygous inversions lead to *lowered fertility* due to the production of *unbalanced gametes*.

29. E is correct.

Nucleolus is the organelle within the nucleus responsible for synthesizing ribosomal RNA (rRNA).

A: *Golgi apparatus* is the organelle responsible for processing, packaging, and distributing proteins.

B: *lysosomes* are organelles with low pH that digest intracellular molecules.

C: *mitochondrion* is a double-membraned organelle where the Krebs (TCA) cycle, electron transport, and oxidative phosphorylation occur.

30. D is correct.

AG mutant flowers not having reproductive organs supports that the AG gene is vital for forming reproductive flower organs in *Arabidopsis*.

31. C is correct.

Glycocalyx refers to extracellular material, such as glycoprotein produced by bacteria, endothelial, epithelial, and other cells.

Glycocalyx consists of several carbohydrate moieties of membrane glycolipids and glycoproteins.

Glycocalyx is composed of a *negatively charged* network of proteoglycans, glycoproteins, and glycolipids on the apical surface of endothelial cells.

Carbohydrate portions of glycolipids on plasma membrane surfaces contribute to cell-cell recognition, communication, and intracellular adhesion.

Glycocalyx plays a significant role in endothelial vascular tissue, including the modulation of red blood cell volume in capillaries and a principal role in the vasculature to maintain plasma and vessel wall homeostasis.

Glycocalyx is on the apical surface of vascular endothelial cells that line the lumen and includes a wide range of enzymes and proteins that regulate leukocyte and thrombocyte adherence.

32. A is correct.

Chromatin (comprising chromosomes) is the combination of DNA and proteins that comprise the genetic contents within the nucleus of a cell.

Primary functions of *chromatin*:

       1) package DNA into a smaller volume

       2) strengthen DNA for mitosis

       3) prevent DNA damage

       4) control gene expression (i.e., RNA polymerase binding) and DNA replication

continued...

Three levels of *chromatin organization*:

> 1) DNA wraps around histone proteins, forming nucleosomes (i.e., *beads on a string*) in uncoiled euchromatin DNA;

> 2) multiple histones wrap into a 30 nm fiber consisting of nucleosome arrays in their most compact form (i.e., heterochromatin);

> 3) higher-level DNA packaging of the 30 nm fiber into the metaphase chromosome (during mitosis and meiosis).

Tandem repeats occur in DNA when a pattern of nucleotides is repeated, and the repetitions are adjacent.

For example, ATCCG ATCCG ATCCG, whereby the sequence ATCCG is repeated three times.

Tandem repeats may arise from errors during DNA replication whereby the polymerase retraces its path (over a short distance) and repeats the synthesis of the same template region of DNA.

33. E is correct.

DNA topoisomerases are nuclear enzymes that regulate DNA supercoiling.

Topoisomerases are essential in DNA replication, transcription, chromosome segregation, and recombination.

Cells have two topoisomerases:

> type I, which makes single-stranded cuts in DNA, and

> type II enzymes, which cut and pass double-stranded DNA.

Gyrase (a subset of topoisomerase II) creates double-stranded breaks between the DNA backbone and relaxes DNA supercoils by unwinding the nicked strand around the other.

B: *helicase* unwinds DNA and induces severe supercoiling in the double-stranded DNA when hydrolyzing the hydrogen bonds between the complementary base pairs and exposing the bases for replication.

C: *DNA polymerase I* is in prokaryotes and participates in excision repair with 3'-5' and 5'-3' exonuclease activity and processing of Okazaki fragments generated during lagging strand synthesis

D: *DNA polymerase III* is in prokaryotes and is the primary enzyme in DNA replication.

34. B is correct.

3' OH of cytosine attacks the phosphate group on the guanine.

35. A is correct.

Introns are intervening sequences in the primary transcript but are excised when RNA is processed into mRNA.

Processed mRNA consists of *exons ligated* (i.e., joined).

Lariat structures are the protein scaffolding used for the splicing of the hnRNA (i.e., primary transcript) into mRNA as the introns are removed, and the exons are ligated.

36. B is correct.

Histone H1 is not in the eight-particle core of a *nucleosome*.

Histone H1 is in the linker regions of about 50 nucleotides between the nucleosomes.

Nucleosome is an *octamer* of the core histones: two H2A, two H2B, two H3, and two H4 histones.

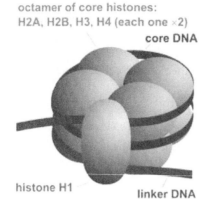

Nucleosome of 8 histones joined by a linker region with histone H1 permit efficient coiling of DNA

37. E is correct.

Cellulose comprises the plant cell wall and is not a chemical component of a bacterial cell wall (*peptidoglycan*).

38. D is correct.

Combinatorial control of gene transcription in eukaryotes is when the presence (or absence) of combinations of transcription factors is required.

39. D is correct.

Once synthesized via transcription, RNA molecules undergo three steps for post-transcriptional processing:

      1) 5' G cap increases RNA stability and resistance to degradation in the cytoplasm;

      2) 3' poly-A-tail functions as a *molecular clock*, and

      3) introns (i.e., non-coding regions) are removed, and exons (i.e., coding regions) are spliced (joined).

40. B is correct.

The second round of transcription can begin before the initial transcript is completed.

41. A is correct.

SP1 is a *transcription factor* that binds nucleic acids.

Therefore, SP1 binds RNA and DNA. Select an organelle that lacks RNA or DNA.

Golgi apparatus is the organelle responsible for processing, packaging, and distributing proteins.

Golgi is not composed of nucleic acids, nor does it process them.

Since no nucleic acids exist within the Golgi apparatus, the transcription factor SP1 would not bind to it.

B: *mitochondrion* is the organelle bound by a double membrane, where the Krebs cycle, electron transport, and oxidative phosphorylation occur.

Mitochondria are the site of most ATP molecules produced during aerobic respiration.

Mitochondria (via the endosymbiotic theory) contain DNA (similar in size and composition to bacterial DNA), and the SP1 transcription factor would bind.

C: *nucleolus* is an organelle within the nucleus where rRNA synthesis occurs.

Thus, SP1 would bind to a nucleic acid (rRNA) within the nucleolus.

D: *ribosomes* contain rRNA and assembled proteins as the translation site (mRNA is converted into proteins).

42. E is correct.

Spliceosome is a large and complex molecular apparatus assembled from snRNP and protein complexes.

Spliceosomes remove introns from pre-mRNA primary transcript (i.e., heteronuclear RNA or hnRNA); catalyze the removal of introns and ligation of exons.

snRNA is a component of the snRNP and provides specificity by *recognizing* the sequences of critical splicing signals at the 5' and 3' ends and branch-site of introns.

Each spliceosome comprises five small nuclear RNAs (snRNA) and a range of associated protein factors.

The spliceosome occurs anew on each hnRNA (pre-mRNA).

hnRNA contains specific sequence elements recognized during spliceosome assembly; the 5' end splice, the branch point sequence, the polypyrimidine (i.e., cytosine and uracil) tract, and the 3' end splice site.

43. B is correct.

Polynucleotides (e.g., DNA) are the only of the four macromolecules (i.e., nucleic acids, proteins, lipids, carbohydrates) repaired rather than degraded.

DNA repair is essential for maintaining cell function and is performed by biological repair systems (i.e., p53 tumor repressor protein).

Uncontrolled cell growth via disruption to the cell cycle regulation may occur by somatic cell mutations.

44. D is correct.

Poly-A tail of RNA is enzymatically added soon after transcription (DNA → hnRNA) is completed.

45. E is correct.

H1 histones are in about 50 nucleotides between the nucleosomes in the linker regions.

Nucleosome is an *octamer* of the core histones: two H2A, two H2B, two H3, and two H4 histones.

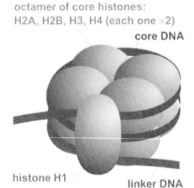

Nucleosome of 8 histones joined by a linker region with histone H1 permit efficient coiling of DNA

46. B is correct.

Splicing process involves snRNA which consists of sugar ribose (like other RNA molecules).

RNA is labile (unstable) and can function as a nucleophile because of the 2'–OH.

47. C is correct.

Chromatin is composed of DNA and histone proteins.

DNA has an overall negative charge because of the negative oxygen (i.e., single-bonded with seven valence electrons) attached to the phosphate group attached to the deoxyribose sugar.

For electrostatic interactions, histones must be *positively charged*.

Histones have a high concentration of basic (positive charge) amino acids (e.g., lysine and arginine).

48. C is correct.

Nucleic acids (e.g., DNA, RNA) elongate via *nucleophilic attack* by 3'–OH of nascent (i.e., growing) strand.

3'–OH undergoes nucleophilic attack on the phosphate group closest to the sugar in the incoming nucleotide.

2'–OH is in RNA (i.e., ribose) compared to a 2'–H for DNA (i.e., deoxyribose, where *deoxy* signifies the absence of O as in OH).

49. A is correct.

Heterochromatin is tightly packed DNA.

Heterochromatin consists of genetically inactive satellite sequences (i.e., tandem repeats of noncoding DNA).

Euchromatin is loosely coiled regions of DNA actively engaged in gene expression because RNA polymerase binds the relaxed region of DNA.

Centromeres and *telomeres* are *heterochromatic*.

Barr body of the second inactivated X-chromosome in females is *heterochromatic*.

50. D is correct.

RNA of the prokaryote does *not* undergo post-transcriptional modifications:

> addition of 5' cap,
>
> removal of introns and ligation of exons, and
>
> addition of a 3' poly-A tail), as does hnRNA (*primary transcript*) in eukaryotes.

Prokaryotes lack a nucleus, so RNA synthesis (i.e., *transcription*) coincides with protein synthesis (i.e., *translation*) in the cytosol.

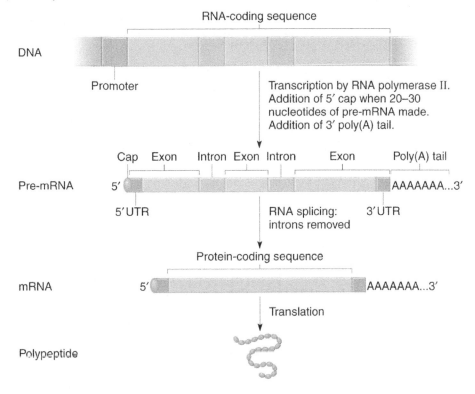

Gene expression with transcription, RNA processing, and mRNA translation into protein.
Nucleotide sequences on chromosomes are transcribed and processed into mRNA within the
nucleus by joining exons (removing introns), adding a 5' cap and a poly-A tail.

51. A is correct.

Recombinant DNA is nucleotides formed in the laboratory through genetic recombination (e.g., molecular cloning) to combine genetic material from multiple sources, creating sequences not in biological organisms.

Recombinant DNA is possible because DNA molecules from organisms share the same chemical structure. They differ in the nucleotide sequence within that identical overall structure.

52. E is correct.

Transformation (i.e., introducing foreign DNA into cells) is successful when foreign DNA is integrated into another organism's genome.

Once integrated, it replicates and divides with the host cell.

53. B is correct.

Restriction enzymes are *endonucleases* that cut DNA at specific *internal sequences*, usually inverted repeat sequences (i.e., palindromes that read the same if the DNA strand is rotated 180°).

54. B is correct.

Restriction enzymes cut DNA at specific sequences.

Endonucleases (i.e., enzyme cutting within the strand) *cleave double-stranded DNA* (dsDNA) between the nucleotides adenosine (A) and guanine (G) palindrome sequences.

Sticky ends are overhangs of TTAA as reading 5' to 3' (by convention, reading top strand left to right).

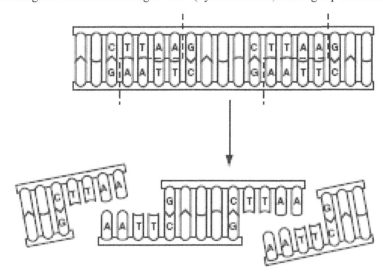

Cellular Metabolism and Enzymes – Detailed Explanations

1. D is correct.

α-helix (alpha helix) is a typical secondary structure of proteins.

α-helix is a *right-handed coiled* or spiral conformation (helix) when each backbone amino (N-H) group donates partial positive hydrogen to form a hydrogen bond with a lone pair of electrons from the backbone carbonyl (C=O) group of another amino acid four residues earlier.

2. A is correct.

ATP is a nucleotide composed of adenosine (A), ribose, and three phosphate groups.

3. C is correct.

Hydrophobic side chain groups (e.g., phenylalanine, methionine, leucine, and valine) interact through hydrophobic interactions, excluding water from the attraction region.

Nine amino acids with hydrophobic side chains are alanine (Ala), glycine (Gly), isoleucine (Ile), leucine (Leu), methionine (Met), phenylalanine (Phe), proline (Pro), tryptophan (Trp), and valine (Val).

B: *hydrogen bonds* require hydrogen to be connected to an electronegative atom of fluorine, nitrogen, oxygen, or chlorine (weaker hydrogen bond due to the larger valence shell size) to establish a δ+ and δ- (partial positive and negative regions that attract).

D: *cysteine* is the only amino acid capable of forming disulfide bonds because the side chain contains sulfur.

E: *dipole-dipole interactions* (collectively Van der Waals) are weak interactions from the close association of permanent or induced dipoles.

Proteins contain many dipole interactions, which vary considerably in strength.

4. B is correct.

Cellular respiration uses enzyme-catalyzed reactions as a catabolic pathway using potential energy of glucose.

While glycolysis yields two ATP per glucose, cellular respiration (i.e., glycolysis, Krebs/TCA cycle, and electron transport chain) produces about 30–32 ATP.

Around 2004, research reduced the estimate of 36-38 ATP due to inefficiencies of ATP synthase.

Cellular respiration is an aerobic process whereby O_2 is the final acceptor of electrons passed from cytochrome electron carriers during the final stage of the electron transport chain.

Glycolysis (glucose to pyruvate) occurs in the cytoplasm.

Krebs cycle (TCA) occurs in the matrix (i.e., the cytoplasm of mitochondria), while the electron transport chain occurs in the intermembrane space of the mitochondria for eukaryotes.

For prokaryotes, both processes occur in the cytoplasm because prokaryotes lack mitochondria.

continued…

Some forms of anaerobic respiration use an electron acceptor other than O_2 (e.g., iron, cobalt, or manganese reduction) at the end of the electron transport chain.

Glucose molecules are entirely oxidized in these cases because glucose products enter the Krebs cycle.

Highly reduced chemical compounds (e.g., NADH or $FADH_2$) establish an electrochemical gradient across a membrane in the Krebs cycle.

The reduced chemical compounds (NADH or $FADH_2$) are oxidized by integral membrane proteins that transfer the electron to the final electron acceptor.

5. E is correct.

K_m is the substrate concentration [S] at half the maximum reaction velocity (V_{max}) and increases when the antibody binds the substrate.

This reaction kinetics follow the profile of a *competitive inhibitor* (visualized by the y-axis intercept) in the Lineweaver-Burke (double reciprocal).

The substrate binds the antibody and is not available to react with the enzyme; therefore, an additional substrate is needed to bind the same amount of enzyme (as a lower substrate concentration in the absence of an antibody).

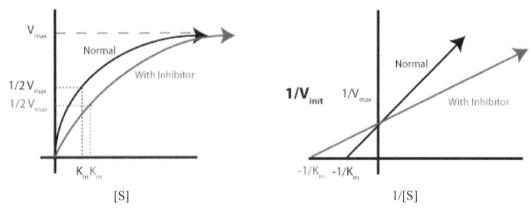

Michaelis-Menten equation (left) and Lineweaver-Burke (double reciprocal) plot

Graph on *left* illustrates the Michaelis-Menten equation for enzyme kinetics.

Graph on *right* is the Lineweaver-Burke (double reciprocal) plot showing the change in K_m when the substrate is subjected to competitive inhibition.

V_{max} does not change when the number of available substrates changes.

Binding to a substrate does not affect V_{max} but affects K_m because the amount of available substrate is reduced, altering the reaction kinetics because it binds the substrate.

6. C is correct.

Metabolism means change and refers to life-sustaining chemical transformations within cells.

Enzyme-catalyzed reactions allow organisms to maintain structures, grow, reproduce, and respond.

Metabolism includes *anabolism* (or *buildup*) and *catabolism* (or *breakdown*).

Catabolism is the breakdown of organic matter and harvests energy from cellular respiration (e.g., glycolysis, Krebs cycle, and the electron transport chain).

Anabolism utilizes energy (e.g., ATP) to *synthesize biomolecules* (e.g., lipids, nucleic acids, proteins).

7. D is correct.

Fermentation is an anaerobic process and occurs in the absence of oxygen.

Purpose of fermentation is to *regenerate* the high-energy nucleotide intermediate of NAD^+.

Oxidative phosphorylation occurs during the electron transport chain as the final stage of cellular respiration.

8. A is correct.

Acid hydrolysis has several effects:

  1) partial destruction of tryptophan prevents the proper estimate of the tryptophan concentration;

  2) conversion of asparagine into aspartic acid prevents the direct measure of asparagine;

  3) conversion of glutamine to glutamic acid.

Therefore, the concentration of glutamic acid is an indirect measure of glutamine.

9. B is correct.

When plasma glucose levels are low, the body utilizes other energy sources for cellular metabolism.

Energy sources are used in preferential order:

  glucose → other carbohydrates → fats → proteins

These molecules are converted to glucose or glucose intermediates degraded in the glycolytic pathway and the Krebs cycle (i.e., citric acid cycle).

Proteins are used last for energy because there is no protein storage in the body.

Catabolism of protein results in muscle wasting and connective tissue breakdown, which is harmful over time.

10. E is correct.

Activation energy is the minimum amount of energy needed for a reaction. It is considered an "energy barrier" because energy must be added to the system.

Enzymes act by *decreasing the activation energy* (or *lowering the energy barrier*), allowing the reaction, and increasing the reaction rate.

11. A is correct.

Phosphate group from ATP is transferred to glucose, creating a *phosphodiester bond*.

ATP + Glucose → Glucose-6-phosphate + ADP

12. D is correct.

Second messengers are common in eukaryotes.

Cyclic nucleotides (e.g., cAMP and cGMP) are second messengers transmitting extracellular signals from the cell membrane to intracellular proteins.

Second messengers are used by hydrophilic protein hormones (e.g., insulin, adrenaline) that cannot cross the plasma membrane.

Steroid hormones (e.g., testosterone, estrogen, progesterone) are lipid-soluble and can pass through the plasma membrane and enter the cytoplasm without second messengers.

13. E is correct.

Greatest direct source of ATP synthesis involves the *electron transport chain*.

Glycolysis occurs in the cytoplasm, the *Krebs cycle* (TCA) in the matrix of mitochondria, and *oxidative phosphorylation* (i.e., the electron transport chain) in the intermembrane space and inner membrane of mitochondria.

Glycolysis produces pyruvate, converted into acetyl CoA, and joined to oxaloacetate in the Krebs cycle, producing citrate as the first intermediate.

Krebs cycle produces two GTP (i.e., ATP) per glucose molecule (or 1 GTP per pyruvate).

Most ATP is formed by *oxidative phosphorylation* when NADH and $FADH_2$ nucleotides are oxidized and donate their electrons to the cytochromes in the electron transport chain.

14. D is correct.

V_{max} is the reaction velocity at a fixed enzyme concentration and depends on the total enzyme concentration. Adding enzymes allows more enzyme reactions per minute.

II: V, not V_{max}, depends on [S]. V_{max} is a constant for a specified amount of enzyme.

III: *competitive inhibition* is when the inhibitor binds reversibly to the active site. Adding enough substrate overcomes competitive inhibition, and the original V_{max} is obtained.

15. B is correct.

Two major models of *enzyme-substrate binding*:

Induced-fit model is when the initial interactions between enzyme and substrate (e.g., hexokinase and glucose) are weak, but the weak interactions induce *conformational changes* that strengthen binding.

Lock-and-key model is when the molecules conform for binding and do not change.

16. D is correct.

Gibbs free energy (ΔG) of a reaction is not dependent on the amount of enzyme.

Gibbs free energy measures the energy difference (Δ) between the reactants and products.

> ΔG is *positive* for endergonic reactions with products higher in energy than the reactants (absorbs energy).

> ΔG is *negative* for exergonic reactions when products are lower in energy than the reactants (releases energy).

17. C is correct.

Zymogens are inactive forms of enzymes and have an ~ogen suffix (e.g., pepsinogen).

From the question, glucokinase has a higher Michaelis constant (K_m).

A higher value for K_m is due to enzymes having a lower affinity for the reactant (e.g., glucose).

Information about K_m does not answer the question and is merely a distraction.

A: *hexokinase* is a control point enzyme (i.e., irreversible steps) regulated by negative feedback inhibition.

B: *hexokinase* and glucokinase catalyze the same reaction (from the question); by definition, *isozymes*.

D: *fructose* is not a reactant in glycolysis.

18. B is correct.

Secondary structure ($2°$) is the repetition of α-helices or β-pleated sheets in the polypeptide backbone.

Primary structure ($1°$) is the linear sequence of amino acids.

Tertiary structure ($3°$) involves interactions between the side chains of the amino acids.

Quaternary structure ($4°$) requires the interaction of two or more polypeptides. $4°$ requires more than one polypeptide chain in the mature protein (e.g., hemoglobin).

19. E is correct.

Cofactors are organic or inorganic molecules classified depending on how tightly they bind to an enzyme.

Coenzymes are loosely bound *organic cofactors* released from the enzyme's active site during the reaction (e.g., ATP, NADH).

Prosthetic groups are tightly bound organic cofactors.

20. B is correct.

Quaternary ($4°$) *structure* of proteins involves two or more polypeptide chains.

Hydrophobic interactions and disulfide bridges between cysteines maintain the quaternary structure between the different polypeptide chains (e.g., 4 chains of 2 α and 2 β in hemoglobin).

21. A is correct.

Mitochondrion is the organelle bound by a double membrane, where the Krebs (TCA) cycle, electron transport, and oxidative phosphorylation occur.

In eukaryotes, the Krebs cycle (i.e., TCA) occurs in the matrix of the mitochondria.

Matrix is an interior space in the mitochondria analogous to the cell cytoplasm.

B: *smooth ER* (endoplasmic reticulum) is connected to the nuclear envelope and synthesizes lipids, phospholipids, and steroids.

Cells secreting lipids, phospholipids, and steroids (e.g., testes, ovaries, skin oil glands) have prominent smooth endoplasmic reticulum.

Smooth ER carries out the metabolism of carbohydrates, drug detoxification, attachment of receptors on cell membrane proteins, and steroid metabolism.

C: *cytosol* is common to eukaryotes and prokaryotes and equivalent to the cytoplasm.

D: *nucleolus* is the organelle within the nucleus responsible for synthesizing ribosomal RNA (rRNA).

E: *intermembrane space of the mitochondria* is where the electron transport chain (ETC) establishes a proton gradient (or chemiosmotic gradient) with concentrated H^+ ions forced into the space in eukaryotes.

22. B is correct.

Pyruvate is the product of glycolysis, converted into acetyl Co-A as the starting reactant for the Krebs cycle.

Pyruvate is *not* a waste product of cellular respiration. Metabolic waste products are from enzymatic processes.

Pyruvate, made during glycolysis (as an intermediate of cellular respiration), is converted to acetyl CoA and enters the Krebs cycle to be oxidized into CO_2 and H_2O or converted into the *waste product of lactate* under anaerobic conditions. Waste products can damage cells and must be removed.

A: *lactate* (2 carbons) is produced from *pyruvate* (3-carbon chain) as the waste product of anaerobic respiration.

Lactate is converted to pyruvate in the liver when O_2 becomes available.

If lactate is not metabolized, it can lead to lactic acidosis (acidification of the blood) and death.

C and D: CO_2 and H_2O are waste products of aerobic respiration.

CO_2 and H_2O are removed from the lungs via expiration during regular breathing.

CO_2 increases lead to acidosis (lowering blood pH) because CO_2 reacts with H_2O to form carbonic acid (H_2CO_3).

E: *ammonia* is the waste product of protein metabolism, converted to the less toxic urea in the liver and removed by the kidneys.

If ammonia is not converted and cleared, the blood becomes alkaline (higher in pH), potentially fatal.

23. A is correct.

V_{max} is proportional to the number of active sites on the enzyme (i.e., [enzyme] or enzyme concentration).

K_m remains constant because it is a measure of the active site affinity for the substrate.

Regardless of the number of enzyme molecules, each enzyme interacts with the substrate similarly.

Models propose mechanisms of enzymatic catalysis.

Michaelis–Menten model describes enzyme-substrate interactions, whereby enzymatic catalysis occurs at a specific site on enzymes – the active site.

Substrate (S) binds the enzyme (E) at the active site for an enzyme-substrate (ES) complex.

ES complex dissociates into enzyme and substrate or moves forward in the reaction to form product (P) and original enzyme.

$$E + S \underset{k_{-1}}{\overset{k_1}{\rightleftharpoons}} ES \overset{k_2}{\rightarrow} P + E$$

Rate constants for different steps in the reaction are k_1, k_{-1}, and k_2.

The overall rate of product formation is a combination of each rate constant.

At constant enzyme concentrations, varying [S] changes the rate of product formation.

At low [S], a small fraction of enzyme molecules is occupied with the substrate.

ES and [P] formation rate increases linearly with substrate concentration.

At high [S], all active sites are occupied with the substrate, and increasing the substrate concentration further does not increase the reaction rate, and the reaction rate is V_{max}.

Relationship between substrate concentration and reaction rate:

$$V = \frac{[S]}{[S] + K_m} V_{max}$$

24. E is correct.

Apoenzyme, with its cofactors, is a *holoenzyme* (an active form).

Enzymes that require a cofactor, but do not have one bound, are *apoenzymes* (or apoproteins).

Cofactors can be inorganic (e.g., metal ions) or organic (e.g., vitamins).

Organic cofactors are coenzymes or prosthetic groups.

Most cofactors are not covalently attached to an enzyme but are tightly bound.

Organic prosthetic groups can be covalently bound.

Holoenzyme refers to enzymes containing multiple protein subunits (e.g., DNA polymerases), whereby the holoenzyme is the complete complex with all subunits needed for the activity.

25. C is correct.

ATP releases about –7.4 kcal/moles.

As an approximation, 1 kcal/mol = ~ 4.2 kJ/mol

Structure of the nucleotide of ATP
(3 phosphates + ribose sugar + adenosine)

ATP contains three phosphate groups and is produced by enzymes (e.g., ATP synthase) from adenosine diphosphate (ADP) or adenosine monophosphate (AMP) and phosphate group donors.

Three central mechanisms of ATP biosynthesis are *oxidative phosphorylation* (in cellular respiration), *substrate-level phosphorylation*, and *photophosphorylation* (in photosynthesis).

Metabolic processes using ATP convert it back into its precursors; ATP is continuously recycled.

26. D is correct.

Cysteine is the only amino acid capable of forming a *disulfide* (S–S covalent) bond and serves an essential structural role in many proteins.

Thiol side chain in cysteine often participates in enzymatic reactions, serving as a nucleophile.

Thiol is susceptible to oxidization to give the *disulfide* derivative *cystine*.

27. C is correct.

Electron transport chain (ETC) uses cytochromes in the inner mitochondrial membrane and is a complex carrier mechanism of electrons that produces ATP through *oxidative phosphorylation*.

A: Krebs (i.e., TCA) cycle occurs in the *matrix* of the mitochondria.

Krebs cycle begins when acetyl CoA (i.e., 2-carbon chain) combines with oxaloacetic acid (i.e., 4-carbon chain) to form citrate (i.e., 6-carbon chain).

A series of additional enzyme-catalyzed reactions result in the oxidation of citrate and the release of two CO_2, and oxaloacetic acid is regenerated to begin the cycle again once it is joined to an incoming acetyl CoA.

B: *long-chain fatty acid degradation* occurs in peroxisomes that hydrolyze fat into smaller molecules fed into the Krebs cycle and used for cellular energy.

D: *glycolysis* occurs in the cytoplasm as the oxidative breakdown of glucose (i.e., 6-carbon chain) into two pyruvates (i.e., 3-carbon chain).

E: *ATP synthesis* occurs in the cytoplasm (glycolysis), the mitochondrial matrix (Krebs cycle), and the inner mitochondrial membrane (ETC).

28. E is correct.

Apoenzyme is an inactive enzyme without its cofactor.

Apoenzyme, with its cofactor(s), is a *holoenzyme* (an active form).

Enzymes that require a cofactor, but do not have one bound, are *apoenzymes* (or apoproteins).

Cofactors are inorganic (e.g., metal ions) or organic (e.g., vitamins).

Organic cofactors are *coenzymes* or *prosthetic groups*.

29. B is correct.

Disulfide bond is a covalent bond derived by coupling two thiols (~S-H) groups as R–S–S–R.

Peptide bonds join adjacent amino acids and make the protein's linear sequence (i.e., primary structure).

30. B is correct.

Enzyme prosthetic groups attach via strong molecular forces (e.g., covalent bonds).

A: *Van der Waals* interactions, like dipole/dipole, are weak molecular forces.

C: *ionic bonds* are powerful in non-aqueous solutions but are not used to attach prosthetic groups because they are weak in aqueous environments such as plasma. For example, NaCl dissociates in water.

D: *hydrogen bonds* (like hydrophobic interactions) are an example of a weak molecular force.

E: *dipole-dipole interactions* are an intermolecular force intermediate in strength between hydrogen bonds and van der Waals interactions that require a dipole (separation in charge) within the bonding molecules.

31. E is correct.

Cellular respiration begins via glycolysis in the cytoplasm but is completed in the mitochondria.

Glucose (six-carbon chain) is cleaved into two pyruvate molecules (three-carbon chain).

Pyruvate is converted to acetyl CoA that enters the Krebs cycle in the mitochondria.

NADH (from glycolysis and the Krebs cycle) and $FADH_2$ (from the Krebs cycle) enter the electron transport chain on the inner membrane of the mitochondria.

32. C is correct.

Primary activity of the thyroid hormone is to *increase* the *basal metabolic rate*.

33. D is correct.

Cofactors are organic or inorganic molecules classified depending on how tightly they bind to an enzyme.

Coenzymes are loosely bound organic cofactors released from the enzyme's active site during the reaction (e.g., ATP, NADH).

Prosthetic groups are tightly bound organic cofactors.

34. B is correct.

Primary structure is the *linear sequence* of amino acids in the polypeptide.

35. D is correct.

Denaturing the polypeptide disrupts the 4°, 3° and 2° structures, while the 1° structure (i.e., linear sequence of amino acids) is unchanged.

In folded proteins, 1° structure determines subsequent 2°, 3° and 4° structures.

36. B is correct.

$FADH_2$ is produced in the Krebs cycle (TCA) in cellular respiration.

A: product of glycolysis is pyruvate (i.e., pyruvic acid), which is converted to *lactic acid* (in humans) or *ethanol* & CO_2 (in yeast) *via* anaerobic conditions.

Yeast is used for alcoholic production and baking for the dough to rise.

C: in glycolysis, the first series of aerobic (or anaerobic) reactions occur in the cytoplasm by breaking the 6-carbon glucose into two 3-carbon pyruvate molecules.

D: two ATP are required, and four ATP are produced = net of two ATP at the end of glycolysis.

E: two NADH are produced by glycolysis and are oxidized (i.e., lose electrons) to compound Q in the electron transport chain within the mitochondria.

37. A is correct.

There are 13 essential (i.e., must be consumed) vitamins: A, B_1 (thiamine), B_2 (riboflavin), B_3 (niacin), B_5 (pantothenic acid), B_6 (pyridoxine), B_7 (biotin), B_9 (folate) and B_{12} (cobalamin), C, D, E and K.

Four fat-soluble vitamins, A, D, E, and K are stored in adipose tissue.

38. D is correct.

Hemoglobin is a *quaternary protein* with two α and two β chains with Fe^{2+} (or Fe^{3+}) as the prosthetic group.

Prosthetic groups are *tightly bound* cofactors (i.e., nonorganic molecules such as metals).

39. E is correct.

Glycine is the only achiral amino acid because hydrogen is the R group (i.e., side chain).

Optical activity is the ability of a molecule to rotate plane-polarized light and requires a chiral center (i.e., carbon atom bound to 4 different substituents).

D: *cysteine* contains sulfur in the side chain and is the only amino acid forming disulfide bonds (i.e., S–S).

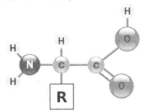

Amino acid structure with the α-carbon attached to the side chain R

40. A is correct.

During glycolysis, two net (four gross = total) molecules of ATP are produced by *substrate-level phosphorylation*, and two molecules of NAD^+ are reduced (i.e., gain electrons) to form NADH.

B: during glycolysis, *two pyruvates* form from each starting molecule of glucose.

C: *glycolysis* is an anaerobic process and does not require O_2.

D: *glucose* is partially *oxidized* (not reduced) into *two pyruvate* molecules during glycolysis.

E: *pyruvate* is produced during glycolysis (not in the Krebs cycle), converted to acetyl CoA (coenzyme A) that enters the Krebs cycle.

41. B is correct.

Krebs (TCA) cycle and the *electron transport chain* are metabolic processes in the mitochondria.

42. C is correct.

Feedback inhibition occurs when a product binds an enzyme to prevent it from catalyzing further reactions.

Since it is *allosteric inhibition*, this product binds a site other than the active site and changes the conformation of the active site to inhibit the enzyme.

Although the allosteric inhibitor can be the same product of the enzyme-catalyzed reaction *or* the product of the metabolic pathway, it is usually the final product that inhibits the entire metabolic pathway, thus saving the energy necessary to produce the intermediates as well as the final product.

When levels of the final product are low, the enzyme resumes its catalytic activity.

43. A is correct.

Obligate anaerobe reactions occur in the *absence* of O_2.

Oxidative phosphorylation occurs during the electron transport chain and requires a molecule of *oxygen* as the final acceptor of electrons shuttled between the cytochromes.

44. E is correct.

Peptide bonds join adjacent amino acids.

The amino acid (written on the left by convention) contributes an amino group ($\sim NH_2$).

The other amino acid (written on the right by convention) contributes a carboxyl group ($\sim COOH$) that undergoes condensation (i.e., joining of two pieces to form a connected unit) *via* dehydration (i.e., removal of H_2O during bond formation).

45. A is correct.

Oxidative phosphorylation (O_2 as substrate/reactant) occurs only in the electron transport chain (the last step for cellular respiration) in the *inner membrane* (i.e., cristae) of the mitochondria.

NADH and $FADH_2$ donate electrons to a series of cytochrome (i.e., protein) molecules embedded in the inner membrane and create an electron gradient, establishing a proton (H^+) gradient within the *intermembrane space* of the mitochondria.

H^+ gradient drives a proton pump coupled with an enzyme, producing ATP via *oxidative phosphorylation*.

Electrons from NADH and $FADH_2$ are transferred to ½ O_2 (i.e., oxidative phosphorylation) to generate ATP and form H_2O as a metabolic waste (along with CO_2) from cellular respiration.

H_2O and CO_2 (as metabolic wastes) are expired from the lungs during breathing.

Each Krebs cycle $FADH_2$ yields two ATP, while each NADH yields three ATP in the electron transport chain.

NADH from glycolysis only produces two ATP because energy is expended to shuttle the NADH from glycolysis (in the cytoplasm) through the double membrane of the mitochondria.

46. C is correct.

Enzymes do not affect free energy (ΔG); decreasing activation energy increases the reaction rate.

Enzymes do *not* affect the position or direction of equilibrium; they only affect the speed of equilibrium.

47. C is correct.

Zymogen (or proenzyme) is an inactive enzyme precursor. Proteolysis (i.e., cleavage) of the zymogen makes it active to catalyze reactions. Changes in substrate concentration regulate enzyme activity; an increase in substrate concentration increases enzyme activity (at saturation, V_{max} is achieved).

Post-translational modifications occur during protein biosynthesis (after translation), and they may involve cleaving proteins or introducing new functional groups to arrive at the mature protein product.

The enzyme may not be functional until post-translational modifications, a crucial regulatory aspect.

48. B is correct.

2° structure consists of numerous local conformations, such as α-helixes and β-sheets.

Secondary conformations are stabilized by hydrogen bonds or the covalent disulfide bonds between S–S of two cysteines to form cystine.

To be classified as 2° structure, the bonds must be formed between amino acids within about 12-15 amino acids along the polypeptide chain.

Otherwise, interactions (e.g., H bonds or disulfide bonds) that connect amino acid residues of more than 15 amino acids along the polypeptide chain qualify as 3° protein structure.

If the bonds occur between different polypeptide strands, the interactions qualify as 4° protein structures (e.g., two α and two β chains in hemoglobin).

49. E is correct.

Glycogen is a polysaccharide (i.e., carbohydrate) storage form with *highly branched glucose monomers*.

Extensive branching in glycogen provides numerous ends to the molecule to facilitate the rapid hydrolysis (i.e., cleavage and release) of individual glucose monomers when needed *via* epinephrine (i.e., adrenaline).

Glycogen is synthesized in the liver because of high plasma glucose concentrations and stored in muscle cells for release during exercise.

A: *glycogenesis* involves the synthesis of glycogen.

B: *glycogenolysis* involves the degradation of glycogen.

D: plants produce *starch* (i.e., analogous to glycogen) as their storage carbohydrate.

50. B is correct.

The fraction of occupied active sites for an enzyme equals V/V_{max} which = $[S]/([S] + K_m)$.

If $[S] = 2K_m$, the fraction of occupied active sites is 2/3.

51. C is correct.

Allosteric regulators bind enzymes at allosteric sites (i.e., other than active sites) with *non-competitive inhibition*.

Once bound to the allosteric site, the enzyme changes its conformational shape.

If the shape change causes the ligand (i.e., molecule destined to bind to the active site) to bind to the active site less efficiently, the modulator is *inhibitory*.

Modulator is excitatory if the shape change causes the ligand to bind to the active site more efficiently (i.e., the active site becomes open and accessible).

52. B is correct.

Biological reactions can be *exergonic* (releasing energy) or *endergonic* (consuming energy).

Biological reactions have *activation energy*, the minimum amount required for the reaction.

These reactions use *enzymes* (i.e., *biological catalysts*) to lower activation energy and increase the reaction rate.

53. C is correct.

Oxidative phosphorylation (in the electron transport chain) uses ½ O_2 as the ultimate electron acceptor.

Electron transport chain (ETC) is on the inner mitochondrial membrane. It uses cytochromes (i.e., proteins) in the inner membranes of the mitochondria to pass electrons released from the oxidation of NADH & $FADH_2$.

Mitochondrial matrix (i.e., the cytoplasm of mitochondria) is the site for the Krebs cycle (TCA).

Outer mitochondrial membrane does not directly participate in oxidative phosphorylation or the Krebs cycle.

Glycolysis and Krebs cycle produce ATP via *substrate-level phosphorylation*, while *oxidative phosphorylation* requires O_2 and occurs during the ETC.

54. D is correct.

Enzymes are often proteins and function as biological catalysts at an optimal temperature (physiological temperature of 36 °C) and pH (7.35 is blood pH).

At higher temperatures, proteins *denature* (i.e., unfolding by disrupting hydrogen and hydrophobic bonds and changing shape) and lose their function.

Proteins often interact with inorganic minerals (i.e., *cofactors*) or organic molecules (i.e., *coenzymes or tightly bound prosthetic groups*) for optimal activity.

Mutations affect *DNA sequences* that encode proteins, resulting in a change in the amino acid sequence of the polypeptide and a change in conformation within the enzyme.

A change in the conformation of enzymes often results in a change in function.

55. D is correct.

Gibbs free energy is:

$$\Delta G = \Delta G° + RT\ln Q$$

where $\Delta G°$ = the Gibbs free energy change per mole of reaction for unmixed reactants and products at standard conditions (i.e., 298K, 100kPa, 1M of each reactant and product), R = the gas constant (8.31 J·mol^{-1}·K^{-1}), T = absolute temperature and Q = [product] / [reactant]

Biomolecules – Detailed Explanations

1. A is correct.

The primary structure of a protein is the linear sequence of amino acids.

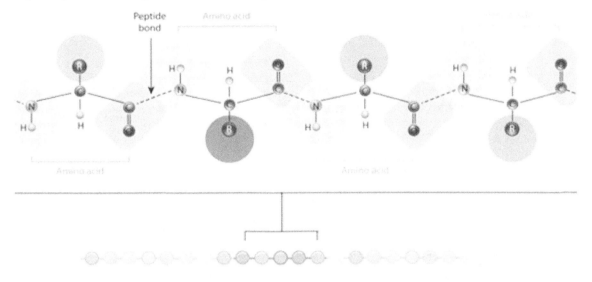

2. B is correct.

All the molecules in the body are divided into four categories. These biomolecular categories are carbohydrates, lipids, nucleic acids, and proteins.

3. A is correct.

Amino acids are linked in peptides by amide bonds. The peptide forms in a condensation reaction *via* dehydration (loss of water) when the lone pair on the nitrogen of an amino group of one amino acid makes a nucleophilic attack on a carbonyl carbon.

Peptide bonds form from the condensation reaction of 2 amino acids

4. B is correct.

The *alpha helix structure* is one of the two common types of secondary protein structure. The alpha helix is held together by hydrogen bonds between every N–H (amino group) and the oxygen of the C=O (carbonyl) in the next turn of the helix; four amino acids along the chain.

The typical alpha helix is about 11 amino acids long.

The other type of secondary structure is the *beta-pleated sheet*.

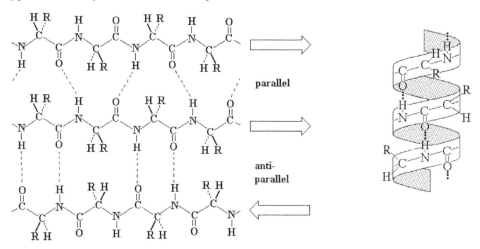

Beta pleated sheets are parallel or anti-parallel (a reference to the amino terminus).

5. C is correct.

The primary structure of a protein is the amino acid sequence, which is formed by covalent peptide linkages.

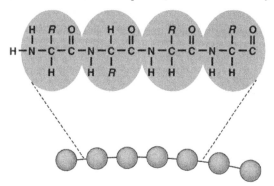

The amino acids (circles) are joined by covalent peptide bonds (lines)

A: only proteins containing more than one peptide subunit have a quaternary structure.

B: proteins are *denatured* by heating, and they lose their conformation above 35-40 °C, not retained.

D: many proteins contain more than one peptide chain (i.e., have a quaternary structure).

6. B is correct.

Amino acids are the building blocks of proteins.

Humans need 20 amino acids, some are made by the body (i.e., nonessential), and others must be obtained from the diet (i.e., essential).

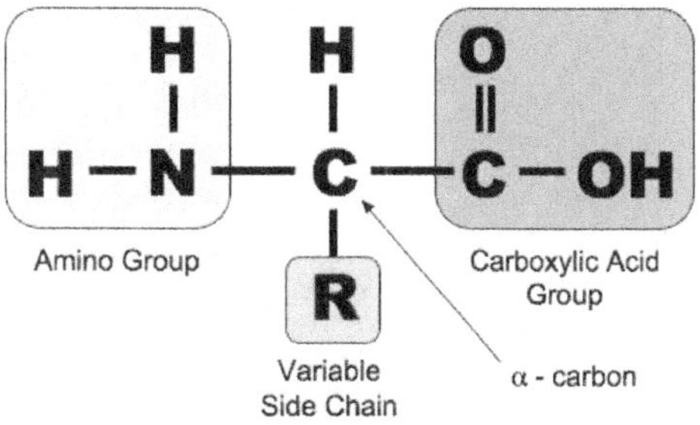

Amino acids contain an amine group, a carboxylic acid, an α-carbon, and an R group.

The following table is shown not for memorization but for identifying characteristics (e.g., polar, nonpolar) for the side chains.

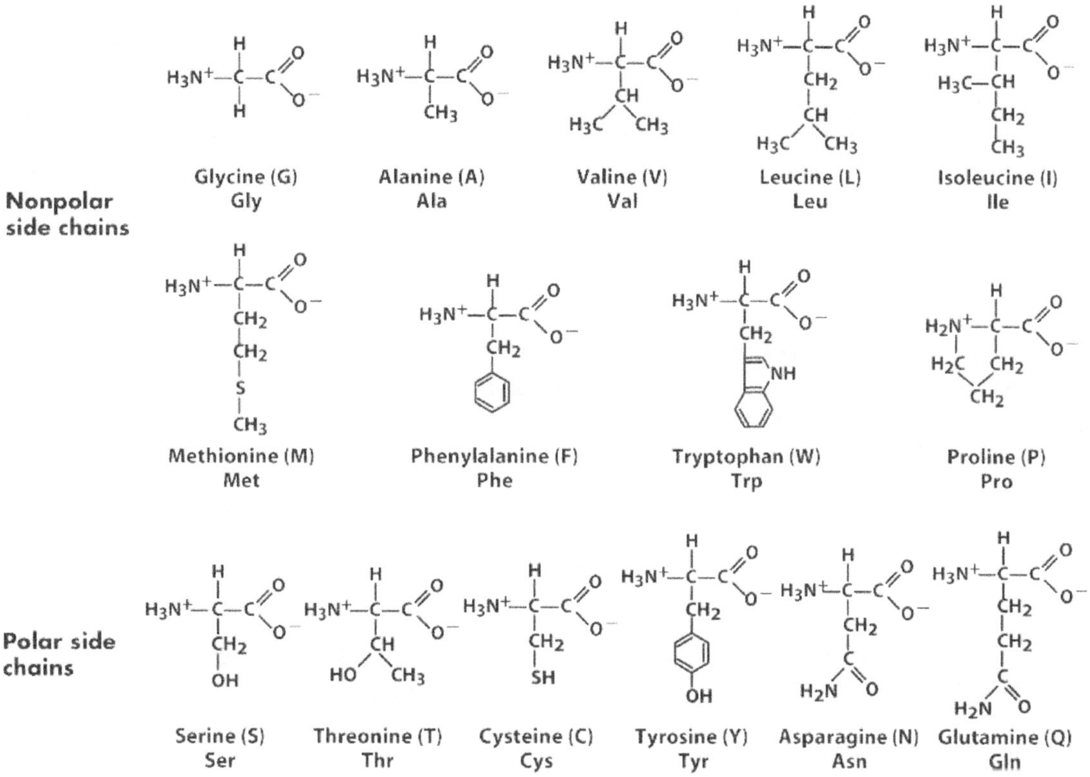

continued...

Acidic   **Basic**

Aspartate (D)   Glutamate (E)   Lysine (K)   Arginine (R)   Histidine (H)
Asp   Glu   Lys   Arg   His

The 20 naturally occurring amino acids.

7. C is correct.

Amino acids are the basic building blocks for proteins.

Two amino acids (dimer) with peptide bonds indicated by arrows

The peptide bond is rigid due to the resonance hybrids involving the lone pair of electrons on nitrogen, forming a double bond to the carbonyl carbon (and oxygen develops a negative formal charge).

8. C is correct.

Protonation or deprotonation of an amino acid residue changes its ionization state: it may become positively or negatively charged or neutral. The process may lead to changes in the interactions among amino acid side chains, as some ionic bonds may be compromised from the lack of opposite charge pairing.

Certain hydrogen bonding interactions may be modulated if Lewis bases are protonated with Brønsted acids, impairing their ability to accept hydrogen bonds from nearby amino acid residues.

9. D is correct.

Collagen is a protein that supports hair, nails, and skin.

Collagen is composed of a triple helix, and the most abundant amino acids in collagen include glycine, proline, alanine, and glutamic acid.

Much of the excess protein consumed in an animal's diet is used to synthesize collagen.

10. B is correct.

Secondary structure for proteins involves localized bonding.

The most important intermolecular interaction is hydrogen bonding, responsible for maintaining the alpha helix and beta pleated (parallel and antiparallel) sheet structures.

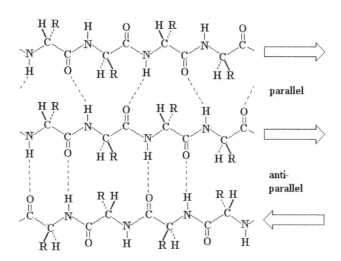

Alpha helix structure with hydrogen bonding shown as dotted lines

Beta pleated sheets (parallel and antiparallel) with hydrogen bonding shown

11. B is correct.

A *polypeptide chain* can undergo short-range bending and folding to form β sheets or α helices.

These structures arise as the peptide bonds can assume a partial double-bond character and adopt different conformations.

The arrangement of groups around the relatively rigid amide bond can cause R groups to alternate from side to side and interact with one another.

The carbonyl oxygen (C=O) in one region of the polypeptide chain could become hydrogen-bonded to the amide hydrogen in another region of the polypeptide chain. This interaction often results in forming beta-pleated sheets or an alpha helix.

Localized bending and folding of a polypeptide *do not* constitute a protein's primary structure.

continued...

A: *primary structure* of a protein is the amino acid sequence; individual amino acids are linked through peptide (i.e., amide) linkages.

C: *tertiary structure* is the 3-D shape that arises by further folding the polypeptide chain. Usually, these nonrandom folds give the protein a particular conformation and associated function.

D: *quaternary structure* is the spatial arrangement between two or more associated polypeptide chains (often linked by disulfide bridges between cysteine residues).

E: *zymogen* (or *proenzyme*) structure refers to an inactive enzyme that requires modification (i.e., hydrolysis to reveal the active site or change in configuration) to become an active enzyme.

12. B is correct.

Proteins are biological macromolecules composed of bonded amino acids with peptide (amide) bonds.

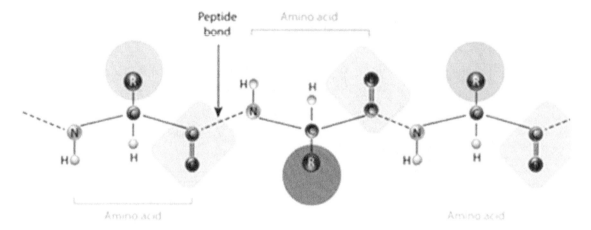

Three amino acids residues of nascent (i.e., growing) polypeptide

13. D is correct.

The plasma membrane is made of phospholipids (i.e., type of lipid). These molecules mostly possess nonpolar characteristics due to the long hydrocarbon chains, making the membrane permeable to nonpolar materials and semipermeable to polar or charged molecules.

14. B is correct.

Although cholesterol plays a pivotal role in the synthesis of other steroids and the integrity of cell membranes, too much cholesterol in the blood results in plaque deposits in blood vessels.

5. D is correct.

Steroid molecules are one of the two kinds of fat molecules, which are composed of fused rings.

Triacylglycerides are composed of long hydrocarbon chains with functionalized head groups.

16. C is correct.

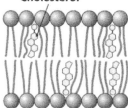

Cholesterol

Cholesterol is a lipid molecule known as a steroid compound.

The fused ring structure of steroid molecules makes them rigid and has fewer degrees of motion due to the few conformations available for cyclic molecules *vs.* acyclic molecules.

Molecules such as phospholipids lack fused-ring structures, and they exist as straight-chained molecules.

Therefore, cholesterol in the cell membrane acts as a bidirectional regulator of membrane fluidity: at high temperatures, it stabilizes the membrane and raises its melting point, whereas, at low temperatures, it intercalates between the phospholipids and prevents them from clustering and stiffening.

17. B is correct.

Triglycerides (or triacylglycerides) are used for storage and exist in the adipose tissue of animals.

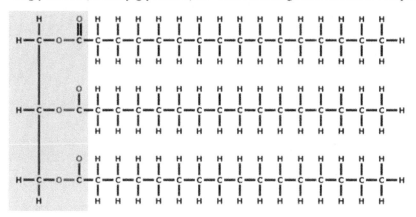

Triglyceride (glycerol and three saturated fatty acid chains)

Phospholipids(below) are the largest component of semi-permeable cell membranes.

Cholesterol

Testosterone

Estradiol

Cholesterol is the precursor molecule for several steroid hormones (e.g., progesterone, aldosterone).

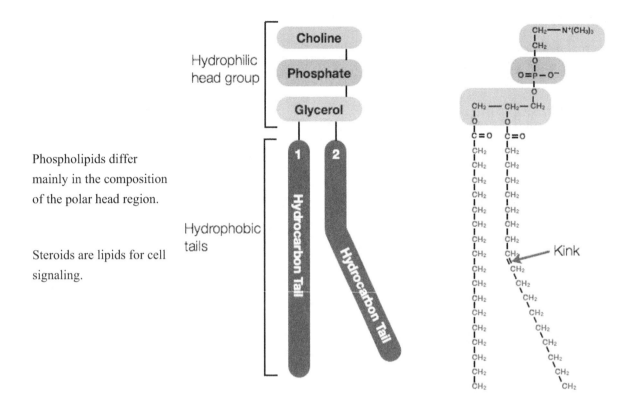

Phospholipids differ mainly in the composition of the polar head region.

Steroids are lipids for cell signaling.

18. B is correct.

An omega-3 is when the alkene (E/Z) double bond is three carbon atoms from the methyl end.

Linoleic acid (top)is ω-6,9 and linolenic acid (bottom) is ω-3,6,9. Note the positions of the double bonds and cis/trans (Z / E) relationships for double bonds

Linolenic acids are omega-3 fatty acids.

Linoleic acids are omega-6 fatty acids.

These molecules contain double bonds and are *unsaturated fats.*

19. D is correct.

Estradiol (shown) is a steroid hormone derived from cholesterol.

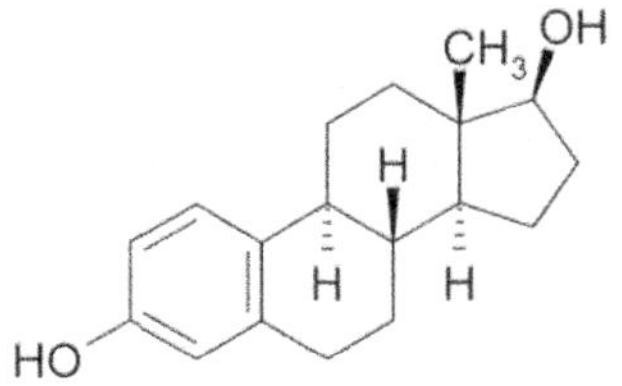

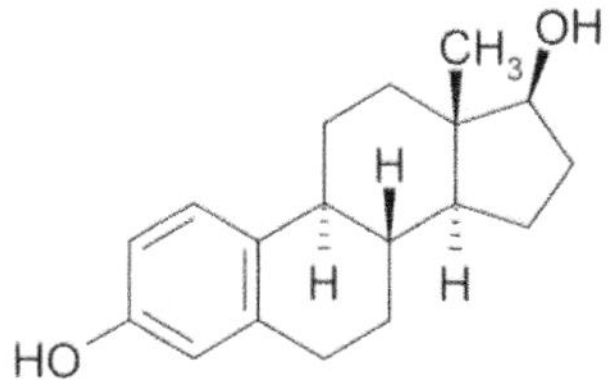

Estradiol is a derivative of cholesterol

Cholesterol is a lipid of four fused rings; three fused rings are six-membered, and the fourth is five-membered.

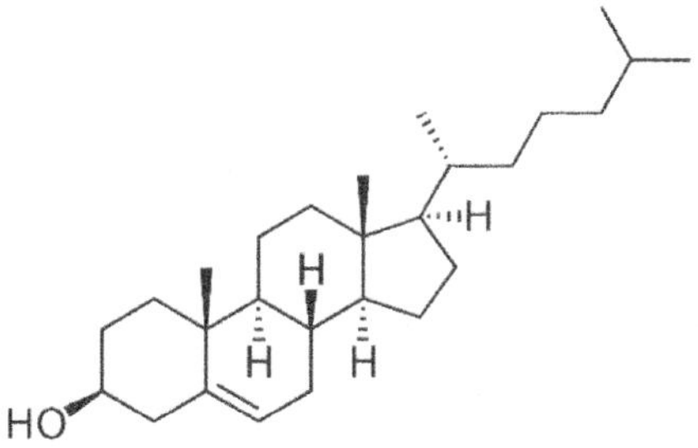

Cholesterol is a four-fused ring structure

Cholesterol is a steroid that makes up one of two types of lipid molecules.

Triglyceride (i.e., glycerol backbone with three fatty acid chains) is the other lipid (shown below).

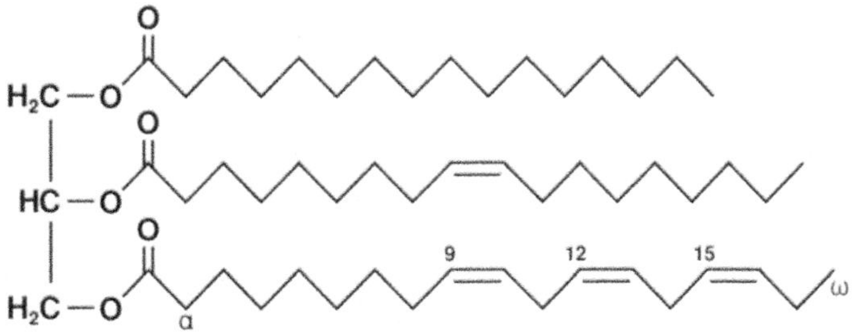

Triglyceride is glycerol backbone with three fatty acid chains

The carbon chain is numbered (example above) from the carboxyl end. Chemists number the double bonds as shown. Nutritionists specify the ω position from the terminal methyl group.

Position *omega* (ω) of the double bond(s) is the number of carbon atoms from the *terminal methyl group*.

20. B is correct.

Not all lipids are entirely hydrophobic. The ionic and polar heads of soaps and phospholipids, respectively, enable the molecules to interact with aqueous or polar environments.

The bulk of these molecules are hydrophobic because they largely consist of hydrocarbon chains or rings.

21. A is correct.

For unsaturated fats, the molecules are more likely to exist as oils (i.e., liquids) at room temperature.

Saturated fats tend to be solid at room temperature because the reduced forms of these molecules have better stacking properties, which allow them to form solid states.

22. B is correct.

The alkene molecules typically found in fatty acids tend to be *Z* alkenes.

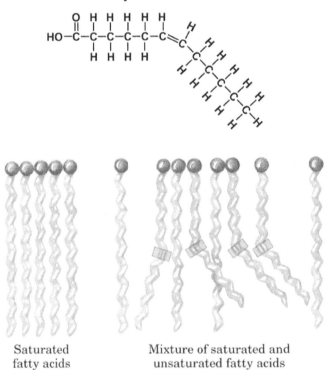

The double bond of the alkene (i.e., unsaturated) prevents the fatty acid molecules from stacking closely. The result is lowering of the melting point for the fat molecule. This may influence the state of matter of the oil, as unsaturated fats tend to be liquid at room temperature, and saturated fats tend to be solids.

Saturated
fatty acids

Mixture of saturated and
unsaturated fatty acids

23. A is correct.

Oils are isolated from plant sources and may consist of several different fatty acids. These oils may contain saturated fat, but other fats present in the mixture are unsaturated fat molecules.

The saturated fats that may be present in oil are palmitic and stearic acid, and the unsaturated fats found in these oils include oleic, palmitoleic, and linoleic acids, as well as others.

24. B is correct.

There are two overall categories of lipids: long-chain lipids (e.g., triglycerides) and smaller, polycyclic lipids, such as steroids (e.g., cholesterol and its derivatives, such as estrogen and testosterone).

Lipid molecules are fat-soluble, and these molecules are largely soluble in organic/hydrophobic.

25. D is correct.

Saturated fats tend to be solid at room temperature because they lack alkene groups. The alkene groups in fat molecules lower the melting point for these compounds.

For example, butter is a dairy product made from the fat of cow's milk, and it is solid at room temperature and is mainly composed of saturated fat molecules.

26. D is correct.

Fatty acids are used to make fat molecules known as triglycerides.

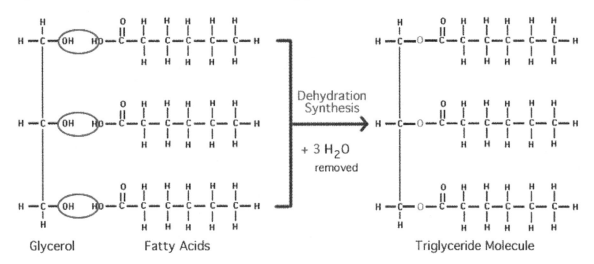

Glycerol   Fatty Acids   Triglyceride Molecule

Formation, via dehydration (removal of H_2O), of triglyceride from glycerol and 3 fatty acids.

Fatty acids are made from one equivalent of a triol known as glycerol and three equivalents of acid-containing groups of fatty acids.

27. C is correct.

Phospholipids are important lipids that make up the bilayer structure of the membranes of cells, organelles, and other enclosed cellular structures.

Phospholipids are two (same or different) fatty acid molecules, a phosphate group, and a glycerol backbone.

The phospholipid contains a hydrophobic (i.e., fatty acid tail) region and hydrophilic (polar head) region.

The hydrophobic regions point toward each other in the membrane bilayer, while the polar heads point towards the inside (i.e., cytosolic) or outside (i.e., extracellular) sides of the bilayer.

28. D is correct.

Fat can be produced from glucose, but glucose is not produced from animal fat.

Excess glucose consumption can lead to increased levels of fat in the body.

29. C is correct.

One exception to the tendency for sugars to have oxygen atoms linked to every carbon is deoxyribose. It is similar to ribose; however, one of the alcohols is replaced with a carbon-hydrogen bond.

30. B is correct.

The ratio of these atoms that compose sugars is typically 1:2:1 (carbon : hydrogen : oxygen).

D-ribose: Fisher projections of an example ribose sugar

31. A is correct.

Monosaccharides cannot be broken down into simpler sugar subunits.

However, monosaccharides can undergo *oxidative degradation* to produce carbon dioxide and carbon monoxide when treated with nitric acid.

32. E is correct.

Lactose is a disaccharide composed of glucose and galactose.

The glycosidic linkage in lactose is a β(1→4) linkage.

33. C is correct.

Glycogen is a polymer of glucose that functions as the energy store of carbohydrates in animal cells (plant cells use starch). Glycogen is common in the liver, muscle, and red blood cells.

Glycogen is a large biomolecule consisting of repeating glucose subunits.

34. D is correct.

Disaccharides contain a glycosidic linkage that is an ether group. The ether can be protonated with Brønsted acids and hydrolyzed in the presence of water.

All polysaccharides can be hydrolyzed to produce monosaccharides (i.e., individual monomers of the polymer).

35. D is correct.

Monosaccharides are the basic unit of carbohydrates.

Subjecting these compounds to acids or bases will not hydrolyze them further. However, they can undergo oxidative decomposition by treating them with periodic acid to form formaldehyde and formic acid.

36. D is correct.

Carbohydrates can be more specifically described as organic compounds that contain carbon, hydrogen, and oxygen. The general molecular formula may vary depending on the type of carbohydrates, but many examples have the formula of $C_nH_{2n}O_n$.

37. C is correct.

The "di" prefix in the name suggests that there are two smaller subunits.

Monosaccharides are linked through glycosidic (i.e., oxygen bonded to two ethers) functional groups.

Lactose is a disaccharide formed by a β(1→4) linkage between galactose and glucose.

38. A is correct.

The *dipole interactions* that join the strands of DNA are specifically hydrogen bonds.

These bonds form from the acid protons between the amides and imide functional groups and the carbonyl and amide Lewis basic sites of the matched nitrogen base pairs.

39. D is correct.

The DNA molecule has a deoxyribose sugar-phosphate backbone with bases (A, C, G, T) projecting into the center to join the antiparallel strand of DNA (i.e., double helix).

The deoxyribose sugar-phosphate backbone is negatively charged due to the formal charge of the oxygen attached to the phosphate group.

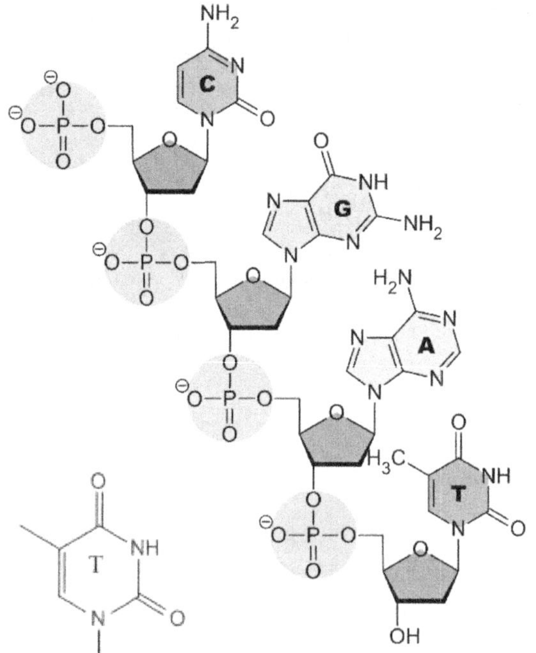

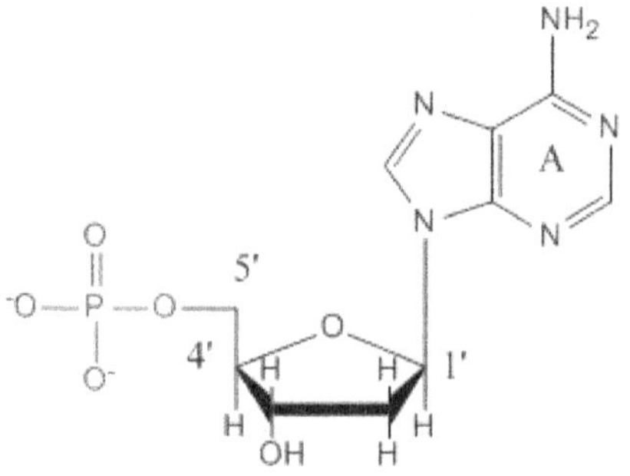

deoxyadenosine 5'-phosphate

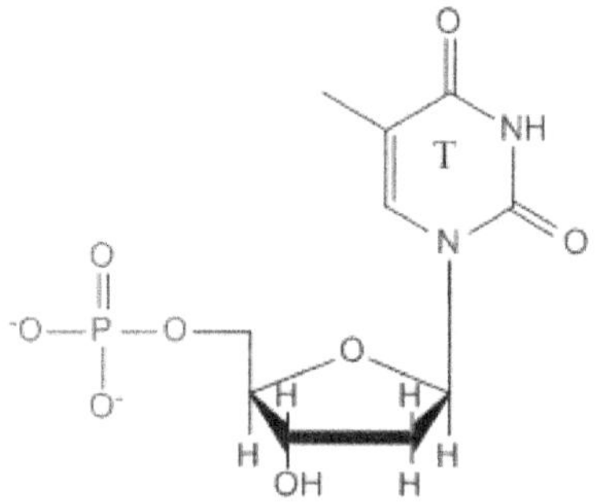

deoxythymidine 5'-phosphate

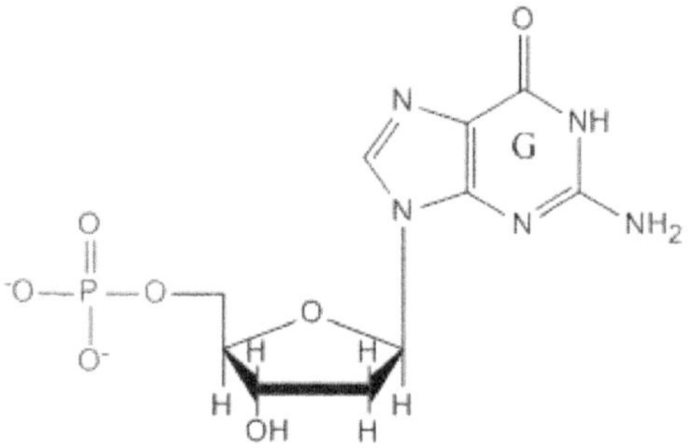

The purines (adenine and guanine) are double-ringed nitrogenous bases, while the pyrimidines (cytosine and thymine) are single-ringed nitrogenous bases.

deoxyguanosine 5'-phosphate

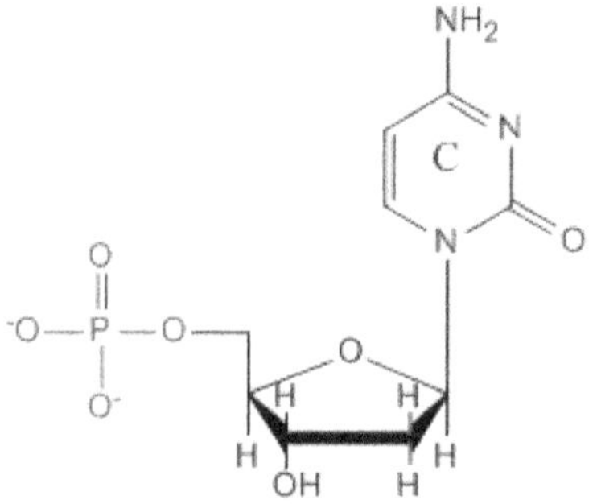

deoxycytosine 5'-phosphate

A nucleotide has a deoxyribose sugar, base, and phosphate, while a nucleoside is a deoxyribose sugar and base without the phosphate group.

40. B is correct.

Four common nucleotides are in DNA molecules:

adenine (A), cytosine (C), guanine (G) and thymine (T)

Four common nucleotides are in RNA molecules:

adenine (A), cytosine (C), guanine (G) and uracil (U)

41. D is correct.

Because adenine forms two hydrogen bonds with thymine, and cytosine forms three hydrogen bonds with guanine. DNA polymerase (in the S phase of interphase) uses the complementary nitrogen base to synthesize the new (daughter) strand.

42. C is correct.

DNA molecules hold the genetic information of organisms.

RNA molecules are synthesized from the DNA strand to make proteins for the cell.

Genes are the sections of DNA responsible for the synthesis of proteins in cells.

The central dogma of molecular biology (designates information flow)

43. D is correct.

There are five nucleotides, four of which appear in DNA.

These nucleotides are cytosine, guanine, adenine, and thymine.

In RNA molecules, the thymine is replaced with another pyrimidine nucleotide known as uracil.

Nucleotides consist of a phosphate group (note the negative charge on oxygens), deoxyribose sugar (lack a 2'-hydroxyl), and a nitrogenous base (adenine, cytosine, guanine, or thymine)

44. D is correct.

DNA	DNA	mRNA	tRNA
A	T	A	U
C	G	C	G
G	C	G	C
T	A	U	A

Complementary base pairing for nucleotides

DNA → DNA (replication); DNA → RNA (transcription); RNA → protein (translation)

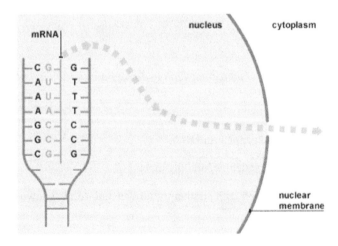

Guanine · · · Cytosine

Adenosine (left) and Uracil (replaces thymine in RNA)

Adenosine (left) and Uracil (replaces thymine in RNA)

A single strand of DNA is the template for RNA synthesis during transcription.

The mRNA (after processing) is translocated to the cytoplasm for translation to proteins.

45. A is correct.

The hexose sugar, nitrogen base, and phosphoric acid group make up nucleotides, and these nucleotides are used to make larger molecules of nucleic acids.

Nucleotides consist of sugar, phosphate, and a nitrogenous base.

46. B is correct.

In any given molecule of DNA, each of the thymine nitrogen bases forms two hydrogen bonds with adenine.

Because each thymine pairs with an adenine residue, there are equal nitrogen bases in the molecule.

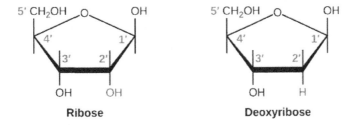

47. D is correct.

Ribose differs from deoxyribose sugars in that ribose lacks one alcohol (i.e., hydroxyl) group.

Ribose sugar (RNA) and deoxyribose sugar (DNA) are used to synthesize nucleic acid polymers.

48. A is correct.

Thymine is a pyrimidine nitrogenous base pair that forms two hydrogen bonds with adenine (purine) in the base-paired structure of DNA.

In RNA molecules, the nitrogenous base thymine is replaced by uracil.

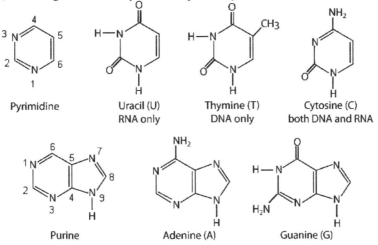

Purines (A, G) are single-ring structures, while pyrimidines (C, T, U) are double-ring structures.

49. B is correct.

There are three general components of nucleotides: a phosphate group, a cyclic five-carbon sugar, and a nitrogenous base.

Fat molecules are biomolecules for phospholipid membranes, storage fat molecules, and lipid molecules.

50. A is correct.

There are three major components of a nucleotide, the subunit that makes up nucleic acids.

All nucleic acids have a nitrogen base used for hydrogen bonding, a hexose sugar (ribose or deoxyribose), and a phosphate group that contains a phosphate linkage with the sugar.

Ester linkages are found in fats, glycosidic linkages are in sugars, and peptide linkages are in proteins.

51. C is correct.

Thymine is a pyrimidine nucleotide base that occurs in DNA but does not occur in RNA. Instead, RNA has uracil.

52. C is correct.

In DNA, thymine (T) hydrogen bonds with adenine (A).

However, in RNA, the thymine is exchanged for uracil (U).

Uracil (RNA)   Thymine (DNA)

53. C is correct.

Nucleic acids determine the sequences of amino acids because of groupings of nucleotides along a sequence corresponding to a particular amino acid.

The information of certain nucleic acids (i.e., mRNA) is translated on ribosomes with the help of tRNA.

Prions are infectious, disease-causing agents of misfolded proteins.

Structure and Function of Systems

Endocrine System – Detailed Explanations

1. A is correct.

Statins are drugs that competitively inhibit the HMG-CoA reductase enzyme that catalyzes the committed step in cholesterol biosynthesis; if the committed step is blocked, cholesterol cannot be made.

*Cholestero*l is the necessary precursor of the five major classes of steroid hormones:

> androgens, estrogens, progestogens, glucocorticoids, and mineralocorticoids.

Insulin is a peptide hormone that causes the liver, skeletal muscles, and fat tissue cells to absorb glucose from the blood.

Glucose is stored as *glycogen* in the liver and skeletal muscles and as *triglycerides* in fat cells (adipocytes).

When blood glucose levels fall below a certain level, the body uses stored sugar as an energy source through *glycogenolysis*, which breaks down the glycogen stored in the liver and muscles into glucose, an energy source.

B: *cortisol* is a steroid hormone.

C, D and E: testosterone, aldosterone, and progesterone have the same (~one) suffix as steroids.

2. D is correct.

Anterior pituitary gland does not produce the hormone thyroxine.

Anterior pituitary secretes *thyroid-stimulating hormone* (TSH) to stimulate the thyroid gland to produce T_4 and then T_3, which stimulate the metabolism of almost every tissue.

Thyroid hormones T_3 and T_4 (triiodothyronine and thyroxine) are derived from the amino acid tyrosine and accelerate oxidative metabolism.

In adults, *thyroid deficiency* (i.e., hypothyroidism) results in a decreased rate of metabolism, which produces symptoms such as weight gain, fatigue, intolerance to cold, and swelling of the thyroid (i.e., goiter).

3. D is correct.

Hormones are steroids or peptides released from a *gland*, traveling via the *blood* to affect a distant target.

A: *paracrine signals* are hormones released by a cell to induce a nearby cell's behavior or differentiation.

C: *autocrine signals* are hormones released from a cell and affect the *same cell* that synthesized the molecule.

Autocrine signals are common during development.

4. A is correct.

Steroid hormones can pass through the cell plasma membrane and enter the nucleus.

Once in the cell cytoplasm, the steroid hormone binds to its cytosolic receptor.

Once bound, the complex migrates into the cell nucleus and binds to the DNA.

Hormone/ receptor complexes function as a transcription factor to activate or inactivate gene transcription.

B: *eicosanoids* are signaling molecules made by the oxidation of 20-carbon fatty acids.

Central nervous system messengers exert complex control over many bodily systems, mainly in inflammation and immunity.

For example, prostaglandins and arachidonic acid are eicosanoids.

C: *peptide* (similar to an amino acid) hormones cannot enter through the cell's plasma membrane but bind (as a ligand) to receptors on the cell's surface via second messengers.

D: *amino acid hormones* (similar to peptide hormones) cannot enter through the cell's plasma membrane but bind (as a ligand) to receptors on the cell's surface via second messengers.

5. D is correct.

Acromegaly is a condition from an over secretion by the anterior pituitary of growth hormone (GH) that decreases the sensitivity of insulin receptors.

Pancreas secretes insulin in response to high blood glucose.

Acromegaly patients do not bind insulin as well as typical cells, and the effects of insulin are diminished.

Excess glucose is not converted into glycogen if insulin cannot exert its effects on the cells.

Hence, the patient has high blood glucose concentrations.

A: *high blood glucose concentrations* lead to the excretion of glucose and the loss of water in the urine, meaning that patients have increased (*not decreased*) urine volume.

B: *cardiac output* is the volume of blood pumped per unit of time, unrelated to insulin receptors' sensitivity.

C: low blood glucose concentration is the opposite effect.

E: glucose in urine increases osmolarity (number of particles), which is compensated by increased urine volume.

6. A is correct.

Posterior pituitary hormones are:

> *oxytocin* (i.e., uterine contraction and lactation) and

> *vasopressin* – an antidiuretic hormone or ADH (i.e., stimulates water retention, raises blood pressure by contracting arterioles, and induces male aggression).

7. E is correct.

Hormones are steroids or peptide molecules released by glands traveling through blood to affect a distant target.

Female reproduction cycle is the primary exception to *negative feedback control* of hormones.

Steroid hormones can pass through the cell plasma membrane and enter the nucleus.

Peptide (similar to an amino acid) hormones cannot enter through the cell's plasma membrane but bind (as a ligand) to receptors on the cell's surface via second messengers.

D: *ducts* are present in the exocrine (not endocrine) system, whereby hormones are released from a gland and distributed throughout the body via the bloodstream.

8. B is correct.

Hypothalamus regulates specific metabolic processes and other activities of the autonomic nervous system.

It synthesizes and secretes certain neurohormones (i.e., releasing hormones), and these, in turn, stimulate or inhibit the secretion of anterior/posterior pituitary hormones.

Hypothalamus regulates many fundamental human functions, including temperature regulation, sleep/wake cycles, water and salt balance, hunger, etc.

Hypothalamus produces hormones such as vasopressin (or ADH) and oxytocin (stored in posterior pituitary).

Hypothalamus produces *releasing factors* that control secretions of the *anterior pituitary*.

A: *cerebrum* regulates memory, conscious thought, voluntary motor activity, and sense interpretations.

Cerebrum refers to the part of the brain comprising the cerebral cortex (two cerebral hemispheres); it includes several subcortical structures such as the basal ganglia, hippocampus, and olfactory bulb.

In humans, the cerebrum is the superior-most region of the central nervous system (CNS).

C: *medulla oblongata* (aka medulla) is the lower half of the brainstem.

Medulla contains the respiratory, cardiac, vomiting, and vasomotor centers and regulates autonomic (i.e., involuntary) functions, such as heart rate, breathing, and blood pressure.

D: *pons* is part of the brainstem that links the medulla oblongata to the thalamus.

Pons relays signals from the forebrain to the cerebellum and primarily involves sleep, respiration, posture, equilibrium, bladder control, hearing, swallowing, taste, eye movement, facial expressions, and facial sensation.

E: *pineal gland* secretes the hormone melatonin, which controls circadian rhythms and may be involved in sexual maturation.

9. A is correct.

Adrenocorticotropic hormone (ACTH) is a tropic polypeptide hormone produced and secreted by the anterior pituitary gland.

ACTH is an essential component of the hypothalamic-pituitary-adrenal axis, often produced in response to biological stress (e.g., long-distance run).

Glucagon is a storage form of glucose that increases blood sugar by releasing glucose molecules in the blood.

Increased heart rate and sympathetic blood shunting away from the intestines are expected during a long-distance run.

10. E is correct.

Cell signaling generally causes a change in *receptor conformation* (i.e., shape).

11. D is correct.

Hormones (steroids and amino acids/peptides) are substances released from *glands and enter the bloodstream* to affect *target tissues*.

12. E is correct.

Parathyroid gland (via PTH) and the thyroid (via calcitonin) are antagonist hormones that regulate blood calcium concentration.

Parathyroid gland secretes PTH to increase blood calcium by removing calcium from bones and calcium-containing tissues.

Humans have four parathyroid glands on the posterior surface of the thyroid gland.

Thyroid gland is mid lower neck, below the *larynx* (i.e., voice box), and above the clavicles (i.e., collarbone).

PTH acts to increase blood $[Ca^{2+}]$, whereas calcitonin (by the C cells of the thyroid gland) decreases $[Ca^{2+}]$.

Parathyroid hormone controls blood Ca^{2+} levels via two mechanisms:

      1) stimulating osteoclasts activity (i.e., bone resorption),

      2) decreasing the Ca^{2+} loss (i.e., renal calcium reabsorption) in urine by the kidney, and therefore,

      3) increasing blood calcium concentration.

Parathyroid hormone (PTH) is a polypeptide hormone with 84 amino acids secreted by the chief cells of the parathyroid glands.

Removal of calcium from bones is primarily done via osteoclasts (i.e., bone-releasing = breakdown bone).

PTH increases blood $[Ca^{2+}]$, whereas calcitonin (by the C cells of the thyroid gland) decreases $[Ca^{2+}]$.

PTH increases $[Ca^{2+}]$ in blood by acting upon parathyroid hormone 1 receptors (high levels in bone and kidney) and parathyroid hormone 2 receptors (high levels in the central nervous system, pancreas, testis, and placenta).

13. D is correct.

Most second messenger systems are initiated by peptide hormones (i.e., ligands), which *cannot pass* through plasma membranes and bind to receptors on the cell surface.

Peptide hormones are hydrophilic, cannot cross the hydrophobic phospholipid bilayer, and bind to a receptor on the target cell's membrane surface.

Ligand-receptor complex may trigger the release of a second messenger (e.g., G-protein or cAMP), or the ligand-receptor complex may be carried into the cytoplasm by receptor-mediated endocytosis.

A series of second messenger events within the cell are responsible for the hormone's activity.

Thus, peptide hormones do *not* directly influence mRNA transcription because they do not enter the nucleus of their target cells and activate transcription.

Cholesterol-derived steroid hormones enter the cell and bind to a cytosolic receptor.

Hormone-receptor complex passes through the nuclear envelope with the receptor and enters the nucleus to function as a transcription factor and increase/decrease gene expression.

14. C is correct.

Posterior pituitary releases *oxytocin* and *antidiuretic hormone* (ADH or *vasopressin*).

A: TSH (*thyroid-stimulating hormone*) is released by the *anterior pituitary*.

B: *prolactin* is produced in the *pituitary gland* and *decidua* (uterine lining – endometrium), *myometrium* (middle layer of the uterine wall), *breasts*, *lymphocytes*, *leukocytes*, and the *prostate*.

D: *progesterone* is produced in *ovaries* (*corpus luteum*), *adrenal glands*, and during pregnancy, in the *placenta*.

Progesterone is synthesized from the precursor – *pregnenolone*.

E: thyroid gland releases *calcitonin.*

15. C is correct.

Anterior pituitary secretes three *gonadotropic hormones* (FSH, LH, placental chorionic gonadotropins hCG).

FSH causes the ova to mature and enlarge.

A: *oxytocin* is synthesized by the hypothalamus and stimulates uterine contractions during birth and milk letdown during lactation.

Prolactin stimulates the production of milk for lactation.

D: LH (*luteinizing hormone*) stimulates ovulation.

16. E is correct.

Estrogen is a steroid hormone (versus peptide hormone).

Steroids are lipid-soluble and diffuse from the blood through cell membranes and into cytoplasm of target cells.

In the cytoplasm, the steroid binds to the *specific receptor*.

Many steroid receptors *dimerize* upon steroid binding to form one functional *DNA-binding unit* that enters the cell nucleus and affects (positively or negatively) gene expression.

Once in the nucleus, the steroid-receptor ligand complex binds to specific DNA sequences and regulates transcription (activates or inactivates) of its target genes.

17. C is correct.

Adrenocorticotropic hormone (ACTH) is produced and released by the anterior pituitary to increase glucocorticoid steroid hormones (corticosteroids) by adrenal cortex cells.

18. B is correct.

Most second messenger systems are initiated by peptide hormones (i.e., ligands) which cannot pass through plasma membranes and instead bind to *receptors on the cell surface*.

Cholesterol-derived steroid hormones (e.g., estrogen) enter the cell and bind to a *cytosolic receptor*.

Together with the receptor, the *hormone-receptor complex* passes through the nuclear envelope and enters the nucleus to function as a transcription factor and increase/ decrease gene expression.

Anterior pituitary (e.g., TSH) and pancreatic (e.g., insulin) hormones are peptides.

Peptide hormones are hydrophilic and cannot cross the hydrophobic phospholipid bilayer.

As a result, peptide endocrine mediators bind as ligands to cell membrane receptors and activate intracellular second messengers (e.g., cAMP).

19. C is correct.

Some cells respond differently to the same peptide hormone because a signal transduction pathway determines a target cell's response.

20. B is correct.

Thyroid hormones T_3 and T_4 (triiodothyronine and thyroxine) are derived from the *amino acid tyrosine* and accelerate oxidative metabolism throughout the body.

Anterior pituitary secretes *thyroid-stimulating hormone* (TSH) to stimulate the thyroid gland to produce T_4 and then T_3, which stimulate the metabolism of tissues.

21. D is correct.

IGF-1 is the primary protein synthesized in response to growth hormones.

Growth hormone (GH) is synthesized by *anterior pituitary* and stimulates tissue growth through *IGF*-1 proteins.

Deletion of both alleles of the IGF-1gene causes a growth deficiency.

A: *parathyroid hormone deficiency* leads to decreased Ca^{2+} levels and brittle bones.

B: *anemia* is an abnormally low level of hemoglobin in the blood.

C: *deficiency of pancreatic lipase* (or bile salts) may result in the inability to digest lipids.

22. E is correct.

Vitamin A is a relatively small, lipid-soluble molecule with a receptor not connected to the plasma membrane.

23. B is correct.

Anterior pituitary secretes GH, PRL, and ACTH hormones.

Eight hormones of the anterior pituitary

Adrenocorticotropic hormone (ACTH) targets the adrenal gland and results in glucocorticoid, mineralocorticoid, and androgens secretions.

Beta-endorphin targets opioid receptors and inhibits the perception of pain.

Thyroid-stimulating hormone (TSH) targets the thyroid gland and results in secretions of thyroid hormones.

Follicle-stimulating hormone (FSH) targets gonads and results in the growth of the reproductive system.

Luteinizing hormone (LH) targets gonads to trigger ovulation, maintain corpus luteum and secrete progesterone (in females) or stimulate testosterone secretion (in males).

Growth hormone (somatotropin or GH) targets the liver and adipose tissue and promotes growth, lipid, and carbohydrate metabolism

Prolactin (PRL) targets the ovaries and mammary glands and results in secretions of estrogens/progesterone; it stimulates milk production.

Leptin targets corticotropic and thyrotropic cells (cell types in the anterior pituitary) and results in secretions of TSH and ACTH.

24. B is correct.

Thyroid hormone increases the *basal metabolic rate* by stimulating protein synthesis and increasing the activity of the Na^+/K^+ ATPase pump.

Thyroid gland dysfunctions are *hyperthyroidism* and *hypothyroidism*.

Typically, the anterior pituitary gland produces thyroid stimulating hormone (TSH) that binds to TSH receptors and stimulates the release of thyroid hormone.

Auto-antibodies bind to TSH receptors and overstimulate the thyroid gland, causing abnormally high thyroid hormone levels.

25. C is correct.

Hormone accumulating inside cells without endocytosis requires diffusion through plasma membranes.

Steroid hormones are hydrophobic and freely diffuse through plasma membranes.

A: *neurotransmitters* are charged molecules that bind to a receptor at the cell surface.

B: *second messengers* transmit signals inside cells but are not hormones.

D: *polypeptides* cannot diffuse through membranes because they are large, hydrophilic molecules.

E: *amines* derive an amino acid (e.g., tyrosine) and include epinephrine, norepinephrine, and dopamine.

Pancreas is an exocrine (via ducts) and endocrine (via the bloodstream) gland.

Exocrine function (via a series of ducts) is performed by cells secreting digestive enzymes (e.g., amylase, lipase, and maltase) and bicarbonate into the small intestine.

Small glandular structures perform endocrine functions of the pancreas called the *islets of Langerhans* (i.e., alpha, beta, and delta cells).

> *Alpha cells* produce and secrete *glucagon*.
>
> *Beta cells* produce and secrete *insulin*.
>
> *Delta cells* produce and secrete *somatostatin*.

27. A is correct.

Luteinizing hormone (LH) surge causes ovulation.

If the anterior pituitary secretes low levels of LH, this inhibits the release of an oocyte and causes infertility.

Oral contraceptives inhibit the release of LH by altering the ratio of estrogen/progesterone levels.

Follicle-stimulating hormone (FSH) stimulates oocyte maturation.

28. C is correct.

Signal transduction pathway:

signal → receptor → responder → effects

29. E is correct.

Cortisol (or *hydrocortisone*) is a steroid hormone produced by the adrenal cortex and released in response to stress and a low level of blood glucocorticoids.

Cortisol is a *glucocorticoid* named for its role in regulating metabolism (glucose levels).

Cortisol's primary functions are to *increase blood sugar* through gluconeogenesis to suppress the immune system, aid in carbohydrate, protein, and fat metabolism, and decrease bone formation.

Cortisol, an important human glucocorticoid, is essential for life and regulates/supports important metabolic, cardiovascular, immunologic, and homeostatic functions.

A: *adrenaline* is known as *epinephrine*.

B: *norepinephrine* (or noradrenaline) is a *catecholamine* (i.e., derived from the amino acid tyrosine) with multiple roles, including being a hormone and a neurotransmitter.

Norepinephrine is a neurotransmitter released from the sympathetic neurons that underlies the *fight-or-flight* response (in conjunction with epinephrine),

increases heart rate,

triggers release of glucose from energy stores,

increases blood flow to skeletal muscle, and

increases oxygen supply to the brain.

Norepinephrine (a stress hormone) affects the brain (e.g., the amygdala), where attention and responses are controlled.

30. D is correct.

Excessive production of epinephrine results in clinical manifestations affecting the sympathetic nervous system (*fight or flight* response) with:

1) elevated blood pressure,

2) increased heart rate,

3) dilation of the pupils, and

4) inhibition of gastrointestinal tract function and motility.

31. C is correct.

Releasing hormone (or releasing factor) is a hormone that controls the release of another hormone.

Hypothalamus is below the *thalamus*.

Hypothalamus links the *nervous and endocrine systems* via the pituitary gland (*hypophysis*).

It is responsible for metabolic processes and other autonomic nervous system activities.

Hypothalamus synthesizes and secretes releasing hormones that modulate the secretion of pituitary hormones.

Hypothalamus controls:

> body temperature,
>
> hunger, thirst,
>
> fatigue, sleep, circadian rhythms, and
>
> essential aspects of parenting and attachment behaviors.

Releasing factors synthesized by the hypothalamus, examples:

> thyrotropin-releasing hormone (TRH),
>
> corticotropin-releasing hormone (CRH),
>
> gonadotropin-releasing hormone (GnRH), and
>
> growth hormone-releasing hormone (GHRH).

Although inhibiting pituitary hormone release, *somatostatin* and *dopamine* are releasing hormones.

32. B is correct.

Parathyroid gland secretes parathyroid hormone to increase blood calcium by removing calcium from bones and other calcium-containing tissues.

Removal of calcium from bones is primarily done via *osteoclasts* (i.e., bone-releasing = breakdown bone).

A: *thyroid glands* secrete *calcitonin* as the antagonist to the parathyroid hormone.

Calcitonin reduces blood $[Ca^{2+}]$ by depositing it onto bone via *osteoblasts* (i.e., building bone).

C: *aldosterone*, secreted by the adrenal cortex, increases Na^+ reabsorption in the kidneys.

D: *glucagon* (α cells of the islets of Langerhans) from the pancreas raises blood glucose.

E: *antidiuretic hormone* (ADH) is known as *vasopressin*; its function is to increase water reabsorption in the collecting tubules of the kidneys.

33. D is correct.

Antagonistic refers to an opposite action, while *agonist* means to mimic the effect.

Antagonistic relationship exists between *insulin and glucagon*.

Pancreas synthesizes insulin that lowers glucose blood levels and glucagon that raises glucose blood levels.

A: ACTH and TSH are unrelated in their actions.

ACTH (*adrenocorticotropic hormone*) is secreted by the anterior pituitary and stimulates the adrenal gland.

TSH (*thyroid-stimulating hormone*) activates the thyroid to produce thyroxine.

B: oxytocin and prolactin are *agonists* (i.e., same effect) of the same process, specifically the production of milk by the mammary gland.

Oxytocin is secreted by the *posterior* pituitary gland and stimulates the *release* of milk during lactation.

Prolactin is secreted by the *anterior* pituitary gland and stimulates *milk production* during lactation.

C: vitamin D and parathyroid hormone (PTH) are *agonists* of the same process because both increase blood calcium levels.

34. E is correct.

Cells receive light, sound, and hormone signals.

35. D is correct.

Endocrine gland synthesizing parathyroid hormone (PTH) is the *parathyroid*.

Parathyroid gland secretes *parathyroid hormone* to increase blood calcium [Ca^{2+}] by removing calcium from bones and other calcium-containing tissues.

Parathyroid gland (via PTH) and the thyroid (via calcitonin) are *antagonist* hormones that regulate blood calcium concentration.

Humans typically have four parathyroid glands, usually on the posterior surface of the thyroid gland.

Parathyroid hormone (PTH) is a polypeptide hormone with 84 amino acids secreted by the *chief cells* of parathyroid glands.

PTH acts to increase blood [Ca^{2+}], whereas calcitonin (by the C cells of the thyroid gland) decreases [Ca^{2+}].

PTH increases [Ca^{2+}] in blood by acting upon:

      parathyroid hormone 1 receptor (elevated levels in bone and kidney) and

      parathyroid hormone 2 receptor (elevated levels in CNS, pancreas, testis, and placenta).

36. B is correct.

Aldosterone is a steroid hormone produced by the outer adrenal cortex in the adrenal gland. Adrenal glands produce aldosterone from low blood pressure in response to *low sodium or elevated potassium*.

Aldosterone increases blood Na^+ levels and decreases blood K^+ concentration.

Aldosterone is vital in regulating blood pressure, mainly by acting on the distal tubules and collecting ducts of nephrons. It increases the reabsorption of ions and water in the kidney, causing the conservation of Na^+, secretion of K^+, increased H_2O retention, and blood pressure.

37. E is correct.

In a positive feedback system, the *output enhances* the original stimulus, while with negative feedback, the output reduces the effect of the stimulus.

Positive feedback system is childbirth, wherein the hormone oxytocin is released, intensifying the contractions.

38. C is correct.

Glucagon is a *peptide hormone* secreted by the pancreas that *raises blood glucose levels*.

Glucagon's effect is opposite to insulin's, which lowers blood glucose levels, and the pancreas releases glucagon when blood glucose levels are too low.

Glucagon causes the *liver to convert stored glycogen into glucose*, which is released into the bloodstream.

Conversely, high blood glucose levels stimulate insulin release, allowing glucose to be taken up and used by insulin-dependent tissues. Thus, glucagon and insulin are part of a feedback system that keeps blood glucose levels within a narrow range.

Glucagon elevates glucose in the blood by promoting gluconeogenesis and glycogenolysis.

Glucose is stored in the liver in the form of glycogen, which is a polymer of glucose molecules.

Liver cells (hepatocytes) have glucagon receptors.

When glucagon binds to the glucagon receptors, the liver cells convert the glycogen polymer into individual glucose molecules and release them into the bloodstream. This process is *glycogenolysis*.

As stores become depleted, glucagon signals the liver and kidney to synthesize additional glucose by gluconeogenesis (i.e., glucose from non-carbohydrate precursors).

Glucagon turns off glycolysis in the liver, causing glycolytic intermediates to be shuttled to gluconeogenesis.

A: *calcitonin* is secreted by the thyroid gland and lowers blood Ca^{2+} levels.

B: *estrogen* is secreted by the ovaries, maintains secondary sex characteristics (i.e., menstrual cycles in females), and is responsible for maintaining the endometrium.

D: *oxytocin* is produced by the hypothalamus and is secreted by the posterior pituitary to stimulate uterine contractions during labor and milk secretion during lactation.

E: *thyrotropin* or thyroid-stimulating hormone (TSH) is an anterior pituitary hormone that stimulates the thyroid to release thyroxine and triiodothyronine, which increase metabolic rate.

---

39. A is correct.

Primary function of *hormone-sensitive lipase* (HSL) is to mobilize stored fats.

When the body needs to mobilize energy stores (e.g., during fasting), HSL is activated through a positive response to catecholamines (i.e., epinephrine, norepinephrine) in the absence of insulin.

Insulin inhibits *hormone-sensitive lipase* (HSL).

Insulin is a peptide hormone (A chain with 21 and B chain with 30 residues) produced by *beta* cells of the pancreas, and it is central to regulating carbohydrate and fat metabolism.

When [glucose] is low, the decreased insulin levels signal the adipocytes to activate hormone-sensitive lipase.

HSL converts – via hydrolysis – the triglycerides into free fatty acids to be utilized as energy by the cell.

B: *epinephrine* (or *adrenaline*) is a hormone and a neurotransmitter.

Epinephrine regulates heart rate, blood vessel and air passage diameters, and metabolism.

Adrenaline release is a crucial component of the fight-or-flight response of the sympathetic nervous system.

Epinephrine is a monoamine called *catecholamines,* produced in some central nervous system neurons and the adrenal medulla (inner region) from the amino acids *phenylalanine* and *tyrosine*.

C: *estrogen* promotes female secondary sex characteristics. Estrogens, in females, are produced primarily by the ovaries and the placenta during pregnancy.

Follicle-stimulating hormone (FSH) stimulates the ovarian production of estrogens by the ovarian follicles and corpus luteum. Other tissues, such as the liver, adrenal glands, breasts, and fat cells, produce some estrogens in smaller amounts. These secondary sources of estrogen are especially important in postmenopausal women.

D: *glucagon* is a peptide hormone secreted by the pancreas and is one of four hormones (e.g., epinephrine, cortisol, and growth hormone) that raise blood glucose levels.

Pancreas releases glucagon when blood sugar (glucose) levels fall too low, and its effect is opposite that of insulin, which lowers blood glucose levels.

Glucagon causes the liver to convert stored glycogen into glucose, which is released into the bloodstream.

High blood glucose levels stimulate *insulin release* and insulin for glucose uptake by insulin-dependent tissues.

Glucagon and insulin are part of a feedback system (i.e., *antagonists*) that keeps blood glucose levels stable.

E: *norepinephrine* (or noradrenaline) is a *catecholamine* (i.e., derived from the amino acid tyrosine) with multiple roles, including being a hormone and a neurotransmitter.

Norepinephrine is a neurotransmitter released from sympathetic neurons that underlies the *fight-or-flight* response (in conjunction with epinephrine),

 increases heart rate,

 triggers release of glucose from energy stores,

 increases blood flow to skeletal muscle, and

 increases oxygen supply to the brain.

40. C is correct.

Molecular signals that bind to receptors of the same cell that synthesize them are *autocrine signals*, common during development.

Paracrine signals are hormones a cell releases to induce a nearby cell's behavior or differentiation.

41. A is correct.

Melatonin is an essential and multifunctional hormone secreted by the pineal gland that has numerous biological effects triggered by the activation of melatonin receptors.

Melatonin affects *circadian rhythms*, mood, the *timing of puberty*, *aging*, and other *biological processes*.

It is a pervasive and powerful *antioxidant* with a particular role in protecting nuclear and mitochondrial DNA.

42. C is correct.

Endocrine islets of Langerhans account for 1–2% of the pancreas and secrete insulin (to lower blood sugar), glucagon (to raise blood sugar), and somatostatin (to inhibit the release of insulin and glucagon).

Islets of Langerhans cells secrete hormones:

> *Alpha cells* produce *glucagon* (15–20% of total islet cells)

> *Beta cells* produce *insulin* (65–80%)

> *Delta cells* produce *somatostatin* (3–10%)

> *Gamma cells* produce *pancreatic polypeptides* (3–5%)

> *Epsilon cells* produce *ghrelin* – hunger-stimulating peptide (<1%)

A: *cortisol* is a hormone released (via the bloodstream) by the adrenal cortex in response to stress.

B: *trypsin* is an exocrine (via duct) pancreatic product necessary for protein digestion.

D: *pepsin* is secreted by chief cells in the stomach to digest protein.

43. D is correct.

When a person starts to perspire profusely, sweat glands are *effectors* in the feedback loop.

44. E is correct.

Epinephrine (or *adrenaline*) is a peptide hormone released by the adrenal medulla and a physiological stimulant (i.e., *EpiPen* for anaphylaxis) that aids in *fight-or-flight* responses.

B: *sympathetic nervous system* stimulates *epinephrine* release.

C: *epinephrine is a peptide hormone* synthesized by the *adrenal medulla*, while the *adrenal cortex* synthesizes *steroid hormones* (e.g., aldosterone and cortisol).

45. C is correct.

Growth-hormone-releasing hormone (GHRH), known as *growth-hormone-releasing factor*, is a 44-amino acid peptide hormone produced in the hypothalamus and carried to the anterior pituitary gland, where it stimulates the secretion of the growth hormone (GH).

Hypothalamic hormones are *releasing* and *inhibiting* because they influence the anterior pituitary.

Eight hormones of the anterior pituitary

Adrenocorticotropic hormone (ACTH) targets the adrenal gland and results in glucocorticoid, mineralocorticoid, and androgens secretions.

Beta-endorphin targets opioid receptors and inhibits the perception of pain.

Thyroid-stimulating hormone (TSH) targets the thyroid gland and results in secretions of thyroid hormones.

Follicle-stimulating hormone (FSH) targets gonads and results in the growth of the reproductive system.

Luteinizing hormone (LH) targets gonads to trigger ovulation, maintain corpus luteum and secrete progesterone (in females) or stimulate testosterone secretion (in males).

Growth hormone (aka somatotropin; GH) targets the liver and adipose tissue and promotes growth, lipid, and carbohydrate metabolism

Prolactin (PRL) targets the ovaries and mammary glands and results in secretions of estrogens/progesterone; it stimulates milk production.

Leptin targets corticotropic and thyrotropic cells (both are cell types in the anterior pituitary) and results in secretions of TSH and ACTH.

46. A is correct.

Ligand signal is not metabolized into useful products, which differs from enzyme-substrate reactions.

47. B is correct.

Gene expression is associated with steroid hormone activity.

48. D is correct.

Hormones are classified as *steroids* (i.e., cholesterol-derived) and *amino acid* (peptide) hormones.

Amino acid hormones include amines (derived from a single amino acid, either tryptophan or tyrosine), peptide hormones (short chains of amino acids), and protein hormones (longer chains of amino acids).

Steroid hormones are corticosteroids (mineralocorticoids and glucocorticoids) or sex steroids (androgens, estrogens, and progestogens).

49. E is correct.

Cyclic AMP (cAMP) is a second messenger derived from ATP and functions for intracellular signal transduction in many organisms by transferring the effects of hormones like glucagon and adrenaline, which cannot pass through plasma membranes.

cAMP activates *protein kinases* that bind to and regulate the function of ion channels (e.g., HCN channels) and some cyclic nucleotide-binding proteins.

cAMP and its associated kinases function in several biochemical processes, including regulating glycogen, sugar, and lipid metabolism.

50. A is correct.

Exocrine glands release secretions through *ducts*, while *endocrine glands* release secretions into the *bloodstream*.

Exocrine secretions of the pancreas are protease, lipase, and amylase (which aid in the digestion of food) and bicarbonate ions (i.e., buffer the pH of chyme) coming from the stomach.

Glucagon is a pancreatic endocrine secretion in response to low blood glucose that increases glucose levels through the degradation of glycogen and by decreasing glucose uptake by muscles.

Nervous System – Detailed Explanations

1. C is correct.

Astrocytes, which collectively form astroglia, are star-shaped glial cells in the brain and spinal cord.

Astrocytes participate in multiple processes and conduct many essential functions.

Schwann cells produce the myelin sheath around neuronal axons in the peripheral nervous system.

2. A is correct.

Sensation is the awareness of changes in the internal and external environments.

For the sensation to occur,

> 1) stimulus energy must match the specificity of the receptor,
>
> 2) stimulus must be applied within a sensory receptor's receptive field (the smaller the receptive field, the greater the brain's ability to correctly localize the stimulus site) and
>
> 3) stimulus energy must be converted into a graded potential (i.e., transduction).

Graded potentials can be *depolarizing* or *hyperpolarizing*.

3. C is correct.

Parasympathetic nervous system maintains *homeostasis* (*rest and digest*), increasing gut motility, modulating heart rate, and constricting the bronchi and pupils.

Sympathetic nervous system prepares for action (*fight or flight*), decreasing digestive tract activity, increasing heart rate, dilating the pupils, and relaxing the bronchi.

4. D is correct.

Autonomic nervous system (ANS) has motor neurons that: innervate smooth and cardiac muscle and glands.

ANS adjusts to ensure optimal support for body activities, operates via subconscious control (involuntary nervous system or general visceral motor system), and has viscera as most of its effectors.

Effectors of the ANS are cardiac muscle, smooth muscle, and glands.

ANS uses a 2-neuron chain for its effectors.

Cell body of the first neuron (i.e., preganglionic neuron) resides in the brain or spinal cord.

The axon of the first neuron (i.e., preganglionic axon) synapses with the second motor neuron (i.e., ganglionic neuron) in an autonomic ganglion outside the central nervous system.

The axon of the ganglionic neuron (i.e., postsynaptic axon) extends to the effector organ.

5. B is correct.

Retinal (or retinaldehyde) is one of the many forms of vitamin A.

Retinal bound to opsin proteins is the chemical basis of vision.

Vision begins with the *photoisomerization of retinal*.

When the 11-*cis*-retinal chromophore absorbs a photon, it isomerizes from the 11-*cis* state to the all-*trans* state.

Absorbance spectrum of the chromophore depends on its interactions with the opsin protein to which it is bound; different opsins produce different absorbance spectra.

6. E is correct.

Frequency of action potentials is related to the *intensity* of the stimulus.

Strength of the stimulus is coded into the *frequency* of the action potentials generated.

The stronger the stimulus, the higher the *frequency* of action potentials.

Thus, the nervous system is *frequency-modulated* and *not amplitude-modulated*.

7. B is correct.

Myopia (i.e., nearsightedness) is when light focuses on the front of the retina, making distant objects blurry.

Image of a distant object is out of focus, while a closer object is in focus, making near objects blurry.

This condition is due to the shape of the eye being too long.

8. E is correct.

Bipolar neurons are neurons that have two extensions.

Bipolar neurons are specialized sensory neurons transmitting certain senses (e.g., sight, smell, taste, hearing, and vestibular functions).

Bipolar neurons are extensively utilized to transmit efferent (motor) signals to control muscles.

Common bipolar neurons are the bipolar cell of the retina and the ganglia of the vestibulocochlear nerve.

Additionally, they are in the spinal ganglia when the cells are embryonic.

9. B is correct.

Smallest distance resolved with the unaided eye is typically 0.2 mm.

10. A is correct.

Blood-brain barrier blocks harmful substances (e.g., bacteria, toxins, metabolic waste products) from entering the brain.

Blood-brain barrier does allow the passage of oxygen, glucose, amino acids, alcohol, and anesthetics.

11. C is correct.

Medulla oblongata controls many vital functions, such as breathing, heart rate, and gastrointestinal activity.

A: *cerebrum* (i.e., cerebral cortex) processes and integrates sensory input and motor responses and participates in memory and creativity.

B: *cerebellum* is vital in coordinating muscles and aids in balance by receiving input from the inner ear, hand-eye coordination, and the timing of rapid movements.

Primary function of the cerebellum is *coordinating unconscious movement*.

D: *hypothalamus* regulates hunger, thirst, sleep, water balance, blood pressure, temperature, and libido.

Hypothalmus is essential in modulating the endocrine system.

E: *pituitary gland* (along with the hypothalamus) is vital for controlling the endocrine system.

12. B is correct.

Acetylcholine (ACh) is the neurotransmitter at *neuromuscular junctions* for *motor* and *memory functions*.

ACh carries signals at neuromuscular (nerve-to-skeletal muscle) connections.

ACh is at synapses in the *ganglia of the visceral motor system*.

13. E is correct.

In anatomy, *decussation* (i.e., crossing) means the same thing as chiasma (or chiasm).

In genetics, *chiasma* is the point where two chromatids are interwoven, when observed between the S phase and anaphase.

In anatomy, *decussation* (i.e., crossing) means the same thing as *chiasma* (or chiasm).

Chiasma is where two chromatids are interwoven in genetics, as observed between the S phase and anaphase.

14. A is correct.

Unlike other body cells, *neurons do not undergo mitosis* (the splitting of cells) because they lack centrioles essential in cell division. This makes diseases affecting the brain and the nervous system particularly crippling.

Some neurons can be generated from neural stem cells preserved in the subventricular zone during development.

Neural stem cells are presumed to be vital for adult brain plasticity.

15. D is correct.

Autonomic nervous system (ANS) is composed of sympathetic and parasympathetic divisions.

Both divisions rely on a two-neuron motor pathway away from the spinal cord and a two-neuron sensory pathway toward the spinal cord.

continued…

ANS is unique because it requires a sequential two-neuron efferent pathway; the preganglionic (first) neuron must first synapse onto a postganglionic (second) neuron before innervating the target organ.

Preganglionic neurons begin at the *outflow* and synapse at the postganglionic neuron's cell body.

Postganglionic neurons synapse at the target organ.

Sympathetic nervous system has *short preganglionic* and *long postganglionic* neurons.

16. D is correct.

Voltage-gated ion channels are transmembrane proteins activated by changes in membrane potential. They are essential to the initiation and propagation of action potentials in neurons.

17. E is correct.

Cerebellum, along with the pons and medulla oblongata, is in the hindbrain. Higher brain sensory neurons and motor neurons pass through the hindbrain. Primary function of the cerebellum is coordinating unconscious movement (e.g., hand-eye coordination, posture, balance).

Cerebellum damage would likely result in *loss of muscle coordination*.

Cerebrum divides into left and right hemispheres, subdivided into *four lobes*.

Cerebrum coordinates most voluntary activities, sensations, and *higher functions* (including speech and cognition). The spinal cord also controls the extremities.

18. A is correct.

Somatic nervous system controls skeletal muscles and consists of sensory and motor nerves.

19. A is correct.

Fovea is in the center of the macula region of the retina. The fovea is responsible for the sharp central vision necessary for reading, driving, and visual detail.

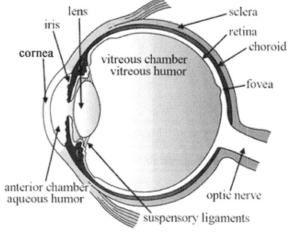

Cone cells are one of two types of photoreceptor cells in the retina and are responsible for color vision and eye color sensitivity.

Cone cells function better in bright light than rod cells, which function better in dim light.

Cone cells are densely packed in the fovea (0.3 mm in diameter, rod-free area) but quickly reduce in number towards the periphery of the retina.

Six to seven million cones in the human eye are concentrated towards the macula.

Rod cells are photoreceptor cells in the eye's retina that function in less intense light than cone cells. One hundred twenty-five million rods are concentrated at the outer edges of the retina and are used in peripheral vision.

Rod cells are more sensitive than cone cells and are responsible for *night vision*.

20. D is correct.

Nucleic acids (e.g., DNA, RNA) are not a chemical class of neurotransmitters.

21. C is correct.

Cell bodies of somatic sensory neurons are not in the CNS but in the *dorsal root ganglia* just behind the spinal cord along the spinal cord.

Peripheral nervous system (PNS) divides into *somatic* and *visceral* components.

Somatic part of PNS consists of the nerves innervating the skin, joints, and muscles.

Somatic sensory neuron cell bodies *lie in the spinal cord's dorsal root ganglia.*

Visceral (*autonomic nervous system*) has neurons innervating internal organs, blood vessels, and glands.

Autonomic nervous system (ANS) consists of *sympathetic* and *parasympathetic nervous systems.*

22. B is correct.

Ganglia are associated with afferent nerve fibers containing cell bodies of sensory neurons.

23. E is correct.

Medulla oblongata monitors CO_2 levels and pH of the blood.

Medula regulates breathing, temperature, heart rate, and reflexes such as sneezing, coughing, and swallowing.

Reticular activating system (RAS) is a network of neurons in the brainstem that receives input from all sensory systems and sends non-specific information to the brain.

Hypothalamus controls hunger, thirst, sleep, water balance, blood pressure, temperature regulation, and libido.

Hypothalamus is vital for modulating the endocrine system.

Cerebral cortex controls vision, hearing, smell, voluntary movement, and memory.

24. D is correct.

Excitatory postsynaptic potential (EPSP) amplitudes can be less than the action potential threshold.

EPSPs are depolarizing currents but do not always sum to threshold due to the dissipation of current or chloride shunting inhibition (IPSP).

25. D is correct.

Eye requires 20–30 minutes to adapt from bright sunlight to complete darkness, becoming ten thousand to one million times more sensitive than at full daylight.

In this process, the eye's perception of color changes as well.

It takes approximately five minutes for the eye to adapt to bright sunlight from the darkness as cones obtain more sensitivity during the first five minutes of entering light.

However, the rods take over after five minutes.   *continued…*

Rhodopsin is a pigment in the retina photoreceptors that immediately photobleached in response to light.

Rods are more sensitive to light and take longer to adapt to light changes.

Rods' photopigments regenerate more slowly and need about 30 min to reach their maximum sensitivity.

However, the sensitivity of rods improves within 5–10 minutes in the dark.

Cones take 9–10 minutes to adapt to the dark.

Sensitivity to light is modulated by intracellular calcium ions and cyclic guanosine monophosphate changes.

26. A is correct.

Synaptic cleft prevents an impulse from being transmitted directly between neurons.

27. C is correct.

Parasympathetic stimulation elicits *rest and digest* responses (i.e., not stress or immediate survival).

Parasympathetic nervous system stimulates saliva production, containing enzymes to digest food.

A: *piloerection* is mediated by small arrector pili muscles at the base of each hair when they contract and pull the hair erect.

This reflex originates from the sympathetic nervous system for most fight-or-flight responses.

B: *contraction of abdominal muscles* during exercise results from somatic nervous system stimulation.

D: increased rate of *heart contractions* is a sympathetic response.

E: *pupil dilation* is a sympathetic response.

28. D is correct.

Graded potentials are changes in membrane potential that vary in size.

In the absence of action potentials, *graded potential decays* as it travels away from the site of origin.

29. E is correct.

Acetylcholine (ACh) is a neurotransmitter that causes depolarization of postsynaptic membranes when released by the presynaptic terminal of another neuron.

ACh is removed from the synapse by the enzyme acetylcholinesterase, which catalyzes the hydrolysis of acetylcholine into choline and acetate.

Insecticides (e.g., Diazinon) are anti-cholinesterases because they block acetylcholinesterase activity, and acetylcholine is not degraded.

This increases the concentration of acetylcholine in the synapse while the presynaptic membrane continues to secrete acetylcholine in response to presynaptic action potentials.

continued...

C: *acetylcholinesterase inactivity* increases (not *decreases*) postsynaptic depolarization because if acetylcholine is not degraded, it continuously binds to its receptors on the postsynaptic membrane and depolarizes it.

D: *anti-cholinesterase* does not affect the activity of other neurotransmitters (e.g., epinephrine or norepinephrine); therefore, the synaptic nervous transmission does *not* cease.

30. A is correct.

Oligodendrocytes are functionally similar to Schwann cells.

31. D is correct.

Cornea is the transparent front eye covering the iris, pupil, and anterior chamber.

With the *anterior chamber* and *lens*, the cornea refracts light, with the cornea accounting for approximately two-thirds of the eye's total optical power (43 diopters).

While the cornea contributes most of the eye's focusing power, its focus is fixed.

Curvature of the lens can be adjusted to focus depending on the object's distance.

Lens is a transparent, biconvex structure in the eye that (with the cornea) refracts light focused on the retina.

In humans, the refractive power of the lens is about 18 diopters (1/3 of the total refractive power).

Lens change shape to adjust the focal distance for objects at various distances, allowing a *real image* of the object to be formed on the retina.

Adjustment of the lens is *accommodation*.

The lens is flatter on its anterior side than on its posterior side.

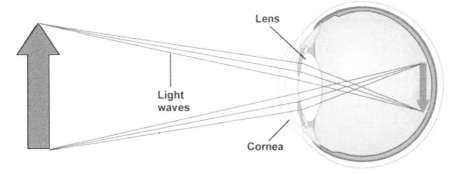

Diopter is a unit of measurement of the optical power of a lens or a curved mirror.

Diopter is equal to the *reciprocal of the focal length* measured in meters (i.e., 1/meters) and therefore is a unit of reciprocal length.

For example, a 3-dioptre lens brings parallel light rays to focus at 0.33 meters.

32. B is correct.

Sodium gates in the membrane can open in response to electrical potential changes.

33. E is correct.

Epinephrine is part of the sympathetic nervous system, and its release prompts the *fight or flight* response.

A: *aldosterone* participates in sodium reabsorption by the kidney.

C: *acetylcholine* is a neurotransmitter. In the heart, acetylcholine neurotransmission has an inhibitory effect, which lowers the heart rate.

Acetylcholine also acts as an *excitatory* neurotransmitter at neuromuscular junctions in *skeletal muscle*.

D: *insulin* causes cells to take up glucose and is *not* part of the sympathetic nervous system.

34. D is correct.

Cerebral cortex is the outer layer of the brain, made of gray matter.

White matter is a different type of nerve fiber in the brain's inner layer.

35. B is correct.

Cerebellum is part of the hindbrain (i.e., the posterior part of the brain) and consists of the pons and medulla oblongata.

Cerebellum receives sensory information from the visual and auditory systems and information about the orientation of joints and muscles.

Cerebellum's primary function is hand-eye coordination.

Cerebellum receives information about the motor signals being initiated by the cerebrum and integrates inputs to produce balance and unconscious coordinated movement.

Damage to the cerebellum compromises these functions, while destruction *impairs coordinated movement*.

A*: thermoregulation* is a function of the hypothalamus (a part of the cerebrum).

C: *sense of smell* (i.e., olfaction) is a cerebrum function.

D: *urine formation* is the primary function of the kidneys, along with some hormonal regulation.

36. C is correct.

A second nerve impulse cannot be generated until the membrane potential has been re-established.

37. E is correct.

Pathway for a beam of light entering the eye:

cornea → aqueous humor → lens → vitreous humor

38. C is correct.

Compared to the external surface of a cell membrane for a resting neuron, the interior surface is negatively charged and contains less sodium.

39. B is correct.

Pressure waves (i.e., sound) are converted into *neural signals* by hair cells in the organ of Corti of the cochlea.

Organ of Corti (in mammals) is part of the cochlea of the inner ear with hair cells (i.e., auditory sensory cells).

Organ of Corti is the structure that *transduces pressure waves into electrical signals* as action potentials.

40. A is correct.

If an electrode is placed at the midpoint along the length of the axon, the impulse will move bidirectionally.

41. C is correct.

Nervous system divides into the *peripheral* (PNS) and *central nervous systems* (CNS).

Peripheral nervous system includes the autonomic nervous system (ANS) and somatic nervous system (SNS).

Autonomic nervous system (ANS) regulates the internal environment through involuntary nervous pathways.

ANS innervates smooth muscle in blood vessels and the digestive tract and innervates the heart, the respiratory system, the endocrine system, the excretory system, and the reproductive system.

Autonomic nervous system divides into *sympathetic, parasympathetic*, and *enteric nervous systems*.

ANS functions divide into *sensory* and *motor subsystems*.

Sensory subsystem consists of those receptors and neurons that transmit signals *to* the central nervous system.

Motor subsystem transmits signals *from* the central nervous system to effectors.

Sympathetic division innervates pathways for immediate action; "*fight-or-flight;*" with heart rate and blood pressure increase, blood vessels in skin constrict (*vasoconstriction*), and those in the heart dilate (*vasodilation*).

Pathways innervating the digestive tract are inhibited, and epinephrine (i.e., adrenaline) is secreted by the adrenal medulla, increasing the conversion of glycogen into glucose to increase blood glucose concentration.

Central nervous system (CNS) consists of the brain and the spinal cord.

Somatic system innervates skeletal muscle, and its nervous pathways are typically under voluntary control.

Parasympathetic system innervates nervous pathways returning the body to homeostasis following exertion.

For example, the PNS decreases heart rate, blood pressure, blood glucose concentrations, blood vessels in the skin dilate, coronary arteries in the heart constrict, and digestive processes resume.

42. E is correct.

Endorphin is a neurotransmitter that works as a chemical process to control and hinder pain perception.

Endorphins release inhibits pain impulses sent to the brain.

43. C is correct.

Photoreceptor cells are specialized neurons in the retina capable of phototransduction (i.e., light converted into electrical signals).

Photoreceptors convert light (visible electromagnetic radiation) into signals that can stimulate biological processes by triggering a change in the cell's *membrane potential*.

Activation of rods and cones involves *hyperpolarization*.

Rods and cones, when not stimulated, depolarize and release *glutamate* (neurotransmitter).

In the dark, cells have a high concentration of cGMP (*cyclic guanosine monophosphate*), which opens ion channels (Na^+ and Ca^{2+}).

Positively charged ions entering cells change membrane potential causing depolarization and glutamate release. Glutamate *depolarizes* or *hyperpolarizes* other neurons.

44. C is correct.

Brain stem is the posterior part of the brain that joins with the spinal cord, consisting of the pons, medulla, and midbrain.

Pons contains neural pathways that carry signals from and to the brain.

Medulla is associated with breathing, heart rate, and blood pressure functions.

Midbrain oversees vision, hearing, motor control, alertness, and temperature regulation.

45. B is correct.

Hypothalamus controls hunger, thirst, sleep, water balance, blood pressure, temperature regulation, and libido.

Hypothalamus is essential in modulating the endocrine system.

Substantia nigra is a small midbrain area that forms a component of the basal ganglia and is involved in Parkinson's disease.

46. D is correct.

Cerebrospinal fluid is a clear fluid in the brain and spinal cord. It acts as a buffer for the brain and provides mechanical and immunological protection.

Red blood cells are usually *not* in cerebrospinal fluid.

47. E is correct.

Otitis is a general term for *inflammation or infection of the ear*.

Glaucoma is increased pressure in the aqueous humor from blockage of aqueous humor outflow.

Myopia (or nearsightedness) causes the image to form in front of the retina, making distant objects blurry.

Hyperopia (hypermetropia or farsightedness) has an image form behind the retina, making near objects blurry.

48. A is correct.

Temporal lobe of the brain is where the *primary auditory cortex* is located.

49. B is correct.

Reflex arc requires one muscle group to contract while the antagonistic muscle group must relax (i.e., inhibitory signal). This excitation/inhibitory response prevents conflicting contractions by antagonistic muscles.

Reflex arcs often are confined to a three-neuron network (i.e., afferent, interneuron, efferent) within spinal cord.

Interneurons (within the spinal cord) integrate the communication between the *afferent and efferent neurons*.

Motor neurons exit the ventral side of the spinal cord.

Reflex arcs do *not* require processing from the brain (i.e., no conscious thought before responding), so the cerebral cortex is *not* involved.

50. D is correct.

Dorsal root ganglia of the spinal cord contain cell bodies of sensory neurons (or *first-order neurons*), which bring information from the periphery to the spinal cord.

51. A is correct.

Reflex arc is a stimulus coupled with a rapid motor response for quickness and protection; it requires no processing (or input) by the brain.

For example, recoiling a finger away from a hot stove, whereby the reflex arc begins when the stove is touched, stimulating a sensory nerve.

Sensory nerves direct a signal *toward* the CNS and synapse with an interneuron, connecting the sensory and motor neurons within the spinal cord.

For example, *interneurons* synapse with a motor neuron that delivers the response signal to an arm and causes movement away from the stove.

Two types of reflex arcs:

       1) *autonomic reflex arc*, which affects internal organs

       2) *somatic reflex arc* that affects muscles

B: a brief delay occurs at the two synaptic junctions because time is necessary for *neurotransmitters to diffuse*.

C: *reflex arc* may consist of only two neurons (one sensory and one motor neuron) and is *monosynaptic* with a single chemical synapse.

In peripheral muscle reflexes (e.g., patellar reflex, Achilles reflex), brief stimulation of the muscle spindle causes the agonist or effector's muscle contraction.

Polysynaptic reflex pathways use interneurons to connect afferent (i.e., sensory) and efferent (i.e., motor) signals. Except for the simplest reflexes, reflex arcs are *polysynaptic*.

D and E: *sensory neurons* can synapse in the brain, but reflex arc neurons synapse in the spinal cord.

52. A is correct.

White matter consists of bundles of myelinated nerve fibers.

Myelin is a white fatty substance enclosing nerve fibers and increasing the transmission speed of neurons.

53. D is correct.

Blood vessels can be directly visualized only during an examination of the eyes, specifically in the retina.

The condition of blood vessels indicates the health of small blood vessels in the nervous system (including signs of *atherosclerosis* or *diabetic vascular disease* that can affect peripheral nerves and the brain).

54. A is correct.

Broca's area is in the frontal lobe of the brain (in the dominant hemisphere – usually the left) and is responsible for speech production.

Damage to Broca's area is commonly associated with speech where the content of the information is correct, but *sentence structure* and *fluidity* are impaired.

55. E is correct.

Organ of Corti and the *semicircular canals* contain hair cells with micro cilia (i.e., small hair) projecting from the apical surface of the cell into the surrounding fluid.

Movement of fluid around the hair cells in the *organ of Corti detects sound*.

Fluid movement around the hair cells in the *semicircular canals* detects changes in body orientation.

Skin hair is different and is formed by keratinized dead epithelial cells.

56. C is correct.

Prefrontal cortex lies at the front of the brain and is responsible for cognitive behavior, personality, decision making, and social behavior.

Limbic association area helps form memories and guides emotional responses.

Primary somatosensory cortex processes sensations such as touch, pain, and temperature.

Posterior association area is where visual, auditory, and somatosensory association areas meet, giving spatial awareness.

Circulatory System – Detailed Explanations

1. B is correct.

*Hemocytoblast cell*s are precursors for the elements of blood.

2. D is correct.

Hemoglobin does exhibit positive, *cooperative binding* (i.e., sigmoid shape O_2 binding curve).

When O_2 binds to the first of four hemoglobin subunits, this initial binding of O_2 changes the shape of Hb and increases the affinity of the three remaining subunits for O_2.

Conversely, as the first O_2 molecule is unloaded, the other O_2 molecules dissociate more easily.

Cooperative binding is necessary for hemoglobin transport of O_2 to the tissues.

Hemoglobin reversibly binds carbon dioxide (CO_2) and transports it to the lungs.

In the lung alveoli, CO_2 dissociates from the hemoglobin and is expired (i.e., exhaled) by the body.

B: *fetal hemoglobin* acquires O_2 from maternal circulation, so fetal hemoglobin has a higher O_2 affinity than adult hemoglobin.

C: *CO poisoning* occurs because this odorless gas has a high hemoglobin affinity and binds tightly, preventing oxygen from binding to the occupied site on hemoglobin.

E: *hemoglobin* reversibly binds carbon dioxide (CO_2) and transports it to the lungs.

In the alveoli of the lungs, CO_2 dissociates from the hemoglobin and is expired (i.e., exhaled) by the body.

3. E is correct.

Arteriole end of the capillary bed has *hydrostatic pressure* (from fluid volume) of 30-36 mmHg, while the opposing *osmotic pressure* (from solute concentration) is 25-27 mmHg.

Hydrostatic pressure forces fluid out of capillaries and into the interstitial space.

Venule end of capillary bed has osmotic pressure greater than hydrostatic pressure, which drops to 12-15 mmHg.

Osmotic pressure draws fluid into the capillaries from the interstitial space and aids liquid returning to the heart.

Most fluid (blood) is forced from the capillaries to the interstitial space at the arteriole end (via *hydrostatic pressure*). The capillaries reabsorb it at the venule end (via osmotic pressure).

4. B is correct.

pH 2 liquid has a greater $[H^+]$ than a pH 7 liquid.

5. A is correct.

Blood volume depends on:

   1) amounts of water and sodium ingested

   2) excreted in the urine, gastrointestinal tract, lungs, and skin

These amounts are highly variable, and it is the function of the kidneys to maintain blood volume within a normal range (i.e., homeostasis) by excreting water and sodium into the urine.

When there is an excess of ingested water and sodium, the kidneys respond by excreting more water and sodium in the urine.

6. A is correct.

O_2 binding to hemoglobin exhibits positive cooperativity with a Hill coefficient greater than 1.

Positive cooperativity is due to the first (of four) O_2 binding weakly to hemoglobin; the binding of the first O_2 increases the affinity of the hemoglobin for additional O_2 binding. Binding curve for cooperativity has a *sigmoid shape*.

Negative cooperativity is when ligand binding to the first site decreases the affinity for additional ligands.

7. E is correct.

Veins are thin-walled inelastic vessels that usually transport *deoxygenated blood* (the pulmonary vein is the exception) *toward* the heart.

Veins do not have a strong pulse because of the fluid exchange in the capillaries.

Because of their low pressure, blood flow in veins depends on compression by skeletal muscles rather than on the elastic, smooth muscles that line the arteries.

Arteries transport blood *away* from the heart and are thick-walled, muscular elastic circulatory vessels.

Blood in the arteries is usually *oxygenated*.

Pulmonary arteries are the *exception,* whereby deoxygenated blood from the heart, returning from the body, is pumped to the lungs.

Mammals have a *four-chambered heart.*

Lymphatic system is an open circulatory system that transports excess interstitial fluid (lymph) to the cardiovascular system and maintains constant fluid levels.

Lymph enters the bloodstream at the *thoracic duct*, connecting to the *superior vena cava.*

8. D is correct.

Blood enters the heart through the *inferior and superior vena cava (see diagram below).*

Right atrium receives the oxygen-poor blood and contracts, bringing blood to the right ventricle. When the ventricle contracts, blood enters the pulmonary artery and lungs, where it is oxygenated

continued...

Pulmonary vein empties blood into the left atrium, which flows into the left ventricle.

Finally, the ventricle contracts, and blood leaves through the aortic valve into the aorta.

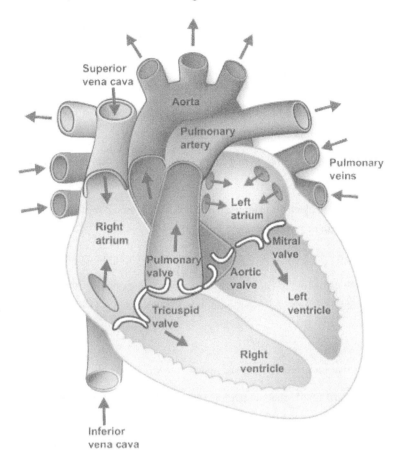

9. C is correct.

Blood has three main functions: transport, protection, and regulation.

Blood transports:

> **Gases** (oxygen and carbon dioxide) between the lungs and tissues
>
> **Nutrients** from the digestive tract and storage sites to the cells
>
> **Waste products** removal by the liver and kidneys
>
> **Hormones** secreted from glands to their target cells

Blood protects by:

> **Leukocytes** (i.e., white blood cells) destroy invading microorganisms and cancer cells
>
> **Antibodies** and other proteins destroy pathogenic substances
>
> **Platelet factors** initiate blood clotting and minimize blood loss

continued...

Blood regulates:

- pH by interacting with acids and bases

- Water balance by transferring water to and from tissues

10. B is correct.

Myoglobin accepts O_2 from hemoglobin because myoglobin has a higher affinity for O_2 than hemoglobin.

Myoglobin releases O_2 into the *cytochrome c oxidase* system because cytochrome c oxidase has a higher affinity for O_2 than myoglobin or hemoglobin.

Cytochrome c oxidase is the last enzyme in the respiratory electron transport chain (ETC) in the mitochondrial (or bacterial) *inner membrane*.

Cytochrome c oxidase receives an electron from each of four cytochrome c molecules and transfers them to one O_2 molecule, converting molecular O_2 into two molecules of H_2O.

In the process, cytochrome c oxidase binds four protons from the inner aqueous phase to make H_2O.

Cytochrome c oxidase translocates four H^+ across the membrane to establish a transmembrane difference of proton electrochemical potential that the ATP synthase uses to synthesize ATP via *oxidative phosphorylation*.

11. E is correct.

Platelets are cell fragments that lack nuclei and participate in *clot formation*.

Platelets (i.e., thrombocytes) are small, disk-shaped clear cell fragments (i.e., do not have a nucleus) 2–3 μm in diameter, derived from the fragmentation of precursor megakaryocytes.

Platelet lifespan is 5 to 9 days. Platelets are a natural source of growth factors circulating in blood and participate in hemostasis (formation of blood clots to stop bleeding).

Low platelet count may result in excessive bleeding.

High platelet count may result in the formation of blood clots (thrombosis), which may obstruct blood vessels and result in stroke, myocardial infarction, pulmonary embolism, or the blockage of blood vessels, for example, in the extremities of the arms or legs.

Erythrocytes (i.e., red blood cells) are the oxygen-carrying components of blood and contain hemoglobin that binds up to four molecules of oxygen.

Macrophages perform phagocytosis of foreign particles and bacteria by engulfing them, digesting the material, and presenting the fragments on their cell surface.

T cells lyse virally infected cells or secrete proteins stimulating B or other types of T cells.

12. A is correct.

AB blood has neither anti-A nor anti-B antibodies, so there is no agglutination reaction when blood is transfused into an AB person.

13. E is correct.

Blood does not carry cells for injury repair. However, blood is essential for wound healing, and special blood cells called *platelets* create clots to stop the bleeding.

Macrophages are blood cells that function as wound protectors by fighting infection and assisting in the repair process by producing chemical messengers (i.e., growth factors) to help repair the wound.

Oxygen-rich red blood cells help build new tissue.

Chemical signals prompt cells to create collagen scaffolding, a scar that starts red and dulls eventually.

14. C is correct.

Myoglobin is a single polypeptide chain with a tertiary (3°) protein structure.

Primary (1°) structure refers to the polypeptide's linear sequence of amino acids.

Secondary (2°) protein structure has alpha (α) helixes and beta (β) sheets.

Quaternary (4°) structure refers to a protein consisting of 2 or more peptide chains.

Hemoglobin is the classic example of a 4° structure protein with 2 α and 2 β chains.

E: highest level of protein structure organization is quaternary (4°). 5° does not exist.

15. C is correct.

CO (carbon monoxide), like O_2, binds to hemoglobin more strongly than O_2, and binding is almost irreversible.

CO forms from incomplete fuel (i.e., hydrocarbons) combustion by faulty space heaters or barbecue grills.

A: CO is not irritating, as it is odorless and colorless.

B: CO does not affect the cytochrome chain.

D: CO does not form complexes in blood.

E: CO does not affect the Na^+/K^+ pump.

16. B is correct.

Arterial hydrostatic pressure (i.e., blood pressure) is higher than hydrostatic at the venous side of capillaries.

Hydrostatic pressure drives fluids *out* of the blood and into the interstitial tissues on the arterial side.

Osmotic pressure is greater in plasma than in interstitial fluid because plasma has a much higher protein concentration (i.e., albumin).

At the venule end, osmotic pressure draws fluids *into* the blood from the interstitial tissues because osmotic pressure is higher than the hydrostatic pressure at the venule.

17. A is correct.

Erythroblast is a red blood cell that retains a cell nucleus and is the immediate precursor of an erythrocyte.

18. B is correct.

Severe combined immunodeficiency (SCID) causes abnormalities in T and B-cells.

B-cells are produced in the *bone marrow*.

T-cells are produced in the *bone marrow* and *mature in the thymus*.

Severe combined immunodeficiency (SCID) is a genetic disorder characterized by the absence of functional T-lymphocytes.

SCID results in an inadequate antibody response due to direct involvement with B lymphocytes or improper B lymphocyte activation due to non-functional T-helper cells.

Consequently, B and T cells are impaired due to a genetic defect.

19. D is correct.

Capillaries have higher hydrostatic pressure at the arteriole and lower hydrostatic pressure at the venule end.

As blood flows from arterioles to capillaries, blood pressure gradually drops due to friction between the blood and the walls of the vessels and the increase in cross-sectional areas provided by numerous capillary beds.

Blood plasma in the capillaries has a *higher osmotic pressure* than the pressure in the interstitial fluid.

Higher osmotic pressure results from *greater number of dissolved solutes* in blood plasma of the capillaries.

Hydrostatic pressure is defined as the force per area that blood exerts on the walls of blood vessels.

The pumping force of the heart through blood vessels creates *hydrostatic pressure*.

20. D is correct.

pH is a log scale:

pH change of 1 unit (e.g., pH 4 *vs.* 5) = 10× difference

pH difference of 2 units (e.g., pH 3 *vs.* 5): $10 \times 10 = 100×$ difference

pH difference of 3 units (e.g., pH 2 *vs.* 5): $10 \times 10 \times 10 = 1,000×$ difference

21. B is correct.

Albumin is the main protein produced in the liver and functions to maintain *osmotic pressure*.

Osmotic pressure is exerted in blood vessels plasma by *pulling water* into the circulatory system.

22. B is correct.

Angiotensin is a peptide hormone derived from the precursor angiotensinogen produced in the liver, which causes vasoconstriction and subsequent increase in blood pressure.

Renin-angiotensin system is a primary target for drugs that lower blood pressure.

continued...

Kidneys secrete renin when blood volume is low, which cleaves angiotensinogen into angiotensin I, which is converted into angiotensin II by the angiotensin-converting enzyme (ACE).

Angiotensin II stimulates the release of aldosterone from the adrenal cortex.

Aldosterone promotes sodium retention in the distal nephron (in the kidney), which increases blood pressure.

Parathyroid hormone (PTH) increases plasma $[Ca^{2+}]$.

Calcitonin (a hormone produced by the thyroid gland) acts to decrease $[Ca^{2+}]$.

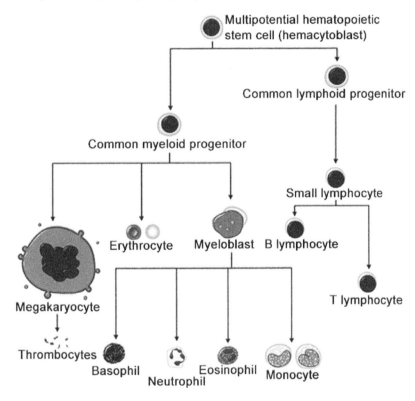

Derivation of principal blood cells (overview for illustrative purposes)

23. C is correct.

Hematopoiesis (i.e., the formation of blood cellular components) occurs in the *bone marrow* in adults.

In the fetus, hematopoiesis occurs in the *fetal liver*.

Spleen is a *reservoir* for red blood cells and *filters* the blood.

Erythrocytes are produced in the bone marrow to replace erythrocytes during their 120-day lifespan.

Erythrocytes (mature red blood cells) are not nucleated to create more space for hemoglobin.

Blood platelets are crucial for the *clotting* of blood.

Leukocytes (i.e., white blood cells), such as macrophages and neutrophils, engulf foreign matter.

Neutrophils are the most abundant white blood cells and account for 50-70% of white blood cells.

E: erythrocytes are produced in the bone marrow to replace erythrocytes during their 120-day lifespan.

24. C is correct.

Blood returns to the heart via the *inferior and superior vena cava* (i.e., hollow veins).

Blood enters the *right atrium* of the heart with the following flow:

superior/inferior vena cava → right atrium → right ventricle → pulmonary artery

→ lungs → pulmonary vein

25. A is correct.

Monocytes are white blood cells with fine granules, making the structures invisible under a light microscope.

26. E is correct.

Surfactants are lipid-based compounds that lower surface tension and form micelles.

Micelle formation requires numerous hydrophobic interactions and minimizes exposure to hydrophilic surfaces.

Micelles are necessary to absorb lipids (i.e., dietary fats) by the small intestine. A lack of micelle formation results in a deficiency of lipid-soluble vitamins (e.g., A, D, E, and K).

27. D is correct.

Blood from the *left ventricle* enters the *aorta* and flows to all body areas (i.e., systemic circulation) *except* the lungs (i.e., pulmonary circulation).

Examples of systemic circulation include blood in the brachiocephalic artery (travels to the head and the shoulders) and blood in the renal artery (travels to the kidney to be filtered).

Superior/inferior vena cava → right atrium → right ventricle → pulmonary artery
(*pulmonary circulation*) → lungs → pulmonary vein → left atrium → left ventricle
→ aorta (*systemic circulation*) → superior/inferior vena cava.

Systemic circulation transports blood from arteries into arterioles, then capillaries, where nutrients, waste, and energy are exchanged.

Blood enters venules, collects in veins, is transported to the superior and inferior venae cavae, enters the right atrium, and flows into the right ventricle.

Pulmonary circulation transports blood to the lungs via the pulmonary artery, where capillary beds around the alveoli exchange gas (O_2 into the blood and CO_2 from the blood).

Pulmonary veins return blood to the left atrium to start systemic circulation.

28. A is correct.

O blood contains neither A nor B antigens, so there is no agglutination reaction when O-type blood is infused.

29. D is correct.

Leukocytes are nucleated.

30. B is correct.

Surfactants are lipid-based compounds that lower the surface tension (or interfacial tension) between two liquids or between a liquid and a solid.

Surfactants may function as detergents, emulsifiers, and foaming agents.

Pulmonary surfactants are secreted by type II cells of the lung alveolar surface in mammals to form a layer over the alveolar surface, which reduces alveolar collapse by decreasing surface tension within the alveolar surface.

31. A is correct.

Alveoli are thin air sacs and sites of gas (e.g., O_2 and CO_2) exchange via *passive diffusion* in the lungs between the air and blood.

Pleura is the outer lining of the lungs filled with pleural fluid that lubricates the lungs.

Bronchi are the two main branches of the air intake pathway, with one bronchus for each lung.

Bronchioles are smaller subdivisions of the bronchi.

Trachea (i.e., windpipe) is the region of the air intake pathway between the glottis and the bronchi.

32. E is correct.

Right atrium is the upper chamber of the right side of the heart.

Blood returns to the right atrium by the superior, inferior vena cava deoxygenated (low in O_2) and passes into the right ventricle to be pumped through the pulmonary artery to the lungs O_2 and removed CO_2.

Left atrium receives oxygenated blood from the lungs through pulmonary vein.

Blood is passed into the muscular left ventricle to be pumped through the aorta to the organs.

Right ventricle pumps blood through the pulmonary arteries to the lungs during *pulmonary circulation*.

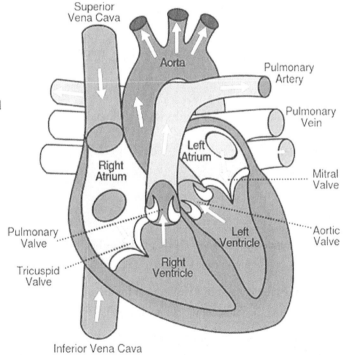

Left ventricle pumps blood through the aorta to the body for *systemic circulation*.

If blood mixes between the ventricles, some blood in the right ventricle (deoxygenated) is mixed with blood in the left ventricle (oxygenated) for systemic circulation. This mixing lowers the O_2 supplied to the tissues.

33. A is correct.

Blood plasma is the liquid part of blood, consisting primarily of water (up to 95%).

Blood plasma holds blood cells in suspension, acting as the extracellular matrix.

34. B is correct.

Antibodies are proteins; therefore, plasma cells have a well-developed rough endoplasmic reticulum.

C: *smooth ER* is responsible for steroid synthesis (e.g., Leydig cells for testosterone synthesis).

D: *mitochondria* function for ATP synthesis via the Krebs cycle and the electron transport chain.

35. A is correct.

Aorta carries oxygenated blood from the heart through systemic (i.e., body) circulation and (like the pulmonary vein) has the greatest partial pressure of O_2.

B: *coronary veins* carry deoxygenated blood to the right side of the heart.

C: *superior vena cava* carries deoxygenated blood from the upper regions to the heart.

D: *pulmonary arteries* carry deoxygenated blood from the heart toward the lungs.

Pulmonary artery is the only artery in adults carrying *deoxygenated* blood.

E: *inferior vena cava* carries deoxygenated blood from the lower regions into the right atrium of the heart.

36. C is correct.

pH of cellular fluids (and blood fluids) is approximately 7. The typical reported value is 7.4.

37. C is correct.

Sequence for forming thromboplastin: prothrombin → thrombin; fibrinogen → fibrin; clot retraction.

38. E is correct.

Major histocompatibility complex (MHC) is a set of cell surface molecules that mediate interactions of *leukocytes* (i.e., white blood cells), immune cells with other cells, and leukocytes.

MHC determines the compatibility of donors for an organ transplant and susceptibility to an autoimmune disease (e.g., type I diabetes, lupus, celiac disease).

Protein molecules—either the host's phenotype or other biologic entities—are continually synthesized and degraded in a cell.

MHC molecules display a protein molecular fraction (i.e., epitope) on the cell surface.

The presented antigen (i.e., an epitope from the degraded protein) can be *self* or *nonself*.

MHC class II can be conditionally expressed by all cell types but occurs typically on *antigen-presenting cells* (APC): macrophages, B cells, and especially dendritic cells (DCs).

continued…

APC uptakes an antigen, processes it, and returns a molecular fraction (i.e., an epitope) to the APC's surface.

Dendritic cells are in tissues in contact with the external environment, such as the skin (i.e., *Langerhans cell*) or the inner lining of the nose, lungs, stomach, and intestines.

Dendritic cells are also in an immature state in the blood. Once activated, they migrate to the *lymph nodes* to interact with T and B cells to initiate an adaptive immune response.

C: *erythrocytes* are not part of the immune system.

D: *macrophages* are part of innate immunity and destroy tissue invaders in a non-specific manner.

39. C is correct.

Deoxygenated blood returns from the systemic circulation and drains into the right atrium from the inferior and superior vena cava.

Blood is pumped through the *tricuspid valve* from the right atrium into the right ventricle, which pumps blood to the lungs via the pulmonary arteries.

CO_2 (carbon dioxide from cellular respiration) is exchanged for O_2 in the lungs' alveoli.

Oxygenated blood is returned to the left atrium via the pulmonary veins.

Blood is pumped through the *mitral valve* into the left ventricle from the left atrium, which ejects it into the aorta for systemic circulation.

A tracer substance injected into the *superior vena cava* would take the longest to reach the left ventricle.

A: *left atrium* receives oxygenated blood via the pulmonary veins.

B: blood with the tracer travels from the right ventricle to the lungs via the pulmonary arteries and returns through the pulmonary veins to the left atrium.

D: blood with the tracer enters the right atrium from the systemic circulation and passes through the tricuspid valve as it is pumped into the right ventricle

E: *tricuspid valve* separates the right atrium from the right ventricle

Tricuspid valve prevents the backflow of blood into the right atrium when the right ventricle contracts, forcing blood into the pulmonary artery.

40. D is correct.

Semi-lunar valves prevent the backflow of blood as it leaves the heart via the aorta (systemic circulation) and pulmonary arteries (pulmonary circulation) because the ventricles have negative pressure once they start to relax before receiving more blood from the atria.

41. C is correct.

Kidneys produce the *erythropoietin (EPO) hormone*, which promotes formation of red blood cells in bone marrow in response to *low oxygen levels*.

42. B is correct.

Atrioventricular (AV) node is at the junction between the atria and ventricles and functions to delay the conduction impulse to the ventricles for a fraction of a second.

Excitation waves spread from the sinoatrial (SA) node through the atria along specialized conduction channels, which activates the AV node, which delays conduction impulses by approximately 0.12s.

Delay in cardiac pulse ensures that *atria eject their blood* into the ventricles before they contract.

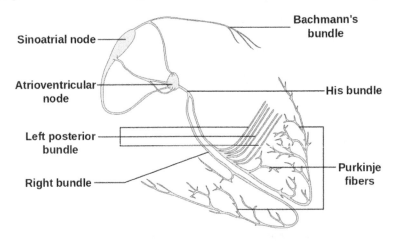

43. D is correct.

Mitral valve is between the left atrium and the left ventricle and prevents the backflow of blood into the left atrium during the left ventricle contraction.

A patient with mitral valve stenosis has impeded blood flow from the left atrium into the left ventricle.

Mitral valve stenosis increases blood volume in the left atrium and reduces the net movement of blood from the left atrium into left ventricle, resulting in *increased left atrial pressure* and *decreased left ventricular pressure*.

A: *right atrium* receives deoxygenated blood by venous circulation and is too far removed for the circulatory process to be affected by mitral valve stenosis.

B: *left ventricle* ejects blood into the aorta as it begins systemic circulation.

Volume/pressure in the left ventricle is reduced due to impeded flow from the left atrium; the patient experiences *decreased pressure* in the *aorta*.

44. C is correct.

pH scale ranges from 1 to 14, with 7 being a neutral pH. pH change of 1 unit changes the ratio by 10 times.

45. E is correct.

Hemorrhage is a loss of blood from the circulatory system.

Hemorrhages can be external (when blood is lost to the outside through a wound or a natural opening) or internal (when blood escapes from blood vessels into other structures).

Moderate blood loss decreases cardiac output (volume of blood pumped by the heart each minute).

---

46. C is correct.

Cardiac conduction pathway begins with the SA node in the right atrium.

Conduction signal travels to the *AV node* between the atria and ventricles before it moves down the bundle of His, which splits into the right/left Purkinje fibers.

Purkinje fibers spread the conduction signal to the ventricles, which contract simultaneously to eject blood.

Blood from the right ventricle enters the pulmonary artery, while blood from the left ventricle enters the aorta.

SA node → AV node → bundle of His → Purkinje fibers

47. B is correct.

Blood in the left ventricle has just returned via the pulmonary vein from the lungs, where it was oxygenated.

Pulmonary vein is the only vein in the adult that carries oxygenated blood.

A: *right atrium* receives blood via the inferior and superior venae cavae returning from systemic circulation.

Blood returning from systemic circulation has low O_2 content when transported to the lungs.

C: *pulmonary artery blood* is pumped to the lungs to be oxygenated and is the least oxygenated blood.

D: *lymph vessels* (e.g., thoracic duct) return lymphatic fluid to venous circulation.

Lymph fluid has an exceptionally low O_2 partial pressure.

E: *superior vena cava* returns deoxygenated blood to the heart from the upper regions.

48. C is correct.

When a swimmer holds their breath, the rising CO_2 blood gases change first and create the urge to breathe.

Chemoreceptors are in the *medulla oblongata*, *carotid arteries*, and the *aorta*.

Chemoreceptors detect and signal the respiratory centers in the medulla to modify the breathing rate when the partial pressure of the respiratory gases is too low or high.

High partial pressure of blood CO_2 causes an *increased breathing rate*.

Chemoreceptors are most responsive to changes in $[CO_2]$ and $[H^+]$, while only extreme changes in $[O_2]$ are relayed to the medulla oblongata.

$[H^+]$ of blood is proportional to the partial pressure of $[CO_2]$.

In erythrocytes, CO_2 combines with H_2O to form H_2CO_3, dissociating into HCO_3^- and H^+.

Increase in $[H^+]$ decreases the pH of the blood.

When chemoreceptors detect an increase in partial pressure of CO_2 or $[H^+]$, the breathing rate increases.

High partial pressure of O_2 in the blood triggers a decrease (not increase) in the breathing rate.

49. B is correct.

Left ventricular wall of the heart is *thick* (i.e., more cardiac muscle) than the right wall because it pumps blood with greater pressure to distribute it in the systemic circulation.

50. E is correct.

Availability of O_2 needed to sustain mental and physical alertness decreases with altitude.

A person at *high altitudes acclimates* to these environmental conditions (i.e., lower partial O_2 concentrations).

O_2 levels decrease as air density (i.e., the amount of O_2 per given volume) drops with increasing altitude.

Dehydration results from high rates of H_2O vapor loss from the lungs, contributing to altitude sickness.

A person at a high altitude needs increased blood flow to deliver more blood to the tissues because the blood carries less O_2.

2,3-BPG is an allosteric effector present in human red blood cells. It interacts with deoxygenated hemoglobin β subunits by decreasing their affinity for O_2, so it allosterically promotes the release of the remaining O_2 molecules bound to hemoglobin, thus enhancing the ability of RBCs to release O_2 near tissues needing O_2 most.

51. C is correct.

Blood from the pulmonary artery is pumped to the lungs to be oxygenated and the least oxygenated blood.

A: *lymph vessels* (e.g., thoracic duct) return lymphatic fluid to the venous circulation.

Lymph fluid has a very low O_2 partial pressure.

B: *left ventricle blood* has just returned via the pulmonary vein from the lungs, where it was oxygenated.

Pulmonary vein is the only vein in the adult that carries oxygenated blood.

D: *inferior vena cava* returns deoxygenated blood to the right atrium from the lower regions of the body.

E: *right atrium* receives blood via the inferior and superior venae cavae returning from systemic circulation.

Blood returning from the body has low O_2 content as transported to the lungs.

52. C is correct.

Afferent arterioles supply blood to the kidneys at the glomerulus.

Efferent arterioles carry blood away from the glomerulus, containing blood filtered and exiting the glomerulus.

Proteins in the filtrate are a clinical indication of kidney abnormalities. Protein does not usually enter the kidney in the filtrate (fluid destined to become excreted as urine).

Loss of blood plasma into the kidney increases the protein concentration (relative to plasma).

D: *vasa recta* form a series of straight kidney capillaries in the medulla and are *parallel to the loop of Henle*.

Vasa recta branch from *efferent arterioles of juxtamedullary nephrons* (nephrons closest to the medulla), entering the medulla and surrounding the loop of Henle.

continued…

Each vasa recta has a *hairpin turn in the medulla* and carries blood at a very slow rate, crucial for supporting *countercurrent exchange* that maintains the concentration gradients established in the renal medulla.

Maintaining this concentration gradient in the renal medulla is one of the components responsible for the kidney's ability to produce concentrated urine.

NaCl and urea are *reabsorbed* into the blood in the *descending portion* of the vasa recta, while H_2O is secreted.

NaCl and urea are *secreted* into the interstitium, while H_2O is reabsorbed in *ascending portion* of the vasa recta.

53. B is correct.

Atrioventricular (AV) valves prevent the backflow of blood from the ventricles into the heart's atria.

Valves are anchored to the walls of the ventricles by *chordae tendineae*.

54. C is correct.

Perspiration is the secretion of water, salts, and urea from the sweat (i.e., sudoriferous) skin pores.

Sweat encounters the air, evaporates, and cools the skin.

Thus, perspiration is a thermoregulatory mechanism involved in heat dissipation, *not* heat conservation.

Eccrine sweat glands are distributed over the body, though their density varies from region to region.

Humans utilize eccrine sweat glands as a primary form of cooling.

Apocrine sweat glands are larger, have a different secretion mechanism, and are mostly limited to the axilla (i.e., armpits) in humans.

A: *constriction* of selective blood vessels at the skin's surface reroutes blood flow from the skin to deeper tissues, which minimizes the loss of body heat.

B: *shivering* is a thermoregulatory mechanism that conserves body heat by intensive, rhythmic, involuntary contraction of muscle tissue that increases internal heat production.

D: *piloerection* (i.e., *goosebumps*) is a reflex contraction of the small muscles at the base of skin hairs, which causes the hairs to stand erect, forming an insulating layer that minimizes the loss of body heat.

55. D is correct.

Platelets are small pieces of large *megakaryocyte cells*.

When a wound occurs, platelets are activated to stick to the edge of the wound and release their contents that stimulate the clotting reaction.

Platelets release several growth factors, including *platelet-derived growth factor* (PDGF), a potent chemotactic agent (direct movement from chemical stimuli), and *TGF beta*, which stimulates extracellular matrix deposits.

Both growth factors have a significant role in repairing and regenerating connective tissues.

A: *leukocytes* (i.e., white blood cells) are immune system cells defending against infectious diseases.

continued…

Leukocytes have common traits, but each is distinct in form and function.

The name "*white blood cell*" derives from the physical appearance of a blood sample after centrifugation.

White cells are in the *buffy coat* (a thin, typically white layer of nucleated cells between the sedimented red blood cells and blood plasma).

Leukocytes are produced and derived from hematopoietic stem cells in the bone marrow.

Leukocytes function for three to four days throughout the body, including the blood and lymphatic system.

A significant distinction is the presence or absence of granules (i.e., granulocytes or agranulocytes).

Granulocytes (or *polymorphonuclear leukocytes*) are characterized by staining cytoplasmic granules.

These granules (*lysozymes*) are membrane-bound enzymes that act primarily to digest endocytosed particles.

According to their staining properties, there are *three granulocytes*: *neutrophils, basophils,* and *eosinophils.*

Agranulocytes (*mononuclear leukocytes*) are characterized by the *absence* of granules in their cytoplasm.

Agranulocytes include *lymphocytes, monocytes,* and *macrophages.*

B: *erythrocytes* (*red blood cells*) are the typical blood cell and the principal means of delivering oxygen (O_2).

C: *lymphocytes* are a white blood cell, a landmark of the adaptive immune system.

Lymphocytes can be categorized into large or small lymphocytes.

Large granular lymphocytes include *natural killer cells* (NK cells), while *small lymphocytes* are T and B cells.

56. A is correct.

Hepatic portal system directs blood from parts of the gastrointestinal tract to the liver.

Inferior vena cava is a large vein that carries *deoxygenated blood* into the heart.

57. E is correct.

Increased pulmonary vascular resistance leads to right-to-left circulation through the foramen ovale and the ductus arteriosus – as in newborns with persistent fetal circulation.

Foramen ovale is a fetal opening connecting the right and left atrium.

Ductus arteriosus is a fetal vessel that allows blood to flow directly from the pulmonary artery to the aorta.

Due to pressure changes, the foramen ovale and the ductus arteriosus normally close at birth.

In newborns with persistent fetal circulation, the *foramen ovale* and *ductus arteriosus* remain open, which causes blood to flow from the *right atrium into the left atrium* and from the *pulmonary artery into the aorta.*

Lymphatic and Immune Systems – Detailed Explanations

1. B is correct.

Thymus is a specialized organ of the adaptive immune system. It is different from other organs (e.g., heart, liver, kidney) because the thymus is at its *largest size during childhood*.

Thymus is the largest and most active during the neonatal and pre-adolescent periods. It provides an inductive environment for the development of T lymphocytes from hematopoietic progenitor cells.

Thymus *atrophies* in the early teens and *thymic stroma* (i.e., connective tissue cells of the organ) is replaced mainly by *adipose* (fat) tissue.

Thymus is the only lymphoid organ that does not *directly* fight antigens.

It is a maturation site for T lymphocyte precursors because they must be isolated from foreign antigens to prevent premature activation.

Cortex and medulla have distinct roles in the development of T-cells.

Histologically, thymus lobes divide into a central medulla and peripheral cortex, surrounded by outer capsule.

Thymus cells are *stromal* and *hematopoietic origin cells* (derived from bone marrow hematopoietic stem cells).

Developing T-cells are *thymocytes*.

Stromal cells include thymic cortical epithelial cells, thymic medullary epithelial cells, and dendritic cells.

2. E is correct.

Antigens are foreign substances that elicit an immune response.

Erythrocytes (red blood cells) deliver O_2 to cells and *not* part of the immune system or an indicator of infection.

A: *plasma cells* are mature B-cells that secrete antibodies.

B: B cells develop in the bone marrow and are part of the humoral immune response.

C: *T-cells* develop in the bone marrow and mature in the thymus to produce cell-mediated immunity.

D: *monocytes* (like macrophages) are phagocytic cells and are part of innate (i.e., non-specific) immunity.

3. B is correct.

Smooth muscle contraction in the lymph capillary walls is *not* involved in lymph transport.

4. D is correct.

Gamma globulins are Y-shaped protein antibodies known as *immunoglobulins* (Ig).

Gamma globulins are produced by B cells and used by the immune system to identify and neutralize foreign objects, such as bacteria and viruses.

Antibodies are secreted by *white blood cells* (i.e., *plasma cells*) and recognize a unique part (i.e., *epitope*) of the foreign target (i.e., *antigen*).

5. B is correct.

Small intestine absorbs nutrients and has a *large surface area* due to the villi and microvilli facing the lumen of the gastrointestinal tract.

6. E is correct.

Thymus has levels of high activity during neonatal development and pre-adolescence.

7. C is correct.

Humoral immunity is *antibody-mediated* because it is regulated by macromolecules (as opposed to cell-mediated immunity) in extracellular fluids (e.g., secreted antibodies, complement proteins, and specific antimicrobial peptides).

Humoral immunity is named because it involves substances in the humor (i.e., body fluids).

Immune system divides into:

   primitive *innate immune* and

   adaptive immune systems (i.e., acquired), each with humoral and cellular components (e.g., phagocytes, antigen-specific cytotoxic T-lymphocytes, and cytokines).

Immunoglobulins (Ig) are glycoproteins that function as antibodies.

Antibodies and *immunoglobulins* are used interchangeably.

Antibodies are synthesized and secreted by plasma cells derived from the immune system's B cells.

Antibodies are large Y-shaped globular proteins in the blood, tissue fluids, and many secretions.

In mammals, five types of antibodies:

   IgA, IgD, IgE, IgG, and IgM

Each immunoglobulin class differs in biological properties and evolved to target specific antigens.

Acquired immune system uses an antibody to identify and neutralize foreign objects (e.g., bacteria, viruses).

Antibodies recognize a specific antigen.

By binding, antibodies can cause agglutination and precipitation of antibody-antigen products, prime for phagocytosis by macrophages and other cells, block viral receptors, and stimulate other immune responses (i.e., complement pathways).

Cytotoxic T cells (or cytotoxic T lymphocytes, T-killer cells, cytolytic T cells, CD8, or killer T cells) function in *cell-mediated immunity*.

Cytotoxic T cells are white blood cells that destroy cancer cells, virally infected cells, or damaged cells.

Most cytotoxic T cells express *T-cell receptors* (TCR) that recognize specific antigen molecules capable of stimulating an immune response often produced by viruses or cancer cells.

8. D is correct.

Lymphatic capillaries are more permeable than blood capillaries.

9. C is correct.

Antibodies are produced in response to antigens (e.g., viral coat proteins, bacterial cell walls) detected by T cells.

T cells stimulate B cells to become plasma cells and secrete antibodies.

B cells mature into *memory cells* (antibody-producing cells) during immune responses, which remain dormant in interstitial fluid and lymphatics until the same antigens are detected and provide a rapid humoral response.

Neurons are not involved in the immune response.

T cells are the immune response organizers and become:

cytotoxic cells (i.e., kill invading cells), helper T cells (i.e., recruit other T and B cells), and

suppressor T cells (i.e., inactivate the immune response when the antigen has been cleared).

Macrophages are phagocytic cells that engulf and digest bacterial cells and foreign material.

Natural killer cells are immune system cells that destroy invading cells.

10. D is correct.

Plasma cells are white blood cells that secrete antibodies that target and bind to antigens (foreign substances).

11. E is correct.

Phagocytosis and *pinocytosis* are movements *into* the cell and are forms of endocytosis.

Phagocytosis is when foreign particles invade the body or minute food particles are engulfed and broken down.

Cell membranes of phagocytes *invaginate to capture particles* and form a *vacuole* with the enclosed material to join a lysosome containing enzymes that hydrolyze the enclosed material.

Pinocytosis is a similar process but describes the ingestion of liquid droplets.

Apoptosis is programmed cell death.

Exocytosis is the transport of membrane-enclosed material *out* of the cell.

Endocytosis is ATP-dependent transport of material into the cell.

12. D is correct.

Lymph leaves a lymph node through *efferent* lymphatic vessels.

13. C is correct.

Lymph flow increases (to a point) in *proportion* to the *increase in pressure* of the interstitial fluid.; determine whether interstitial fluid protein increases fluid pressure.

Proteins *move out* of the capillaries and into the interstitial space, increasing solute concentration.

Fluid flows out of capillaries and into the interstitial space, increasing interstitial fluid volume and fluid pressure.

A: *fluid movement* from interstitial spaces into capillaries *decreases interstitial fluid pressure*, but an increase of proteins in the interstitial causes fluid movement out of the capillaries.

D: *increasing interstitial fluid pressure* increases lymph flow (until point 0 – see graph).

14. B is correct.

Phagocytes function to eliminate foreign invaders (e.g., particles, microorganisms, dying cells) by digestion.

Macrophages and *neutrophils* are essential in the inflammatory response by releasing proteins and other substances that control infection and damage the host tissue.

15. A is correct.

Lymph transport depends on the movement of adjacent tissues, such as skeletal muscles.

16. A is correct.

Monocytes and *macrophages* are non-specific immune system cells that phagocyte foreign matter.

Platelets are produced by bone marrow and are part of the clotting cascade.

T-cells are part of the cell-mediated immune response and do not phagocytize other cells.

B-cells are part of adaptive immunity, secreting antibodies and do not phagocytize other cells.

17. D is correct.

B cells (or B lymphocytes) are a type of lymphocyte that matures in the bone marrow.

B lymphocytes participate in the humoral immunity of the adaptive immune system.

Activated B cells undergo a two-step differentiation process producing short-lived plasmablasts (for immediate immune response) and long-lived *plasma cells* and *memory B cells* (for persistent protection).

Plasma cells release into blood and lymph antibody molecules closely modeled after the receptors of the precursor B cell.

When released, antibodies bind to the target antigen (i.e., foreign substance) and initiate destruction.

18. E is correct.

Erythroblastosis fetalis (or Rh incompatibility) occurs when a Rh⁺ fetus develops within an Rh⁻ mother and requires a Rh⁺ father.

Subsequent children between an Rh⁻ mother and a Rh⁺ father are affected because the first child sensitizes the mother to Rh protein and stimulates the production of antibodies to Rh⁺ antigens.

If exposed to the Rh⁺ antigens, the Rh– mother produces antibodies against the Rh proteins of the fetus.

Anti-Rh antibodies are present when the second Rh⁺ fetus develops.

Usually, maternal and fetal blood systems are separate, but incompatibility may occur late in the pregnancy because of the mixing of maternal and fetal blood.

19. B is correct.

Spleen function does *not* include forming crypts that trap bacteria.

20.   A is correct.

Bone marrow synthesizes B and T cell lymphocytes.

B cells mature in the bone marrow, while *T cells migrate to the thymus for maturation.*

T cells have three functions:

> 1) activating B-cells to respond to antigens,
>
> 2) stimulating the growth of phagocytic macrophages, and
>
> 3) destroying antigens (i.e., foreign invaders) and abnormal tissue (e.g., cancer).

Thymus is vital for immunity in children and adults.

E: erythrocytes develop in bone marrow and circulate for 120 days before macrophages recycle components.

21. D is correct.

Peyer's patches are lymphoid follicles named after the Swiss scientist Johann Conrad Peyer (1653-1712).

Peyer's patches are gut-associated lymphoid tissue, usually in the small intestine, mainly in the *distal jejunum* and *ileum*.

Peyer's patches are essential for the *immune response* within the gut.

Pathogenic microorganisms (or antigens) entering the gastrointestinal (GI) tract encounter *macrophages, dendritic cells, B-lymphocytes,* and T-*lymphocytes* in *Peyer's patches.*

22. A is correct.

Erythrocytes have antigens expressed on their cell surfaces and are classified by the type of antibody elicited.

Four major blood types are A, B, AB, and O.

Three alleles determine the four groups because alleles for A and B are *codominant*, while allele O is *recessive*.

> A alleles encode for A antigens on erythrocytes

> B alleles encode for B antigens

> O alleles do not encode for an antigen

For example, a person with

> type A blood has the genotype AA or AO

> type B blood is BB or BO

> type AB blood is AB, and type O blood is OO

The presence (or absence) of specific antibodies determines blood groups.

Blood serum does not contain antibodies to endogenous blood type antigens but produces antibodies to the other blood antigens.

For example, a patient with:

> type A blood has antibodies to B antigens

> type B blood has antibodies to A antigens

> type AB blood has neither anti-A nor anti-B antibodies since their red blood cells carry both antigens

Patients with type O blood have anti-A and anti-B antibodies; red blood cells with neither A nor B antigens.

Agglutination (i.e., clumping of blood) is when anti-A or anti-B antibodies react with antigens on blood cells.

Type A blood mixed with another blood type (except AB), antibodies from other blood types agglutinate.

Precipitation does not occur in the test tube that contains type AB blood.

23. D is correct.

Pancreas is *not* classified as a lymphatic structure.

24. D is correct.

Lymph capillaries are in digestive organs and the central nervous system (CNS).

25. B is correct.

Innate immune system responds to foreign antigens with white blood cells (i.e., granulocytes) and inflammation.

Granulocytes include *neutrophils*, *eosinophils*, and *basophils* because of granules in their cytoplasm.

Granulocytes are *polymorphonuclear cells* (PMNs) due to their distinctive lobed nuclei.

Neutrophil granules contain toxic substances that destroy or inhibit the growth of bacteria and fungi.

Like macrophages, neutrophils attack pathogens by activating a respiratory burst of *potent oxidizing agents* (e.g., hydrogen peroxide, free oxygen radicals, and hypochlorite).

Neutrophils are the *most abundant phagocyte* (i.e., 50 to 60% of the total circulating leukocytes) and are usually the first cells at the site of infection.

Innate immunity does *not* involve humoral immunity (B cell) or cell-mediated immunity (T cell).

26. A is correct.

Thymus is a lymphoid organ where T-cells and lymphocytes mature in the immune system with a *cortex* and *medulla*, which help the development of T-cells.

Thymus produces *thymosin*, which is the hormone responsible for creating T-cells.

27. E is correct.

Type A and B alleles are codominant to the O allele.

For example,

       genotype AA or AO has type A blood

       genotype BB or BO has type B blood

       genotype OO has type O blood

Type AB blood has the genotype AB and produces gametes with A or B alleles.

Type O blood has the genotype OO and produces gametes with O alleles.

Two genotypes for mating AB × OO are AO or BO (type A or B blood)

28. A is correct.

Islets of Langerhans are pancreatic regions containing endocrine cells (alpha, beta, delta, PP, and epsilon cells) separated from the surrounding pancreatic tissue by a thin fibrous connective tissue capsule.

Endocrine islets of Langerhans account for 1–2% of the pancreas and secrete insulin (to lower blood sugar), glucagon (to raise blood sugar), and somatostatin (to inhibit the release of insulin and glucagon).

continued...

Islets of Langerhans cells secrete hormones:

    Alpha cells produce *glucagon* (15–20% of total islet cells)

    Beta cells produce *insulin* (65–80%)

    Delta cells produce *somatostatin* (3–10%)

    Gamma cells produce *pancreatic polypeptides* (3–5%)

    Epsilon cells produce *ghrelin* – hunger-stimulating peptide (<1%)

Cortisol is a hormone released (via the bloodstream) by the *adrenal cortex* in response to stress.

Trypsin is an exocrine (via duct) pancreatic product necessary for protein digestion.

Pepsin is secreted by chief cells in the stomach to digest protein.

29. B is correct.

CD4$^+$ cells (or *T helper cells*) are white blood cells essential for human immunity.

CD4$^+$ cells are *helper cells* because they send signals to other immune cells, including CD8 killer cells that destroy the pathogen (e.g., bacteria or virus).

CD4$^+$ depletion (e.g., an untreated HIV infection or following immune suppression before an organ transplant) makes the body vulnerable to infections that would otherwise be innocuous.

CD4$^+$ cells are activators of both *cell-mediated* and *humoral* responses.

AIDS is a form of *severe combined immunodeficiency* (SCID).

Loss of an adequate CD4$^+$ response leads to the suppression of both humoral and cell-mediated responses.

Immune system divides into non-specific (*innate*) and adaptive (i.e., *acquired*) immunity.

    Innate immune system consists of physical barriers (e.g., skin and mucous membranes) and cells that non-specifically remove invaders (e.g., mast cells, macrophages, neutrophils).

    Adaptive immune system synthesizes cells directed against specific pathogens and can respond rapidly if a similar pathogen is encountered.

Innate system responds with the same mechanisms (and efficiency) to infection.

30. D is correct.

Lymphoid tissue functions include:

    1) lymphocyte and macrophage activities and

    2) storing and providing a proliferation site for lymphocytes.

31. B is correct.

Lymph nodes are linked by lymph vessels and contain phagocytic cells (*leukocytes*) that filter lymph and remove and destroy foreign particles (i.e., pathogens).

Lymphatic fluid absorbs fat and fat-soluble vitamins.

Liver breaks down hemoglobin and uses its components to produce bile salts.

Amino acids are not absorbed from the digestive tract by the lymphatic system or lymph nodes.

Glucagon is produced by the pancreas and increases glucose blood concentration.

O_2 is carried to the tissues for cellular respiration by the hemoglobin protein in red blood cells.

32. D is correct.

Antigens are foreign substances (e.g., bacteria) that induce an immune response, specifically the production of antibodies to destroy the antigen.

33. A is correct.

Lymph circulates throughout the lymphatic system formed when lymph capillaries collect interstitial fluid.

Lymph derives from interstitial fluid; its composition changes as blood and surrounding cells exchange substances with interstitial fluid.

Lymph *returns protein and excess interstitial fluid* to the circulation.

Lymph *collects bacteria* and brings them to *lymph nodes*, where they are degraded.

34. E is correct.

Vaccine effectiveness depends on the organism's immune system.

Plasma cells (a differentiated form of a B cell) secrete antibodies (i.e., immunoglobulin).

Acquired immunity consists of humoral (i.e., antibodies) and cell-mediated (i.e., T cells) responses.

Humoral response is mediated by B cells synthesized and matured in the bone marrow.

When stimulated by antigens, B cells differentiate into *memory B* and *plasma B cells* that secrete antibodies.

Cell-mediated immunity is T cells originating in bone marrow (as B cells do) but migrate and mature in thymus.

T-helper cells regulate the activity of other T and B cells.

Macrophages are *non-specific immune cells* released by bone marrow and participate in *phagocytosis* but do *not* synthesize or release immunoglobulin (antibodies).

Thymus is the structure where *T cells mature*.

T cells start as *hematopoietic precursors* and migrate from the bone marrow to the thymus and undergo maturation, ensuring that the cells react against antigens (i.e., *positive selection*) and do not react against antigens on body tissues (i.e., *negative selection*).

Once mature, T cells leave the thymus to perform their vital functions in the immune system.

35. D is correct.

Antibodies are composed of *heavy and light polypeptide chains* with a *constant domain* and *variable domain* of each heavy and light chain at the *amino-terminal end* of the monomer.

Two variable domains bind the *epitope* on specific antigens.

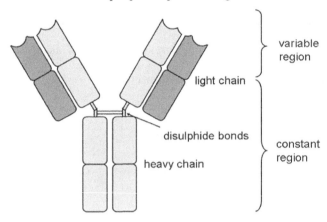

36. B is correct.

Small intestine is lined with villi (i.e., finger-like projections), increasing the absorptive surface area.

Villi are capillaries and lacteals within the core of the small intestine (i.e., lymphatic vessels).

Amino acids and glucose pass through the walls of the villi into the capillary.

Fatty acids and glycerol pass into the lacteals and are reconverted into lipids.

Lymph and absorbed lipids empty into the central circulatory system via the *thoracic ducts* that join the *superior vena cava* at the *left subclavian* and *left jugular vein* (near the shoulders and below the clavicle).

37. E is correct.

IgG antibodies pass from a pregnant mother to her fetus and are not associated with passive immunity.

38. B is correct.

Anemia is a decreased red blood cell count.

Spleen is similar in structure to a large lymph node and acts primarily as a blood filter; it removes old red blood cells, recycles iron, and holds a reserve of blood, which can be valuable in hemorrhagic shock.

Spleen *synthesizes antibodies* in its white pulp and removes antibody-coated bacteria and antibody-coated blood cells via blood and lymph node circulation.

Anemia results from fragile red blood cell abnormalities, making them susceptible to rupture by the spleen.

Typically, the spleen destroys red blood cells about every 120 days.

Adenoids (*pharyngeal* or *nasopharyngeal tonsils*) are masses of lymphatic tissue posterior to the nasal cavity in the roof of the nasopharynx, where the nose blends into the throat.

39. D is correct.

T cells are categorized as:

helper, cytotoxic (killer), memory, regulatory (suppressor), or natural killer T cells.

40. A is correct.

Lymphatic system transports excess fluid and proteins from the interstitial space into the circulatory system.

It functions to *remove proteins from interstitial spaces*.

Lymphatic system is essential in absorbing nutrients (particularly lipids) from the small intestine via lacteals (i.e., specialized lymph vessels).

Lymphatic system does *not* regulate erythropoiesis.

Macrophages in lymph nodes engulf bacteria and other foreign particles.

Erythropoiesis is red blood cell production and occurs in the bone marrow.

Erythropoiesis is stimulated by decreased O_2 detected by the kidneys, which secrete erythropoietin (hormone).

41. A is correct.

Liver is involved in several vital metabolic roles.

Red blood cell synthesis occurs in the bone marrow and is not associated with the liver.

B: *liver deaminates amino acids* by removing the amino terminus so amino acid remnants can enter the metabolic pathways to provide energy.

C: *liver* is involved in fat metabolism.

If glycogen stores are high, glucose is converted into fatty acids and stored as triglycerides.

D: *liver stores carbohydrates* as *glycogen* when carbohydrates and energy are abundant.

42. B is correct.

B-lymphocytes (or B-cells) are white blood cells creating antibodies.

B-cells develop from stem cells in the bone marrow.

43. B is correct.

Antibodies bind to antigens through interactions between the antibody's variable region and the antigen.

Fragment antigen binding (or Fab fragment) region on an antibody binds to antigens.

It is composed of one constant and variable domain of heavy and light chains at the amino-terminal end of the monomer. The two variable domains bind the epitope on their specific antigens.

A: antibodies (or *immunoglobulins*) *do not assist in the phagocytosis* of cells.

D: *antibodies* are produced by *plasma cells* derived from stem cells in the bone marrow.

continued...

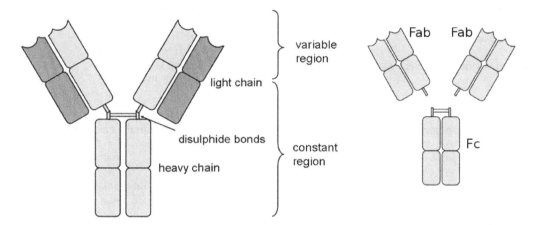

44. D is correct.

Tissue repair after an injury is not part of the inflammatory response; it is the restoration of tissue structure and function via two separate processes: *regeneration* and *replacement*.

Regeneration is when the destroyed cell type must replicate.

Replacement is when tissue is replaced with connective (scar) tissue.

45. B is correct.

Agglutinins are antibodies recognizing blood types and cause agglutination (i.e., clumping or sticking) of blood.

Blood type is determined by antibodies (i.e., *agglutinins*) to A or B antigens on red blood cells (*erythrocytes*).

A or B antigens are two types on the surface of red blood cells.

For example, a person with:

        A antigen produces agglutinins to type B blood (*anti-B antibodies*);

        B antigen produces agglutinins to type A blood (*anti-A antibodies*).

Type A blood has A antigens and makes *anti-B agglutinin*.

Type B blood has B antigens and makes *anti-A agglutinin*.

Type AB blood has both antigens and makes no agglutinins (otherwise, the blood would coagulate itself).

Type O blood has neither A nor B antigens on the surface of the red blood cells but has antibodies (i.e., agglutinins) to type A and B blood.

Rh factor (discovered in rhesus monkeys) is a red blood cell antigen independent of ABO blood types.

Agglutinin is a substance that causes particles to coagulate (i.e., causing the particles to change from fluid-like to a thickened-mass state).

Agglutinins can be antibodies that bind to the antigen-binding sites of antibodies.

Also, agglutinins can be any other substance, for example, a lectin (sugar-binding protein).

46. E is correct.

Disulfide bonds (quaternary structure between cysteine residues) hold antibody molecules together.

47. C is correct.

Fluid from lymphatic tissues is returned to the circulation at the *right and left lymphatic ducts* that feed into veins in the upper portion of the chest.

Lymphatic system is part of the circulatory system, comprising a network of conduits called lymphatic vessels that carry clear lymph fluid toward the heart.

Lymph system is *not a closed system.*

Circulatory system processes about 20 liters of blood per day through capillary filtration, which removes plasma while leaving blood cells.

17 liters of filtered plasma are reabsorbed into blood vessels, while 3 liters remain in the interstitial fluid.

Lymph system provides an accessory route for an excess of 3 liters per day to return to the blood.

Lymph is essentially recycled blood plasma.

Lymphatic organs are essential in the immune system, having considerable overlap with the lymphoid system.

Lymphoid tissue is in many organs, particularly the lymph nodes and lymphoid follicles associated with the digestive system, such as the tonsils.

Lymphoid tissues contain lymphocytes and other cells for support.

Lymphatic system includes structures dedicated to the circulation and production of *lymphocytes* (the primary cellular component of lymph), including bone marrow, thymus, spleen, and lymphoid tissue associated with the digestive system.

48. D is correct.

Lymphocytes have *membrane-bound immunoglobulin receptors* specific to a particular antigen.

When the receptor is engaged, the lymphocyte cell proliferates, resulting in a clone of antibody-producing cells (plasma cells). This occurs in secondary lymphoid organs (i.e., spleen and lymph nodes).

Clonal selection theory explains the mechanism for generating diversity of antibody specificity.

49. C is correct.

B lymphocytes (B cells) differentiate and divide into *memory* (or *plasma cells*) when stimulated by antigens.

Plasma cells make antibodies recognizing and binding specific antigen that activate precursor B lymphocytes.

Cytotoxic T cells originate from T cells (T lymphocytes), not B lymphocytes, and bind and destroy antigens.

Lymphokines originate from T cells (T lymphocytes), not B lymphocytes.

Lymphokines are secreted by helper T cells and activate T cells, B cells, and macrophages.

Macrophages specialize in removing decayed cells and cellular debris. They *do not* originate from lymphocytes.

Monocytes enter damaged tissue through the *endothelium* (single layer) of blood vessels (i.e., leukocyte extravasation); it changes to become a *macrophage*.

Monocytes are attracted to a damaged site by *chemotaxis* (i.e., chemical signals) triggered by stimuli (e.g., damaged cells, pathogens, and cytokines released by macrophages).

50. E is correct.

Antigens displayed by *dendritic cells* activate *helper T cells*.

51. B is correct.

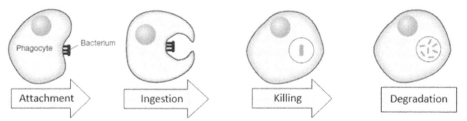

Stages of phagocytosis from the attachment of bacterium to degradation by phagocyte

52. C is correct.

Memory B cells form after primary infection and differentiate into plasma cells (i.e., B lymphocytes) when exposed to a specific antigen.

Phagocytosis is an example of nonspecific (innate) immunity and includes

      1) *monocytes* (large white blood cells)

      2) *macrophages* (stimulate lymphocytes and immune cells to respond to pathogens)

      3) *neutrophils* (first responders of inflammatory cells migrating toward the site of inflammation)

      4) *mast cells* (wound healing and defense against pathogens and for allergy and anaphylaxis)

      5) *dendritic cells* (antigen-presenting cells bridging innate and adaptive immune systems)

Stomach acid is an example of innate (i.e., nonspecific) immunity.

Skin is an example of innate (i.e., nonspecific) immunity.

Digestive System – Detailed Explanations

1. C is correct.

Liver is a multi-function organ necessary for proper physiology within humans.

Red blood cells are formed primarily in the *red bone marrow* in adults.

Liver does not manufacture red blood cells in adults, but it is a source of red blood cells in the developing fetus.

A: *glycogen* is stored in the *liver* and *muscle cells* for release when blood glucose levels are low.

B: *liver detoxifies* compounds such as alcohol, drugs, and metabolites.

For example, the liver hydrolyzes pharmaceutical compounds and prepares them for excretion by the kidneys.

D: liver forms *urea* from the metabolism of excess *dietary amino acids*.

Deamination removes amino groups combined with CO_2 via reactions to form *urea* as moderately toxic waste.

E: liver *regulates blood sugar levels* by removing glucose from the blood and storing it as glycogen.

Conversely, the liver releases glycogen to increase plasma glucose when levels are low.

2. E is correct.

Insulin decreases blood sugar levels in several ways, including inhibiting *glycogenolysis*.

A: *aldosterone* is a steroid hormone produced by the outer adrenal cortex in the adrenal gland. Adrenal glands produce aldosterone from low blood pressure in response to *low sodium or elevated potassium*.

B: *glucagon* is a peptide hormone secreted by the pancreas that raises blood glucose levels as an antagonist to the actions of insulin.

Pancreas releases glucagon when blood glucose levels fall too low.

Glucagon causes the liver to convert stored glycogen into glucose, released into the bloodstream.

C: *adrenaline* (or *epinephrine*) is involved in the sympathetic response of *fight or flight*.

3. B is correct.

In mammals, *epiglottis* prevents food from entering the trachea.

4. D is correct.

Epiglottis is a cartilaginous structure that diverts food into the *esophagus* and not the trachea.

Epiglottis closes the *respiratory tract* (*trachea*) and covers the glottis (i.e., opening at the top of the trachea).

A: *tongue* is a muscle that manipulates food for mastication but does not close off the trachea.

B: *larynx* is the voice box and is below the glottis.

C: *glottis* is the opening at the top of the trachea (windpipe), between the vocal cords, covered by the epiglottis.

E: *esophageal sphincter* (also known as *cardiac sphincter*) separates the esophagus from the stomach.

5. D is correct.

Digestion is aided by *mechanical* and *chemical* stimuli.

Mechanoreceptors and *chemoreceptors* embedded in the lining of the GI tract respond to stimuli (e.g., stretching of organs, osmolarity, pH, substrates, and end products of digestion) to initiate reflexes.

Reflexes may *activate or inhibit* glands from secreting substances (e.g., digestive juices, hormones), blood, or mixing contents and moving them along the GI tract.

Walls of alimentary canal (digestive system; esophagus, stomach, intestines) have sensors to regulate digestion.

6. E is correct.

Herbivores cannot digest plant cell walls (i.e., cellulose) but have *long digestive systems*.

Microorganisms digest cellulose (i.e., dietary fiber) and provide the herbivores with the nutrients (i.e., cellulose is composed of glucose monomers) from degradation products.

7. B is correct.

Esophagus is a muscular tube through which food (i.e., bolus) passes from the pharynx to the stomach.

Glottis is the opening of the *trachea* (i.e., windpipe), between the vocal cords and covered by the *epiglottis*.

Trachea (i.e., windpipe) connects the pharynx and larynx to the lungs, allowing *air passage*.

Larynx (i.e., voice box) manipulates pitch and volume and is below the *glottis*.

E: *fundus* is the upper part of the stomach, which forms a bulge higher than the opening of the esophagus (farthest from the pylorus).

8. E is correct.

Collecting absorbed nutrients for metabolic processing or storage is a function of the hepatic portal circulation.

Hepatic portal circulation collects absorbed nutrients for metabolic processing or storage.

9. D is correct.

Lipid production and *deposition* depend on hormones and genetic predisposition.

Liver is the *largest organ* (i.e., glandular functions) and participates in:

       detoxification (e.g., drugs, alcohol)

       bile production for dietary *lipids emulsification*

       storage of fat-soluble vitamins (A, D, E & K)

       synthesis of lipids

       metabolism of cholesterol

       production of urea

10. C is correct.

Liver produces bile stored in the gallbladder before being released into the small intestine *duodenum*.

Bile contains no enzymes but emulsifies fats, breaking down large globules into tiny fat droplets.

Bile is released upon stimulation from the hormone *cholecystokinin* (CCK),

I-cells synthesize *cholecystokinin* (CCK) in the *mucosal epithelium* of the small intestine.

A: *large intestine* absorbs water, vitamins K, B_1 (*thiamine*), B_2 (*riboflavin*), and B_{12} (*cobalamin*).

B: *small intestine* completes chemical digestion and absorbs nutrients (i.e., monomers of proteins, carbohydrates, and lipids).

D: *gallbladder* receives bile from the liver and stores it for release into the small intestine.

E: *pancreas* produces digestive enzymes (e.g., amylase, trypsin, lipase) and hormones (e.g., insulin, glucagon).

11. A is correct.

Alimentary canal is the digestive tract through which food enters and wastes are expelled.

Alimentary canal has the same structure throughout – a wall consisting of *four main layers*.

Mucosa is the layer closest to the lumen (*tubular space*), then *submucosa, muscularis externa,* and *serosa*.

 Mucosa participates in absorption and secretion.

 Submucosa absorbs the internalized elements from the blood.

 Muscularis externa is responsible for gut movement and causes food to travel the gastrointestinal tract.

 Serosa (outside layer) secretes a fluid that reduces muscle movement friction.

12. D is correct.

Type 1 diabetes can occur from a deficiency of insulin produced by *beta cells* of the pancreas.

With a deficiency (or absence) of insulin, plasma glucose rises to dangerously elevated levels, and patients excrete excess glucose in the urine.

A: *insulin* is not stimulated by decreased blood glucose levels.

B: *insulin* is not produced by the *thyroid gland*.

C: decreased levels of *circulating erythrocytes* (i.e., anemia) are *not* related to diabetes.

E: *hematocrit* is volume percentage (%) of red blood cells in blood, typically 40% for women and 45% for men.

Hematocrit is an integral part of complete blood count results, along with hemoglobin concentration, white blood cell count, and platelet count.

13. B is correct.

Large intestine absorbs water from indigestible food matter, secretes K^+ and Cl, and passes waste for excretion.

Some salts and minerals are reabsorbed with this water, and bacteria in the large intestine produce vitamin K.

Large intestine consists of the *cecum, appendix, colon, rectum,* and *anal canal.*

Sixteen hours are needed for the large intestine to complete the digestion of food, removing water, and absorbing the remaining nutrients from food before indigestible matter moves to the rectum.

Colon absorbs vitamins created by colonic bacteria, such as vitamin K (essential, as daily ingestion of vitamin K is not usually enough to maintain adequate blood coagulation), vitamin B_{12}, thiamine, and riboflavin.

Chloride secretions increase in *cystic fibrosis.*

Recycling nutrients (e.g., carbohydrate fermentation, short-chain fatty acids, urea cycling) occurs in the colon.

A: *duodenum* is the anterior (and shortest) section of the small intestine, connecting the posterior end of the stomach and precedes the jejunum and ileum, where most *chemical digestion* occurs.

Duodenum uses *enzymatic breakdown* of food in the small intestine and regulates the *rate of emptying* of the stomach *via* hormonal pathways.

Duodenum villi are leafy-looking and secrete mucus (found only in the duodenum).

Secretin and *cholecystokinin* are released from cells in the duodenal epithelium in response to acidic and fatty stimuli present when the *pylorus* (from the stomach) opens and releases *gastric chyme* (i.e., dietary food products mixed with gastric juices) into the duodenum for further digestion.

Liver and gallbladder release *bile.*

Pancreas releases *bicarbonate* and *digestive enzymes* (e.g., *trypsin, amylase,* and *lipase*) into the duodenum.

C: *jejunum* is the second section of the small intestine, connecting the duodenum (i.e., anterior end) and ileum (i.e., posterior end).

Jejunum lining (i.e., enterocytes) is specialized to absorb small nutrient particles, which enzymes have previously digested in the duodenum.

Once absorbed, nutrients (except fat, which go to the lymph) pass from enterocytes into the enterohepatic circulation and enter the liver via the *hepatic portal vein*, where blood is processed.

D: *ileum* mainly absorbs vitamin B_{12} and bile salts and products of digestion not absorbed by the jejunum.

Ileum walls have folds, each with many tiny finger-like projections, known as *villi*, on their surface. Epithelial cells lining these villi possess even more microvilli.

Ileum lining secretes *proteases* and *carbohydrases* for the final stages of protein and carbohydrate digestion.

E: *mouth* does *not* absorb water but masticates (chews) and moistens food. It converts a small amount of starch into maltose using salivary amylase (enzyme).

14. E is correct.

Cholecystokinin (CCK) is a hormone that increases the output of enzyme-rich pancreatic juice and stimulates *contractions of the gallbladder* to release bile.

Cholecystokinin is released by I cells in the *duodenum* and *proximal jejunum mucosal epithelium* of the small intestine in response to dietary fat and protein.

CCK stimulates the release of *pancreatic lipase* to digest fat, *trypsin,* and *chymotrypsin* for proteins.

Salivary amylase is produced in the mouth and digests carbohydrates unrelated to cholecystokinin.

15. D is correct.

Proteins are denser than lipids, and lipoproteins with higher protein content are denser.

Lipoproteins with low-density transport mainly lipids and contain little protein.

For example, VLDL transports more lipids and less protein than LDL.

Small intestine forms chylomicrons with the lowest density and highest lipid and lowest protein lipoproteins.

16. D is correct.

Oral cavity begins mechanical (i.e., *mastication*) and chemical digestion (i.e., *salivary amylase* and *lingual lipase*) of *bolus* (i.e., food with saliva).

Mechanical digestion breaks down large particles into smaller particles through the searing actions of teeth, thus increasing the total surface area of the ingested food.

Chemical digestion begins in the mouth when the salivary glands secrete *saliva* containing *salivary amylase*, which hydrolyzes starch into simple sugars.

Saliva lubricates the bolus to facilitate swallowing and provides a solvent for food particles.

Muscular tongue manipulates food during chewing (*mastication*) and pushes *bolus* (food mixed with saliva) into the pharynx.

17. B is correct.

Bile does not contain digestive enzymes.

Bile is an emulsifying agent released by the gallbladder that *increases the surface area* of dietary fats, allowing more contact with *lipase* to cleave fats into smaller particles.

18. C is correct.

Salts (e.g., K^+Cl^- and Na^+Br^-) and *acids* (e.g., H_2SO_4 dissociates into H^+ and HSO_4^-) are *electrolytes* that dissociate into ions.

Cations are *positive* charges, and *anions* are *negative* charges.

Molecules with *ionic bonds* (i.e., differences in electronegativity) dissociate in aqueous solutions such as blood.

Glucose, sucrose, and fructose have *covalently* bonded carbon backbones and are *not* electrolytes.

19. E is correct.

Sodium bicarbonate ($NaHCO_3$) buffers the blood to maintain a slightly basic pH (7.35) of the blood.

$NaHCO_3$ is the conjugate base of H_2CO_3 (i.e., carbonic acid) from combining carbon dioxide (CO_2) and water:

$$CO_2 + H_2O \leftrightarrow H_2CO_3 \leftrightarrow H^+ + HCO_3^-$$

20. B is correct.

Saliva includes *electrolytes*, *digestive enzymes*, *mucin*, *lysozyme*, and *IgA*.

21. A is correct.

Muscular sphincters subdivide the digestive tract: the esophagus-stomach (*lower esophageal sphincter*), stomach-duodenum (*pyloric sphincter*) and ileum-colon (*ileocecal sphincter*).

Small intestine is the only organ with a high concentration of *villi*.

Peristalsis is the process of wave-like contractions that move food along the GI tract and occurs along the entire length of the digestive system.

Peyer's patches are organized lymphoid follicles in the submucosa and the mucosal layers of the lowest portion of the small intestine, primarily in the *distal jejunum* and the *ileum*.

However, Peyer's patches can also be in the duodenum.

Peyer's patches are essential in the immune system of the intestinal lumen and the generation of the immune response within the mucosa.

22. C is correct.

Low pH of the stomach (~2 to 3) is essential for the function of the protease enzymes (e.g., pepsin) that hydrolyze proteins into their amino acids.

A: *peristalsis* propels food (i.e., chyme) and indigestible waste (i.e., feces) through the system.

B: *amylases*, *lipases*, and *bicarbonate* (HCO_3^-) are released through the *pancreatic duct*.

D: glucose and amino acids are absorbed into the blood, while *dietary lipids*, separated into glycerol and free fatty acids, are absorbed by *lacteals* (special vessels within the villi of the small intestine) that transport the ingested components into the lymphatic system.

E: *cholecystokinin* (CCK) stimulates the release of enzymes needed to digest fat (i.e., pancreatic lipase) and protein (i.e., trypsin and chymotrypsin).

Cholecystokinin is released in I cells in the duodenum and proximal jejunum mucosal epithelium.

23. A is correct.

Hydrochloric acid (HCl) released in the stomach denatures proteins, unfolding their three-dimensional shapes.

Pepsin (enzyme) hydrolyzes proteins into peptide fragments (i.e., linear sequences of amino acids).

24. B is correct.

Parietal cells are epithelial cells of the stomach that secrete *gastric acid* (HCl) and *intrinsic factors*.

Tagamet, *cimetidine*, and *nizatidine* are H_2-receptor antagonists inhibiting parietal cells from releasing HCl, and the pH of the stomach increases.

Chief cells produce pepsin (enzyme), which digests protein.

25. E is correct.

Carbohydrates absorbed into the blood via the *small intestine* must be *hydrolyzed* (degraded by adding water) to monosaccharides before absorption.

Starch digestion (i.e., plant polymer of glucose) begins with salivary alpha-amylase (*ptyalin*).

Starch (or amylum) is a polymeric carbohydrate with numerous glucose units joined by *glycosidic bonds*.

Salivary amylase activity is minimal compared with *pancreatic amylase* in the small intestine.

Alpha-amylase digestion products and dietary disaccharides are hydrolyzed to their corresponding monosaccharides by enzymes (e.g., maltase, isomaltase, sucrase, lactase) in the small intestine's brush border.

Amylase hydrolyzes starch to *alpha-dextrin*, which is digested into *maltose*.

Maltose is the disaccharide of two glucose monomers produced when amylase catabolizes starch.

26. C is correct.

Gastrin is a digestive hormone that stimulates stomach acid secretions by the presence of peptides and proteins.

27. B is correct.

Positively charged and negatively charged compounds are filtered at a higher rate for the same molecular weight than neutral compounds.

Negative charge on cellulose filtration membranes attracts positively charged and repels negatively charged compounds.

28. B is correct.

Lactase is an enzyme released into the small intestine that hydrolyzes lactose (i.e., a disaccharide) into its *glucose* and *galactose* monomer sugars.

A: *kinase* (enzyme) phosphorylates (i.e., adds phosphate) its substrate.

C: *lipase* (enzyme) hydrolyzes lipids into glycerol and free fatty acids.

D: *zymogen* (ending in ~ogen) is the inactive enzyme cleaved by physiological conditions into its active form.

For example, pepsin*ogen*, trypsin*ogen*, and chymotrypsin*ogen* are cleaved in the small intestine into the active enzymes of pepsin, trypsin, and chymotrypsin.

E: *phosphatase* removes phosphate from its substrate (i.e., opposite action to kinase, which adds).

29. E is correct.

Pepsinogen (inactive digestive enzyme) is secreted by the *chief cells* in the stomach.

30. C is correct.

Gastrointestinal tract is lined with *involuntary smooth muscle* controlled by the *autonomic nervous system*.

Esophagus is the exception;

upper 1/3 consists of voluntary skeletal muscle (e.g., for swallowing),

middle 1/3 consists of a mixture of skeletal and smooth muscle, and

lower 1/3 is smooth muscle.

31. C is correct.

Lipids are the primary means of food storage in animals.

Lipids release more energy per gram (9 kcal/gram) than carbohydrates (4 kcal/gram) or proteins (4 kcal/gram).

Lipids provide insulation and protection against injury as the primary component of *adipose* (fat) tissue.

A: *proteins* are composed of *amino acids* with C, H, O, and N but may contain S (i.e., sulfur in cysteine).

B: α helices and β pleated sheets are protein *secondary structures*.

D: C:H:O ratio of carbohydrates is 1:2:1 ($C_nH_{2n}O_n$).

E: *maltose* is a disaccharide composed of two molecules of glucose.

32. A is correct.

Hepatocytes (liver cells) are the primary tissue of the liver and 70-85% of the liver's cytoplasm.

Hepatocytes participate in:

protein synthesis; storage,

modification of carbohydrates,

synthesis of cholesterol, bile salts, and phospholipids,

detoxification, modification, and excretion of substances.

Hepatocytes initiate the *formation and secretion of bile*.

33. E is correct.

Acinar cells synthesize and secrete pancreatic enzymes.

Pepsinogen and *pancreatic proteases* (e.g., trypsinogen) are secreted as *zymogens* (i.e., inactive precursors).

Proteases must be inactive while secreted because they would digest the pancreas and the GI tract before reaching their target location.

A: *protease* is a general term for enzymes that digest proteins.

B: *salivary amylase* digests carbohydrates in the mouth and is secreted in its active form.

D: *bicarbonate* (HCO_3^-) is not an enzyme but buffers the pH of the gastrointestinal system and blood.

Centroacinar cells of the *exocrine pancreas* secrete *bicarbonate, secretin,* and *mucin*.

34. D is correct.

Small intestine is where enzymatic digestion is completed, and food monomers (i.e., amino acids, sugars, glycerol, and fatty acids) are absorbed.

Small intestine is adapted for absorption because of its large surface area of *villi* (i.e., finger-like projections).

Amino acids and *monosaccharides* pass through the villi walls and enter the capillary system.

In contrast, after hydrolysis into *glycerol and free fatty acids*, *dietary lipids* are absorbed by *lacteals* within the small intestine villi connected to the *lymphatic system*.

A: *stomach* is a large muscular organ that stores, mixes, and partially digest dietary proteins.

B: *gallbladder stores bile* before its release in the small intestine.

C: *large intestine* functions in the absorption of *salts and water*.

E: *rectum* provides for the temporary storage of feces before elimination through the anus.

35. C is correct.

Vitamin B_{12} requires *intrinsic factor* for absorption.

36. E is correct.

Bicarbonate (HCO_3^-) is not a digestive enzyme but is an important compound that buffers (i.e., resists changes in pH) both the blood and fluids of the gastrointestinal tract.

HCO_3^- is released into the duodenum as a weak base to increase the pH of chyme entering the small intestine.

If the small intestine is too acidic, the protein lining of the small intestine (i.e., mucus of the stomach lining is absent in the small intestine) would be digested.

Pancreatic enzymes would *denature* (disrupt secondary and tertiary structure) and be unable to digest chyme (food mixed with gastric juices) in the small intestine.

37. A is correct.

Carbohydrates (e.g., glucose, fructose, lactose, maltose) and proteins provide 4 calories per gram (4 kcal/gram).

Fats (lipids) are energy-dense and provide 9 calories per gram.

38. C is correct.

Goblet cells are *glandular simple columnar epithelial cells* that secrete *mucin*, which forms mucus when dissolved in water.

Goblet cells use *apocrine* (i.e., bud secretions) and *merocrine* (i.e., exocytosis via a duct) secretion.

Goblet cells are scattered among the epithelial lining of organs (i.e., intestinal and respiratory tracts) and inside the trachea, bronchus, and larger bronchioles in the respiratory tract, small intestines, the colon, and conjunctiva in the upper eyelid (i.e., goblet cells supply the mucus tears).

39. B is correct.

Proper digestion of *macromolecules* is required to absorb nutrients from the small intestine.

Carbohydrates must be broken down into monosaccharides like glucose, fructose, and galactose.

Lactose is a disaccharide of glucose and galactose; sucrose is glucose and fructose; maltose is two glucose.

Disaccharide digestion into sugar monomers occurs at the *intestinal brush border of the small intestine* via enzymes, including *lactase, sucrase,* and *maltase.*

A: *amino acids* are the *monomers* of proteins.

Proteins must be hydrolyzed into mono-peptides, dipeptides, or tripeptides for absorption in the duodenum of the small intestine.

D: *lipids* are degraded into *free fatty acids* and *glycerol* for absorption in the small intestine.

40. D is correct.

Liver uses vitamin K to produce *prothrombin*, a clotting protein involved in the cascade, to form a *fibrin* clot.

Hemorrhagic diseases result from a deficiency of dietary vitamin K.

Vitamins A, D, E, and K are *fat-soluble.*

Essential means that the nutrient *cannot* be produced by the body and must be ingested from the diet.

Necessary means that nutrient is required (without reference source – dietary or synthesized from precursors)

A: *vitamin A* is necessary for skin, hair, mucous membranes, night vision, and bone growth.

B: *vitamin B_{12}* is an essential (i.e., must be ingested from food) water-soluble vitamin for red blood cell formation and the proper functioning of the nervous system.

C: *vitamin D* is necessary for bone and tooth development and dietary calcium and phosphate absorption.

E: *vitamin E* is an antioxidant that protects cell membranes and prevents degradation of vitamin A.

41. A is correct.

Large intestine (i.e., colon) absorbs vitamins created by bacteria (e.g., vitamin K, B$_{12}$, thiamine, and riboflavin).

B: many plants and animals synthesize vitamin C from carbohydrate precursors (e.g., glucose and galactose).

Ascorbic acid (vitamin C) is synthesized within the tissues of mammals, except primates (e.g., humans) and guinea pigs, which lack an enzyme necessary for the last step of vitamin C biosynthesis.

Bacteria residing in the gut of people with Chron's disease can gain the ability to produce vitamin C to reduce inflammation; this is not a typical biological process for most individuals.

C: bacteria in the large intestine produce gas, which is not essential.

D: *bilirubin* is the yellow breakdown product of heme catabolism from aged red blood cells. It is responsible for the yellow color of bruises, the background straw-yellow color of urine, the brown color of feces, and yellow discoloration in jaundice (i.e., resulting from liver disease).

*Heme i*s in hemoglobin as the principal component of red blood cells; bilirubin is excreted in bile and urine, and elevated levels indicate diseases.

42. B is correct.

Saliva is a complex mixture of water, mucus, electrolytes, enzymes, and antibacterial compounds.

Saliva lubricates *bolus* (food mixed with saliva) and buffers the oral cavity pH to 6.2-7.4.

Saliva contains *lingual lipase* and *salivary amylase* (enzymes) that digest lipids and carbohydrates. These enzyme classes are produced in the pancreas and secreted into the duodenum of the small intestine.

A: *chymotrypsin* (along with trypsin) is secreted by the pancreas to digest proteins.

C: *pepsin* is produced by gastric chief cells to initiate protein breakdown.

D: *trypsin* (along with chymotrypsin) is secreted by the pancreas to digest proteins.

E: *secretin* regulates pH in the duodenum through inhibiting gastric acid secretion by parietal cells of the stomach and by stimulating bicarbonate production by centroacinar cells and intercalated ducts of the pancreas.

43. D is correct.

Cardiac sphincter (or *lower esophageal sphincter*) regulates the flow of material (i.e., *bolus*) from the esophagus into the stomach.

Food substance is *bolus* in the mouth or esophagus and *chyme* (food mixed with gastric juices) upon entering the stomach.

A: *gallbladder* is a small storage organ for bile (digestive secretion of the liver) before it is released into the duodenum of the small intestine via *cholecystokinin* (CCK) to emulsify dietary fats.

B: *pyloric sphincter* regulates the flow of chyme from the stomach into the small intestine.

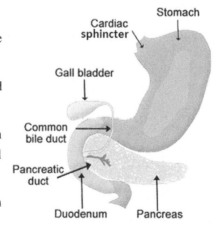

C: *epiglottis* is the structure that blocks the opening to the trachea (i.e., windpipe) during swallowing.

44. B is correct.

Hemoglobin production in RBCs requires *intrinsic factor* stomach secretions.

45. E is correct.

Cholecystokinin (CCK) stimulates the release of enzymes needed to digest fat (i.e., pancreatic lipase) and protein (i.e., trypsin and chymotrypsin).

Salivary amylase is produced in the mouth and digests carbohydrates.

Cholecystokinin is released in I cells in the duodenum and proximal jejunum mucosal epithelium.

Bile is synthesized by the liver and released from the gallbladder as an emulsifying agent to increase the surface area of lipids and facilitate their digestion in the duodenum.

46. C is correct.

A patient develops a peptic ulcer when gastric mucosa overproduces HCl or when mucosal defenses are inadequate to protect the stomach mucosa lining from the expected concentration of HCl.

pH in the stomach is about 2 because of the secretion of HCl, and this acidic environment is needed by the gastric (stomach) enzyme pepsin, which functions optimally at pH 2.

Peptic ulcers can be treated with antacids, which neutralize the HCl and raise the pH.

Pepsin becomes nonfunctional with increasing pH; therefore, pepsin is most affected by an overdose of antacid.

Small intestine has a pH of between 6 and 7 and is alkaline due to bicarbonate (HCO_3^-) secretions.

Trypsin, procarboxypeptidase, and lipase are enzyme products of *exocrine pancreas* secretions into the small intestine and function best in the alkaline environment.

A: *procarboxypeptidase* is an enzyme that *hydrolyzes proteins*.

B: *trypsin* is an enzyme that *hydrolyzes protein*.

D: *lipase* is an enzyme that *hydrolyzes lipids*.

47. A is correct.

Most nutrients are absorbed through the *mucosa* of the intestinal *villi* by *active transport*.

48. E is correct.

Intrinsic factor is secreted as a glycoprotein produced by the parietal cells of the stomach and is required for the absorption of vitamin B_{12} (cobalamin) in the small intestine.

Stomach secretes gastrin as a peptide hormone that stimulates the secretion of _gastric acid_ (HCl) by _parietal cells_ of the stomach and _pepsin_ produced by the _chief cells_ in the stomach to digest dietary proteins.

Stomach absorbs caffeine and ethanol (i.e., alcohol).

B: _pancreas_ produces several digestive enzymes, including proteases (e.g., trypsin and chymotrypsin) and fat-digesting enzymes (e.g., pancreatic lipase and pancreatic amylase).

Pancreatic enzymes function within the small intestine and not within the pancreas itself.

49. B is correct.

Continuous muscle contraction depletes O_2 and causes the muscle fiber to depend on anaerobic respiration for energy (ATP) production.

Anaerobic respiration converts pyruvate into lactic acid to regenerate NAD^+ as a necessary component for glycolysis in the absence of O_2.

50. D is correct.

In the small intestine, chemical digestion needs _cholecystokinin_ (CCK), an intestinal hormone that stimulates gallbladder contraction.

Cholecystokinin is released by the small intestine I cells in response to _dietary fat and protein_.

CCK stimulates the release of enzymes needed to digest fat (i.e., _pancreatic lipase_) and protein (i.e., _trypsin_ and _chymotrypsin_). _Salivary amylase_ is produced in the mouth and digests carbohydrates.

CCK is released in I cells in the duodenum and proximal jejunum mucosal epithelium.

Cholecystokinin is a hormone released by the small intestine wall due to acidic chyme from the stomach. It stimulates the _gallbladder to release bile_ and the _pancreas to release digestive enzymes_ into the duodenum.

51. A is correct.

Intrinsic factor is secreted by _parietal cells_ with HCl and is essential for vitamin B_{12} absorption in the ileum.

Chief cells release pepsinogen (i.e., zymogen), converted into pepsin.

Mucus cells protect the stomach lining from damage by pepsin and HCl.

Erosion of mucous cells by gram-negative _Helicobacter pylori_ (_H. pylori_) is the primary cause of gastric ulcers.

52. E is correct.

Bile is an emulsifying agent that increases the surface area of dietary lipids (i.e., fats), allowing an increase in contact with *lipase* (i.e., enzyme) to dissociate fats into smaller particles.

Bile is *not an enzyme* and does not catalyze a chemical change in fats.

Lipids are separated into smaller micelles after interaction with bile.

Bile is made from *bile salts*, *cholesterol derivatives*, and *pigments* from the breakdown of hemoglobin.

B: proteins are large polymers of amino acids linked by *peptide bonds*.

C: enzymes *catalyze chemical reactions* by *lowering the energy of activation*.

D: *hormones* are *chemical messengers* released into the *blood* that signal target cells.

53. A is correct.

Pepsin functions at an optimum pH of about 2.0 but becomes denatured in the small intestine, where pH has been increased to between 6 and 7 by bicarbonate (HCO_3^-) ions.

B: *pancreatic amylase* (i.e., small intestine) and salivary amylase (i.e., mouth) digest starch.

D: *pepsinogen* is a zymogen converted into pepsin by HCl in the stomach.

54. C is correct.

Cholecystokinin (CCK) is a hormone released by the small intestine wall due to acidic chyme from the stomach.

CCK stimulates the gallbladder to release bile and the pancreas to release digestive enzymes into the duodenum.

55. B is correct.

Most chemical (i.e., enzymatic) digestion occurs in the *small intestine*.

Small intestine provides most digestion of starch, lipids (fat), most protein, and all absorption of monomers.

Some starch is digested into the *disaccharide maltose* in the mouth by *salivary amylase*.

Within the stomach is a small amount of protein digestion, in which the stomach enzyme *pepsin* splits proteins into smaller chains of amino acids (i.e., *peptides*).

However, digestion occurring before the small intestine is incomplete, and most of the digestive process occurs within the small intestine.

A: *liver* is not part of the alimentary (i.e., gastrointestinal) canal, and food does not pass through the liver.

Liver does produce *bile* (i.e., an *emulsifying agent*), which increases the *surface area* of fats and mixes them within the watery enzyme environment of the small intestine.

E: *pancreas* produces several digestive enzymes, including the proteases (e.g., trypsin and chymotrypsin) and fat-digesting enzymes (e.g., pancreatic lipase and pancreatic amylase).

Pancreatic enzymes function within the *small intestine* and not within the pancreas itself.

Excretory System – Detailed Explanations

1. A is correct.

Renin regulates the *mean arterial blood pressure* by mediating the extracellular volume (i.e., blood plasma, lymph, and interstitial fluid) and *arterial vasoconstriction*.

2. C is correct.

Individual collecting ducts empty into larger ducts called *minor calyces*, joining to form a *major calyx*.

Major calyces join in the kidney to form the *renal pelvis*.

Two ureters originate from the *renal pelvis* and connect to the *urinary bladder* to store urine.

Single urethra transports urine from the bladder for discharge from the body.

3. E is correct.

Adrenal cortex produces *aldosterone*.

Aldosterone stimulates the reabsorption of Na^+ from collecting ducts and secretion of K^+ because aldosterone activates the Na^+/K^+ pumps at the distal convoluted tubule.

Na$^+$ reabsorption draws H_2O, increasing blood volume and pressure and producing concentrated urine.

Aldosterone release is stimulated by angiotensin II, influenced by renin (i.e., renin-angiotensin system).

Vasopressin (ADH, antidiuretic hormone) is secreted by the hypothalamus and stored in the posterior pituitary.

Vasopressin increases H_2O reabsorption by *opening water channels* in the collecting ducts of the nephron (compared to the indirect action of *aldosterone* that increases *salt reabsorption*).

4. C is correct.

Permeability properties of the *loop of Henle* allow the kidney to establish the *medullary osmotic gradient*.

5. B is correct.

Fluid accumulates and decreases renal function because it interferes with blood filtration.

Obstruction of urine discharge from the nephron *increases hydrostatic pressure* (i.e., the pressure of liquid) in Bowman's capsule.

Increase in kidney hydrostatic pressure impedes blood passage into Bowman's capsule as putative filtrate.

Humans have two kidneys, but a kidney stone in the *urethra* (single tube out of the bladder) results in a fluid backup in the urinary bladder, ureters, and, effectively, both kidneys.

6. E is correct.

Water reabsorption in kidneys is directly proportional to the *osmolarity* of interstitial tissue compared to filtrate.

If osmolarity of the filtrate is *higher* than kidney tissue, water diffuses *into* the nephron.

If osmolarity of the filtrate is *lower* than kidney tissue, water diffuses *out* of the nephron.

Infusing the nephron of a healthy person with a concentrated NaCl solution increases the filtrate osmolarity, and water diffuses *into* the nephron.

Since the volume of urine excreted is *inversely proportional* to the amount of water reabsorption, there is an *increase in urine volume*.

7. D is correct.

ADH (*antidiuretic hormone*) is known as *vasopressin*.

Vasopressin's primary functions are to retain water and constrict blood vessels.

ADH regulates water retention by *increasing water absorption* in the nephron's *collecting ducts*.

8. B is correct.

Glucose, amino acids, and phosphate are reabsorbed in the *proximal convoluted tubule* by *secondary active transport*.

Urea is a waste that may (or may not) be reabsorbed by the kidney but does not involve active transport.

Reabsorption Site	Reabsorbed nutrient	Notes
Early proximal tubule	Glucose (100%), amino acids (100%), bicarbonate (90%), Na^+ (65%), Cl^-, phosphate and H_2O (65%)	PTH inhibits *phosphate excretion* AT II stimulates Na^+, H_2O, and HCO_3^- *reabsorption*
Thin descending loop of Henle	H_2O	Reabsorbs via medullary hypertonicity for *hypertonic urine*
Thick ascending loop of Henle	Na^+ (10–20%), K^+, Cl^-; indirectly induce paracellular reabsorption of Mg^{2+}, Ca^{2+}	Region is impermeable to H_2O, and the urine becomes *less concentrated* as it ascends
Early distal convoluted tubule	Na^+, Cl^-	PTH causes Ca^{2+} reabsorption
Collecting tubules	Na^+ (3–5%), H_2O	Na^+ is reabsorbed in exchange for K^+, and H^+, regulated by aldosterone ADH acts on V2 receptors and increases aquaporin-2 channels in the renal collecting duct

9. D is correct.

An unusually long loop of Henle maintains a steep osmotic gradient, allowing the excretion of hypertonic urine.

Compared to the human kidney, the kidney of an animal living in an arid environment can produce more concentrated urine because it maintains a greater osmolarity gradient in the medulla.

High osmolarity of the medulla produces hypertonic urine.

The greater the osmolarity within the medulla (i.e., a longer loop of Henle), the more concentrated the urine.

10. A is correct.

Eliminating solid waste is the function of the digestive system; the respiratory system eliminates CO_2.

11. C is correct.

Hydrostatic (i.e., blood) *pressure* assists diffusion of waste removal by Bowman's capsule.

12. B is correct.

Descending limb of the nephron contains filtrate that becomes *concentrated* as it moves into the medulla.

13. E is correct.

Glomerulus is the capillary portion of the nephron where glucose, water, amino acids, ions, and urea pass through the capillary bed and enter Bowman's capsule.

Larger plasma proteins and cells *remain* within the glomerulus and do not enter Bowman's capsule.

Glucose and amino acids pass into the filtrate (i.e., the urine) but are *entirely reabsorbed* into the blood.

Urea is filtered and excreted in the urine, and Na^+ and other salts are filtered but partially reabsorbed.

14. B is correct.

A: *ureter* is innervated by *parasympathetic* and *sympathetic nerves*.

C: *urinary bladder* has transitional epithelium and does not produce mucus.

D: urine exits the bladder when the autonomically controlled *internal sphincter* and the voluntarily controlled *external sphincter* open.

Incontinence results from problems with these muscles.

E. *detrusor muscle* is a layer of urinary bladder wall with smooth muscle

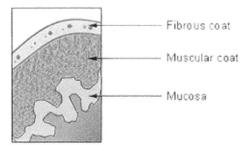

Ureter wall

15. E is correct.

Glucose usually is reabsorbed from the filtrate and is *not excreted* in the urine.

Presence of glucose in urine signifies that glucose transporters in the *proximal convoluted tubule* (not the loop of Henle) cannot reabsorb glucose from the filtrate.

16. A is correct.

Glomerular hydrostatic pressure is the primary force moving solutes and water out of blood across the filtration membrane.

17. C is correct.

Hypertonic refers to a solution of greater solute concentration.

Hypertonic solution has a higher concentration of solutes outside the cell than inside the cell.

When a cell is placed in a hypertonic solution, water flows out to balance the concentration of solutes.

Hypotonic refers to a solution of lesser solute concentration.

Hypotonic solution has a lower concentration of solutes outside the cell than inside.

Water flows into a hypotonic solution when a cell is placed into it, causing it to swell and burst (i.e., plasmolysis).

Depending on their environment, organisms have unique needs to maintain their H_2O balance.

Evolution results in renal structures for osmoregulation based on habitat.

For example, fish living in saltwater maintain hypotonic body fluids because the hypertonic environment they live in draws H_2O out by osmosis.

Fish obtain H_2O by ingesting ocean water, raising internal osmolarity, so they excrete salt to lower osmolarity.

18. C is correct.

Water reabsorption by the *descending limb of the loop of Henle* is by *osmosis*.

19. C is correct.

Gout results when uric acid is not adequately eliminated.

Kidneys are the main organs that secrete, eliminate, filter, and reabsorb compounds to maintain *homeostasis*.

Thus, gout may be caused by a renal (kidney) problem.

A: *spleen* is a *lymphoid organ* that *filters blood* for pathogens.

B: *large intestine reabsorbs water* and is the site of *vitamin K synthesis* by symbiotic bacteria.

Distal end of the colon stores indigestible material as feces.

D: *liver synthesizes blood proteins* (e.g., albumins, fibrinogen, some globulins), *produces bile*, *detoxifies metabolites*, and *stores fat-soluble vitamins* (A, D, E & K).

Vitamin K is *fat-soluble* but is excreted.

20. A is correct.

Proximal tubule of the nephron divides into initial *convoluted* and *straight (descending) portions*.

Proximal convoluted tubule reabsorbs into the peritubular capillaries approximately two-thirds of the salts (i.e., electrolytes), water, and filtered organic solutes (e.g., glucose and amino acids).

21. A is correct.

Solute concentration varies depending on the region of the kidney.

Nephron is the functional unit of the kidney.

Cortex (as a descriptive term) is the kidney's outer region with the lowest solute concentration.

Filtrate (putative urine) entering the nephron moves through the proximal convoluted tubule, loop of Henle, distal convoluted tubule, collecting duct, renal pelvis, out of the kidney, and into the bladder (for storage).

Convoluted tubules are within the cortex.

Loop of Henle, collecting ducts, and the pelvis are in the medulla (i.e., middle region).

Filtrate travels from the cortex to the medulla, increasing gradients to reabsorb water and concentrate urine.

Pelvis (in the medulla) has a high concentration gradient and reabsorbs H_2O and salts.

Medulla has a high concentration gradient to produce concentrated urine.

Epithelium does not refer to any region of the kidney.

22. E is correct.

Urea is the primary nitrogenous waste (e.g., deamination of amino acids) product of humans.

24. B is correct.

Alcohol is a diuretic because it inhibits the release of ADH.

25. C is correct.

Passive diffusion of Na^+ occurs at the loop of Henle.

Descending limb is permeable to H_2O and less impermeable to salt and thus indirectly contributes to the concentration of the interstitium.

As filtrate descends into the medulla, *hypertonic interstitium osmosis* causes H_2O to flow *out* of the *descending limb* until the osmolarity of the *filtrate and interstitium* equilibrate.

Longer descending limbs allow more H_2O to flow out, so a *longer loop of Henle* creates *hypertonic filtrate*.

> *Thin ascending loop* of Henle is *impermeable to H_2O*.
>
> *Thick segment of the ascending loop* of Henle uses *active transport for Na^+*.
>
> *Distal convoluted tubule* uses *active transport for Na^+*.
>
> *Proximal convoluted tubule* uses *active transport for Na^+*.

26. D is correct.

Angiotensin II acts at the Na^+/H^+ exchanger in the kidney's *proximal tubules* to stimulate *Na^+ reabsorption* and *H^+ excretion*, coupled with *bicarbonate reabsorption*, increasing blood volume, pressure, and pH.

ACE (i.e., *angiotensin-converting enzyme*) inhibitors are major *anti-hypertensive drugs*.

27. A is correct.

Sodium-hydrogen exchange carrier moves Na^+ ions out of the urine and into epithelial cells and H^+ ions as an *anti-port carrier* (i.e., in the opposite direction) into the urine.

H^+ ions move out of epithelial cells, the pH inside cells is basic (~7.35), and the expected pH of urine is acidic.

Urine pH varies between 4.6 and 8, with 7 being average.

28. D is correct.

Polyuria is excessive urine production (i.e., greater than 2.5L/day).

Diabetes mellitus (i.e., lack of insulin) is a common cause of polyuria, which causes osmotic diuresis.

In the absence of *diabetes mellitus*, the causes are:

> *primary polydipsia* (i.e., intake of excessive fluids),
>
> *central diabetes insipidus* (i.e., deficiency of vasopressin), and
>
> *nephrogenic diabetes insipidus* (i.e., the improper response of the kidneys to ADH).

29. E is correct.

Metabolism of amino acids by the liver involves deamination (i.e., removal of the amino group).

Depending on the organism, *nitrogenous wastes* are excreted as *ammonia, urea*, or *uric acid*.

Organisms where H_2O is abundant (e.g., fish) excrete dilute urine as ammonia.

In contrast, organisms in arid conditions excrete uric acid (e.g., some birds desiccate urine to a pellet).

30. D is correct.

Elevated hydrostatic pressure in Bowman's capsule *lowers net filtration*.

31. C is correct.

Kidneys and the *respiratory system* maintain body fluids near a pH of 7.35.

Respiratory system regulates the level of CO_2, while kidneys control $[HCO_3^-]$ (brackets for concentration).

$$CO_2 + H_2O \leftrightarrow H_2CO_3 \leftrightarrow H^+ + HCO_3^-$$

Lungs release (via expiration) excess CO_2 to maintain blood pH at about 7.35.

CO_2 levels increase the reaction shifts to the right, increasing [H+] in the blood and *decreasing pH*.

32. B is correct.

Tubular reabsorption is not only a passive transport process.

33. A is correct.

Urethra is a tube that connects the urinary bladder to the male or female genitals to remove urine.

During ejaculation, sperm travels from the *epididymis* through the *vas deferens* and *urethra* that opens to the outside from the tip of the penis.

In males, the *urethra* functions in the reproductive and excretory systems.

In females, the reproductive and excretory systems do not share a common (i.e., urethral) pathway.

Sperm enters the vagina and travels through the *cervix, uterus, and fallopian tubes*.

Urine leaves the body through the *urethra*.

Vagina and urethra do not connect in females because they are separate openings.

B: *ureters* serve the excretory function. The ureter is the duct connecting the kidney to the bladder.

Urine is formed in the kidneys, travels to the bladder *via ureters*, and is stored until excreted by the urethra.

C: *prostate gland* (only in males) contributes most ejaculated fluid to semen; a prostatic fluid, which is *alkaline* and neutralizes the acidity of residual urine in the urethra.

Prostatic fluid protects sperm from acidic conditions in the female reproductive tract.

D: *vas deferens* (or *ductus deferens*) transports sperm from the epididymis to ejaculatory duct for ejaculation.

E: *epididymis* is a collection of coiled tubes on top of seminiferous tubules in the male reproductive tract.

Sperm are produced in the seminiferous tubules. Sperm mature and acquire motility in epididymis, where they are stored until ejaculation.

34. E is correct.

Secondary active transport (i.e., coupled or co-transport) uses energy for transport across a membrane.

It uses electrochemical potential differences created by pumping ions out of the cell to drive the process.

In contrast to *primary active transport*, there is no direct coupling of ATP.

Movement of ions (or molecules) from the side where it is *more concentrated to where it is less concentrated* increases *entropy* and serves as a source of energy for metabolism (e.g., H^+ gradient in the electron transport chain for oxidative phosphorylation via the ATP synthase).

35. C is correct.

Vasopressin (or *anti-diuretic hormone*, ADH) is released from the posterior pituitary to *reduce plasma volume* or *increase osmolarity*.

Aldosterone is a *mineral corticoid* released by the *adrenal cortex* in response to *low blood pressure*.

Aldosterone regulates *blood pressure* mainly by acting on the *distal tubules* and *collecting ducts*.

36. B is correct.

High osmolarity of the medulla produces *hypertonic urine.*

The greater the osmolarity within the medulla (i.e., a longer loop of Henle), the more concentrated the urine is.

A: animals living in an arid environment produce *hypertonic urine.*

C: *greater hydrostatic pressure* does *not* affect urine osmolarity.

D: *increasing rate of filtrate* does not affect urine osmolarity.

37. C is correct.

Loop of Henle recovers *water and sodium chloride* from the filtrate to produce a small volume of *concentrated urine* for excretion.

Water is reabsorbed in the descending limb, while electrolytes are actively reabsorbed in the ascending limb.

38. E is correct.

Nephron is the functional renal unit composed of the *proximal convoluted tubule, descending and ascending loops of Henle, distal convoluted tubule,* and the *collecting duct.*

Nephron eliminates wastes, regulates *blood volume and pressure,* controls levels of *electrolytes and metabolites,* and *regulates blood pH.*

Proximal convoluted tubule reabsorbs 2/3 of H_2O entering the nephron.

Descending loop of Henle passively reabsorbs H_2O.

Distal convoluted tubule reabsorbs H_2O when stimulated by aldosterone.

Collecting duct reabsorbs H_2O when stimulated by antidiuretic hormone (ADH).

Thin ascending loop (unlike the descending loop of Henle) is impermeable to H_2O and is critical for *countercurrent exchange* that concentrates urine.

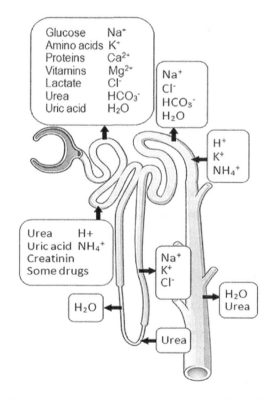

Secretion and reabsorption of solutes in the nephron

39. B is correct.

Renal clearance is the maximum concentration for a solute in plasma when its *concentration is greater* than the capacity for the nephron to reabsorb the solute, so it is excreted in the urine.

For example, the renal clearance threshold for *glucose* is about 180mg/100 ml.

40. B is correct.

Plasma osmolarity is detected by osmoreceptors of the hypothalamus that signal the pituitary gland to secrete ADH (or *vasopressin*).

ADH acts on nephrons to *increase H_2O permeability*; increasing H_2O reabsorption decreases plasma osmolarity.

Therefore, increased ADH secretion *lowers plasma osmolarity*.

A: *dehydration* results from an *excess excretion of dilute urine* (i.e., *diuresis*) that may result from an excessive fluid loss or increased plasma osmotic pressure.

C: decreased H_2O permeability in the nephron increases plasma osmolarity, increasing ADH secretion.

ADH increases H_2O reabsorption by increasing the H_2O permeability of the nephron.

Therefore, decreasing water permeability increases plasma osmotic pressure.

D: *excretion of dilute urine* results from *low plasma osmolarity* or *inhibition of ADH secretions* (e.g., by alcohol or caffeine).

Low solute concentration (i.e., osmolarity) of blood *decreases* pituitary secretion of ADH.

Low ADH levels reduce H_2O reabsorption and excretion of dilute urine, raising plasma osmolarity because of the loss of H_2O from the blood.

41. A is correct.

Renal clearance is the amount of liquid filtered out of the blood or the amount of substance cleared per time (i.e., volume/time).

Kidneys do not entirely remove a substance from the renal plasma flow.

Clearance is the rate of waste substances cleared from the blood (e.g., *renal plasma clearance*).

Substances have a *specific clearance rate* depending on their filtration characteristics (e.g., glomerular filtration, secretion from the peritubular capillaries, and reabsorption from nephrons).

Constant fraction of the substance is eliminated per unit of time.

Overall clearance is variable because the amount of substance eliminated per unit of time changes with the *concentration of the substance in blood.*

42. C is correct.

For females, the anatomy of the *excretory system* from the urethra and into the body:

urethra → bladder → opening to the ureter → ureter → renal pelvis of the kidney

43. D is correct.

Adrenal cortex synthesizes cortisol and aldosterone.

Aldosterone deficiency reduces the reabsorption of Na^+ and H_2O from urine, *increasing volume* of urine excreted.

A: *sex steroids* are synthesized primarily by the *gonads* (i.e., ovaries and testes).

C: decreased resistance to stress results from a *deficiency of cortisol*.

44. E is correct.

For males, the anatomy of the *excretory system* from the urethra and into the body:

urethra → prostate → ejaculatory duct → vas deferens → epididymis → seminiferous tubules

45. B is correct.

Renin is part of the *renin-angiotensin system* that *influences blood pressure*.

Renin is formed by the *juxtaglomerular apparatus* near the distal convoluted tubule of the nephron and acts indirectly on the adrenal cortex but does *not* act on the pituitary gland.

When blood pressure falls (e.g., heavy bleeding), renin is released by the kidneys and converts the zymogen of angiotensinogen to angiotensin I by the *angiotensin-converting enzyme* (ACE).

Angiotensin II causes vasoconstriction (to increase blood pressure) and aldosterone release from the adrenal cortex that opens ion channels in convoluted tubules (to *increase H_2O reabsorption*).

46. C is correct.

Transport epithelial cells in the ascending loop of Henle in humans have membranes impermeable to water.

47. A is correct.

Antidiuretic hormone (ADH) is released from the posterior pituitary and stimulates the collecting duct in the kidneys to reabsorb H_2O to concentrate the urine.

Diabetes insipidus does not respond to ADH despite having average plasma concentrations of ADH.

Patient's urine remains diluted because the *collecting ducts fail to reabsorb H_2O*.

Diabetes mellitus affects the *pancreas* and elevates blood glucose levels.

48. C is correct.

Excretion of *dilute urine* requires the impermeability of the collecting tubule to water.

49. D is correct.

Glucose is reabsorbed in the proximal convoluted tubule, and H_2O is reabsorbed along the nephron except for the ascending limb, where only salt (e.g., Na^+, K^+ and Cl^-) is reabsorbed.

K^+ is secreted into the filtrate (i.e., solution destined to be urine) and reabsorbed in *proximal convoluted tubule* and *ascending loop of Henle*.

Cl^- and Na^+ are reabsorbed along the nephron, *except in the descending limb* and *collecting ducts*.

Amino acids are reabsorbed in the proximal convoluted tubule.

50. E is correct.

Brush border increases the surface area to reabsorb solutes from the filtrate.

Brush border is composed of *villi* and does not influence the direction or rate of fluid movement, unlike cilia.

51. B is correct.

Distal convoluted tubules within the nephron are the site of *aldosterone* function.

Aldosterone is produced by the adrenal cortex and stimulates the reabsorption of Na^+ from the collecting duct and secretion of K^+ because aldosterone activates the *Na^+/K^+ pump* at *distal convoluted tubules*.

Na^+ reabsorption draws H_2O, increasing blood volume and pressure and producing *concentrated urine*.

Aldosterone release is stimulated by angiotensin II, influenced by renin (i.e., renin-angiotensin system).

Vasopressin (ADH; antidiuretic hormone) is secreted by the *hypothalamus* and stored in the *posterior pituitary*.

Vasopressin *increases H_2O reabsorption* by *opening water channels* in the *collecting ducts* of the nephron (compared to the indirect action of *aldosterone that increases salt reabsorption*).

52. A is correct.

When the glomeruli cannot filter adequate amounts of fluid, the primary physiological effect is the retention of salt and H_2O since the kidneys can no longer excrete these.

Blood travels via the *interlobular artery* to the *afferent arteriole* and the glomerulus through a network of capillaries.

Blood flows *out* of the glomerulus via the *efferent arteriole*.

Bowman's capsule is part of the kidney and is a round, double-walled structure.

Plasma (i.e., the liquid component of blood) is filtered through the *glomerular membrane* and *epithelial layer* of Bowman's capsule and drains into *efferent arterioles*.

Filtered blood leaves through the tubule at the top and rejoins the *interlobular vein*.

B: *urinary output* decreases significantly to less than 500 mL/day compared to the average of 1-2 L/day.

continued…

C: *glomerulus inflammation* results in the inability of urea to be excreted and causes excessive accumulation of urea in the blood (i.e., uremia).

D: *salt and H_2O excretion* in the extracellular fluid increases drastically and decreases in the filtrate (i.e., urine), which leads to an excess of extracellular fluid in body tissue (i.e., edema).

53. E is correct.

Thick segment of ascending limb of the nephron loop moves ions out into interstitial spaces for reabsorption.

54. A is correct.

Renin secretion catalyzes the conversion of angiotensin I to angiotensin II, increasing aldosterone secretion.

Without renin secretion, the production of angiotensin II decreases.

If renin is blocked, aldosterone cannot cause the increased synthesis of Na+ absorbing proteins, and Na+ absorption decreases.

B: blood pressure decreases, which reduces the amount of blood entering Bowman's capsule.

D: blood pressure would decrease.

E: *platelets* are involved in blood clotting and are not related to the production of angiotensin II.

55. B is correct.

An example of a properly functioning homeostatic control system is when kidneys excrete salt into the urine when dietary salt levels rise.

56. E is correct.

Posterior pituitary releases the antidiuretic hormone (ADH) and causes the collecting tubule to become more permeable to H_2O.

Therefore, more H_2O is reabsorbed, and urine volume decreases while it becomes concentrated.

B: salts, glucose, and amino acids are reabsorbed via *active transport*, while H_2O is reabsorbed via *diffusion*.

C: *ammonia* is converted into urea in the liver and excreted by the kidney.

D: glomerulus, Bowman's capsule, proximal and distal convoluted tubules are in the nephron's cortex.

Descending convoluted tubules and collecting ducts span the *cortex, outer medulla, and inner medulla*.

Loop of Henle is in the *inner medulla*.

Muscle System – Detailed Explanations

1. C is correct.

Sarcolemma (or myolemma) is the cell membrane of striated muscle fiber cells; it is a lipid bilayer plasma membrane and an outer coat with a thin polysaccharide layer (glycocalyx).

Glycocalyx contacts the basement membrane that contains thin collagen fibrils and specialized proteins (e.g., laminin) to function as a scaffold for the muscle fiber to adhere.

Neuromuscular junction connects the nervous system to the muscular system via synapses between efferent nerve fibers and muscle fibers (i.e., muscle cells).

When an action potential reaches the end of a motor neuron, voltage-dependent calcium channels open, and calcium enters the neuron.

Calcium binds to a sensor for vesicle fusion with the plasma membrane and subsequent neurotransmitter release (e.g., acetylcholine) from the motor neuron into the synaptic cleft.

On the post-synaptic membrane surface, the sarcolemma has invaginations (i.e., postjunctional folds), which increase the surface area of the post-synaptic membrane at the boundary of the synaptic cleft.

Postjunctional folds form the motor endplate that has numerous acetylcholine receptors.

Acetylcholine binding to the post-synaptic receptor on muscle cells depolarizes the muscle fiber and causes a cascade, resulting in muscle contraction.

2. A is correct.

Cardiac muscle exhibits cross striations formed by alternating myosin thick and actin thin protein filaments.

Like skeletal muscle, the primary structural proteins of cardiac muscle are actin and myosin.

In contrast to skeletal and smooth muscle, *cardiac muscle* cells are often *branched* rather than linear and longitudinal.

Histologically, *T-tubules in cardiac muscle*, compared to skeletal muscle, are *larger and broader* and run along the Z-discs; there are *fewer T-tubules in cardiac muscle* than in skeletal muscle.

3. D is correct.

Phosphocreatine and *ATP* are energy-storage molecules in muscle fibers that release energy for contraction.

A: *lactose* (i.e., milk sugar) is a disaccharide composed of *glucose* and *galactose*.

B. ADP (*adenosine diphosphate*) is a lower energy form of ATP (adenosine triphosphate).

C: *lactic acid* is a product of anaerobic respiration and is not a direct energy source.

E: cAMP is a second messenger in target cells of peptide hormones.

4. E is correct.

Tropomyosin in skeletal muscle is a contraction inhibitor, blocking *myosin-binding sites* on actin molecules.

5. A is correct.

Actin thin filaments and myosin thick filaments do *not* change in length during muscle contractions.

Muscle contraction is via the *sliding filament model* by increasing the overlap of actin and myosin filaments.

6. A is correct.

Sarcolemma (or myolemma) is the cell membrane of a striated muscle fiber cell.

Motor endplate is a large terminal formation at the juxtaposition of the axon of a motor neuron and the striated muscle cell it connects to.

7. D is correct.

Slow-twitch fibers produce 10 to 30 contractions per second, while *fast-twitch fibers* produce 30 to 70.

8. E is correct.

Permanent sequestering of Ca^{2+} in the sarcoplasmic reticulum (i.e., storage compartment in muscle) prevents Ca^{2+} from binding to troponin, which causes a conformational (shape) change in tropomyosin to move and expose the *myosin-binding sites* on the thin actin filament.

A: Ca^{2+} depletion does not cause depolymerization of thin actin filaments because this would occur when Ca^{2+} is sequestered into the sarcoplasmic reticulum as the contraction is complete and the muscle relaxes.

B: *permanent muscle contraction* occurs if ATP is absent (e.g., death) because ATP hydrolysis is necessary to release myosin cross-bridges from the thin actin filament.

C: resorption of Ca^{2+} from bone (via osteoclast activity) decreases bone density.

9. C is correct.

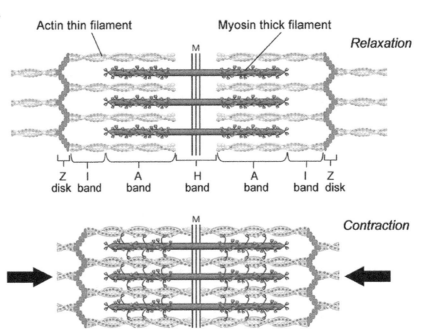

Sliding filament model of skeletal muscle with myosin thick and actin thin filaments

10. A is correct.

Treppe stimulus is the gradual increase in muscular contraction following rapidly repeated stimulation.

11. A is correct.

Vagus nerve is part of the parasympathetic nervous system.

Heart rate is set by the *SA node* innervated by the vagus nerve (i.e., parasympathetic).

Rhythmic pace of SA nerve is faster than the rate of typical heartbeats; *vagus nerve slows* heart contractions.

Without inhibition from the vagus, the heart would typically beat between 100 – 120 beats per minute.

12. C is correct.

Continuous muscle contractions deplete available O_2 (i.e., stored on myoglobin) during strenuous activity and cause the muscle fiber to rely on anaerobic respiration for energy.

Reducing pyruvate to lactic acid regenerates NAD^+ needed for glycolysis without O_2 (i.e., anaerobic conditions).

13. D is correct.

Neuromuscular junction is a synapse between the motor neuron and the muscle fiber.

14. A is correct.

Motor units with larger, less excitable neurons are used later in muscle stimulation when contractile strength increases.

15. E is correct.

Relaxation of smooth muscles that line the circulatory system causes the *dilation of blood vessels*.

16. A is correct.

Cardiac muscle does *not* require stimulation by the autonomic nervous system (ANS).

17. B is correct.

Muscle cells use *creatine phosphate* to store energy transferred to ADP to synthesize ATP.

18. A is correct.

Shivering is a protective mechanism of increases in muscle contractions, which raises core body temperature.

19. C is correct.

Muscle cells share:

> *extensibility* (ability to be stretched)
>
> *contractility* (ability to shorten forcefully)
>
> *excitability* (ability to respond to a stimulus)
>
> *elasticity* (ability to contract to the original length after being stretched)

Communication is *not* a property of muscle tissue.

20. E is correct.

Individual muscle cells are surrounded by *endomysium*.

21. A is correct.

Involuntary muscles contract *without* conscious control.

I: *cardiac muscle* is another involuntary muscle only in the heart.

II: *smooth muscle* is in the walls of organs such as the intestines and stomach.

III: *skeletal muscle* has voluntary muscles attached to the skeleton.

22. B is correct.

Myoglobin is a small protein that carries and stores oxygen in muscle cells.

Myoglobin traps oxygen, allowing cells to produce the energy required for muscle contractions.

23. C is correct.

Heart ventricles require long contraction periods to pump the viscous blood.

B: *gap junctions* permit rapid communication in adjacent cardiac muscle cells contracting simultaneously.

D: Na^+ is *outside* the resting neuron and flows into the cell during an action potential.

E: K^+ is *inside* the resting neuron and flows out of the cell during an action potential.

24. C is correct.

Intercalated discs are microscopic identifying features of cardiac muscle.

Cardiac muscle consists of individual heart muscle cells (or *cardiomyocytes*) connected by intercalated discs to work as a single functional organ or syncytium.

Intercalated discs support *synchronized contraction of cardiac tissue* and occur at the Z line of the sarcomere.

25. A is correct.

After death, *cellular respiration ceases*, depleting oxygen used to make ATP.

The corpse hardens and becomes stiff (in humans, it commences after 3-4 hours, reaches maximum stiffness after 12 hours, and gradually dissipates by approximately 24 hrs. after death).

Unlike normal muscular contraction, after death, the body cannot complete the cycle and release the coupling between myosin and actin, creating a state of muscular contraction until the breakdown of muscle tissue by enzymes during decomposition.

26. E is correct.

Muscles move by contracting, bringing the *origin and insertion closer*, often moving the insertion while the origin remains fixed.

27. A is correct.

Titin is necessary for contractions of striated muscle tissues; it connects the Z to M line in sarcomeres and contributes to force at the Z line, and resting tension in I band region.

28. D is correct.

T tubules function to facilitate cellular communication during muscle contraction.

29. D is correct.

During muscle contraction, *Ca^{2+} binds to troponin*, causing tropomyosin strands to move and expose *myosin-binding sites on actin thin filaments*.

30. E is correct.

Peristalsis is a contractile process of smooth muscle that propels chyme (food mixed with gastric juices) through the intestines and takes place along the entire length of the digestive system.

31. C is correct.

Myofilaments are microscopic, thread-like structures in myofibrils, giving muscle its striped appearance.

Muscles contract by sliding thick and thin myofilaments along each other.

32. D is correct.

Antagonistic muscles move bones in opposite directions relative to a joint and require one muscle to relax while the other contracts.

33. E is correct.

Slow-oxidative skeletal muscle fiber type is most *resistant* to fatigue.

34. D is correct.

During muscle contraction, the *thick filament cross-bridges attach to actin filaments*.

35. E is correct.

Tendons connect *muscle to bone*, while *ligaments* connect *bone to bone*; tendons are *not cartilage*.

36. C is correct.

Muscle contractions:

      motor neuron action potential → neurotransmitter release → muscle cell action potential →
      release of calcium ions from SR → ATP-driven power stroke → sliding of myofilaments

37. A is correct.

Calcium release from the sarcoplasmic reticulum is usually required to contract a muscle.

Permanent sequestering of Ca^{2+} in the sarcoplasmic reticulum (storage compartment in muscle) prevents Ca^{2+} from binding to troponin, which causes the conformational change in tropomyosin to move and expose the myosin-binding sites on the thin actin filament.

Skeletal muscle has *multinucleated fibers* with a striated appearance from the repeating motifs of actin and myosin filaments.

Actin and myosin filaments slide past each other and shorten during contraction.

Intercellular conductivity of action potentials is *not* present in a skeletal muscle.

Contraction does *not* require energy, but ATP is needed to *release cross-bridges* between actin and myosin for a subsequent contraction.

Each muscle fiber is innervated by neurons from the somatic division of the PNS.

Axon releases an action potential to each muscle fiber, but this action potential cannot pass from one muscle fiber to another.

When an action potential reaches the muscle fiber, it causes the release of Ca^{2+} from the sarcoplasmic reticulum to permit the sliding of the actin and myosin filaments.

38. B is correct.

Enteric nervous system (ENS) is a division of the autonomic nervous system (ANS) and controls the gastrointestinal (GI) tract.

Peristalsis is a contractile process of smooth muscle that propels a ball of food through the intestines.

A: *contraction of the diaphragm* is under the control of the *autonomic nervous system*.

As diaphragm contracts, the volume of the *thoracic cavity increases*, and the air is drawn into the lungs.

C: *gap junctions* conduct cardiac muscle action potentials.

D: *knee-jerk reflex* contracts skeletal muscles innervated by the somatic nervous system.

39. A is correct.

ATP breaks bonds between two contractile proteins for myosin-actin cross-bridges.

Skeletal muscle has *multinucleated fibers* with a striated appearance from the repeating motifs of actin and myosin filaments.

Actin and myosin filaments *slide* past each other and shorten during contraction.

Contraction does not require energy, but *ATP is needed to release cross-bridges* between actin and myosin for a subsequent contraction.

Muscle fiber is innervated by neurons from the *somatic division* of the PNS.

Axons release an action potential to muscle fibers, but this action potential cannot pass between muscle fibers.

When an action potential reaches the muscle fiber, it causes the release of Ca^{2+} from the sarcoplasmic reticulum to permit the sliding of the actin and myosin filaments.

40. B is correct.

Unlike skeletal and cardiac muscle, smooth muscle does not contain the *calcium-binding protein troponin*, and *calmodulin* has a regulatory role in *calcium levels*.

In skeletal muscle, calcium is stored in the *sarcoplasmic reticulum* within the cell, while in smooth muscle, calcium is stored when bound to *calmodulin* within the cell.

Contraction for smooth muscle is initiated by *calcium-regulated phosphorylation of myosin* rather than by *calcium-activated troponin* mechanisms.

41. D is correct.

Skeletal muscle has multinucleated fibers with a striated appearance from repeating *actin and myosin filaments*.

Actin and myosin filaments *slide* past each other and shorten during contraction.

Contraction does *not* require energy, but ATP is needed to release cross-bridges between action and myosin for a subsequent contraction.

Each muscle fiber is innervated by neurons from the *somatic division* of the PNS.

Axons release an action potential to muscle fibers, but action potential cannot pass between muscle fibers.

Action potential reaching muscle fiber causes the release of Ca^{2+} from the sarcoplasmic reticulum to permit the sliding of actin and myosin filaments.

42. D is correct.

Excitation-contraction coupling requires ATP and Ca^{2+}.

43. B is correct.

Smooth muscle contains *thin actin and thick myosin filaments* (albeit not striated) and requires Ca^{2+} for contraction.

44. C is correct.

Synaptic vesicles release acetylcholine into the synaptic cleft for skeletal muscles.

45. E is correct.

Specific smooth muscle cells divide to increase their numbers.

46. C is correct.

Diaphragm is a *skeletal muscle innervated by the phrenic nerve* of the somatic nervous system.

Smooth and cardiac muscles are involuntary because the autonomic nervous system innervates them.

47. A is correct.

Thick filament of skeletal muscle fibers is composed of *myosin*.

48. E is correct.

It is not characteristic of a smooth muscle that they are thicker than thin filaments.

49. B is correct.

Characteristics of smooth muscle:

      involuntary

      without T-tubules

      lacking troponin and tropomyosin

      without repeating striations (Z disks) of sarcomeres

      single unit with the whole muscle contracting or relaxing

Smooth muscle cells undergo involuntary contractions in:

      1) blood vessels for regulating blood pressure,

      2) gastrointestinal tract to propel food during digestion, and

      3) bladder to discharge urine.

50. A is correct.

Glycogen is abundant in the sarcoplasm and provides stored energy for muscle cells during exercise.

51. A is correct.

Striated muscle cells (i.e., skeletal muscle) are responsible for the mobility of the body and limbs.

Striated muscle cells are *long and cylindrical* with *many nuclei*.

Cardiac muscle cells (i.e., cardiomyocytes) are only in the heart.

Cardiac muscle is primarily *single nucleated* but may have up to four nuclei.

T tubules are in *striated and cardiac muscle* cells.

Smooth muscle cells are involuntary and primarily in the reproductive, digestive, and endocrine systems.

52. E is correct.

Cardiac muscle, unlike other muscle types, undergoes *spontaneous depolarization* for contractions.

Smooth and skeletal muscle requires stimulation (e.g., neurotransmitter) for depolarization and contractions.

Cardiac muscle cells (i.e., *cardiomyocytes*) are *single-nucleated* but can have four central nuclei.

Cardiomyocyte (cardiac muscle) is *striated*.

Cardiac muscle is innervated by the *autonomic* nervous system (ANS).

Somatic motor system innervates skeletal muscle and controls voluntary actions (e.g., walking, standing).

53. A is correct.

Somatic nervous system innervates skeletal muscles and has myelinated axons without synapses.

Activity of neurons leads to excitation (i.e., contraction) of skeletal muscles; therefore, they are motor neurons.

Motor neurons are never inhibitory.

Somatic fibers are responsible for voluntary movement.

54. D is correct.

Multiunit smooth muscle has one nucleus, no sarcomeres, and rare gap junctions.

55. E is correct.

Myoglobin is an iron- and oxygen-binding protein in the muscle tissue of vertebrates and most mammals, like hemoglobin, the iron- and oxygen-binding protein in red blood cells.

Myoglobin is the primary oxygen-carrying pigment of muscle tissues.

High concentrations of myoglobin allow organisms to hold their breath for longer periods (e.g., diving animals).

56. C is correct.

Muscle is a bundle of parallel fibers, and each fiber is a multinucleated cell created by the fusion of several mononucleated embryonic cells.

Skeletal muscle is responsible for voluntary movement and is innervated by the somatic nervous system.

Skeletal muscle is composed of individual components known as *myocytes* (i.e., muscle cells).

Long cylindrical multinucleated cells are *myofibers* and composed of *myofibrils*.

Myofibrils are actin and myosin filaments repeated as sarcomeres – functional (contractile) unit of muscle fiber.

Sarcomere give skeletal muscle's striated appearance and forms the necessary structure for muscle contraction.

A: *cardiac muscle* composes the muscle tissue of the heart. These muscle fibers possess characteristics of skeletal and smooth muscle fibers.

As in skeletal muscle, cardiac muscle has a *striated appearance*, but cardiac muscle cells have predominantly one or two centrally located nuclei.

Cardiac muscle is innervated by the *autonomic nervous system* (ANS), modulating heartbeat rates.

B: *smooth muscle* in the digestive tract, bladder, uterus, and blood vessel walls are responsible for involuntary action and is innervated by the autonomic nervous system.

Smooth muscle is not striated and has one centrally located nucleus.

57. D is correct.

Skeletal muscle cells use the *sarcoplasmic reticulum for calcium storage*.

58. D is correct.

Cardiac muscle contains actin & myosin filaments as in striated skeletal muscle.

Syncytium is a multinucleated cell resulting from the fusion of several individual cells.

Cardiac muscle is not a true *syncytium* (i.e., a cell with several nuclei).

Adjoining cardiac cells are linked by *gap junctions* that communicate action potentials directly from the cytoplasm of one myocardial cell to another.

Sympathetic nervous system increases heart rate.

Parasympathetic nervous system stimulation (via the vagus nerve) decreases heart rate.

Skeletal System – Detailed Explanations

1. C is correct.

Vertebral column consists of 31 bones, known as *vertebrae*.

Spinal curves help withstand stress by providing an even distribution of body weight and movement flexibility

2. D is correct.

Tendons connect bone to muscle, while *ligaments connect bone to bone*.

Aponeuroses are layers of broad flat tendons.

3. C is correct.

Synovial fluid functions as a lubricant, decreasing friction between the ends of bones moving past each other.

Bone cells (i.e., *osteocytes*) receive blood circulation for adequate nutrition and hydration, but the synovial fluid is not involved.

4. B is correct.

Lumbar region is in the lower back and bears the most body weight.

Cervical region supports the head.

Thoracic region supports the ribs.

Sacral and *coccyx* connect the spine to hip bones and muscles of the pelvic floor.

5. E is correct.

Osteocytes are derived from *osteoprogenitors*; some differentiate into active *osteoblasts* that do *not divide* and have an average half-life of 25 years.

Osteocytes reside in *lacunae spaces* in mature bone, while their *processes are inside canaliculi spaces*.

Osteoblasts trapped in the matrix they secrete become *osteocytes*.

Osteocytes are networked via *long cytoplasmic extensions* that occupy *tiny canals* (i.e., *canaliculi*) and exchange nutrients and waste through *gap junctions*.

Osteocytes occupy the *lacuna space*.

Osteocytes have reduced synthetic activity and (like osteoblasts) do not undergo mitotic division; they are actively involved in the *dynamic turnover of bone matrix*.

6. D is correct.

Five types of bones:

> *long, short, flat, irregular,* and *sesamoid.*

Short bones are as wide as long, with a primary function to provide support and stability with little to no movement (e.g., *tarsals* in feet and carpals in hands).

Two bone tissue types:

> *cancellous bone* (i.e., *trabecular,* or *spongy bone*)

> *cortical bone* (i.e., *compact bone*).

7. A is correct.

Axial skeleton supports and protects the brain, spinal cord, and internal organs.

Axial skeleton consists of the skull, neck bones, vertebral column, and rib cage.

Appendicular skeleton is the part of the skeleton consisting of bones that support limbs.

8. E is correct.

Skeletal system functions to produce blood cells, storage of minerals, protection of the viscera (internal organs), and toxin removal.

Skeletal system is vital in regulating *energy metabolism* through the endocrine system.

Vitamin C is an essential nutrient in citrus fruits, leafy greens, and other foods; deficiency leads to *scurvy.*

9. D is correct.

Cartilage does *not* contain nerves.

Unlike other connective tissues, cartilage does *not* contain blood vessels.

Cells of the cartilage (*chondrocytes*) produce a large extracellular matrix composed of *collagen fibers, elastin fibers,* and abundant *ground substances* rich in *proteoglycan.*

Elastic cartilage, hyaline cartilage, and *fibrocartilage* differ in relative amounts of the three main components.

10. A is correct.

Compact bone is a dense material used to create the hard outer shell of most bones.

Compact bone is the main structure for support, protection, and movement.

Spongy bone is lighter and used for more active functions, filling the inner layer of most bones.

Trabecular bone is another term for spongy bone.

Long bone is a classification of bone by its shape (e.g., femur), as is irregular bone (e.g., vertebra).

11. C is correct.

Rickets is a disease in children resulting in soft and pliable bones due to vitamin D deficiency.

12. C is correct.

Middle ear contains *malleus*, *incus*, and *stapes* bones which amplify vibrations of the tympanic membrane (i.e., eardrum) and transmit them to the *oval window* leading to the inner ear and receptors on the *auditory nerve*.

Larynx, nose, outer ear, and skeletal joints are composed of *cartilage*.

Cartilage is neither innervated nor vascularized.

13. D is correct.

Bone marrow is *red marrow* (mainly hematopoietic tissue) and *yellow marrow* (mainly fat cells).

Red and yellow bone marrow contain blood vessels and capillaries.

Bone marrow is *red at birth*, but more is converted to yellow with age until half of adult bone marrow is yellow.

Red marrow is mainly in flat bones (e.g., sternum, pelvis, vertebrae, cranium, ribs, and scapulae) and cancellous (i.e., spongy bone) material at the *epiphyseal ends of long bones* (e.g., femur and humerus).

Red marrow gives rise to *red blood cells*, *platelets,* and most *lymphocytes* (i.e., white blood cells).

Yellow marrow is in the *medullary cavity* (i.e., the hollow interior of the middle portion of long bones).

Body converts *yellow marrow back to red marrow* in severe blood loss to increase blood cell production.

14. B is correct.

Parathyroid hormone (PTH) increases plasma Ca^{2+} by increasing the activity of *osteoclast cells*.

Osseous tissue forms the rigid part of the bones making up the skeletal system.

15. E is correct.

Osteon is the structural unit of compact bone with *lamellae* (i.e., concentric bone layers) surrounding *Haversian canals* (i.e., hollow passages).

16. B is correct.

*Parathyroid hormone*s maintain the appropriate calcium levels in the blood, often at the expense of bone loss.

17. A is correct.

Cartilage is a connective tissue with a flexible and strong matrix.

18. A is correct.

Growth hormone deficiency during bone formation can cause decreased epiphyseal plate activity.

Epiphyseal plate is the area of the long bone where new bone growth occurs.

19. E is correct.

Ligaments attach bone to bone.

A: *osteocyte* is typical in mature bone cells derived from *osteoprogenitors*.

Some osteocytes differentiate into active *osteoblasts*.

In mature bone, osteocytes and their processes reside inside lacunae and canaliculi.

Osteocytes contain a nucleus with a thin ring of cytoplasm.

Osteoblasts trapped in the matrix it secretes become osteocytes.

Periosteum is the membrane covering the surface of bones.

20. B is correct.

Secondary ossification centers produce the ossification of the ends of long bones.

21. A is correct.

Kyphosis is an abnormal curvature of the thoracic spine from compression fractures of weakened vertebrae.

22. C is correct.

Thyroid hormones (e.g., thyroxine) have significant metabolic effects but not bone remodeling.

Thyroid hormones increase basal metabolic rate, affect protein synthesis, and regulate long bone growth and neural maturation.

Thyroid hormones increase sensitivity to *catecholamines* (e.g., adrenaline).

Thyroid hormone is essential to developing and differentiating human body cells.

It regulates protein, fat, and carbohydrate metabolism, affecting how cells use energetic compounds and stimulating vitamin metabolism.

Calcitonin, vitamin D, and parathyroid hormone (PTH) participate in Ca^{2+} metabolism and bone remodeling.

23. A is correct.

Until adolescence, diaphysis of bone increases in length due to epiphyseal plates.

24. E is correct.

Bones store *calcium* and *phosphate*, support and protect the body, produce blood cells, and store fat within the yellow bone marrow.

Bones do *not* regulate the temperature of blood.

25. B is correct.

Growth hormone is the most important stimulus for *epiphyseal plate activity* during infancy and childhood.

26. C is correct.

Osteon is the functional unit of compact bone with cylindrical structures typically several millimeters long and 0.2mm in diameter.

Each osteon has concentric lamellae layers of compact bone tissue surrounding a central *Haversian canal* with nerves and blood supplies.

Boundary of an osteon is the *cement line*.

A: *periosteum membrane* covers the outer surface of bones, except joints of long bones.

B: *endosteum* lines the inner surface of bones.

D: *trabeculae* are tissue elements forming a small mechanical strut or rod (e.g., femur head), usually composed of dense collagenous tissue (e.g., trabecula of spleen).

Trabecula can be composed of other materials.

For example, trabeculae consist of muscles forming *trabeculae carneae* of heart ventricles.

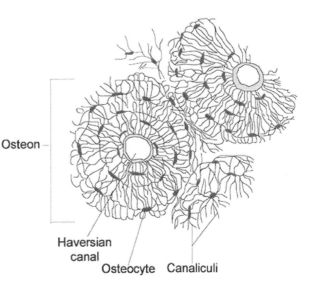

Compact bone from a transverse section of a long bone's cortex

27. D is correct.

Parathyroid hormone (PTH) elevates blood calcium levels by increasing the number and activity of osteoclasts.

28. E is correct.

Bones are covered and lined by *periosteum* (i.e., protective tissue), dense irregular connective tissue.

Periosteum divides into an *outer fibrous layer* and an *inner osteogenic* (or *cambium*) *layer*.

Fibrous layer contains fibroblasts, while the *osteogenic layer* contains progenitor cells that develop into osteoclasts and osteoblasts.

Osteoblasts increase the width of long bones and the overall size of other bone types.

29. A is correct.

Yellow bone marrow is usually in the *medullary* cavity of long bones.

Red blood cells, platelets, and most white blood cells arise in red marrow. Red and yellow bone marrow contain blood vessels and capillaries.

At birth, bone marrow is red. With age, more is converted to yellow; around half of adult bone marrow is red.

Red marrow is mainly in flat bones (e.g., pelvis, scapulae, sternum, cranium, ribs, vertebrae) and spongy material at the epiphyseal ends of long bones (e.g., femur and humerus).

Haversian canals are a series of tubes around narrow channels formed by lamellae; this region is *compact bone.*

Osteons are arranged in parallel to the long axis of the bone.

Haversian canals surround blood vessels and nerve cells throughout the bone to communicate with osteocytes in *lacunae* (i.e., spaces within a dense bone matrix containing living bone cells) through *canaliculi* (i.e., canals between the lacunae of ossified bone).

Volkmann's canals are microscopic structures in compact bone. They run within osteons *perpendicular* to Haversian canals, interconnecting the canals and periosteum (i.e., membrane covering bone surfaces).

Volkmann's canals carry *small arteries throughout bones.*

30. B is correct.

*Haversian canal*s run through the core of each osteon and are the site of blood vessels and nerve fibers.

31. D is correct.

Endochondral ossification, with cartilage, is one of two processes during fetal development of the mammalian skeletal by which bone is created.

Endochondral ossification is essential for the rudimentary formation of long bones, lengthening long bones, and healing bone fractures.

Appositional growth is when the cartilage grows in thickness (i.e., diameter) due to the extracellular matrix on the peripheral cartilage surface, accompanied by chondroblasts developing from the *perichondrium*.

Intramembranous ossification is essential for rudimentary bone tissue creation during fetal development.

Intramembranous ossification is for healing bone fractures and the rudimentary formation of bones of the head.

Unlike endochondral ossification, cartilage is not present during intramembranous ossification.

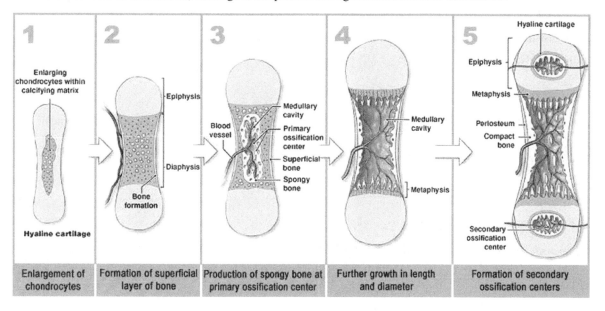

32. C is correct.

Ligaments are fibrous connective tissue that joins bone to bone.

Synovium is the smooth lining of synovial joints that produces synovial fluid.

Osteoprogenitor cells become osteo*blasts* (not osteo*clasts*).

Sockets are joints (e.g., ball and socket joints of hips).

E: muscles do connect bones *via* their origin and insertion points, but they are *not connective tissue* (i.e., contractile tissue).

33. B is correct.

Failure of the *lamina of the vertebrae* to fuse correctly in the lumbar region during development can produce an exposed spinal cord, known as *spina bifida*.

34. E is correct.

Epiphyseal plate is the area of growth in long bones; a *hyaline cartilage plate* in the metaphysis of long bones.

Appositional growth is when the cartilage grows in thickness (i.e., diameter) due to the extracellular matrix on the peripheral cartilage surface, accompanied by chondroblasts developing from the *perichondrium*.

35. D is correct.

Up to 50% of bone by weight is modified *hydroxyapatite* with calcium and phosphate in a compound that includes hydroxyl (i.e., ~OH) groups.

Bones store *calcium* and *phosphate*.

36. B is correct.

Osteoclast activity releases calcium ions into the bloodstream and is stimulated by parathyroid hormone (PTH).

37. E is correct.

Osseous tissue (or *bone tissue*) is structural and supportive connective tissue forming a rigid skeletal system.

38. D is correct.

Bone is *connective tissue* that stores calcium.

39. B is correct.

Bone growth and healing from a fracture are impossible without osteoblasts.

40. D is correct.

Osteoclasts are progenitor cells for *white blood cells* derived from *monocytes* and *macrophages*.

Osteoclasts and macrophages participate in nonspecific phagocytosis.

Osteoclasts degrade their surrounding matrix.

Parathyroid hormone (PTH) promotes osteoclast activity, while *calcitonin* inhibits the activity of osteoclasts.

Erythrocytes (or *red blood cells*) are *terminally differentiated*

Chondrocytes are terminally differentiated and the only cells in cartilage that produce and maintain the *cartilaginous matrix, collagen,* and *proteoglycans*.

Mesenchymal stem cells are progenitors of *chondrocytes* but differentiate into several cell types, including osteoblasts.

41. B is correct.

For interstitial growth, chondrocytes in *lacunae divide* and secrete a matrix, allowing cartilage growth from within.

42. D is correct.

Diaphysis is the main shaft of long bone made of cortical bone, bone marrow, and adipose tissue.

Diaphysis comprises compact bone surrounding a central cavity with red or yellow marrow.

Primary ossification occurs in the *diaphysis*.

43. E is correct.

Parathyroid glands are four small pea-shaped structures embedded in the posterior surface of the thyroid.

Parathyroid glands synthesize and secrete parathyroid hormone (PTH) that (along with *calcitonin* and *vitamin D*) regulates plasma $[Ca^{2+}]$ via negative feedback.

PTH raises plasma $[Ca^{2+}]$ by increasing *bone resorption* and decreasing Ca^{2+} excretion in the kidneys.

Parathyroid hormone converts vitamin D to its active form, stimulating intestinal *calcium absorption*.

Insulin lowers plasma glucose levels and increases glycogen storage in the liver.

Glucagon stimulates the conversion of glycogen into glucose in the liver and increases plasma glucose levels.

Anti-diuretic hormone (ADH) stimulates the reabsorption of H_2O in kidneys by increasing the permeability of the nephron to H_2O.

Aldosterone regulates plasma $[Na^+]$ and $[K^+]$ and the total extracellular H_2O volume.

Aldosterone stimulates active reabsorption of Na^+ and passive reabsorption of H_2O in the nephron.

44. C is correct.

Epiphyseal plate has cartilage growth by pushing the *epiphysis away from the diaphysis*.

45. E is correct.

Spongy bone (i.e., *cancellous bone*) is at the ends of long bones, proximal to joints, and within vertebrae.

Spongy bone contains blood stem cells for differentiation into mature blood cells.

Cancellous bone is highly vascular and frequently contains red bone marrow where hematopoiesis (i.e., production of blood cells) occurs.

Long bones participate in fat storage.

Erythrocyte (or red blood) cell storage occurs in the liver and spleen.

46. A is correct.

Trabeculae are thin rods and plates of bone tissue at the ends of long bones.

Despite being porous, the structure provides strength and allows *significant mechanical stresses* on the bones.

Osteons are the functional unit of compact bone rather than spongy bone.

Osteons consist of concentric layers called *lamellae*.

Haversian canals are microscopic tubes in a bone that allow blood vessels and nerves to travel through them.

47. C is correct.

Calcitonin is a peptide hormone secreted by the thyroid gland.

Osteoclasts (i.e., bone *degradation*) inhibit activity in bones.

Osteoblasts (i.e., bone *formation*) do not have calcitonin receptors, so calcitonin does not directly affect them.

Bone resorption and formation are interdependent.

Inhibition of osteoclastic activity by calcitonin indirectly leads to increased osteoblastic activity.

48. B is correct.

Osteoporosis is a progressive bone disease characterized by decreased bone mass and density, increasing fracture risk.

Osteoporosis reduces bone mineral density, where bone microarchitecture deteriorates, and the amount and variety of proteins in bone are altered.

Trabecular bone (i.e., spongy bone in the ends of long bones and vertebrae) is more prone to turnover due to a higher concentration of *osteoclasts* (breakdown bone) and *osteoblasts* (deposit bone) and remodeling of calcium/phosphate within the bone.

Calcitonin stimulates osteoblasts to build bone mass.

Menopause contributes to osteoporosis by reducing estrogen levels, thereby reducing osteoblast activity.

49. C is correct.

Bursae are connective tissue sacs lined with *synovial membranes* acting as cushions where friction develops.

50. B is correct.

Epiphyseal plate is a hyaline cartilage plate in the metaphysis at each end of a long bone.

Epiphyseal plate is present in children and adolescents.

In adults, the epiphyseal plate is replaced by an *epiphyseal line*.

Respiratory System – Detailed Explanations

1. B is correct.

Circulatory system transports gases to and from tissues and cells.

Respiratory system conducts gas exchange in the alveoli of the lungs.

2. A is correct.

Sound intensity (i.e., loudness) is controlled primarily by the force of air from the lungs passing the *larynx*.

Size of vocal folds affects the *pitch* of the voice.

3. D is correct.

Autonomic nervous system (i.e., sympathetic, and parasympathetic) regulates internal environments (i.e., maintains homeostasis via parasympathetic division) by controlling involuntary processes.

ANS innervates the heart, smooth muscle around blood vessels, digestive tract, and endocrine, reproductive, excretory, and respiratory systems.

Sympathetic division of ANS controls *vasoconstriction of arterioles* in response to changes in temperature.

Somatic nervous system innervates skeletal muscles in response to external stimuli.

Sensory nervous system innervates skin, taste, and olfactory receptors.

4. A is correct.

Alveoli walls are composed of two types of cells, type I and type II.

>   *Type I cells* form the structure of the alveolar wall.

>   *Type II cells* secrete *surfactant*.

5. E is correct.

Inspiratory and expiratory centers are in the *medulla oblongata*.

6. B is correct.

Pressure in lungs *exceeds atmospheric pressure* causing air *out* of the lungs to flow down the pressure gradient.

7. C is correct.

Unlike inspiration, *expiration is passive* because no muscular contractions are involved.

Air is expelled from the lungs when the *diaphragm relaxes* and pushes up on the lungs.

8. E is correct.

Diaphragm is an internal skeletal muscle sheet extending across the bottom of the rib cage.

Diaphragm separates the thoracic cavity (heart, lungs, and ribs) from the abdominal cavity and is vital in respiration – as the diaphragm contracts, the volume of the thoracic cavity increases, and air enters the lungs.

9. A is correct.

Many animals do not have sweat glands, so sweating is not a method of heat loss.

Panting mechanism serves as a substitute for sweating. When a large amount of air comes into the upper respiratory passages, it permits *water evaporation* from the *mucosal surfaces* to aid in heat loss.

Preoptic area of the anterior hypothalamus is the *thermoregulatory center* that monitors blood temperature.

B: *rapid breaths* during panting are not deep enough to affect the rate of CO_2 expiration.

C: *surface moisture* of the respiratory mucosa is dehydrated via evaporation.

D: *respiratory muscles* move faster and are engaged during panting.

10. B is correct.

C-shaped rings of cartilage form the *trachea*, allowing it to *maintain openness*.

11. B is correct.

Hyaline cartilage rings help support the trachea while simultaneously being flexible during breathing.

12. D is correct.

Intrapulmonary pressure is pressure within the lungs, which varies between inspiration and expiration.

Intrapulmonary pressure must fall *below atmospheric pressure to initiate inspiration*.

During inspiration, increased lung volume decreases intrapulmonary pressure to sub-atmospheric levels, and air enters the lungs.

Decrease in lung volume raises intrapulmonary pressure above atmospheric pressure, expelling air (i.e., exhalation) from the lungs.

13. E is correct.

Fenestrated capillaries (i.e., openings between cells) are *single-layer endothelial cells*.

Blood (with the erythrocytes) moves under *hydrostatic pressure* for oxygen exchange.

14. B is correct.

Surfactant prevents alveoli from collapsing by disrupting the cohesiveness of H_2O, thereby *reducing the surface tension* of the alveolar fluid.

15. E is correct.

[CO_2] in blood affects Hb's affinity for O_2 and therefore affects the location of the curve on the O_2-dissociation graph, but [CO_2] is not the reason for the sigmoidal shape.

High [CO_2] in the blood decreases Hb's affinity for O_2 and shifts the curve to the right (i.e., *Bohr effect*).

Bohr effect (graph) is a physiological observation in which Hb's O_2 binding affinity is inversely related to [CO_2] and blood acidity. Increased blood [CO_2] or a decreased pH (more H^+) results in Hb releasing O_2 at the tissue.

Decrease in CO_2 (or an *increase in pH*) causes hemoglobin to bind O_2 and load more O_2.

CO_2 reacts with water to form carbonic acid, causing a decrease in blood pH.

Carbonic anhydrase (erythrocyte enzyme) accelerates the formation of bicarbonate and protons, decreasing pH in tissue and promoting dissociation of O_2 to tissue.

In the lungs, where PO_2 is high, binding of O_2 causes Hb to release H^+, combining with bicarbonate to release CO_2 via exhalation; reactions are closely matched, so homeostasis of blood pH is about 7.35.

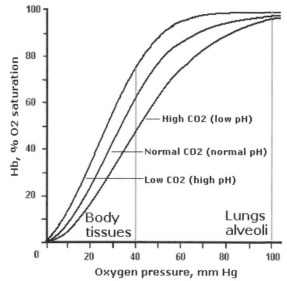

16. D is correct.

Increased carbon dioxide [CO_2] in blood is detected by respiratory centers in the *pons* and *medulla*, which signal the body to breathe more deeply and frequently.

Decreased concentration carbon dioxide [CO_2] levels decrease the frequency and depth of breathing.

17. A is correct.

Type II alveolar cells produce pulmonary surfactants.

18. D is correct.

Ductus arteriosus fails to close; less O_2 is in the systemic circulation blood because O_2 is shunted from the aorta to lower pressure pulmonary arteries.

Pulmonary circulation carries more oxygenated blood than usual because highly oxygenated blood from the aorta mixes with deoxygenated blood in the pulmonary circulation.

Heart pumps more forcefully to compensate for reduced O_2 delivery by bringing more blood to the tissues.

19. C is correct.

Alveolar ventilation rate is directly proportional to the partial pressure of O_2 in the blood. The greater the ventilation rate, the greater the amount of O_2 available in the alveoli to diffuse across the respiratory membrane and enter the pulmonary capillaries.

continued...

Alveolar ventilation increases proportionally with increased O_2 consumption, increasing during exercise (e.g., deeper and rapid breathing) because metabolism is accelerated, and there is a greater need for O_2.

Arterial partial pressure of O_2 remains (more or less) steady because increased demand offsets increased supply of O_2 during exercise.

A: P_{O_2} does not decrease because of increased alveolar ventilation.

B: only if alveolar ventilation did not increase with metabolism.

D: ventilation increases as metabolism increases.

20. C is correct.

In respiration, inhalation stretches the lungs, and *elastic recoil* refers to the ease with which the lungs rebound.

Intrapleural pressure (i.e., the pressure within the pleural cavity) decreases during inhalation.

Diaphragm relaxes during expiration, the lungs recoil, and the intrapleural pressure restores.

Lung compliance (i.e., the lung's ability to stretch and expand) is inversely related to elastic recoil.

Elastic recoil of the lungs occurs because:

1) elastic fibers in the connective tissue of the lungs and

2) surface tension of the fluid that lines alveoli.

Due to cohesion, water molecules bond (via *hydrogen bonding*), pull on alveolar walls, and cause alveoli to recoil and become smaller.

Two factors *prevent lungs from collapsing*:

1) *surfactant* (i.e., *surface-active lipoprotein complex* formed by type II alveolar cells) and

2) *intrapleural pressure*.

21. B is correct.

Chemoreceptors are in the *medulla oblongata*, on the *carotid arteries*, and the *aorta*.

Chemoreceptors detect and signal the respiratory centers in the *medulla* to modify *breathing rate* when the partial pressure of respiratory gases changes (i.e., low, or high).

Chemoreceptors respond to changes in $[CO_2]$ and $[H^+]$, while extreme changes in $[O_2]$ are relayed to the *medulla oblongata*.

$[H^+]$ of blood is *directly proportional to the partial pressure of [CO_2]*.

CO_2 combines with H_2O in erythrocytes to form H_2CO_3, dissociating into HCO_3^- and H^+.

Increase in $[H^+]$ decreases the pH of the blood.

Chemoreceptors detect increases in partial pressure of CO_2 or increases in $[H^+]$, increasing breathing rate.

High partial pressure of O_2 in the blood triggers a decrease (not increase) in the breathing rate.

22. A is correct.

Lung compliance measures the lung's ability to stretch and expand.

Surface tension of alveolar fluid is the force created by films of molecules, *reducing surface area,* thus affecting *lung compliance*.

23. D is correct.

Bronchodilation is the expansion of bronchial air passages caused by sympathetic stimulation, increasing muscle blood flow.

24. E is correct.

Tidal volume is *air entering* the lungs during regular inhalation at rest; same amount leaves during exhalation.

Average tidal volume is 500ml.

Inspiratory reserve volume is the amount of air inhaled above tidal volume during a *deep breath*.

Expiratory reserve volume is the air exhaled above tidal volume during a *forceful breath*.

Residual volume is the air remaining in the lungs after a maximal exhalation; some air remains to prevent the lungs from collapsing.

Vital capacity is the most air exhaled after taking the deepest breath; this amount can be up to ten times more than customarily exhaled.

Total lung capacity is the vital lung capacity, plus residual volume equaling the total air the lungs can hold.

Average total lung capacity is 6000 ml, varying with age, height, gender, and health status.

25. B is correct.

Excess plasma H+ is removed to raise the pH.

Exhalation of CO_2 is increased because of low pH.

Therefore, the reaction *shifts left* to produce CO_2 expired.

26. C is correct.

Respiration performs *gas exchange* which relies on the laws of partial pressure.

Partial pressure is the respective pressure of each gas in two connected regions.

Gases equalize pressure, affecting the direction of movement.

Gas moves from areas of higher to lower partial pressure.

Greater pressure differences cause rapid *gas diffusion*.

27. D is correct.

Fetal circulation differs from adult circulation, whereby in fetal circulation, blood is oxygenated by the placenta because fetal lungs are nonfunctional before birth.

Umbilical vein carries oxygenated blood from the placenta to the fetus.

Three shunts in fetal circulation divert blood from the fetal liver and lungs:

1) *ductus venosus* diverts blood from the fetal liver before converging with the inferior vena cava, returning deoxygenated blood to the right atrium.

   Oxygenated blood from the umbilical vein mixes with deoxygenated blood of the venae cavae; blood entering the fetal right atrium is partially oxygenated.

2) *foramen ovale* diverts blood away from the right ventricle and pulmonary artery; most blood bypasses pulmonary circulation and enters the left atrium directly from the right atrium.

   Remaining blood in the right atrium empties into the right ventricle and is pumped to the lungs via the *pulmonary artery*.

3) *ductus arteriosus* reduces blood to the lungs by diverting it from the pulmonary artery to the aorta.

Gas exchange occurs in the placenta (not fetal lungs).

In the fetus, *pulmonary arteries carry partially oxygenated blood to the lungs*, which are further deoxygenated because blood unloads oxygen to the fetal lungs.

Deoxygenated blood returns to the left atrium via the *pulmonary veins*.

Blood mixes with partially oxygenated blood crossing the right atrium (via *foramen ovale*) before being pumped into systemic circulation by the left ventricle.

Blood delivered (via *aorta*) has lower partial pressure blood for O_2 delivered to lungs.

Deoxygenated blood returns to the placenta via *umbilical arteries*.

Ductus arteriosus obstruction increases blood supply to fetal lungs because blood pumped into the pulmonary arteries by the *right ventricle flows through the lungs*.

Ductus venosus obstruction dramatically increases blood supply to the fetal liver because oxygenated blood from the *umbilical vein* passes through the liver before the heart.

Pulmonary artery obstruction decreases blood supply to the fetal lungs.

Aorta obstruction diminishes blood supply to tissue but not the volume of blood delivered to the fetal lungs.

28. C is correct.

Hypoxia is a pathological condition whereby tissue is deprived of adequate oxygen supply.

29. C is correct.

Sensory organs of the brain, aorta and carotid arteries monitor oxygen and CO_2 levels in blood.

Carbon dioxide must be eliminated from blood continuously to maintain acid-base balance.

Chemoreceptors near the respiratory center in the brain control acid-base balance by sensing the changes in the pH of cerebrospinal fluid.

Increased concentration of CO_2 is the most potent stimulus to breathe more deeply and more frequently to remove excess CO_2.

Chronic hypoventilation (e.g., patients with chronic obstructive pulmonary disease) is when chemoreceptors lose sensitivity and inadequately respond to increases in CO_2 peripheral chemoreceptors attempt to regulate respiratory function to restore the acid-base balance.

Peripheral chemoreceptors detect the concentration of oxygen in peripheral blood.

Therefore, the stimulus to breathe is low oxygen rather than increased carbon dioxide levels.

If oxygen level is significantly increased by administering supplemental oxygen, the peripheral chemoreceptors will not stimulate breathing, resulting in *apnea* (i.e., *cessation of airflow*).

Supplemental oxygen must be given to patients with chronic obstructive pulmonary disease at very low levels.

Elevated blood pressure does not encourage breathing or cause external symptoms.

30. E is correct.

Lower respiratory tract begins at the trachea and extends into the primary bronchi and the lungs.

31. C is correct.

Esophagus is part of the digestive system and is not a part of the respiratory tract.

Respiratory tract begins with the trachea, which divides into the two main bronchi.

Main bronchi subdivide into branching *bronchioles*, leading to *alveoli* (i.e., site of gas exchange in lungs).

32. D is correct.

*Respiratory cente*rs are in the medulla oblongata and pons, brain stem structures.

Respiratory centers have receptors for *neural, chemical,* and *hormonal signals* to control the depth and rate of breathing via *movements of the diaphragm* and *respiratory muscles*.

33. E is correct.

Exhalation begins in *alveoli;* air moves through *bronchioles* to *bronchi* and passes through the *trachea* towards the *larynx* and then the *pharynx*.

34. A is correct.

CO_2 is carried in blood in three ways; % concentration depends on whether it is venous or arterial blood.

1) 70-80% of CO_2 is converted to bicarbonate ions HCO_3^- by carbonic anhydrase in the red blood cells via the reaction:

$$CO_2 + H_2O \rightarrow H_2CO_3 \rightarrow H^+ + HCO_3^-$$

2) 5-10% is dissolved in blood plasma.

3) 5-10% is bound to hemoglobin as carbamino compounds.

Hemoglobin is the primary oxygen-carrying molecule in the RCB and carries carbon dioxide.

CO_2 does *not* bind to the same site as O_2; it combines with N-terminal groups on the four globin chains.

Due to allosteric effects on hemoglobin, binding CO_2 lowers O_2 bound for a given partial pressure of oxygen.

Deoxygenation of the blood increases its ability to carry carbon dioxide – *Haldane effect*.

Oxygenated blood has reduced capacity for CO_2, affecting blood's ability to transport CO_2 from tissues to lungs.

Rises in partial pressure of CO_2 cause offloading oxygen from hemoglobin (*Bohr Effect*).

35. B is correct.

Nasal conchae are long, spongy, curled shelves of bone protruding into the breathing passage of the nose.

36. C is correct.

Diffusion is how O_2 and CO_2 are exchanged in the lungs and through cell membranes.

37. B is correct.

Capillaries have extensive blood exchange networks, the greatest cross-sectional area, and the highest resistance to blood flow.

Blood pressure is highest in *aorta* and drops as blood returns to heart via the *inferior and superior venae cavae*.

38. C is correct.

CO_2 is transported in blood as *bicarbonate ions* in plasma after entering the erythrocytes.

39. E is correct.

Gas exchange is a passive process whereby gases diffuse down partial pressure gradients.

Inhalation is an active process requiring contraction of the diaphragm and the external intercostal muscles.

Exhalation is passive from the elastic recoil of the lungs and relaxation of the diaphragm and external intercostal muscles.

During vigorous exercise, *active muscle contractions* assist in exhalation.

40. A is correct.

CO_2 transport does *not* include an attachment to the heme of hemoglobin.

41. C is correct.

Carina is a cartilage ridge in the trachea's lower part, dividing the two main *bronchi*.

42. B is correct.

Erythrocyte number is *not* a factor promoting oxygen binding to and dissociation from hemoglobin.

43. E is correct.

Hypovolemic shock is a state of decreased blood plasma from such conditions as hemorrhaging and dehydration.

Loss of blood plasma would be more rapid during arterial bleeding (i.e., high *hydrostatic* pressure) than during venous bleeding (i.e., low hydrostatic pressure).

44. A is correct.

When an individual goes from a low to high altitude, erythrocyte count increases after a few days because the concentration of O_2 or total atmospheric pressure is lower at high altitudes.

45. A is correct.

Air pressure within the lungs less than atmospheric pressure causes air to rush into the lungs.

B: *thoracic cavity* enlargement causes the pressure of air within the lungs to fall.

C: low pressure inside the thoracic cavity is due to expansion of thoracic volume from diaphragm contractions.

D: when the pressure drops, air rushes in, and ciliated membranes warm, moisten, and filter inspired air.

Air travels through the bronchi, into the bronchioles, and alveoli, where diffusion occurs to oxygenate blood and release CO_2.

46. D is correct.

Mucus in the nose traps dust and microbes carried by *cilia* (tiny hairs) lining the inside nasal passages.

DAT Biology Practice Questions and Detailed Explanations

47. E is correct.

Larynx is the organ that connects the lower portion of the pharynx and the trachea.

Larynx functions as a valve to close air passages while swallowing, maintaining a patent airway and vocalization.

Pharynx divides into the nasopharynx, oropharynx, and laryngopharynx.

Pharynx is part of the digestive and respiratory systems and is vital for vocalization.

Laryngopharynx (or *hypopharynx*) is part of the throat connecting to the esophagus.

It is inferior to (below) the epiglottis and extends to where the pharynx diverges into the *respiratory* (*larynx*) and *digestive* (*esophagus*) pathways.

Laryngopharynx, like the oropharynx above it, is a passageway for food and air.

Oropharynx (or *mesopharynx*) lies behind the oral cavity, extending from the uvula to hyoid bone level.

Food and air pass through the oropharynx, and a flap of connective tissue (i.e., *epiglottis*) closes over the glottis when food is swallowed to prevent aspiration.

Nasopharynx (or *epipharynx*) is the higher portion of the pharynx that extends from the skull base to the upper surface of the soft palate and lies above the oral cavity.

Pharyngeal tonsils (or *adenoids*) are lymphoid tissue structures in the posterior wall of the nasopharynx.

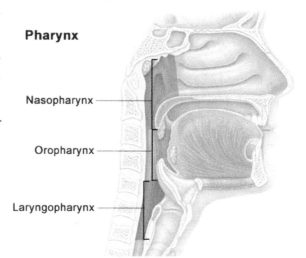

48. B is correct.

Surfactant helps increase alveolar surface tension as a physical factor influencing pulmonary ventilation; as alveolar surface tension increases, additional muscle action is required.

                                      Copyright © Sterling Test Prep.

Integumentary System – Detailed Explanations

1. B is correct.

Melanin is a natural pigment in most organisms.

Melanogenesis produces melanin in the skin after exposure to UV radiation, causing the skin to appear tan.

Melanin is an effective absorber of light, whereby the pigment dissipates over 99.9% of absorbed UV radiation and protects skin cells from UVB radiation damage, thereby reducing the risk of cancer.

2. A is correct.

Subcutaneous tissue (or *hypodermis*, *subcutis*, or *superficial fascia*) is the lowermost layer of the integumentary.

Subcutaneous tissue is *not* part of skin but lies below the dermis.

Subcutaneous tissue attaches skin to the underlying bone and muscle and supplies blood vessels and nerves.

Hypodermis consists of loose connective tissue and elastin.

3. C is correct.

Skin sensations are due to *nerve endings* in (mostly) the dermis.

4. E is correct.

Tactile cells (i.e., *Merkel cells*) are epithelial mechanoreceptor cells for light touch sensation.

Nociception (i.e., *pain receptors*) detects *mechanical*, *thermal*, and *chemical changes*.

Nociception is a *neural process* for perceiving stimuli.

5. B is correct.

Apocrine glands develop at puberty under hormonal influence and are *not* crucial for thermoregulation.

Odor from sweat is due to bacterial activity on oily compounds, which acts as pheromones from *apocrine sweat glands* (i.e., axillary parts of external genitalia).

Armpits (i.e., underarms) are referred to as *axillary*.

6. A is correct.

Reticular dermis is the lower layer of skin under the papillary dermis, composed of *densely packed collagen fibers* comprising *irregular connective tissue*.

Reticular dermis *strengthens* skin and provides *structure* and *elasticity*.

Reticular dermis supports *sweat glands* and *hair follicles*.

7. E is correct.

Eccrine glands are major sweat glands of humans responsible for thermoregulation through cooling by evaporation of sweat.

8. C is correct.

Arrector pili are small muscles attached to hair follicles that occasionally contract, causing hairs to stand on end. This can involuntarily occur when a person is cold or experiences strong emotions such as fear.

9. B is correct.

Sebaceous glands in the skin secrete an oily/waxy matter (i.e., *sebum*) to lubricate and waterproof skin and hair.

Sebaceous glands are abundant on the face and scalp but distributed within the skin (*except palms and soles*).

In eyelids, *meibomian sebaceous glands* secrete a type of *sebum* into tears.

10. D is correct.

Cortex is the part of the hair cells with *pigment granules* responsible for hair color.

11. D is correct.

Loss of skin (e.g., severe burn) increases the risk of dehydration, bacterial infection, and inadequate body temperature maintenance.

12. A is correct.

Sweat glands (or *sudoriferous glands*) are small tubular structures of the skin that produce sweat.

Two main types of sweat glands:

> **Eccrine sweat glands** are distributed over the body, though their density varies from region to region.
>
> Humans utilize eccrine sweat glands as a *primary method of cooling*.
>
> **Apocrine sweat glands** are larger, have a different secretion mechanism, and are limited to the *axilla* (armpits) and perianal areas. Apocrine glands contribute little to human cooling but are effective sweat glands in *hoofed animals* such as cattle, camels, horses, and donkeys.

Eccrine designates merocrine secretions from sweat glands (eccrine sweat glands).

Merocrine is the typical manner of secretion.

Merocrine classifies exocrine glands and their secretions for histology.

Merocrine cell secretions are via *exocytosis* from secretory cells into an epithelial-walled duct or ducts and onto a bodily surface (or into a lumen).

Glands release products and no part is lost or damaged (compare *holocrine* and *apocrine*).

continued…

B: *apocrine cells* release secretions via exocytosis of plasma membranes. Secretions are less damaging to glands than *holocrine secretions* (which destroy a cell) but more damaging than merocrine secretion (*exocytosis*).

Mammary glands are *apocrine glands* for secreting breast milk.

C: *ceruminous glands* are specialized subcutaneous *sudoriferous* (i.e., sweat) glands in the external auditory canal, producing cerumen (earwax) by mixing secretions with sebum and dead epidermal cells.

Cerumen *waterproofs* canals, kills bacteria, keeps eardrums pliable, lubricates and cleans external auditory canals, and traps particles (e.g., dust, fungal spores) by coating guard hairs of the ear, making them sticky.

D: *sebaceous glands* in the skin secrete oily/waxy matter (sebum) to lubricate and waterproof skin and hair.

Sebaceous glands are abundant on the face and scalp, though they are distributed throughout the skin (*except for the palms and soles*).

E: *holocrine secretions* are produced in the cytoplasm and released by plasma membrane rupture, which destroys the cell and results in the secretion of the product into the lumen.

Sebaceous gland is a *holocrine* because its secretion product (*sebum*) is released with remnants of dead cells.

13. D is correct.

Carotene, melanin, and *hemoglobin* are pigments that contribute to skin color.

14. C is correct.

Burn Type	Layers affected	Sensation	Healing time	Prognosis
Superficial (1°)	Epidermis	Painful	5–10 days	Heals well; repeated sunburns increase the risk of skin cancer later in life
Superficial partial thickness (2°)	Extends into the superficial (papillary) dermis	Very painful	less than 2–3 weeks	Local infection/cellulitis but no scarring typically
Deep partial thickness (2°)	Extends into the deep (reticular) dermis	Pressure and discomfort	3–8 weeks	Scarring, contractures (may require excision and skin grafting)
Full thickness (3°)	Extends through the entire dermis	Painless	Prolonged (months) and incomplete	Scarring, contractures, amputation (early excision recommended)
Fourth degree (4°)	Extends - entire skin and into underlying fat, muscle, and bone	Painless	Requires excision	Amputation, significant functional impairment, and in some cases, death

15. C is correct.

Epidermis contains no blood vessels, and cells in the deepest layers are nourished by diffusion from blood capillaries that extend to the upper layers of the dermis.

16. B is correct.

Integumentary (or *skin*) system functions in thermoregulation, UV protection, and infection resistance. It is the site of vitamin D synthesis but does not function in synthesizing vitamin E; plants synthesize vitamin E.

17. E is correct.

Dermis is a skin layer between the *epidermis* (i.e., cutis) and *subcutaneous tissues* that consists of connective tissue and cushions the body from stress and strain.

Dermis divides into two layers:

> *superficial area* adjacent to the epidermis (i.e., *papillary region*) and

> *reticular dermis* (deep, thicker area).

Dermis is tightly connected to the epidermis through a *basement membrane*.

Structural components of the dermis are *collagen, elastic fibers*, and *extrafibrillar matrix*.

Dermis contains *mechanoreceptors* (i.e., sense of touch and heat), *sweat glands, hair follicles, sebaceous glands, apocrine glands, blood vessels*, and *lymphatic vessels*.

Blood vessels provide nourishment and waste removal for *dermal* and *epidermal cells*.

18. A is correct.

Skin has three layers:

> *epidermis* (outermost layer)

> *dermis* (beneath the epidermis)

> *hypodermis* (fat and connective tissue)

19. E is correct.

Sweat is mainly composed of water.

20. A is correct.

Dermis lies beneath the epidermis and contains connective tissue, sweat glands, and hair follicles.

Epidermis is the outermost layer and physical barrier protecting the body against microbes, UV light, and chemical compounds.

21. D is correct.

Eccrine skin glands are essential for body temperature regulation.

22. A is correct.

Stratum corneum is the outer layer of the five layers of the epidermis, consisting of dead cells (corneocytes).

It comprises numerous layers of flattened cells with no nuclei or cellular organelles. These cells contain a dense network of keratin, a protein that helps keep the skin hydrated by preventing water evaporation.

Epidermis consists of five layers of cells, each with a distinct role in the skin's health and functioning.

Stratum basale is the deepest layer of the five layers of epidermis and a continuous layer of cells.

It is described as one-cell thick (but two to three cells thick in hairless skin and hyperproliferative epidermis).

Stratum basale is primarily basal keratinocyte cells that divide to form the keratinocytes of the stratum spinosum, which migrate superficially.

Melanocytes (pigment-producing cells), *Langerhans cells* (immune cells), and *Merkel cells* (touch receptors) are other cells within the stratum basale.

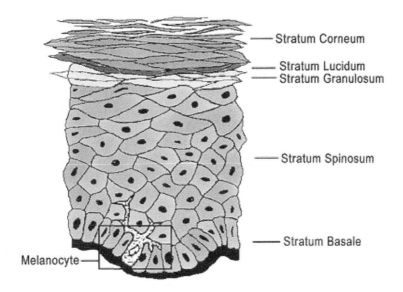

Stratum spinosum is where keratinization begins. It comprises polyhedral keratinocytes that synthesize fibrillar proteins (*cytokeratin*), which build up within the cells by aggregating to form *tonofibrils*.

Tonofibrils form the desmosomes allowing strong connections to form between adjacent keratinocytes.

Stratum granulosum is a thin layer of cells as keratinocytes migrate from the underlying stratum spinosum to become granular cells containing keratohyalin granules.

These granules are filled with proteins and promote hydration and crosslinking of *keratin*.

At the transition between the *stratum granulosum* and *stratum corneum* layers, cells secrete *lamellar bodies* (containing lipids and proteins) into the extracellular space to form the hydrophobic lipid envelope responsible for the skin's barrier properties.

Simultaneously, cells lose their nuclei and organelles, causing granular cells to become non-viable corneocytes in the *stratum corneum*.

23. E is correct.

Holocrine secretions are produced in the cytoplasm and released by plasma membrane rupture, which destroys the cell and results in the secretion of the product into the lumen.

Sebaceous gland is a *holocrine* because its secretion product (*sebum*) is released with remnants of dead cells.

24. D is correct.

Melanin is a group of natural pigments derived from the amino acid tyrosine but is not an amino acid or protein.

Skin pigment is produced in a specialized group of cells known as *melanocytes*.

25. D is correct.

Sebaceous, *mammary*, and *ceruminous glands* are accessory glands of the skin.

26. A is correct.

Friction ridges give rise to the distinctive fingerprints of humans.

27. B is correct.

Dense irregular connective tissue is the principal tissue in *the dermal layer*.

28. C is correct.

Adipose tissue (comprised mainly of lipids) is not a derivative of the epidermis.

29. E is correct.

Keratin protein provides the epidermis with protective properties.

30. A is correct.

Cuticle is not a zone of the hair along its length.

31. B is correct.

Lunula (or *lunulae*) is the whitish crescent-shaped area of fingernail bed (or toenail) and visible part of nail root.

32. B is correct.

Integumentary system refers to the skin and appendages (i.e., hair, nails, glands, nerves).

Adipose tissue (comprised mainly of lipids) accumulates in the deepest, subcutaneous layer of skin.

33. A is correct.

People accumulate fat in the *hypodermis* when gaining weight.

34. C is correct.

Apocrine sweat glands are in specific locations on the body associated with hair.

35. B is correct.

Melanomas are a rare form of skin cancer but must be removed quickly to prevent metastasizing.

36. A is correct.

Skin cancer is often due to exposure to UV light.

37. B is correct.

Needles pierce skin epidermal layers by *corneum*, *lucidum*, *granulosum*, *spinosum*, and the *basale*.

Epidermis consists of five layers, each with a distinct role in the skin's health, well-being, and functioning.

Stratum corneum is the outermost layer of the epidermis, consisting of dead cells (*corneocytes*). Its purpose is to form a barrier to protect underlying tissue from infection, dehydration, chemicals, and mechanical stress.

Stratum lucidum is a thin translucent layer of dead skin cells in the epidermis.

It comprises three to five layers of dead, flattened keratinocytes, which do not feature distinct boundaries and are filled with an intermediate form of keratin (*eleidin*).

Stratum granulosum is a thin layer of cells where keratinocytes migrate from the underlying stratum spinosum to become *granular cells* containing keratohyalin granules.

These granules are filled with proteins and promote hydration and *crosslinking of keratin*.

At transitions between *stratum granulosum* and *stratum corneum* layers, cells secrete lamellar bodies (containing lipids and proteins) into extracellular spaces.

This forms the hydrophobic lipid envelope responsible for the skin's barrier properties. Cells lose their nuclei and organelles, causing the granular cells to become non-viable corneocytes in the stratum corneum.

Stratum spinosum is where keratinization begins. This layer comprises polyhedral keratinocytes active in synthesizing fibrillar proteins (cytokeratin), built up within the cells by aggregating to form tonofibrils.

Tonofibrils form the desmosomes allowing strong connections to form between adjacent keratinocytes.

Stratum basale is the deepest layer of the five epidermis layers and a continuous layer of cells. It is one cell thick (though it may be two to three cells thick in hairless skin and hyperproliferative epidermis).

Melanocytes (pigment-producing cells), *Langerhans cells* (immune cells), and *Merkel cells* (touch receptors) are within the stratum basale.

38. E is correct.

Stratum basale layer of the epidermis would be affected first by inhibiting cell division (e.g., chemotherapy).

Epidermis has five layers of cells.

Each epidermal layer has a distinct role in skin health, well-being, and functioning.

Stratum basale is the deepest layer of the five epidermis layers and a continuous layer of cells.

It is often described as one cell thick (though it may be two to three cells thick in hairless skin and hyperproliferative epidermis).

Stratum basale is primarily made of basal keratinocyte cells that divide to form the keratinocytes of the stratum spinosum, which migrate superficially.

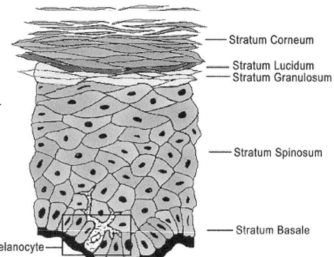

Melanocytes (pigment-producing cells), *Langerhans cells* (immune cells), and *Merkel cells* (touch receptors) are within the stratum basale.

B: **stratum spinosum** is where keratinization begins. This layer comprises polyhedral keratinocytes active in synthesizing fibrillar proteins (i.e., cytokeratin) built up within the cells by aggregating to form tonofibrils.

Tonofibrils form the desmosomes allowing strong connections to form between adjacent keratinocytes.

C: **stratum corneum** is the outermost layer of the epidermis, consisting of dead cells (*corneocytes*).

It forms a barrier to protect underlying tissue from infection, dehydration, chemicals, and mechanical stress.

D: **stratum lucidum** is a thin, translucent layer of dead skin cells in the epidermis.

It comprises three to five layers of dead, flattened keratinocytes, which do not feature distinct boundaries and are filled with an intermediate form of keratin (*eleidin*).

Stratum granulosum is a thin layer of cells where keratinocytes migrate from underlying stratum spinosum to become granular cells containing *keratohyalin granules*.

These granules are filled with proteins and promote hydration and crosslinking of keratin.

At the transition between the *stratum granulosum* and *stratum corneum* layer, cells secrete lamellar bodies (containing lipids and proteins) into the extracellular space.

This forms the hydrophobic lipid envelope responsible for the skin's barrier properties.

Cells lose nuclei and organelles, causing granular cells to become non-viable *corneocytes* in stratum corneum.

39. D is correct.

Mitosis occurs primarily in the *basale stratum* of the epidermis.

Stratum basale is the deepest layer of the five epidermis layers and a continuous layer of cells.

Often described as one cell thick, but two to three cells thick in hairless skin and hyperproliferative epidermis.

Stratum basale is primarily made of basal keratinocyte cells that divide to form the keratinocytes of the stratum spinosum, which migrate superficially.

Cells within the stratum basale are melanocytes (pigment-producing cells),

Langerhans cells (immune cells), and Merkel cells (touch receptors).

A: **stratum spinosum** is where keratinization begins. This layer comprises polyhedral keratinocytes active in synthesizing fibrillar proteins (cytokeratin), which build up within the cells by aggregating to form tonofibrils.

Tonofibrils form the desmosomes allowing strong connections to form between adjacent keratinocytes.

B: **stratum granulosum** is a thin layer of cells where keratinocytes migrate from underlying stratum spinosum to become granular cells containing *keratohyalin granules*.

Keratohyalin granules are filled with proteins and promote hydration and *crosslinking of keratin*.

At the transition between *stratum granulosum* and *stratum corneum* layers, cells secrete lamellar bodies (containing lipids and proteins) into extracellular spaces, forming a hydrophobic lipid envelope responsible for skin's barrier properties.

Simultaneously, cells lose nuclei and organelles, causing granular cells to become non-viable corneocytes in the stratum corneum.

C: **stratum corneum** is the outermost layer of the epidermis, consisting of dead cells (*corneocytes*). It forms a barrier to protect underlying tissue from *infection*, *dehydration*, *chemicals*, and *mechanical stress*.

40. B is correct.

Fingerprints result from the unique structure of the *papillary dermis*, the uppermost layer of the dermis.

41. C is correct.

Mechanoreceptor is a sensory receptor that responds to mechanical pressure or distortion.

Pacinian corpuscles, Meissner's corpuscles, Merkel's discs, and *Ruffini endings* are four mechanoreceptors

Meissner's (i.e., tactile) *corpuscles* are mechanoreceptors and nerve endings in the skin responsible for sensitivity to light touch.

Merkel discs are mechanoreceptors in skin and mucosa (i.e., the lining of endodermal organs) that detect pressure and texture and relay information to the brain.

A: *Ruffini endings* are mechanoreceptors in deep layers of skin, registering *mechanical deformation in joints*.

B: *bulboid corpuscles* (or *end bulbs of Krause*) are *thermoreceptors*, sensing *cold temperatures*.

D: *Pacinian corpuscles* are mechanoreceptor nerve endings in the skin, sensing *vibrations* and *pressure*.

42. D is correct.

Aging of the integumentary system involves changes in the hair, sebaceous glands, and blood vessels.

43. E is correct.

Integument functions with resident macrophage-like cells ingesting antigenic invaders and presenting them to the immune system.

44. D is correct.

Glands only found in the *auditory canal are ceruminous glands.*

Ceruminous glands are specialized subcutaneous sudoriferous (i.e., sweat) glands in the external auditory canal.

They produce cerumen (or earwax) by mixing their secretion with sebum and dead epidermal cells.

Cerumen waterproofs canals, kills bacteria, keeps eardrums pliable, lubricates and cleans the external auditory canal, and traps particles (e.g., dust, fungal spores) by coating the guard hairs of the ear, making them sticky.

45. C is correct.

External root sheath is not a major region of a hair shaft.

46. D is correct.

Oil glands that are typically associated with hair shafts and provide lubrication for hair and skin are sebaceous glands.

Sebaceous glands are in skin and secrete an oily/waxy matter (sebum) to lubricate and waterproof the skin and hair.

Sebaceous glands have highest abundance on face and scalp, though distributed throughout the skin (except palms and soles).

47. A is correct.

Ceruminous glands are sudoriferous (sweat) glands located subcutaneously in the external auditory canal.

Ceruminous glands produce *cerumen* (or *earwax*) by mixing secretions with sebum and dead epidermal cells.

Cerumen waterproofs the canal, kills bacteria, keeps eardrums pliable, lubricates and cleans external auditory canals, and traps foreign particles (e.g., dust, fungal spores) by coating guard hairs of ears, making them sticky.

48. E is correct.

Free nerve endings are customarily associated with the hair shaft for tactile sensations.

Reproductive System – Detailed Explanations

1. D is correct.

Menstrual cycle is regulated by the hypothalamus, anterior pituitary, and ovaries.

Follicle-stimulating hormone (FSH) is released by the anterior pituitary, stimulating the maturation of an ova.

Progesterone, synthesized by the ovary and corpus luteum, regulates the development and shedding of the endometrial lining of the uterus.

Adrenal medulla synthesizes epinephrine (adrenaline) and norepinephrine, which assist the sympathetic nervous system in stimulating the *fight or flight* response but are *not* involved in the menstrual cycle.

2. A is correct.

Oogenesis produces one viable egg and (up to) three polar bodies resulting from the cytoplasm's unequal distribution during meiosis.

Gametes (e.g., egg and sperm) become haploid (1N) through reductive division (i.e., meiosis), in which a diploid cell (2N) gives rise to four haploid sperm or one haploid egg and (up to) three polar bodies.

B: *interstitial cells* are stimulated by luteinizing hormone (LH) to produce testosterone, stimulating sperm development within the seminiferous tubules, along with FSH.

C: *follicle-stimulating hormone* (FSH) stimulates eggs to develop in follicles within the ovaries.

D: *follicle-stimulating hormone* (FSH) participates in gamete production for males and females.

3. E is correct.

Anterior pituitary secretes *follicle-stimulating hormone* (FSH) and *luteinizing hormone* (LH) to influence the maturation of the follicle. *Follicle-stimulating hormone* (FSH) stimulates the maturation of gametes (e.g., ova and spermatids).

Follicle-stimulating hormone (FSH) stimulates estrogen production, which aids in maturing the primary follicle.

Luteinizing (LH) stimulates ovulation and the development of the corpus luteum.

Mature corpus luteum secretes progesterone, causing the uterine lining to thicken and become vascular in preparation for the implantation of the fertilized egg (i.e., zygote).

4. A is correct.

Sperm synthesis begins within the seminiferous tubules of the testes.

Sperm undergoes maturation and storage in the *epididymis*.

During ejaculation, sperm are released from the *vas deferens*.

Seminal vesicles are a pair of male accessory glands that produce about 50-60% of the liquid of the semen.

Mnemonic SEVEN UP — sperm path during ejaculation:

Seminiferous tubules > **E**pididymis > **V**as deferens > **E**jaculatory duct > **N**othing > **U**rethra > **P**enis

5. C is correct.

Hypothalamus secretes releasing factors (tropic hormones), so the anterior pituitary releases LH and FSH.

Follicle-stimulating hormone (FSH) stimulates ovaries to produce mature *ovarian follicles*.

During the follicular stage, the ovary produces estrogen.

As estrogen is released, FSH levels drop, and LH levels increase, which triggers the follicle to release the ovum (i.e., ovulation).

Luteinizing hormone (LH) affects the corpus luteum (i.e., formerly the follicle) that secretes progesterone.

Estrogen is first secreted by ovaries (under the influence of FSH) during the follicular stage (day 1 to 14), decreasing FSH secretions.

Decrease in FSH, along with an increase in LH, causes rupture of the follicle (i.e., ovulation) and formation of the *corpus luteum*.

As the corpus luteum matures, *progesterone levels increase*.

6. D is correct.

At day 14, LH surges, causing a mature follicle to burst and release the ovum from the ovary (i.e., ovulation).

Following ovulation, luteinizing hormone (LH) induces the ruptured follicle to develop into the corpus luteum, secreting progesterone and estrogen.

Prolactin stimulates milk production after birth.

Ovaries secrete estrogen and progesterone, while the *anterior pituitary secretes LH*.

Progesterone and estrogen *inhibit GnRH release*, inhibiting the release of FSH and LH, preventing additional follicles from maturing.

Progesterone stimulates development and maintenance of endometrium in preparation for embryo implantation.

7. B is correct.

Luteinizing hormone (LH) stimulates the release of testosterone in males by Leydig cells.

Testosterone is necessary for proper development of the testes, penis, and seminal vesicles.

Testosterone surges between the first and fourth months of life, and testosterone inadequacy is a primary cause of *cryptorchidism*.

During puberty, testosterone is needed for *secondary male sex characteristics* (e.g., growth of body hair, broadening of shoulders, enlarging of larynx, deepening voice, and increased secretions of oil and sweat glands)

Cortisol is a stress hormone that elevates blood glucose levels.

E: FSH stimulates the maturation of the gametes (e.g., ova and spermatids).

8. C is correct.

Leydig cells are *androgens* (i.e., male hormones such as 19-carbon steroids) that secrete testosterone, androstenedione, and dehydroepiandrosterone (DHEA) when stimulated by luteinizing hormone (LH) released by the pituitary gland.

Leydig cells are adjacent to *seminiferous tubules* in testicles.

Luteinizing hormone (LH) increases conversion of cholesterol to pregnenolone leading to testosterone synthesis and secretion by Leydig cells.

Prolactin (PRL) increases the response of Leydig cells to LH by increasing the number of LH receptors expressed on Leydig cells.

9. B is correct.

Spermatozoon development produces motile, mature sperm, fusing with an ovum to form the zygote.

Eukaryotic *cilia* are structurally like eukaryotic flagella, but distinctions are based on function and length.

Microtubules form the sperm's flagella, which is necessary for movement through the cervix, uterus, and along the fallopian tubes (i.e., oviducts).

Acrosomal enzymes digest the outer zona pellucida (a glycoprotein membrane surrounding the plasma membrane of an oocyte) to permit the fusion of sperm and egg.

Sperm midpiece (diagram below) has many mitochondria used for ATP production for the sperm's movement (via the flagellum) through the female cervix, uterus, and Fallopian tubes.

D: *testosterone* is necessary for *spermatogenesis*.

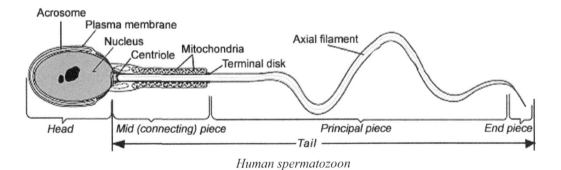

Human spermatozoon

10. A is correct.

Seminiferous tubules are in the testes where meiosis occurs to create gametes (e.g., spermatozoa).

Epithelium of *seminiferous tubules* consists of *Sertoli* (i.e., *nurse cells*) cells that nourish developing sperm and function as phagocytes by consuming residual cytoplasm during spermatogenesis.

Between the Sertoli cells are spermatogenic cells, which differentiate through meiosis into sperm cells.

11. C is correct.

Chlamydia and other infections may scar the reproductive tract, preventing the ova from reaching the uterus and resulting in infertility.

12. E is correct.

Seminal vesicles secrete a considerable proportion of the fluid that ultimately becomes semen.

50-70% of the seminal fluid originates from the seminal vesicles but is not expelled in the first ejaculate fractions dominated by spermatozoa and zinc-rich prostatic fluid.

13. A is correct.

Estrous cycle (i.e., sexual desire) comprises the recurring physiologic changes induced by reproductive hormones in most mammalian females.

Estrous cycles start after sexual maturity in females and are interrupted by anestrous phases or pregnancies.

Menstrual cycle (diagram below) changes the uterus and ovary for sexual reproduction. The menstrual cycle is essential for producing eggs and preparing the uterus for pregnancy.

In humans, the length of a menstrual cycle varies significantly among women (ranging from 21 to 35 days), with 28 days designated as the average length.

Each cycle has three phases based on the ovary (ovarian cycle) or the uterus (uterine cycle).

Ovarian cycle consists of the *follicular, ovulation, and luteal phases*, whereas the uterine cycle has *menstruation, proliferative,* and *secretory phases*.

Endocrine system controls both cycles, and the regular hormonal changes can be interfered with using hormonal contraception to prevent reproduction.

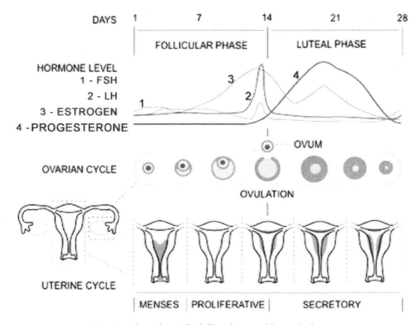

Menstrual cycle with follicular and luteal phases

14. C is correct.

Estrogen is a steroid hormone necessary for typical female maturation.

Estrogen stimulates the development of the female reproductive tract and contributes to *secondary sexual characteristics* and *libido*.

Estrogen is secreted by the *follicle* during the menstrual cycle and is responsible for the thickening of the endometrium in preparation for the implantation of the fertilized egg.

A: *luteinizing hormone* (LH) induces the ruptured follicle to develop into the *corpus luteum*.

B: *luteinizing hormone* stimulates testosterone synthesis in males.

D: *follicle-stimulating hormone* (FSH) is released by the anterior pituitary and promotes the development of the follicle, which matures and begins secreting estrogen.

E: *insulin* is a peptide hormone secreted in response to high blood glucose levels, and it stimulates the uptake of glucose by muscle and adipose cells and the conversion of glucose into the storage molecule of glycogen.

15. A is correct.

Increased estrogen secretions initiate the luteal surge that increases LH secretion → ovulation.

16. B is correct.

Sperm mature and are stored until ejaculation in the *epididymis*. During ejaculation, sperm flows from the lower portion of the epididymis. Products from the prostate gland have not activated them, and they cannot swim.

Sperm is *transported via peristaltic action* of muscle layers within the *vas deferens* and forms *semen* mixed with diluting fluids of the seminal vesicles and other accessory glands before ejaculation.

Seminiferous tubules secrete testosterone.

Primary functions of the testes are to produce sperm (i.e., spermatogenesis) and androgens (e.g., testosterone).

Leydig cells are localized between seminiferous tubules and produce and secrete testosterone and other androgens (e.g., DHT, DHEA) necessary for sexual development and puberty, secondary sexual characteristics (e.g., facial hair, sexual behavior, and libido), supporting spermatogenesis and erectile function.

Luteinizing hormone (LH) results in testosterone release.

Testosterone and follicle-stimulating hormone (FSH) are needed to support spermatogenesis.

17. B is correct.

Inner lining of the Fallopian tubes is covered with cilia, helping the egg move towards the uterus, where it implants if fertilized.

Fertilization usually happens when sperm fuses with an egg in the Fallopian tube.

C: cilia lining the respiratory tract perform this function.

D: *Fallopian tubes* are isolated from the external environment, so pH fluctuations are not an issue.

18. B is correct.

In males, *testosterone* is primarily synthesized in *Leydig cells* in the testis.

Testosterone synthesis is regulated by the *hypothalamic–pituitary–testicular axis*.

When testosterone levels are low, the hypothalamus releases *gonadotropin-releasing hormone* (GnRH), which stimulates the pituitary gland to release FSH and LH.

FSH and LH stimulate the testis to produce testosterone.

Testosterone acts on the hypothalamus and pituitary with elevated levels inhibiting GnRH and FSH/LH release through a negative feedback loop.

19. B is correct.

If fertilization of the ovum does not occur, the *corpus luteum stops secreting progesterone and degenerates*.

Menstruation phase follows decreased progesterone secretion but does not result from increased estrogen levels.

Increased estrogen secretion (not LH) causes luteal surge, which occurs earlier in the cycle.

Thickening of the endometrial lining occurs while estrogen and progesterone levels are high.

20. A is correct.

Vasectomy procedures prevent the movement of sperm along the vas deferens.

Genetics

Mechanisms of Reproduction – Detailed Explanations

1. B is correct.

Gametes form via *meiosis* and are double-stranded haploids.

A single chromosome consists of two hydrogen-bonded complementary antiparallel DNA strands.

2. C is correct.

Let C designate wild-type and c designate the color bind allele.

Mother is Cc, and the father is CY (a normal allele with a single copy of the X gene).

From mating, the mother's gamete (as a carrier due to her dad) is C or c, with a 50% probability of the gamete inheriting the C or c allele.

Assuming a boy (i.e., the father transmits Y and not X), the father's allele of Y (boy) is 100%, and the probability of the mother passing a c (colorblind) is 50%.

Probability of a son being color blind is 50% or ½.

If the question had asked, "what is the probability that they will have a color-blind child?" the analysis changes to determine the probability for all children (not just boys in the original question).

Gametes produced by the mother are C and c with a 50% probability each.

Affected child is a boy.

What is the probability that the father passes the X or Y gene to the offspring? – Probability is 50%.

Individual event probabilities are multiplied to determine the overall probability: $½ × ½ = ¼$

3. C is correct.

Seminiferous tubules are in the testes and are the site of sperm production. *Spermatozoa* are the mature male gametes in many sexually reproducing organisms. *Spermatogenesis* is how spermatozoa are produced from male primordial germ cells by mitosis and meiosis. Initial cells in this pathway are spermatogonia, which yield 1° spermatocytes by mitosis.

1° spermatocyte divides via meiosis into two 2° spermatocytes.

Meiosis converts 1° spermatocyte (2N) into four spermatids (1N).

2° spermatocytes complete meiosis by dividing into 2 spermatids as mature spermatozoa (i.e., sperm cells).

1° spermatocyte gives rise to two 2° spermatocytes that, by further meiosis, produce four spermatozoa.

continued...

Seminiferous tubules are in the testes and the location of meiosis and subsequent creation of gametes (e.g., spermatozoa for males or ova for females).

Epithelium of the tubule consists of *Sertoli cells* whose primary function is to nourish the developing sperm cells through the stages of spermatogenesis.

Sertoli cells function as phagocytes, consuming the residual cytoplasm during spermatogenesis.

Spermatogenic cells differentiate between the Sertoli cells, which differentiate through meiosis into sperm cells.

4. E is correct.

Primary oocytes are arrested in meiotic prophase I from birth until ovulation within the ovaries.

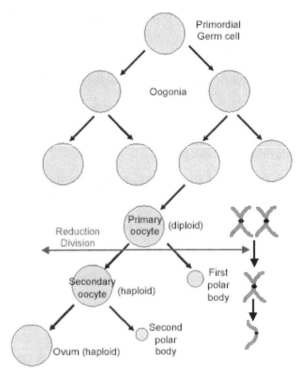

Diploid primordial germ cell undergoes two rounds of meiosis to form haploid ovum and polar bodies

5. C is correct.

A human cell after the first meiotic division is 1N with 2 chromatids.

6. D is correct.

Genetic recombination is when two DNA strand molecules exchange genetic information (i.e., a base composition within the nucleotides), resulting in new combinations of alleles (i.e., alternative forms of genes).

In eukaryotes, the natural process of genetic recombination during meiosis (i.e., the formation of gametes – eggs and sperm) results in genetic information passed to progeny.

Genetic recombination in eukaryotes involves pairing homologous chromosomes (i.e., a set of maternal and paternal chromosomes), which may involve nucleotide exchange between the chromosomes.

Information exchange may occur without physical exchange when a section of genetic material is duplicated without a change in the donating chromosome or by breaking and rejoining the DNA strands (i.e., forming new molecules of DNA).

continued...

Mitosis may involve recombination, where two sister chromosomes form after DNA replication. New combinations of alleles are often not produced because the sister chromosomes are usually identical.

In meiosis and mitosis, recombination occurs between similar DNA molecules (homologous chromosomes or sister chromatids, respectively).

In meiosis, non-sister (i.e., same parent) homologous chromosomes pair with each other, and recombination often occurs between non-sister homologs. For somatic cells (mitosis) and gametes (meiosis), recombination between homologous chromosomes or sister chromatids is a common DNA repair mechanism.

7. C is correct.

Primary oocytes (2N cells) are arrested in prophase I of meiosis I until puberty. There is additional development into secondary oocytes that occurs prior to ovulation.

After ovulation, the oocyte is arrested in metaphase of *meiosis II until fertilization*.

8. B is correct.

Pseudoautosomal regions are named because any genes within them are inherited, like autosomal genes.

Pseudoautosomal regions allow males to pair and segregate X and Y chromosomes during meiosis.

Males have two copies of genes: one in the pseudoautosomal region of their Y chromosome and the other in their X chromosome's corresponding portion.

Typical females possess two copies of pseudoautosomal genes, as each X chromosome contains pseudoautosomal regions.

Crossing over (during prophase I) between the X and Y chromosomes is usually restricted to the pseudoautosomal regions.

Pseudoautosomal genes exhibit an *autosomal*, rather than sex-linked, inheritance pattern.

Females can inherit an allele initially on the Y chromosome of their father, and males can inherit an allele initially on the X chromosome of their father.

9. E is correct.

Primary spermatocyte completes the synthesis (S) phase of interphase, not the first meiotic division, and remains diploid (2N) with 46 chromosomes (i.e., 23 pairs).

10. B is correct.

Chromosomes (not chromatids) *segregate* during mitosis to produce identical somatic (body) 2N (diploid) cells from the parental cell. Meiosis is the process for germline cells (i.e., egg, sperm).

Mutations are inheritable changes in the cell's genetic (DNA) material; recombination occurs during prophase I (at the chiasma of the tetrad) of meiosis, and homologous chromosomes segregate during meiosis I

During meiosis I, homologous chromosomes separate. Subsequently, during meiosis II, the sister chromatids separate to produce four 1N (haploid) products, each with half the number of chromosomes as the original cell.

11. E is correct.

In females, secondary oocytes are haploid (i.e., single copies of 23 chromosomes, each with pair of chromatids).

Secondary oocytes do not complete meiosis II (i.e., haploid with a single chromatid) until fertilized by sperm.

Each month during puberty, one primary oocyte (i.e., diploid, each with a pair of chromatids) completes meiosis I to produce a secondary oocyte (1N) and a polar body (1N).

The 1N secondary oocyte (i.e., 23 chromosomes each with a pair of chromatids) is expelled as an ovum from the follicle during ovulation, but meiosis II does not occur until fertilization.

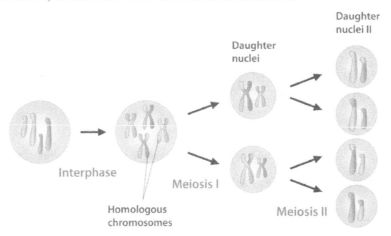

Chromosomes replicate in S phase of mitosis to produce homologous chromosomes. Meiosis I daughter cells are diploid (2N), while the gametes formed from meiosis II (reductive phase) are haploid (1N).

Menarche is marked by the onset of menstruation and signals the possibility of fertility.

Menstruation is the sloughing of the *endometrial lining* of the uterus during the monthly hormonal cycle.

Menopause is when menstruation ceases.

12. D is correct.

Klinefelter syndrome describes the symptoms from additional X genetic material in males.

Turner syndrome is the condition in females with a single X (monosomy X) chromosome.

XYY syndrome is a genetic condition in which a human male has an extra male (Y) chromosome, giving 47 chromosomes instead of 46. XYY is not inherited but usually occurs during the formation of sperm cells.

Nondisjunction error during anaphase II (meiosis II) results in sperms with an extra Y chromosome.

If an atypical sperm contributes to genetic makeup, the child has an extra Y chromosome in each somatic cell.

Triple X syndrome is not inherited but usually occurs during the formation of gametes (e.g., ovum and sperm) because nondisjunction in cell division results in reproductive cells with additional chromosomes.

During cell division, errors (non-disjunction) can result in gametes with additional chromosomes.

An egg or sperm may gain an extra X chromosome due to non-disjunction, and if one gamete contributes to the zygote, the child will have an extra X chromosome in each cell.

---

13. C is correct.

In males, diploid spermatogonia (2N) cells undergo meiosis I to produce 1° diploid spermatocyte (2N), which undergoes meiosis II to yield 2° haploid spermatocytes (1N).

2° spermatocytes undergo meiosis II to produce four spermatids (1N) that mature into spermatozoa (i.e., sperm).

In females, 1° oocyte is (2N), whereby 2° oocyte undergoes the second meiotic division to produce two (1N) cells – a mature oocyte (i.e., ovum – female gamete) and another polar body.

Primary oocyte is diploid (2N).

During fertilization, a (1N) ovum and a (1N) sperm fuse to produce a (2N) zygote.

Spermatogonium is a diploid (2N) cell.

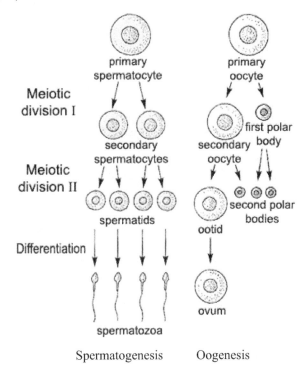

Diploid primary oocytes and oocytes undergo two rounds of meiosis forming haploid spermatozoa and ovum

14. D is correct.

Probability that a child will be male (or female) is ½.

Each event is *independent*; the first (or second or third) child does *not* affect future events.

Probability for 4 children is;

$$½ × ½ × ½ × ½ = 1/16$$

Same probability if the first and third child are female, with the second and fourth as male (or combination).

15. D is correct.

Unequal division of cytoplasm occurs during the meiotic process of oogenesis (i.e., production of an egg cell). Meiotic divisions occur in two stages.

First stage produces precursor (2N) cells when a daughter cell (precursor egg) receives most of the cytoplasm; the other is devoid of sufficient cytoplasm (but genetically identical) and a nonfunctioning polar body.

Second division of oogenesis is when the large (2N) daughter cell divides again, and again one (1N) daughter cell receives the most cytoplasm (i.e., putative *ovum*).

The other daughter eggs become small nonfunctional (1N) *polar bodies*.

Polar bodies (from meiosis I) may divide (via meiosis II) to form two nonfunctional (1N) polar bodies.

The result is a potential of four (1N) cells.

However, only one—the one with a greater amount of cytoplasm during each meiotic division—becomes a functional egg (i.e., ovum) cell along with (up to) three (1N) polar bodies.

Bacterial cells divide for reproduction, and cytoplasmic division is equal.

Mitosis of kidney cells distributes cytoplasm equally.

Spermatogenesis is when one (2N) precursor cell forms four functional (1N) sperm cells because both meiosis divisions are equal and contain an equal amount of cytoplasm.

16. B is correct.

Dyneins are motor proteins (or *molecular motors*) using ATP to perform movement as *retrograde transport*.

Dynein transports cellular contents by *walking* along cytoskeletal microtubules towards the *minus-end* of the microtubules, usually oriented towards the cell center (i.e., *minus-end directed motors.*)

Kinesins are motor proteins that move toward the *plus-end* of the microtubules (i.e., *plus-end directed motors*).

Ovulation is the phase of the female menstrual cycle. A partially mature ovum that has yet to complete meiosis II is released from the ovarian follicles into the Fallopian tube (i.e., oviduct).

After ovulation, the egg can be fertilized by sperm during the *luteal phase*.

Ovulation is determined by circulating hormone levels and is not affected by a defect in dynein motor proteins.

Lungs require cilia to remove bacteria and other particulates.

Kartagener's syndrome males would be *infertile due to sperm immobility*.

Ova would not typically enter the Fallopian tubes (i.e., oviduct) because of the lack of cilia, which would cause an increased risk of ectopic pregnancy.

E: *epithelium lining* the tube of the middle ear is ciliated.

Beat is directed from the cavity to the pharynx, which clears mucus and pathogens.

Therefore, interference with the ciliary function would increase middle ear infections.

17. E is correct.

DNA replication occurs during the synthesis (S) phase of interphase (i.e., G1, S, G2) to form *sister chromatids* joined by a centromere.

Replication occurs during the cell cycle *S* phase (i.e., interphase).

Transcription (in the nucleus) and *translation* (in the cytoplasm) occur during the S phase.

18. C is correct.

Progesterone is a steroid hormone involved in the female menstrual cycle, pregnancy (supports *gestation*), and embryogenesis.

Progesterone levels are relatively low in women during the pre-ovulatory phase of the menstrual cycle, rise after ovulation, and are elevated during the luteal phase.

During pregnancy, human chorionic gonadotropin (HCG) is released, maintaining the corpus luteum and allowing it to maintain progesterone levels.

At 12 weeks, the placenta begins to produce progesterone in place of the corpus luteum – this process is the *luteal-placental shift*.

After the luteal-placental shift, progesterone levels start to rise further.

After delivery of the placenta and during lactation, progesterone levels are very low.

Progesterone levels are low in children and postmenopausal women.

Adult males have levels like those in women during the follicular phase of the menstrual cycle.

19. A is correct.

During meiosis, the gamete (e.g., ovum and sperm) reduces its genetic component from diploid (2N) to haploid (1N) with half the typical chromosome number for somatic (i.e., body cells).

When a haploid egg and sperm unite, they form a diploid zygote.

Ova contains an X chromosome, while sperm contains an X or a Y chromosome.

Gametes form in meiosis (i.e., two reduction divisions) without intervening chromosome replication.

During prophase I of meiosis I, *tetrads* form, and *sister chromatids* (i.e., a chromosome replicated in a prior S phase) undergo homologous recombination as *crossing over*.

Crossing over increases genetic variance within the progeny and is a driving force in the evolution of a species.

20. E is correct.

Meiosis is cell division in sexually reproducing eukaryotes (animals, plants, and fungi), whereby the chromosome number is reduced by half, resulting in four genetically distinct haploid daughters.

DNA replication is followed by mitosis and *two rounds of cell division* in meiosis to produce four (1N) cells.

continued...

Two rounds of meiotic divisions are Meiosis I and Meiosis II.

Meiosis I is a *reductive division*, as the cells are reduced from diploid (2N) to haploid (1N).

Meiosis II (only G phase separates I and II) is an *equational division*, as the cells begin and end as haploids.

21. D is correct.

Crossing over occurs during prophase I of meiosis. During prophase I, the *chromatin condenses* into chromosomes, the centrioles migrate to the poles, the spindle fibers begin to form, and the nucleoli and nuclear membrane disappear.

Homologous chromosomes physically pair and intertwine in the process of *synapsis*.

Prophase I: *chromatids* (i.e., a strand of the replicated chromosome) of *homologous chromosomes* break and exchange equivalent pieces of DNA via *crossing over*.

Metaphase I: *homologous pairs align* at the equatorial plane, and each pair attaches to a separate spindle fiber by its *kinetochore* (i.e., protein collar around the centromere of the chromosome).

Anaphase I: *homologous chromosomes separate* and are pulled by the spindle fibers to opposite cell poles.

Disjunction (i.e., separation of homologous chromosomes) is essential for segregation, as described by Mendel.

Telophase I: *nuclear membrane forms* around each new nucleus, and chromosomes consist of sister chromatids joined at the centromere.

The cell divides into two daughter cells, each receiving a haploid nucleus (1N) of chromosomes.

Interkinesis is a brief period between the two reduction cell divisions of meiosis I and II and during which the chromosomes partially uncoil.

22. A is correct.

In prophase I, *tetrads form*, genetic recombination occurs, and the spindle apparatus forms.

Chromosomes migrate to the poles of the cell during anaphase from the *splitting of the centromere*.

23. E is correct.

Spermatogenesis and *oogenesis* are *gametogenesis*.

Haploid (1N) gametes (i.e., ova and sperm) are produced by diploid (2N) cell reductive divisions (i.e., meiosis).

Spermatogenesis occurs in the gonads, whereby the cytoplasm equally divides during meiosis with the production of four viable sperm 1N cells.

Oogenesis occurs in the gonads, whereby the cytoplasm divides unequally. One 1N ovum (e.g., egg) receives the bulk of the cytoplasm and (up to) three additional 1N polar bodies.

Polar bodies contain a 1N genome (like sperm and egg) but lack sufficient cytoplasm for a viable gamete.

continued...

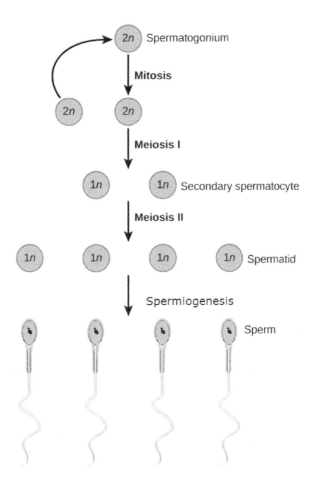

Diploid primary oocytes and oocytes undergo two rounds of meiosis forming haploid spermatozoa and ovum

24. B is correct.

Barr body is an *inactive X chromosome* in a female somatic cell rendered inactive by *lyonization* for species in which sex is determined by the Y chromosomes (i.e., humans and other species).

Lyon hypothesis states that cells with multiple X chromosomes inactivate all but one X randomly during mammalian embryogenesis.

In humans with more than one X chromosome, the number of Barr bodies visible at interphase is one less than the total number of X chromosomes.

For example, a man with Klinefelter syndrome of 47, XXY karyotype has a single Barr body.

A woman with a 47, XXX karyotype has two Barr bodies.

25. A is correct.

Polar bodies form in females as 1N, nonfunctional cells during meiosis.

Meiosis is a two-stage process whereby a 2N cell undergoes a reduction division to form two 1N cells.

Each 1N cell forms two 1N cells for four 1N cells from a parental 2N germ cell in the *second meiotic* division.

For sperm cells, four functional, unique 1N gamete sperm cells form.

For egg cells, the first meiotic division involves an *unequal division of cytoplasm* that results in one large cell and one small cell (i.e., the first polar body).

The large cell divides (second meiotic division) to generate *one functional egg* (1N ovum containing most of the cytoplasm) and another polar body.

First polar body divides again to form two other polar bodies. One large ovum (i.e., functional egg cell) and three polar bodies form during a female meiotic division.

Polar bodies form in mitosis, which is how somatic (i.e., body cells) cell divisions occur; equal cells do not form gametes (i.e., germline cells).

26. E is correct.

Turner syndrome (i.e., 45, X) describes several conditions in females, of which monosomy X (i.e., the absence of the entire sex (X) chromosome, the Barr body) is the most common.

Turner syndrome is a chromosomal abnormality when all or part of a sex chromosome is absent or abnormal.

27. D is correct.

Dolly, the sheep, was cloned in 1996 by fusing the *nucleus* from a mammary gland cell of a Finn Dorset ewe into an *enucleated egg cell* from a Scottish Blackface ewe.

During gestation, Dolly was carried to term in the uterus of another Scottish Blackface ewe.

She was a genetic copy of the Finn Dorset ewe from the somatic mammary gland cell.

Dolly's creation showed that somatic (i.e., body cell) cell DNA in a differentiated (*vs. pluripotent* or *totipotent*) could be induced through nuclear transfer (i.e., transplantation) to expand developmental fate (e.g., like a germ cell) in progression from a zygote.

Development – Detailed Explanations

1. A is correct.

Respiratory exchanges during fetal life occur through the *placenta*.

Placenta connects the developing fetus to the uterine wall and allows nutrient uptake, waste elimination, and gas exchange via the mother's blood supply.

Umbilical cord connects the developing embryo (or fetus) and the placenta. During prenatal development, the umbilical cord is physiologically and genetically part of the fetus and contains two arteries (the umbilical arteries) and one vein (the umbilical vein).

Umbilical veins supply the fetus with oxygenated, nutrient-rich blood from the placenta. Conversely, the fetal heart pumps deoxygenated, nutrient-depleted blood through the umbilical arteries back to the placenta.

Fetal circulatory systems change at birth as the newborn uses its lungs. After the infant's first breath, the newborn's cardiovascular system constricts the ductus arteriosus (i.e., connects the pulmonary artery to the aorta) and converts it to the *ligamentum arteriosum*. Resistance in the pulmonary blood vessels decreases, increasing blood flow to the lungs.

At birth, umbilical blood flow ceases, and blood pressure in the inferior vena cava decreases, causing a decrease in pressure in the *right atrium*. *Left atrial pressure* increases due to increased blood flow from the lungs. Increased left atrial pressure, coupled with decreased right atrial pressure, causes *closure* of the *foramen ovale*.

Ductus venosus, which shunts blood from the left umbilical vein directly to the *inferior vena cava* to allow oxygenated blood from the placenta to bypass the liver, completely closes within three months after birth.

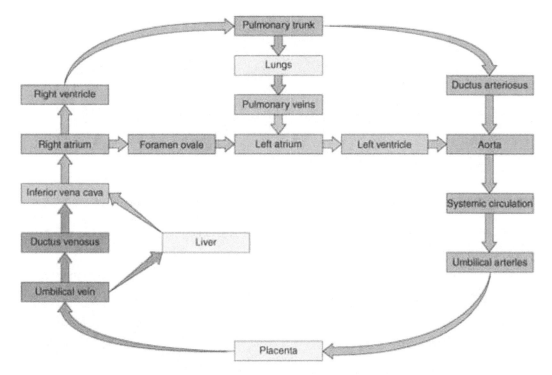

Adult and fetal circulatory systems with ductus arteriosus and ductus venosus provide shunt pathways

2. D is correct.

Indeterminate cleavage cells maintain the ability to develop into a complete organism.

Zygote implantation into the uterus causes cell migration transforming the blastula from a single-cell layer into a three-layered gastrula (i.e., ectoderm, mesoderm, and endoderm).

Blastulation begins when the morula develops the blastocoel as a fluid-filled cavity that (by the fourth day) becomes the blastula as a hollow sphere of cells.

Determinate cleavage results in cells whose differentiation potential is determined early in development.

3. B is correct.

Mutations in *Drosophila*, transforming one body segment into a different one, are in homeotic genes.

Homeotic genes encode the related homeodomain protein involved in developmental patterns and sequences.

Homeotic genes influence the development of specific structures in plants and animals, such as the Hox and ParaHox genes, which are essential for segmentation.

Homeotic genes determine where, when, and how body segments develop. For example, alterations in homeotic genes in laboratory flies cause changes in patterns of body parts, sometimes producing dramatic effects, such as legs growing in place of antennae or an extra set of wings.

Hox genes are *homeotic transcription factors* are crucial for controlling the body plan along the *anterior-posterior axis* (i.e., craniocaudal axis) and specify the segment identity of tissues within the embryo.

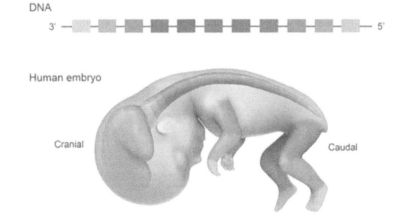

HOX genes encode homeodomain proteins as developmental regulators of the anterior-posterior axis

Homeodomain is a protein structural domain that binds DNA or RNA and is a transcription factor (i.e., facilitates polymerase binding and activation).

Homeodomain proteins fold with a 60-amino acid helix-turn-helix structure in which the short loop regions connect three alpha-helices.

N-terminus of the two helices is *antiparallel,* and the longer C-terminal helix is roughly perpendicular to the axes established by the first two.

Third helix functions as a *transcription factor* and interacts directly with DNA

4. E is correct.

Ectoderm gives rise to hair, nails, skin, brain, and nervous system.

Ectoderm forms "outer linings," including the epidermis (i.e., outermost skin layer) and hair.

Ectoderm is the precursor to *mammary glands* and *central* (CNS) and *peripheral nervous systems* (PNS).

Connective tissue is derived from *mesoderm.*

Rib cartilage is derived from *mesoderm.*

Epithelium of the digestive system is derived from *endoderm.*

5. D is correct.

Chorion is a membrane between the developing fetus and mother in humans and most mammals.

Chorion consists of two layers:

> *outer layer* formed by the *trophoblast*

> *inner layer* formed by the *somatic mesoderm* (in contact with the amnion).

6. A is correct.

The embryo does *not* support the maintenance of the *corpus luteum* when an embryo lacks the synthesis of human chorionic gonadotropin (hCG).

Human chorionic gonadotropin interacts with a receptor on the ovary, producing progesterone secretion.

Progesterone creates a thick lining of blood vessels and capillaries in the uterus to sustain the fetus.

Thus, the corpus luteum is supported during pregnancy.

7. C is correct.

Mesoderm develops into the circulatory, musculoskeletal, and excretory systems, outer coverings of internal organs, gonads, and various types of muscle tissue.

Ectoderm develops into the brain and nervous system, hair and nails, lens of the eye, inner ear, sweat glands, the lining of the nose and mouth, and skin epidermis.

Endoderm develops into the epithelial lining of the digestive tract, respiratory tracts, lining of the liver, bladder, pancreas, thyroid, and alveoli of the lungs.

Epidermis is not an embryonic germ layer but the layer of the skin covering the dermis.

8. B is correct.

Gastrulation is a phase early in animal embryonic development, during which the single-layered blastula is reorganized into a trilaminar (*three-layered*) structure of the *gastrula*.

Three germ layers are:

>   *ectoderm, mesoderm,* and *endoderm.*

Gastrulation occurs after cleavage, formation of the blastula, and primitive streak, followed by organogenesis when individual organs develop within the newly formed germ layers.

Following gastrulation, cells are organized into sheets of connected cells (e.g., epithelial) or mesh of isolated cells (i.e., *mesenchyme*).

Each germ layer gives rise to specific tissues and organs in the developing embryo.

Ectoderm gives rise to the epidermis and other tissues that will form the nervous system.

Mesoderm is between the ectoderm and the endoderm.

Mesoderm gives rise to somites that form muscle, cartilage of the ribs and vertebrae, dermis, notochord, blood and blood vessels, bone, and connective tissue.

Endoderm gives rise to epithelium of the respiratory system, digestive system, and organs associated with the digestive system (e.g., liver and pancreas).

Gastrulation occurs when a blastula of one layer folds inward and enlarges to create the *three primary germ layers* (i.e., endoderm, mesoderm, and ectoderm).

Archenteron gives rise to the digestive tube.

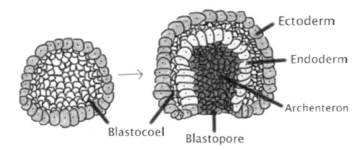

Blastula (left) becomes the gastrula (right) with the formation of the three primary germ layers

9. A is correct.

During the first *eight weeks* of development, myelination of the spinal cord does not occur.

Myelination of the *corticospinal tract* starts around 36 weeks and finishes around two years.

Most major developmental milestones before two years are due to myelination of nerve fibers.

10. E is correct.

Ectoderm germ layers give rise to the skin epidermis and the nervous system.

Endoderm germ layer gives rise to the lining of the digestive system, its associated glands, organs (e.g., liver and pancreas), and the lungs.

Mesoderm gives rise to most organs and systems, including excretory, reproductive, muscular, skeletal, and circulatory systems. If tissue is not specifically endoderm or ectoderm, it is likely to *be mesoderm derived*.

The incorrect choices are *mesoderm-derived* tissues or structures.

11. C is correct.

Fate mapping traces the embryonic origin of tissues in adults by establishing the correspondence between individual cells (or groups of cells) at one stage of development and their progeny at later stages.

When conducted at single-cell resolution, this process is *cell lineage tracing*.

Phylogenetic tree (i.e., an evolutionary tree) is a branching diagram showing the inferred evolutionary relationships (phylogeny) among species or other entities based upon similarities and differences in their physical or genetic characteristics.

Taxa joined in the tree are implied to have descended from a *common ancestor*.

Pedigree diagram shows the occurrence and appearance (i.e., *phenotypes*) of a gene in ancestors.

A pedigree presents family information in an easily readable chart.

Pedigrees use *standardized symbols*: *squares* represent males and *circles* females.

Pedigree construction is *family history*; details about an earlier generation may be uncertain as memories fade.

For unknown sex, a diamond is used.

Phenotype in question is represented by a filled-in (darker) symbol.

Heterozygotes are indicated by a shaded dot inside a symbol or a half-filled symbol.

Linkage map is a genetic diagram of an experimental population that shows the relative position of its known genes or genetic markers based on recombination frequency rather than the physical distance on chromosomes.

Genetic linkage is the tendency of genes proximal on a chromosome to be inherited together during meiosis.

Genes whose loci (i.e., position) are closer are *less likely* to be separated onto different chromatids during chromosomal crossover (i.e., during prophase I) and are genetically *linked*.

12. A is correct.

Hyaline cartilage tissue is the precursor of long bones in the embryo.

Fibrous cartilage is in intervertebral discs.

Dense fibrous connective tissue generally forms *tendons* and *ligaments*.

Elastic cartilage provides internal support and recoil to the external ear and epiglottis.

13. D is correct.

Gene expression changes as development proceeds; proteins are encoded by expressed genes.

During development, cells change their ability to respond to signals from tissues and induce changes in other cells. These changes during development are inherited by daughter cells.

Microtubules are involved in mitosis but do not change during development.

Somatic cells have the same genes (exceptions include gametes and B and T cells).

14. C is correct.

*Acrosome*s are at the tip of the sperm and contain specialized secretory molecules.

Acrosomal reaction is a signaling cascade involving the glycoproteins on the egg's surface.

Acrosin digests the zona pellucida and membrane of the oocyte.

Part of the sperm cell membrane fuses with the egg cell's membrane, and the contents of the head enter the egg fused with the plasma membrane. This allows the sperm to release its degradation enzymes, penetrate the egg's tough coating, and bind and fuse.

Pronucleus is the nucleus of a sperm or an egg cell after the sperm enters the ovum but before they fuse.

15. E is correct.

Three primary germ layers form during gastrulation in embryogenesis: *ectoderm, mesoderm,* and *endoderm.*

Ectoderm is the external germ layer giving rise to the skin, fingernails, and nervous system (including the eye).

Mesoderm is the middle germ layer and gives rise to most organ systems, including the musculoskeletal, cardiovascular, reproductive, and excretory systems.

Endoderm is the innermost germ layer and gives rise to the gallbladder, liver, pancreas, and epithelial lining of luminal structures and accessory digestive organs.

16. D is correct.

Ductus arteriosus is a blood vessel connecting the pulmonary artery to the proximal descending aorta in the developing fetus. It allows most blood from the right ventricle to bypass the fetus's fluid-filled non-functioning lungs. Upon closure at birth, the *ductus arteriosus* becomes the *ligamentum arteriosum.*

Ligamentum teres (i.e., round ligament) refers to several structures:

       ligamentum teres *uteri* (i.e., round ligament of the uterus)

       ligamentum teres *hepatis* (round ligament of the liver)

       ligamentum teres *femoris* (i.e., ligament of the head of the femur)

17. C is correct.

Blastula invagination forms *mesoderm* as the third primary germ layer during gastrulation.

---

18. E is correct.

Homeotic genes encode homeodomain proteins involved in developmental patterns and sequences.

Homeodomain is a protein structural domain that binds DNA or RNA and is often transcription factors.

Homeodomain protein folding consists of a 60-amino acid helix-turn-helix structure in which short loop regions connect three alpha-helices. N-terminus of the two helices is antiparallel, and the longer C-terminal helix is perpendicular to the axes established by the first two.

Third helix functions as a *transcription factor and interacts directly with DNA.*

19. D is correct.

Neurulation and *organogenesis* follow gastrulation.

Mitosis continues throughout development, but *cleavage* is a specific term reserved for *the first few cell divisions* when the *zygote* becomes the *morula.*

During *cleavage*, no growth occurs, and the morula is the same approximate size as the zygote.

Blastula formation precedes gastrulation.

Blastocoel is the fluid-filled central region of a blastula and forms early after fertilization when the zygote divides into many cells.

E: once *differentiated* (i.e., morphological, and biochemical distinct), a cell does not reverse this differentiation process unless it is a cancerous cell.

20. A is correct.

Trophoblast cells give rise to the outer layer of a blastocyst, provide nutrients to the embryo and develop into a large part of the placenta.

Trophoblasts form during the first stage of pregnancy and are the first cells differentiating from the fertilized egg.

21. B is correct.

Placenta connects the developing fetus to the uterine wall and allows nutrient uptake, waste elimination, and gas exchange via the mother's blood supply.

Umbilical cord connects the developing embryo (or fetus) and the placenta.

During prenatal development, the *umbilical cord* is physiologically and genetically part of the fetus and contains two arteries (the *umbilical arteries*) and one vein (the *umbilical vein*).

Umbilical veins supply the fetus with oxygenated, nutrient-rich blood from the placenta.

Fetal heart pumps deoxygenated, nutrient-depleted blood through the umbilical *arteries* to the placenta.

22. E is correct.

For vertebrates, *induction* is how a group of cells cause *differentiation* in another group of cells.

For example, cells that form the notochord induce the formation of the neural tube.

For example, induction in vertebrate development is eye formation, where the optic vesicles induce the ectoderm to thicken and form the lens placode (i.e., thickened portion of ectoderm becoming lens), which induces the optic vesicle to form the optic cup, which induces the lens placode to form the cornea.

Neural tube does develop into the nervous system but is not induced by another group of cells or tissue.

Thyroxin stimulating hormone (TSH) stimulates thyroxine secretion but is not induction.

Neurons synapse with other neurons via neurotransmitters (i.e., chemical messengers), but they do not induce changes in other tissues, as does induction.

23. D is correct.

Acrosomal reaction by the sperm is hydrolytic enzymes degrading the plasma membrane.

Acrosome is at the tip of sperm and contains specialized secretory molecules.

Acrosomal reaction is due to a signaling cascade involving the glycoproteins on the egg's surface.

Acrosin digests the zona pellucida and membrane of the oocyte, and the sperm releases its degradation enzymes to penetrate the egg's tough coating and allow the sperm to bind and fuse with the egg.

24. C is correct.

Endoderm is the innermost germ layer and gives rise to the inner lining of the respiratory and digestive tracts and associated organs.

Blastula refers to a hollow ball of embryonic cells arising from the morula. The blastula is *not* a germ layer.

Ectoderm is the outermost germ layer and gives rise to the hair, nails, eyes, skin, and central nervous system.

25. E is correct.

Inner cell mass is the cells inside the primordial embryo that forms before implantation and gives rise to the definitive structures of the fetus.

Primitive streak is a structure that forms in the blastula during the initial stages of embryonic development.

Primitive streak establishes:

>   *bilateral symmetry*
>
>   determines the *site of gastrulation*
>
>   *initiates germ layer formation*

26. D is correct.

Fetal circulatory system changes as newborns begin using their lungs at birth.

Resistance in the pulmonary blood vessels decreases, causing an increase in blood flow to the lungs.

Umbilical blood flow ceases at birth, and blood pressure in the inferior vena cava decreases, which causes a decrease in pressure in the right atrium.

In contrast, the left atrial pressure increases due to increased blood flow from the lungs.

Increased left atrial pressure, coupled with decreased right atrial pressure, causes closure of the foramen ovale.

> *Ductus arteriosus* (i.e., connects the pulmonary artery to the aorta) constricts and subsequently is sealed.

> *Ductus venosus*, which shunts blood from the left umbilical vein directly to the inferior vena cava to allow oxygenated blood from the placenta to bypass the liver, completely closes within three months after birth.

Fetus produces adult hemoglobin a few weeks before birth (2 α and 2 β chains; alpha and beta) though lower amounts of fetal hemoglobin continue until the production completely stops.

After the first year, low fetal hemoglobin levels (2 α and 2 γ chains; alpha and gamma) are in the infant's blood.

27. B is correct.

Homeotic genes encode the related homeodomain protein involved in developmental patterns and sequences.

Homeobox is a stretch of DNA about 180 nucleotides long that encodes a homeodomain (i.e., protein) in vertebrates and invertebrates.

Exons (expressed sequences) are retained during RNA processing of the primary transcript (hnRNA) into mRNA for translation into proteins.

28. A is correct.

Somatic cells have the same genome, but individual cells express different genes.

Differences in expression are *spatial* (i.e., cell type) or *temporal* (i.e., stages of development).

Ectoderm tissue arises after gastrulation as a primary germ layer.

Each germ layer retains its *determination*.

Somatic cells have identical genomes compared to their parents.

Gametes (via segregation and recombination during prophase I) have unique 1N genomes compared to their parents.

29. C is correct.

Yolk sac in humans gives rise to *blood cells* and *gamete-forming cells*.

Chorion is a double-layered membrane formed by trophoblast and extra-embryonic mesoderm.

Chorion gives rise to the fetal part of the placenta.

Luteal placental shift (7-9 weeks) is when the placenta develops enough to produce hormones to sustain the pregnancy.

Before this shift, the *placenta secretes progesterone* instead of the *corpus luteum*.

In humans, waste goes to the placenta and is received by the mother.

Non-placental organisms use allantois to collect waste.

30. A is correct.

Trophoblast is primarily responsible for forming placental tissue.

Trophoblast gives rise to the outer layer of a blastocyst, provides nutrients to the embryo, and develops into a large part of the placenta.

Trophoblasts form during the first stage of pregnancy and the first cells to *differentiate* from the fertilized egg.

31. C is correct.

Spina bifida is a bone abnormality that arises from the embryonic mesoderm germ layer.

A lesion to the mesoderm would affect the development of other structures based on different connective tissue (e.g., blood, blood vessels, muscles, and connective tissue of organs).

Thus, this lesion affects the development of blood vessels and muscles.

I: *intestinal epithelium* develops from *endoderm*.

II: skin, hair, and the nervous system develop from *ectoderm*.

32. B is correct.

Homeotic genes encode the related homeodomain protein involved in *developmental patterns and sequences*.

Homeotic genes are involved in developmental patterns and sequences.

For example, homeotic genes determine where, when, and how body segments develop.

Alterations in these genes cause changes in body parts and structure patterns, sometimes resulting in dramatic effects.

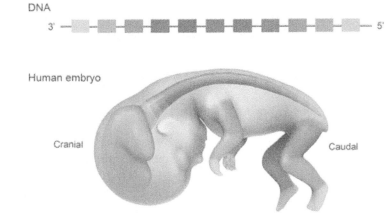

HOX genes encode homeodomain proteins as developmental regulators of the anterior-posterior axis. The linear sequence of genes on the chromosome corresponds to the cranial-caudal orientation

Homeodomain is a protein structural domain that binds DNA or RNA and is a transcription factor (i.e., facilitates polymerase binding and activation).

33. D is correct.

Mesoderm forms muscles, blood, bone, reproductive organs, and kidneys.

34. C is correct.

Primitive streak is a transitional structure formed at the onset of gastrulation.

Inner cell mass is converted into the trilaminar embryonic disc comprised of the three germ layers: ectoderm, mesoderm, and endoderm.

Primitive streak formation is not part of implantation but an early process of embryonic development.

35. A is correct.

During labor, the *oxytocin* hormone stimulates contractions of uterine smooth muscle.

36. D is correct.

Ectoderm cells are determined but not differentiated because they have the potential to develop into more than one type of tissue, but not any type.

Experimentally, ectoderm development was influenced (i.e., induced) by changing locations within the developing embryo. The underlying *mesoderm* differentiated because it released the molecular inducers as signals to the overlying ectoderm (undifferentiated).

Ectoderm cell *location* is essential because their development (i.e., differentiation into specific tissue/structures) is induced by the underlying mesoderm cells that send chemical substances (i.e., inducers) specific to the position of the mesoderm.

Mesoderm, not ectoderm, determines cellular differentiation at this stage of development.

Differentiated fate of the cells has not yet been determined because the transplanted cells would develop into wing feathers instead of claws.

Ectoderm cells cannot develop into any tissue because location influences the development of transplanted ectoderm cells.

37. D is correct.

Recognition of the sperm by the *vitelline envelope* (i.e., a membrane between the outer zona pellucid and inner plasma membrane) triggers the cortical reaction, transforming it into the hard *fertilization membrane* as a physical barrier to other spermatozoa (i.e., *slow block to polyspermy*).

Cortical reaction within the egg is analogous to the acrosomal reaction within the sperm.

38. C is correct.

Polyspermy in humans results in a nonviable zygote.

39. E is correct.

Mesoderm germ layer gives rise to many tissues.

Intestinal mucosa is derived from *endoderm*

Nerve is derived from *ectoderm*.

Lung epithelium is derived from *endoderm*.

40. C is correct.

Genomic imprinting is *epigenetic* (i.e., *heritable change*) when specific genes are expressed in a parent-of-origin-specific manner.

Genomic imprinting is an *epigenetic process* involving *DNA methylation* and *histone modulation* to achieve single-allelic gene expression without altering the original genetic sequence.

41. C is correct.

Embryos require *greater protein translation rates* using ribosomes to read mRNA transcripts.

42. E is correct.

Zygote (i.e., fertilized egg) is the first structure to form during human fertilization that undergoes rapid cell divisions without significant cellular growth to produce a cluster of cells of the same size as the original zygote.

Cells derived from cleavage are *blastomeres* and form a solid mass known as a *morula*.

Cleavage ends with the formation of the *blastula*.

> Ovulation → fertilization (sperm and oocyte) → diploid zygote (undergoes cleavage) → morula (solid ball of cells) → blastocoel (undergoes invagination) → blastopore (ectoderm and endoderm)

43. A is correct.

Capacitation is the final step in spermatozoa maturation. It is required for competence to fertilize oocytes.

Capacitation destabilizes the acrosomal sperm head membrane, allowing greater binding between sperm and oocyte by removing steroids (e.g., cholesterol) and non-covalently bound glycoproteins, which increases membrane fluidity and Ca^{2+} permeability.

Ca^{2+} influx produces intracellular cAMP levels and increased sperm motility.

44. C is correct.

Endoderm develops into *epithelial linings* of the digestive and respiratory tracts, parts of the liver, thyroid, pancreas, and bladder lining.

45. E is correct.

Homeotic genes influence the development of specific structures in plants and animals, such as the Hox and ParaHox genes, which are essential for segmentation.

Homeotic genes determine where, when, and how body segments develop in organisms.

Alterations in these genes cause changes in patterns of body parts, sometimes causing dramatic effects, such as legs growing in place of antennae or an extra set of wings.

Loss-of-function mutations result in the gene product with less or no function.

An allele with loss of function (i.e., null allele) is an *amorphic* (i.e., complete loss of gene function) mutation.

Phenotypes associated with such mutations are often recessive.

Exceptions are haploid or *haploinsufficiency* (i.e., a diploid organism has a single copy of the functional gene) when the reduced dosage of a normal gene product is not enough for a typical phenotype.

46. A is correct.

Cells may assume several fates and are not yet terminally *differentiated*.

Gastrula cells influenced by their surroundings are *competent*.

Ectoderm layer gives rise to the eye, among other structures.

Cells can become other ectoderm tissue (e.g., gills).

47. B is correct.

Proteases and *acrosin* enzymes degrade the protective barriers around the egg and allow the sperm to penetrate.

Acrosomal reaction by the sperm is hydrolytic enzymes degrading the plasma membrane.

*Acrosome*s are at the tip of the sperm and contain specialized secretory molecules.

Acrosomal reaction is due to a signaling cascade involving the glycoproteins on the egg's surface.

Acrosin digests the zona pellucida and membrane of the oocyte, and the sperm releases its degradation enzymes to penetrate the egg's tough coating and allow the sperm to bind and fuse with the egg.

48. A is correct.

Human blastocyst implants in the uterine wall about a *week* after fertilization.

49. B is correct.

Ectoderm develops into the nervous system, the epidermis, the eye lens, and the inner ear.

Endoderm develops into the lining of the digestive tract, lungs, liver, and pancreas.

Mesoderm develops into the connective tissue, muscles, skeleton, circulatory system, gonads, and kidneys.

50. A is correct.

After the infant's first breath, the newborn's cardiovascular system constricts the *ductus arteriosus* (i.e., connects the pulmonary artery to the aorta) and converts it to the *ligamentum arteriosum*.

Fetal circulatory systems change at birth as the newborn uses its lungs.

Resistance in pulmonary blood vessels decreases, increasing blood flow to the lungs.

At birth, umbilical blood flow ceases, and blood pressure in the inferior vena cava decreases, which causes a decrease in pressure in the right atrium.

In contrast, the left atrial pressure increases due to increased blood flow from the lungs.

Increased left atrial and decreased right atrial pressure causes *closure* of the *foramen ovale*.

Ductus venosus, which shunts blood from the left umbilical vein directly to the inferior vena cava to allow oxygenated blood from the placenta to bypass the liver, completely closes within three months after birth.

Diagram below

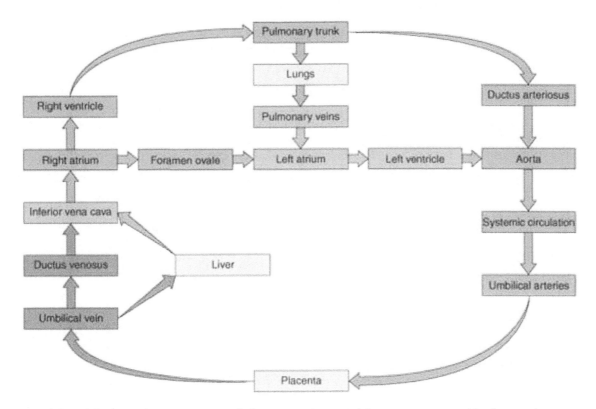

Adult and fetal circulatory systems with ductus arteriosus and ductus venosus provide shunt pathways

51. C is correct.

Genomic imprinting is an *epigenetic* (i.e., heritable changes in gene activity) process involving DNA methylation and histone remodeling for monoallelic (i.e., single allele) gene expression without altering the genetic sequence within the genome.

Epigenetic changes are established in the germline (i.e., cells that give rise to gametes of egg/sperm) and can be maintained through mitotic divisions.

52. E is correct.

Amniotic fluid, surrounded by the amnion, is a liquid environment around the egg that protects it from shock.

Embryonic membranes include:

1) ***chorion*** lines the inside of the shell and permits gas exchange;

2) ***allantois*** is a saclike structure developed from the digestive tract and functions in respiration, excretion, and gas exchange with the external environment;

3) ***amnion*** encloses *amniotic fluid* as a watery environment for embryogenesis and shock protection;

4) ***yolk sac*** encloses the yolk and transfers food to the developing embryo.

53. A is correct.

Mesoderm gives rise to the *entire circulatory system, muscle*, and most other tissue between the *gut and skin* (excluding the nervous system).

Ectoderm gives rise to skin, the nervous system, the retina, and the lens.

Differentiated endoderm has a restricted fate that does not include heart tissue.

Endoderm gives rise to the *inner lining of the gut*.

54. C is correct.

At the end of the *first trimester*, an ultrasound can determine the sex of the fetus.

55. E is correct.

Eggs are viable and can be fertilized 12-24 hours after ovulation.

56. B is correct.

Blastulation begins when the *morula* develops a fluid-filled cavity (i.e., blastocoel). By the fourth day, it becomes a hollow sphere of cells (i.e., blastula).

Gastrula is the embryonic stage characterized by the three primary germ layers (i.e., endoderm, ectoderm, and mesoderm), the blastocoel, and the archenteron.

Early gastrula is two-layered (i.e., ectoderm and endoderm); shortly afterward, a third layer (i.e., mesoderm) develops.

Gastrulation is followed by organogenesis, when individual organs develop within newly formed germ layers.

Morula is the solid ball of cells from the early cleavage stages in the zygote.

Zygote is the (2N) cell formed by the fusion of two (1N) gametes (e.g., ovum and sperm).

57. B is correct.

Proteases and *acrosin* enzymes degrade the protective barriers around the egg and allow the sperm to penetrate.

Acrosomal reaction by the sperm is hydrolytic enzymes degrading the plasma membrane.

Acrosomes are at the tip of the sperm and contain specialized secretory molecules.

Acrosomal reaction is due to a signaling cascade involving the glycoproteins on the egg's surface.

Acrosin digests the zona pellucida and membrane of the oocyte, and the sperm releases its degradation enzymes to penetrate the egg's tough coating and allow the sperm to bind and fuse with the egg.

58. C is correct.

Regarding fertilization, the *vagina's acidic environment* destroys millions of sperm cells.

DNA and Protein Synthesis – Detailed Explanations

1. D is correct.

Histones are basic (i.e., positively charged) proteins associated with nuclei DNA to condense chromatin.

Nuclear DNA does not appear in free linear strands; instead, it is highly condensed and wrapped around histones (i.e., positively-charged proteins) to fit inside the nucleus and form chromosomes.

Three major types of RNA engage in gene expression:

1) *messenger* RNA (mRNA) molecules carry the coding sequences (i.e., "blueprints") for protein synthesis and are transcripts;

2) *ribosomal* RNA (rRNA) forms the core of a cell's ribosomes (i.e., macromolecular cellular particles where protein synthesis takes place);

3) *transfer* RNA (tRNA) molecules transport amino acids (i.e., protein building blocks) to the ribosomes during protein synthesis.

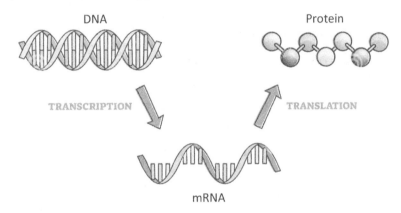

Gene expression with DNA transcribed into mRNA, which is translated into protein

2. D is correct.

Frederick Griffith (1928) reported an early experiment suggesting that bacteria transfer genetic information through *transformation*.

Griffith observed a *transforming principle*, where heat-killed S (smooth) bacteria was destroyed, and (now known) its DNA survived the process and was incorporated by R (rough) strain bacteria.

S genetic fragments protected R strain bacteria from host immunity and killed the host.

3. E is correct.

Depurination is the hydrolysis of the glycosidic bond of DNA and RNA purine nucleotides guanine or adenine.

Nucleotides have sugar, phosphate, and base (A, C, G, T or U).

For DNA, the sugar is deoxyribose, while RNA contains ribose.

Glycosidic bonds are hemiacetal groups of a saccharide (or an amino acid) and the hydroxyl group of an organic compound (e.g., alcohol).

Glycosidic bond formation from the nucleophilic attack of alcohol on the anomeric carbon of a hemiacetal

4. A is correct.

Unequal crossing over is a gene duplication (or deletion) event that deletes a sequence in one strand of the chromatid. It replaces it with duplication from its sister chromatid in mitosis, or homologous chromosomes recombine during prophase I in meiosis.

5. D is correct.

Sulfur is in the amino acid cysteine but is absent in nucleic acids.

Hershey-Chase (i.e., associate *blender*) experiment in 1952 used radiolabeled molecules of phosphorus (^{32} P for nucleic acids) and sulfur (^{35}S for proteins) to determine whether nucleic acids (phosphorus) or protein (sulfur) carried the genetic information.

Nucleic acids contain C, H, O, N and P and are polymers of *nucleotide* subunits.

Nucleic acids (e.g., DNA, RNA) encode cellular information for protein synthesis and replication.

6. D is correct.

mRNA is the subclass of RNAs molecule translated into proteins.

7. A is correct.

Aging of normal cells is associated with a loss of *telomerase activity*.

8. C is correct.

Translation is initiated on ribosomes within the cytoplasm.

A: *transcription* (not translation) occurs in the nucleus.

B: *Golgi* receives proteins from the rough endoplasmic reticulum for processing and sorting.

Golgi modifies (e.g., adds carbohydrate groups) and sorts proteins in the *secretory pathway*.

D: proteins destined for the *lumen of the rough endoplasmic reticulum* have at their amino terminus a particular sequence of amino acids referred to as a *leader sequence* (about 6 to 10 amino acids).

Signal recognition protein (SRP) recognizes the leader sequence and binds a receptor on the rough ER, attaching the ribosome and the nascent polypeptide to the endoplasmic reticulum (ER) membrane.

9. E is correct.

When a gene is duplicated by crossing over between chromatids, the gene on the other chromatid is deleted.

Unequal crossing over is a gene duplication (or deletion) event that deletes a sequence in one strand of the chromatid. It replaces it with duplication from its sister chromatid in mitosis, or homologous chromosomes recombine during prophase I in meiosis.

10. C is correct.

To show that DNA, not RNA, protein, or other cell components, was responsible for transformation, Avery, MacLeod, and McCarty (1944) used several biochemical tests.

Trypsin, chymotrypsin, and ribonuclease (enzymes digesting proteins or RNA) did not affect the transforming agent causing the disease.

DNase treatment degrades DNA and destroys the extract's ability to cause disease.

Streptococcus pneumoniae (i.e., pneumococcus) is a Gram-positive pathogenic bacterium.

S. pneumoniae was recognized as a major cause of pneumonia in the late 19th century and has been the subject of numerous humoral immunity (i.e., antibody-mediated) studies.

11. B is correct.

Western blotting separates proteins by electrophoresis and is commonly used to identify the presence of HIV antibodies (proteins).

Blotting techniques rely on gel electrophoresis to separate DNA, RNA, or proteins based on size.

After resolution (separation) by electrophoresis, the gel (containing resolved products) is blotted (i.e., transferred to nitrocellulose).

After transferring the macromolecules (DNA, RNA, or proteins) from the gel to the blotting paper by capillary action, the blotting paper is probed by specific markers that hybridize with complementary sequences fixed on the blotting paper.

A: *Eastern blotting* does not exist.

C: *Northern blotting* uses RNA in gel electrophoresis.

D: *Southern blotting* uses DNA in gel electrophoresis.

12. C is correct.

Position C represents the ribose sugar's 3' hydroxyl (~OH).

As in DNA, *the 3' hydroxyl is the site of attachment.*

RNA and DNA require a free 3' OH for the nucleic acid to increase length.

Position D contains a 2' hydroxyl (~OH) that distinguishes this sugar as ribose, as opposed to DNA which would lack the 2' hydroxyl (deoxyribose = without oxygen) at the 2' position of the sugar.

13. E is correct.

Adenine and guanine are *purines*.

C**y**tosine and th**y**mine/uracil are *pyrimidines*; note the presence of *y* for pyrimidines.

A: DNA strands are *antiparallel*: one strand has a 5' → 3' polarity, and its complementary strand 3' → 5'.

B: DNA consists of nucleotides, which have a phosphate group, a deoxyribose sugar, and a base (A, C, G, T).

D: cytosine binds guanine with three hydrogen bonds.

Adenine binds thymine (in DNA) or uracil (in RNA) with two hydrogen bonds.

14. C is correct.

Tumor suppressor gene protects a cell from aberrant cell cycles.

When this gene mutates to cause a loss (or reduction) in its function, the cell can progress to cancer, usually with other genetic changes.

The loss of *tumor suppressor genes* may be more important than *proto-oncogene* activation for forming many types of human cancer cells.

Apoptosis is the process of programmed cell death (PCD) that may occur in multicellular organisms.

Biochemical events lead to characteristic cell changes (morphology) and death, including blebbing, cell shrinkage, nuclear fragmentation, chromatin condensation, and chromosomal DNA fragmentation.

In contrast to necrosis (i.e., traumatic cell death that results from acute cellular injury), apoptosis confers advantages during an organism's lifecycle.

For example, a human embryo separates fingers and toes because cells between the digits undergo *apoptosis*.

Unlike necrosis, apoptosis produces cell fragments called *apoptotic bodies* that phagocytic cells can engulf and quickly remove before the cell contents spill onto surrounding cells and cause damage.

A: *telomerase* is an enzyme that adds DNA sequence repeats (i.e., TTAGGG) to the 3' end of DNA strands in the telomere regions at the ends of eukaryotic chromosomes.

This region of repeated nucleotides as telomeres with noncoding DNA hinders the loss of essential DNA from chromosome ends. When the chromosome is copied, 100–200 nucleotides are lost, causing no damage to the coding region of the DNA.

Telomerase is a reverse transcriptase that carries its RNA molecule used as a template when it elongates telomeres that have been shortened after each replication cycle.

Embryonic stem cells express telomerase, allowing them to divide repeatedly.

In adults, telomerase is highly expressed in cells that divide regularly (e.g., male germ cells, lymphocytes, and specific adult stem cells). Telomerase is not expressed in most adult somatic cells.

15. B is correct.

Aminoacyl tRNA synthetase (enzyme) uses energy from ATP to attach a specific amino acid to tRNA.

16. C is correct.

DNA was the transforming principle verified in experiments by Avery, MacLeod, and McCarty (1944) and Hershey and Chase (1952).

17. D is correct.

There are 4 different nucleotides (adenine, cytosine, guanine, and thymine/uracil).

Each codon is composed of 3 nucleotides.

Therefore, there must be 64 (4^3) possible variations of codons to encode for the 20 amino acids.

Genetic code is *degenerate* (i.e., redundant) because several codons encode for the same amino acid.

61 codons encode for amino acids and 3 stop codons that terminate translation.

18. E is correct.

Signal sequence at the N-terminus of the polypeptide targets proteins to organelles (e.g., chloroplast, mitochondrion).

19. C is correct.

Adenine pairs with thymine *via* 2 hydrogen bonds, while guanine pairs with cytosine *via* 3 hydrogen bonds.

Treatment of DNA with 2-aminopurine causes the adenine-thymine (A-T) base pair to be replaced with a guanine-thymine (G-T) base pair (before replication).

Thymine is replaced by cytosine: G-C base pair after replication.

This single-point mutation is incorporated into future generations.

If the mutation had been corrected before replication (via proofreading mechanisms during replication), there would be no change in the DNA base sequence.

20. D is correct.

Codons with two bases would be insufficient because the four bases in a two-base codon would form $4^2 = 16$ pairs, less than the 20 combinations needed to specify the amino acids.

A triplet is sufficient because four bases in a three-base codon can form $4^3 = 64$ pairs, enough to encode the 20 amino acids.

21. B is correct.

After one replication, the DNA was at an intermediate density between ^{14}N and ^{15}N.

After two replications, there were two densities – one band in the centrifuge tube was an intermediate between the ^{14}N and ^{15}N, while the other consisted of ^{14}N.

The *semiconservative* DNA replication model was one of three tested by the Meselson-Stahl (1958) experiment.

> ***Semiconservative replication*** would produce two copies containing one original and one new strand.

> ***Conservative replication*** would leave the two original template DNA strands in a double helix and produce a copy composed of two new strands containing the new DNA base pairs.

> ***Dispersive replication*** would produce two copies of the DNA, each containing distinct regions of DNA composed of either original or new strands.

In the Meselson-Stahl (1957-58) experiments, *E. coli* were grown for several generations in a medium with ^{15}N.

When DNA was extracted and separated by centrifugation, the DNA separated according to density.

The E. coli cells with ^{15}N in their DNA were transferred to a ^{14}N medium and divided.

The DNA of the cells grown in a ^{15}N medium had a higher density than cells grown in a standard ^{14}N medium.

Since *conservative replication* would result in equal amounts of DNA of the higher and lower densities (but no intermediate density), conservative replication was excluded.

This result was consistent with *semiconservative* and *dispersive replication*.

Semiconservative replication yields one double-stranded DNA with ^{15}N DNA and one with ^{14}N DNA.

Dispersive replication would result in double-stranded DNA, with both strands having mixtures of ^{15}N and ^{14}N DNA, which would have appeared as DNA of an *intermediate density*.

22. C is correct.

DNA microarray (or *DNA chip*) collects microscopic DNA spots attached to a solid surface. DNA microarrays measure the expression levels of many genes or genotype multiple regions of a genome.

Each DNA spot contains picomoles (10^{-12} moles) of a specific DNA sequence.

Short sections of a gene (or other DNA element) hybridize cDNA *probes*.

An array simultaneously uses tens of thousands of probes; microarrays evaluate many genetic tests in parallel.

23. B is correct.

Avery, MacLeod, and McCarty (1944) demonstrated that DNA was the *transforming principle* for nonvirulent strains of pneumococcus.

Enzymes that destroyed nucleic acids destroyed the transforming activity, strengthening their hypothesis.

24. A is correct.

Codon-anticodon hybridization (i.e., bonding interaction) occurs between mRNA (*codon*) and tRNA (*anticodon*) during translation for protein synthesis.

25. B is correct.

Northern blot is a molecular biology technique to study gene expression by detecting RNA expression levels. Northern blotting uses electrophoresis to separate RNA samples by size. It involves the capillary transfer of RNA from the electrophoresis gel to the blotting membrane. It uses a hybridization probe via complementary hydrogen bonding to target expressed RNA fragments (i.e., expressed genes).

Eukaryotic mRNA is isolated using oligo (dT) cellulose chromatography to hybridize mRNA with a poly-A tail. The sample is resolved (i.e., separated) by gel electrophoresis.

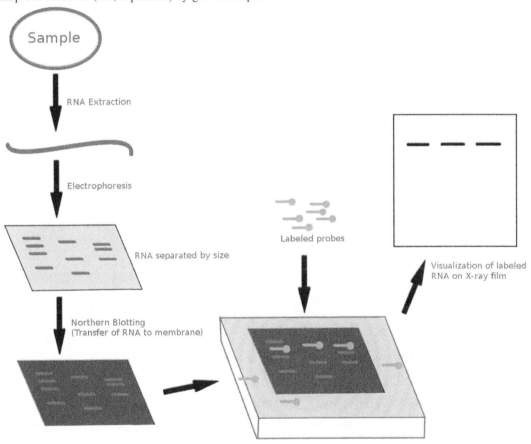

Northern blot uses RNA resolved by electrophoresis to evaluate gene expression using specific probes

Electrophoresis gels are fragile, and probes cannot enter the gel matrix. After resolution by electrophoresis, the size-separated RNA sample is transferred to a positively charged nylon (or nitrocellulose) membrane through capillary blotting. The negatively-charged mRNA adheres to the positive charge on the nylon.

In situ hybridization uses labeled probes of complementary DNA (cDNA) or RNA to localize a specific DNA or RNA sequence in a tissue section (*in situ*). Probes hybridize to the target sequence at an elevated temperature, and the excess probe is washed away.

26. E is correct.

Chromosomes replicate during the synthesis (S) phase of interphase.

27. E is correct.

DNA contains T, which is replaced with U in RNA.

28. B is correct.

Duplicated genes are closely related but diverged in sequence and function over evolutionary time.

29. D is correct.

Hershey and Chase showed in 1952 that when bacteriophages (i.e., viruses), composed of DNA and protein, infect bacteria, their DNA enters the host bacterial cell while their protein does not.

Hershey and Chase grew separate populations of viruses and incorporated radioactive sulfur (^{35}S to label protein) or phosphorus (^{32}P to label DNA) into the bacteriophages.

Two groups of viral progeny contained either ^{32}P or ^{35}S radioactive isotopes.

Separate aliquots of the labeled progeny were allowed to infect unlabeled bacteria. The viral ^{35}S protein coats remained outside the bacteria, while the ^{32}P DNA entered the bacteria.

Centrifugation separated the phage protein coats from the bacteria.

Bacteria were lysed to release the phages.

Hershey and Chase experiment demonstrated that the DNA, not protein, was the *transforming* molecule that entered the bacteria from a viral infection.

30. C is correct.

Replication forks open double-stranded DNA by disrupting hydrogen bonds between complementary nucleotide base pairs (e.g., A bonded to T and C bonded to G).

Gyrase cuts one strand of the DNA backbone and relaxes the positive supercoil that accumulates as helicase separates the two strands of DNA.

Ligase seals the backbone of DNA (i.e., joins Okazaki fragments) by forming phosphodiester bonds between deoxynucleotides in DNA.

31. A is correct.

Four atoms in the peptide bond are in the box.

Note that the oxygen on the carbonyl is oriented 180° from the H (antiperiplanar) on the nitrogen because the lone pair on the nitrogen participates in resonance, and the peptide bond is rigid (i.e., double bond like character).

32. D is correct.

DNA and ribozymes of RNA (discovered in 1982) are capable of self-replication.

Protein functions include:

1) peptide hormones as chemical messengers transported within the blood,

2) enzymes that catalyze chemical reactions by lowering the energy of activation,

3) structural proteins for physical support within the cells, tissues, and organs,

4) transport proteins as carriers of important materials, and

5) immune system antibodies bind foreign particles (i.e., antigens).

33. B is correct.

Eukaryote RNA polymerase needs *transcription factors* (i.e., DNA binding proteins) to bind the promoter (on mRNA) and initiate basal-level transcription.

34. E is correct.

Percent of adenine cannot be determined because RNA is a single-stranded molecule.

Base-pairing rules for DNA (i.e., Chargaff's rule) are for double-stranded DNA but not single-stranded RNA.

35. A is correct.

I: AUG sequences are not only the initial start codon downstream of the initial *start codon* (AUG). If this sequence is not the start codon, this change could result in a stop codon (UAA).

II: *genetic code* is read 5′ to 3′ and AUG (encoding methionine) is a start codon.

A change in the start sequence in the mRNA (AUG to AAG) causes a failure in initiating translation.

III: changes in the first, second, or third amino acid may change U to A in the resultant amino acid.

The third position of the codon is the *wobble position* because the specified amino acid often does not change.

Nucleotide changes may not change the specified amino acid because the genetic code is redundant (i.e., most amino acids are encoded by more than one codon).

For example, AUU and AUA codons both encode isoleucine.

Genetic code is *degenerate*, whereby changing a nucleotide (often in the 3rd position) does not change the amino acid encoded by the triplet codon.

Each codon (three nucleotides) encodes for one amino acid, and there is no ambiguity in the genetic code.

36. B is correct.

Genetic code (mRNA into protein) has several amino acids specified by more than one codon, three stop codons, and each is 3 nucleotides (bases) long.

37. D is correct.

Polymerase I (Pol I) adds nucleotides at the RNA primer-template junction (i.e., the origin of replication) and is involved in excision repair with 3'-5' and 5'-3' exonuclease activity and processing of Okazaki fragments generated during lagging strand synthesis.

B: *primase* adds the first two RNA primers at the start of DNA replication because the DNA polymerase must bond to double-stranded molecules.

RNA primer is removed by DNA polymerase I after the newly synthesized DNA strand has been replicated via DNA polymerase III.

a: *template strand* of parental DNA

b: *leading strand* of newly synthesized DNA

c: *lagging strand* (Okazaki fragments) of newly synthesized DNA

d: *replication fork* with helicase opening and unwinding the double-stranded DNA

e: *RNA primer* synthesized by primase

f: *direction* of DNA strand synthesis

DNA replication

38. E is correct.

Okazaki fragments are associated with the lagging DNA strand and (like all DNA) are synthesized in a 5'→ 3' direction by DNA polymerase III.

A: DNA polymerase I removes the short sequence RNA primers deposited by primase needed for the anchoring of the polymerase III to DNA for the synthesis of DNA in a 5'→ 3' direction.

B: Okazaki fragments are used to replicate the lagging strand and are covalently linked by *DNA ligase* (not DNA polymerase I), forming a continuous DNA strand.

D: Okazaki fragments are not synthesized to fill in gaps after removing the RNA primer by DNA polymerase I.

Diagram below

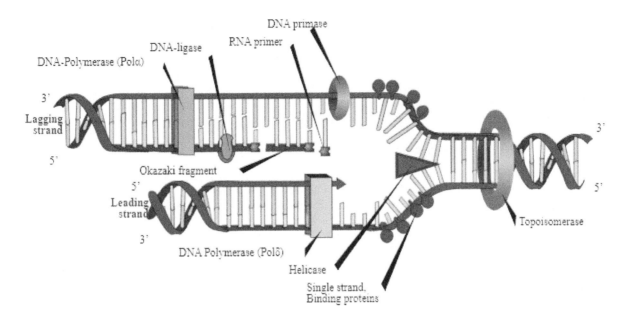

DNA semiconservative replication with associated proteins for leading and lagging strands. DNA polymerase proceeds from 5' to 3' along parental strands.

39. C is correct.

Ribosomal RNAs (rRNA) form a large subunit and a small subunit.

During translation, mRNA is between the small and large subunits, and the ribosome catalyzes the formation of a peptide bond between the two amino acids held by the rRNA.

A single mRNA can be translated simultaneously by multiple ribosomes.

Ribosomes catalyze the formation of a *peptide bond* between two amino acids tethered by rRNA.

Ribosomes have three binding sites: A, P, and E.

Peptidyl transferase catalyzes this reaction.

A site binds an aminoacyl-tRNA (i.e., a tRNA bound to an amino acid).

Amino (NH_2) group of the aminoacyl-tRNA, with the new amino acid, attacks the ester linkage of peptidyl-tRNA (in the P site), the last amino acid of the growing chain, forming a new peptide bond.

tRNA holding the last amino acid moves to the E site, and the aminoacyl-tRNA is now the peptidyl-tRNA.

40. A is correct.

Protein synthesis does require energy.

B: rRNA is part of the ribosome and is necessary for proper binding of the ribosome to mRNA.

C: tRNA brings an amino acid to the ribosome, where it interacts with the mRNA of the proper sequence.

D: tRNA does have the amino acid bound to its 3' end.

41. B is correct.

Polymerase chain reaction (PCR) requires the sequence at the ends of the fragment to be amplified.

From the ends, primers use complementary base pairing to anneal the target fragment and permit amplification.

No knowledge of the region between the ends is required because the parent strands will be the template used by the DNA polymerase.

42. D is correct.

Shape of tRNA is determined primarily by *intramolecular base pairing*.

43. E is correct.

In prokaryotic cells, methylated guanine contributes to correcting mismatched pairs of bases.

44. A is correct.

Magnesium is a *divalent* mineral that DNA and RNA polymerases use as a cofactor (i.e., catalyst not consumed in the reaction) to stabilize interactions between polymerase and negative charge on the nucleic acid backbone.

45. C is correct.

Ribosome structure is created by the internal base-pairing of rRNA and ribosomal proteins.

46. A is correct.

Three types of RNA are *mRNA*, *tRNA*, and *rRNA*, which DNA encodes.

rRNA is synthesized in the nucleolus within the nucleus.

tRNA functions as a carrier of amino acid molecules.

Unlike mRNA, tRNA is a comparatively short ribonucleotide polymer of RNA subunits.

Although tRNA is single-stranded, there are double-stranded segments where the nucleotide chain loops back (i.e., hairpin turns) with hydrogen bonds between complementary base pairs; like DNA, two hydrogen bonds between A and U and three hydrogen bonds between C and G.

mRNA is the template for protein synthesis and has a poly-A tail, which functions as a *molecular clock* for mRNA degradation.

47. D is correct.

Phosphate group is the chemical group at the 5' end of a single polynucleotide strand.

48. E is correct.

Puromycin is an analog with a similar shape to tRNA.

Puromycin joins the ribosome, forms one peptide bond, and becomes covalently attached to the nascent protein.

However, since it lacks a carboxyl group, it cannot be linked to the next amino acid, and protein synthesis terminates prematurely.

A: *initiation* requires binding a single aminoacyl-tRNA (the initiator) to the ribosome and is unaffected.

Puromycin

B: *aminoacyl-tRNA* enters the large subunit of the ribosome at the A site during elongation.

D: *puromycin* lacks a carboxyl group and can only form one bond, so peptide synthesis stops prematurely.

49. C is correct.

In *E. coli* cells, DNA polymerase I degrades the RNA primer portion of Okazaki fragments.

50. D is correct.

DNA polymerase I proofreading increases replication fidelity by monitoring for mismatched pairs originating from the high processivity of polymerase III that rapidly replicates DNA.

Bacteria have a much lower DNA replication rate of about 1 in 1,000, increasing the mutation rate of bacteria.

51. C is correct.

DNA is a nucleotide polymer of the deoxyribose sugar, a phosphate group, and a nitrogenous base (e.g., A, C, G, T). Phosphodiester bonds join the nucleotides in DNA's backbone.

52. A is correct.

In *E. coli* cells, DNA polymerase III synthesizes most of the Okazaki fragments.

53. E is correct.

All the molecules, except cysteine, are nitrogenous bases – the component molecules of DNA and RNA (e.g., mRNA, rRNA & tRNA).

Nitrogenous bases guanine (G) and adenine (A) are purines, while cytosine (C) and thymine (T is in DNA) or uracil (U is in RNA) are pyrimidines.

Cysteine is an amino acid (not a nitrogenous base), and amino acids are the monomers for proteins.

54. A is correct.

Restriction enzyme (*restriction endonuclease*) cut DNA at specific nucleotide sequences (i.e., restriction sites).

Restriction enzymes are a defense mechanism against invading viruses in bacteria and archaea.

Prokaryotes have restriction enzymes that selectively cleave foreign DNA.

Host DNA is protected by a modification enzyme (i.e., methylase) that alters the prokaryotic DNA and prevents cleavage by the endogenous restriction enzyme.

55. C is correct.

RNA polymerase is an enzyme that produces primary transcript RNA in transcription.

Molecule C has a phosphodiester bond from the 3' of the base to the 5' downstream base and a triphosphate at the 5' end of the molecule.

A: represents DNA because of the absence of hydroxyl at the 2' position of the sugar.

B: contains a monophosphate at the 5' position.

D: shows a phosphodiester bond at the 2' position (not the 3').

E: shows a phosphodiester bond between two 5' ends.

First step, the two strands of the DNA double helix are physically separated at a high temperature in DNA melting.

Second step, the temperature is lowered, and two DNA strands become templates for DNA polymerase to selectively amplify the target DNA.

Third step, reaction mechanism uses RNA polymerase to synthesize a complementary strand to the template.

Selectivity of PCR results from using *primers complementary* to the DNA region targeted for amplification under specific *thermal cycling conditions*.

The process continues for 30 to 40 cycles, doubling the amount of DNA each cycle.

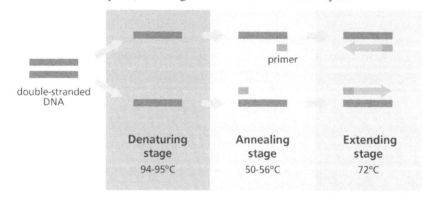

PCR amplification uses three steps for denaturing, annealing, and replicating DNA

57. A is correct.

DNA is double-stranded with A, C, G and T, while RNA is single-stranded with U replacing the T of DNA.

DNA uses the sugar of deoxyribose (i.e., the absence of ~OH group at the 2' in RNA), while RNA uses ribose (i.e., the presence of ~OH group at the 2').

58. B is correct.

Ligase is an enzyme used by the cell during DNA replication (and in other biochemical processes) that catalyzes the joining of two large molecules (e.g., DNA nucleotides) by forming a new chemical bond.

Newly formed bond is *via* a condensation reaction (joining) and usually involves dehydration with the loss of H_2O when the molecules (e.g., DNA, amino acids) are linked.

59. E is correct.

In DNA, thymine (T) base pairs with adenine (A) with two hydrogen bonds, while cytosine (C) base pairs with guanine (G) with three hydrogen bonds.

More energy is required to break three hydrogen bonds than two hydrogen bonds. A DNA sequence with increased C-G pairs has a higher melting point and requires more energy to denature (i.e., separate).

When bonded to its complementary strand, the DNA strand with GCCAGTCG has two T-A and six C-G pairs:

(2 pairs × 2 H bonds = 4) + (6 pairs × 3 bonds = 18) = 22 H bonds

Thus, this DNA strand has the most hydrogen bonds and the highest melting point.

A: five T-A pairs and three C-G pairs:

(5 pairs × 2 H bonds = 10) + (3 pairs × 3 bonds = 9) = 19 H bonds

C: four A-T pairs and four C-G pairs:

(4 pairs × 2 H bonds = 8) + (4 pairs × 3 bonds = 12) = 20 H bonds

D: four A-T pairs and four C-G pairs:

(4 pairs × 2 H bonds = 8) + (4 pairs × 3 bonds = 12) = 20 H bonds

60. C is correct.

Reverse genetics analyzes the function of a gene by observing the phenotypic effects of specific gene sequences obtained by DNA sequencing.

Reverse genetics seeks to find *which phenotypes* arise due to genetic sequences.

It proceeds in the opposite direction of classical genetics, which investigates the genetic basis of a phenotype.

61. D is correct.

Protein synthesis requires biochemical energy from ATP or GTP.

Two high-energy phosphate bonds (from ATP) provide the energy required to form one aminoacyl-tRNA involving the attachment of each amino acid to its tRNA.

> *Initiation complex* formation requires energy from one GTP.

> *Initiation* requires one high-energy phosphate bond (ATP) is required.

> *Elongation* with the delivery of each new tRNA to the A site requires one GTP.

> *Translocation* of the peptidyl-tRNA requires one GTP.

> *Termination* does not require the hydrolysis of a high-energy phosphate bond (e.g., ATP, GTP).

For each amino acid added to the polypeptide chain, two high-energy phosphate bonds are used for "charging" the tRNA with the correct amino acid (2 GTP × 50 amino acids = 100).

For chain formation, one high-energy phosphate bond is required to carry the amino acid to the ribosome and another to translocate the ribosome (2 GTP × 49 peptide bonds = 98).

> Total: 1 + 100 + 98 = 199

62. E is correct.

mRNA in *E. coli* cells is composed primarily of phosphodiester linkages between ribonucleotides.

63. B is correct.

DNA repair is a collection of processes by which a cell identifies and corrects damage to the DNA molecules encoding its genome.

Before replication of DNA, the cell methylates the parental strand for reference during any potential errors introduced during replication.

Normal metabolic activities and environmental factors such as UV light and radiation can cause DNA damage, resulting in many individual lesions per cell per day.

Many lesions cause structural damage to the DNA molecule and can alter the cell's ability to transcribe genes for the survival of its daughter cells after mitosis.

DNA repair process is constantly active as it responds to damage in the DNA structure, and methylation references the original strand when mismatches are detected during replication.

64. A is correct.

Methionine is the *start codon* of mRNA and is the first amino acid in eukaryotic proteins.

Mature protein may excise a portion of the original polypeptide, so methionine is not always the first amino acid in the mature protein after modification in the Golgi.

Genetics and Inheritance Patterns – Detailed Explanations

1. A is correct.

Model organism for *genetic studies* (e.g., pea plants, Drosophila, zebrafish) has common features. The organism must be bred in *large numbers*, and *ease of cultivation* favors viable offspring that *transmit genetic information* between generations.

Genetic studies rely upon statistics that favor *large sample numbers*. Therefore, a short generation time (i.e., the span between birth and fecundity) is preferred.

There should be *discreet phenotypic differences* among alleles (alternative forms of the gene).

For example, among the seven traits Mendel (1822-1884) observed, he inventoried tall *vs.* short plants, round *vs.* smooth seeds, and green *vs.* yellow seeds.

Mendel controlled the crosses by manually transferring pollen from the anther of a mature pea plant of one variety to the stigma of a separate mature pea plant of the second variety.

Organisms should have a *well-characterized genome* (gene identity and function have been studied).

Increasing *numbers of chromosomes* increase the genes that can influence the observable phenotypic outcomes.

Fewer chromosomes facilitate statistical analysis and causation when the genome is manipulated.

2. C is correct.

Sex-linked genetic disease, hemophilia, causes excessive bleeding because the blood does not clot. Tom, Mary, and their four daughters do not exhibit symptoms of hemophilia.

However, their son exhibits symptoms of hemophilia because Mary is heterozygous.

3. C is correct.

Eye color is sex-linked in *Drosophila*.

Determine the phenotype of parents.

Red-eyed flies with red-eyed and sepia-eyed parents must be heterozygous because a sepia-eyed parent only contributes recessive sepia alleles.

When a heterozygous (Rr) red-eyed fly is crossed with a homozygous recessive (rr) sepia-eyed fly, ½ of the offspring are red-eyed (Rr) because of the dominant (red) allele from the heterozygous fly.

Punnett Square:

Red eyed parent

	R	r
r	Rr (red)	rr (sepia)
r	Rr (red)	rr (sepia)

(left label: Sepia eyed Parent)

continued...

Since the question does not assign gender to the sepia and red-eyed parents, the Punnett squares for two combinations for sex-linked traits are:

Red eyed female (♀)

		R	r
Sepia eyed male (♂)	r	Rr (red)	rr (sepia)
	y	Ry (red)	ry (sepia)

Red eyed male (♂)

		R	y
Sepia eyed female (♀)	r	Rr (red)	ry (sepia)
	r	Rr (red)	ry (sepia)

4. E is correct.

Color blindness pertains to cone photoreceptors in retinas, as the cones can detect the color frequencies of light.

About 8 percent of males, but 0.5 percent of females, are colorblind, whether it is one color, a color combination, or another mutation.

Males are at a greater risk of inheriting an X-linked mutation because males have one X chromosome (XY) while females have two (XX).

Men lack a second X chromosome to compensate for the X chromosome that carries the gene mutation.

If a woman inherits a typical X chromosome in addition to the one that carries the mutation, she does not display the mutation.

5. C is correct.

Microscopy is the laboratory technique of magnifying objects that cannot be seen with the unaided eye.

Gregor Mendel (1822-1884) performed crossbreeding experiments with pea plants to study inheritance patterns and introduced the terms *dominant* and *recessive* for phenotypic traits (or *alleles*).

6. E is correct.

AAbbCc produces 2 gametes:

AbC and Abc = 1/2

AaBbCc produces 8 gametes:

ABC, ABc, AbC, Abc, aBC, aBc, abC, abc = 2/8 possible = 1/4

From probability: $1/2 \times 1/4 = 1/8$

	ABC	ABc	AbC	Abc	aBC	aBc	abC	abc
AbC	X	X	X	X	X	**Yes**	X	X
Abc	X	X	X	X	**Yes**	X	X	X

7. B is correct.

Afflicted children are aa = 1 of 4 possibilities = ¼ or 25%.

	A	a
A	AA	Aa
a	Aa	**aa**

8. C is correct.

Tumor suppressor genes protect a cell from aberrant cell cycles.

When this gene's function is lost or reduced due to mutation, the cell can progress to cancer (usually combined with other genetic mutations).

Loss of tumor suppressor genes may be more critical than proto-oncogene/oncogene activation to form many kinds of human cancer cells.

Both alleles of the tumor suppressor gene encoding a particular protein must be affected before an effect is manifested.

If one allele is damaged, the second can produce the correct protein.

9. D is correct.

Color blindness is a *sex-linked trait* because the gene is on the X chromosome.

Mother is a carrier (not afflicted with condition) and is heterozygous for the recessive allele (color blindness).

Father has the allele on his X chromosome (Y chromosome lacks the gene).

Genotype and *phenotype* of an XY son depend entirely on the mother (afflicted vs. carrier) since the afflicted father transmits the gene on his X.

Mother is heterozygous; a son has a 50% probability of receiving the color-blindness allele from his mother.

10. B is correct.

If two strains of true-breeding plants with different alleles are crossed, their progeny is the F_1 generation.

11. C is correct.

   AaBbCcDdEe × AaBbCcDdEe

From probability;

   ½ × ½ × ½ × ½ × ½ = 1/32

12. A is correct.

Autosomal recessive inheritance is the product of mating two carriers (i.e., heterozygous parents).

In mating two heterozygotes for an autosomal recessive gene, there is a:

25% (1/4) probability of a homozygous *unaffected* child

25% (1/4) probability of a homozygous *affected* child

50% (1/2) probability of a heterozygous (*carrier*) child

75% of children are phenotypically normal (25% AA and 50% Aa).

Of all children, 50% are phenotypically normal but carry the mutant gene (Aa).

13. D is correct.

If the dominant allele frequency is three times that of the recessive allele,

$$p = 3q$$

Hardy-Weinberg equilibrium:

$$p + q = 1$$

so

$$3q + q = 1$$

Solving for q

$$4q = 1$$

$$q = 0.25$$

$$p = 0.75$$

Allele frequency:

$$p^2 + 2pq + q^2 = 1$$

Heterozygote allele = 2pq

Substituting for p and q,

$$2(0.75) \cdot (0.25) = 0.375 \text{ or } 37.5\%$$

14. E is correct.

Loss of heterozygosity is a chromosomal event resulting from losing the gene and surrounding region.

Diploid cells (e.g., human somatic cells) contain *two copies* of the genome, one from each parent.

Each copy contains approximately 3 billion bases, and for most positions in the genome, the base is consistent between individuals. However, a small percentage may contain different bases.

These positions are *single nucleotide polymorphisms* (or SNP). The region is heterozygous when the genomic copies from each parent have different bases for these regions.

Most chromosomes within somatic cells are paired, allowing SNP locations to be potentially heterozygous.

One parental copy of a region can be lost, resulting in the region with just one copy.

If the copy lost contained the dominant allele, the remaining recessive allele would appear in a phenotype.

15. A is correct.

Maternal inheritance involves all progeny exhibiting the phenotype of the *female* parent.

B: not maternal inheritance because the progeny exhibits the phenotype of the *male* parent.

C and D: Mendelian 1:1 segregation and not maternal inheritance.

Maternal inheritance is uniparental when all progeny have the genotype and phenotype of the female parent.

16. E is correct.

Gene is a fundamental physical, functional unit of heredity transferred from a parent to offspring and determines some offspring characteristics.

Genes are DNA sequences encoding proteins.

Alleles are forms of the same gene with slight differences in their sequence of DNA bases.

Genome is the *complete set of genetic information* for an organism.

Genome has the genetic information needed for an organism and allows it to develop, grow and reproduce.

17. B is correct.

GC base pairs converted to AT base pairs in the promoter will likely lose gene function completely.

18. A is correct.

Mutations affect proteins but not lipids or carbohydrates.

In proteins, the effects on the protein are no change (i.e., silent mutation), abnormal protein production, loss of protein (enzyme) function, or gain of protein (enzyme) function.

Loss of function of a gene product may result from mutations encoding a regulatory element or the loss of critical amino acid sequences.

continued...

Gain-of-function mutations are changes in the amino acids resulting in enhancement of the protein function.

There may be an increase in the level of protein expression (affecting the operator region of the gene) or an increase in each protein molecule's ability to perform its function (change in the shape of the protein).

19. A is correct.

The desired phenotype is green smooth peas, and green and smooth are dominant phenotypes.

Therefore, the genotypes selected for the cross must avoid the two recessive alleles (g and s).

For GgSs × GGSS, one parent (GGSS) is a double dominant, and therefore all offspring have the dominant phenotype (G and S) regardless of the other parent's genotype.

B: Gg × gg yields 1/2 yellow (g) phenotype offspring

C: ss × Ss yields 1/2 wrinkled (s) phenotype offspring

D: Gg × Gg yields 1/4 yellow (g) phenotype offspring

20. C is correct.

Retinoblastoma (Rb) is a rapidly developing cancer in immature cells of the retina, the light-detecting tissue of the eye. It is a common malignant tumor of the eyes in children. A single allele is inherited (i.e., dominant) for the phenotype.

21. E is correct.

Phenotype of the first child does not influence the probability of the second child.

For example, the probability of getting a tail on the first toss of a coin does not influence the probability of getting a head on the second toss.

Punnett square determines possible gametes and their combinations.

If ½ of the woman's gametes carry the trait and ½ of the father's gametes carry the trait, the probability of a child receiving the allele from each parent is ½ × ½ = ¼.

22. C is correct.

In Mendel's experiment, the cross of spherical-seeded and wrinkled-seeded pea plants inherited alleles (or *gene variants*) from each parent.

However, only spherical-seeded plants resulted from the cross.

Wrinkled-seed gene is a recessive allele compared to the spherical-seed gene (i.e., the dominant gene).

Dominant allele is a genetic variant expressed more strongly than other variants (or alleles) of the gene (i.e., recessive) for many reasons.

23. B is correct.

Notation 2N indicates that a given cell line is diploid, two homologous versions of each chromosome.

Human somatic cells are diploid with 23 different chromosome pairs (N = 23) for 46 chromosomes (2N = 46).

Gamete cells (eggs and sperm) are haploid (i.e., 1N).

Mitosis is the mode of cell division used by somatic cells, resulting in two diploid daughter cells genetically identical to the diploid parent cell.

24. D is correct.

Degree of genetic linkage measures the physical distance of two genes on the same chromosome.

Probability of crossover and corresponding exchange between gene loci (location on the chromosome) is generally proportional to the distance between the loci.

Genes far apart on a chromosome are more likely to be separated during crossover than genes physically close.

Thus, *frequency of genetic recombination* between two genes is *related to their distance.*

Recombination frequencies are used to construct genetic maps.

One map unit (Morgan units) is defined as a 1 percent recombinant frequency.

Recombination frequencies are roughly *additive* and are a good approximation for small percentages.

Largest percentage of recombinants cannot exceed 50%, resulting when the two genes are at the opposite ends of the same chromosome.

Crossover events result in an exchange of genes.

However, an odd number of crossover events (a 50% probability between an even and an odd number of crossover events) results in a recombinant product.

25. A is correct.

Epigenetic inheritance results from changes in gene activity, *not* caused by changes in the DNA sequence.

It studies stable, long-term alterations in the transcriptional potential that are not necessarily heritable.

Unlike simple genetics based on changes to the DNA sequence (genotype), the changes in gene expression or cellular phenotype of epigenetics have other causes.

For example, *cellular differentiation* is an epigenetic change in eukaryotes cells.

During *morphogenesis*, totipotent (i.e., all potent) stem cells become pluripotent (i.e., highly potent, but with limited determinate potential) cells of the embryo, which become fully differentiated cells.

Gene expression is when a single fertilized egg cell (zygote) divides, and the resulting daughter cells change into different cell types (e.g., neurons, muscle cells, epithelium, endothelium of blood vessels) by activating some genes while inhibiting the expression of others.

26. C is correct.

Female children receive one X from their mother and one X from their father.

X from the father must carry the color-blindness allele because the father is colorblind.

X from the mother has a wild-type and a color blindness allele because she is heterozygous recessive.

50% of female children are homozygous colorblind, and 50% are heterozygous carriers.

27. D is correct.

True breeding means that the organism is homozygous (e.g., AA or aa) for the trait.

All progeny are heterozygous Aa (below) and exhibit the dominant phenotype.

	A	A
a	Aa	Aa
a	Aa	Aa

28. C is correct.

	A	A
a	Aa	Aa
a	Aa	Aa

	A	a
A	AA	Aa
a	Aa	aa

F$_1$: all tall   F$_2$: ¾ are tall, and ¼ is short

29. B is correct.

Frameshift mutation is when 1 or 2 base pairs are added or deleted. A 3 base pair addition or deletion causes an *in-frame* mutation because 3 nucleotides encode each codon.

Frameshift mutation (i.e., addition/deletion of other than multiples of 3 nucleotides) causes the ribosome to read all downstream codons in the wrong frame. They usually result in truncated (i.e., *nonsense* mutation) or non-functional proteins (i.e., *missense* mutation).

An altered base pair (i.e., *point* mutation) is not a frameshift mutation because it substitutes (not adds or deletes) and does not cause the ribosome to read codons out of frame.

Point mutations can result in nonsense (i.e., premature stop codon) or missense (i.e., improperly folded protein) mutations.

Base pair additions/deletions (other than in multiples of 3) cause frameshift mutations.

30. D is correct.

Mendel's *law of independent assortment* states that the probability of a cross resulting in a genotype equals the *product* of individual probabilities.

Crosses by two heterozygous individuals for the three genes (A, B, and C) produce homozygous dominant offspring for each trait.

Each parent is heterozygous for A, genotype = Aa.

Ratio of offspring equals 1/4 AA, 1/2 Aa, and 1/4 aa; a typical 1:2:1 ratio for heterozygous crosses.

Parents are heterozygous for genes B and C, the probability of offspring being BB is 1/4, and CC is 1/4.

Probability that offspring are genotype AABBCC = *product of individual probabilities*:

$$1/4 \times 1/4 \times 1/4 = 1/64$$

31. E is correct.

Nonsense mutation is a DNA point mutation resulting in a premature stop codon in the transcribed mRNA and a truncated (i.e., incomplete) protein, usually nonfunctional.

Missense mutation is a point mutation where a nucleotide is changed and substitutes for a different amino acid.

Genetic disorders of sickle cell anemia, thalassemia and Duchenne muscular dystrophy arise from *nonsense mutations*.

32. B is correct.

Recessive trait is expressed when present in both copies (i.e., alleles) or is the single copy of the gene.

Human Y chromosome confers maleness.

Recessive (single copy) alleles on the X are expressed (e.g., hemophilia).

Recessive X-linked allele is expressed in unaffected females with two (homozygous) alleles.

33. B is correct.

Mendelian *Laws of inheritance* explain patterns of disease transmission.

Inheritance patterns of single-gene diseases are *Mendelian* after Augustinian friar Gregor Mendel (1822-1884), who first reported different gene segregation patterns for specific garden peas traits.

Mendel calculated *probabilities* of inheritance for traits in the next generations.

Because of mutations or polymorphisms, most genes have more versions (i.e., alleles).

Individuals carry normal, mutant, or rare alleles, depending on mutation/polymorphism and allele frequency within a population.

Single-gene diseases are usually inherited depending on gene location and whether one or two regular copies of the gene are needed for the disease to manifest (i.e., affected individuals).

continued...

Expression of a mutated allele is *dominant*, *co-dominant*, or *recessive*.

Five basic *patterns of inheritance for single-gene diseases*:

Autosomal dominant:

each affected person has an affected parent

manifests in each generation

Autosomal recessive:

parents of an affected person are carriers (i.e., unaffected)

typically, NOT seen in each generation

X-linked dominant:

females affected more frequently

can affect males and females in the same generation

X-linked recessive:

males affected more frequently

often affects males in each generation

Mitochondrial:

males and females can be affected but passed by females

can appear in each generation

An accurate family history is essential to determine inheritance pattern when a family is affected by a disease.

34. A is correct.

Two traits are *unlinked* when inherited on separate chromosomes or because the genes are apart greater than 50 centimorgans.

At large distances, double-crossing over occurs, and the genes appear unlinked.

35. D is correct.

Let T = tall and t = short; B = brown eyes and b = blue eyes.

Father is *homozygous tall* and *blue-eyed*; his genotype is TTbb.

Mother is *heterozygous tall* and *heterozygous brown-eyed*; her genotype is TtBb.

Determine the probability that parents produce a tall child with blue eyes (T_bb).

The genes for height and eye color are unlinked.

Father (TTbb) contributes T and b alleles, so his gametes have T and b alleles.

Mother (TtBb) contributes T or t and B or b, so her gametes are (in equal amounts): TB, tB, Tb, or tb.

continued...

Genotypes of the offspring:

> TTBb, TTbb, TtBb, Ttbb

Half the offspring are tall and brown-eyed (T_B_), and half are tall and blue-eyed (T_bb).

Therefore, the probability of a tall child with blue eyes is ½.

A faster method is calculating phenotype ratios for height and eye color separately and then combining them.

> Mating TT × Tt = 100% tall

> Mating Bb × Bb = ½ blue and ½ brown

> Multiplying 1 tall × ½ blue = ½ tall blue

36. A is correct.

Recombination is the exchange of genetic information between homologous chromosomes and occurs during prophase I of meiosis.

Crossing over between non-sister homologs in *meiosis r*esults in a new combination of alleles, for example:

> AB / ab can yield Ab / aB

Recombination occurs in eukaryotes during *mitosis* but between *sister chromatids* which are copies (replicated during the S phase) and therefore do *not* lead to novel genotypes.

Recombination is a *DNA repair mechanism* between homologous chromosomes.

Research supports that recombination is not a random event.

Recombination hotspots include chromosome regions with *high GC content* and particular architecture (e.g., genome size, haploid chromosome number, chromosome size, and chromosome rearrangements).

Enzymes catalyze recombination (e.g., rec A, rec B, rec C, and rec D) by initiating and *facilitating strand invasion* and *strand transfer* during recombination.

High recombination frequency means the genes are *farther apart.*

Each percent frequency of recombination equals one map unit between the genes. So, 2.5% recombination frequency equals genes 2.5 map units apart.

Largest recombination frequency is 50%, as if the genes were on different chromosomes (consistent with Mendel's Law of Independent Assortment).

Recombination frequency would be the same for *cis-* and *trans*-heterozygotes because the distance is the same between the genes regardless of whether they are on the same (*cis*) or homologous (*trans*) chromosomes.

Recombination frequency is *not* a completely random event.

Specific regions within the chromosome have differences in the propensity to undergo recombination; the presence of *hotspots* and architectural features (e,g, histones) increase or decrease recombination frequencies.

Recombination frequency increases (not decreases) with *distance.*

Genes have different distances; with different distances, the recombination frequency changes.

37. C is correct.

There are two possible alleles for each of the three genes.

If the genes assort independently (not linked):

$2^3 = 8$ combinations exist

38. A is correct.

Each affected person has an affected parent in the *autosomal dominant* inheritance pattern.

Autosomal dominant inheritance is a way a genetic trait can be passed from parent to child.

One parent's copy of a mutated (changed) gene can cause genetic conditions.

A child who has a parent with the mutated gene has a 50% chance of inheriting that mutated gene.

Men and women are *equally likely* to have these mutations.

Sons and daughters are *equally likely* to inherit them.

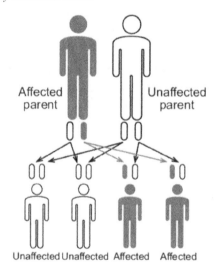

Autosomal dominant inheritance pattern with presence in each generation

39. C is correct.

Parents are Aa × Aa (carriers but not afflicted with the disease).

Progeny could be AA, Aa, Aa, or aa.

From the Punnett square, eliminate aa because this is the disease state.

The question asks the probability that she is heterozygous (Aa) but not homozygous (AA) = 2/3.

40. E is correct.

Anticipation is associated with an earlier onset of symptoms and increased disease severity in each generation.

Anticipation is observed in autosomal dominant diseases by *trinucleotide repeat expansions* (e.g., Huntington's disease, myotonic dystrophy) because increased-length triple repeats are unstable during cell division.

A: *codominance* is when a gene has more than one dominant allele. In the ABO blood group system, the I^A and I^B alleles are codominant.

Heterozygous individual for *two codominant alleles* expresses the phenotypes associated with both alleles.

Heterozygous individuals for the I^A and I^B alleles express the AB blood group phenotype, A- and B-type antigens are on the surface of red blood cells.

Codominance occurs at the locus for the beta-globin component of hemoglobin.

Three molecular phenotypes of Hb^A/Hb^A, Hb^A/Hb^S, and Hb^S/Hb^S are detectable by protein electrophoresis.

B: *penetrance* is the proportion of individuals carrying the variant of a gene (allele or genotype) and expressing the trait (phenotype).

In medical genetics, the penetrance of a disease-causing mutation is the proportion of individuals with the mutation who exhibit clinical symptoms.

For example, if a mutation in the gene responsible for an autosomal dominant disorder has 95% penetrance, 95% of those with the mutation develop the disease, while 5% do not.

D: *gain of function mutations* change the gene product to gain a new and abnormal function.

These mutations usually have dominant phenotypes and are expressed with a single allele.

41. B is correct.

Hardy-Weinberg equation:

$$p^2 + 2pq + q^2 = 1$$

where p equals gene frequency of dominant allele, and q equals gene frequency of recessive allele

Hence, in the population:

p^2 is the frequency of *homozygous dominants*

2pq is the frequency of *heterozygotes*

q^2 is the frequency of *homozygous recessives*

For a trait with two alleles, p + q must equal 1 since the combined frequencies of the alleles – 100%.

If the frequency of the recessive allele for a trait is 0.6,

q = 0.6

continued...

Since

$$p + q = 1$$

$$p = 0.4$$

To calculate the frequency of individuals expressing the *dominant phenotype* (not the dominant genotype), determine the number of individuals *homozygous for the dominant trait* (p^2) and add the *number of heterozygotes* (2pq) exhibiting the dominant phenotype:

$$p^2 = (0.4) \times (0.4)$$

$$p^2 = 0.16$$

$$2pq = 2 \times (0.6) \times (0.4)$$

$$2pq = 0.48$$

So,

$$p^2 + 2pq = 0.16 + 0.48$$

$$p^2 + 2pq = 0.64$$

A: 0.48 = frequency of *heterozygous* individuals.

C: 0.16 = frequency of *homozygous dominant* individuals.

D: 0.36 = frequency of *homozygous recessive* individuals.

42. C is correct.

Maximum recombination frequency between two genes is 50%.

43. B is correct.

For a recessive trait to appear in a phenotype of an offspring (e.g., long hair), offspring inherit a recessive allele (Mendel called it *traits*) from each parent (i.e., two copies of the recessive gene).

Short-haired parents carry one copy (i.e., heterozygous) of the recessive long-haired allele (or *gene*).

Combined with the second copy from the other long-haired parent, it produced the long-haired offspring.

44. D is correct.

Meiosis in males produces four haploid (1N) unique cells genetically different from the parental cell.

45. D is correct.

Point mutations occur when a single nucleotide base (A, C, G, T) is substituted by another.

Silent mutation is a point mutation that

       1) occurs in a noncoding region or

       2) does not change the amino acid sequence due to the degeneracy of the genetic code.

Frameshift mutation is the insertion or deletion of some nucleotides. These mutations severely affect the coded protein since nucleotides are read as triplets.

Addition or loss of nucleotides (except in multiples of three) changes the reading frame of the mRNA and often gives rise to premature polypeptide termination (i.e., nonsense mutation).

Missense mutation results from the insertion of a single nucleotide that changes the amino acid sequence of the specified polypeptide.

46. E is correct.

Two reciprocal crossing-over events appear in progeny at an approximate ratio of 1:1.

47. C is correct.

EEBB × eebb produces offspring of single genotype EeBb, as determined by the Punnett square for the cross between a homozygous dominant by a homozygous recessive.

58. D is correct.

Mutations may cause *premature translation termination* (i.e., *nonsense* mutation) and nonfunctional protein.

49. E is correct.

	A	a
A	AA	Aa
a	Aa	aa

Afflicted children are AA, Aa or Aa (not aa) = 3 of 4 possibilities = ¾ or 75%.

50. D is correct.

Recombinant frequencies of linked genes map the relative locations of genes on a single chromosome.

Recombinant frequencies are determined by crossing individuals that differ in alleles for the genes in question and determining the genotypes of their progeny.

Recombinant frequencies equal frequencies of nonparent genotypes since these genotypes arise by crossover.

Mapping is based on the *probability* of a crossover between two points; the probability of crossover *increases* as the distance between the genes *increases*.

continued…

Farther away, genes have a *greater* recombinant frequency.

Probability that two genes are inherited together (i.e., linked) *decreases* as the distance between them on a chromosome *increases*.

One map unit = 1% recombination frequency, and recombinant frequencies are (roughly) additive.

However, if the genes are far apart, the recombination frequency reaches a *maximum of 50%*, at which point the genes are considered to be sorted independently.

There are four genes (D, E, F, and G), and the recombinant frequencies between each pair are given.

To construct the map, *start* with the allele pair with the *highest recombinant frequency*: between G and E (23%), which means that G and E are 23 map units apart and on the two ends.

Determine the intervening genes by finding the genes closest to the two endpoints.

G and D are 8 map units apart, closest to G. Thus, D must be next to G.

Genes on this chromosome must be G, D, F, and E by elimination.

EFDG is equally correct if the map started from the opposite direction, but this is not an answer choice.

To verify, D and E are 15 map units apart because the distance from G to D, which is 8, plus the distance from D to E, which is 15, is the distance from G to E, which equals 23.

G and F are 15 map units apart, while F and E are 8 units apart.

The numbers add, whereby the distance from G to E equals G to D + the distance from D to E.

The observed numbers may be off by one or two map units (not a mistake) because map distances are roughly additive (i.e., based on rounding for the probabilities).

> Questions **51** through **57** are based on the following:

The pedigree illustrated by the schematic shows the inheritance of albinism, a homozygous recessive condition manifested in a total lack of pigment. Specify the genotypes using *A* and *a* to indicate dominant and recessive alleles.

Note: solids are albino individuals.

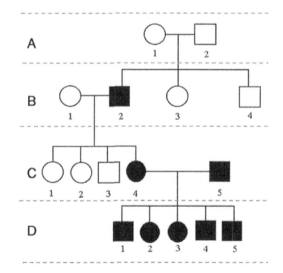

51. C is correct.

Individual A-1 in the pedigree is *Aa*.

52. C is correct.

Individual A-2 in the pedigree is *Aa*.

---

53. C is correct.

Individual B-1 in the pedigree is *Aa.*

54. B is correct.

Individual B-2 in the pedigree is *aa.*

55. C is correct.

Individual C-3 in the pedigree is *Aa.*

56. B is correct.

Individual C-4 in the pedigree is *aa.*

57. B is correct.

Individual D-4 in the pedigree is *aa.*

58. E is correct.

BBss × bbss produces gametes Bbss.

Then crossed:

> Bbss × Bbss and produce the four gametes:

> BBss, Bbss, bBss and bbss

Phenotypically,

> ¾ (BBss, Bbss, bBss) are black and spotted

> ¼ (bbss) is red and spotted

59. A is correct.

X-linked recessive inheritance is a mode of inheritance whereby a mutation in a gene on the X chromosome causes the phenotype to be expressed

> 1) *hemizygous males* with a single allele of the mutation because they have one X chromosome and

> 2) *homozygous females* who are homozygous for the mutation (i.e., a copy of the gene mutation on each of two X chromosomes).

X-linked inheritance indicates that the gene is on the X chromosome.

Females have two X, while males have one X and one Y.

Carrier females have one allele and do not usually express the phenotype.

continued...

X-linked gene mutations are more common in males (i.e., a single allele of the X chromosome) than in females (i.e., two X chromosomes).

Gene appears to *alternate generations* because heterozygous phenotypically normal females transmit it.

Affected males transmit the gene to their daughters, carriers for the trait.

There is no father-to-son transmission because the sons inherit the father's Y chromosome.

Males carrying the mutant gene show the trait.

60. C is correct.

X-inactivation (i.e., lyonization) is when one of two X chromosomes in female mammals is inactivated.

Inactive X chromosome is silenced by transcriptional inactivity within heterochromatin (i.e., condensed DNA).

Females have two X chromosomes, and X-inactivation prevents them from having twice as many X chromosome gene products as males (XY) for dosage compensation of the X chromosome.

Which X chromosome becomes inactivated is random in humans.

Once an X chromosome is inactivated, it remains inactive throughout life and in descendants.

Calico and tortoiseshell-colored cats are phenotypic examples of *X-inactivation* because the alleles for black and orange fur coloration reside on the X chromosome.

For a patch of fur, inactivation of an X chromosome carries one gene resulting in the fur color of the allele for the active gene.

Calico cats are almost always female because the X chromosome determines the color of the cat, and female cats (like all female mammals) have two X chromosomes.

Male mammals have one X and one Y chromosome.

Y chromosome lacks color genes; there is no probability a male cat could have orange and non-orange.

One prominent exception is when, in rare cases, a male has XXY chromosomes (Klinefelter syndrome).

61. D is correct.

Autosomal dominance is typical Mendelian inheritance.

An individual needs a single copy of the mutant gene to exhibit the disease for *autosomal dominant* traits.

Autosomal dominance usually,

> equal numbers of males and females affected
>
> traits do not skip generations
>
> father-to-son transmission

Diversity of Life

Microbiology – Detailed Explanations

1. E is correct.

The *major* distinction between prokaryotic and eukaryotic cells is that prokaryotic cells do not have a nucleus, but eukaryotic cells do.

2. B is correct.

Penicillin prevents bacterial peptidoglycan cell wall formation by covalently binding to a serine residue at the transpeptidase active site.

Binding the enzyme's active site is characteristic of an *irreversible competitive* inhibitor.

Irreversible binding with a covalent bond creates a stable and permanent attachment.

Competitive because it competes with the substrate for the active site.

Penicillin (*β*-lactam antibiotic) inhibits the formation of peptidoglycan cross-links in the *bacterial cell wall*.

Enzymes hydrolyzing the peptidoglycan cross-links continue to function, but those that form crosslinks do not; this weakens the bacterium cell wall, and osmotic pressure rises, causing cell death (cytolysis).

A: *reversible competitive inhibitors* utilize weak molecular attachment (i.e., van der Waals or hydrogen bonds) when attaching to the enzyme's active site.

C: penicillin does *not digest* the cell wall but prevents cross-linking bacterial *cell wall peptidoglycan*.

The effect inhibits the bacteria's ability to remodel their cell wall or prevent progeny from forming a necessary cell wall to counter osmotic pressure.

E: *noncompetitive inhibitors* bind to an allosteric site, which is different from the active site.

Binding of a molecule to the allosteric site of the enzyme causes a conformational change (i.e., three-dimensional shape change), affecting the shape (i.e., function) of the active site.

3. D is correct.

Viruses are simple, non-living organisms that take on living characteristics when they infect a host cell.

Their genetic material is RNA or DNA; not arranged into chromosomes but associated with a complex of nucleic acids and histone proteins.

Viruses contain DNA or RNA and a protein coat (i.e., capsule).

Cellular machinery and biomolecules in a host cell (prokaryotic or eukaryotic) are required for viral replication.

4. D is correct.

Replica plating technique of Joshua and Esther Lederberg demonstrated (in 1952) that streptomycin revealed the presence of streptomycin-resistant bacteria.

5. B is correct.

Operon is a functional unit of genomic DNA with a cluster of genes under the control of a single regulatory signal or promoter.

Genes (i.e., nucleotide sequences) are transcribed together into mRNA strands.

The genes contained in the operon are expressed together or not at all.

Several genes must be *co-transcribed* and *co-regulated* to be defined as an operon.

6. C is correct.

Neurospora is a fungus and haploid for most of its life cycle.

For fungus, a brief diploid (2N) stage after fertilization transitions via meiosis to produce haploid (1N) cells, which repeatedly divide via mitosis before entering another sexual cycle.

A: most fungi undergo meiosis and a sexual cycle.

B: separation of fertilization and meiosis is characteristic of the life cycle of plants.

D: *fertilization* immediately following meiosis is characteristic of diploid organisms.

7. D is correct.

Enzymes are biomolecules in prokaryotic cells.

8. A is correct.

Endomembrane system extends the nuclear envelope and includes endoplasmic reticulum and Golgi apparatus.

Golgi receives proteins within vesicles from the RER and modifies, sorts, and packages proteins destined for the secretory pathway (i.e., plasma membrane, exocytosis from the cell, or organelles within the cell).

Golgi is essential for synthesizing *proteoglycans* (i.e., components of connective tissue) in the extracellular matrix of animal cells.

Golgi primarily modifies proteins delivered from the rough endoplasmic reticulum.

It participates in lipid transport and the synthesis of lysosomes and is the site of carbohydrate synthesis.

B: *lysosomes* are organelles with low pH that function to digest intracellular molecules.

C: *peroxisomes* are organelles in most eukaryotic cells.

Peroxisomes function in the breakdown of very-long-chain fatty acids through *beta-oxidation*.

In animal cells, the very-long-chain fatty acids are converted to medium-chain fatty acids and subsequently shuttled to mitochondria.

They are degraded, via oxidation, into *carbon dioxide* and *water*.

continued...

D: *smooth endoplasmic reticulum* connects to the nuclear envelope and functions in metabolic processes (i.e., synthesis of lipids, phospholipids, and steroids).

It carries out the metabolism of carbohydrates, drug detoxification, attachment of receptors on cell membrane proteins, and steroid metabolism.

Cells secreting lipids, phospholipids, and steroids (e.g., testes, ovaries, skin oil glands) have a robust, smooth endoplasmic reticulum.

Smooth endoplasmic reticulum contains *glucose-6-phosphatase* (enzyme), which converts glucose-6-phosphate to glucose during *gluconeogenesis.*

9. C is correct.

Hfr (high-frequency recombination) cell is a bacterium with a conjugative plasmid (F factor) integrated into its genomic DNA instead of being in an autonomous circular DNA element in the cytoplasm (i.e., a plasmid).

F^+ denotes cells with the F plasmid, while F^- denotes cells that do not.

Unlike a typical F^+ cell, Hfr strains attempt to transfer their *entire* DNA through the mating bridge (pili).

The F factor tends to transfer during conjugation, and often, the entire bacterial genome is dragged along, but the transfer is often aborted before the complete plasmid is transferred.

Hfr cells are useful for studying gene linkage and recombination.

Because the genome's transfer rate through the mating bridge is constant, investigators can use the Hfr strain of bacteria to study genetic linkage and map the chromosome.

A: during conjugation, the transfer of Hfr DNA is interrupted by spontaneous breakage of the DNA molecule at random points.

F^+ denotes cells with the F plasmid, while F^- denotes cells that do not.

Typically, the chromosome is broken before the F factor is transferred to the F^- cell.

Therefore, the conjugation of a Hfr cell with an F^- cell does not usually result in an F^+ cell, and the F factor usually remains in the Hfr cell.

B: Hfr cells produce sex pili (i.e., mating bridge in this example), and the F^- cell is the transfer recipient.

D: F factor is integrated into the bacterium's chromosome, and the F factor is replicated along with the cells' genome before conjugation.

continued...

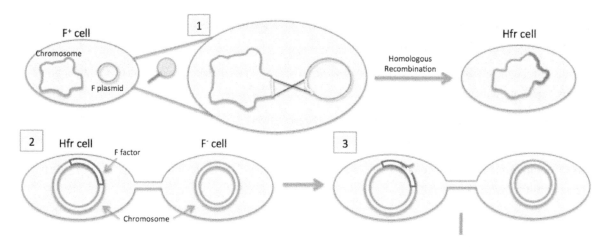

F⁺ cell integrates plasmid to form Hfr cell that transfers the F factor by conjugation to an F⁻ cell

10. E is correct.

Ames test (developed in the 1970s) uses bacteria to evaluate whether a chemical likely causes cancer.

It assesses the mutagenic potential of chemical compounds.

Positive test indicates that the chemical is *mutagenic* and may function as a *carcinogen* because cancer is often linked to genetic mutations.

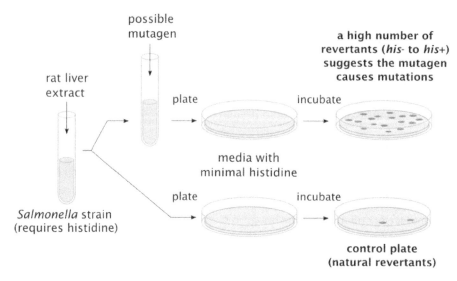

Ames test evaluates potential mutagens for the ability to transform nutrient-deficient cells upon exposure

11. A is correct.

Plants are generally autotrophs; animals are heterotrophs, and bacteria can be either.

Auxotrophs are unable to synthesize an organic compound required for growth.

In genetics, a strain is auxotrophic if it has a mutation that renders it unable to synthesize an essential compound (i.e., *essential* is needed for growth but cannot be synthesized).

continued...

For example, a uracil auxotroph is a yeast mutant with an inactivated uracil synthesis pathway gene.

Such a strain cannot synthesize uracil and will grow if uracil can be taken up from the environment.

B: *chemotrophs* obtain energy by oxidation of electron donors in their environments.

These molecules can be organic (e.g., chemoorganotrophs) or inorganic (e.g., chemolithotrophs).

Chemotroph designation contrasts with phototrophs, which utilize solar energy.

Chemotrophs can be autotrophic or heterotrophic.

C: *heterotrophs* use energy derived from another organism's metabolism (*hetero* means other).

D: *prototrophs* are characterized by synthesizing the compounds needed for growth.

12. B is correct.

Endospore is a dormant, tough, non-reproductive structure produced by certain bacteria.

Endospore consists of bacterium DNA and cytoplasm, surrounded by a tough outer coating.

Endospores can survive without nutrients.

Lack of nutrients usually triggers endospore formation.

13. E is correct.

Fungi are a large group of eukaryotes, including microorganisms such as mold, yeasts, and mushrooms.

Fungi are a kingdom (Fungi) separate from plants, animals, protists, and bacteria.

One significant difference is that fungal cells have cell walls with chitin.

The cell walls of plants and some protists contain cellulose, while bacterial cell walls contain peptidoglycan.

Fungi reproduce by sexual and asexual means and produce spores like basal plant groups (e.g., ferns, mosses).

Like algae and mosses, fungi typically have haploid (1N) nuclei with a small percentage of their life cycle in a diploid (2N) phase.

14. C is correct.

Cyanide is a poison interfering with the electron transport chain (ETC) of the inner plasma membrane (for prokaryotes) or the inner mitochondrial membrane (for eukaryotes) by binding to cytochromes (mainly *cytochrome c oxidase*) of the electron transfer complexes.

Cyanide inhibits the flow of electrons down their reduction potential and effectively inhibits the transport chain.

Consequently, the proton pump stops, and ATP cannot be generated aerobically.

Electron carriers such as NADH and FADH$_2$ cannot be oxidized and yield high-energy electrons to the electron transport chain because they are blocked.

NAD$^+$ and FAD are not regenerated, and aerobic *respiration ceases*.

continued...

DNA replication, RNA transcription, and protein synthesis require energy (ATP or GTP) and are processes necessary for host cell functions and viral replication.

If aerobic ATP formation is inhibited, there will be a deficiency of ATP for cell functions and viral replication.

Energy is required for a bacteriophage (a virus that infects bacteria) to replicate.

15. E is correct.

Transformation is the genetic alteration of a cell resulting from the direct uptake, incorporation, and expression of exogenous genetic material (exogenous DNA) from its surroundings and passes through the cell membrane.

Transformation introduces genetic material into nonbacterial cells, including animal and plant cells.

B: *conjugation* transfers genetic material (plasmid) between bacterial cells by direct cell-to-cell contact or a bridge-like connection between two cells (i.e., pili).

Conjugation is a mechanism of *horizontal gene transfer*, as are transformation and transduction.

The other gene transfer mechanisms do not involve cell-to-cell contact (conjugation uses a pilus).

C: *transduction* is how a virus transfers DNA from one bacterium to another.

In molecular biology, foreign DNA is introduced via a viral vector into another cell.

D: *recombination* is when DNA molecules exchange genetic information, forming new allele combinations.

In eukaryotes, genetic recombination between homologous chromosomes during prophase I of meiosis leads to a novel set of genetic information passed on to progeny.

Most recombination occurs spontaneously to increase genetic variation.

16. E is correct.

Viruses can have a genome consisting of double-stranded DNA (dsDNA).

Retroviruses have RNA genomes (single-stranded or double-stranded).

After infecting the host cell, the retrovirus uses *reverse transcriptase* to convert its RNA into DNA.

17. B is correct.

Cells of the same strain transfer their genomes in the same order and at the same rate.

Transfer is interrupted at times, and by matching the genes transferred to the length of time necessary for the transfer, the linear order of the genes is mapped.

A: *polycistronic* refers to the expression of bacterial genes on a single mRNA in an operon.

C: *rate of chromosome (i.e., F factor) transfer* must be constant because differences in the transfer rate would obscure the results.

D: F factors and the bacterial chromosome replicate using the same conjugation method (bacterial mating).

18. C is correct.

Prokaryotic ribosomes (30S small & 50S large subunit = 70S complete ribosome).

Eukaryotic ribosomes (40S small & 60S large subunit = 80S complete ribosome).

19. A is correct.

Retroviruses are a family of enveloped viruses that use reverse transcription to replicate within a host cell.

Retrovirus is a single-stranded RNA virus with nucleic acid as a single-stranded mRNA genome (including 5' cap and 3' poly-A tail).

Retrovirus is an obligate parasite within the host cell. Once inside the host cell cytoplasm, the virus uses its reverse transcriptase (enzyme) to produce DNA from its RNA genome. *Retro* describes this backward flow of genetic information.

Integrase (enzyme) incorporates this new reverse-transcribed DNA into the host cell genome. *Provirus* is the integrated retroviral DNA.

The host cell treats the viral DNA as part of its genome, translating and transcribing the viral genes and the cell's genes, producing the proteins required to assemble new copies of the virus.

20. C is correct.

Virus is a simple non-living organism that takes on living characteristics when it enters host cells.

Since viruses are not free-living organisms, they must replicate within a host cell.

Viruses contain DNA (single-stranded or double-stranded) or RNA (single-stranded or double-stranded) and have a protein coat.

Bacteriophage (i.e., a virus that infects bacteria) injects its genome into the bacterium while leaving the protein coat on the cell surface.

However, the entire virus (including the protein capsid) may enter the host cell in eukaryotes.

After entering the cytoplasm, the protein coat is removed (i.e., a virus is unencapsulated).

21. A is correct.

Bacterial conjugation transfers genetic material (plasmid) between bacterial cells by direct cell-to-cell contact or a bridge-like connection between two cells (i.e., pili).

Conjugation is *horizontal gene transfer*, as are transformation and transduction.

The other mechanisms do not involve cell-to-cell contact (conjugation requires a pilus).

B: *transformation* is the genetic alteration resulting from the direct uptake, incorporation, and expression of exogenous genetic material (exogenous DNA) from its surroundings and through the cell membranes.

In molecular biology, transformation introduces genetic material into nonbacterial cells, including animal and plant cells.

continued…

C: *transduction* is how a virus transfers DNA from one bacterium to another.

In molecular biology, *transduction* is when foreign DNA is introduced into another cell via a viral vector.

D: *recombination* is when DNA molecules exchange genetic information, resulting in a new combination of alleles.

Most recombination occurs spontaneously to increase genetic variation.

In eukaryotes, *genetic recombination* between *homologous chromosomes* during prophase I of meiosis leads to a novel set of genetic information passed on to progeny.

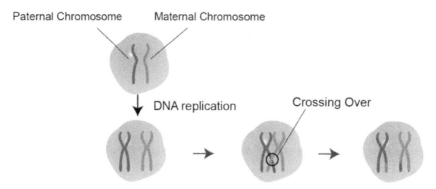

Crossing over occurs during prophase I at the tetrad during prophase I of meiosis as the product of recombination

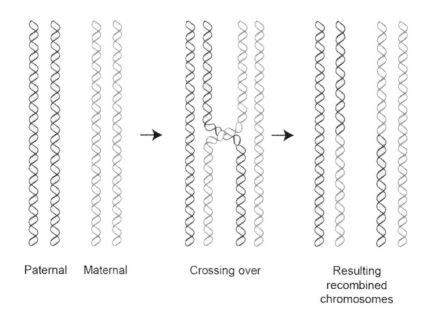

Recombination between homologous chromosomes during prophase I of meiosis

22. D is correct.

E. coli on the soft agar produces a solid growth (i.e., lawn) covering the agar.

Phages lyse cells, releasing phages (i.e., viruses).

Clear spots on the agar plate correspond to where the bacteria were lysed and are *plaques* (i.e., clear spots).

A: *viral replication* produces clear spots on the lawn of *E. coli* growth.

B: *colonies* on the agar surface indicate *E. coli* growth, not locations where the virus lysed the bacteria cells.

C: *smooth layer* of bacterial growth on the agar plate indicates the absence of the virus.

23. E is correct.

Gram staining differentiates bacterial species into Gram-positive and Gram-negative by the chemical and physical properties of peptidoglycan cell walls.

Gram stain is usually the first assay in identifying a bacterial organism.

Gram-negative bacteria are more resistant to antibiotics than Gram-positive bacteria, despite their thinner peptidoglycan layer.

Pathogenic capability of Gram-negative bacteria is often associated with specific components of their membrane, in particular, the lipopolysaccharide layer (LPS).

Penicillins are β-lactam antibiotics to treat bacterial infections by, usually, Gram-positive organisms.

Penicillin core structure, where "R" is the variable group

Gram-positive bacteria take up the violet stain used in Gram staining.

This differential staining distinguishes them from the other large group of bacteria, Gram-negative bacteria that cannot retain the crystal violet stain.

Gram-negative bacteria take up the counterstain (e.g., safranin or fuchsine) and appear red or pink.

Gram-positive bacteria retain crystal violet stain by a thick *peptidoglycan layer* superficial to cell membranes.

In Gram-negative bacteria, this peptidoglycan layer is thinner and between two cell membranes.

The cell membrane, peptidoglycan layer, and cell wall are three distinct structures.

Cell walls provide structural support, protection, and rigidity to the cell.

Gram-positive bacteria have a *thicker peptidoglycan cell wall*, giving them a *purple-blue color* from staining.

Gram-negative bacteria stain a pink-red color.

continued…

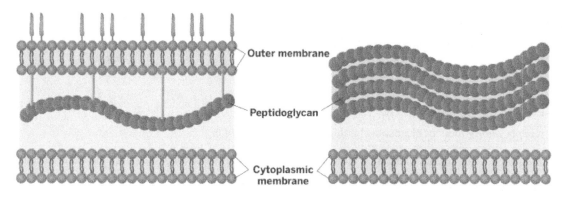

Gram-negative (left) comparison with gram-positive (right) cell walls

24. B is correct.

Viral genomes are single-stranded or double-stranded DNA, single-stranded or double-stranded RNA.

Retroviruses contain a single-stranded RNA (i.e., mRNA as its genome).

Retroviruses have *reverse transcriptase* and *integrase* to facilitate their infective ability within the host cell.

25. E is correct.

Operons are mainly in prokaryotes and encode for clusters of related (i.e., similar function) genes.

Lac operon of *E. coli* allows the digestion of lactose and consists of a set of control and structural genes.

Three structural genes are controlled by an operator on another part of the genome.

Lac genes encoding enzymes are *lacZ, lacY,* and *lacA.*

The fourth *lac* gene is *lacI,* encoding the lactose repressor—"I" stands for *inducibility.*

Without lactose, a repressor protein (*lacI*) is bound to the operator, preventing RNA polymerase from binding.

The binding of the repressor protein prevents the translation of the structural genes (*lacZ, lacY,* and *lacA*).

When lactose is present (i.e., glucose is absent), *lacI* binds the repressor dissociating from the operator region.

RNA polymerase (i.e., *inducible system*) attaches to the promoter, and translation occurs.

26. D is correct.

Prophage is a viral genome inserted and integrated into the circular bacterial DNA chromosome or as an extrachromosomal plasmid.

Lysogenic phase (i.e., latent form) of a bacteriophage is when viral genes are in bacterium without disrupting the cell.

continued…

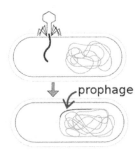

Prophase formation with a virus infecting a bacterial cell

Lytic cycle is one of the two cycles of viral reproduction, the other being the lysogenic cycle.

Lytic cycle destroys the infected cell and its membrane.

A critical difference between the lytic and lysogenic phage cycles is that in the *lytic phage*, the viral DNA exists as a separate molecule within the bacterial cell and *replicates separately from host bacterial DNA*.

The location of viral DNA in the lysogenic phage cycle is within the host DNA (i.e., integrated); the virus (phage) replicates using the host DNA machinery.

Phage is a free-floating separate molecule to the host DNA in the lytic phage cycle.

27. C is correct.

Retrovirus has an RNA genome transcribed (by the virus-encoded reverse transcriptase enzyme) into single- and then double-stranded DNA incorporated into the host cell genome.

B: *reverse transcriptase* (enzyme) converts the RNA of the virus into DNA when infecting host cells.

28. B is correct.

E. coli are normal flora of the human gut and are adapted to live in the human intestine.

Therefore, the optimal temperature for growth is 37 °C, whereby enzyme activity is optimal.

A: temperature of the human intestine is 37 °C. Bacteria growing optimally at this temperature exhibit the typical phenotype.

C: *conjugation* by bacteria is not necessary for growth.

Conjugation is mediated by a small genetic element (i.e., fertility or F factor) as independent or integrated into the bacterial chromosome.

F factor encodes for the F pili, which forms a conjugation bridge and allows genetic material transfer between mating cells.

Cells carrying the F factor are F$^+$ and transfer to an F$^-$ cell.

Part of the bacterial chromosome can be transferred during conjugation, but the point of origin and the gene order are the same.

D: oxygen utilization is irrelevant to the growth temperature of bacteria.

29. A is correct.

Some bacteria can propel themselves through liquid using a *flagellum*.

30. C is correct.

When a virus infects a cell (eukaryotic or prokaryotic), it must attach to a host cell via specific proteins on the viral capsid or envelope. These proteins bind to receptor proteins on the membrane of the target cell.

Following this process, the virus enters cells via one of the three mechanisms: membrane fusion, endocytosis, or viral penetration. The latter mechanism is specific to bacteriophages.

Membrane fusion is the most well-known mechanism for enveloped viruses to enter eukaryotic cells.

The viral envelope fuses with the host cell's membrane, and the contents of the virus are released into the cell.

Endocytosis is utilized by enveloped and non-enveloped viruses that infect eukaryotic cells.

In endocytosis, the virus is engulfed by the cell and shuttled by cellular vesicles to the cytoplasm.

31. C is correct.

Bacteria are prokaryotes and have *no membrane-bound organelles* such as peroxisomes or nucleolus.

32. E is correct.

Lysogen is a bacterial cell where a phage (i.e., virus) exists as DNA in its dormant state (prophage).

Prophage is integrated into the host bacterial chromosome (i.e., lysogenic cycle) or (rarely) exists as a stable plasmid in the host cell.

The prophage expresses genes that repress the phage's lytic action until this repression is disrupted.

The virus enters the *lytic life cycle*, ultimately rupturing the cell and releasing virions.

B: *temperate* refers to the ability of some bacteriophages to enter the lysogenic lifecycle.

33. D is correct.

Protein synthesis (like for eukaryotes) occurs in three phases: initiation, elongation, and termination.

For translation, hydrogen bonds join codons on mRNA and anticodons on tRNA, not amino acid and mRNA.

The prokaryotic cellular translation machinery is the 70S ribosome (30S small and 50S large subunits).

F-met is used only in prokaryotic translation initiation.

First, an *initiation complex* forms with the 30S subunit, mRNA, initiation factors, and a special initiator formyl methionine F-met tRNA.

50S subunit binds the initiation complex to form the 70S ribosome.

The complete large subunit of the ribosome complex has two binding sites: the P (peptidyl transferase) site and the A (aminoacyl) site.

continued...

Initiator formyl methionine (F-met) tRNA is in the P site.

Elongation begins with binding a second tRNA (charged with its corresponding amino acid) to the vacant A site of the large ribosomal subunit.

The appropriate amino acid is determined by the complementary hydrogen bonding between the anticodon of the tRNA and the next codon of mRNA.

The orientation for the mRNA (from 5' to 3') is E-P-A (ribosomes move towards the 3' end of mRNA).

Peptide bonds are catalyzed by peptidyl transferase (at the P site) with a nucleophile attack from the lone pair of electrons on the N of the amino terminus on the carbonyl of the C terminus (at the A-site).

tRNA in the P site, now uncharged (without amino acid), moves to the E site and dissociates.

tRNA in the A site (after peptide bond formation and the ribosome translocates) is now in the P site, the A site is vacant, and this is where the incoming tRNA (carrying the next amino acid to join the polypeptide) binds.

This binding cycle to the A site, peptide bond formation, and translocation create a growing polypeptide chain.

Termination occurs when one of the three tRNA stop codons (i.e., not charged with an amino acid) hybridizes to the mRNA in the A site.

Termination factors catalyze the hydrolysis of the polypeptide chain from the tRNA, and the ribosomal complex dissociates.

N-Formylmethionine (fMet) is a derivative of methionine whereby a formyl group adds to the amino group

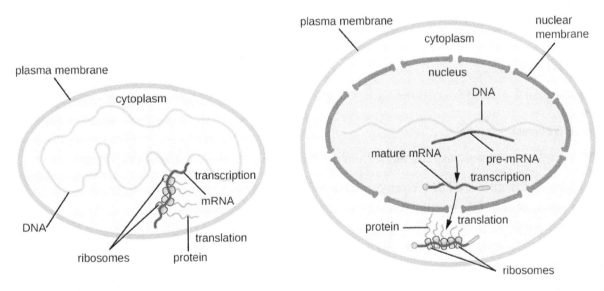

Prokaryotic cell (left) and eukaryotic cell (right). Prokaryotes have concurrent transcription and translation, while eukaryotes separate the processes by the presence of a nucleus.

A: prokaryote mRNA does not undergo splicing to remove introns.

B: *translation* in prokaryotes uses N-terminal formyl methionine (F-met) as the initiator amino acid.

continued…

C: *prokaryotes* have no nucleus, the mRNA has no nuclear membrane to cross, and translation begins before its synthesis is complete.

Eukaryotic mRNA must be processed (5' G-cap, 3' poly-A tail, and splicing of exons with the removal of introns) and transported across the nuclear membrane before translation begins in the cytoplasm.

34. B is correct.

Surface-to-volume ratio limits the size of biological cells because when the volume increases, so does the surface area, but the surface area increases at a slower rate.

Eukaryotes grow beyond the apparent limitation of surface-to-volume ratios because of organelles (specialized environment) and extensive cytoplasmic matrix, utilizing microfilaments and motor proteins for cargo transport.

35. D is correct.

Prokaryotes have *peptidoglycan cell walls*, 30S and 50S ribosomes, and plasma membranes without cholesterol.

36. E is correct.

Viruses consist of genetic material with single-stranded DNA, double-stranded DNA, single-stranded RNA, or double-stranded RNA packaged within a protein coat.

A: viruses do not have membrane-bound organelles but consist entirely of nucleic acid (RNA or DNA) and, for retroviruses, reverse transcriptase (enzyme).

C: bacteria have *peptidoglycan* (i.e., N-linked glucose polymers) cell walls.

D: viruses do not have a phospholipid bilayer membrane.

37. A is correct.

Episome is an F⁻ plasmid that can integrate into the bacterial chromosome by homologous recombination.

38. B is correct.

Reverse transcriptase (enzyme) converts RNA of the virus into ds-DNA when infected into host cells.

The host cell treats the viral DNA as part of its genome, translating and transcribing the viral genes and the cell's genes, producing the proteins required to assemble new copies of the virus.

Newly synthesized DNA is incorporated into the host cell genome by integrase (enzyme), at which point the retroviral DNA is a *provirus*.

Retrovirus flow of genetic information:

RNA (virus) → DNA (from virus template) → RNA (host cell machinery) → polypeptide

39. A is correct.

T4 has a DNA genome transcribed and translated by the host's machinery.

Transcription and translation occur in the cytoplasm since the bacterial cell does not contain a nucleus.

Therefore, both processes occur in the same locations and are concurrent.

B: a late gene encodes lysozyme enzymes because the host is not lysed until the viruses are assembled and packaged into their protein capsids to be released for infection of other host cells.

C: the assembly must be complete before lysis.

D: bacterial cells have a *peptidoglycan cell wall*, so budding cannot occur.

The cell wall is lysed by lysozyme, and the host cell ruptures, which causes the release of the virus.

40. C is correct.

Gram-positive bacteria take up the violet stain used in the Gram staining.

Differential staining distinguishes them from the other large group of Gram-negative bacteria that cannot retain the crystal violet stain.

Gram-negative bacteria take up the counterstain (e.g., safranin, fuchsine) and appear red or pink.

Gram-positive bacteria retain the crystal violet stain due to a *thick peptidoglycan layer* superficial to the cell membrane.

In Gram-negative bacteria, this peptidoglycan layer is much thinner between cell membranes.

The cell membrane, peptidoglycan layer, and cell wall are three distinct structures.

Cell walls provide structural support, protection, and rigidity to the cell.

D: *teichoic acids* are in the cell walls of Gram-positive bacteria (e.g., *Staphylococcus*, *Streptococcus*, *Bacillus*, *Clostridium, Listeria*) and extend to the surface of the peptidoglycan layer.

Teichoic acids are not in Gram-negative bacteria.

41. C is correct.

A bacterium with an outer lipopolysaccharide layer is Gram-negative and protects against penicillin.

A: *fimbriae* (i.e., a proteinaceous appendage in many Gram-negative bacteria) is thinner and shorter than a flagellum and allows a bacterium to attach to solid objects.

B: *bacterial cell membranes* have a phospholipid bilayer like eukaryotes, except it lacks cholesterol.

D: *Gram-negative bacteria* have a thinner peptidoglycan cell wall that does not retain Gram stain.

42. E is correct.

DNase is an enzyme that degrades DNA by hydrolysis of the DNA molecule.

Bacterial cells treated with DNase die because bacteria have DNA genomes, while RNA viruses are unaffected by DNase and continue to synthesize proteins following treatment with DNase.

A: having multiple copies of a gene is not enough to prevent DNase from degrading the DNA.

C: *viral genomes* typically contain multiple reading frames to use their limited nucleic acid efficiently, but multiple reading frames do not prevent DNA hydrolysis.

D: viral protein coat is not able to denature DNase.

Denaturation breaks weak (e.g., hydrogen, dipole, and hydrophobic) bonds by heat or chemical treatment.

43. C is correct.

F⁻ recipient remains F⁻ in mating between Hfr and F⁻ cells.

44. A is correct.

Translation in prokaryotes uses the *initiation* amino acid of N-terminal formyl methionine (F-met).

Specific cells in the human immune system can identify f-MET and release local toxins to inhibit bacterial (i.e., prokaryote) infections.

45. C is correct.

Dextran is a large polysaccharide and does *not pass* through the cell membrane.

Osmotic pressure of the solution increases, H_2O moves out of the cell to reduce the osmotic pressure difference, and the cell undergoes crenation (i.e., shrinking).

46. A is correct.

Gram staining differentiates bacterial species into two large groups: Gram-positive and Gram-negative.

Gram staining differentiates the chemical and physical properties of *peptidoglycan cell walls*.

Gram-positive bacteria have a thicker peptidoglycan cell wall which gives Gram-positive bacteria a purple-blue color from staining, while Gram-negative result in a pink-red color.

Gram staining is usually the first assay in identifying a bacterial organism.

47. A is correct.

DNA polymerase replicates DNA strands by synthesizing new strands from a template strand.

DNA polymerase replicates the DNA F factor in F⁺ cells before conjugation.

B: *reverse transcriptase* is a retroviral enzyme synthesizing DNA from an RNA (virus) template.

C: *DNA ligase* catalyzes the formation of phosphodiester bonds that link adjacent DNA bases.

D: *integrase* is a retroviral enzyme that integrates provirus DNA into host genomes.

48. B is correct.

Conjugation occurs between bacterial cells of different mating types.

"Maleness" in bacteria is determined by the presence of a small extra piece of DNA that can replicate independently of the larger chromosome.

Male bacteria having this *sex factor* (the *F factor*) are denoted F⁺ if the sex factor exists as extrachromosomal.

F⁺ bacteria can conjugate only with F⁻ bacteria, the "female" that do not possess the F factor.

Genes on the F factor determine the formation of *sex pili* (hair-like projections) on the surface of the F⁺ bacterium, which forms cytoplasmic bridges to transfer genetic material. The pili aid the F⁺ cell in adhering to the F⁻ cell during conjugation.

During conjugation (bacterial mating) of an F⁺ cell with an F⁻ cell, and before the transfer, the F factor replicates, and the F factor is the DNA likely to be transferred to the female. F⁻ becomes an F⁺ by receiving one copy of the F factor, while the original F⁺ retains a copy.

If this were the only genetic exchange in conjugation, all bacteria would become F⁺ and cease conjugation. In F⁺ bacterial cultures, a few bacteria with the F factor incorporated into their chromosome can be isolated and are *Hfr* bacteria, which may conjugate with F⁻ cells.

They do not transfer their F factor during conjugation but often transfer linear portions of their chromosomes; the transfer is interrupted by the spontaneous breakage of the DNA molecule at random sites, usually, before the F factor crosses to the F⁻ cell.

This process is *unidirectional*, and no genetic material from the F⁻ cell is transferred to the *Hfr* cell.

49. E is correct.

Retrotransposons (or transposons via RNA intermediates) are a subclass of transposons. They are endogenous genetic elements that amplify in a genome as ubiquitous components of DNA in many eukaryotic organisms.

Around 42% of the human genome is retrotransposons.

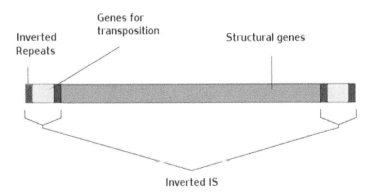

Bacterial DNA transposon with flanking inverted sequences encompassing structural genes

Retrotransposons are copied into RNA and back into DNA which may integrate into the genome.

The second step of forming DNA may be catalyzed by a reverse transcriptase encoded by the retrotransposon.

50. B is correct.

Plasmids are small circular double-stranded DNA in bacteria carrying extrachromosomal genetic information.

Plasmids (with an origin of replication) are replicated by bacterial proteins and inherited by progeny.

Proteins encoded by genes on plasmids often provide resistance to antibiotics by degrading the antibiotic.

Through recombinant DNA technology, plasmids are engineered to carry genes not typically in bacteria.

Plasmids are introduced into cells by transforming DNA across the cell wall and plasma membrane without killing bacterial cells.

After transformation, exposure to the specific antibiotic allows the selection of bacteria that received plasmid.

Bacteriophages, such as bacteriophages λ are viruses that infect bacterial cells.

Bacteriophage λ are engineered to carry novel genes, not in bacteria or bacteriophages.

I: *plasmids* are extra-chromosomal circular DNA molecules and not organelles because organelles are membrane-bound cellular components present only in eukaryotes.

II: like the bacterial genome, plasmids are in the cytoplasm.

Without a nucleus, prokaryotic ribosomes translate plasmid mRNA into proteins while transcribed into mRNA from DNA.

III: plasmids rely on bacterial machinery for metabolic processes (e.g., replication, transcription, translation).

51. B is correct.

Fungi are members of a large group of eukaryotic organisms that includes microorganisms such as yeasts, molds, and mushrooms.

These organisms are classified as a Fungi kingdom (separate from plants, animals, protists, and bacteria).

One major difference is that fungal cells have cell walls with *chitin.*

The cell walls of plants contain *cellulose*), some protists contain *cellulose,* and bacteria contain *peptidoglycan.*

A: *protoplasts* are plant, bacterial or fungal cells that lose their cell wall by mechanical or enzymatic means.

C: L forms are strains of bacteria that lack a cell wall.

D: viruses do not have cell walls.

A virus particle (i.e., virion) has nucleic acid enclosed in a capsid as a protective protein coat.

E: *mycoplasma* is a genus of bacteria that lack a cell wall (they have cell membranes only).

Mycoplasma are unaffected by many common antibiotics, such as penicillin or other beta-lactam antibiotics, targeting peptidoglycan cell wall synthesis without a cell wall.

52. E is correct.

Prokaryotes do *not* have membrane-bound organelles (e.g., nuclei, mitochondria, lysosomes).

Prokaryotes have *peptidoglycan* cell walls.

Fungi have cell walls with *chitin*.

53. C is correct.

Bacteriophages are viruses that infect bacteria and typically consist of a protein coat (i.e., head) and a core containing nucleic acid.

Like viruses, bacteriophages contain host-specific protein tail fibers for attachment.

Upon infection, bacteriophages can enter one of two life cycles (image below).

In the *lytic cycle*, the viral nucleic acid enters the bacterial cell.

Lytic cycle begins using host machinery to produce new virions (i.e., virus particles), lysing the host cell and infecting other cells.

Lysogenic cycle is when viral DNA integrates into the bacterial chromosome, replicating with it and being passed to daughter cells (integrated into their genome) in this inactive form.

Lytic cycle destroys the infected cell and its membrane.

A critical difference between the lytic and lysogenic phage cycles is that in the lytic phage, the viral DNA exists as a separate molecule within the bacterial cell and replicates separately from the host bacterial DNA.

The location of viral DNA in the lysogenic phage cycle is within the host DNA (i.e., integrated); the virus (phage) replicates using the host DNA machinery.

Phage is a free-floating separate molecule to the host DNA in the lytic phage cycle.

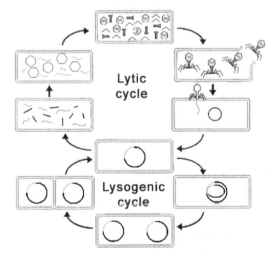

Lytic phase lysis the cell and releases virions while lysogenic cycles involve the integration of the viral genome into the host cell

continued…

When an integrated virus (i.e., prophage) becomes activated, it exits the lysogenic and enters the lytic cycle.

Activation triggers for the virus to enter the lytic cycle include *cellular or metabolic stresses* such as UV light, depleted nutrients, or cellular abnormalities.

Retroviruses are RNA-containing viruses replicating by reverse transcriptase (enzyme) through a DNA intermediate via a viral-coded *RNA-dependent DNA polymerase*.

For example, human immunodeficiency virus (HIV), the causative of AIDS, is a retrovirus.

Retroviral life cycle consists of four main events:

> 1) virus binds its host and injects its RNA and a few viral enzymes;
>
> 2) RNA is converted to DNA by reverse transcriptase;
>
> 3) DNA integrates into the host cell's genome; and
>
> 4) viral genes are expressed, and virions are assembled and released from the cell by budding.

Bacteriophage and retrovirus integrate into the host genome (i.e., lysogenic) or lyse cells (i.e., lytic cycle).

A: *bacteriophage*s have host-specific protein tail fibers and infect bacteria.

B: bacteria (the target of bacteriophage) have no immune system.

Bacteria have a defense against infection by nucleotide-specific *restriction enzymes* used for molecular biology and biotechnology.

D: *retroviruses* contain an RNA genome (ss-RNA or ds-RNA) and reverse transcriptase, not in bacteriophages.

54. E is correct.

Integration of phage DNA into bacterial chromosomes uses *site-specific recombinase* encoded in the phage.

55. A is correct.

Sequences recognized by most restriction enzymes are *inverted repeats* (i.e., palindromes) that read the same if inverted (i.e., rotated by 180°).

Sticky ends for DNA fragments are the same in either orientation, so ligation occurs from either orientation.

B: DNA strands do serve as primers for DNA polymerase

C: DNA *ligase* creates a phosphodiester bond that covalently links sticky ends of DNA.

D: *plasmid DNA*, like bacterial DNA, is double-stranded.

56. D is correct.

Virulence describes disease severity or a pathogen's infectivity.

The virulence factors of bacteria are typically proteins or other molecules synthesized by enzymes.

Virulent viruses use the *lytic* lifecycle.

Proteins are coded by genes in chromosomal DNA, bacteriophage DNA or plasmids.

Classification and Diversity – Detailed Explanations

1. D is correct.

Mnemonic: **D**arn **K**ing **P**hillip **C**ame **O**ver **F**or **G**ood **S**oup:

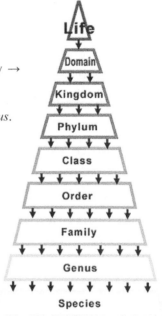

Domain → Kingdom → Phylum → Class → Order → Family → Genus → Species

Canis lupus indicates that the wolf's genus is *Canis,* and the species is *lupus.*

Family is more inclusive than genus or species, so any member of the species *lupus* is in the genus *Canis* of the Canidae family.

2. A is correct.

Class encompasses several orders.

Mnemonic: **D**arn **K**ing **P**hillip **C**ame **O**ver **F**or **G**ood **S**oup:

Domain → kingdom → phylum → class → **order** → family → genus → species

3. E is correct.

Homology serves as evidence of common ancestry.

Homology is a relationship between structures or DNA derived from a common ancestor.

Homologous traits are traced by descent from a common ancestor.

Analogous organs have similar functions in two taxa, not in the last common ancestor but evolved separately.

Homologous sequences are *orthologous* if they descend from the same ancestral sequence separated by a speciation event.

When a species diverges into two species, the copies of a single gene in the resulting species are orthologous.

Orthology is strictly defined by ancestry.

Orthologs (i.e., orthologous genes) are genes in distinct species that originated by vertical descent from a single gene of the last common ancestor.

Due to gene duplication and genome rearrangement, the ancestry of genes is difficult to ascertain.

Strongest evidence that two similar genes are orthologous is usually a phylogenetic analysis of the gene lineage.

Orthologous genes often, but not always, have the same function.

4. A is correct.

Homology is a relationship between structures or DNA derived from a common ancestor.

Homologous traits descend from a common ancestor (e.g., the forelimb of a human and a dog).

Analogous organs, the opposite of homologous organs, have similar functions in two taxa, not in the last common ancestor but instead evolved separately.

Homologous sequences are *orthologous* if they descend from the same ancestral sequence separated by a speciation event.

When a species diverges into two separate species, the copies of a single gene in the two resulting species are orthologous.

Orthologues (i.e., orthologous genes) are genes in distinct species that originated by *vertical descent* from a single gene of the last common ancestor.

Orthology is strictly defined by ancestry.

Due to gene duplication and genome rearrangement, the ancestry of genes is difficult to ascertain.

Strongest evidence that two similar genes are orthologous is through phylogenetic analysis of gene lineage.

Orthologous genes often, but not always, have the same function.

	Analogous leg	Analogous flipper
Homologous mammals	Cat leg	Whale flipper
Homologous insects	Praying mantis leg	Water boatman flipper

Homologous (common ancestor) vs. analogous structures (similar function but evolved separately)

5. C is correct.

Homology is a relationship between structures or DNA derived from a common ancestor.

Homologous traits descend from a common ancestor (e.g., the forelimb of a human and a dog).

Analogous organs are the opposite of homologous organs and have similar functions in two taxa that were not in the last common ancestor but instead evolved separately.

Homologous sequences are *orthologous* if they descend from the same ancestral sequence separated by a speciation event.

When a species diverges into two species, copies of a single gene in the two resulting species are orthologous.

Orthologs (i.e., orthologous genes) are genes in distinct species that originated by vertical descent from a single gene of the last common ancestor.

Orthology is strictly defined by ancestry.

Strongest evidence that two similar genes are orthologous is usually a phylogenetic analysis of the gene lineage.

Orthologous genes often, but not always, have the same function.

D: wings of a pigeon and a bat represent *analogous structures*.

6. B is correct.

Taxonomy of humans:

> Domain: Eukaryota → Kingdom: Animalia → Phylum: Chordata → Subphylum: Vertebrata →
> Class: Mammalia → Order: Primates → Family: Hominidae → Genus: Homo →
> Species: *H. sapiens* → Subspecies: *H. s. sapiens*

7. B is correct.

Ants are not chordates.

Tunicates are marine invertebrates and members of the subphylum Tunicata within Chordata (i.e., the phylum includes all animals with dorsal nerve cords and notochords).

Tunicates live as solitary individuals or replicate by budding and becoming colonies (each unit is a zooid).

Tunicates are marine filter feeders with a water-filled, sac-like body structure and two tubular openings, known as *siphons*, through which they draw in and expel water.

They take in water through the *incurrent siphon* during respiration and feeding and expel filtered water through the *excurrent siphon*.

Most adult tunicates are sessile and permanently attached to rocks or other hard surfaces on the ocean floor; others swim in the pelagic zone (i.e., open sea) as adults.

8. E is correct.

Echinoderms are invertebrate predecessors of the chordates and include starfish, sea urchins, and cucumbers.

They are characterized by a primitive vascular system known as the water vascular system.

Adult echinoderms have radial symmetry, while larvae are bilaterally symmetrical.

They move with structures known as tube feet, have no backbone, and are heterotrophic (i.e., they do not synthesize food).

Crayfish are in the phylum Arthropoda, which includes insects.

Arthropods are characterized by segmented bodies covered in a chitin exoskeleton and jointed appendages.

9. B is correct.

Kingdom encompasses many phyla.

Mnemonic: **D**arn **K**ing **P**hillip **C**ame **O**ver **F**or **G**ood **S**oup:

> Domain → kingdom → **phylum** → class → order
> → family → genus → species

10. D is correct.

Homo sapiens belong to the phylum Chordata. *Taxonomy of humans*:

> Domain: Eukaryota → Kingdom: Animalia → Phylum: Chordata → Subphylum: Vertebrata →
> Class: Mammalia → Order: Primates → Family: Hominidae → Genus: Homo →
> Species: *H. sapiens* → Subspecies: *H. s. sapiens*

11. B is correct.

Organisms of phylum *Chordata* have a dorsal notochord, while subphylum Vertebrata has a backbone.

Nonvertebrate chordates include amphioxus (lancelet) or unrelated tunicate worm.

Lancelet (or *amphioxus*) is the modern subphylum Cephalochordata and is vital in zoology – it provides indications about the origins of the vertebrates.

Lancelets are comparison points for tracing vertebrates' evolution.

They are the archetypal vertebrate form.

Lancelets split from vertebrates more than 520 million years ago; their genomes hold clues about evolution, specifically how vertebrates have adapted old genes for new functions.

Vertebrates include most of the phylum Chordata with about 64,000 species.

Vertebrates include amphibians, reptiles (e.g., lizards), mammals, birds, jawless and bony fish, sharks, and rays.

Shark and lamprey eel are vertebrates with cartilaginous skeletons.

12. A is correct.

Cell, tissue, organ, organism, population, and community represent the correct ordering of the levels of complexity at which life is studied, from simplest to complex.

13. A is correct.

Notochord is *ventral* to the *neural tube* and forms during gastrulation.

The notochord induces *neural plate formation* (during neurulation) to synchronize neural tube development (precursor to the central nervous system).

Notochord is a flexible rod-shaped structure in embryos of all chordates.

It is composed of cells derived from the mesoderm and defines the primitive axis of the embryo.

In lower chordates, this chord remains throughout the life of the animal.

In higher chordates (e.g., humans), the notochord exists during embryonic development and disappears.

If the notochord persists, it functions as the primary axial support. In most vertebrates, it becomes the nucleus pulposus of the intervertebral disc.

B: *notochord remains* in the lower chordates, such as the amphioxus and the tunicate worm.

It is not vestigial (not a genetically determined structure that lost its ancestral function) because it disappears.

D: *echinoderms* are the invertebrate predecessors of chordates and include starfish, sea urchins, and cucumber.

Echinoderms do *not* possess a notochord.

E: *notochord is not* part of the nervous system.

14. E is correct.

Chordates are animals that, for at least some of their life cycle, possess:

> 1) a notochord
>
> 2) a dorsal neural tube
>
> 3) pharyngeal slits
>
> 4) an endostyle
>
> 5) a post-anal tail

Chordate phylum includes the subphyla Vertebrata (e.g., mammals, fish, amphibians, reptiles, birds),

Tunicata (e.g., salps, sea squirts), and Cephalochordata (e.g., lancelets).

Vertebrata subphylums have a backbone, but it is not a shared characteristic of chordates.

continued….

Chordates are a phylum that shares a bilateral body plan and have, at some stage:

Notochord is a relatively stiff rod of cartilage extending inside the body.

Among vertebrate sub-group chordates, the notochord develops into the spine.

This helps the animal swim by flexing its tail in aquatic species.

Dorsal neural tube (for vertebrates, including fish) develops into the spinal cord, the leading communications trunk of the nervous system.

Pharyngeal slits comprise the throat immediately behind the mouth (modified fish gills).

In some chordates, pharyngeal slits are part of a filter-feeding system extracting food from its environment.

Endostyle groove in the ventral wall of the pharynx stores iodine and a precursor of the vertebrate thyroid gland.

In filter-feeders, it produces mucus to gather food particles, transporting food to the esophagus.

Post-anal tail is a muscular tail extending behind the anus.

15. B is correct.

Migratory birds nesting on islands is not behavioral, temporal, or geographical isolation leading to speciation.

The birds are migratory and are not geographically isolated.

16. D is correct.

Sponges are Porifera (i.e., pore or Ostia-bearing) phylum animals.

Like other animals, they are multicellular, heterotrophic, and lack cell walls.

Sponges lack tissues and organs and have no body symmetry, differentiating them from other animals.

Heterotrophy means obtaining food and energy by consuming other organic substances rather than sunlight or inorganic compounds.

17. B is correct.

Homology is a relationship between structures or DNA derived from a common ancestor.

Homologous traits are explained by descent from a common ancestor.

Analogous organs have similar functions in two taxa, not in the last common ancestor but evolved separately.

Homologous sequences are *orthologous* when descended from ancestral sequences separated by speciation.

When a species diverges into two species, copies of a single gene in the two resulting species are *orthologous*.

Orthologues (i.e., orthologous genes) are genes in distinct species that originated by vertical descent from a single gene of the last common ancestor.

continued...

Orthology is defined by ancestry.

Due to gene duplication and genome rearrangement, the ancestry of genes is difficult to ascertain.

Strongest evidence that two similar genes are orthologous is usually a *phylogenetic analysis* of *gene lineage*.

Orthologous genes often, but not always, have the same function.

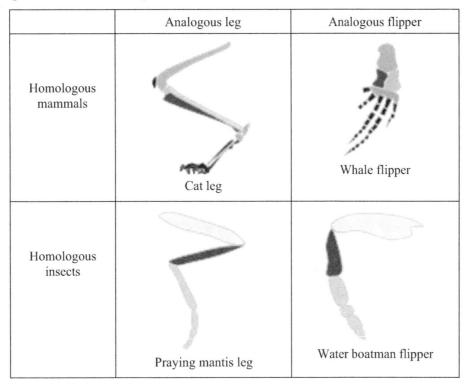

	Analogous leg	Analogous flipper
Homologous mammals	Cat leg	Whale flipper
Homologous insects	Praying mantis leg	Water boatman flipper

Homologous (common ancestor) vs. analogous structures (similar function but evolved separately)

18. C is correct.

*Arthropod*s are invertebrate animals with an exoskeleton, segmented body, and jointed appendages and include insects, arachnids, myriapods, and crustaceans.

19. E is correct.

Animal cells do *not* have cell walls, distinct from plant cells.

Another distinct feature of plant cells is the presence of chloroplasts in the structure.

20. C is correct.

Annelids are a large phylum of segmented worms, each segment having the same set of organs.

Coelom is a cavity lined by a mesoderm-derived epithelium.

Organs formed inside a coelom can grow, freely move, and develop independently of the body wall while protected by fluid cushions.

Organisms are classified into three groups: *continued...*

1) *Coelomates* are animals with a fluid-filled body cavity (i.e., coelom) and complete lining (peritoneum derived from mesoderm), allowing organs to be attached and suspended while moving freely within the cavity.

Coelomates include most bilateral animals, including all vertebrates.

2) *Pseudocoelomates* are animals with a pseudocoelom fully functional body cavity (e.g., roundworm).

Pseudocoelomate *organ*s are held loosely and not as well organized as coelomates.

Mesoderm-derived tissue partly lines the fluid-filled body cavity.

Pseudocoelomates are *protostomes*, but not all protostomes are pseudocoelomates.

3) *Acoelomates* are animals with no body cavity (i.e., flatworms). Semi-solid mesodermal tissues between the gut and body wall hold their organs in place.

21. B is correct.

From embryological studies, ancient chordates were closely related to the ancestors of echinoderms, marine animals such as sea stars, and sea urchins.

Sea anemones are a group of water-dwelling, predatory animals.

22. C is correct.

Echinoderms are marine animals such as sea stars, sea urchins, and sand dollars characterized by radial (usually five-point) symmetry.

Most echinoderms can regenerate tissue, organs, and limbs and reproduce asexually.

23. A is correct.

Cnidaria is a phylum of animals with over 10,000 species exclusively in aquatic and marine environments.

Cnidaria bodies consist of a *non-living jelly-like substance* sandwiched between two layers of epithelium that are mostly one cell thick.

Their distinguishing feature is *cnidocytes*, specialized cells mainly for capturing prey.

Cnidaria has two basic body forms: *swimming medusae* and *sessile polyps*; each is radially symmetrical, with mouths surrounded by tentacles that bear cnidocytes.

Both forms have a single orifice and body cavity used for digestion and respiration.

Many cnidarian species form colonies of single organisms with Medusa-like or polyp-like zooids or both.

B: *echinoderms* are a phylum of marine animals, and adults have radial (usually five-point) symmetry (e.g., sea urchins, sand dollars, starfish, and sea cucumbers).

24. C is correct.

Chordates are animals with a *notochord* (stiff rod of cartilage that extends inside the body), *dorsal neural tube*, and *pharyngeal slits*, which are openings of the pharynx to allow aquatic organisms to extract oxygen from water and excrete carbon dioxide (i.e., gills).

25. E is correct.

A hollow *nerve cord* (a single hollow nerve tissue tract) constitutes the central nervous system of chordates.

26. B is correct.

Cephalization is an evolutionary trend when nervous tissue becomes concentrated toward one end of an organism over many generations. This process produces a head region with sensory organs.

Cephalization is intrinsically connected with a change in symmetry.

Cephalization accompanied the shift to bilateral symmetry in flatworms.

In addition to a concentration of sense organs, annelids place the mouth in the head region. This process is tied to developing an anterior brain in the chordates from the notochord.

An exception to the trend of cephalization throughout evolutionary advancement is the phylum Echinodermata.

Echinodermata, despite having a bilateral ancestor, developed with 5-point symmetry) and no concentrated neural ganglia or sensory head region.

Some echinoderms have developed bilateral symmetry secondarily.

27. E is correct.

Deuterostomes differ from protostomes in embryonic development.

In deuterostomes, the first opening (i.e., blastopore) becomes the anus. In protostomes, it becomes the mouth.

Chordates, echinoderms, and hemichordates are deuterostomes.

28. A is correct.

Pharyngeal pouches are filter-feeding organs in fish that develop into gills used for respiration.

29. D is correct.

Corals are marine invertebrates (phylum Cnidaria), typically in compact colonies with identical individual *polyps*.

Coral includes reef builders of tropical oceans secreting calcium carbonate, forming a hard skeleton.

A coral "head" is a colony of myriad genetically identical polyps.

Each polyp is a spineless animal, typically a few millimeters in diameter and a few centimeters in length.

Tentacles surround a central mouth opening, and an *exoskeleton* is excreted near the base.

Over many generations, colonies create a large skeleton structure.

Individual heads grow by the asexual reproduction of polyps.

Corals breed *sexually* by *spawning:* polyps of the same species release gametes simultaneously for several nights, cycling around full moons.

30. B is correct.

First amphibians developed from lobe-finned fish about 370 million years ago during the Devonian period.

Lobe-finned fish had multi-jointed leg-like fins that allowed crawling at the bottom of the sea.

Their bony fins evolved into limbs, ancestors of tetrapods, including amphibians, reptiles, birds, and mammals.

31. E is correct.

Notochord is a flexible rod essential in vertebrate development and the skeletal element of developing embryos.

Notochord is related to cartilage, serving as the axial skeleton of the embryo until other elements form.

32. D is correct.

Chordates are animals that, for at least some period of their life cycles, possess the following: a notochord, a dorsal neural tube, pharyngeal slits, an endostyle, and a post-anal tail.

Notochord is a flexible rod-shaped structure in embryos of chordates.

It is composed of mesoderm-derived cells that define the embryo axis.

Notochord is a relatively stiff cartilage rod extending along the inside of the body.

Among the vertebrate sub-group of chordates, the notochord develops into the spine, and in aquatic species, this helps the animal swim by flexing its tail.

In lower chordates, the notochord remains throughout life.

In higher chordates (e.g., humans), the notochord exists only during embryonic development and disappears.

If it persists throughout life, it functions as the primary axial support, while in most vertebrates, it becomes the nucleus pulposus of the intervertebral disc.

Notochord is ventral to the neural tube and forms during gastrulation.

The notochord *induces neural plate formation* (during neurulation) to synchronize neural tube development (precursor to the central nervous system).

33. C is correct.

Earthworms are part of the Annelid phylum.

Pseudocoelom is a fluid-filled cavity between the body wall and intestine of certain invertebrates, such as roundworms and hookworms.

All other statements are true.

34. C is correct.

Notochords are similar to cartilage, made of type II collagen. Collagen makes notochords soft and flexible.

Notochord is a flexible rod between the nerve cord and the digestive tract.

35. B is correct.

Cnidaria bodies consist of a non-living jelly-like substance sandwiched between two layers of epithelium that are mostly one cell thick.

Cnidaria has two body forms: swimming medusae and sessile polyps, each *radially symmetrical* with mouths surrounded by tentacles with cnidocytes.

Echinoderms are a phylum of marine animals, and adults have radial (usually five-point) symmetry (e.g., sea urchins, sand dollars, starfish, and sea cucumbers).

36. A is correct.

Chordates share several key features, such as a notochord, a dorsal hollow nerve cord, pharyngeal slits, and a post-anal tail.

Of the characteristics visible on a cat, a tail extending beyond the anus makes it a chordate.

37. B is correct.

Vertebral column is the backbone or spine, a segmented series of bones separated by intervertebral discs.

38. E is correct.

Ovoviviparous fish (e.g., guppies and angel sharks) have eggs that develop inside the mother's body after *internal fertilization*, whereby each embryo develops within its egg.

Yolk nourishes the embryo, which receives little or no nourishment from the mother.

Viviparous fish retain the eggs and nourish the embryos. They have a structure analogous to the placenta (mammals), connecting the mother's blood with the embryo.

39. C is correct.

Chordates are defined by the presence of a *notochord*.

Not all chordates are vertebrates, have paired appendages, or have backbones.

Chordates are *deuterostomes* where the first opening (i.e., blastopore) becomes the anus.

Chordates are a phylum that shares a bilateral body plan and have, at some stage:

Notochord is a relatively stiff rod of cartilage extending inside the body.

Among vertebrate sub-group chordates, the notochord develops into the spine. This helps the animal swim by flexing its tail in aquatic species.

Dorsal neural tube (for vertebrates, including fish) develops into the spinal cord, the leading communications trunk of the nervous system.

Pharyngeal slits comprise the throat immediately behind the mouth (modified fish gills). In some chordates, they are part of a filter-feeding system extracting food from the environment.

Endostyle groove in the ventral wall of the pharynx stores iodine and a possible precursor of the vertebrate thyroid gland. In filter-feeders, it produces mucus to gather food particles, which help transport food to the esophagus.

Post-anal tail is a muscular tail extending behind the anus.

40. A is correct.

Chordates are animals with a notochord, a dorsal neural tube, pharyngeal slits, an endostyle, and a post-anal tail for at least some of their life cycles.

41. B is correct.

Hominoids are called *apes*, but *ape* is used differently.

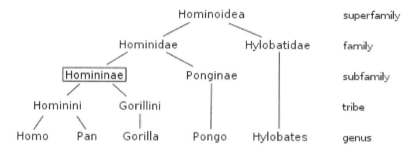

Homininae cladogram divides into genus homo, pan and gorilla

Until 1970, Hominidae meant humans only, with non-human great apes assigned to the family Pongidae.

Later discoveries led to revised classifications, with the great apes then united with humans (now in subfamily Homininae) as members of the family Hominidae

By 1990, molecular biology techniques classified gorillas and chimpanzees as more closely related to humans than orangutans.

Gorillas and chimpanzees are in the subfamily Homininae.

Hominines are a subfamily of Hominidae that includes humans, gorillas, chimpanzees, bonobos, and hominids which arose after the evolutionary split from orangutans.

Homininae cladogram has three main branches, which lead to gorillas, chimpanzees, bonobos, and humans.

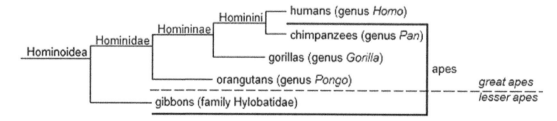

Homininae cladogram includes gorillas, chimpanzees, and humans

42. D is correct.

Fish evolved with *jawless fish*, followed by *bony fish with a jaw*.

Lastly, fish with leg-like fins, which allowed for movement along the seabed, evolved into limbs of *tetrapods*.

43. E is correct.

Jaws and limbs are characteristic of *vertebrates*.

44. A is correct.

Yolk nourishes the embryo, which receives little or no nourishment from the mother.

Amniotic fluid, surrounded by the amnion, is a liquid environment around the egg, protecting it from shock.

Embryonic membranes include:

> 1) **chorion** lines the inside of the shell and permits gas exchange;

> 2) **allantois** is a saclike structure developed from the digestive tract and functions in respiration, excretion, and gas exchange with the external environment;

> 3) **amnion** encloses *amniotic fluid* as a watery environment for embryogenesis and shock protection;

> 4) **yolk sac** encloses the yolk and transfers food to the developing embryo.

45. E is correct.

External fertilization is male sperm fertilizing an egg outside the female's body, as seen in amphibians and fish.

Mammals, further in the evolution of vertebrate groups, use internal fertilization for reproduction.

46. A is correct.

Prehensile refers to an appendage or organ adapted for holding or grasping.

47. D is correct.

Mammals are *endothermic* (warm-blooded) vertebrates with *body hair* and the ability to feed babies with *milk*.

In the embryonic development of vertebrates (e.g., mammals), *pharyngeal pouches* develop into essential structures such as the eardrum and thymus gland.

48. E is correct.

Hominoids are called *apes*, but *ape* is used differently.

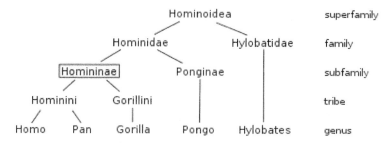

Homininae cladogram divides into genus homo, pan and gorilla

Until 1970, Hominidae meant humans only, with non-human great apes assigned to the family Pongidae.

Later discoveries led to revised classifications, with the great apes then united with humans (now in subfamily Homininae) as members of the family Hominidae

By 1990, molecular biology classified gorillas and chimpanzees as more closely related to humans than orangutans.

Gorillas and chimpanzees are in the subfamily Homininae.

Hominines are a subfamily of Hominidae that includes humans, gorillas, chimpanzees, bonobos, and hominids which arose after the evolutionary split from orangutans.

Homininae cladogram has three main branches, which lead to gorillas, chimpanzees, bonobos, and humans.

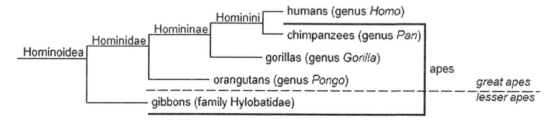

Homininae cladogram includes gorillas, chimpanzees, and humans

49. C is correct.

Cartilaginous fishes have a skeleton made of cartilage rather than bone.

Sharks, skates, rays, and sturgeons have cartilaginous skeletons, while hagfish have cartilaginous skulls.

50. A is correct.

Old World monkeys are primates in the clade of Catarrhini.

They are native to Africa and Asia today, inhabiting environments from tropical rainforest to savanna, shrubland, and mountainous terrain.

Old World monkeys include familiar species of nonhuman primates (e.g., baboons, macaques).

They are medium to large and range from arboreal (i.e., locomotion in trees) to fully terrestrial (e.g., baboons).

New World monkeys are the five families of primates in Central and South America and portions of Mexico. They are small to mid-sized primates.

New World monkeys differ from Old World monkeys in several aspects.

The prominent phenotypic distinction is the nose, commonly used to distinguish between groups.

New World monkeys have noses flatter than the narrow noses of Old-World monkeys and have side-facing nostrils.

New World monkeys are the only monkeys with prehensile tails.

Old-World monkeys have shorter, non-grasping tails.

51. C is correct.

A reptile's body temperature is determined by the temperature of its surrounding environment, meaning it could fluctuate more often than endothermic (*warm-blooded*) animals.

Birds are *endothermic*, so their body temperature remains constant and is warmer than reptiles.

52. D is correct.

Earthworms are soft-bodied segmented worms with nephridia, paired organs in each worm segment.

Nephridia remove nitrogenous waste.

53. E is correct.

Monotremes are mammals laying eggs instead of birthing live young like marsupials and placental mammals.

The surviving species of monotremes are indigenous to Australia and New Guinea, though evidence suggests they were once widespread.

The existing monotreme species are the *platypus* and four species of echidnas (i.e., spiny anteaters).

54. B is correct.

Legs and limbs indicate that the animal is *segmented*.

55. D is correct.

Lemurs are a clade of *strepsirrhine primates* characterized by a *moist nose tip*.

Lemurs are primarily *nocturnal animals* and are on the island of Madagascar.

56. E is correct.

Birds have a *complex respiratory system*.

Upon inhalation, 75% of the fresh air bypasses the lungs and flows directly into a posterior air sac extending from the lungs, connects with air spaces in the bones, and fills them with air.

25% of the air goes directly into the lungs.

When birds exhale, the used air flows out of the lung, and the stored fresh air from the posterior air sac is simultaneously forced into the lungs.

Bird's lungs receive fresh air during inhalation and exhalation.

Sound production uses the *syrinx*, a muscular chamber incorporating multiple tympanic membranes that diverge from the trachea's lower end.

In some species, the *trachea* is elongated to increase *vocalization volume* and *perceived size*.

57. D is correct.

Grasping hands of primates (i.e., having opposable thumbs) are an adaptation to life in the trees.

Thumbs help primates grasp objects (e.g., tree branches) firmly.

58. B is correct.

Chordates are both vertebrates and invertebrates.

Chordates share features:

> *notochord,*
>
> *dorsal hollow nerve cord,*
>
> *pharyngeal slits,* and
>
> *post-anal tail.*

In vertebrate chordates, the notochord is replaced by a *vertebral column*.

59. B is correct.

Radial symmetry is present in organisms with symmetry around a central axis.

Radial symmetry is in *starfish* or *sea urchins*, whose body parts extend outward from a center point.

Ecosystems and Biomes – Detailed Explanations

1. A is correct.

Ecosystem is a community of organisms (e.g., plants, animals, microbes) with nonliving (i.e., *abiotic*) components of their environment (e.g., air, water, minerals). It is the network of interactions among organisms and between organisms and their environment.

Nutrient cycles and *energy flows* link *biotic* (i.e., living) and *abiotic* (i.e., nonliving) components.

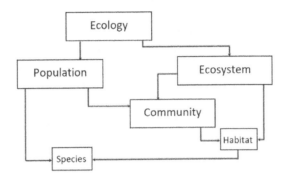

Relationship between organisms and their environment. Population, ecosystem, community, habitat, and species relationship are highlighted.

Ecology is the study of relationships between living organisms and between their environments.

Population is a group of organisms of the same species living in the same area.

Community is a group of populations living and interacting in an area.

Habitat is the environment in which a species lives.

Species are a group of organisms that can breed and produce fertile offspring.

2. B is correct.

Weather is the immediate conditions (e.g., hourly, daily, weekly), while *climate* is the average conditions.

3. A is correct.

Symbiosis is the close and often long-term interaction between species.

Historically, some biologists proposed symbiosis as *persistent mutualisms* (i.e., all organisms benefit).

Biologists and ecologists now propose symbiosis as *persistent biological interactions*; mutualistic (+/+), commensalism (+/0), or parasitic (+/−).

4. C is correct.

Climate zones are distinct in an east-west direction around Earth and are classified by climate parameters.

Climate zones are primarily determined by *variations in temperature* related to *latitude* and *altitude*.

Angle of the sun's rays contributes to differences in climate zones.

5. E is correct.

Greenhouse effect is a natural phenomenon that maintains Earth's temperature range.

Greenhouse gases on Earth are water vapor (36–70%), CO_2 (9–26%), methane (4–9%), and ozone (3–7%).

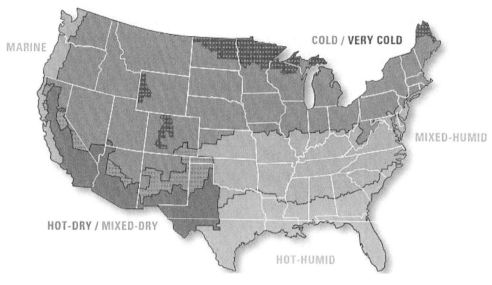

U.S. climate zones

6. D is correct.

Convection is movement caused by hotter (i.e., less dense) air rising and colder (i.e., denser) air sinking under the influence of gravity, consequently resulting in heat transfer.

Global wind patterns in the atmosphere are created by *convection* (i.e., air movement based on density).

When *warm air rises* and cools in a low-pressure zone, it may not hold the water it contains as vapor.

Some water vapor condenses to form clouds or precipitation.

When *cool air descends*, it warms.

7. E is correct.

Wetlands ecosystems have saturated ground surfaces either permanently or temporarily.

8. C is correct.

Niche describes when each species has separate, unique physical and environmental conditions.

Biological aspects of an organism's niche are *biotic factors* (i.e., living) required for survival.

Abiotic factors (i.e., nonliving) include soil, sunlight, water, and minerals.

Ecological niche is how organisms (or populations) respond to the distribution of resources and competitors (e.g., growing with abundant resources while predators are scarce) and how it alters those factors (e.g., limiting access by other organisms, being a food source for predators and a consumer of prey).

9. C is correct.

Niche is when each species has separate, unique physical and environmental conditions.

Niche is the range of *physical and biological conditions* in which an organism lives and how it obtains resources for survival and reproduction.

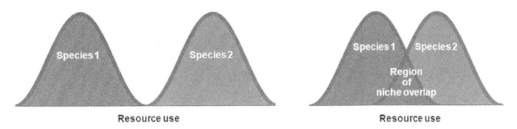

Resource partitioning results in competition for scarce resources when niche regions overlap

10. B is correct.

Competitive exclusion principle (*Gause's law of competitive exclusion* or *Gause's law*) states that two species competing for the same resources cannot coexist when ecological factors are constant.

Domination occurs when one species has even a slight advantage.

One competitor overcomes another, leading to extinction or behavioral shift toward a different ecological niche.

11. D is correct.

Primary producers (i.e., *autotrophs*) produce energy from inorganic compounds in an ecosystem.

Primary producers often use *photosynthesis* (e.g., plants and cyanobacteria).

Autotrophs (e.g., plants) support the ecosystem and feed heterotrophs.

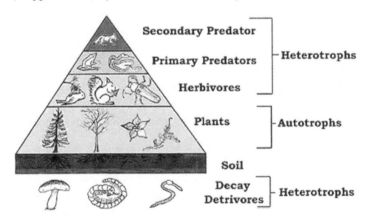

Trophic levels as positions on a food web. Autotrophs support the ecosystem and feed heterotrophs.

12. E is correct.

Primary producers (i.e., *autotrophs*) produce energy from inorganic compounds in an ecosystem.

Primary producers often use *photosynthesis* (e.g., plants and cyanobacteria).

Plants are primary producers.

Autotrophs support the ecosystem and feed heterotrophs.

Autotrophs create organic compounds using energy from the sun or inorganic compounds.

Autotrophs divide into *photoautotrophs* and *chemoautotrophs*.

Photoautotrophs (e.g., algae, plants, cyanobacteria) use photosynthesis, converting solar energy into organic compounds.

Chemoautotrophs are bacteria that oxidize inorganic compounds such as ammonia, nitrite, and sulfide to generate organic compounds.

They are rare and typically found in caves, hydrothermal ocean vents, and other environments lacking light.

Archaea (single-cell prokaryotes) may produce biomass from oxidizing inorganic compounds (i.e., chemoautotrophs).

For example, *archaea* produce biomass in *deep ocean hydrothermal vents*.

Decomposers are fungi and other organisms that produce biomass from oxidizing organic materials.

They absorb and metabolize nutrients (i.e., saprotrophic nutrition from dead or decaying material).

13. A is correct.

Open ocean waters are separated from cold, nutrient-rich interior water by *density differences* restricting water mixing and reducing nutrient supply, which becomes the limiting factor for productivity.

Open oceans have negligible nutrients from land and little upwelling to supply nutrients from deep oceans.

14. B is correct.

Habitat is an ecological area inhabited by a species.

Habitat is the natural environment where an organism lives or the physical environment encompassing a population.

Niche describes when each species has separate, unique physical and environmental conditions.

Niche is the range of *physical and biological conditions* in which an organism lives and how it obtains resources for survival and reproduction.

Niche breadth is the range of habitat by an organism.

continued...

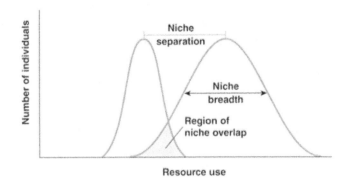

Niches may overlap and introduce competition for scarce resources

15. A is correct.

Food web is a graphical model depicting linked *food chains b*y feeding relationships in an ecosystem.

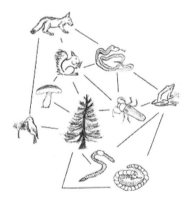

Food web and energy flow relationship examples

Food chain is a *linear succession* whereby another eats each species.

16. E is correct.

Mutualism is when two organisms of distinct species exist in a relationship, each benefit.

B: *parasitism* is a non-mutual symbiotic relationship between species, where one species (i.e., the parasite) benefits at the expense of the other (i.e., the host).

C: *commensalism is* when two organisms of distinct species exist in a relationship, each benefit.

D: *omnivorism* is a human diet consuming meat, eggs, dairy, and produce traced to an organic farm.

17. A is correct.

Predation is a biological interaction when a predator (i.e., a hunting organism) feeds on prey.

A predator may (or *may not*) kill its prey before feeding, but the act of predation often results in the prey's death and the eventual absorption of the prey's tissue through consumption.

Given an alternative, *predators* (e.g., lions, tigers, wolves) may engage in *scavenging* feeding.

Mutualism (+/+) is a symbiosis of *persistent biological interactions.*

18. B is correct.

Biomass is the mass (i.e., a body of matter without defined shape) of living organisms in an area (or ecosystem).

Biomass can include microorganisms, plants, or animals.

The mass can be expressed as the average mass per unit area or as the total mass in the community.

How biomass is measured depends on why it is being measured.

Species biomass is the mass of one or more species.

Community biomass is the mass of the species in the community.

Trophic levels show a succession of the flow of *food energy* and *feeding relationships*.

It is a food chain or ecological pyramid occupied by groups with similar feeding modes.

Trophic level 1	Producers
Trophic level 2	Primary consumers
Trophic level 3	Secondary consumers
Trophic level 4	Tertiary consumers

Food chain is the hierarchy in which organisms in an ecosystem are grouped into trophic (nutritional) levels.

Ecological pyramid represents the biomass or the energy flow in an ecosystem.

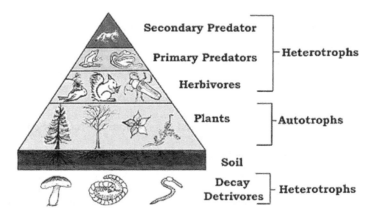

Trophic levels as positions on a food web. Autotrophs support the ecosystem and feed heterotrophs.

19. C is correct.

Herbivory is an animal anatomically and physiologically adapted to eating plants.

As a result of their plant diet, herbivorous animals typically have mouthparts adapted to rasping or grinding.

For example, foliage or marine algae are the main component of herbivores.

20. D is correct.

Parasitism (+/–) is a non-mutual symbiotic relationship between species, where one species (i.e., the parasite) benefits at the expense of the other (i.e., the host).

A: *synnecrosis* is a rare symbiosis when the interaction between species is detrimental to both.

It is short-lived because the interaction eventually causes death.

Evolution selects against synnecrosis and is uncommon.

B: *predation* is a biological interaction when a predator (i.e., hunting organism) feeds on prey.

Predators may not kill their prey before feeding, but predation often results in the prey's death and eventual absorption of their tissue through consumption.

The remains of prey may become a food source for scavengers.

Scavengers feed on dead organisms that they did not kill.

Organisms (e.g., lions, tigers, wolves) considered predators may engage in scavenging feeding behavior when given the alternative.

C: *mutualism* (+/+) is when two organisms of different species exist in a relationship, each benefit.

E: *commensalism* is a relationship between organisms where an organism benefits without affecting the other.

21. C is correct.

Omnivores consume meat, eggs, dairy, and produce.

Autotrophs support the ecosystem and feed heterotrophs.

Autotrophs create organic compounds using energy from the sun or inorganic compounds.

Autotrophs divide into photoautotrophs and chemoautotrophs.

Photoautotrophs (e.g., algae, plants, cyanobacteria) use photosynthesis to convert solar energy into organic compounds.

Chemotrophs are organisms that obtain energy by oxidation of electron donors in their environments.

These molecules can be organic or inorganic.

Chemotrophs can be either *autotrophic* or *heterotrophic*.

Herbivores are animals anatomically and physiologically adapted to eating plants.

As a result of their plant diet, herbivorous animals typically have mouthparts adapted to rasping or grinding.

22. D is correct.

Ecosystems include food production, solar energy (photosynthesis), and O_2 production (e.g., photosynthesis).

They are the network of interactions among organisms and between organisms and their environment.

23. E is correct.

Autotrophs support the ecosystem and feed heterotrophs.

Autotrophs create organic compounds using energy from the sun or inorganic compounds; they are divided into *photoautotrophs* and *chemoautotrophs*.

Photoautotrophs (e.g., algae, plants, cyanobacteria) use photosynthesis, converting solar energy into organic compounds.

Heterotrophs obtain nutrients and energy by consuming organic substances.

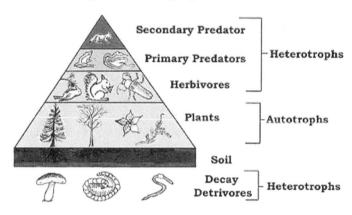

Trophic levels as positions on a food web. Autotrophs support the ecosystem and feed heterotrophs.

24. C is correct.

Primary succession is one of two biological and ecological successions of plant life, occurring in an environment devoid of vegetation and usually lacking soil (e.g., lava flow).

It is the gradual growth of an ecosystem over a longer period.

Secondary succession occurs on a substrate that supports vegetation before an ecological disturbance from less cataclysmic events (e.g., floods, hurricanes, tornadoes), which destroy plant life.

25. B is correct.

Heterotrophs obtain nutrients and energy by consuming organic substances.

Autotrophs are *producers*.

Heterotrophs are *consumers* and rely on producers.

26. E is correct.

Primary succession is one of two biological and ecological successions of plant life, occurring in an environment devoid of vegetation and usually lacking soil (e.g., lava flow).

Primary succession is the gradual growth of an ecosystem over a more extended period.

Secondary succession occurs on a substrate that supports vegetation before an ecological disturbance from less cataclysmic events (e.g., floods, hurricanes, tornadoes), which destroy plant life.

27. B is correct.

The snail is a typical detritivore.

Detritivores are heterotrophs that obtain nutrition from decomposing (waste or detritus) plants, dead organisms, and feces and contribute to decomposition and the nutrient cycles.

Detritivores are not to be confused with other decomposers, such as bacteria, fungi, and protists, which cannot ingest minute lumps of matter.

Decomposers absorb and metabolize nutrients (i.e., saprotrophic nutrition from dead or decaying material).

28. A is correct.

Matter recycles through the biosphere because biological systems do not deplete it but transform it.

29. D is correct.

Clearing and farming are physical disturbances to the ecosystem.

Climax community is a biological community of plants, animals, and fungi that has reached a *steady-state* through ecological succession (i.e., vegetation in an area over time).

Equilibrium occurs because the climax community has species best adapted to average conditions in that area.

30. A is correct.

Ecosystems include food production, solar energy (photosynthesis), and O_2 production (e.g., photosynthesis).

They are the network of interactions among organisms and between organisms and their environment.

Biomes are geographically and climatically defined as contiguous with similar conditions, such as communities of plants, animals, and soil organisms.

31. B is correct.

Tundra is a biome where low temperatures and short growing seasons hinder tree growth.

Vegetation includes dwarf shrubs, grasses, mosses, and lichens.

Desert is a barren land where little precipitation occurs, and consequently, living conditions are hostile to plant and animal life.

32. C is correct.

The bird is the carnivore, while the insect is the consumer (heterotroph).

33. B is correct.

Tundra is a biome where low temperatures and short growing seasons hinder tree growth. The vegetation includes dwarf shrubs, grasses, mosses, and lichens.

Desert is a barren land where little precipitation occurs, and consequently, living conditions are hostile to plant and animal life.

Boreal forest (or *taiga*) is a biome characterized by coniferous (i.e., softwood) forests mainly consisting of pines, spruces, and larches and is the world's largest terrestrial biome.

34. A is correct.

Decomposers are fungi and other organisms that produce biomass from oxidizing organic materials.

They absorb and metabolize nutrients (i.e., saprotrophic nutrition from dead or decaying material).

Scavengers feed on dead organisms that they did *not* kill.

Often, the remains of the prey become a food source for scavengers.

35. D is correct.

Climate is the average conditions, *while the weather* is the immediate conditions (e.g., hourly, daily, weekly).

36. E is correct.

Nitrogen fixation is when atmospheric nitrogen (N_2) is converted into ammonium (NH_4).

Nitrogen fixation is necessary for life because nitrogen is required for nucleotides of DNA and RNA and amino acids of proteins.

Diazotrophs are prokaryotic (i.e., bacteria and archaea) microorganisms that can fix nitrogen.

Some higher plants and animals (e.g., termites) have symbiotic relationships with diazotrophs.

37. C is correct.

Primary productivity is the rate at which producers (autotrophs) produce organic matter.

38. B is correct.

Biomes are climatically and geographically defined as *contiguous areas* with *similar climatic conditions,* such as communities of animals, plants, and soil organisms and are often called ecosystems.

Factors such as plant structures define biomes (e.g., shrubs, trees, and grasses), leaf types (e.g., broadleaf and needleleaf), plant spacing (e.g., forest, woodland, savanna), and climate.

Biomes, unlike ecozones, are not defined by genetic, taxonomic, or historical similarities.

Biomes are often identified by patterns of ecological succession and climax vegetation.

39. A is correct.

North Pole and the South Pole are not classified into major biomes.

40. E is correct.

Predation is a biological interaction when a predator (i.e., a hunting organism) feeds on prey. A predator may (or may not kill) its prey before feeding on them, but the act of predation often results in the prey's death and the eventual absorption of the prey's tissue through consumption.

Scavengers feed on dead organisms that they did not kill. Often, the remains of the prey become a food source for scavengers.

Organisms (e.g., lions, tigers, wolves) considered predators may engage in scavenging feeding behavior when given the alternative.

41. B is correct.

Aphotic zone is the area of a lake or ocean with little or no sunlight, the depths beyond which less than 1 percent of sunlight penetrates.

Below the photic zone is the dark aphotic zone, where photosynthesis cannot occur.

Benthic zone is the lowest ecological zone in water bodies and usually involves sediments on the seafloor.

These sediments are essential in providing nutrients for the organisms that live in the benthic zone.

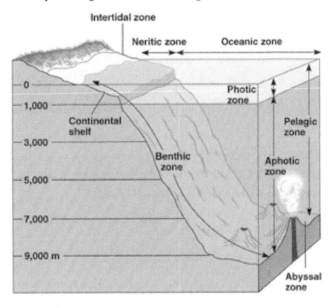

Deep ocean zones include photic, pelagic, aphotic, and abyssal zones

Phytoplankton (microalgae), like terrestrial plants, contain chlorophyll and require sunlight to live and grow.

Most phytoplankton is buoyant and floats in the ocean's upper layers, where sunlight penetrates the water.

Phytoplankton is the base of many aquatic food webs whereby shrimp, jellyfish, and whales feed on them.

Zooplankton is heterotrophic (sometimes detritivores) plankton – organisms drifting in oceans, seas, and freshwater bodies.

Individual zooplankton is usually microscopic but may (e.g., jellyfish) be larger and visible to the unaided eye.

42. C is correct.

Transpiration is when water moves in a plant and evaporates from aerial parts, such as leaves, stems, and flowers.

43. D is correct.

In aquatic ecosystems, *nitrogen* and *phosphorus* are the most important, often in short supply relative to the needs of plants, algae, and microbes.

Elements like iron, manganese, and copper are needed in lesser amounts.

44. A is correct.

Phytoplankton (microalgae), like terrestrial plants, contain chlorophyll and require sunlight to live and grow.

Most phytoplankton is buoyant and floats in the ocean's upper layers, where sunlight penetrates the water.

Phytoplankton is the base of many aquatic food webs whereby shrimp, jellyfish, and whales feed on them.

Zooplankton is heterotrophic (sometimes detritivores) plankton – organisms drifting in oceans, seas, and freshwater bodies.

Individual zooplankton is usually microscopic, but may (e.g., jellyfish) be larger and visible to the unaided eye.

45. C is correct.

Energy flows in one direction while nutrients recycle.

Nutrient cycles and *energy flows* link *biotic* (i.e., living) and *abiotic* (i.e., nonliving) components.

46. B is correct.

Boreal forest (or *taiga*) is a biome characterized by coniferous (i.e., softwood) forests mainly consisting of pines, spruces, and larches, and is the world's largest terrestrial biome.

47. E is correct.

Freshwater ecosystems naturally share resources between habitats.

At lower elevations, rivers and streams bring salt and nutrients from the mountains to lakes, ponds, and wetlands. Eventually, they bring those nutrients to the ocean.

48. A is correct.

Wetlands are areas filled with water most of the year. It might not always be wet.

Ponds and *lakes* are usually kept filled with water from many sources. They receive more water than they give off through evaporation.

Lake and ponds are distinguished by *depth* and *surface area*.

Lakes usually are much deeper than ponds and have a larger surface area.

Ponds have water in the photic zone, meaning ponds are shallow enough to allow sunlight to reach the bottom.

49. D is correct.

Estuaries are partly enclosed coastal bodies of brackish water (i.e., saline levels of 0.05 to 3% between fresh and saltwater).

Estuaries form when rivers or streams flow in and connect freely to the open sea.

Estuaries form a transition zone between the river and maritime environments and have marine influences (e.g., tides, waves, and saline water) and river influences (e.g., freshwater and sediment).

Inflows of seawater and freshwater provide nutrients in the water column and sediment, making *estuaries* among the most *productive natural habitats*.

50. A is correct.

Aphotic zone is the area of a lake or ocean with little or no sunlight, the depths beyond which less than 1 percent of sunlight penetrates.

Below the photic zone is the dark aphotic zone, where photosynthesis cannot occur.

51. C is correct.

Abiotic factors (i.e., nonliving) include soil, sunlight, water, and minerals.

Biotic factors are living components affecting other organisms. Biotic factors need food and metabolic energy for proper growth.

52. D is correct.

Estuaries are partly enclosed coastal bodies of brackish water (i.e., saline levels of 0.05 to 3% between fresh and saltwater).

Estuaries form when rivers or streams flow in and connect freely to the open sea.

Estuaries form a *transition zone* between rivers and maritime environments and have marine influences (e.g., tides, waves, and saline water) and river influences (e.g., freshwater and sediment).

Inflows of seawater and freshwater provide nutrients in the water column and sediment, making estuaries among the most *productive natural habitats*.

53. E is correct.

Scavengers feed on dead organisms that they did not kill.

Often, the remains of the prey become a food source for scavengers.

Detritivores are heterotrophs that obtain nutrition from decomposing (waste or detritus) plants, dead organisms, and feces and contribute to decomposition and the nutrient cycles.

Detritivores are not to be confused with other decomposers such as bacteria, fungi, and protists, which cannot ingest minute lumps of matter.

Decomposers absorb and metabolize nutrients (i.e., saprotrophic nutrition from dead or decaying material).

Notes for active learning

Evolution and Ecology

Evolution and Natural Selection – Detailed Explanations

1. D is correct.

Charles Darwin (1809-1882), during his trip to the Galapagos Islands in the 1830s, observed several species of finches that differed among islands.

2. A is correct.

Evolutionary relationships classify organisms:

Kingdom → Phylum → Class → Order → Family → Genus → Species

Largest group (i.e., kingdom) divides into smaller subdivisions.

Each smaller group has common characteristics. Of the answers, a genus is the smallest subdivision, and organisms in the same genus are more similar than organisms classified as the same family, order, class, or kingdom.

3. E is correct.

Mutations are the source of genetic variation for natural selection.

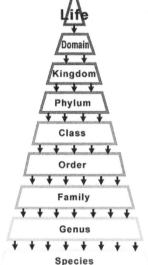

4. A is correct.

Chloroplast is a plant cell organelle that may have originated from cyanobacteria through *endosymbiosis*.

Endosymbiotic theory proposes that a eukaryotic cell engulfed a photosynthesizing cyanobacterium about one billion years ago. Photosynthesizing cyanobacterium became a permanent resident in the cell because it escaped the phagocytic vacuole in which it was contained.

Chloroplasts contain their DNA and ribosomes (like prokaryotic ribosomes) and undergo autosomal replication (i.e., replicating independently of the cell cycle), supporting this theory.

Cyanobacteria obtain energy through photosynthesis and have the color of the bacteria (i.e., blue).

Named blue-green algae, this is a misnomer as cyanobacteria are prokaryotes, while algae are eukaryotes.

By producing oxygen as a by-product gas of photosynthesis, cyanobacteria converted Earth's early reducing atmosphere into an oxidizing one, dramatically changing the composition of life by stimulating biodiversity and leading to the near-extinction of oxygen-intolerant organisms.

Endosymbiotic theory proposes that chloroplasts in plants, mitochondria in eukaryotes, and eukaryotic algae evolved from prokaryotic cyanobacterial ancestors.

Mitochondria evolved from free-living prokaryotic heterotrophs that, similarly to chloroplasts, entered eukaryotic cells and established a symbiotic relationship with the host (the theory of *endosymbiosis*).

Mitochondria contain circular DNA (similar in size and composition to prokaryotes), ribosomes (like prokaryotic ribosomes), and unique proteins in the organelle membrane (similar in composition to prokaryotes) and replicate independently, providing further evidence to support this theory.

5. D is correct.

Evolution is the long-term changes in a population's gene pool caused by environmental selection pressures.

I: *random mutation* creates new alleles selected for (or against) as a phenotypic variation for natural selection (i.e., survival of the fittest).

II: *reproductive isolation* of a population is a crucial component of speciation.

Geographically isolated populations often diverge to yield reproductive isolation leading to speciation.

III: *speciation* might happen in a population with no specific extrinsic barrier to gene flow.

For example, a population extends over a broad geography, and mating in the population is not random.

Individuals in the far west would have zero probability of mating with individuals in the far east range.

This results in reduced *gene flow* but not total isolation.

Such a situation may (or not) be sufficient for speciation.

Speciation would be promoted by different selective pressures at opposite ends of the range, which would alter gene frequencies in groups at different ranges so they would not be able to mate if they were reunited.

6. C is correct.

Charles Darwin (1809-1882) hypothesized that the mechanism of evolution involves natural selection.

7. E is correct.

Prokaryotes are primarily *unicellular* organisms, although a few, such as mycobacterium, have multicellular stages in their life cycles or create large colonies like cyanobacteria.

Eukaryotes are often *multicellular* and are typically much *larger than prokaryotes*.

Eukaryotes have *internal membranous structures* (i.e., organelles) and a cytoskeleton composed of microtubules, microfilaments, and intermediate filaments, essential for cellular organization and shape.

8. D is correct.

Archaean Eon contains the oldest known fossil record, dating to about 3.5 billion years.

9. A is correct.

Urey and Miller demonstrated in 1953 that organic molecules might be created from inorganic molecules under the primordial earth conditions. They designed an experiment that simulated conditions thought at the time to be on the early Earth and assessed for the occurrence of chemical origins of life.

Urey-Miller did not prove the existence of life on earth. However, experiments showed over 20 different amino acids produced in Miller's original experiments.

10. B is correct.

Nature uses many methods for fertilization, development, and care of offspring.

Internal fertilization involves internal development and much care for offspring.

These organisms (e.g., humans and many mammals) produce few offspring, but a substantial percentage reach adulthood.

External fertilization involves external development and little care for offspring.

These organisms (e.g., many species of fish) produce large numbers of sperm and eggs because few sperm and eggs interact to produce a zygote.

Few zygotes survive without physical protection from predators, and millions of eggs and sperm must be released to perpetuate the species.

A: *protective coloring* might help for survival against predators, but not related to caring for the young.

C: *laying eggs* is not related to not caring for the young (most birds care for their young).

D: not relevant to the survival rate of the offspring.

11. C is correct.

Mutualism is when two species live in close association and both benefits.

Parasitism is a relationship between two organisms where one organism benefits while the other is harmed.

Commensalism involves a relationship between organisms where one benefits without affecting another.

Mimicry (in evolutionary biology) is the similarity of species, which protects one or both and occurs when a group (the mimic) evolves to share common characteristics with another group (the models).

Similarity can be in appearance, behavior, sound, scent, or location, mimicking similar places to their models.

Amensalism is a relationship where one species is inhibited or wholly obliterated while the other is unaffected.

For example, consider a sapling growing under the shadow of a mature tree.

The mature tree can deprive the sapling of sunlight, rainwater, and soil nutrients. Throughout the process, the mature tree is unaffected.

Additionally, if the sapling dies, the mature tree will gain nutrients from the decaying sapling.

Since the nutrients become available due to the dead sapling's decomposition (as opposed to living sapling), this would not be a case of parasitism.

12. D is correct.

Disruptive selection shifts allele frequencies towards variants of extremes, leading to two subpopulations.

These subpopulations do not favor the intermediate variants of the original population and grow disparate over time, likely leading to speciation.

A: *sexual selection* gives an individual an advantage in finding a mate.

Sexual selection often acts opposite to the effects of natural selection (e.g., a brighter plume may make a bird vulnerable to predators but gives it an advantage during reproduction).

It is hypothesized that sexual selection leads to sexual dimorphism (i.e., phenotypic differences between males and females of the same species).

B: *stabilizing selection* is a shift in phenotypes towards intermediates by disfavoring variants at extremes.

Stabilizing selection reduces variation within the species and perpetuates similarities between generations.

C: *directional selection* is the population shift in allele frequencies towards variants of one extreme.

13. D is correct.

Similarity among the embryos of fish, amphibians, reptiles, and humans is evidence of *common ancestry*.

14. E is correct.

Mutualism (i.e., symbiotic) is a relationship between two organisms where both benefits.

For example, soybeans depend on humans to survive while humans are provided with food.

Both species benefit from mutualism relationship.

Commensalism is a class of relationships where one organism benefits without affecting the other.

Mutualism (i.e., symbiotic) is a relationship between two organisms where both benefits.

Parasitism is a relationship between two organisms where one benefits while the other is harmed.

15. B is correct.

Natural selection leads to a population most adapted (*fittest*) to its current environment.

16. A is correct.

From an evolutionary perspective, *passing genetic information* to progeny is paramount.

17. E is correct.

Inherited traits determined by heredity are genes.

18. D is correct.

The evolutionary process of natural selection *works on existing genetic variation* within a population.

19. C is correct.

Genetic drift changes allele frequency within a population due to random sampling.

Allele frequency of a population is the fraction of the same alleles.

Offspring have the same alleles as parents, and probability determines if an individual survives and reproduces.

Genetic drift may cause allele variants to disappear and thereby reduce genetic variation.

20. A is correct.

Human height characteristics result from *polygenic* (i.e., many genes contribute) inheritance.

21. C is correct.

The oldest known *fossilized prokaryotes* were laid down approximately 3.6 billion years ago, about 1 billion years after the formation of the Earth's crust.

Eukaryotes appear in the fossil record later and may have formed from the aggregation of multiple prokaryotes.

The oldest known *fossilized eukaryotes* are about 1.7 billion years old.

However, some genetic evidence suggests eukaryotes appeared as early as 3 billion years ago.

Protists are a large and diverse group of eukaryotic microorganisms which belong to the kingdom Protista.

There have been attempts to remove the kingdom from the taxonomy, but it is commonly used.

Some professional organizations and institutions prefer the name Protista.

Protists are unicellular or they are multicellular without specialized tissues.

Besides their relatively simple levels of organization, protists do not have much in common.

The straightforward cellular organization distinguishes protists from other eukaryotes (e.g., fungi, animals).

Protists live in almost any environment with liquid water.

Many protists, such as algae, are photosynthetic and are vital primary producers in ecosystems, particularly in the ocean as part of the plankton.

Protists include pathogenic species, such as the kinetoplastid *Trypanosoma brucei,* causing sleeping sickness, and species of the apicomplexan *Plasmodium,* causing malaria.

22. D is correct.

Morphological or physical similarity between organisms is insufficient for classifying the same species.

Species are organisms that mate and produce *viable* and *fertile* offspring (give rise to additional offspring).

Organisms appearing different (e.g., dog breeds) are the same species if they mate and produce *fertile offspring*.

A: organisms can be the same species yet have different gene varieties (i.e., alleles) at the same gene locus.

For example, blue-eyed and green-eyed individuals can mate and produce fertile offspring.

B: *no relationship* between producing viable, fertile offspring and blood type.

C: *somatic cells* are body cells, not reproductive cells (i.e., gametes) or haploid (i.e., 1N or monoploid).

Somatic cells are diploid (2N) and undergo *mitosis* for cell division.

Gametes are haploid (1N) and undergo *meiosis* for cell division.

23. C is correct.

Gene pool is the population's total collection of alleles.

24. E is correct.

A pivotal point in Darwin's explanation of evolution is that any trait that confers an increase in the *probability* of its possessor surviving and reproducing is favored and spread through the population.

25. C is correct.

If an allele's frequency in a population is 0.7, the alternate allele is 0.3.

26. E is correct.

Natural selection is how mutations are selected for (or against) in the environment.

If the resulting phenotype offers some degree of fitness, the genes are passed to the next generation.

A: *natural selection* includes selection pressures and needs a population with genetic variation (random mutations) to select the fittest organisms.

C: *Darwin's theory* depends on more than mere mutations. It is based on over-reproduction. Offspring are selected for (or against) when their genetic makeup is fit for the local environment.

Organisms most fit (for their environment) and pass their genes (i.e., gametes) to the next generation.

The result is survival (greatest reproduction) of the *fittest organisms in the environment*.

D: *Lamarck* proposed that if traits were used (e.g., stretching of a giraffe's neck), these acquired traits are passed to the next generation.

Acquired characteristics (phenotypic changes) do not affect the genes and are not passed to the next generation via the gametes (e.g., sperm and egg).

27. B is correct.

Fewer copies of an allele magnify the effect of *genetic drift*.

Genetic drift is negligible when there are many copies of an allele.

28. D is correct.

A population that survived a bottleneck and recovered to its original size has *less genetic variation* than before.

29. B is correct.

Founder effect and *population bottleneck* differ because founder effect requires isolating a small group from a larger population.

30. B is correct.

Life originated in an atmosphere with *little or no oxygen.*

Until the Great Oxygenation Event (GOE) about 2.4 billion years ago, there was no atmospheric free oxygen.

Cyanobacteria appeared about 200 million years before the GOE began producing oxygen by photosynthesis.

Before the GOE, free oxygen produced was chemically captured by dissolved iron or organic matter.

The GOE was when oxygen sinks became saturated with oxygen produced by cyanobacterial photosynthesis.

Excess free oxygen accumulated in the atmosphere after the GOE.

Free oxygen is toxic to obligate anaerobic organisms. The rising concentrations eradicated most of Earth's anaerobic organisms.

Cyanobacteria were responsible for one of Earth's most significant extinction events.

Free oxygen reacts with atmospheric methane (a greenhouse gas), which is oxidized to CO_2 and H_2O.

Free oxygen has been an essential constituent of the atmosphere ever since.

Periods with much oxygen in the atmosphere are associated with the rapid development of animals.

Today's atmosphere contains about 21% oxygen, which is enough for the rapid development of animals.

31. B is correct.

Founder effect is the likely explanation that a population of humans has a higher rate of polydactyly (extra fingers or toes) than the human population.

32. E is correct.

Gene flow occurs through migration.

33. C is correct.

The first organisms had nothing else to eat. Even with millions of organisms, one organism must eat many, which would have exhausted the supply.

34. B is correct.

Evolutionary fitness measures *reproductive success* (i.e., the hereditary succession of gene pools).

35. A is correct.

Lamarck's theory of evolution proposed that enhanced structures (e.g., a giraffe's neck) arise based on use.

Lamarck (1744-1829) had a false premise that favorable characteristics obtained by use were inheritable.

For example, giraffes stretch their necks to reach leaves on branches.

Lamarck proposed that offspring inherit the trait (longer necks) based on use. However, only changes in the DNA of gametes (e.g., egg or sperm) are inherited.

B: de Vries (1848-1935) confirmed Mendel's observations with different plant species.

C: Mendel (1822-1884) defined classical genetics by experiments with inheritable traits (e.g., seed color, wrinkled vs. round seeds) in pea plants.

Mendel described the principles of dominance, segregation, and independent assortment. The unit of inheritance (i.e., genes) was unknown.

D: *Darwin's Theory of Natural Selection* states that *environmental pressures select the fittest organism* to survive and reproduce.

Natural Selection by Mendel is based on six principles.

1) **Overpopulation**: more offspring are produced than can survive with insufficient food, air, light, and space to support the population;

2) **Variations**: offspring have differences (i.e., variations) in characteristics than the population.

Darwin did not know why, but de Vries later suggested that *genetic mutations* cause variations.

Some mutations are *beneficial* fittest), but most are *detrimental*;

3) **Competition**: developing populations compete for necessities (e.g., food, air, light).

Many young die, while the number of adults remains constant for generations;

4) **Natural selection**: some organisms have phenotypes (i.e., variations) conferring an advantage over others;

5) **Inheritance of variations**: individuals reproduce and transmit favorable phenotypes.

Favored alleles (i.e., variations of genes) eventually dominate the gene pool;

6) **Evolution of new species**: natural selection (fittest) propagates favorable genes and phenotypes over generations.

Favorable changes result in significant changes in the gene pool for the evolution of a new species (i.e., organisms that reproduce and yield fertile offspring).

E: Morgan induced mutation in *Drosophila,* studied the inheritance of these mutations and described sex-linked inheritance (i.e., Morgan unit for the frequency of recombination within an organism).

36. D is correct.

Non-poisonous butterflies evolve color changes to look like poisonous butterflies in *directional selection*.

37. E is correct.

Genetic variation would likely be decreased by stabilizing selection.

38. C is correct.

Asexual reproduction is more efficient than sexual reproduction in the number of offspring produced per reproduction, in the amount of energy invested in this process, and in the amount of time invested in the development of the young (before and after birth).

Asexual reproduction relies on *genetic mutation* for phenotypic variability to be passed to future generations since it produces genetic clones of the parent.

Sexual reproduction involves the process of meiosis – two rounds of cell division and the likelihood of crossover (during prophase I).

A: new phenotype may be disadvantageous *or* advantageous.

B: a much greater probability of a mutation occurring with sexual reproduction (i.e., at the chromosomal level), known as chromosomal aberrations.

D: *sexual reproduction* requires more *energy* and *time* per progeny (i.e., offspring).

Species reproducing sexually have a selective advantage because of *gene recombination* during fertilization.

Fusing two genetically unique nuclei (haploid sperm and haploid egg nucleus) yields a unique (2N) zygote.

Fertilizing two unique gametes introduces phenotypic variability into a population.

This genetic and phenotypic variability may benefit or harm individuals in their environment.

Advantageous phenotypes survive and pass genes to future generations consistent with natural selection (i.e., survival of the fittest).

39. D is correct.

Birds laying an intermediate number of eggs have the highest reproductive success, likely resulting from stabilizing selection.

40. E is correct.

Nucleotides are sugar (ribose for RNA or deoxyribose for DNA), a phosphate group, and a base.

Nitrogenous bases are guanine, adenine, cytosine, thymine (for DNA), or uracil (for RNA).

Adenine and guanine are purines, while thymine, cytosine, and uracil are pyrimidines.

A: *lipids* (i.e., fats) are composed of glycerol (i.e., 3-carbon chain) and (up to) three fatty acids.

B: *monosaccharides* are the monomers (e.g., glucose, fructose) of carbohydrates (e.g., glycogen, cellulose).

C: *nucleosides* have a nitrogenous base and sugar (without phosphate).

Nucleotides have a phosphate group, nitrogenous base, and sugar.

D: amino acids are monomers for proteins that do not contain sugar, phosphate or bases.

41. A is correct.

Sexual selection likely results from a female deer choosing to mate with males with the biggest antlers.

42. A is correct.

Embryos indicate that fossilized organisms reproduce sexually.

Development of an embryo involves two distinct reproductive cells fusing, characteristic of sexual reproduction.

This single-cell zygote results from fertilizing the female egg cell with a male sperm cell.

43. D is correct.

Cambrian Explosion occurred 542 million years ago with the rapid appearance of most major animal phyla.

This was accompanied by significant diversification of other organisms, as the fossil record shows.

Before about 580 million years ago, most organisms were simple, composed of individual cells occasionally organized into colonies.

Over the following 70-80 million years, the rate of evolution accelerated by order of magnitude, and the diversity of life became similar to today.

44. C is correct.

During evolution, primates needed to walk on two legs (i.e., *bipedal*) to free their hands for other tasks.

Hands were used in creating weapons and tools to gather food and protect the young.

45. B is correct.

Eyes facing forward allow two fields of vision to overlap, enabling the perception of depth.

Animals without facing forward eyes could not likely judge the distance to objects (e.g., tree branches) due to flawed depth perception.

As primates moved into trees to escape predators, they needed to navigate tree branches, meaning evolution favored good depth perception.

46. D is correct.

Sexual reproduction increases fitness and allows for modifications in traits, which can help adapt to new living conditions in a changing environment.

Sexual reproduction adds to the diversity of the offspring.

All other answer choices characterize asexual reproduction.

47. D is correct.

Arboreal locomotion is the movement of animals in *trees*.

Some animals have evolved to move in habitats where trees are present.

Animals may only scale trees occasionally or become exclusively arboreal.

48. A is correct.

Australopithecus afarensis is an extinct species with hip, knee, and foot morphology distinctive to bipedalism.

Footprints show *Australopithecus afarensis* walked with an upright posture and a decisive heel strike, which is early evidence of bipedalism.

49. E is correct.

Amniotic eggs are laid on land by certain reptiles, birds, and mammals.

Amniotic eggs differ from *anamniotic* eggs, typically laid in water (by fish and amphibians).

50. A is correct.

Gluteus muscles of the pelvis are important for propulsion and stability while walking.

Bipedal humans are different from quadrupedal apes in the lateral orientation of the ilium, which constitutes the bowl-shaped pelvis.

51. C is correct.

Homo sapiens evolved after the *Homo erectus* and are *modern humans*.

52. B is correct.

Neanderthals are closely related to modern humans, with differences based on DNA by 0.3%, but twice the greatest DNA difference among contemporary humans.

Genetic evidence suggests Neanderthals contributed to the DNA of anatomically modern humans, probably through interbreeding between 80,000 and 30,000 years ago.

Recent evidence suggests that Neanderthals practiced burial behavior and buried their dead.

Archaeological remains by Neanderthals include bones and stone tools.

53. B is correct.

r/K selection refers to traits whereby the parental investment is related to the quantity and quality of offspring.

A higher quantity of offspring with decreased parental investment, or a lower quantity of offspring with increased parental investment, promotes reproductive success in different environments.

r-selected species emphasize *high growth rates and typically exploit less-crowded ecological niches*. They produce many offspring, which may die before adulthood (i.e., high *r*, low *K*).

This strategy fares better in an environment with *density-independent factors* (e.g., harsh environment, short seasons). The species withstand predation better because they produce more offspring than needed for population survival.

K-selected species display traits associated with living at *densities close to carrying capacity* and are typically strong competitors in crowded niches. They invest heavily in *fewer offspring*, most of which will mature (i.e., low *r*, high *K*). *K*-strategists fare better with *density-dependent factors* (e.g., limited resources) and exploit limited resources by *specializing*.

Species that use r-selection are *opportunistic,* while K-selected species are described as *equilibrium*.

54. D is correct.

The decimating fire was a random event unrelated to the apparent fitness of the fly in its typical environment.

Genetic drift is the random change over time in the allele frequency within a population, such as the one caused by the decimating fire in the loss of allele(s) for the altered structure.

Reproduction is not involved in the loss of the advantageous modification.

Natural selection is not the cause since the death of the flies was unrelated to their fitness, and a decimating fire would likely have killed all flies, regardless of their advantageous modification.

Hardy-Weinberg equilibrium describes ideal circumstances which do not apply to this situation.

Animal Behavior – Detailed Explanations

1. A is correct.

Potato washing requires learning.

Learning behavior includes habituation, sensitization, classical conditioning, operant conditioning, observational learning, play, and insight learning.

Innate behaviors do not need prior experience or learning.

2. E is correct.

Behavior is the *internally coordinated responses* (i.e., actions or inactions) of organisms (individuals or groups) to internal or external stimuli. Behaviors can be *innate* (instinct) or *learned.*

Behavior is an act of an organism that changes its relationship to its environment; it provides outputs from the organism to the environment.

3. B is correct.

Evolution is the long-term changes in a population's *gene pool* caused by environmental selection pressures.

Mutations are the source of genetic variation for natural selection.

Random mutations create new alleles selected for (or against) as a phenotypic variation for natural selection (i.e., survival of the fittest).

4. C is correct.

Operant conditioning is behavior modified by *antecedents* (i.e., before trained behavior) and consequences.

Operant conditioning is distinguished from *classical conditioning* (or *respondent conditioning*) because operant conditioning addresses reinforcement and punishment to change behavior.

Imprinting is *phase-sensitive* learning (learning during a life stage) rapid and independent of the consequences of behavior.

Imprinting has a critical period.

Insight learning is the faculty of reason or rationality and involves a sudden realization distinct from cause-and-effect problem-solving. It manifests *spontaneously* and is a noteworthy event in the learning process.

Insight learning is *problem-solving* occurring suddenly by understanding relationships between parts of a problem rather than through test and error.

Classical conditioning differs from *operant conditioning* because the behavior is strengthened or weakened, depending on its consequences (i.e., reward or punishment).

Classical conditioning involves reflexive (reflex) behaviors elicited by prior exposure. It occurs when a conditioned stimulus is paired with an unconditioned stimulus.

Consequences do not maintain behaviors conditioned through classical conditioning.

5. A is correct.

Innate (or *instinct*) behavior is the inherent inclination towards a particular complex behavior.

A truncated sequence of actions, without variation, is conducted in response to a clearly defined stimulus.

Instinctive behavior is *without prior experience* (i.e., absence of learning) and uses innate biological factors.

6. D is correct.

Innate (or *instinct*) behavior is the inherent inclination towards a particular complex behavior; a truncated sequence of actions, without variation, is conducted in response to a clearly defined stimulus.

Instinctive behavior is performed *without prior experience* (i.e., absence of learning) and expresses innate biological factors.

7. B is correct.

Moths communicate with predators, in this example, by sight. Animals communicate using four primary methods: visual, auditory, tactile, and chemical.

8. D is correct.

Classical conditioning differs from *operant conditioning* because the behavior is strengthened or weakened depending on its consequences (i.e., reward or punishment).

Classical conditioning involves reflexive (reflex) behaviors elicited by prior exposure.

Classical conditioning occurs when a conditioned stimulus is paired with an unconditioned stimulus.

Consequences do not maintain behaviors conditioned through classical conditioning.

9. C is correct.

Imprinting is *phase-sensitive* learning (learning during a life stage) that is rapid and independent of the consequences of behavior.

Imprinting has a critical period.

10. E is correct.

Imprinting is *phase-sensitive* learning (learning during a life stage) that is rapid and independent of the consequences of behavior. Imprinting has a critical period.

11. A is correct.

Habituation diminishes a physiological or emotional response to a frequently repeated stimulus.

12. D is correct.

Classical conditioning differs from *operant conditioning* because the behavior is strengthened or weakened depending on its consequences (i.e., reward or punishment).

Classical conditioning involves reflexive (reflex) behaviors elicited by prior exposure.

Classical conditioning occurs when a conditioned stimulus is paired with an unconditioned stimulus.

Consequences do not maintain behaviors conditioned through classical conditioning.

13. C is correct.

Animals secrete *pheromones* (e.g., sex attractants) to influence the behavior of species members.

Animals *communicate* using four methods: visual, auditory, tactile, and chemical.

14. B is correct.

Imprinting is *phase-sensitive learning* (i.e., during a life stage), independent of the consequences of behavior.

Imprinting has a critical period.

15. E is correct.

Learning occurs when an external stimulus causes an animal to change behavior (e.g., response to stimuli).

16. A is correct.

Circadian rhythms are biological processes reoccurring every 24 hours.

Circadian clock drives these rhythms widely observed in plants, animals, fungi, and cyanobacteria.

17. D is correct.

Migrating birds that nest in the Northern Hemisphere tend to fly northward in the spring for the burgeoning insect populations, budding plants, and abundance of nesting locations.

As winter approaches and the availability of insects and other food drops, the birds move south again.

Migration is based on seasons.

18. C is correct.

Kin selection is the evolutionary strategy favoring the reproductive success of an organism's relatives, even at a cost to the organism's survival and reproduction.

Kin altruism is unselfish behavior driven by *kin selection*.

Kin selection is *inclusive fitness*, combining the number of offspring produced with the number an individual can produce by supporting others (e.g., siblings).

For example, kin selection includes honeybees that do not reproduce by deferring to relatives, adopting orphans in animal populations, and familial caring for the young.

19. E is correct.

Hibernation is how animals conserve energy to survive adverse weather conditions or food scarcity.

Hibernation involves *physiological changes* such as decreased body temperature, heart rate, respiration rate, and slowed metabolism.

It is a form of torpor (lethargy); metabolism is less than five percent.

20. B is correct.

Operant conditioning is behavior modified by *antecedents* (i.e., before trained behavior) and consequences.

It is distinguished from *classical conditioning* (or *respondent conditioning*) because operant conditioning addresses reinforcement and punishment to change behavior.

Insight learning is problem-solving occurring suddenly by understanding relationships between parts of a problem rather than through test and error.

Insight learning is the faculty of reason or rationality and involves a sudden realization distinct from cause-and-effect problem-solving.

Insight learning manifests spontaneously and is a noteworthy event in the learning process.

Classical conditioning differs from *operant conditioning* because the behavior is strengthened or weakened depending on its consequences (i.e., reward or punishment).

Classical conditioning involves reflexive (reflex) behaviors elicited by prior exposure. It occurs when a conditioned stimulus is paired with an unconditioned stimulus.

Consequences do not maintain behaviors conditioned through classical conditioning.

Habituation diminishes a physiological or emotional response to a frequently repeated stimulus.

21. E is correct.

Fertility and reproduction in animals follow circadian and seasonal rhythms.

Reproductive rhythm aims to maximize mating opportunities and offspring birth during favorable seasons for climate and food availability.

Their purpose is to increase offspring survival.

Chronobiology studies the rhythms of organisms and how external conditions influence them.

22. A is correct.

Courtship is mate-selection behavior (i.e., *rituals*).

Animal courtship occurs outside human observation, so it is the least documented animal behavior.

Animals *communicate* using four methods: visual, auditory, tactile, and chemical.

Courtship may include complicated protocols, vocalizations, beauty, or prowess.

23. D is correct.

Members of a society belong to the same species and interact closely.

Social animals (e.g., ants, termites) live together in large groups and often cooperate in many tasks.

24. B is correct.

Insight learning is the faculty of reason or rationality and involves a sudden realization distinct from cause-and-effect problem-solving. It manifests *spontaneously* and is a noteworthy event in the learning process.

Insight learning is *problem-solving* occurring suddenly by understanding relationships between parts of a problem rather than through test and error.

25. C is correct.

Animals require resources (e.g., food, water, biotic factors) for survival. An animal may benefit most by defending a territory if that area has more resources than the surrounding areas.

Competitive exclusion principle (*Gause's law of competitive exclusion* or *Gause's law*) states that two species competing for the same resources cannot coexist when ecological factors are constant.

26. D is correct.

Innate (or *instinct*) behavior is the inherent inclination towards a particular complex behavior.

A truncated sequence of actions, without variation, is conducted in response to a clearly defined stimulus.

Instinctive behavior is performed *without prior experience* (i.e., absence of learning) and expresses innate biological factors.

27. E is correct.

Social animals (e.g., ants, termites) live together in large groups and often cooperate in conducting many tasks.

Groups offer advantages such as greater protection from predation.

28. C is correct.

Nocturnality is an animal behavior characterized by *activity during the night* and *sleep during the day*.

Nocturnal creatures have advanced senses of hearing to avoid predators and communicate.

Diurnal animals are awake during the day and sleep at night.

29. A is correct.

Animals *communicate* using four methods: visual, auditory, tactile, and chemical.

Some species rely more on one form to communicate; however, all use methods to show affection, ward off threats or attract mates.

Animals often use chemical communication (e.g., *pheromones*) to mark territory.

For example, animals (e.g., dogs, lions) make *scent posts* to mark their territory and set territory boundaries.

30. B is correct.

Operant conditioning is behavior modified by *antecedents* (i.e., before trained behavior) and consequences.

Operant conditioning is distinguished from *classical conditioning* (or *respondent conditioning*) because operant conditioning addresses reinforcement and punishment to change behavior.

Imprinting is *phase-sensitive* learning (learning during a life stage) that is rapid and independent of the consequences of behavior.

Imprinting has a critical period.

Habituation diminishes a physiological or emotional response to a frequently repeated stimulus.

Classical conditioning differs from *operant conditioning* because the behavior is strengthened or weakened depending on its consequences (i.e., reward or punishment).

Classical conditioning involves reflexive (reflex) behaviors elicited by prior exposure.

It occurs when a conditioned stimulus is paired with an unconditioned stimulus.

Consequences do not maintain behaviors conditioned through classical conditioning.

31. A is correct.

Animals *communicate* using four methods: visual, auditory, tactile, and chemical.

For example, changes in skin color and patterns are visual signals.

Animals secrete *pheromones* (e.g., sex attractants) to influence the behavior of species members.

32. C is correct.

Animals *communicate* using four methods: visual, auditory, tactile, and chemical.

For example, changes in skin color and patterns are visual signals.

Pheromones are *chemical signals* released by animals to influence other animals.

33. A is correct.

Imprinting is when environmental patterns (or objects) presented to a developing organism during a *critical period* in early life become accepted as permanent aspects of their behavior.

For example, a duckling passes through a critical period when its mother is the first large moving object it sees.

B: *instrumental conditioning* involves reward or reinforcement to stimuli to establish a conditioning response.

C: *discrimination* involves learning organisms that respond differently to slightly different stimuli.

D: *pheromones* (e.g., sex attractants) are secreted by animals to influence the behavior of species members.

Populations and Community Ecology – Detailed Explanations

1. D is correct.

Sustainable development minimizes environmental impact. Sustainable buildings preserve precious natural resources and improve the quality of life. Buildings should consider design, construction, or operation, reducing or eliminating negative impacts and positively impacting climate and the natural environment.

Features can make a development *green*, including:

Efficient use of energy, water, and other resources; renewable energy, such as solar energy

Pollution and waste reduction measures and enabling re-use and recycling

Good indoor environmental air quality

Use of materials that are non-toxic, ethical, and sustainable

Consideration of the environment in design, construction, and operation

Design enables adaptation to a changing environment

2. A is correct.

Community is a population of species occupying the same geographical area. In ecology, a community is an association of populations of two or more species simultaneously occupying the same geographical area.

Ecosystem is a community of organisms (e.g., plants, animals, microbes) with nonliving (i.e., *abiotic*) components of their environment (e.g., air, water, minerals).

Ecosystems are the network of interactions among and between organisms and their environment.

Habitat is an *ecological area* inhabited by a species. It is the natural environment in which an organism lives or the physical environment encompassing a population.

3. B is correct.

Population density measures population per unit area.

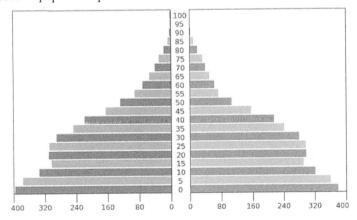

Population density plots age vs. population (in thousands) with male (left) and female comparison

4. D is correct.

Sustainable development meets people's needs without compromising future generations' ability to meet their natural resources and environmental quality needs.

Preventing long-term environmental harm ensures that people can benefit from its use in the future.

5. C is correct.

Range (or *distribution*) of a population is the geographical area.

Dispersion is the variation in local *density* within a range.

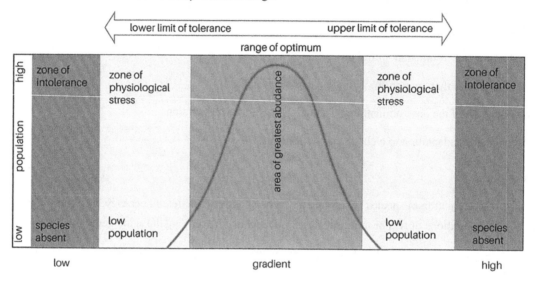

Range of tolerance plots population vs. bifurcated range of optimum stress

6. E is correct.

Observation involves noting characteristics *without* engagement or intervention by the researcher.

7. A is correct.

Demography uses statistics such as births, deaths, income, the incidence of disease, and education, illustrating the changing structure of human populations.

Population growth rate is how the number of people changes in a given period; the flow of people in and out, births, and deaths affect the number of individuals within a population.

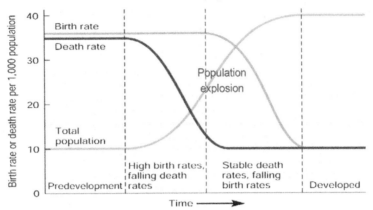

Birth rate and death rate affect population size transitioning from high to low rates with increasing population

8. B is correct.

Population density measures population per unit area (e.g., people per square mile).

9. C is correct.

Biotic factors are living components affecting other organisms.

For example, animals consume other organisms and organic food. Biotic factors need food and metabolic energy for proper growth.

Biotic factors include human influence.

10. E is correct.

Coal, natural gas, oil, and energy are derived from fossil fuels, including minerals (e.g., copper, magnesium). Non-renewable resources are not replenished at a sufficient rate for sustainable economic extraction.

Non-renewable resources require tens of thousands to millions of years and specific conditions to form.

Renewable resources are replenished over time through biological reproduction or other naturally recurring processes. They are integral to Earth's natural environment and the largest components of its ecosphere.

Renewable resources may be the source of power for renewable energy.

However, renewal and sustainability will not be sustainable when resource consumption exceeds the renewal rate.

11. A is correct.

Ecological models trace the interaction between and interdependence of factors within and across all population levels. It highlights people's interactions with physical and environmental factors.

12. B is correct.

The Dust Bowl was a period of severe dust storms that significantly damaged the ecology and agriculture of the American and Canadian prairies during the 1930s; severe drought and a failure to apply dryland farming methods to prevent the aeolian processes (wind erosion) caused the phenomenon.

Crops began to fail with the onset of drought in 1931, exposing the bare, over-plowed farmland. It began to blow away without deep-rooted prairie grasses to hold the soil in place. The eroding soil led to massive dust storms and economic devastation—especially in the Southern Plains.

13. C is correct.

Immigration is moving *into* an area.

Carrying capacity is the maximum population size the environment can sustain based on resources. If a population grows larger than the carrying capacity, species may die due to a lack of environmental resources.

Emigration is moving *out* of an area.

14. D is correct.

Animal training is not a method used by ecologists to study the environment.

15. E is correct.

Slower growth rate means fewer new individuals in a population. Increased birth rate and decreased death rates lead to a rise in growth rate, whereas decreased birth rate slows down the population growth rate.

	High stationary	**Early expanding**	**Late expanding**	**Low stationary**	**Declining**
	Stage 1	Stage 2	Stage 3	Stage 4	Stage 5
Birth rate	High	High	Falling	Low	Rising again
Death rate	High	Falls rapidly	Falls slowly	Low	Low
Natural output	Stable or slow increase	Very rapid increase	Increase slows down	Falling and then stable	Stable or slow increase

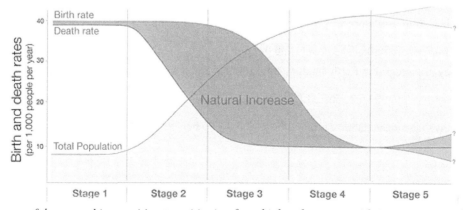

Five stages of demographic transition transitioning from high to low rates with increasing population

16. E is correct.

Desertification is land degradation when a relatively dry land region becomes increasingly arid, typically losing its bodies of water and vegetation, and wildlife.

Desertification is caused by factors such as climate change and human activities.

Removal of most vegetation is the immediate cause of desertification.

Desertification is driven by drought, climatic shifts, agriculture tillage, overgrazing, fuel deforestation, and construction materials harvesting.

Desertification is a global ecological and environmental problem.

B: *monoculture* is the agricultural practice of growing a single crop for many consecutive years.

Monocultures are widely used in industrial agriculture, and its implementation has allowed for large harvests from minimal labor.

However, monocultures quickly spread pests and diseases, making a uniform crop susceptible to a pathogen.

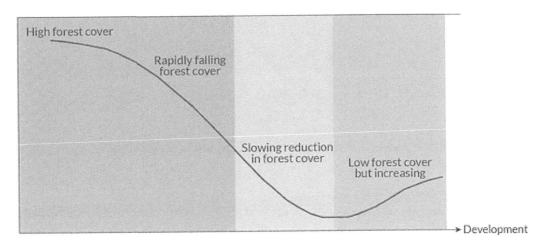

Four stages of forest transition model plotting forest cover vs. development

Stage 1 *Pre-transition*: high forest cover. No or slow loss of forest. (left panel on the graph)

Stage 2 *Early transition*: deforestation rates increasing.

Stage 3 *Late transition*: low forest cover but a slowing rate of deforestation

Stage 4 *Post-transition*: low forest cover but increasing through reforestation. (right panel on the graph)

17. A is correct.

Exponential growth is a process that increases quantity over time.

Exponential growth graphs exhibit *a steep curve up*.

Animals require resources (e.g., food, water, biotic factors) for survival.

Number of microorganisms in the culture increases *exponentially* until an essential nutrient is exhausted, which impedes the organisms' growth.

Typically, the first organism divides into two, who split to form four, eight, etc.

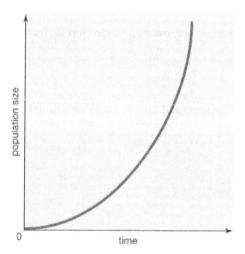

Exponential growth plotting population size vs. time with a steep positive slope indicating increasing numbers

18. C is correct.

Desertification is land degradation when a relatively dry land region becomes increasingly arid, typically losing its bodies of water and vegetation, and wildlife.

Desertification is caused by factors such as climate change and human activities. The immediate cause of desertification is the removal of most vegetation.

Desertification is driven by factors (alone or in combination) such as drought, climatic shifts, tillage for agriculture, overgrazing, deforestation for fuel, and harvesting of construction materials.

Desertification is a significant global ecological and environmental problem.

B: *monoculture* is the agricultural practice of growing a *single crop* for many consecutive years. It is widely used in industrial agriculture, and its implementation has allowed for large harvests from minimal labor.

However, monocultures quickly *spread pests and diseases*, making a uniform crop susceptible to a pathogen.

   Stage 1 Pre-transition: high forest cover. No or slow loss of forest.

   Stage 2 Early transition: deforestation rates increasing.

   Stage 3 Late transition: low forest cover but a slowing rate of deforestation

   Stage 4 Post-transition: low forest cover but increasing through reforestation.

19. B is correct.

Decreased birth rate and *emigration* (i.e., outflow) cause population size to *decrease*.

20. D is correct.

Soil erosion gradually removes the top layer of soil by natural elements such as water, wind, and farming.

Irrigation controls the amount of water released by supplying it at regular intervals for farming, which is an effective way of maintaining the quality of the soil.

21. D is correct.

Demographic transition is the shift from high birth and death rates to low birth and death rates as a country develops from a pre-industrial to an industrialized economic system.

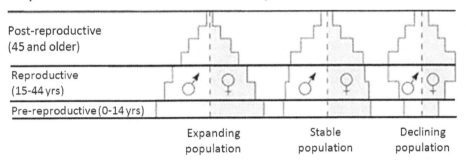

Age structure diagrams: pyramid (left) for expanding, bell-shaped (center) for stable, urn-shaped (right) for declining population profiles

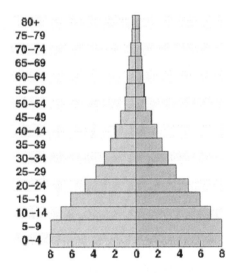

An expansive population pyramid plots age vs. percent. Males on the left. The graph is skewed towards younger members when the demographic transition is incomplete

22. A is correct.

Births and *immigration* (inflows) *increase* population size.

23. E is correct.

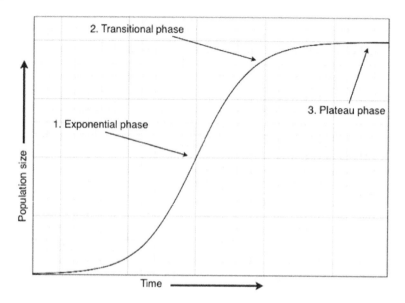

Sigmoidal (S)-shaped logistic growth curve of population growth with environmental resistance. The exponential phase has an accelerating growth rate. Exponential phase is marked by a steep positive slope, the transitional phase with a slightly positive slope, and the plateau phase with flat curve profiles

Exponential growth is a process that increases quantity over time; the graph exhibits a steep curve upward.

Logistic curve (or *function*) is a common *sigmoid function* (S-shape) concerning population growth.

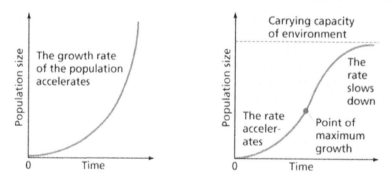

Exponential (unrestricted) growth (left) has accelerating growth patterns, and logistic (restricted) growth (right) where the rate decreases as environmental carrying capacity is achieved

Animals require resources (e.g., food, water, biotic factors) for survival.

Number of microorganisms in culture increases exponentially until an essential nutrient is exhausted, which impedes the organisms' growth.

24. A is correct.

Using predators and parasites for pest management is a sustainable resource in ecology.

25. B is correct.

Exponential growth is a process that increases quantity over time.

Exponential growth graph exhibits a steep curve upward.

Animals require resources (e.g., food, water, biotic factors) for survival.

The number of microorganisms in the culture increases exponentially until an essential nutrient is exhausted, which impedes the organisms' growth.

Typically, the first organism divides into two, forming four, eight, etc.

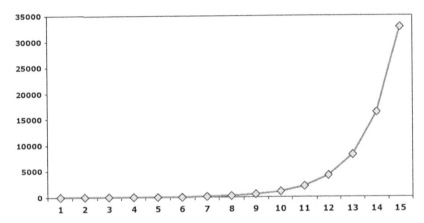

Exponential growth with population vs. generation plotted shows accelerated growth rates

26. C is correct.

DDT (or d*ichlorodiphenyltrichloroethane*) was a modern synthetic pesticide used in the United States (beginning in the 1940s) to control insects on food crops and in buildings for pest control.

DDT was discontinued in 1972 because of its harmful effects on humans and wildlife.

27. D is correct.

Renewable resources can be regenerated or replenished.

A renewable resource is a natural resource that can replenish over time through biological reproduction or other naturally recurring processes.

Renewable resources are a part of Earth's natural environment and the largest component of its ecosphere.

They may be the source of power for renewable energy.

Renewal and sustainability are not ensured if the renewable resource consumption exceeds its renewal rate.

28. C is correct.

Density-dependent limiting factors affect the size or growth due to variation in population density.

Dense populations are more strongly affected than less crowded ones.

Density-dependent limiting factors include food availability, disease, living space, predation, and migration.

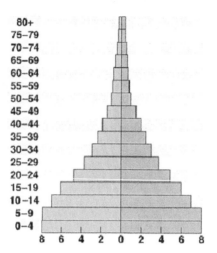

An expansive population pyramid plots age vs. percent. Males on the left. The graph is skewed towards younger members when the demographic transition is incomplete

29. E is correct.

Carrying capacity is the maximum population size the environment can sustain indefinitely based on the available resources.

If a population grows larger than the carrying capacity, species may die due to a lack of environmental resources.

30. B is correct.

Biological magnification is any concentration of a toxin, such as pesticides, in the tissues of tolerant organisms at successively higher levels in a food chain.

Biomagnification is when an organism's chemical concentration exceeds its food concentration when the primary exposure route occurs from the diet.

Higher-level predators (e.g., fish, birds, marine mammals) build up greater dangerous amounts of toxic materials than animals lower on the food chain.

DDT was banned in 1972 as a suspected carcinogen (i.e., cancer causing agent).

31. B is correct.

Exponential growth is a process that increases quantity over time.

Graph of exponential growth exhibits a steep curve upward.

Animals require resources (e.g., food, water, biotic factors) for survival.

Number of microorganisms in culture increases exponentially until an essential nutrient is exhausted, which impedes the organisms' growth.

Typically, the first organism divides into two, who split to form four, eight, etc.

32. E is correct.

Photochemical smog is air pollution from the interaction of sunlight with certain chemicals in the atmosphere.

Ozone is one of the primary components of photochemical smog.

Smog is air pollution that reduces visibility, labeled in the early 1900s to describe a mix of smoke and fog.

Smoke usually came from burning coal, while smog was common in industrial areas and remains a familiar sight in cities today.

The atmospheric pollutants or gases that form smog are released into the air when fuels are burnt.

Smog is formed when sunlight and its heat react with these gases and fine particles in the atmosphere.

Particulate matter is a mixture of tiny particles and liquid droplets.

Particle pollution comprises several components: acids (nitrates and sulfates), organic chemicals, metals, and soil or dust particles.

Greenhouse gas absorbs infrared radiation (net heat energy) emitted from Earth's surface and reradiates it back to Earth's surface, thus contributing to the greenhouse effect.

Carbon dioxide, methane, and water vapor are the most important greenhouse gases.

Ozone layer is a region in the Earth's stratosphere that contains high ozone (O_3) concentrations and protects the Earth from the sun's harmful ultraviolet radiations.

33. A is correct.

Acid rain is any form of precipitation when acidic components (e.g., sulfur dioxide, nitrogen oxides) fall to the ground from the atmosphere.

These compounds rise into the atmosphere, reacting with water and oxygen and falling to the ground as precipitation.

34. C is correct.

Logistic curve (or *function*) is a standard *sigmoid function* (S-shape) concerning population growth.

Initial growth stage is exponential.

As saturation begins, growth slows, and at maturity, growth stops.

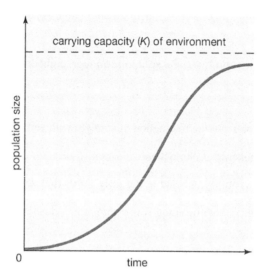

Logistic growth plotting population size vs. time where the rate decreases at carrying capacity

Exponential growth is a process that increases quantity over time; graph exhibits a *steep curve upward*.

35. C is correct.

Limiting factors in an ecosystem are typically food, water, habitat, and mate. The availability factors will affect the carrying capacity of an environment. As the population increases, food demand increases as well. Since food is a limited resource, organisms will begin competing for it.

36. A is correct.

Acid rain is a chemical reaction with sulfur dioxide, and nitrogen oxides are released into the air. These compounds rise into the atmosphere, reacting with water and oxygen and falling to the ground as precipitation.

37. D is correct.

The vapors given off when gasoline evaporates and the substances produced when gasoline is burned (carbon monoxide, nitrogen oxides, particulates, and unburned hydrocarbons) contribute to air pollution.

Burning gasoline produces carbon dioxide (CO_2), a greenhouse gas.

Lead gasoline (prohibited in 1996) releases suspended particles into the air. Motor-vehicle emissions have been reduced by banning lead gasoline for motor vehicles.

However, lead is used in general-aviation gasoline for piston-engine aircraft.

Lead poisoning causes brain damage, chronic illness, lowered IQ, and elevated mortality.

38. D is correct.

Density-dependent limiting factors affect the size or growth due to variation in population density.

Dense populations are more strongly affected than less crowded ones.

Density-dependent limiting factors include food availability, disease, living space, predation, and migration.

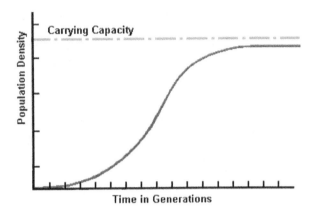

Logistic growth plotting population size vs. time where the rate decreases at carrying capacity

39. E is correct.

Particulate matter is a mixture of tiny particles and liquid droplets.

Particle pollution comprises several components: acids (nitrates and sulfates), organic chemicals, metals, and soil or dust particles.

40. B is correct.

Carrying capacity is the maximum population size the environment can sustain indefinitely based on the available resources. If a population grows larger than the carrying capacity, species may die due to a lack of environmental resources.

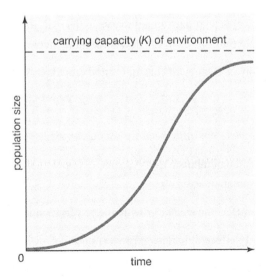

Logistic growth plotting population size vs. time where the rate decreases at carrying capacity

41. A is correct.

Species diversity is the adequate number of different species represented in a collection of individuals.

B: *genetic diversity* refers to the total number of genetic characteristics in the genetic makeup of a species.

It is distinguished from genetic variability, which describes the tendency of genetic characteristics to vary.

Genetic diversity serves as a way for populations to adapt to changing environments.

C: *ecosystem diversity* refers to the diversity of a place at the level of ecosystems (i.e., biotic, and abiotic factors).

D: *biodiversity* refers to variation in species rather than ecosystems.

42. B is correct.

Density-dependent limiting factors affect the size or growth due to variation in population density.

Dense populations are more strongly affected than less crowded ones.

Density-dependent limiting factors include food availability, disease, living space, predation, and migration.

43. D is correct.

Species diversity is the adequate number of different species represented in a collection of individuals.

B: *genetic diversity* refers to the total number of genetic characteristics in the genetic makeup of a species.

Genetic diversity is distinguished from *genetic variability*, which describes the tendency of genetic characteristics to vary. It serves as a way for populations to adapt to changing environments.

44. E is correct.

Drought is a prolonged period of abnormally low rainfall, leading to a water shortage. This limiting factor does not apply to marine animals.

45. A is correct.

Introduced species (or exotic species) is an organism not native to the place or area it is introduced. Instead, it has been accidentally or deliberately transported to the new location by human activity.

Introduced species may be predators or ecological consumers and crowd out native species.

46. B is correct.

Density-independent limiting factors are *not* influenced by population size.

Factors include weather, climate, and natural disasters. All species populations in the ecosystem will be similarly affected, regardless of population size.

Density-dependent limiting factors affect the size or growth due to variation in population density.

Dense populations are more strongly affected than less crowded ones.

Density-dependent limiting factors include food availability, disease, living space, predation, and migration.

47. D is correct.

Higher birth and lower death rates increase the number of individuals, thus increasing competition.

Fewer resources and higher population density lead to increased competition.

A decrease in population size can reduce competition.

48. C is correct.

Habitat is the natural environment in which an organism lives or the physical environment encompassing a population.

Habitat is an ecological area inhabited by a species.

Habitat fragmentation divides large habitats into smaller, isolated patches due to *habitat loss* by human activity and natural causes. This negatively affects biodiversity and reduces the suitable habitat for certain species.

49. C is correct.

Habitat is an ecological area inhabited by a species. It is the natural environment in which an organism lives or the physical environment encompassing a population.

50. E is correct.

Density-independent limiting factors are *not* influenced by population size.

Density-independent factors include weather, climate, and natural disasters.

Species populations in the ecosystem are similarly affected, regardless of population size.

The spray program affected the mosquito population as a density-independent limiting factor.

51. D is correct.

Density-dependent limiting factors affect the size or growth due to variation in population density.

Dense populations are more strongly affected than less crowded ones.

Density-dependent limiting factors include food availability, disease, living space, predation, and migration.

Density-independent limiting factors are *not* influenced by population size. Factors include weather, climate, and natural disasters.

All species populations in the ecosystem will be similarly affected, regardless of population size.

52. A is correct.

Hot spots are regions of species in a single geographic region (i.e., endemism).

Ecological hot spots tend to occur in tropical environments where species richness and biodiversity are higher than in ecosystems closer to the poles.

For example, biodiversity hotspots are forest habitats, as they constantly face destruction and degradation due to illegal logging, pollution, and deforestation.

53. B is correct.

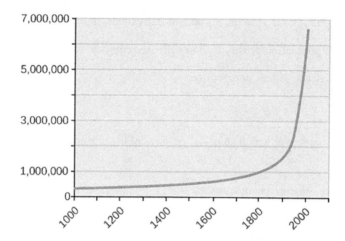

World population from 1000 AD. Graph plots population (in thousands) vs. year

DAT Biology Subject Review provides a comprehensive review of biology topics tested on the DAT. The content covers foundational principles and theories necessary to answer test questions.

This review book will increase your score.

Visit our Amazon store

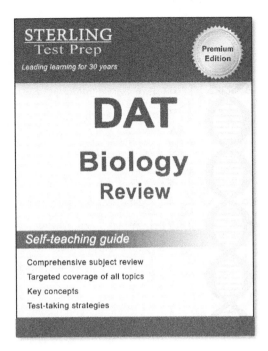

DAT online practice questions

Our advanced online testing platform allows you to practice these and other DAT questions on the computer and generate Diagnostic Reports for each test.

Assess your knowledge of subjects and topics via Diagnostics Reports with your performance analysis

Learn important scientific topics and concepts for comprehensive DAT preparation

Improve your test-taking skills by simulating testing under time constraints

To access these and other DAT questions online
at a special pricing for book owners visit:
http://dat.sterling-prep.com/bookowner.htm

If you benefited from this book, we would appreciate if you left a review on Amazon, so others can learn from your input. Reviews help us understand our customers' needs and experiences while keeping our commitment to quality.

Frank J. Addivinola, Ph.D.

Dr. Frank Addivinola is the lead author and chief editor for Sterling Education. With his outstanding education, laboratory research, and university science and humanities teaching, he guided the development of this book.

Frank Addivinola earned his BA in biology from Williams College, Master of Liberal Arts with a concentration in biology at Harvard University, Masters in Biotechnology at Johns Hopkins University, Masters of Science in Technology Management, and Masters of Business Administration at the University of Maryland, Juris Doctorate and Masters of Laws at Suffolk University, and Doctorate in Law and Public Policy at Northeastern University.

Dr. Addivinola conducted original research in developmental biology as a doctoral candidate in Molecular and Cell Biology and a pre-IRTA fellow at the National Institutes of Health (NIH), Bethesda, MD. Nobel laureate Marshall W. Nirenberg, Chief of the Biochemical Genetics Laboratory at the National Heart, Lung, and Blood Institute (NHLBI), was his dissertation advisor. His doctoral research focused on sequencing *OG*-2 genomic DNA, cloning and sequencing full-length *OG*-2 cDNAs with splice sites, and determining the cognate nucleotide binding site of the expressed homeodomain and flanking amino acids.

Before his research training at the NIH, Dr. Addivinola researched prostate cancer in the Cell Growth and Regulation Laboratory of Dr. Arthur Pardee at the Dana Farber Cancer Institute of Harvard Medical School. He participated in identifying early genetic markers for prostate cancer.

Frank Addivinola was a teaching fellow in Organic Chemistry at Harvard University and has taught at Johns Hopkins, the University of Maryland, and other universities. Professor Addivinola taught undergraduate and graduate-level courses, including biology, biochemistry, organic chemistry, inorganic chemistry, anatomy and physiology, medical terminology, nutrition, medical ethics, math, and law and public policy. He received several awards for teaching, research, and presentations.

Made in the USA
Coppell, TX
01 November 2024

39456293R00326